Becoming Visible

Becoming Visible
Women in European History
THIRD EDITION

edited by

Renate Bridenthal
Brooklyn College, CUNY

Susan Mosher Stuard
Haverford College

Merry E. Wiesner
University of Wisconsin—Milwaukee

Houghton Mifflin Company　　Boston　New York

Editor-in-Chief: Jean Woy
Assistant Editors: Keith Mahoney/Leah Strauss
Associate Project Editor: Gabrielle Stone
Associate Production Coordinator: Deb Frydman
Senior Manufacturing Coordinator: Marie Barnes
Marketing Manager: Sandra McGuire

Cover Image: A Balloon Site, Coventry by Dame Laura Knight. Imperial War Museum.
Cover Design: Sarah Melhado

Credits:

Page 20: From Miriam Lichteim, *Ancient Egyptian Literature II: The New Kingdom*. Copyright © 1976. Reprinted by permission of the University of California Press.

Page 108: Kuno Meyer, ed. and trans., "Eve's Lament" from ERIU 3 (1907), p. 148; as found in Patrick L. Henry, trans., *Danta Ban: Poems of Irish Women, Early and Modern* (Cork, Mercier Books, 1991), p. 81. Reprinted by permission of Mercier Books.

Page 140: Christiane Klapisch-Zuber, *Women, Family, and Ritual in Renaissance Florence,* translated by Lydia Cochrane. Copyright 1984 by the University of Chicago Press. Reprinted by permission of the publisher.

Printed in the U.S.A.

Library of Congress Catalog Number: 97-72450

ISBN: 0-395-79625-3

10 11 12 13 14 15-FFG-11 10 09 08 07

*Dedicated to the women's movement
to which this book owes its own visibility.*

Contents

Preface

Since the publication of the first edition of *Becoming Visible: Women In European History* two decades ago, the question of women's visibility has become moot. The questions now are multiple: which women are visible? when? in what way? To what degree have women been limited by gender ascriptions, how have these changed, and to what degree have women both shaped and overcome these notions of gender? Over the five thousand years of European history here surveyed, ever more research has increased the complexity of the questions and answers.

As our Introduction indicates, the volume as a whole develops several main themes. One is a new appreciation of the fact that Europe is not an isolated enclave, and that the history of European women has always linked them with that of people in the rest of the world. European women traveled in various capacities and those who did not profited from the goods and services and people that returned. With accelerating speed, globalization has transformed the European subcontinent and the women who inhabit it. Other themes carried through in these essays are the differentiation among women, the historical construction of gender, women's work experiences and their changing political possibilities. Differences of social status, of ethnicity, of familial relations affect all other experiences that women have: in work, in love, in play, and in politics. The fact that women are differently affected from men in these areas is a product of gender constructions that have varied over time. These essays show the wide variety of sexual and other behaviors evinced by women through the centuries.

In this third edition, we have again drawn on the most recent research, and we have also reconceptualized some periodization, not only to make room for updated material, but also to account for some new thinking. We have dropped any discussion of prehistoric times and begin instead with recorded history. We have rectified the previous neglect of early northern Europe with a new chapter on that subject. We have dealt with early modern Europe topically, and the new chapters on the Renaissance, Reformation and Enlightenment are less abstract and take a closer look at the actual experience of women in those historical periods. The chapter on the interwar period has been replaced by one that takes both world wars into account as well, and is complemented by an expansion of the chapter on fascism. Finally, two new chapters bring the volume up to the date of publication: one on women in Eastern

Europe and another on women in contemporary Europe. In all, this volume contains seven new chapters and thirteen revised from the previous edition.

Although these essays present a fairly continuous story, the contributors have, as before, brought their own individual interpretations to this volume. We welcome the diversity, which itself is an important pedagogical tool.

We thank the following readers for their insightful comments on the second edition of the book in preparation for the third: Judith Coffin, University of Texas–Austin; Susan Conner, Central Michigan University; Joan Francis, Atlantic Union College; Anne Meyering, Michigan State University; Susan Pederson, Harvard University; Cynthia Truant, University of California–San Diego. We especially thank our editor at Houghton Mifflin, Jean Woy, for her support, careful reading, and helpful suggestions, which have made this third edition live up to our best expectations.

Introduction

In 1976 *Becoming Visible* challenged readers with the message that, indeed, women had a history of great complexity with significant change over the centuries. In 1987 a second edition of *Becoming Visible* incorporated the findings of a remarkably fruitful decade of research on women's history into the revised volume. Now in 1998 another extraordinary decade of historical research demands a third edition, but, ironically, the project of women's history is again under attack, as it was when it was first born. Women's history ought to be incorporated with men's, critics have argued recently; it is "lop-sided" to view women alone. However, through investigating the realm of the discounted, where women have so frequently lived out their lives, our imaginations are engaged to adopt a more expansive view of what constitutes history. This volume carefully limns in the lives of men and children who surround women, but women remain the major focus of the twenty-one authors of the essays. The editors believe this is necessary, because women's lack of a history has so often left women with the mistaken impression that they were alone, or the first, or the only, women in their chosen field of endeavor. Only an adequate knowledge of our past can prevent us from constantly reinventing the wheel.

The third edition goes beyond the first two in several ways. First, this edition queries how women responded to Europe's permeable boundaries and to influences and interactions from abroad. What affects women abroad affects women at home, and the opposite is true as well. European women migrated, crusaded, colonized, and traveled. Europe has profited from people, goods, and services from around the globe. Today women live in a global society and struggle with problems that are interrelated and universal. In particular, this third edition queries how women responded to Europe's permeable boundaries and to influences and interactions from abroad that contributed to Europe's successive transformations.

Second, the third edition adds newer knowledge on women's sexuality, the symbolism of female sexuality, and its prescriptive capacity for determining women's lives.

And third, the explosion in scholarly research in the last decade has allowed us to discriminate more finely among different groups of women. We can also tell more stories about the extraordinarily diverse lives of women over the past five thousand years. Readers will meet remarkable women from all walks of life, backgrounds, religions, and ethnic groups in these pages.

1

As in earlier editions, the essays consider whether European women's history follows the same trajectory as men's over the long term. Certain topics ground the volume as in the past: the interplay of gender and class, women's work, legal rights, intellectual and religious life, and social power.

GENDER RELATIONS

Of necessity the history of men and powerful institutions comes into play where authors consider gender, the system of relations between women and men. The earliest centers of civilization differed on assumptions about gender five thousand years ago. The supremely confident Egyptians found it less necessary to create an ideology that subordinated women than did their neighbors in western Asia, where constant attacks, a resulting militarism, and an increasingly large-scale commerce led to what Barbara Lesko characterizes as a blatant form of patriarchy with accompanying assumptions about women's weakness and need for protection. Marilyn Katz explains the system of opposition and alignment of qualities that Aristotle employed to link women to men. In the juxtaposition of ideology with social practice a notion of the polis as a cultural totality emerged. While elite women of ancient Greece experienced both privileges and restrictions within gender systems, poorer women who worked for a living often escaped the dictates of a cultural ideal that associated the female with the inner spaces of the home.

JoAnn McNamara makes it clear that within the Roman Empire another aspect of Aristotelian thinking, that of a continuum of qualities assigned to gender, came into play. Thus, in a biological universe, a gender continuum according to varying degrees of virility and effeminacy characterized a world where a patrician Roman woman could be more generously endowed with virtue than men of lesser races and classes. Lisa Bitel explains how early Europe inherited a system of gender assumptions from ancient and classical times that assumed women were weaker, more stupid, and more sinful than men. However, stories that men wrote about women acknowledged a strange discrepancy between a fairly limited set of formal ideas about women and the mind-boggling variety of actual and fictional women. Although authors might explain away prominent women by describing them as manly, monstrous, or extraordinarily virtuous, they took for granted that ordinary women could be useful, welcome, and influential members of the community.

Susan Stuard argues that scholastic thinking and university-trained theologians of the twelfth and thirteenth centuries revived the rigid system of polarities first forwarded by Pythagoras and Aristotle in ancient Greece. These notions juxtaposed woman's nature to man's, and a more systematic construction of gender emerged. However, polar notions were never applied to medieval women's lives in a wholly consistent manner. Society relied so heavily on women's essential contributions and hard work that at times gendered assumptions were not brought to bear at all. Carole Levin continues the story of the social construction of gender through stating that while Renaissance men described woman's nature as morally weak and intellectually feeble, Christine de Pizan, in *The Book of the City of Ladies*, stoutly denounced the misogyny of the learned men of the Renaissance by articulating an alternate perspective of women's worth, a view that women had intellectual and human dignity.

Though many aspects of scholastic thought were challenged by the Protestant Reformation of the sixteenth century, notions of gender polarities were not. As Susan C. Karant-Nunn demonstrates, they were actually given added reinforcement in both Protestant and Catholic teaching. Protestants rejected the notion of a celibate clergy and held up a new model of the best possible Christian life: the pious pastor's family. Though this model validated marriage, it meant that wifehood, housekeeping, and motherhood were held as women's only legitimate vocations, and unmarried women were regarded as increasingly suspect. This model shaped the Catholic Reformation as well, for women were expected to show their Christian devotion as members of either male-headed households or enclosed convents; while Christian men might travel as missionaries or help aid the poor and suffering out in the world, women were to serve God by serving their husbands or by prayer. There were some women who chafed against these expectations among both Protestants and Catholics, who preached, published, traveled, and even died for their faith, but they were few in number. The message promoting women's inferiority and subordination was relentlessly preached on Sundays and at weddings and taught to both boys and girls in school; not surprisingly, it was accepted by most women as well as men.

In the same way that they agreed about women's "nature" as inferior and domestic, Protestants and Catholics agreed about the need to impose order and discipline on their societies and to reform human behavior to bring it into line with what were seen as divine injunctions. The desire for order was also one of the contributing factors in the witch craze, during which tens of thousands of people, most of them women, who were viewed as particularly vulnerable to the devil's wiles, were tried and executed in Europe and some European New World colonies.

In modern times some women learned to instrumentalize historical notions of gender difference to gain power. Margaret Strobel shows that women of imperial nations could argue that their very femininity enabled them better to understand and "reform" colonized women. Of necessity this involved accepting the notion of being the inferior sex within a superior race and did not directly challenge inequality. Similarly, Claudia Koonz shows that twentieth-century right-wing dictatorships created rigidly sex-segregated social institutions, which enabled a few women to administer a hierarchy of institutions, albeit under male supervision. Such women also tended to believe that their very difference from men made separate organizations appropriate, although the argument of female particularity removed any basis for equal empowerment. Richard Stites and Barbara Einhorn, investigating the most advanced attempts in socialist countries to prioritize social class over gender, reveal the enormous lasting power of traditional notions of femininity. Legislation for political and economic equality did not alter the assumption that women had primary responsibility for child and family care, with the result that they carried a huge double burden of work. While sometimes their productive and sometimes their reproductive contribution was emphasized, support for both remained insufficient, leading to exhaustion among would-be heroic "superwomen." A third expectation of political involvement therefore remained anemic. After the fall of socialism in 1989, most attempts at equalization fell away and gender roles became sharply divided once more, in part to ward off any competition for privatized and increasingly scarce resources and employment.

In Western Europe, however, two decades after World War II, thanks to accelerating changes in women's work and education, a new feminist movement challenged gender distinctions at their very root and made total liberation a goal for women.

WOMEN'S WORK

For most of recorded European history there have been surprising similarities in women's work: indeed, these similarities provide one reason historians now emphasize how gender shapes the economy, for many aspects of women's work have remained stubbornly the same despite vast economic change. Women have always worked as well as performed the essential tasks of child bearing and raising and home making. In ancient Egypt work performed by women was sustained by laws that gave women authority over the property they inherited or produced. A woman received a dowry from her parents and handled that wealth independently. If she was divorced, the law compelled her husband to grant her that part of his wealth that had been pledged to her upon marriage. Many occupations were open to women, including some of the most powerful ones within the priesthood. Coupled with the occasional woman's reign as pharaoh, ancient Egypt offered women great opportunity.

Marilyn Katz notes that spinning and weaving were, above all, the province of women. In the fifth-century Athenian household wives displayed their artistic skills through weaving, while slaves performed the grueling household labor and more tedious tasks of cloth making. Poorer women were not enclosed in the home but were market vendors, wool workers, wet-nurses, and grape pickers. Although Hellenistic women had greater access to public space than their Hellenic forebears, propriety, or adherence to widespread social ideals, was always and everywhere contingent upon property status in ancient Greece. The Roman Empire continued this pattern, although

Christianity and changes in Roman law accorded women more authority over time. Christian women of the fourth century of the Common Era contributed wealth and political connections to doctrinal or political causes espoused by the men. Christian men in turn brought their female friends into the inner decision-making circles of the Church. This presents a picture of collaboration rather than of separate spheres of work and authority.

Lisa Bitel notes that women in early medieval northern Europe were primarily wives and mothers. This was an age when the household was the major economic, social, and political unit of society. Through households both women and men rendered their labor to the great task of settling Europe and building an economy. Laws declared that it was a wife's responsibility to assist her husband when agricultural tasks were most pressing, at ploughing and harvesting. Generally, because women worked in the farmyard and house, close to children and spinning, while men's place was in the fields, a sexual division of labor pertained. However, women also moved out of the home to participate in trade and profit-making ventures. In the High Middle Ages women brought their hard-working habits and flexible division of labor to emerging towns and the work of crafts and a trading economy. But their very attitudes, which helped in the creation of a commercial revolution in Europe, were soon met by an erosion in the rights of inheritance and control of property. Vast amounts of new wealth were at stake, and gender ideology was invoked to limit women's control of property. The Renaissance saw a continuation of this trend. Margherita Datini was trusted by her husband to manage the family business at home in Prato while he traveled abroad, but he expected her newly acquired skills at writing letters to keep him informed, and her reading skills to assure him that she followed his orders.

All early Mediterranean societies were slave-keeping societies, and no religious tradition of the region—Judaism, Christianity, or Islam—outlawed slavery. In a traditional world with a constant high ratio of unskilled labor to skilled work, a slave's contribution to the welfare of all was great. Slavery was encouraged by Rome's political consolidation of the Mediterranean region and persisted through the early Middle Ages to be revived again in the thirteenth century. Women slaves were preferred in the medieval revival of the trade. Their presence in Western Mediterranean cities and on the islands of the sea was a prelude to the overseas transport of slaves to New World plantations. Slavery persisted in parts of Eastern Europe alongside serfdom at least until the seventeenth century. The Roma, popularly known as Gypsies, for example, were slaves in Romania from the sixteenth to the nineteenth centuries, before they were set free to roam again.

As economic and social historians began to analyze women's work twenty years ago, they tended to focus on the ways in which economic change—such as the development of first mercantile and then industrial capitalism—shaped the gender division of labor, the meaning of the work that men and women performed, and aspects of family structure such as age at marriage, number of children, and patterns of residence. Both Merry E. Wiesner and Laura L. Frader investigate these changes, Wiesner focusing on the preindustrial period, 1350–1750, and Frader on the industrial economy, 1750–1900. They also explore a newer area of investigation, the ways in which gender structures shaped economic change. For example, laws regulating women's rights to own property, notions of women's intellectual and physical capability, ideas about female and male honor and sexuality, and regional marriage patterns all influenced the way in which the European economy developed. Traditional explanations for regional variations in development have focused on economic and political factors such as the presence of coal and iron, strong systems of banking, policies that favored trade, or navigable rivers; it is now clear that regional differences in family patterns and notions of gender also played a role.

Investigating women's work provides extensive evidence for what has become a key assertion in women's history over the last decade, that of vast differences in women's experience, which make generalizations difficult. A woman's marital status might shape both the work available to her and the way that work was paid and valued. For example, though wages were low and working conditions horrendous, factory work offered new opportunities for young unmarried women at the same time it often destroyed married women's contribution to family income by destroying the demand for homespun thread. By the late nineteenth century, unmarried women also found work in retail stores, banks, primary schools, offices, and telephone companies, positions usually closed to married women. Thus even within one family, marital status may have made a significant difference in women's work experience. When variations resulting from social class, age, family size, place of residence, and ethnicity are added to this, the range was enormous.

Whether in 1350 or 1900, women were paid less than men—often for the same job—and the work they did was defined as less skilled and less taxing physically or mentally. These definitions of skill and of the effort needed for certain jobs were based more on gender than on the actual work; tasks such as lace making or silk spinning (both female occupations) actually involve a great deal of skill, and the work of gathering and binding grain (another female occupation) is actually harder on the body than cutting it with a scythe (a male occupation). At times notions of gender worked to exclude women's activities from concepts of work completely, with women who took in boarders, ironed clothing, sold beer, or made and sold butter and cheese not considered "workers" (to say nothing of women's unpaid labor of housekeeping and child rearing, which were totally excluded from definitions of work). In the preindustrial economy, women appear only rarely to have objected to the devaluation of their work, with their protests limited to disobeying laws or individually demanding the right to work at tasks usually restricted to men, but in the industrial economy they acted more forcefully to protest exploitation, organizing in unions and leading strikes. Such actions took them into the world of politics and at times were accompanied by more purely political actions such as joining socialist or worker's parties.

The essays by Stuard, Wiesner, and Frader note that European economic developments must be placed in a worldwide context, for international trade, the spread of slavery, colonization, and the growth of empires provided Europe with capital, raw materials, and consumer goods. European women were both producers and consumers in this web of trade; black wool cloth spun by women in Germany could be found on middle-class Filipinos as early as the seventeenth century, and by the eighteenth century even factory workers and domestic servants in Europe might own a tea set and drink tea imported from India. The essay by Dena Goodman points out that although Europeans rarely questioned the economic merits of colonialism, a few did recognize that their civilization, which seventeenth- and eighteenth-century writers argued was the most rational and moral in the world, was increasingly dependent on slavery and the trade in human beings.

The nineteenth century's rush to colonize the rest of the world involved women in more complex ways, as Margaret Strobel shows. For some, the new colonies offered opportunities of careers as missionaries, ethnographers, anthropologists, travelers, and reforming reporters. Such work held an intrinsic contradiction. On the one hand, it furthered the cause of empire by remolding colonial people in the European image. This could challenge local oppression of women, as in the case of *sati* (widow immolation on the husband's funeral pyre) in India, or disempower them where domestic ideology replaced productive labor, as in Africa. On the other hand, some colonizing women critiqued empire by reporting its brutalities and "softened" it through ameliorative acts that also served to ensconce it. Rarely, though, did they oppose the "civilizing mission" that supposedly justified imperial exploitation of people and resources.

Imperialism soon led the European nations to war. Tragically, two world wars at the cost of about 50 million lives mark the first half of the twentieth century. Not only did the wars engage the major European powers and their colonies, making them global, but they also involved civilian populations to an unprecedented degree, leading to a concept of "total war," the full involvement of state and society for warfare. Sandi Cooper shows how women were mobilized on every level in World War I: at the front for communications and nursing, on the home front replacing men at their jobs, and carrying on as before in "women's work," including family care.

Women's proven capability at men's work during World War I both opened new possibilities and led to a backlash. Where in the past religion had functioned to impose social discipline, as in the Protestant and Catholic Reformations, now the secular nation-state performed that function. The reality of blurred gender roles led to a demand for renewed clarity, which meshed with the need for women to replace the slaughtered populations, in part with an eye to future cannon fodder. Both Sandi Cooper and Claudia Koonz discuss the pronatalist policies that cajoled and coerced women to raise the birthrate that urbanization had pressed downward. Cooper shows how politicized women resisted nationalist militancy and formed international organizations for peace. Koonz, by contrast, finds right-wing dictatorships wooing women to the nationalist cause by glorifying their traditional role as mothers.

And yet, when World War II broke out, women's nonproductive labors again had to be enlisted. Cooper and Koonz show women actively, if differently, engaged on both sides of the war. The Axis powers enlisted women in the sex-segregated hierarchy focused on the home front: the Allies achieved some integration, especially among partisan forces and in the military of the Soviet Union. Once again, women proved how much greater was their equality than their difference with men.

This point had been made most forcefully by socialist feminists discussed by Charles Sowerwine. After World War I, full egalitarianism, of gender as well as class, could be tested in the first country to experiment with socialism. Richard Stites shows how the Bolshevik revolution in Russia drew on earlier utopian movements as well as on Marxism in trying to transform customary behaviors. In the early headiness of revolution, divorce was eased, abortion made readily available, Moslem women unveiled, and a Women's Department of the Communist Party set up to counsel women about their new rights. Soon after, industrialization programs pushed women into higher education and new occupational structures formerly dominated by men.

However, here, too, the ideal failed to be realized. Moslem men resisted the unveiling of women, easy divorce was abused and then rescinded, pronatalist policies prevailed as the country prepared for the expected aggression from Nazi Germany, and women rarely cracked the glass ceiling of higher economic management and politics. These were only some of the disappointments that led to the disintegration of socialism in Russia in the 1980s.

Similar disappointments marked the experience of women in Central and East European countries where socialism was instituted after World War II. Despite constitutional commitments to equality and some success in bringing women into formerly male-dominated occupations, job segregation and wage inequality persisted. As in capitalist countries, once an occupation became feminized, like medicine, it tended to be devalued monetarily and in terms of status. Most women could only glimpse the apex of career hierarchies through the glass ceiling that separated them from it. However, the revolutions against socialism in 1989 and the transition to capitalism have so far proved a disaster for most women, who are much more frequently unemployed than men. Some manufacturing has left the countries in search of cheaper labor sources elsewhere in the global economy. The public sector, which employed many women, has been decimated. Child care facilities have been vastly reduced. Prostitution is on the rise. In a unifying Europe, women of Central and Eastern Europe have joined the ranks of those who face major economic and social restructuring.

In Western Europe, the two world wars accelerated the entrance of women, including married women with children, into the paid work force. Jane Jenson shows how the male breadwinner role was supplanted by the dual-earner family, with married women often accepting part-time work at low pay and with few benefits. To ameliorate these conditions, to buffer families against the vicissitudes of economic cycles, and to prevent social unrest during the Cold War, the welfare state emerged in Western Europe. "Welfare" meant an interconnected set of social programs, indicating state commitment to society's reproductive well-being. Some feminist groups sought to extend even this by demanding wages for the hitherto unpaid labor of housework, though the idea did not take hold.

Meanwhile, advanced capitalist economies continued to expand until they connected globally, a process that continues to this day. Some multinational corporations have even cut loose from their national base, decentralizing their production and offices. Renate Bridenthal shows how the competitive search for an even cheaper work force has vastly increased women's employment in the world. A small elite of educated women have joined jetsetting management in organizing far-flung assemblies of manufactured goods, produced in unregulated tax-free export zones employing young unmarried women or in the homes of married women responsible for child care. Office work, too, has been "exported" via the new communications technology; now women at home can process data for companies in countries other than their own.

In one way, gender thus continues to structure work: however, in another way, work has begun to change family structures and gender roles. The expectation that women will work for pay may account for the fact that Western European women have become less conformist. There has been a freeing up of the sexual double standard and an increase in cohabitation before marriage, later marriage, increasing divorce, and declining birthrates. Population decline is offset by new immigrants from Eastern Europe and from former colonies. The new mobile economy has set populations moving too, and migrant women also confront new challenges that foster independence, despite the tug of anxious traditionalists.

WOMEN AND POLITICS

To turn to the issue of political power and authority, the modern world has seen nothing quite like the power of supreme women rulers in the ancient world. The Pharaoh Hatshepsut of the New Kingdom (1567–1085 B.C.) may possibly be the most powerful woman the world has seen. However, women exerted political power throughout western Asia, Egypt, and Europe in the ancient world. Extraordinary women helped create the institutions of the Roman Empire and the conversion of a Roman elite of influential women created social acceptance for the new religion of Christianity. Women of the sagas like Mebd (Maeve) inspired followers, and royal women of the High Middle Ages followed their own policies apart from those of royal fathers, husbands, and sons. Few women have wielded such authority as can be found among the abbesses of the great double monastic houses of Europe. These women escaped the strictures of gender ideology that saw women as passive while men are active, but they became increasingly rare over the centuries in Europe.

In the early modern era the exclusion of women—except for a few queens, noblewomen, and abbesses—from position of political power in Europe was debated from time to time, usually in very theoretical milieus such as academies and law schools, but it occasionally became a topic of more general concern. One of these times was the mid-sixteenth century, a point at which dynastic accidents left a number of women—Mary and Elizabeth Tudor, Mary Stuart—as rulers, causing some writers to question the validity of all women's rule, including that of a hereditary monarch. Rule became an act of legerdemain for a woman; for example, Queen Elizabeth I (Elizabeth Tudor) presented herself to the English people not only as both virgin and mother, but as both male and female, as both king and queen. The issue of a woman's incapacity to rule took on new life in France of the seventeenth and eighteenth centuries, as thinkers began to develop new ideas about citizenship, rights, and political authority that, combined with other factors, would eventually lead to the French Revolution. As the merits of hereditary monarchies and aristocratic social hierarchies were called into question, some thinkers also questioned the well-established hierarchy based on gender. As Dena Goodman points out, the intellectual movement of the Enlightenment developed two competing interpretations of gender, one that emphasized the equality of men and women based on their equal possession of reason and one that emphasized differences between them. Like the thinkers of the Reformation, the thinkers of the Enlightenment who emphasized difference saw a maintenance of gender distinctions as essential to a well-ordered society.

The discussion of equality and difference in terms of the relationship between men and women was continually related during the Enlightenment to discussion of other axes of difference—racial, economic, social—and particularly to notions of how enlightened "modern" Europe differed from its own past and from the rest of the world, both of which were viewed as barbarous. This discussion was carried out in new types of places where men and women gathered, such as salons, reading clubs, circulating libraries, coffeehouses, and bookshops, and also in a much broader world of print, forming a major theme in poetry, pamphlets, periodicals, and the new literary form of the novel. These spaces, whether physical places or the pages of a book, became part of a new public sphere, broader than simply the more traditionally understood public sphere of political institutions, and one that included women.

Though ideas about gender complementarity may have been more popular than those of gender equality in the nineteenth century, in the late eighteenth century, particularly in France, equality was literally the battle cry. As Darlene Levy and Harriet Applewhite point out, *equality* was accompanied, in the slogan of the French Revolution, not only by *liberty,* but also by *fraternity,* a word whose gender ambiguities express more general gender ambiguities in the legacy of the Revolution. During the course of the Revolution, many women (and a few men) claimed through their writings and actions that "liberty, equality, fraternity" applied equally to men and women, that women were (or should be) full, active citizens with rights to political representation and an obligation to defend the nation. Every revolutionary code or constitution drafted during the course of the Revolution, however, excluded women, and most men who supported revolutionary aims generally saw women's proper roles as teaching their children or at most exercising surveillance. This ambiguity has also shaped recent discussions by historians of the long-term effects of the French Revolution, with some historians viewing it as the beginning of women's involvement in the public sphere and conceptual inclusion in the world of political rights, and others as an event that firmly established the notion that the "citizen," the political individual, was male.

The nineteenth-century feminist movement has also provoked a range of opinion among historians, which is reflected in this volume in the essays by Karen Offen and Charles Sowerwine. Both essays demonstrate that, indeed, the "woman question" would not go away, that the failure of nineteenth-century governments to grant women political rights or to end institutionalized sexual inequality in terms of law, property rights, or employment led to political activities and movements and to theoretical critiques of women's subordinate status. Both the movements and the debates eventually encompassed every country of Europe, and eventually linked European women with those in other parts of the world through international organizations of women working for suffrage, women's education, peace, or the rights of workers.

Offen stresses the great variety within the feminist movement, noting that an emphasis on individual rights is strongest in Anglo-American understandings, whereas continental feminists more often stressed women's duties to, and links to, their community in a more relational form of feminism that viewed gender distinctions—though not gender inequality—as natural and desirable. Nineteenth-century feminists agreed on many things—that women's experience and values were important, that injustices were institutionalized and should be changed—but they often disagreed with one another sharply over tactics, solutions, and priorities. Some chose to put their energies into working for women's access to formal education, others into ensuring women's rights to own property, and still others into winning the vote for women. A few radicals advocated free love as the purest emancipation from the patriarchal family, but many more feminists emphasized women's responsibilities as mothers within the family, creating an image of the citizen-mother-educator that would be very useful in arguments for women's rights, although it was also an argument used by those who opposed women's rights.

Individual feminists and feminist organizations were often pragmatic, connecting with other groups to achieve an aim. The most prominent example of this in the nineteenth century was the connection with the socialist movement, which Offen views primarily as a rivalry, whereas Sowerwine views the connection much more positively, noting the ways in which early-nineteenth-century writers such as Flora Tristan linked the goals of workers and women. As industrial development changed the European economy, some socialist leaders did grow hostile to women's labor, viewing it as a threat to men's higher-paid skilled labor. Others, however, such as August Bebel and Karl Marx, developed theories of economic and political development in which both women's work and their political equality were goals. Some women leaders, such as Clara Zetkin, rejected alliances with nonsocialist women's groups, whereas others were ready to work with them.

Both the socialist and feminist movements were often sharply divided among themselves about priorities, tactics, and philosophy, so that it is not surprising that those who advocated the liberation of both workers and women would also disagree about such issues as whether there should be separate women's organizations or how strongly to support women's suffrage. The nineteenth-century socialist women's movement provides an excellent example of what has been a main contention of women's history in the last decade: that class and gender intersect in extremely complex ways for both individuals and groups.

This new intersection was fully acted out in 1917 when cold and hungry women workers of Petrograd marched through the city on International Women's Day and thereby inaugurated the Russian Revolution. Marxist theory was committed to women's emancipation, if not to an earlier counterculture of gender-egalitarianism popular among the radical intelligentsia, and so Bolshevik women fanned out into the countryside teaching literacy and counseling women about their new rights. Richard Stites explores the successes and failures of Russian women to achieve political power: in local governance bodies they were better represented than in many capitalist countries, but the top echelons remained tightly closed to women.

Barbara Einhorn finds the same to be true of the post–World War II socialist countries of Central and East Europe. Despite quotas that ensured around one-third women's participation in Communist parties and other mass organizations, women had diminishing visibility in top decision-making bodies. However, with the rejection of state socialism came dramatic drops in the level of female representation in the earliest democratic elections, and the new parties boasted almost no female leaders.

In many capitalist countries of post–World War I Europe, women achieved the vote after nearly a century of struggle, now referred to as the "first wave" of feminism. Sandi Cooper shows how the notion of democracy and mass mobilization worked to empower women in other ways as well. The ravages of war especially motivated women to organize for peace, including establishment of the enduring Women's International League for Peace and Freedom.

But the exponentially increasing number of women reached through earlier organizational efforts and through improved means of mass communication and transportation led to ever widening circles of involvement until the emergence, in the 1960s and 1970s, of a Women's Liberation Movement. It was this movement that gave rise to books like this one, validating the importance of women as subjects of history. Renate Bridenthal and Jane Jenson discuss the 'second-wave" feminism that contested gender inequalities and even questioned gender roles and heterosexuality itself. Bridenthal shows how, continuing in the tradition of Cooper's post–World War I pacifists, women organized on behalf of nuclear disarmament and ecology after World War II. Jenson explains that, drawing on and advancing the earliest demands of Levy and Applewhite's revolutionaries to citizenship claims, feminists achieved considerable state commitment to society's reproductive well-being.

Unfortunately, the new mobile economy has contributed to the relative impoverishment of states' public sectors, and most welfare states are now reducing their social supports. Nevertheless, women's mobilization continues to defend and expand women's rights. Beyond the nation-state, the European Union offers a new venue for transnational organizing through its representative bodies, special committees, and Women's Lobby. Finally, the United Nations Decades for Women, 1975–1995, made it possible for feminism to go global. Hundreds of thousands of women have come together at international women's meetings in Mexico City, Copenhagen, Nairobi, and Beijing to forge bonds of solidarity. Women have become fully visible for their share of doing the world's work, and now demand recognition for it and empowerment in directing it. We hope that readers of this volume will carry the torch.

Hatshepsut, the greatest of the female pharaohs
of Egypt, governed a united and prosperous
kingdom for twenty years during the brilliant
Eighteenth Dynasty.   THE METROPOLITAN MUSEUM
OF ART, ROGERS FUND & EDWARD S. HARKNESS, GIFT
1929 (29.3.3).

1

Women of Ancient Egypt and Western Asia

Barbara S. Lesko

What was life like for women in the first civilizations? For many decades the modern interpretation of women's roles in the earliest societies has been influenced by biblical accounts and classical writers. Scholars accepted the "male" as norm and paid little heed to what the female half of the population contributed to history. But women do have a history. Only in recent years have scholars taken a fresh look at the earlier ancient western Asiatic documents in order to locate women and to learn about their lives and contributions to the earliest civilizations. Findings differ as widely as the varied geography, resources, and values of western Asiatic lands themselves.

History is based on the written record, and women's (like men's) earliest records appear along the banks of the great rivers of western Asia—the Nile, the Euphrates, and the Tigris—at about the same time: 3100 B.C. This chapter tells the story of those women's lives from records of their day.

For many decades the modern interpretation of women's roles in the earliest societies was influenced by biblical accounts and by what is known of the classical (Indo-European) cultures of later periods. The celibate philosophers and churchmen who preserved, edited, and handed on the writings and ideologies of these cultures thought of the "male" as norm and paid little heed to what the female half of the population contributed to human and cultural evolution and political history. Only in recent years have scholars taken a fresh look at the earlier ancient western Asiatic documents in order to find women and to evaluate in a thoughtful manner how they lived and what they contributed to the earliest civilizations. The findings are not similar for all of ancient western Asia, however, partly because the lands under discussion varied greatly in geography, resources, and values.

Because they are the writings of men, ancient texts also must be viewed with an eye to possible biases. The same is true of paintings in Egyptian tombs. No longer can they be viewed as windows into an actual world when women are either underrepresented or shown only in the role of entertainer or wife.

Of all the civilizations, Egypt's lasted the longest (three thousand years in the ancient world), but Sumer on the Euphrates passed on aspects of its culture, such as the writing system (cuneiform), artistic and literary themes, and some religious beliefs, to the Semitic peoples who gradually replaced the Sumerians and whose city-states grew into empires further to the north in Mesopotamia. Whereas Egypt enjoyed a unified, wealthy, and stable government under a "divine" monarchy for much of its history, its eastern neighbors, whether in Palestine, the Levant, or Mesopotamia, were generally a fragmented group of small city-states sometimes joined in short-lived confederations under a strong ruler. Interstate warfare was endemic; it was encouraged by poor soil, limited resources, and a perceived need to control waterways and trade routes.

EGYPT

The value system of a group strongly affects the roles and rights of its women. One overriding characteristic of Egypt's eastern neighbors—Babylonia and Assyria especially—was an avid interest in trade and the accumulation of private wealth. In Egypt, however, the divine king and his family (including wives and daughters) oversaw industries, collected taxes from the harvests throughout the country, and controlled natural resources and long distance trade. Thus prestige for people in Egypt depended not so much on material wealth as on a closeness and usefulness to the royal family, which bestowed positions, wealth, and tombs upon their trusted officials. Roles in government demanded literacy, and the literate man, rather than the fighting man, became the most valued citizen in Egypt. Egypt did not even have a professional army until about 1500 B.C. This in turn meant that even great Egyptian generals had themselves depicted in civilian dress and even as scribes. The literate constituted a tiny percentage of the population and used their special knowledge as an insignia of their eliteness, thus excluding most men and women from the government bureaucracy. This affected women especially. The small ancient populations, faced with high infant and child mortality, gave enormous importance to a woman's childbearing ability; motherhood therefore meant prestige for women of all classes.

However, many women worked outside the home, serving in the palace households and its factories. Some women gained status as wet nurses for future kings; others trained and supervised weavers, who were themselves largely women. Female musicians and dancers were very much a part of court and temple life. Among workers, roles tended to be determined by gender, but men and women were also found in some of the same crafts and services. However, because this varied over time, it is difficult to make absolute statements about the activities of women. We are unfortunately dependent, more than we should be, on the view of women held by men who were professional writers and sages. Private letters and legal documents have proved to be the most reliable sources of information on Egyptian women, but since they were written on fragile papyrus paper, very few have survived the centuries. Thus every scrap of evidence is precious in the quest for the ancient woman. At the same time, the possible biases of the original writer and the modern translator and interpreter must be kept in mind.[1]

In a pre-industrial society, all functions, indeed all work, depended on human labor, and children were not only society's future but also their parents' social security, or the "staff of old age," as the Egyptians said. High infant mortality and plagues necessitated large families and frequent pregnancies. Women's role as perpetuator of the family and the nation was of overriding importance. Girls married young, but because of the dangers of childbearing, there was great attrition, and most women did not live to experience menopause. Men, because they lived longer, often had more than one wife serially in this monogamous society. This does not mean that women exercised no power at home or in the greater society, but women's greatest gift to society and her family was understood to be her fertility. Whereas men were depicted in ways that stressed their trade or their literacy and rank in the government, women in ancient Egypt invariably appear in art as sensual, young, and healthy—attributes that suggest their potential as sexual and fecund beings. Deities associated with sex and fertility were very popular, and both men and women served in their temples or brought them votive offerings seeking aid in finding a mate or in conception.

Among the Egyptian elite, both sexes enjoyed important roles in the religious cults, and they often were portrayed in such a way as to indicate their piety or their religious rank (by their recorded titles and cultic implements).

From very early in Egyptian history women enjoyed the same full legal status as men.[2]

Some queens of the first dynasties possessed enormous tombs—as large as kings' tombs—and one, Meritneit, may well have ruled Egypt, at least on behalf of an underaged son. A document of the Second Dynasty stated that a woman did have the right to rule the country. One Fifth Dynasty (ca. 2300 B.C.) tablet, now in Palermo, Italy, records the names of the mothers of some of the first kings of Egypt who reigned centuries before the inscription was carved— surely good evidence for the prime importance of those royal women. Egypt also had five female pharaohs in later centuries: Nitokerty, Sobekneferu, Hatshepsut, Nefertiti, and Tawosret. These were exceptional, however, since the succession traditionally ran from father to son. In order to keep the throne in the ruling family, siblings or half-siblings often married each other, but new men could claim or be given the throne if no royal male heir survived. In that case the newcomer's rule was strengthened by marriage to a daughter or sister of the previous ruler.

In the Old Kingdom (ca. 2686–2181 B.C.) the royal family held all major posts in the government and temples, and the queens recorded their priestly titles in the cults of major deities. The king was acknowledged as the living incarnation of the sky god Horus, and a son of Re, the sun god. His wife was the earthly manifestation of the goddess Hathor, wife of Re. Both kings and principal queens were the only persons originally to enjoy a full panoply of burial equipment that permitted them to unite after death with the gods in the sky: pyramid tombs, solar boats, and magical funerary spells known today as the Pyramid Texts. But after the building of the largest pyramids we find that nonroyalty participated more in the government and in the cults.

Women's Rights

Egyptian women's place was definitely not restricted to the home. Among the nonroyal but elite people of the late Old Kingdom, women were found as priestesses in important cults, and the titles *King's Acquaintance* and *Decorated by the King* were held by many elite women, some of whom were shown in tomb art receiving awards of jewelry from the state.[3]

The state called upon women as well as men for the national service, which means that women worked part of the year in factories or on construction sites as part of the tax program. Thus women were as much citizens as men, and indeed shared equal legal rights. Women were fully independent legal personalities and never needed a legal guardian or cosignatory to enter into any activity such as selling or buying property, adopting, suing, or freeing slaves. Daughters inherited equally with their brothers unless one child could prove that all the burial expense involved with the parent's funeral was born by him or her alone. In this case he or she was entitled to a greater share of the inheritance, unless a parent's will stated that the children should share equally. At the other end of society, paintings depicting agriculture show peasant women working alongside men in the fields, gleaning grain, pulling flax, and carrying heavily loaded baskets. Women were also shown in the marketplace selling and buying—proof of their purchasing power. In the Old and Middle Kingdom, spinning and weaving seem to have been exclusively women's activities; indeed after agriculture, weaving was surely Egypt's most important industry. Egypt's fine and silklike linen cloth was valued throughout the ancient world. It served as a principal commodity of exchange in this barter economy and was used for diplomatic gifts and divine offerings as well as for home consumption. Heavier linen was used for sails and other more utilitarian purposes.

The Egyptians depended upon their king to uphold *ma'at:* the essence of justice and right order in the kingdom and in nature itself. With the belief that their divine ruler could ensure the desired annual flood of the Nile and rich harvests, they felt themselves a secure and elect people. Egypt's nearest neighbors were primitive tribes of the desert to the east and west, and the Old Kingdom had good trading relations with states much further away. With little to fear, Egyptians accomplished much in architecture, engineering, mathematics, and medicine.

In time, the expanding civil service required leaders from outside the ranks of royalty to take on roles. By the beginning of the next major historical period in Egypt, the Middle Kingdom, provincial governors had power and wealth, built fine tombs in their home towns, and commissioned life-sized statues for themselves and their wives in the style of royalty.[4] Even lower-class women and men could acquire the proper religious books, offering tables, and coffins that helped them share in the afterlife, which was once a royal prerogative. The provincial governors also began to imitate royalty by tracing the inheritance of their local rule through the women of their family line. Some women of ranking families were titled "ruler of the city," and some were buried with the staffs and weapons generally associated with men. It may be that the greater autonomy of provincial aristocratic families allowed more flexibility in the powers their members could exercise.

During the Middle Kingdom, women filled a variety of professional positions. On the grand private estates they had responsibilities such as major-domo, sealer, and treasurer. In general, fewer administrative titles appear in the documentary records of the Middle Kingdom than in those of the large central government of the Old Kingdom. However, several titles were recorded that were held in common by both sexes: one such was that of *scribe,* showing that some women were literate. Whether they read from texts or recited stories and myths from memory, women with the title of *reciter* appear in wealthy households; these women provided entertainment while preserving their culture's traditions.[5] The title *Nebet Per,* or "mistress of the house," appears as the title for women of property, and the title that translated as "citizen," *'ankhet en niut,* is believed to designate a free woman. Women could bring suit in court (the sage Ptahhotep warned against contending with one's wife in court), and one Middle Kingdom woman even sued her father. Many prominent men only listed the name of their mother on their monuments. Such mothers were revered and obviously played an important and recognized role in socializing the young. This is stressed by the New Kingdom sage Ani, who also pointed out that wives had skills and feelings that should be respected:

Do not control your wife in her house
When you know that she is excellent
Do not say to her "where is it? Bring (it)!"
When (she) has put it in the best place
Behold her proficiency![6]

On the other hand, men still dominated in the government and perhaps in the home as well. With some notable exceptions, family tombs feature the male head of family far more than anyone else in scenes and inscriptions. A man of renown in his community would boast about how he looked after all weaker folk, including widows, who were at a disadvantage if they had no wealth of their own. Egypt, like every known civilization, was dominated by men. In other words, there was a distinction between women's legal status and their public or social status.[7] The first was firm and the second quite variable. Personalities, personal wealth, or even locale could affect a woman's power, influence, and freedom. Changes in opportunities occurred over the vast span of Egypt's ancient history. For instance, there was a noticeable exclusion of women from the clergy as the Old Kingdom gave way to the Middle Kingdom, and by late in the Twelfth Dynasty, few women outside the royal family held high priestly positions; these had been seized by men.

Royal Women

Royal wives and daughters played important cultic roles and had vital religious functions for the nation, and there is clearly an absence of king's sons from the monuments. Political power could be inherited, as when Sobekneferu survived as the last of her line and became a monarch at the end of the Twelfth Dynasty. At other times, women of the harem might plot to advance their sons over those of the chief queen's. The assassination of Amenemhet I at the beginning of the Twelfth Dynasty was plotted in the harem, and we are told that "women marshaled troops." State *execration* texts (a religious curse) of the Twelfth Dynasty name some Egyptian women as enemies of the state.[8]

A poorly understood but intriguing historical period intervenes between the Middle and New Kingdoms. During this time Egypt was under the rule, at least in the north, of a foreign people who had ties with the Aegean as well as the eastern Mediterranean worlds. These Hyksos rulers tried to adapt to Egyptian ways, but the Upper Egyptians were determined to wrest back the country. They did this with a series of war campaigns in which their womenfolk played vital roles in rallying the troops during desperate times. Years later, the ancestresses of the victorious Eighteenth Dynasty family were repeatedly honored and even deified.[9]

In the New Kingdom (1567 to 1085 B.C.), queens achieved an apogee of power and possessed great wealth in the form of extensive estates. They had their own palaces and administrations that could collect tax revenues. Pharaoh's Great Royal Wife often lived apart from her husband, and some of the most prominent men of the kingdom served her as stewards, tutors, and advisors. Pharaoh had to travel to his consort's palace if he wished her company. As one male scholar has commented rather disparagingly: "Here was matriliny and matrilocal residence with a vengeance!"[10]

While they ruled from the capital of Memphis, at the apex of the Nile Delta, Pharaoh's family turned their home town and local temple in Upper Egypt into the prime religious center of the country. Karnak is the world's largest temple. The queen of Egypt now became the wife of its god Amun-Re, and the holders of this chief sacerdotal role gained in power and independence as time passed. The first god's wife was Ahmose-Nefertari, who had a temple dedicated to her and who was worshiped for generations.

Ahmose-Nefertari's granddaughter, Hatshepsut, was one of the most powerful women of ancient history. The daughter of the great warrior king Thutmose I, who marched Egypt's armies to the banks of the Euphrates River and created the first "world empire" in Egypt's history, Hatshepsut claimed divine sanction and her father's approval when she seized the rule from her royal charge, the young prince Thutmose III, son of her husband's concubine. Hatshepsut was a strong-willed and capable ruler who vigorously continued the policies of her father to strengthen Egypt's defenses. She bolstered the economy through trading expeditions to foreign lands. Contemporary texts tell of her leading Egyptian armies south into Nubia to secure that southern flank (and incidentally ensure the flow of Africa's tribute into Egypt). Her fleet sailed south through the Red Sea to the equatorial African land of Punt (modern Eritrea). Hatshepsut's brilliant reign saw the improvement of Egypt's landscape through many splendid building projects, including her impressive terraced temple at Deir el-Bahri, the greatest surviving monument from antiquity to a woman. Hatshepsut originally intended that her only child and daughter Neferure should succeed her as king, but when the girl died Hatshepsut bowed to political expediency and accepted Thutmose III as her heir. She gave him control of the army; this arrangement did not disturb their cooperative arrangement. Years after his stepmother's death, however, Thutmose attempted to destroy the memory of the woman who had kept him so long in the shadows. He had her figure chiseled from the wall reliefs that decorate her temples.

Later in the dynasty, royal women are again prominent in the records. Queen Tiy, the common-born wife of Amenhotep III, shared in his colossal statuary as an equal figure and also carried on diplomatic correspondence with foreign rulers. This participation by the Great Royal Wife appears again in the next dynasty, when Ramses II and the Hittite ruler in Anatolia concluded a peace treaty with the names of their queens attached to it and with letters exchanged between the royal ladies of both lands. Whether in the realm of religion or in diplomacy, the queens of these leading nations were clearly part of the process of ensuring the welfare of their countries. Indeed, the Hittite consort queens of this period were so important in the realm that they held on to power after the death of their husbands.[11]

The Eighteenth Dynasty continued to produce important women. Queen Tiy's daughter-in-law was the famous beauty Nefertiti, whose career, although imperfectly understood, seems to indicate considerable prominence, not only in the monotheistic sun cult of her husband Akhenaten, but in the government as well. She was a coregent with her husband and may well have succeeded him as a short-reigned pharaoh, since some surviving art of her period depicts her as aging and wearing a crown similar to that of kings.[12]

Such political power for queens was destined to end, however, and a backlash occurred, precipitated by Nefertiti's third daughter, Ankhesenamun. Widowed by Pharaoh Tutankhamun, she tried to stay in command of Egypt by means of an unprecedented political and personal alliance with a prince of the far-off powerful kingdom of the Hittites, Egypt's chief rival in western Asia. The discovery of this plot had unhappy consequences for the ambitious queen, diminishing the glory of the formidably female Eighteenth Dynasty. As if in response, some Nineteenth Dynasty literati wrote satirical pieces that reflect badly on the character of highly placed women.[13] Nevertheless, Pharaoh Ramses II (1304–1237 B.C.) honored his queen Nefertari with a lovely rock-cut temple at Abu Simbel, which was adorned by colossal images of the royal couple. He erected a 31-foot-high statue of his daughter Merytamun at one of his other temples in Middle Egypt. At the end of the Nineteenth Dynasty another queen, Tausert, reigned as pharaoh for a few years.

Other Women in Political and Religious Life

Denied actual positions in the state's bureaucracy, New Kingdom women had to resort to plots and rebellions to have a political role. In the Twentieth Dynasty, palace women retained their ambitions and their influence with others. A harem conspiracy against Ramses III may have ended his life and thirty-year reign. Three papyrus documents tell of this plot and the investigation into it, describing highly placed men who conspired with a secondary queen named Tiy and other women of the harem. A male overseer of the treasury and chief of the chamber apparently carried messages for harem women to their mothers and brothers urging them to gather and incite groups of people to rebellion. The sister of a troop commander in Nubia asked him to return to Egypt and attempt a military insurrection. Surviving records do not clarify whether the plot was successful, but they do record the eventual punishment of accused persons.[14]

From the last years of Ramses III's reign, records show that women of the popular classes participated in the first labor strike in recorded history against this government on behalf of their civil servant husbands. From about the same time comes a record of a highly placed woman in religious circles plotting with a general in the murder of two policemen.

The priesthood became quite professional in the New Kingdom, and priest's wives held both sacerdotal and administrative positions in the temples. Many elite women were chantresses or musicians in temples, serving both gods and goddesses. However, the wives of priests also looked after the gathering, storaging, and arranging of offerings. They headed the choirs and were much involved in temple life. Some records show these women acting authoritatively in the greater community. For instance, one tells of a chief concubine of Amun Re acting on behalf of those civil servants in the royal necropolis who had not received their government pay regularly and who went on strike to protest the fact. There are suggestions that elite women of the New Kingdom had the leisure time to become educated, and there is the distinct possibility that some daughters of priests were among those who edited and painted the miniature vignettes for the Books of the Dead that Egyptian temples sold to any who could afford these collections of spells that would help them gain entrance into the blessed hereafter.[15] In the villages, "knowing women," diviners or shamans, played an important, if poorly documented, community role, helping to solve problems, find missing items, and aiding the sick.[16]

During the first millennium B.C., daughters of the royal family attained higher ecclesiastical powers than ever before. While the political capital remained in the north of the country, a princess was sent south to be her father's representative in Upper Egypt. She ruled from the temple of Karnak, seat of Amun-Re, king of the gods, as a celibate *pontifix maximus*, overseeing all cultic matters and temple personnel and, in general, maintaining the greatest temple in the world. The title of *god's wife of Amun* had been borne by either queens or princesses beginning in the Eighteenth Dynasty, but under none, so far as we know, had the position assumed so independent and political a role as now in the Twenty-third Dynasty under the Libyan-descended rulers of Egypt. King Osorkon III (777–749 B.C.), the fourth king of that dynasty, transferred estates and property away from the high priest of Amun to the "god's wife" and consecrated his own daughter in that office. She would ensure her succession by adopting a successor who would carry the title *divine adoratrice*. These women, whose line spanned many reigns of this and subsequent dynasties, were a source of moral and political stability and leadership in the South, where they would probably have won credibility and loyalty from the Upper Egyptians far more readily than any military prince. Judging from texts and iconography, these women enjoyed many perquisites of a ruling monarch, including great wealth and large administrative staffs.

In religious matters, the "god's wife" was very like a female pope who ruled by the word of Amun and the transmission of his oracle. The one who reigned the longest was Nitocris, a daughter of King Psammetichus or Psamtik of the Twenty-sixth Dynasty, a new royal line that came to power following both Kushite and Assyrian invasions of Egypt. This young princess was escorted from the Delta to Thebes with a large flotilla of boats and a large dowry. Her vast wealth was administered for her by a major-domo appointed by her father (and thus answerable to him for major expenditures). However, once her father died, Nitocris appointed her own men who were loyal to her: men of Upper Egypt whom she knew. This independent woman reigned for over fifty years without even adopting a successor and in that way kept the kings of Egypt from exerting influence in the South. Finally, in 594 B.C., when she was in her eighties, Nitocris adopted her great niece Ankhnesneferibre, who was given the title of first prophet (or high priest) of Amun, the only woman known to have held this high clerical office. This was another indication of the interest that Nitocris had in keeping her high ecclesiastic staff at Karnak female.[17]

How the more ordinary ancient woman confronted and participated in power is interesting as well. This issue can be explored through legal documents like wills (one Twentieth-Dynasty woman disinherited half of her children for not looking after her in old age) and by resorting to court records, where women testified in important state tribunals, such as those that investigated the robbing of royal tombs during the Twenty-first Dynasty.[18] These show that women were treated exactly like men; that is, they were questioned under torture. The female testifiers were quite bold and verbose in their answers to questions, and some exhibited considerable *sang-froid* although under oath and subject to the terrible punishment of impalement if found guilty.

There also survive some remarkable letters in which women administrators (in weaving factories) addressed the king himself, either complaining of his lack of support or boasting of their abilities.[19] Indeed, the bold rhetoric of the women stands in sharp contrast to what was urged by the instructional texts that taught school boys proper speech, etiquette, and how to get ahead in the world of the bureaucrats.[20]

Love and Marriage

Love poetry first appeared in the New Kingdom along with a new class of wealthy and literate knights, some of whom composed courtly love poetry that treated a lady as an object of veneration.[21] Adoration and respect for high-ranking women may also be seen in a letter written by an officer to his deceased wife. In this letter he recalls to her how his young charioteers used to come and prostrate themselves before her and bring her many pretty gifts.

The husband also tells his wife that, in proof of his devotion to her memory, he has abstained from sexual relations for three years after her death.[22] The respect shown the lady in question by her husband's subordinates was due to her husband's rank, yet it also shows that wives in Egypt were not secluded or kept apart from male company. Tomb paintings depict banquets attended by women as well as men.

The Egyptian language had no word for virginity, and ancient Egyptian love songs suggest a free mingling of young men and women prior to marriage: love affairs with the boy next door and secret trysts in a garden or field. After marriage, loyalty was expected, and murder might be sanctioned in the case of any couple caught in adultery. However, documents reveal that divorce more often followed. Either a man or woman could initiate divorce, and a wife was entitled to receive support from her husband even if she initiated the divorce and left his house. If the husband repudiated his wife, the law compelled him to grant her that part of his wealth that had been pledged upon marriage to her, except in cases of adultery. Often brides were in a better position economically than their husbands because a woman received a dowry from her parents, which represented her possible inheritance, and she was free to handle wealth independently. Meanwhile her husband had to wait for his parents to die to gain his inheritance. Since Egyptians of both sexes tended to marry young, the wife might be the wealthier of the two for a number of years. The expression used for marriage was *gereg per*, "to establish a house," and young couples could set off on their own rather than move into the household of one of their parents.

Wives shared everything acquired by the husband and inherited one-third of the estate at his death, with children receiving two-thirds. If no children survived, a husband could "adopt" his wife legally to make her his sole heir and recipient of his entire estate. Of course, many couples were poor and, in an agricultural community, probably lived with parents and other relatives in one household so that they could better manage their farm. This is reflected in letters surviving from a Middle Kingdom household that show that each member of the extended family received a salary.[23]

Marriages among people of property were often documented by property settlements or marriage contracts. Sometimes deeds of marriage dated from years after a couple had lived together and brought children into the world, so that such a document could serve as important proof of a settlement on behalf of the wife and her children. In this way the rights of those children would be protected after their mother's death against the claims of any other progeny of their father. A grandmother's marriage document might serve years later as proof of a family's rightful claim to property. Two documents, each concerning settlement of a wife's property, survive from the late New Kingdom (Twentieth Dynasty). In the first, a husband made a settlement of his own property on his wife at the time of their marriage. In the case of his death or their divorce, his wife kept this property. The second document concerned the case of a father who settled two-thirds of his estate upon his daughter on the occasion of her marriage. She and her husband shared this property but were later divorced. The woman retained half of the settlement, although her father went on record as saying she should have received more. The most advantageous arrangement for a bride developed around 563 B.C. with the *sankh* deed, which obligated the husband to provide a regular income for his wife. She gave him a substantial sum, repayable on demand, and as security the husband pledged his entire wealth. Such a marriage could not terminate without the wife's agreement.[24] This may have been the policy that horrified a Greek traveler in Egypt in the first century B.C. Diodorus Siculus shook a disapproving head over marriage among the Egyptians when he told his readers, "The wife lords it over the husband, as in the deed about the dower, the men agree to obey the wife in everything" (Diod. 1,27,2).

Certainly, a woman did maintain her status as a completely independent legal personality and did not give up her rights to her husband upon marriage. After the conquest of Egypt by Alexander the Great in 323 B.C., two parallel legal systems functioned in the country—the original Egyptian and the imported Greek. One crucial difference between the two was that under the Egyptian system a woman continued to hold the same position as the Egyptian man, whereas under the Greek system a woman required a guardian in order to perform many legal acts. Whether in the marketplace, at labor service, on the picket line, or at social events, the Egyptian woman, throughout her history, took her place beside her menfolk. The Greek author Herodotus, who traveled to Egypt in the mid–fifth century B.C., was so struck by the oddity of seeing women in public that he scoffed: "The Egyptians themselves, in their manners and customs, seem to have reversed the ordinary practices of mankind. For instance, women attend market and are employed in trade, while men stay at home and do the weaving" (Book II, 35). Thus it is clear that Egyptian women continued to enjoy a basic equality with men regardless of differences in work or occupation. Several factors could have contributed to the Egyptian woman's equal status, including the basic optimistic and secure outlook of the Egyptian people, the preservation and respect for age-old traditions, and the state's official view that women could be depended upon to perform useful work for the greater society outside the home.

In retrospect, the ancient Egyptian woman stands out as the first documented example of relative equality. Although not totally equal, these ancient women provide important precedents for today's goals. Records themselves are sparse, but when they are available they reveal evidence of active lives outside the home, equal legal status, and leadership positions in religion and in the work force with authority over others.

On the other hand, women were kept out of the civil bureaucracy, and when royal women actually gained control of the supreme power in the land, resentment arose, manifested in attempts to erase the memory of that female rule. The defacement of Hatshepsut's monuments and the official eradication of Nefertiti's memory demonstrate the threat men felt when women took power in the political arena and strove to fill roles traditionally played by males. These Egyptian women ruled during relatively secure times, and other women pharaohs took command in times of crisis, perhaps when no man wished for responsibilities in what seemed impossible economic or political situations. It is gratifying to find women at the helm of the world's most powerful nation, but one must recall that ancient Egypt's history is 3000 years long, and the female examples of pharaonic rule remain in the distinct minority. However, even the desecrations of monuments did not totally eradicate historical memory, and a thousand years after they died, the female rulers of the Eighteenth Dynasty were still found in the records used by the historian Manetho.

Egypt endured as a practical and successful civilization for so long that the amount of source material for it far exceeds that from the shorter-lived civilizations of Sumer, Old Babylonia, or Assyria. However, turning away from Africa toward western Asia and societies contemporary with ancient Egypt can further elucidate women's earliest history. The other peoples, the Sumerians, Babylonians, and Assyrians, are introduced for purposes of comparison and therefore will receive briefer treatment.

WESTERN ASIA: AN INTRODUCTION

The vast area of the "fertile crescent," encompassing the eastern Mediterranean coast and its forested mountains, southern Iraqi swamplands, fertile river valleys, deserts, and northern steppe, saw the arrival of numerous peoples of varying ethnolinguistic backgrounds and several short-lived empires. Some basic similarities in technology and customs were pervasive in the area. For example, the scarcity of timber led to the wide use of mud brick for building and writing material. When baked, the small inscribed tablets became indestructible nuggets of information. The family and society were more blatantly patriarchal than in Egypt, although the degrees of this male dominance in the family varied. It may be seen in the description of institutions like marriage from a man's point of view: marriage was called "the taking of a wife" (rather than the establishment of a house, as in Egypt). Marriage was arranged between senior males of the two families, and the placing of a monetary value on the virginity of the bride was also characteristic of western Asiatic society, as was the view that adultery is only a female crime and punishable by death. Marriage was often monogamous, but many western Asiatic cultures used the Levirate for a widow, which, by forcing her to marry her dead husband's kin, helped keep the line of her dead husband alive and his estate within his family. The importance of accumulating private fortunes marked the societies of western Asia, and primogeniture, or an advantage in inheritance going to the eldest son, is also marked. Generally women were regarded as the purer of the sexes and were given the duty to care for their family's gods and pray for their kin's welfare.

Although hundreds of thousands of clay tablets have been recovered by archeologists from western Asiatic sites, many have not been published, at least not in translation, and until recently relatively few have been studied for the information they can supply on ancient women's roles and rights.[25] The most spectacular archeological finds, like royal burials, often provoke more questions than answers.[26] Although new publications of the last decade have contributed to a better understanding of Sumerian women, a trustworthy picture has not yet emerged, and thus the following reconstruction is subject to future adjustments and additions.

SUMER

Sumer, on the Euphrates River in what is now Iraq, had four major city-state groupings in the third millennium B.C. There was frequent intercity warfare, at least during the middle centuries. From the records it is clear that through-out the third millennium B.C. elite women (the wives and daughters of Sumer's rulers and high officials) owned real estate and maintained their own households and estates, with complex administrations of their own.[27] Records indicate that, at least at the top levels of society, women had the same legal rights as men and went to court to protect them.

The wife of the Sumerian city ruler was definitely active in the economic life of her city and thus played a public role. At the city-state of Lagash, its first lady, as well as being a major property owner (possessing fields, orchards, livestock, and slaves), oversaw commodity transactions in wool, leather, gold, and grain. This was comparable to the rights of Egyptian royal women, who also collected taxes, and may have been widespread. A Sumerian governor's wife definitely had a religious cultic role to play in the temples of her city-state, just as did royal wives and daughters and governor's wives in Egypt.

That private property emerged early on is clear from deeds of sale of both fields and houses. The household was the basic unit of society in Sumer, and it was the mother of the family who processed and stored the food and cloth-ing or oversaw a staff of servants if the family were wealthy. Private land-holdings appeared among all classes of society; even the humblest owned houses and gardens, although land belonging to ordinary citizens, actually belonged to the larger family unit rather than to any individual member.

Certainly many women did lead lives outside the confines of their homes. Among the laborers, large numbers of women were organized in groups work-ing under a female supervisor (as weavers in the house of the governor's wife, for instance), and they apparently took their young children to work with them.[28] Thousands of women were involved in weaving, but they also milled flour, pressed olive oil, and produced pottery. Free women, not slave laborers, have been called the backbone of the Sumerian industries. Women in Sumer worked outdoors in agriculture, dug irrigation canals, and towed boats.

Even if such women were deemed capable of doing what we regard as "men's work," they were paid less than men. Perhaps this indicates that some women had slave status, because many war captives were put to work for the state institutions. Sumerian records are difficult to interpret because the language often does not distinguish between masculine and feminine names, nor does it exhibit gendered pronouns. This may indicate an original sense of equality between the sexes. Women were employed outside the home in large numbers, and widows could head the household, at least if their children were young. On the other hand, among the poor, wives and even mothers could be sold into slavery to pay off debts incurred by their menfolk.[29] Obviously, great differences existed among women according to their social class. Besides working for estates of the governor and his wife, many people in the city-state, both men and women, worked for the temple and its resident deity, while the temple in its turn supported the skilled artisans and craftspeople. Women could also participate in the cult as musicians and singers in temples and palaces.

Marriage

Once private property became an issue, marriage became an economic concern for the clan or family, and a betrothal, arranged by parents, was often sealed officially by a contract inscribed on a tablet. However, a Sumerian proverb speaks of a young girl having the right to choose her own spouse, and love songs suggest freedom of association between young men and women, as in Egypt. Other texts reveal that an older woman, as a legal adult, could marry the man of her own choice. A bride received a gift of jewelry from the groom and a dowry from her parents. The groom's family brought food provisions to the wedding; the concept of paying for the bride was unknown to the Sumerians. A wife could be divorced on very slim grounds, however, and, if she did not bear children, her husband was allowed to take a second wife.[30] As was true of other ancient western Asiatic societies, women's independence shows up in economic matters but not in family life.

In some respects, a woman in Sumer had certain legal rights equivalent to those of the men of her society. She might own property, engage in business, and act as a witness for legal documents. As private property increased, however, so did debts. The temple, a source of financing, made loans at high interest. To pay off those debts, parents often resorted to selling their children into slavery to the local temple for up to three years of labor. Daughters were more often liable to be so sold because a son was expected to train for, and inherit, his father's trade and was therefore more essential to the family's future.

Women in Political and Religious Life

As changes in the economy seriously affected women's freedom, so did changes in political life. War became increasingly common among the Sumerian city-states as populations expanded and disputes arose over water and boundary rights. These crises brought about a demand for a permanent and strong leadership, and kingship as an institution soon appeared in Kish and then in Uruk and Ur. Once monarchy appeared, royal women helped legitimate the king's succession to the throne. Lists of rulers compiled later remain the only historical records of the earliest reigns, but in some of the oldest cities the highest officeholders were listed, along with their fathers *and* their wives. A ruler of Umma claimed that city by virtue of his marriage to the daughter of a previous ruler. Two successive queens of Lagash held their own court and had their own ministers and attendants. They dated documents by the year of their own reigns (as kings did), and one of these queens kept up a diplomatic exchange with the king's wife of another city-state. Each had her own official seals, as did the queens of Ur.[31]

The first woman ruler known in western Asiatic history—Ku-bau—ruled the city of Kish in its Third Dynasty (ca. 2450 B.C.). That she began her career as a tavern keeper or "alewife" indicates not only the existence of private enterprise for women but also the height to which an ordinary woman could rise within her community. However, as happened in Egypt, after her death the reign of this woman was disparaged.

Some women reached high status in religious life as female priestesses serving male deities (and male priests served goddesses). At Ur the richest of the so-called royal graves, which feature the remains of numerous male and female retainers slain to accompany their deceased mistress, probably belonged to the priestesses who served Ur's moon god. The elaborate graves of these ranking women at Ur clearly demonstrate their predominance in that early state where cult and daily life were tightly intermeshed.

In time, the emergence of permanent kingship in response to continuing crises changed ordinary women's status in Sumer. Royalty grew in wealth and abused its tax-gathering privileges. Before long, however, the citizens' militia gave way to a standing army loyal to the king, which was supplied with a heavily armed chariotry and supported by a regular system of tax collecting. Next private property became more heavily taxed, and the crown appropriated temple lands to support the king and his expensive policies. The redistribution of wealth that ensued led to sharp social stratification and ultimately to a class struggle. The class of commoners was reduced to the status of clients of the palace or a nobleman's estate, reducing some free citizens to debt slavery. Fortunately, a good ruler, in the person of Uru'inimgina of Lagash, arose, who determined to re-establish "divine law," or a just way of conducting the affairs of his kingdom. He removed tax collectors and unjust administrators and gave the temples back their old lands. Under his reforms, citizens imprisoned for debts went free and the desperate plight of orphans and widows received the king's attention. Among his reform statements was an enigmatic reference to women having once had two husbands at a time, a practice he now prohibited. This reference conjures up visions of unusual sexual freedoms permitted to women in earlier Sumerian society; this same king also passed a severe penalty against women saying certain banned or evil words to men.[32]

Woman could not bear arms, but in times of crisis they stayed at home tending the children, the sick, and the wounded. They were not trained to defend the city or their family's private property. In times of crisis, then, the women's status slipped to that of dependent, to be protected along with property by a professional military elite.

AKKAD

The reformer Uru'inimgina in time fell victim to the imperialistic ambitions of the ruler of the state of Umma, and this strong man was in turn conquered by the first true empire builder in world history—Sargon of the Semitic city of Akkad to the north of Sumer. He ushered in a number of social, religious, and artistic changes that had lasting significance in ancient western Asia. We know little about this Sargon or how he accomplished his successes, although he seems to have had a high regard for women and for goddesses, at least for Ishtar, whom he credited for his rise to power. Especially interesting is his enlightened attitude toward his daughter, Enheduanna, whom he appointed as chief priestess of the gods at the cities of Ur and Uruk. Sargon entrusted her not only with high religious responsibilities but also with representing his authority in conquered territory; in this way he sealed the cultural and political union of the Akkadians and Sumerians.[33]

One Sumerologist called Enheduanna "the first systematic theologian." An intelligent woman who took her position seriously, the princess became proficient in the Sumerian language. She may have written at least two great cycles of Sumerian hymns and started a collection of Babylonian hymns dedicated to her father's patron goddess Ishtar. As demanded by her office, the priestess-princess remained celibate, but the practice of kings sharing responsibility with these royal princesses continued for many years in Sumer and Akkad. As in Egypt during the first millennium with the "god's wife of Amun," priestesses outlasted some rulers and proved to be a force for continuity and unity in the realm. Thirteen royal priestesses followed Enheduanna over the next five hundred years. Each held the office for life.

The earliest extant list of female professions from Sumer (ca. 2400 B.C.) names prostitutes along with scribes, doctors, and cooks, with no apparent stigma attached. Originally, the prostitutes may have been exclusively cultic, that is, employed by the temples, where the entire populace celebrated the annual sacred marriage rite between the city's ruler and goddess. Like the

Egyptians, the Sumerians had viewed sexuality and procreation as mystical and even divine acts and the sexual embracing of the high priestess by the ruler of the city-state was a vital civic duty to ensure bounteous harvests and prosperity for all. The *Epic of Gilgamish* attributes a civilizing effect to a harlot who cohabited with the barbarian "wild man" and thus humanized him and instilled him with wisdom. In time, however, attitudes about prostitution changed, possibly with its increasing commercialization and spread, and perhaps the result of the desperate indebtedness that befell many families after the rise of kingship and its severe taxation. Society's first attempts to regulate women's sexual life appear in the reform text of Uru'inimgina and continue with intensity in the law code of Hammurabi, the Babylonian ruler.

From the end of the history of the Sumerians comes the extensive legal text composed of the judgments of the last king of the city-state of Isin, who speaks of seeking to establish justice for the daughters and sons of the cities.[34] This judicial code ranks as the first full surviving text pertaining to family law. Old Sumerian practices continued: a daughter inherited and lived in her father's house if she remained unmarried; children inherited equally; a mother's dowry passed to her children; and a childless wife could not be set aside in favor of another. Neither childless wives nor divorced wives could be forced out; they were owed support from their former husbands, even if the husbands remarried.

In the code of Eshnunna, another Sumerian city-state of this period, the law also protected women against unjust husbands.[35] If a man divorced a wife by whom he had children, the law stated: "He shall be driven from his house and from whatever he owns." In this law code, a man convicted of the rape of a betrothed girl or a married woman was sentenced to death, as was a wife caught in adultery or a husband found in a homosexual relationship. A raped slave girl won the recompense of a payment in silver. A prostitute who bore a child to an otherwise childless man would get his support—food and clothing—but would not be allowed to share the domicile with his legal wife. In general, fines formed the punishments in these codes, but the king decided the punishment in capital offenses.

It appears that this society divided along class lines. Men and women of the same class had some similar rights and opportunities, but people of lower classes did not enjoy as many privileges. If a class system is very much in evidence here, so is the state's intrusion into private matters in order to protect and regulate private lives.

THE AMORITE KINGDOMS OF BABYLONIA AND ASSYRIA

Sumerians as a cultural group disappeared from history early in the second millennium after a combination of catastrophes that included famine and invasion from Iran. Meanwhile, in the north large cities were prospering, homes to sophisticated populations of the Semitic language. These people engaged in long-distance trade and manufacturing. They were kin to the Amorite sheiks from the steppes who conquered the old city-states of Sumer and Akkad and established dynasties. Texts by the thousands have been recovered from Ebla, but it is the city of Mari that has been known long enough for scholars to have deciphered and studied its texts. The site of Mari on the middle Euphrates yields significant information about Amorite women in public life, especially from the letters of the royal family from the eighteenth century B.C. Included are letters from female relatives and acquaintances of the king who hold honors and influence in the kingdom. Such status, however, depended upon the goodwill of the king, who maintained a patriarchal rule that reflected his tribal heritage. Generally, male functionaries had charge of the administration of the land; all actual authority was in the hands of the king. Male correspondence predominates in the Mari archive, often peppered with disparaging remarks about the weak and unheroic character of women. Nevertheless, two powerful administrators at Mari were the king's chief wife, Sabitu, and the intelligent and capable official Addudirri. The queen appears to have been designated by her husband as a substitute for him during his prolonged absences; as such, she played a significant role as quasi-official head of state and was active in palace, religious, and governmental affairs. Secondary wives administered at lesser palaces, overseeing the concubines of their royal husbands. At Mari domestic concerns were largely left to highly placed women in the royal household while the king and his men fought many an armed and diplomatic battle.[36]

Economic Implications for Women

This period illustrates new developments in the status of women and documents the re-emergence of private property and a middle class based on trade unconnected to temple or palace. Independent merchants carrying on long-distance trade increased in numbers, but family farms, inns, and small businesses of various types flourished. Private fortunes increased.

To conserve their wealth, the families of the newly propertied classes came up with an ingenious solution. Under an earlier social system that sent their daughters to other men's households equipped with a sizable dowry, fathers had often lost a good part of their fortunes. Since a mother's dowry property passed to her children, the marriage of several daughters seriously depleted a father's holdings. To avoid this, prominent families dedicated one or more daughters to be "brides of the god" of their city. Young women inducted into cloisters under the supervision of clergy lived chaste, celibate lives until death.[37] To be sure, they received dowries, as in any marriage arrangement, but these *naditu* women died without issue and their dowry did not pass into the temple's treasury but reverted back to their own families. These women pursued business themselves, leasing land and loaning out their money at good interest, and this income added to the original dowry and eventually enlarged the family fortune. Clearly the daughters of the capitalist and royal families were subordinated to the commercial interests of those families. Freed from the burdens of childrearing, however, such *naditu* women could participate more fully in economic activities and often enjoyed longer-than-average life spans. Many had time to learn to read and write, as is evidenced by the correspondence of women who served as scribes in the cloister at the great commercial city of Sippar. Among the celibate priestesses, the daughter of the king of Uruk wrote a long letter that became a classic text for use in schools. Women filled some secular positions too: a woman doctor practiced at the palace at Larsa, and at Mari a female administrative assistant served the king.

Legal Changes Affecting Women

The political predominance of the Semitic people in Mesopotamia brought about cultural changes with far-reaching outcomes. The widespread notion of a hopeless hereafter not only meant that grave goods—food, weapons, jewelry buried with the dead—disappeared, but may well account for harsher penalties in the law code. The Babylonian elaboration upon the Sumerian Gilgamish epic stresses the finality of death, holding out no hope of eternal life for mankind (tablet 10). This Semitic-speaking people's lack of faith in a final judgment with good rewarded and evil punished may help explain why their law codes stand out as so much harsher than the Sumerians', and why monetary fines were replaced by corporal punishment.

The most famous collection of legal pronouncements from ancient western Asia is that of Hammurabi of Babylon, successor to a family line established by an Amorite chieftain who had come to power in the region of old Ur around 1894 B.C. Hammurabi (1792–1750 B.C.) exerted his control over a number of city-states and by his thirtieth year of reign claimed sovereignty over all of ancient Sumer and Akkad. His legal text of 280 judgments attributed to the sun god dealt with both civil and criminal law and sought to protect the weak from the strong.[38] It differs markedly from earlier codes of the Sumerian tradition by introducing the principle of *lex talionis* (eye for an eye; tooth for a tooth), which was based on the more conservative law of the desert. Hammurabi tried to establish fair dealing among the people of his kingdom and to protect the rights of women to their property (forbidding its use by a husband or father to pay his debts). The code acknowledged a wife's or daughter's right to receive an inheritance from a male relative if he willed it to her. A mother's dowry automatically descended to her children. As with the Sumerians, a marriage was legally solemnized and recorded with a deed, and the bride received a dowry from her father and gifts from her intended. The code affirmed her right to keep property even in cases of divorce, and this might well befall her if she could not bear children, unless she adopted children when faced with childlessness.

In their rights to inherit and own property and to testify in court, women enjoyed the same advantages as men. The code reveals a definite class system, however; for instance, the wife of a wealthy free man was protected, not only from the disrespectfulness of his concubine, but even from the maliciousness of the town gossip, whereas the wives of poor men could be sold into slavery for up to three years to pay off a husband's debts. Still, a woman who could demonstrate to the authorities just cause for leaving a husband had hope of a legal separation supported by the return of her dowry, but a widow who wished to remarry, if she had young children, had to gain the consent of judges, who first investigated the late husband's estate and then formally granted the right. This was to protect the children of the first marriage and ensure their rights of inheritance. By contrast, the children of a poor debtor could be sold into slavery. The code reveals a definite class structure as well as a deep ambivalence toward woman's capacities and her societal role.

Apparently face-saving was very important for husbands; if a wife embarrassed him, she could be divorced. If the husband proved that his wife had been adulterous, she could be killed; if she had been a spendthrift, she could be divorced and given no settlement. If she wished to engage in business on her own, this too was deemed a humiliation to her husband; the wife had to leave him in order to have her independence, and she forfeited her divorce settlement. It is possible that those women who still engaged in business were widows who no longer had to fear a husband's or society's disapproval. Later Neo-Babylonian texts reveal that women generally married as teenagers men about ten years older, and that the average life span during the Babylonian Empire was about 55 years. Thus, if a woman was widowed around the age of 45, she still had a good ten years or more in which to handle her estate on her own.[39] A wife accused by another of adultery, even though known to be innocent, had to throw herself into the river "for the sake of her husband" (for his good name?), but if accused only by her husband she need take only an oath of innocence, unless he could prove otherwise. Respectability was legislated for the upper classes, and women maintained their respectability at the cost of self-expression and freedom. A definite double standard of sexual behavior had emerged.[40]

On the whole, the judgments of Hammurabi startle the modern reader by their severity. For instance, if a pregnant woman died after being struck by a man, that man's daughter could be put to death, just as could the son of a builder if his building collapsed and killed another's son. The principle of an eye for an eye and a tooth for a tooth extended to families, not just individuals.

Assyria: Patriarchy in Extreme

One society, however, does stand out for its repression of women: the Assyrians, who were another people of western Semitic stock who dominated northern Syria from their capital Assur on the northern Tigris river. Hammurabi's ideas of justice seem enlightened when compared to the cruel intolerance and misogyny evident in the Assyrian law codes.[41] These codes seem obsessed with subjugating women to men.

A vigorous mercantile people, the Assyrians maintained foreign trading colonies, and during the second half of the second millennium Assyria often went to war to open up or protect trade routes. In the first millennium the Assyrians founded an empire that reached briefly to Egypt. Because of the tremendous influx of war captives, chattel slavery became a highly significant economic factor during this era and during the subsequent Neo-Babylonian era of the first millennium B.C. These societies also saw the development of the greatest commercial centers in history up to this time.

From the beginning, the Assyrian kingdom was vulnerable to invasion on three fronts, and its survival depended on ceaseless military vigilance. Records are more plentiful for its later history, when the brutality of the Neo-Assyrians in war was proverbial and brought vilification in the Hebrew Bible. Even their art had a remarkable brute strength: its human and animal forms are heavy and muscular, and the themes of warfare and lion hunts predominate on the bas reliefs at the palaces of Nineveh and Nimrud. Assyrians expressed little, if any, faith in a future life beyond the grave.

Economics and Women's Rights

The importance of commerce in this society colored official attitudes, which regarded women as the property of men. Girls did not inherit from their parents, but parents received payment for the young daughters they gave in marriage. Girls were married during their teens, but were possibly betrothed much earlier. Men married at a later age, and thus husbands always enjoyed a distinct superiority over their wives. The young Assyrian bride was a passive object in an agreement between her father and the groom's father. Indeed, marriages resembled business alliances between two families, with the virginity of the daughter gaining her father a handsome price. It is not surprising that Levirate marriage, which preserved the integrity of a man's estate and household, prevailed among the Assyrians. Because betrothals were prolonged, a girl betrothed to a man who died had to marry his father or brother, even if this meant that she became a secondary wife.

Unlike her other western Asiatic sisters, Assyrian women could not own property. Even goods brought into a marriage could be taken away by the husband and given to whomever he pleased. If a woman's husband divorced her, she had to leave everything behind, including their children. A wife could be held responsible for her husband's debts, and a daughter could be enslaved with no time limit to pay for her father's debts. A wife left abandoned because of her husband's disappearance had to wait five years before remarrying.

When a woman was the victim of crime, she still suffered at the hands of justice. An unmarried woman who had been raped could be given to her tormentor in marriage, presumably because her monetary value to her family was now diminished through loss of her virginity. The rapist of a virgin was punished by his own wife being ravished by his victim's father; the rapist of a married woman was put to death. Casual romantic attention paid by a man to another's wife could mean his disfigurement, and adultery meant death to both parties.

Regulation of Female Sexuality

In a society where women were not entrusted with wealth, Assyrian women were totally dependent upon their menfolk, and the state concerned itself with regulating women's sexuality as well as their status. There were laws against abortion that carried the penalty of impalement on a stake with no burial after death and a law mandating the veiling of all respectable women. Respectable women were defined as those under the protection of a man—wives, daughters, concubines, and even the maids of married ladies. The veil (unknown among the Egyptians and Sumerians) became an enforced badge of respectability and social standing. Women not under a man's protection went unveiled in public places and, like slave women and professional prostitutes, were fair game for all comers. Men attempting to protect these "non-respectable" women by veiling them were themselves severely and publicly punished. Thus the state tried to discourage anything but the most casual of encounters with such women, possibly as a way to make marriage essential for all women and would-be respectable men. The placing of a monetary value on virginity may be read in two ways: either it made a transferable commodity out of a daughter, or it was the society's way of protecting young women from incestuous rape, since it was to her family's advantage for her to be a virgin in order to command the highest price in a marriage contract.

Surviving Assyrian antiwitchcraft literature shows that this society considered women to be far more prone to sorcery than men. The average Assyrian woman's social role was so circumscribed that any activity outside familial controls was suspect.[42]

It seems likely that meaningful relationships of all types could only be built between members of the same sex in such a segregated society. Assyrian society, which like ancient Greece was exclusively obsessed with male importance, even had corps of male prostitutes. This is revealing, not only of Assyrian male's sexual preferences, but of the complete absence of women from all types of social life outside the home. It speaks of the dehumanizing effect of the arranged marriage system, in which personal choice may not have figured even for prospective grooms.[43] Never before had a civilization commanded so narrow a role for its average free woman, rendering her completely dependent on the males of her family. Where the norm—a repressive, patriarchal double standard in which women had almost no civil rights—is so extreme, the causes are correspondingly evident: the vital importance of trade and wealth enhanced conservative patriarchic attitudes inherited from the nomadic past, and a highly sophisticated military organization made possible such a strictly regulated society.

After some political setbacks, the Assyrian empire underwent rapid expansion and spread over the entire "fertile crescent" westward to include Egypt (between 934 and 610 B.C.). The Neo-Assyrian rulers claimed to be the heirs in unbroken succession of the earlier Assyrian state. The state was made up of peasants, slaves, and a noble class from which both civic and military officials were drawn. That women had a bit more freedom of movement under this powerful state than that which wrote the earlier Middle Assyrian law code may be guessed from the claim of Ashurnasirpal that he invited women as well as men to his banquet for tens of thousands celebrating the inauguration of his new palace city of Kalhu (Nimrud). The king had several wives, but they were not often portrayed.

It was the king's mother who usually exerted the greatest power and influence in this and other ancient western Asiatic kingdoms. Not only did she command the legions of palace workers, but she had the ear of her son and thus considerable unofficial power. A queen-mother was important as a protector of the proper succession, and two famous queens are known from Neo-Assyrian history: Shammuramat/Semiramis early in the reign of Adadnirari III, and Naqi'a-Zakutu, mother of Esarhaddon and grandmother of Ashurbanipal. They used their influence to ward off possible dynastic crises and to ensure the proper succession of the heirs apparent. The latter caused the court and royal family to renew their oaths of loyalty to uphold Ashurbanipal's right to accede to the Assyrian throne in 668 B.C.

ANCIENT ISRAEL

For Israel, social historians have as source material bountiful writings by the "People of the Book." The texts of the Hebrew Bible include several literary genres—proverbs and hymns, sermons and instructions, law and history—that span almost one thousand years. Not surprisingly, the texts reveal some diversity in attitudes about women, yet all reflect the male point of view of their writers. Thus some researchers have recently turned to archeology and the reconstruction of private households for insights into women's lives.[44]

The Israelites by the late thirteenth century B.C. inhabited the hill country on both sides of the Jordan River. They supported themselves by farming and pasturing. Warfare with other peoples in the region and along the coastal plain dominated their history. Poor agricultural land contributed to the frail economic state of the nation, which remained on the defensive or dependent on a more powerful neighbor and at the mercy of the armies of the conquerors who crossed the region over the centuries. Assyria conquered the northern tribes in 722 B.C. and Babylon the southern tribes in 587 B.C. Even periods of strong centralized rule, as in the tenth century under King David, who founded the capital, created a standing army, and forced the quarrelsome tribes into a united kingdom, were marked by political coups. For example, his successor Solomon came to power by means of a harem conspiracy. Poor land and fragmentation constantly plagued the Israelites. Occasional weak leadership by authorities meant that prophets did not hesitate to berate kings.

Religious law handed down by Moses was the basis of this society. While mothers were revered and were doubtless the socializers of the young and the managers of the household, membership in the greater society, whether in the sociopolitical or religious realms, fell exclusively to men. Only men were deemed responsible individuals in public life and, as such, were considered responsible for the acts of their dependents. When the "people" were exhorted, as when Moses warned them not to approach a woman lest they be defiled before a religious act, only males were addressed. The rite of male circumcision was of central importance. Purity laws, which deemed a woman impure for seven days each month (Lev. 12:1; 15:18–33), made the priesthood a male profession (Exod. 23:17; 28:1), as did the especially long and complex postparturient purification that followed each pregnancy. Home provided the only environment in which the women of the Hebrew Bible functioned. Only there, as the mother of children, did she exercise her authority over others, but she remained always subject to the authority of some male relative. While theologians disdained the old fertility cults, this society gave reverence to the reproductive role of its mortal women.[45]

The Hebrew Bible (Prov. 31:10) describes the "good wife" as industrious, prudent, wise, and gracious. She taught her children, produced the food and clothing for her family, helped the poor, and, through her virtue, enhanced her husband's reputation. Regarded as a natural and god-ordained helpmate, the good wife was called the "crown of her master." Children owed mothers honor, love, and respect and the same burial rites accorded to their fathers.

Sex, for women, belonged in the marriage bed, and even a girl who had been raped had to become, or be treated as, the wife of her attacker (Exod. 21:7-11; Deut.21:10-14). The Bible tells of a bride found not to be a virgin being stoned to death by the elders of the town. Death was also the ordained punishment for the adulterous wife, whereas infidelity by the husband with prostitutes won toleration (although not encouragement), and polygamy gained acceptance (although not enthusiastically). A woman could never divorce her husband (as she could in Egypt), but divorce lay within the husband's rights, and texts say nothing about any obligation of the husband toward the wife he set aside. The arranged and Levirate marriage predominated in the early period (Gen. 38). The male commanded higher value than the female: the votive offering of the male in the temple had a higher monetary value in the eyes of the priests (Lev. 27), and some laws treated women as the property of men (Exod. 20:17; Deut. 5:21). For instance, a man might sell his daughter to pay his debts for a period of up to six years (Exod. 21:2; 21:7).

Only a few women (those without brothers) might inherit property, since sons, if there were any, inherited everything from their parents. The woman who did inherit still had to marry within her tribe, so the inheritance fell to her husband (Num. 36: 1-9). Although society subordinated the woman economically and socially to the man (the word for husband was *master*), wives were not legally chattels. Husbands could not sell their wives, nor could they divorce them without substantial cause (Deut. 22:15ff.), and nowhere does the Hebrew Bible state that a wife must obey her husband. Indeed, when Proverbs describes a wife finding and purchasing good land and planting it with a vineyard herself (Prov. 31:10, 16–18), it suggests that some independence and initiative were allowed the "good wife."

Although mothers taught their children the Torah, within the family the father represented the religious authority for his wife and children in the sacrificial rites. Only men of the community were bidden to come before the Lord (Exod. 23:17; 34:23, and Deut. 16:16).

As among the Egyptians, references appear to "wise women" or diviners who may have practiced the occult, and prophetesses like Miriam, Deborah, and Huldah spoke for Yahveh and received honor for this. However, unlike earlier priestesses in Babylon or Egypt, these prophetesses cannot be considered cultic authorities or connected with the sanctuary and officiating in the ritual. For this reason, perhaps, foreign cults from Babylon attracted the veneration of some women in ancient Israel (Jer. 7:8; 44:15-19; and Is. 17:10). Indeed, especially among women, the cults of the god Tammuz and the goddess Asherah were very popular until the Babylonian captivity.[46]

Despite the strong patriarchal bent to this society, Hebrew Bible history does include stories of women who saved their people or their cities from catastrophe through leadership and acts of courage. Abigail, Esther, Judith, and Jael all play this strong female role. In times of crisis women found identity and inspiration independent of gender roles. Normally, however, when the Hebrew Bible woman became visible, it was, in the words of Phyllis Bird, "as a dependent and usually an inferior in a male-centered and male-dominated society."[47]

The Hebrew Bible was a male-edited and published compilation and may not leave us with a complete picture of Israelite or Canaanite women. It was the product of an urban elite and has been criticized for reflecting poorly the life of women in the countryside. Obviously, in any agrarian society, where slave labor was at a minimum, vital roles in food production and household management were played by the women. However, Israel was almost constantly at war with her neighbors, and male strength, vigilance, and domination doubtless appeared necessary for the security of the state throughout its long tumultuous history. Constant preparation for war left little space for creative self-development within the general female population, whose singular contribution as replenisher of the race was deemed most essential. Individual women might give advice and might rally the people, but women, as a group, were the least effective members of this often poor and war-torn society.

CONCLUSION

In ancient times, it is clear that women of royal families often enjoyed influence and power, great wealth, and important duties whatever the conditions were that prevailed for the women of their states. When comparing nonroyal women of Egypt to those of western Asia, one finds in general a more marked tendency to male control in the family (and state control of women outside the home as well) evident in western Asia. What was the real cause of the rise of patriarchy there? Several reasons suggest themselves. The first is militarism. In an early agrarian society like Egypt where internal disputes were effectively handled by the strong, centralized government, where wars usually took place beyond the borders, where no standing army existed during the first fifteen hundred years of recorded history, and where invasion seldom affected the country at large, women continually shared the burdens, rights, and obligations of citizens. However, in societies where warfare between cities was frequent and invasion by outside hostile forces familiar, militarism developed, excluding women and rendering them dependents. Second, where commercialism held sway at the same time, as in Assyria, the most blatant examples of patriarchy were found. Commerce based on private initiative first appeared well developed in the Old Babylonian period, when the first concerted effort by men to control women for financial gain is also documented. This may be seen, not only in the laws of Hammurabi, but in institutions like that of the cloistered *naditu* women. Coupled with virulent militarism, as in Assyria, the rise of large-scale commerce had a devastating effect on women's rights. Because in Egypt commerce long remained a major concern of the state, which controlled trade with foreigners, its impact on the wider society remained less significant. In Egypt prestige was based, not on wealth, education and closeness to the rulers. Thus very different value systems prevailed in the societies of ancient western Asia, resulting in differing attitudes toward women.

We might further point out, however, that, even during the somewhat militaristic Egyptian empire of the New Kingdom, women's status and freedoms did not diminish significantly. This introduces a third factor: confidence. A supremely confident nation can afford tolerance. Egypt, a wealthy and fertile country, had confidence in its gods, in the eternity of life, in the bounty of its land, and in its superiority over its neighbors. Sumer, in its early formative years, shared these advantages as well. Not so the subsequent societies with their poorer resources and indefensible borders. It is the threatened male and the threatened society—like Middle Assyria, surrounded on three sides by deadly enemies, and weak impoverished Israel—that created a restricted role for their women.

NOTES

1. Barbara S. Lesko, "Researching the Role of Women in Ancient Egypt," *KMT: A Modern Journal of Ancient Egypt.* 5, no. 4 (1994–1995), pp. 14–23.
2. Barbara S. Lesko, ed., *Women's Earliest Records from Ancient Egypt and Western Asia* (Brown Judaic Studies, 166), Scholars Press, Atlanta, 1989.
3. Del Nord, "Hkrt-nswt = 'king's concubine?,'" *Serapis* 2 (1970), pp. 10–11.
4. Barbara S. Lesko, "Women's Monumental Mark on Ancient Egypt," *Biblical Archaeologist*, 54, no. 1 (1991), pp. 4–15.
5. William A. Ward, *Essays on Feminine Titles*, American University of Beirut, Beirut, 1986.
6. Miriam Lichtheim, *Ancient Egyptian Literature II: The New Kingdom*, University of California Press, Berkeley, 1976, p. 135.
7. Janet H. Johnson, "The Legal Status of Women in Ancient Egypt," *Mistress of the House, Mistress of Heaven: Women in Ancient Egypt,* Catalogue by Anne K. Capel and Glenn E. Markoe, Cincinnati Art Museum, Hudson Hills Press, New York, 1997, pp. 175–186.
8. John A. Wilson, *The Culture of Ancient Egypt*, University of Chicago Press, Chicago, 1956, p. 156.
9. Donald B. Redford, *History and Chronology of the Eighteenth Dynasty of Egypt: Seven Studies,* University of Toronto Press, Toronto, 1967, p. 30.
10. *Ibid.,* p. 72. Matriliny refers to descent traced through the mother, and matrilocality refers to mother-centered establishments, as in Egyptian queens having their own palaces, estates, and staffs.
11. Amélie Kuhrt, *The Ancient Near East c. 3000–330 B.C.,* vol. 1, Routledge, London and New York, 1995, pp. 263, 268, 279.
12. Julia Samson, *Nefertiti and Cleopatra: Queen-Monarchs of Ancient Egypt*, The Rubicon Press, London, 1985, pp. 95–97; James P. Allen, "Nefertiti and Smenkh-ka-re," *Göttinger Miszellen*, 1994, 141, pp. 7–13.
13. Leonard H. Lesko, "Three Late Egyptian Stories Reconsidered," in *Egyptological Studies in Honor of Richard A. Parker*, ed. L. H. Lesko, University Press of New England, Hanover and London, 1986, pp. 98–103.
14. John A.Wilson, "Results of a Trial for Conspiracy," *Ancient Near Eastern Texts Relating to the Old Testament*, ed. James B. Pritchard, 2d ed., Princeton University Press, Princeton, 1955, pp. 214–216; and Hans Goedicke, "Was Magic Used in the Harem Conspiracy Against Rameses III?" *Journal of Egyptian Archaeology* 49 (1973), pp. 71–92.
15. Betsy M. Bryan, "Evidence for Female Literacy from Theban Tombs of the New Kingdom," *Bulletin of the Egyptological Seminar* 6 (1984), pp. 17–32; Leonard H. Lesko, "Some Remarks on the Books of the Dead Composed for the High Priests Pinedjem I and II," in *For His Ka: Essays Offered in Memory of Klaus Baer* ed.

D. Silverman *(Studies in Ancient Oriental Civilization,* 55), The Oriental Institute, Chicago, 1994, pp. 179–186.

16. Joris Borghouts in *Pharaoh's Workers: The Villagers of Deir el Medina,* ed. L. H. Lesko, Cornell University Press, Ithaca, 1994, pp. 129–130.
17. Ricardo Caminos, "The Nitocris Adoption Stela," *Journal of Egyptian Archaeology* 4 (1964), pp. 107–118.
18. Barbara S. Lesko, "The Rhetoric of Women in Ancient Egypt," in *Essays on the Rhetorical Activities of Historical Women,* ed. M. M. Wertheimer, University of South Carolina Press, Columbia, forthcoming 1997.
19. Edward F. Wente, *Letters from Egypt* (Society of Biblical Literature Writings from the Ancient World, 1), Scholars Press, Atlanta, 1990, pp. 36, 82.
20. B.S. Lesko, *op. cit.*
21. Barbara S. Lesko, "True Art in Ancient Egypt," *Egyptological Studies in Honor of Richard A. Parker,* ed. L. H. Lesko, University Press of New England, Hanover and London, 1986, pp. 85–97.
22. Wente, *op. cit.,* pp. 216–217.
23. T. G. H. James, *The Hekanakhte Papers and Other Early Middle Kingdom Documents,* Metropolitan Museum of Art, New York, 1962, p. 34.
24. J. Cerny and T. Eric Peet, "A Marriage Settlement of the Twentieth Dynasty," *Journal of Egyptian Archaeology* 13 (1927), pp. 30–39; Alan H. Gardiner, "Adoption Extraordinary," *Journal of Egyptian Archaeology* 26 (1941), pp. 23–29; and P. W. Pestman, *Marriage and Matrimonial Property in Ancient Egypt* (Papyrologica Lugduno-Batava, IX), Leiden, 1961.
25. For bibliography, see Barbara S. Lesko, ed., *Women's Earliest Records from Ancient Egypt and Western Asia* (Brown Judaic Studies 166), Scholars Press, Atlanta, 1989.
26. P. R. S. Moorey, "What Do We Know About the People Buried in the Royal Cemetery?" *Expedition,* 20, no. 1 (1977), p. 40.
27. Marten Stol, "Private Life in Ancient Mesopotamia," *Civilizations of the Ancient Near East,* ed. J. M. Sasson, Charles Scribners, New York, Vol. 1, pp. 485–501; Marc Van de Mieroop, "Women in the Economy of Sumer," in *Women's Earliest Records,* ed. Barbara Lesko, pp. 55–62.
28. Van de Mieroop, *op. cit.,* pp. 63, 67.
29. Stol, *op. cit.,* p. 133; Kuhrt, *op. cit.,* p. 62.
30. Samuel Noah Kramer, *The Sumerians, Their History, Culture, and Character,* University of Chicago Press, Chicago, 1963, p. 78.
31. William W. Hallo, in *The Legacy of Sumer,* ed. Denise Schmandt Besserat (Bibliotheca Mesopotamica, 4), Undena Press, Malibu, 1979, p. 27.
32. However, see S. N. Kramer in *Legacy of Sumer,* p. 12, where he points out that Urukagina's wife, Queen Shagshag, "was the mistress of vast estates and ran her affairs every bit her husband's equal" and further, that Urukagina (Uruimgina) made an attempt to equalize wages between men and women in one known instance, so that he should not be regarded as antiwomen (pp. 12–13).
33. Hallo, *op. cit.,* p. 29; and William W. Hallo and J. J. A. Van Dyk, *The Exaltation of Inanna,* Yale University Press, New Haven, 1968, pp. 1–11.
34. S. N. Kramer, "Lipit-Ishtar Lawcode," in Pritchard, *op. cit.,* pp. 159–161.
35. Albrecht Goetze, "The Laws of Eshnunna," in Pritchard, *op. cit.,* pp. 161–163.

36. Bernard Frank Batto, *Studies of Women at Mari,* Johns Hopkins University Press, Baltimore, 1974, pp. 8–36, 64–73.

37. Rivkah Harris, "Independent Women in Ancient Mesopotamia?" in B. S. Lesko, *op. cit.,* pp. 150–156.

38. Theophile Meek, "The Code of Hammurabi," in Pritchard, *op. cit.,* pp. 161–180; and Elizabeth Mary Mac Donald, *The Position of Women as Reflected in Semitic Codes of Law,* University of Toronto Press, Toronto, 1931, pp. 11–32.

39. Martha T. Roth, "Age at Marriage and the Household: A Study of the Neo-Babylonian and Neo-Assyrian Forms," *Compositive Studies in Society and History* 29 (1987), pp. 715–747.

40. Kuhrt, *op. cit.,* p. 337.

41. Theophile Meek, "The Middle Assyrian Laws," in Pritchard, *op. cit.,* pp. 180–188.

42. Sue Rollin, "Women and Witchcraft in Ancient Assyria," in *Images of Women in Antiquity,* ed. Averil Cameron and Amélie Kuhrt, Wayne State University Press, Detroit, 1983, pp. 65–78.

43. Jean Bottero, "La femme dans l'Asia Occidentale Ancienne: Mesopotamie et Israel," in *Histoire Mondiale de la femme,* ed. P. Grimal, Nouvelle Librarie de France, Paris, 1957, p. 176.

44. Carol Meyers, "Women and the Domestic Economy of Early Israel," in B. S. Lesko, *op. cit.,* pp. 265–278.

45. Phyllis Bird, "Images of Women in the Old Testament," in *Religion and Sexism,* ed. Rosemary Radford Reuther, Simon and Schuster, New York, 1974; and P. Trible, "Women in the Old Testament," *Interpreter's Dictionary of the Bible,* supplementary volume, K. Crim general editor, Abingdon Press, Nashville, 1976, pp. 963–966; and Carol Meyers, "The Roots of Restriction: Women in Early Israel," *Biblical Archaeologist,* 41, no. 1 (1978), pp. 91–103.

46. Peter R. Ackroyd, "Goddesses, Women and Jezebel," in Cameron and Kuhrt, *op. cit.,* pp. 245–259.

47. Bird, *op. cit.,* p. 56.

SUGGESTIONS FOR FURTHER READING

The most reliable source for reconstructing the social history of ancient peoples is surely their own writings. Fortunately, published anthologies of texts are available in English to the student, the most comprehensive of these being *Ancient Near Eastern Texts Relating to the Old Testament,* which contains literary and nonliterary works from the Egyptian, Sumerian, Babylonian, Hittite, and Assyrian cultures. Now in its third edition (1969) and accompanied by a volume of plates illustrating monuments from these civilizations, *Ancient Near Eastern Texts* was edited by James B. Pritchard; its contributors are an impressive roster of leading orientalists, and it is published by Princeton University Press. Since its publication, more specialized anthologies representing single cultures include, for Egypt, three volumes of *Ancient Egyptian Literature* by Mirian Lichtheim, published by the University of California Press (1973–1980); and *Letters from Ancient Egypt,* translated by Edward Wente for the Society for Biblical Literature series *Writings from the Ancient World,* published by Scholars Press of Atlanta in 1990. For the same series Martha T. Roth published *Law*

Collections from Mesopotamia and Asia Minor in 1995. In 1967 A. Leo Oppenheim produced *Letters from Mesopotamia* (University of Chicago Press, 1967), and Benjamin R. Foster published *Before the Muses: An Anthology of Akkadian Literature* in two volumes (Bethesda, Md., 1993).

The 1970s saw the publication of the third revised edition of *The Cambridge Ancient History*, a monumental work of several volumes with contributions by many leading scholars of that decade. This has now been followed by the two-volume work *The Ancient Near East c. 3000–330 B.C.* by Amélie Kuhrt for the Routledge History of the Ancient World (London, 1995).

The number of books on women in ancient Egypt in particular and on women in antiquity generally has increased markedly in the decade following the publication of the second edition of *Becoming Visible: Women's Earliest Records,* edited by Barbara S. Lesko. This volume published the proceedings of an international conference on women in the ancient Near East held at Brown University in 1987, including contributions from nineteen scholars and containing a comprehensive bibliography (Scholars Press, Atlanta, 1989).

More specifically focused studies in English are Barbara S. Lesko's *The Remarkable Women of Ancient Egypt,* now in its third edition (B. C. Scribe Publications, Providence, 1996); and Gay Robins's *Ancient Egyptian Women* (Harvard University Press, 1993). Numerous articles in scholarly journals and encyclopedias, such as Scribners' four-volume *Civilizations of the Ancient Near East,* Jack Sasson editor-in-chief (New York, 1995), have expanded the bibliography considerably in recent years.

On this bell-shaped krater bowl for mixing wine and water, the only vase attributed to the "Persephone painter," Persephone returns to her mother from the Underworld. Hermes and Hecate accompany Persephone and help her to effect the transition from the rocky earthen terrain beneath which lies the Underworld to reunion with her mother, Demeter. Persephone is dressed as a bride and raises her hand in greeting. Hecate, holding torches like those used in the bridal procession, guides Persephone toward Demeter, who stands waiting solemnly, grasping the scepter that marks her status as goddess and queen, divine mistress of agriculture and growth (ca. 440 B.C.).   THE METROPOLITAN MUSEUM OF ART, FLETCHER FUND, 1928 (28.57.23).

CHAPTER 2

Daughters of Demeter: Women in Ancient Greece

Marilyn A. Katz

Demeter's Olympian world was a patriarchal one governed by Zeus, "father of gods and men." But in her myth, Demeter successfully resists the arbitrary and tyrannical exercise of patriarchal power, circumscribes her own areas of potency and authority, and celebrates her affinity with other female divinities.

Similarly, the women of ancient Greece inhabited a polis ("city-state") that was governed by male authority but in whose social, economic, and religious dimensions they participated actively. The ideology of women's place, along with representations of women in myth, literature, and art, sometimes conforms to this social reality but just as often contradicts it. A comprehensive under-standing of women's role in the ancient Greek polis and of the particularity of ancient Greek patriarchy thus requires that we juxtapose ideology with social practice and attempt to recover a notion of the polis as a cultural totality. Within it, elite women of all periods enjoyed special privileges. Women of the poorer classes, who were required to work for a living, escaped the dictates of a cultural ideal that associated the female with the inner spaces of the home. And women whose lives conformed to the cultural ideal nevertheless enjoyed the pleasures of formally sanctioned and informal associations with other women.

Crowning the high, rocky pre-eminence of the Athenian acropolis lie the remains of the Parthenon. It was constructed as part of the building program begun around 450 B.C. under the direction of Pericles to commemorate the Greeks' triumph over the Persians and to celebrate the achievements of Athenian democracy. Divine and mythical females figure prominently in the Parthenon's architectural program, to which those of a number of other Greek temples are similar. Their representation reveals much about the ideology of women's incorporation into the ancient Greek polis ("city-state").

The temple was dedicated to Athena Parthenos ("Virgin"), who as Athena Polias was "guardian of the city." Her miraculous birth from Zeus's head was celebrated in the center of the east pediment, just over the temple's main entrance. Athena's special powers of military prowess and wisdom derived from her special relationship to Zeus and symbolize the magnitude and beneficence of female potency when submitted to benign male control.

In the sculpted panels (metopes) on the western end of the temple—the side first visible on approach—appeared the battle between the Greeks and Amazons, mythical warrior women who lived at the boundaries of the civilized world free of men and male domination. Metopes on the other three sides represented battles between gods and giants (east), Greeks and Trojans (north), and Lapiths and centaurs (south). Amazons were thus associated by analogy with the monstrous opponents of the Olympian order (giants), the traditional eastern enemies of the western Greeks (Trojans), and the drunken half-animals (centaurs) who disrupted the wedding feast of the horse-taming Lapiths.

A festival procession leading up to the Parthenon was part of a yearly polis celebration commemorating Athena's birth, which was celebrated with special grandeur every fourth year. Girls and women were part of this Panathenaic festival, in which they presented to the goddess the robe they had woven for her and carried the sacred implements for sacrifice. Their participation testifies to the centrality of women's role in religious celebrations, which were themselves a major aspect of the city's public life. In Athens, major religious celebrations occupied approximately one-third of the year, and some of these, like the Thesmophoria in honor of Demeter, were restricted to women; in others, like the Lenaia in honor of Dionysus, women played a prominent part.

To the north of the acropolis, in the plain stretching out below, was the agora or civic center; on a hill to the west was the Pnyx, site for the meeting of the Athenian assembly; and on the southern slope of the acropolis was the theater of Dionysus. From the first of these two centers of civic life women were excluded, and they may also have been restricted from the third, for women were prohibited by law from transacting business exchanges in significant amounts, and they were also barred from appearing as witnesses or litigants in the many law courts located in and around the agora. Thus only poor women, noncitizen women, or slaves formed part of the daily hustle and bustle of the agora. Furthermore, citizen women were not voting members of the body politic and so did not participate in the assembly deliberations about which we read so much in our ancient sources. And although women were represented freely on the dramatic stage by male actors, they may not have attended the performances of the tragedies that form such a prominent part of the ancient Athenians' cultural legacy.

Thus women were part of ancient Greek communal life but not of its political or judicial dimensions. Women and the category of the female, however, were central to what might be called the communal imagination of the ancient Greeks. This ideological space of the polis was structured according to the principles of polarity and analogy, and the opposition between male and female was one of its governing categories.

For example, among fourth-century B.C. Pythagorean philosophers, who were organized as philosophical and religious societies in the southern and Greek parts of Italy, one group taught that there was not one principle underlying the sensible universe, but ten, and that these were organized in contrasting pairs:

Limit and Unlimited
Odd and Even
One and Plurality
Right and Left
Male and Female
Rest and Motion
Straight and Crooked
Light and Darkness
Good and Evil
Square and Oblong[1]

The Pythagorean Table of Opposites articulates the opposition between male and female starkly, but the distinction in the Parthenon sculptures between the warrior-goddess Athena and the warrior-women Amazons expresses similar ideas in a subtler and more complex way: the goddess who acknowledges submission to the male is contrasted with the mythical females who refuse it.

The women who took part in the Panathenaic procession were neither Athenas nor Amazons, of course, but in our ancient sources we encounter the divine, mythical, or generic female far more often than we do actual women. Attempts to distinguish the lived reality of women's lives from ideological representations of the female inevitably compromise our understanding of the ancient Greek cultural totality, in which, with some exceptions noted in the following text, remarkable similarities in our information about women persist across time, space, and genre. Accordingly, in this chapter I discuss representations of women in myth, literature, and art along with the social realities that conditioned their lives. Sources for the latter are almost exclusively

Athenian, and although the situation of Athenian women cannot be regarded as typical, it is also equally unlikely to have been unique in the world of the ancient Greeks. Moreover, it is the situation of Athenian women that has been regarded, from antiquity to the present day, as paradigmatic for the women of ancient Greece generally.

GENESIS AND GENERATION

Hesiod's *Theogony* ("Birth of the Gods") was the ancient Greek creation epic, and its narrative is organized around a progression from a world dominated by the generative power of the female to one governed by the moral authority of the male. In the first stage of the myth the goddess Gaia ("Earth") comes into being and generates Ouranos ("Sky") out of herself; together they produce the Titans, the generation of monstrous and primordial deities. But when Ouranos attempts to secure his primacy by confining the Titans in Gaia's womb, Gaia arms her youngest son Kronos with a sickle and he castrates his father. Kronos impregnates the Titan goddess Rhea with the Olympian gods, but swallows them down as they issue from her womb until Rhea substitutes a stone wrapped in swaddling clothes for her youngest son Zeus. Zeus then forces Kronos to disgorge the Olympians, and after a fierce battle in which the Titans are defeated, establishes the Olympian order. In order to escape his predecessors' fates, Zeus swallows his first wife Mêtis ("Cunning Wisdom") and gives birth to Athena from his head. Once this act establishes the principle of male control over female reproductive power, generation can proceed normally, and among the many children born to Zeus from his union with goddesses of the older and younger generation are those whose names symbolize the beneficence of his rule (e.g., Justice, Good Order, Peace).

The human world of the polis, too, was governed by the principle of male authority over females, and the laws regulating succession and inheritance authorized men's appropriation of women's reproductive potential. Women in the polis were subject to *kyrieia* ("guardianship"), which gave fathers, husbands, brothers, or adult sons both the authority to act on their behalf and the responsibility for their support and well-being. Children were also subject to their fathers' guardianship—the boys until they reached majority, and the girls until it was transferred to their husbands. A woman's chief civic privilege and duty was to bear legitimate children to her husband—the sons who would become his heirs and citizens of the polis, and the daughters through whose marriages alliances would be forged with other households.

When a man had a daughter but no sons, then his daughter became an *epiklêros* ("heiress"), endowed like Athena with the authority to transmit his legacy. She was married to her father's nearest male relative (usually his brother and her paternal uncle), and her sons became their maternal grandfather's heirs.

Only in myth and legend could men reproduce without women, but on the tragic stage male characters like Jason in Euripides' *Medea* express the wish that it were possible to "procreate children otherwise" than with women.[2] The myth of Pandora, who was represented on the base of Athena's cult statue in the Parthenon, explicitly embodies this theme of woman as curse. In Hesiod's *Theogony* and *Works and Days* she is "a beautiful evil"[3] created from clay by the potter god Hephaestus on Zeus's orders, bedecked by Aphrodite, Athena, and Hermes and transferred to earth by Hermes, who gives her to the unsuspecting Epimetheus to be "a curse to men who eat bread."[4] In the *Works and Days*, Pandora uncaps the jar and releases upon the earth evils for men who, before her advent, had lived "apart from evils and difficult toil and without the painful diseases which cause death for men."[5]

As in the Bible, agricultural labor and sexual reproduction are analogous necessities that define the human condition and set it apart from that of the gods. These imperatives testify to man's mortality at the same time that they remedy it, by supplying nourishment to sustain life on a daily basis and heirs to ensure continuity through time. In the Hesiodic view, the "race" (*genos*) of women is both the cause and effect of the human condition, and the establishment of civilized order is contingent on the regulating power of patriarchal authority.

HEROES AND HEROINES

Homer's epic poems, the *Iliad* and the *Odyssey* (which were composed in the eighth or seventh century B.C.), represent the world of the heroes, traditionally believed to have lived ten generations before the historical era. But its cultural spaces are configured much as we find them many centuries later when, as a late author explains: "Man's job is in the fields, the agora, the affairs of the city; women's work is spinning wool, baking bread, keeping house."[6] The *Iliad* is a poem of war, and its battlefield is an exclusively masculine domain, into which women enter only as the spoils of war, captured and enslaved when their city falls, or as prizes distributed among the men when they engage in competition among themselves. Within this world of men, the affective focus is the relationship between its hero Achilles and his companion-in-arms Patroclus, and their close friendship foreshadows the homoerotic associations between men that were a customary aspect of men's communal life in the polis.

The *Iliad*'s "inner" space is the world of Troy, the domain of old men, women, and children: it is glimpsed only briefly in the poem, when Hector returns home from the battlefield. Upon leaving, Hector admonishes his wife Andromache to return home and attend to her spinning and weaving, while he concerns himself with battle.[7] And the same lines recur in the *Odyssey*, on two occasions when Telemachus sends his mother Penelope from the great hall, so that the men may occupy themselves with male pursuits.[8] But both poems also idealize the marriage relationship as a union of complementarities. Hector, taking leave of Andromache, formulates a heroic ideal in which he fights on behalf of her and their young son, and she rejoices in their prowess.[9] And the plot of the *Odyssey* centers on its hero's return to a wife whose cleverness and perspicacity match his own.

Achilles is a figure of *mênis*, of the "vengeful wrath" that sends him from the battlefield when his honor is insulted and drives him back to it when Patroclus is killed. But Odysseus is a man of *mêtis*, of the "cunning wisdom" personified by Zeus's first wife in the *Theogony* and associated with the wiles of women. The world of the *Odyssey* is one dominated by its female figures—the goddess Athena, who protects its hero, the women both divine and human who attempt to detain him from his goal or to help him reach it, and above all Penelope, the wife celebrated for her steadfast faithfulness to her absent husband. The reunion of Odysseus and Penelope is the emotional highpoint of the poem, and their relationship embodies Odysseus's praise of marriage spoken earlier in the poem: "For nothing is finer than this: / when a husband and wife live together in their home, / alike in mind and thought—a great distress to their enemies / but a joy to their friends, as they themselves know best."[10]

When their husbands are present the aristocratic women of the *Odyssey* join the men in the great hall, whereas in the classical period respectable women did not appear in the *andrôn*, or men's quarter of the house where men gathered for feasting and entertainment. And in the utopian world of the *Odyssey*'s Phaeacia, its queen Arete is celebrated as a woman "of noble intelligence," honored outstandingly by her husband, children, and people, among whom she circulates freely, giving counsel and "dissolving quarrels, even among men."[11]

Penelope's loyalty to her husband in the *Odyssey* is configured against the paradigms of the faithless Helen, who caused the Trojan War by succumbing to the seductions of Paris, and of the treacherous Clytemnestra, who took a lover and conspired with him to kill her husband upon his return from the war. And Penelope's faithfulness is imbued with the authority of an autonomous moral choice by the combination of Odysseus's absence with Telemachus's youth: Penelope is married, and thus not under her father's guardianship; her husband, who would normally be her guardian, is absent; her son is too young to assume control of the household. Penelope is thus anomalously exempted from male control and free to make her own decisions about her marital status. Once Odysseus returns, however, the customary boundaries reassert themselves: Penelope is entrusted with guardianship of the stores within, and Odysseus goes off to replenish the household herds and flocks.[12]

We are not in a position to determine how well the representations of men and women in Homer's poems accorded with the social realities of the time when they were composed, in the eighth or seventh century B.C. But discounting the archaic and aristocratic ambience of their settings, women's principal activities and concerns in the epic are the same as those of the classical era: they are preoccupied with spinning and weaving, with safeguarding the household stores, and with the care of their children; they are responsible for petitioning the gods in times of war and for mourning over the dead; and they are the victims consigned to slavery when the city falls.

MAIDEN SONGS AND MARRIAGE RITUALS

Sappho is the best known of ancient Greek women poets, and many of her songs commemorate the pleasures of the female circles with which her name is traditionally associated. These relationships were both highly aestheticized and highly eroticized, although the fragmentary character of the poetic remains and the absence of a context makes it impossible to specify their setting with certainty.

In all likelihood Sappho's lyrics, like those of the contemporary Spartan poet Alcman's maiden songs, reflect the existence in her time of ritual associations in which girls were trained in singing and dancing in preparation for their transition into adulthood and marriage. In one of the lyric fragments, Aphrodite is invited to appear in "a lovely grove of apple trees" and invited to "gently pour forth in golden cups / nectar mingled with our festivities."[13] Several of the fragments elaborate the vocabulary of physical beauty and erotic desire. Recalling one departed companion, Sappho remarks: "But now she stands out among the Lydian women / as after sunset / the rosy-fingered moon / Surpasses all the stars."[14] And in a fragment of Alcman, the erotic effect of one girl's touch is described: ". . . and with desire that looses the limbs, but she looks glances more melting than sleep and death. . . ."[15]

In the classical period, too, girls in both Athens and Sparta participated in ritual associations. Spartan girls competed in athletic contests at Olympia in honor of Hera, goddess of marriage, and Athenian girls took part in races in honor of Artemis at her sanctuary at Brauron, on the east coast of Attica. Representations of choral dance on vases from both the archaic and classical periods suggest that such activities were a persistent feature of citizen women's lives.

A number of Sappho's fragments lament the departure of one of its members, most likely for marriage, and in one remarkable fragment of a hexameter poem by the fourth-century Erinna, the poet appears to recall her beloved friend Baucis's abandonment of childhood games for marriage and subsequent death.[16] In poetry as well as in sepulchral epigrams, a girl's marriage is commonly represented as an abrupt transition from childhood joys to adult responsibilities, and the death of a young maiden is frequently figured as marriage to the god of the Underworld. The formulations of these themes may have been conditioned by the young age (fourteen) at which girls usually married a man some fifteen years their senior, but they also reflect a proclivity to configure rituals of separation and transition using metaphors of death and rebirth.

Marriage in the polis was virilocal (centered in the husband's house), and so entailed a woman's transfer from both her father's house and his authority to those of her husband. The wedding was an event celebrated with feasting, dance, and song; its highlight was the torchlight evening procession that brought the bride to the groom's house, accompanied by special attendants for each and by the bride's mother. The groom's mother awaited the couple's arrival in the marital home, and the bride's entrance into her new home was celebrated with a special ritual of incorporation performed at the hearth. On the following morning, another day of festivities began, in which friends and relatives brought gifts to the new husband and wife.

Although the fact that a wedding feast had taken place could be cited later as proof of the marriage's legitimacy, its legally binding moment was the betrothal, a contract between the groom and the bride's father, which also fixed the terms of the dowry. For example: "Father: I give you this woman for the procreation (literally, "ploughing") of legitimate children. Young Man: I take her. Father: And three talents as dowry. Young Man: Fine."[17]

Procne in Sophocles' *Tereus* claims that "we women live most happily as young girls in our fathers' homes, where innocence is our nursemaid."[18] And it is true that for women the passage into adulthood brought accommodation to new social circumstances and to the authority of a man who might have been a relative stranger. Thus the literary theme that represents marriage as rape or associates it with death may also attest to one aspect of the lived reality of women's lives in ancient Greece. It might just as well, however, reflect the convention of modesty that required women to disavow sexual desire and eagerness for the privileges of an adult status that, even as children, they practiced to assume: among collections of bridal vases, we find some miniature examples depicting little girls dressed up as brides, and these were doubtless girls' toys.

FARMING AND FERTILITY

As the betrothal formula indicates, the field and furrow were metaphors for the female body in Greek thought: Plato, for example, claimed that it was "not earth which imitates woman in the matter of pregnancy and childbirth, but woman who imitates earth."[19] Plato went on to praise Athens, maintaining that her earth was the first to have brought forth wheat and barley, and that Athens had benefited mankind generally by dispensing her gift of grain.

Plato is alluding to the myth of Demeter, goddess of grain who, in the seventh century B.C. Homeric hymn that canonized her attributes and achievements, afflicted the earth with a devastating drought and famine when her daughter Persephone was carried off by Hades, god of the Underworld, to be his bride. Zeus, Persephone's father, had given her to Hades, arrogating to himself the same prerogative that belonged to mortal fathers in the polis. Other, later authors, like Xenophon, writing in the late fifth and early fourth centuries B.C., adopted a more enlightened view, regarding it as normal for both parents to choose their daughter's husband together.[20]

But in the Homeric hymn, Demeter only hears her daughter's shrieks as she is carried off from the field where she had been playing with the daughters of Ocean, and Demeter wanders the earth searching for Persephone. Helios, god of the sun, explains to Demeter that Zeus "gave the slender-ankled girl to Hades, his own brother, to be his blossoming bedmate and wife."[21] Enraged, Demeter abandons the heavenly company of the Olympians and, disguising herself as an old woman, lives among mortals. Later, she withdraws further, into her luxurious temple, and, "wasting away with longing for her deep-girdled daughter, brought on a harsh and most terrible year for mortal men, all over the all-nourishing earth: no seed sprouted in the earth, for fair-wreathed Demeter kept it concealed."[22] The oxen draw their ploughs in vain; men sow their seeds of grain fruitlessly. The whole race of mortals is threatened with extinction, and Demeter would have deprived the Olympians too of "the glorious privilege of their honors and sacrifices"[23] if Zeus had not intervened. Hermes is sent to retrieve Persephone, and she is reunited with Demeter in a celebration that includes Rhea, Demeter's mother, and Hecate, a kindly goddess of the older generation of Titans who "ever after is [Demeter's] attendant and follower."[24]

Zeus promises that Persephone will spend two-thirds of the year with her mother and the other immortals, and one-third in the Underworld, as Hades' bride. And so Demeter "swiftly brought forth grain from the dark, rich fields, and the whole expanse of earth blossomed with leaves and flowers."[25]

In the hymn, Demeter goes on to instruct Triptolemus and the other princes of Eleusis in her rites, the Eleusinian mysteries, which were celebrated every year over the course of a week at Eleusis, an Attic town about 10 miles northwest of Athens. But in other myths, on several vase paintings, and in Plato's allusion referenced previously, Triptolemus is an Athenian culture hero to whom Demeter taught the art of agriculture and who transmitted it to other peoples.

The Eleusinian mysteries were open to all Greeks, male and female, citizen and noncitizen, Athenians and foreigners, free and slave. We know little about their content and meaning except that they held out to initiates the promise of immortality. Other cults of Demeter, however, were concerned more directly with agriculture and fertility, and were celebrated in tandem with important events in the farming year.[26] These were widespread throughout the Greek world and were open only to citizen wives.

At Athens, the Stenia, Thesmophoria, and Skira were exclusively women's festivals; the first two were held in October and November, just before the autumn ploughing and sowing of grain and vegetables, and the third occurred in June and July, just after the harvesting of the winter barley and wheat. The Stenia was a nocturnal festival in which women sought to distract Demeter from her grief with jesting and ritual insults. It was a preliminary to the Thesmophoria, a major, three-day festival that celebrated the reunion of Demeter and Persephone; and in the Skira, the women observed rites that prepared the threshing-floors for the processing of the harvested grain.

Thus, at the times when men occupied themselves with "the works of Demeter"—ploughing, sowing, reaping, and threshing—the women of the polis assumed responsibility for soliciting divine benevolence from Demeter and Persephone so that the crops of wheat, barley, and vegetables would sprout, grow, and flourish. These foods formed the staple of the Greeks' everyday diet, and women's rites, evoking divine solicitude for the prosperity of the crops, complemented men's agricultural labors. Furthermore, this cultural discourse between male and female spheres of responsibility for cereal cultivation and agricultural growth was overseen and sanctioned by the polis: the state council offered sacrifices to Demeter and Persephone on the occasion of the Stenia, and during the Thesmophoria the women appropriated the assembly meeting place for the celebration of their rites.

Such celebrations were an important aspect of women's participation in the communal life of the polis; they also provided occasions when the women of the city gathered together on their own in "assemblies" that were apart from the male assemblies in the political arena, from which women were excluded. Participation in such religious rituals, then, represented the public life of the Athenian wife. Through the festivals of Demeter and Persephone, Athenian women confirmed their own associations with fertility, enacted their own reunions with married daughters, and endowed their procreative capacities with both cosmic and political significance.

THE DRAMA OF SOCIAL LIFE

The predominance of women on the Athenian tragic stage has often seemed perplexing when contrasted with their exclusion from other arenas of communal life, including perhaps, the dramatic performances themselves. But the theater was first and foremost a ritual space dedicated to the god Dionysus, in whose honor the tragedies were enacted as part of his spring festival. And Dionysus himself was above all lord of transgressive behavior, whose entourage included both satyrs, male symbols of bestiality and phallic excess, and maenads, female embodiments of divine possession and of wild and ecstatic transport.

Furthermore, the conventions of the Greek tragic stage required mimetic disguise, and its male actors assumed the masks and costumes of both gods and heroes, men and women, in tribute perhaps to the god's power as master of transformations, and especially to his androgynous character as "the double god," at once both masculine and feminine. Both by its ritual setting and its conventions, then, the world of Greek tragedy was marked as anomalous from the perspective of ordinary social life.

But these same features also combined to transform the tragic stage into a realm of the imaginary: a site where the tensions, ambiguities, and contradictions of the polis and its ideals could be freely explored. And among these, none was so fraught with complex meaning as the dimorphic social organization that divided male from female within the polis, consigning women to subordinate social status and reserving for men the privileges of autonomy and power.

From this perspective, then, it is not surprising that the drama of the Athenian tragic stage focuses on conflict, and that its clash of opposites often sets male against female—a conflict that frequently serves as the vehicle for dramatizing larger social and cultural discontinuities within the polis. Orestes' acquittal of the murder of his mother Clytemnestra, for example, becomes the founding act through which the blood vendetta is displaced for the rule of law in Aeschylus's *Oresteia.* In Sophocles' *Antigone,* its heroine defies the edict against her brother's burial issued by Creon, her uncle and the city's ruler, by invoking her allegiance instead to the customs of religious practice; these called for family members to bury their dead, and Antigone claims they are sanctioned by "the gods' unwritten and unfailing laws."[27] And in Euripides' *Bacchae,* it is the women of Thebes led by their king's mother who succumb to the power of the new god Dionysus, but who also, in the throes of their ecstatic transport, dismember the young ruler who had opposed the god's advent.

In these tragedies, social, judicial, and religious issues are played out as family dramas, and their polarities are expressed in the language of sexual conflict. Athena, for example, casts the deciding vote for Orestes on the principle, as she says, of male superiority: "I am wholly for the male . . . and entirely on the father's side."[28] Creon refuses to bend in the face of public opposition because, as he says, "she is the man and not I [if I yield]."[29] And Pentheus is outraged that, under the influence of Dionysus, the women have "left their looms and spindles" and "abandoned their homes."[30]

Greek drama also explored the cultural ambiguities that conditioned a wife's status within the polis. A new bride, for example, upon entering her husband's home for the first time, was incorporated into its domestic cult through a ritual of adoption performed at the hearth that duplicated the rite through which both strangers and slaves were welcomed. A wife, then, was in some respects an outsider in her husband's home, and indeed legally she never abandoned her ties to her natal family, into which she might be recalled if she became an *epiklēros* ("heiress") and to which she, along with her dowry, returned in the event of divorce (and also if she was widowed and childless). And, although its particulars are disputed, the institution of *aphaeresis* ("carrying-off") apparently permitted a father under certain circumstances to remarry his daughter to a more desirable husband. A free man, incidentally, would employ the same institution (*aphaeresis*) to assert the freedom of a friend who had been seized as a slave.

In Euripides' *Alcestis*, these issues are played out as the problem of the wife's proper role in the hierarchy of outsiders: strangers, guest-friends, and slaves. The faithful Alcestis undertakes to die in place of her husband, but when Admetus's period of mourning is interrupted by the arrival of Heracles, he abandons grief for the role of host, explaining that the one who has died was a "stranger" or "outsider" (*othneios*), not a *sungenês* or relative.[31] Heracles, upon discovering the truth, undertakes to retrieve Alcestis from the dead, and at the end of the play hands over to Admetus a slave, the veiled woman whom he has won as a prize, and who may or may not be Alcestis herself: the play leaves her status ambiguous.

Greek tragedy, then, addressed itself to the sociopolitical ideals of the polis, but through its characters, subjects, and setting it was also removed from ordinary social life. Greek comedy, by contrast, reintroduces the common-place into dramatic performance through its focus on the particulars of con-temporary social and political debate, its irreverent treatment of the gods, its free recourse to both the fantastic and grotesque in plot and costume, and above all its rampant use of vulgarity and interest in the elemental aspects of bodily functions. Comedy was performed both at the City Dionysia and also at the Lenaea, a midwinter Dionysiac festival in which women played a prominent role.

Several of Aristophanes' plays exploit the cultural preoccupation with the opposition between male and female by staging a full-scale battle of the sexes in which women vanquish men in the service of the polis. Here, citizen women, far from representing alienation from, or hostility to, the structures of civilized life, can claim plausibly to embody them better than the men. In the *Lysistrata*, for example, women occupy the acropolis to carry out a sex strike and force an end to the Peloponnesian War. They lay claim to special prestige within the city on account of their history of religious service to Athena and to a particular wisdom in guiding its affairs because of their expertise in handling wool: just as they clean the wool and pick out burrs and thistles from it, they will purge the city of all worthless elements and pluck out all the political cabals and conspiratorial coteries.[32]

In the *Ecclesiazusae* ("Women in the Assembly"), the women of Athens contrive to take over the masculine preserve of the assembly on the Pnyx and vote through a revolution abolishing the family and private property, but not, significantly, slavery. And an ancient myth preserved in a late source explains the etiology of the name of Athens by referring to the time when Cecrops, Athens's first legendary king, called an assembly of all the citizens, "male and female," to decide between Athena's and Poseidon's claims to serve as the city's tutelary deity. When the women, who outnumbered the men by one, voted for Athena, Poseidon took revenge by flooding the countryside and was only appeased when the women of Athens were disenfranchised.[33]

The ancient Greeks took account, then, in both myth and drama, of the disparities in civil status between men and women and of the ambiguities of women's role in the family. In the political sphere, where thoughts and ideas had practical consequences, the status quo was never, apparently, questioned. But in tragedy, comedy, and myth—in the realm of the imaginary—Athenian dramatists and their audiences explored freely both the dangers of female "otherness" and the potential remedies for women's subordination.

THE POLITICS OF PUBLIC LIFE

The women of Aristophanes' *Ecclesiazusae* know enough about the rules and conventions governing assembly for public debate and decision to misuse them for their own purposes. Is this an example of comic exaggeration or a sign of women's familiarity with customary practices in even those cultural domains from which they were excluded? Or, perhaps, a veiled reference to that mythical time when women had the vote but lost it, along with their own names, after electing Athena over Poseidon as tutelary deity of the acropolis?

Other myths and stories, to be sure, testified to women's capacities as rulers and warriors, even as they consigned such peoples and exploits to the geographical borders of the Greek world or the margins of its historical memories. Among these, none exercised such fascination as the Amazons, those warrior women "more men for their courage than women for their sex"[34] whom every hero, from Achilles to Heracles, was required to vanquish, and whose defeat by Theseus, when they invaded Attica, was central to his role as the legendary founder of Athenian democracy. Amazons figured prominently in the public iconography of the polis in Athens and elsewhere, but their representation found its way into the private domain as well, including on the ceramic implements with which Athenian women protected their knees when they carded the wool.

Several of these knee guards represented Amazons armed, arming, or on horseback. On one of them, Amazons arming in preparation for battle are shown on one side, and the other side of the knee guard depicts proper Athenian wives working wool in the women's quarters of the home. We find analogous juxtapositions of contradictory themes on other vases, too: one, for example, represents a scene of homosexual courtship between boys and men in the gymnasium on one side, and the other side depicts a scene of heterosexual courtship between men and, apparently, respectable women (i.e., not hetaeras or courtesans).

Mythical, legendary, and some historical women appear frequently in Herodotus's *Histories*. But in Herodotus's historical vision neither events nor their causes were limited to either the human realm or to the public domain of strictly political action. And the *Histories*, consequently, are a repertory for the many myths, legends, and stories that conditioned the Greeks' understanding of their historical past, as well as for ethnographic particulars about the social and sexual mores of those peoples who constituted the "other" of the known world.

But in the account of the military campaigns and battles of the Persian War itself, only one Greek woman appears—Artemisia, the Carian queen of Herodotus's native city Halicarnassus (in Asia Minor), who fights on the Persian side.[35] Other Greek women do not figure in the account except incidentally, as when, for example, they are evacuated from Attica before the battle of Salamis.[36] And women generally are even more strikingly absent from Thucydides' *History of the Peloponnesian War,* whose concept of historically significant action was restricted to the domain of military and political events, and for whom women's chief glory in respect to the historical record, as with regard to the public arena generally, consisted in being "talked about least among men, whether for praise or blame."[37]

Nevertheless, women were the ones who provided the polis with its soldiers, and among the Spartans this contribution was marked by the construction of an equivalence between the warrior who perished in battle and the woman who died in childbirth, providing exemption for both from the normal prohibition against named tombstones. In Athens, women's contribution of their sons to war was commemorated most visibly in the many scenes of the warrior's farewell on vase paintings, where a woman helps him arm or, even more frequently, holds the pitcher and bowl for the ritual libation at the family's altar preceding the warrior's departure.

When their city fell, as we have noted, its women suffered enslavement, the fate of the women of Troy in myth, but no less that of the historical women of Melos, when their island was reduced to submission by the Athenians in 416 B.C., during the Peloponnesian War.[38] And when the city was under siege, women did not hesitate to take up whatever arms were available. On Achilles' shield in the *Iliad* they and their children defend the city from atop its walls,[39] and this generic scene has a correlate in the historical record when, during the siege of Plataea, the women pelted the invaders with stones and tiles from the roof tops.[40] And although the women of Sparta were especially renowned for the fierceness of their patriotism,[41] Athenian women too, on one occasion at least, imitated their husbands' public action: the men in the assembly had stoned a councilman to death when he proposed capitulation to Persia during the Persian Wars; the women ran to the councilman's home and killed his wife and children by the same means.[42]

When warriors fell in battle, women in epic poetry and art joined in the public lamentations in the archaic period, both as family members and as professional mourners, and they are often depicted tearing their hair and lacerating their flesh in grief. Both sumptuary legislation in the sixth century, and the fifth-century custom of a communal burial and commemoration of the war dead in Athens, restricted women's public roles in funerary ritual, but family members, including especially its women, played an important part in the *prothesis* ("laying out") and *ekphora* ("funeral procession") of their own dead, as well as in periodic commemorative rites for ancestors. And women appear frequently on the many funerary vases of the fifth century, which represent visits to the tomb and offerings left in memory of its occupant.

Greek women did not, then, participate directly in the political and military affairs of the city. And during their lives, even their public visibility was circumscribed by a number of restrictions both formal and informal, such as the custom observed by the orators of not identifying respectable women by name. When women died, however, both their names and their lives were celebrated and enshrined on marble grave steles erected and sometimes inscribed by husbands, children, and other family members. On them, the dead woman frequently clasps her husband's or mother's hand in a gesture of last farewell, and inscriptions, when they appear, proclaim her virtue and record the grief of those she leaves behind.

THE PHILOSOPHY OF PRIVATE LIFE

The agora and the assembly meeting place (the Pnyx) were the centers of communal civic life in the polis, but there were other institutionalized places and occasions for male gatherings—the gymnasia where they came together for sports and other forms of recreation, and the symposia, drinking parties after the evening meal. The names of two of the gymnasia, however, the Academy and the Lyceum, are better known for the philosophical schools associated with them. And indeed, several of Plato's dialogues are set beside or within the gymnasium, where men socialized and, in the fourth century at any rate, explored philosophical issues.

Among these issues was the proper relationship between men and women in the polis, conceptualized often as the appropriate relation of *oikos*, the private space of the household, to the public domain of the polis. In Xenophon's *Oeconomicus* ("Household Management") and in the *Oeconomica* attributed to Aristotle, men and women are provided by nature with opposite faculties that nevertheless tend toward the same end, the "partnership" of the household.[43] Men, for example, are naturally adapted for movement, whereas women's nature is sedentary and patient; courage is assigned to men and fear to women so that he can defend the household and she can preserve and protect it.[44]

In the *Politics* and *Ethics* Aristotle defends the subordination of wife to husband on the basis of the principle that the male is by nature superior and the female inferior.[45] Consequently, he is made to rule and she to be ruled, but not, however, in the manner of a slave; Aristotle frequently takes pains to distinguish the status of slave from that of women.[46]

Plato, Aristotle's predecessor and teacher, had argued differently in the *Republic,* where, as in Aristophanes' *Ecclesiazusae,* the proposal of equality for women is contingent upon the abolition of private property and the family.

Justice, in both the human soul and in the state, he claims, is genderless, and although differences in the capacity for it exist, they are correlated more closely with distinctions of class or type rather than sex.[47]

Plato's ideal state has much in common with Spartan political institutions, where both the private and public lives of the citizen were organized communally, with public education (the *agôgê*) structured around a system of age-grades, and military training provided in the *syssitia* ("dining clubs") to which men of twenty were elected and where they dined daily even after marriage. The upbringing of girls in Sparta was also state-supervised and included institutionalized training in dancing and athletics. In Plato's *Republic*, boys and girls are given the same education with an emphasis on mathematics, but we have no evidence that girls in the historical Sparta learned to read and write.

The Spartan polis was possibly less idiosyncratic in the ancient Greek world than our sources on the subject, which are uniformly biased and tendentious, would have us believe. Women in Athens, for example, though not trained in athletics, seem nevertheless to have had opportunities for sport and exercise. And it is certain that, among the wealthy at any rate, they learned to read and gathered in private homes to share music and poetry. On a series of vases beginning in the mid–fifth century B.C., women are depicted reading together from papyrus book rolls, playing the lyre while deciphering the notes from a papyrus "score," and checking boys' recitations against a papyrus text. On other vases, groups of women appear to be holding contests in singing and recitation among themselves.

The *syssitia* at Sparta were public, compulsory, and universal. Their analogue in Athens was the symposium, a private and voluntary institution that, like the gymnasium, provided the setting also for philosophical dialogue. The symposium more commonly, however, provided an occasion for drinking, music, dancing girls, and sexual encounters. The women whose presence at symposia is attested on numerous vases were exclusively *pornae* ("prostitutes"), slave women, or *hetaerae* (courtesans, literally, "female companions"), who were usually either free foreigners or resident aliens.

Slave boys, too, were available to satisfy men's sexual desires, but at Athens sexual relations between citizen men were institutionalized by a ritualized form of courtship that encouraged homoerotic and pederastic relations between an older and younger man (the *erastês* or lover and *erômenos* or beloved). And in Sparta, institutionalized pederasty functioned both as a general political phenomenon and as a feature in the formation of political alliances. The form of intercourse practiced between Athenian men was ideally intracrural ("between the thighs") and did not involve penetration, submission to which violated bodily integrity and was regarded as appropriate for only women or slaves. Male citizens who prostituted themselves by accepting payment in return for sex suffered the penalty of partial disenfranchisement.

Communal life for men in Athens was not restricted to its centers of political activity but included institutions where the physical, intellectual, and aesthetic aspects of their lives might also find expression. Communal associations among women, except in the sphere of religion, were not institutionalized. Among the wealthy, however, where the daily drudgery of child care and household labor could be entrusted to slaves, opportunities for informal social gatherings seem to have been exploited freely.

THE DISORDERS OF THE BODY

A citizen woman's sexual life was legally restricted to relations with her husband, but as represented by Aristophanes, at any rate, sexuality was a source of lively enjoyment for wives. From the medical writers' perspective, however, the woman's body was exclusively a reproductive one, and for them the female orgasm, like its male version, was associated with the release of "seed."[48]

Furthermore, intercourse was regarded as beneficial to women because the uterus (hystera), which was naturally light, dry, and liable to desiccation, was then suffused with the moisture of the man's semen. Deprived of wetness, the womb would seek to restore the imbalance by wandering throughout the body and lodging itself near moister organs, producing the condition known as "hysteria." The physician could coax it back into place through the use of foul-smelling fomentations applied from above, or sweet-smelling ones burned below.[49]

But as Plato described it, hysteria resulted when the womb (the "animal" within women), desirous of procreation and frustrated by infertility, "becomes furiously angry and wanders everywhere throughout the body." It is cured when "desire and passion" bring man and woman together in sexual intercourse, through which "tiny formless animals" are sown in the womb.[50]

For Aristotle, the male endows the fetus with form through his semen in conception and generation, and the female supplies it with matter from her menstrual blood.[51] Semen, in Aristotle's view, is a more refined form of blood, "concocted" through the male's greater bodily heat to a higher state of purity than menstrual blood. Menstrual blood is also "concocted" but remains impure, lacking the constituent of "soul."[52] For the female, Aristotle claims, endowed by nature with less bodily heat, is thereby "a kind of incapacitated male."[53]

A similar view of conception and generation appears in Aeschylus's *Oresteia*, where Apollo, defending the primacy of father over mother, argues that "the mother is not parent of her child, / but nurse only of the new-planted seed that grows; / the parent is he who mounts."[54] Medical writers, however, saw things differently; some claimed that seed was contributed by both parents and that it was drawn from all the parts of the body.[55] Nevertheless, from the point of view of their bodies, women were constituted by the medical writers principally through their reproductive capacities. The treatises on women address only this aspect of their bodily functioning, whereas "the patient" in Hippocratic writings on such topics as "regimen in acute diseases" is generically male. Thus, for the medical writers, women's anatomical form followed their sociological function.

THE CONVENTIONS OF EVERYDAY LIFE

A woman's *hystera* or womb, in its tendency to wander and in its insatiable longing for sexual intercourse, was the polar opposite of Hestia ("Hearth"), virgin goddess of the inner spaces of the home around whose symbolically circular and immobile altar the sacred rituals of the household were performed. Like Hestia, who in Plato's *Phaedrus* "stays at home alone"[56] when the other Olympians go out in procession, the Athenian wife was ideally a home-keeping woman, for whom, as Xenophon remarks, it was better "to remain within rather than wander about outside."[57]

We have seen something of her domestic duties already, chief among which was the care of her children, whose upbringing she oversaw until her sons reached the age of seven, when their education was taken over by the men, and until her daughters departed for marriage. As wives in their turn, daughters performed the tasks they had watched their mothers doing and which they had learned by practicing at their sides.

Spinning and weaving were, above all, the province of women, an activity that might be performed by slaves as grueling household labor, by wives to exercise and display their artistic skills, or by heroines and goddesses— Penelope as proof both of her virtue and her wiliness, Athena Erganê ("Worker") in her function as patron of the women's craft, or the Moirae ("Fates"), who spun out the thread of life and cut it at life's end. Socrates advised Aristarchus, burdened with the support of his female relatives, to set them to work at the loom,[58] but for a citizen woman spinning and weaving was creative as well as practical, both a daily occupation in the home and an act endowed with religious significance.

In the *Republic*, Socrates catalogues (only to dismiss as trivial) women's customary occupations: "weaving and baking and cooking."[59] And whereas the variety of tasks involved in wool-working is represented frequently on vases, kitchen tasks appear only in the more humble medium of terracotta figurines, which may have served as toys.

Meat was normally consumed only on festival occasions, and its consumption was always preceded by sacrifice. An extensive series of ritual actions—in some of which women participated—governed the preparation and slaughter of the domestic animal, as well as the cooking and distribution of its parts. The transformation of flour into bread, by contrast, was an everyday task, although religious celebrations of various kinds also called for the preparation of ritual cakes, and some vase paintings depict women patting them into form.

"We have hetaerae for pleasure, concubines for the daily care of the body, but wives to bear us legitimate children and to be the trusted guardians of our household."[60] So proclaims one speaker in a fourth-century oration, and another reports that "after the birth of my child, I had every confidence [in my wife] and entrusted all of my affairs to her, presuming that there was complete intimacy between us."[61] A woman's interest in her husband's household was thought secure only once it was consolidated through the birth of children, but thereafter she became guardian of the household stores and was entrusted with oversight of its day-to-day functioning.

We have seen what this entailed, and most of this activity was not performed as solitary labor but in the company of slaves or sometimes freed women, like the one who was found lunching in the courtyard with a citizen wife and her children when some men came to collect a debt.[62] On vase paintings representing a variety of other activities in the women's quarters, women are often shown as a group, and usually without signs of status distinction. We have noted that they are represented together spinning and weaving and reading and singing, and they are also shown washing, grooming, dressing, and adorning themselves.

During the day, the house was the province of women, and both in town, where private homes were close together, and in the country, where dwellings were further apart, there would have been many occasions for socializing. Chief among these were daily excursions to the well, and a large number of the vases used for water carrying were decorated with women gathered at the fountain house. On some vases we see also the unsupervised encounters with men against which women's restriction to indoors, enshrined in countless proverbs and adages, was intended to safeguard.

And indeed it was when she went to the river with her maids to launder the clothes that Nausicaa came across Odysseus,[63] although we hear of only one occasion in the classical period when a chance meeting outdoors led to subsequent adultery, and that was during a funeral procession.[64]

A man who committed adultery with another man's wife could be killed on the spot, whereas rape was punishable by a fine. For adultery, which required a wife's collusion, brought into question the legitimacy of her husband's children. A husband was required to divorce an adulterous wife, and she was punished further by exclusion from the city's religious rituals.[65] This dual sanction was the equivalent of disenfranchisement for women, since the citizen women's entitlements in the polis involved principally the rights to bear legitimate children, to participate in religious festivals for women, and to assume an honored place in other public religious celebrations.

Aristotle reports that in democracies it was impossible to keep poor women from going out,[66] and it was in fact not just a sign of immodesty, but also of poverty for free women to circulate in the public spaces of the polis. They are found there in our sources as vendors of bread, garlands, vegetables, perfumes, and other goods, and Demosthenes talks about a time when poverty forced citizen women into wet-nursing, wool working, or grape picking.[67] Some of these working women appear on vases engaged with men in commercial encounters, and although those represented on drinking cups are probably hetaerae ("courtesans"), others may be poor citizen women supporting themselves by their labor. In extreme circumstances, citizen women might be forced to sell themselves, and we hear of one who became a hetaera because of poverty, and another because she was "bereft of guardian and relatives."[68]

The sanction against adultery for women, as we saw, amounted to a kind of excommunication, and participation in the religious life of the polis was not just a woman's chief public function, but also a part of her daily life in the home. Upon entering her husband's *oikos* (household) for the first time, a wife was initiated into its cult, and she maintained it on a regular basis thereafter, sacrificing either by herself or with her family at the many shrines that were to be found both within the home and at the point of its boundary with the world outside.

In the ancient polis, no domain of the secular was marked off from that of the religious, and no activity was too mundane to be exempt from supervision by one or another of the many divinities of the Greeks in one or another of their many embodiments. The same was true of the *oikos,* which, organized ritually like the polis around its central shrine, was not only a site for many religious observances but a sacred space whose ritual integrity was maintained by means of the daily activities that took place within it. Women's confinement to the household in the ancient Greek polis, then, did not entail the kind of exile from the centers of significant social, political, and economic activity that it has for Western women in the modern era. At the same time, it was also the unmistakable sign of women's inferiority within a cultural order constructed around a complex system of analogies and polarities, that is, complementaries and oppositions between male and female.

PROPERTY AND PROPRIETY

After 338 B.C, when Athens was defeated by Philip of Macedon, Athens was still a polis, but, as with other Greek city-states of the Hellenistic period (323 B.C. to A.D. 19), her independence was overshadowed by her relationship to the great Hellenistic kingdoms. In 322, for example, an Athenian revolt against Macedonian domination was put down and a Macedonian garrison was established in the city, along with a revision of the constitution restricting the franchise to the wealthy. Then, after a brief restoration of democracy, the city was recovered by a Macedonian general and its administration was handed over to Demetrius of Phaleron, nephew of Aristotle and his successor as head of the Lyceum, which was founded by Aristotle in 335. Under Demetrius of Phaleron, property qualifications for citizenship were slightly broadened, but it was not until Demetrius Poliorcetes ("Beseiger of Cities") drove out Demetrius of Phaleron in 307 that full democracy was restored. But instability remained a regular feature of Athenian political life throughout the fourth century and after.

By the end of the fourth century the political landscape of the polis had been transformed in ways that were to remain permanent: power and prestige were concentrated in the hands of the rich, and political offices were increasingly monopolized by a propertied elite who expended their wealth conspicuously in public benefactions. Among the members of this urban elite women are to be counted as well, especially in the Greek cities of Asia Minor, where women held public offices, acted as benefactors of their cities, and were rewarded for their generosity with public dedications of statues, honorific inscriptions, and the like.[69]

Evidence for such public activity derives mostly from the second century B.C. and later. For example, several decrees dating to the second half of the second century from Cyme, in the province of Aeolis on the west coast of Asia Minor, honor Archippe, the daughter of Dicaeogenes, for her distributions to the populace and her construction of a council house, and reward her with the dedication of a statue in the agora.[70] But beginning with the late fourth century, there is also evidence that respectable women were artists, musicians, poets, philosophers, actresses, and physicians.[71]

Most of this evidence attests to women's activities in parts of the Greek world other than Athens, but one fourth-century Athenian epitaph for Phanostrate records that she was a midwife and physician who "caused pain to none, and was mourned by all upon her death."[72] A biographer of Plato includes two women among his disciples, neither of whom, however, was herself an Athenian.[73] And Arete, the daughter of Aristippus who came to Athens from Cyrene to study with Socrates, was one of her father's disciples; she reportedly trained her son herself, so that he bore the nickname *Metrodidaktos* ("Mother-taught").[74]

Inscriptions and other testimony to women's activities in the public sphere proliferate in the Hellenistic period. These cannot, however, be regarded as a secure basis for asserting that women's status or roles generally underwent a significant transformation. For this evidence must be evaluated in the context of the political transformations of the period, the persistence of traditional ideology, and continuities with inscriptional evidence from the earlier periods.

Thus wealth combined with the new political prominence of urban elites to make it possible for the women of propertied families to play a role as benefactors in the public domain. But in the Hellenistic kingdoms generally, women of royal families often assumed public duties. And, one might add, they sometimes met with death as a result.

The example of Mania, wife of Zenis of Dardanus, a Greek city on the Hellespont, is a case in point, and it dates from the early fourth century. Zenis had been appointed governor of the Persian province of Aeolis in 399 B.C., and upon his death Mania approached the satrap Pharnabazus and asked to be appointed in her late husband's place. Pharnabazus agreed and Mania served him well, using a Greek mercenary force to subdue the independent Greek cities on the coast. During the battles, she herself "looked on from a carriage." Later, however, her son-in-law, stung by gossip claiming that it was shameful for a woman to rule while he was a mere private person, murdered both Mania and her son.[75]

Throughout this period, just as in the late fifth century, philosophical arguments that some virtues were common to both men and women were combined with advocacy of traditional role divisions. Among Pythagoreans in the third and second centuries B.C., for example, seventeen women were numbered as members of the community. But Phintys, in her treatise "On Chastity," claims that "serving as generals, public officials, and statesmen is appropriate for men," whereas "keeping house, remaining within, and taking care of husbands belongs to women."[76]

And women of all periods offer dedications of money, statues, crowns, ritual vessels, and the like, although less frequently than men. In the early fifth century B.C., a washerwoman offered a tithe of her earnings in a dedication recorded on the acropolis of Athens[77]; a woman of the early fourth century claimed in a dedication that she was a "thrifty worker"[78]; and in the second half of the fourth century Melinna dedicated a share of her earnings to Athena Erganê ("Worker") in thanks for the goddess's beneficence, proclaiming that by her own handiwork and skill she had raised her children.[79]

The ideology that restricted women to the private and men to the public sphere did not, then, restrict either the minority of elite women of the Hellenistic age from engaging in public benefactions or the majority of women of modest means in all periods from working for their livelihoods. Propriety, or adherence to widespread social ideals, was always and everywhere contingent upon property status.

CONCLUSION

Our literary sources and other sources abound in contradictory evaluations of the quality of women's lives in ancient Athens. The anonymous young wife mentioned in a dramatic fragment, for example, objects to her father's plans to divorce her from her now impoverished husband and marry her to a wealthier man, protesting that "my husband has been to me everything I wanted, and all that pleases him, father, pleases me."[80] The heroine of Euripides' *Medea,* by contrast, complains bitterly about woman's lot, claiming that, as for the complementarity between bearing children and bearing arms for the city, she for her part "would rather stand in battle three times than bear one child."[81]

These lines were written by men, of course, but even if we had access to the voices of ancient Greek women themselves, it is not clear that this would settle the much-debated question of women's status. Comparisons with the situation of women in Western democracies, traditional societies, or sex-segregated modern states are easy, but they are inevitably misleading, since the position of women in a given society is meaningful only with reference to the overall social, political, and economic character of the cultural order in which it is inscribed.

From the perspective of its constitution and political institutions, the ancient polis was unquestionably a "male club" from which women were excluded and to which their only significant contribution was through child-bearing. But the city was also a sociocultural, religious, and economic community, and women had an important role to play in each of these domains. Even the homekeeping women of the wealthier classes were active and regular participants in the broadly comprehensive sociocultural arena of the city's rituals and festivals. Women's confinement to the household in the ancient Greek polis, then, did not entail a wholesale exile from the city's institutionalized communal life.

Nevertheless, ancient Greek cultural ideals, as we have seen, insisted upon a strict polarity between male and female and upon a hierarachy that elevated men over women. Cultural ideals have a power of their own, and we have no reason to think that Greek citizen women did not, in their own way and for their own reasons, subscribe to an ideology that proclaimed a person fortunate if he had been born "human instead of beast, man instead of woman, and Greek instead of barbarian."[82]

NOTES

1. Aristotle, *Metaphysics* I.v.6; 986 a 23–27. Hugh Tredennick, *Aristotle XVII, Metaphysics, Books I–IX*, p. 35 (LCL 271). All citations from Greek texts are translated by the author unless otherwise indicated. But in each case references to the most easily available English texts are also included. For most authors, the reader is directed to the appropriate volume of the Loeb Classical Library edition (LCL), published by Harvard University Press, which is cited by the name of the editor and/or translator, and for which the series number is given in parentheses. Many of the Loeb Classical Library translations are available on line at http://www.perseus.tufts.edu/Texts/chunk_TOC.html. And many of the passages may also be found conveniently in Fant and Lefkowitz 1992, some sections of which are available on line at http://www.uky.edu/ArtsSciences/Classics/wlgr/wlgr-index.html.
2. Euripides, *Medea*, lines 573–574. D. Kovacs, *Euripides, Cyclops, Alcestis, Medea*, p. 345 (LCL 12).

3. Hesiod, *Theogony,* line 585. Hugh G. Evelyn-White, *Hesiod, The Homeric Hymns and Homerica,* p. 123 (LCL 57).
4. Hesiod, *Works and Days,* line 82. Evelyn-White, *op. cit.,* p. 9.
5. Hesiod, *Works and Days,* line 82. Evelyn-White, *op. cit.,* p 9.
6. Hierocles (from the *Oeconomicus*) apud Stob. *Flor.* IV.28.21 (= von Arnim, *Frag. Eth.* 62.21). No English translation available.
7. Homer, *Iliad,* Book VI, lines 490–493. A. T. Murray, *Homer, The Iliad,* Vol. I. Books 1–12, p. 297 (LCL 170).
8. Homer, *Odyssey,* Book 1, lines 356–359 Book 21, lines 350–353. A. T. Murray, *Homer, The Odyssey,* Vol. I. Books 1–12, p. 29, Vol. II, Books 13–24, p. 329 (LCL 104, 105).
9. Homer, *Iliad,* Book VI, lines 476–481. A. T. Murray, *Homer, The Iliad,* Vol. I. Books 1–12, p. 297 (LCL 170).
10. Homer, *Odyssey,* Book 6, lines 182–185. A. T. Murray, *Homer, The Odyssey,* Vol. I. Books 1–12, p. 219 (LCL 104).
11. Homer, *Odyssey,* Book 7, lines 67–74. A. T. Murray, *Homer, The Odyssey,* Vol. I. Books 1–12, p. 237 (LCL 104).
12. Homer, *Odyssey,* Book 23, lines 350–358. A. T. Murray, *Homer, The Odyssey,* Vol. II. Books 13–24, p. 399 (LCL 105).
13. Sappho, fragment 2, lines 2–3, 14–16, trans. Jane McIntosh Snyder, *The Woman and the Lyre: Woman Writers in Classical Greece and Rome* (Carbondale, Illinois, and Bristol, Great Britain: Southern Illinois University Press and Bristol Classical Press, 1989), p. 16. D. M. Campbell, *Greek Lyric, Vol. I. Sappho and Alcaeus,* p. 57 (LCL 142).
14. Sappho, fragment 96, lines 6–9, trans. Snyder, *op. cit.,* p. 28. Campbell, *op. cit.,* p. 121.
15. Alcman, fragment 3, lines 61–62, trans. Charles P. Segal, "Archaic Choral Lyric," in *The Cambridge History of Classical Literature,* Vol. I, ed. P. E. Easterling and B. M. W. Knox (Cambridge and New York: Cambridge University Press, 1985), pp. 165–185, citation p. 178. D. M. Campbell, *Greek Lyric, Vol. II. Anacreon, Anacreontea, Choral Lyric from Olympus to Alcman,* p. 379 (LCL 143).
16. See Snyder, *op. cit.,* pp. 92–97. D. L. Page, *Select Papyri, Vol. III. Literary Papyri: Poetry,* pp. 487, 489 (LCL 360).
17. Menander, *Perikeiromene,* lines 435–437 (lines 1013–1014). W. G. Arnott, *Menander, Vol. II, Heros, etc.,* p. 465 (LCL 459).
18. Sophocles, fragment 524 Nauck. H. Lloyd-Jones, *Sophocles, Vol. III, Fragments,* pp. 293, 295 (LCL 483).
19. Plato, *Menexenus* 237e. R. G. Bury, *Plato, Vol. IX. Timaeus, etc.,* p. 343 (LCL 234).
20. Xenophon, *Oeconomicus* vii.11. E. C. Marchant and O. J. Todd, *Xenophon, Memorabilia and Oeconomicus, etc.,* p. 417 (LCL 168).
21. *Homeric Hymn to Demeter,* lines 78–80. Evelyn-White, *op. cit.,* p. 295.
22. *Homeric Hymn to Demeter,* lines 304–307. Evelyn-White, *op. cit.,* p. 311.
23. *Homeric Hymn to Demeter,* line 311. Evelyn-White, *op. cit.,* p. 311.
24. *Homeric Hymn to Demeter,* line 440. Evelyn-White, *op. cit.* p. 321.
25. *Homeric Hymn to Demeter,* lines 471–473. Evelyn-White, *op. cit.,* p. 323.
26. The interpretation of these festivals in this and the following paragraphs is based on Foxhall, "Women's Ritual and Men's Work," in R. Hawley and B. Levick, *Women in Antiquity: New Assessments,* London, 1995.

27. Sophocles, *Antigone*, lines 454–455. H. Lloyd-Jones, *Sophocles, Vol. II, Antigone, etc.*, p. 45 (LCL 21).
28. Aeschylus, *Eumenides*, lines 738–739. Herbert Weir Smyth, *Aeschylus, Vol. II, Agamemnon, etc.*, p. 345 (LCL 146).
29. Sophocles, *Antigone*, line 484. Lloyd-Jones, *op. cit.*, p. 47.
30. Euripides, *Bacchae*, lines 119, 218, 1237. A. S. Way, *Euripides, Bacchanals, etc.*, pp. 15, 21, 105 (LCL 11).
31. Euripides, *Alcestis*, lines 532–533. D. Kovacs, *Euripides, Cyclops, Alcestis, Medea*, pp. 215, 217 (LCL 12).
32. Aristophanes, *Lysistrata*, lines 574–586. B. B. Rogers, *Aristophanes, Vol. III. Lysistrata, etc.*, pages 59, 61 (LCL 180).
33. Varro, cited in Augustine, *City of God*, Book 18.8–10. Eva M. Sanford and W. M. Green, *St. Augustine, City of God, Vol. V. Books XVI–XVIII.35*, pp. 391, 393 (LCL 415). See also Apollodorus, *Library* III.xiv.1, where a different version of the contest appears. J. G. Frazer, Apollodorus, *The Library, Vol. II. Book III. Chapter x*, pp. 77, 79, 81 (LCL 122).
34. Lysias, *Oration II* (Funeral Oration) Section 4. W. R. M. Lamb, *Lysias*, p. 33 (LCL 244).
35. Herodotus, *Histories*, Book 7.99. A. D. Godley, *Herodotus, The Persian Wars, Vol. III. Books V–VII*, pp. 401, 403 (LCL 119).
36. Herodotus, *Histories*, Book 8.40. A. D. Godley, *Herodotus, The Persian Wars, Vol. IV. Books VIII–IX*, p. 39 (LCL 120).
37. Thucydides, *History of the Peloponnesian War*, Book II.45.2. C. F. Smith, *Thucydides, History of the Peloponnesian War, Vol. I. Books I–II*, p. 341 (LCL 108).
38. Thucydides, *History of the Peloponnesian War*, Book V.116.4. Smith, *op. cit., Vol. III. Books V–VI*, p. 179 (LCL 110).
39. Homer, *Iliad*, Book XVIII, lines 514–515. A. T. Murray, *Homer, The Iliad, Vol. II. Books 13–24*, p. 327 (LCL 171).
40. Thucydides, *History of the Peloponnesian War*, Book II.4.2. Smith, *op. cit., Vol. I. Books I–II*, pp. 263, 265 (LCL 108).
41. Plutarch, "Sayings of Spartan Women," *Moralia* 240C–242D. Frank C. Babbitt, *Plutarch, Moralia, Vol. III. Sayings of Kings and Commanders, etc.*, pp. 455–469 (LCL 245).
42. Herodotus, *Histories*, Book 9.5. A. D. Godley, *Herodotus, The Persian Wars, Vol. IV. Books VIII–IX*, pages 161, 163 (LCL 120).
43. Xenophon, *Oeconomicus* vii.18. E. C. Marchant and O. J. Todd, *Xenophon, Memorabilia and Oeconomicus, etc.*, p. 419 (LCL 168). Aristotle, *Oeconomica* I.ii.3, 1343b15–24. G. Cyril Armstrong, *Aristotle, Vol. XVIII, Oeconomica, Magna Moralia*, pp. 331, 333 (LCL 287).
44. Xenophon, *Oeconomicus* vii.23–25. Marchant and Todd, *op. cit.*, pp. 421, 423 (LCL 168). Aristotle, *Oeconomica* I.ii.4, 1343b24–1344a8. G. Cyril Armstrong, *Aristotle, Vol. XVIII. Oeconomica, Magna Moralia*, p. 333 (LCL 287).
45. Aristotle, *Politics* I.ii.12, 1254b13. H. Rackham, *Aristotle, Vol. XXI. Politics*, p. 21 (LCL 264); Aristotle, *Ethics* VIII.x.5, 1160b40. H. Rackham, *Aristotle, Vol. XIX. Nicomachean Ethics*, p. 493 (LCL 73).
46. Aristotle, *Politics* I.v.1, 1259a40. H. Rackham, *Aristotle, Vol. XXI. Politics*, p. 59 (LCL 264). Cf. Aristotle, *Rhetoric* I.v.6, 1360b. J. H. Freese, *Aristotle, Vol. XXII. The*

Art of Rhetoric, p. 51 (LCL 193); and Aristotle, *Ethics* VIII.x.4–5, 1160b25–40. H. Rackham, *Aristotle, Vol. XIX. Nicomachean Ethics*, p. 493 (LCL 73).

47. Plato, *Republic* V.5, 455D. Paul Shorey, *Plato, Volume V, The Republic, Books I–V*, p. 447 (LCL 237). Cf. Plato, *Meno* 72C–73C. W. R. M. Lamb, *Plato, Vol. II, Laches, etc.*, pp. 271, 273 (LCL 165).

48. See A. E. Hanson, "The Origin of Female Nature," in "Conception, Gestation, and the Origin of Female Nature in 'Corpus Hippocraticum,'" *Helios* 19, 1993, pp. 31–71. 1993, pp. 41–44; G. E. R. Lloyd, ed., *Hippocratic Writings* (New York: Penguin Books, 1978) pp. 319–320; and http://www.uky.edu/ArtsSciences/Classics/wlgr/wlgr-medicine.html.

49. See Hanson, *op. cit.*, p. 36; G. E. R. Lloyd, *Science, Folklore, and Ideology* (New York: Cambridge University Press, 1983), pp. 58–94, esp. 83–84; and http://www.uky.edu/ArtsSciences/Classics/wlgr/wlgr-medicine.html.

50. Plato, *Timaeus* 91c. R. G. Bury, *Plato, Vol. IX, Timaeus, etc.*, pp. 249, 251 (LCL 234).

51. Aristotle, *Generation of Animals* I.xx, 729 a10. A. L. Peck, *Aristotle, Vol. XIII. Generation of Animals*, p. 109 (LCL 366); see also http://www.uky.edu/ArtsSiences/Classics/wlgr/wlgr-medicine.html.

52. Aristotle, *Generation of Animals* II.iii, 737 a29–30. Peck, *op. cit.*, p. 175; see also http://www.uky.edu/ArtsSciences/Classics/wlgr/wlgr-medicine.html.

53. *Ibid.* The participle *incapacitated* (*pepêrômenon*) is sometimes translated as "deformed," but "incapacitated" is a more likely meaning in this context. The participle derives from a verb meaning "to maim," "cripple," "mutilate," "castrate," "be defective," or "be incapacitated" in some other way. In the *Ethics*, for example, Aristotle says that virtue can be achieved through study and practice by all who are not "incapacitated" (*pepêrômenois*) for it. Aristotle, *Ethics* I.ix.4, 1099b19. H. Rackham, *Aristotle, Vol. XIX. Nicomachean Ethics*, p. 493 (LCL 73). See also G. E. R. Lloyd, "Aristotle on the Difference Between the Sexes," in *Science, Folklore and Ideology* (New York: Cambridge University Press, 1983), pp. 94–105.

54. Aeschylus, *Eumenides*, lines 659–661. Herbert Weir Smyth, *Aeschylus, Vol. II. Agamemnon, etc.*, p. 335 (LCL 146).

55. See Hanson, "The Origin of Female Nature," in Konstan *op. cit.*, p. 44; G. E. R. Lloyd, ed., *Hippocratic Writings* (New York: Penguin Books, 1978) pp. 321–322; and http://www.uky.edu/ArtsSciences/Classics/wlgr/wlgr-medicine.html.

56. Plato, *Phaedrus* 247a. H. N. Fowler, *Plato, Vol. I. Euthyphro, etc.*, page 475 (LCL 36).

57. Xenophon, *Oeconomicus* vii.30. E. C. Marchant and O. J. Todd, *Xenophon, Memorabilia and Oeconomicus, etc.*, p. 423 (LCL 168).

58. Xenophon, *Memorabilia* II.vii.7–12. Marchant and Todd, *op. cit.*, pp. 151, 153, 155 (LCL 168).

59. Plato, *Republic*, Book V.455 C–D. Paul Shorey, *Plato, Vol. V. The Republic, Books I–V*, p. 447 (LCL 237).

60. Demosthenes 59 (Neaera) 122. A. T. Murray, *Demosthenes, Vol. VI. Private Orations (L–LIX)*, pp. 445, 447 (LCL 351).

61. Lysias 1.6. W. R. M. Lamb, *Lysias*, p. 7 (LCL 244).

62. Demosthenes 47 (Evergus) 55. A. T. Murray, *Demosthenes, Vol. VI. Private Orations (XLI–XLIX)*, p. 311 (LCL 346).

63. Homer, *Odyssey*, Book 6, lines 25ff. A. T. Murray, *Homer, The Odyssey, Vol. I. Books 1–12*, pp. 209ff. (LCL 104).

64. Lysias 1.20. W. R. M. Lamb, *Lysias*, p. 13 (LCL 244).

65. Demosthenes 59 (Neaera) 85–87. A. T. Murray, *Demosthenes, Vol. VI. Private Orations (XLI–XLIX)*, pp. 417, 419 (LCL 346).
66. Aristotle, *Politics* IV.xii.9, 1300a9. H. Rackham, *Aristotle, Volume XXI. Politics*, p. 361 (LCL 264).
67. Demosthenes 57 *Eubulides* 45. A. T. Murray, *Demosthenes, Vol. VI, Private Orations (XLI–XLIX)*, p. 265 (LCL 346).
68. Antiphanes, *Hydria*, fragment 212. J. M. Edmonds, *The Fragments of Attic Comedy after Meineke, Bergk, and Kock* (Leiden: E.J. Brill, 1957–1961), Vol. II, p. 275. Charles Burton Glick, *Athenaeus, The Deipnosophists, Vol. VI. Books XIII–XIV.653b*, p. 89 (LCL 327).
69. For the particulars of this Hellenistic system of "euergetism," see Van Bremen, "Women and Wealth," in A. Cameron and A. Kuhrt, *Images of Women in Antiquity*, London, 1983 pp. 223–242.
70. H. W. Pleket, *Epigraphica. Vol. II. Texts on the Social History of the Greek World* (Leiden: E. J. Brill, 1969), Chap. I, no. 3. No English translation available.
71. Sarah B. Pomeroy, "*Technikai kai Mousikai*: The Education of Women in the Fourth Century and in the Hellenistic Period," *American Journal of Ancient History* 2 (1977) pp. 51–68.
72. H. W. Pleket, *Epigraphica. Vol. II. Texts on the Social History of the Greek World* (Leiden: E. J. Brill, 1969), chap. I, no. 1. No. 376 in M. B. Fant and M. R. Lefkowitz, *Women's Life in Greece and Rome: A Sourcebook on Translation*, Baltimore, Johns Hopkins Press, 1992.
73. Diogenes Laertius, III (Plato) 46. R. D. Hicks, *Diogenes Laertius, Lives of Eminent Philosophers, Vol. I. Books I–V* (LCL 184). No. 216 in Fant and Lefkowitz, *op. cit.*
74. Diogenes Laertius, II (Aristippus) 86. R. D. Hicks, *Diogenes Laertius, Lives of Eminent Philosophers, Vol. I. Books I–V*, pp. 215, 217 (LCL 184).
75. Xenophon, *Hellenica* III.i.10–15. Carleton L. Brownson, *Xenophon, Hellenica I–V*, pp. 181–185 (LCL 88).
76. H. Thesleff, *The Pythagorean Texts of the Hellenistic Period* (Abo, 1965), pp. 151–154. No. 208 in Fant and Lefkowitz, *op. cit.* electronic version: http://www.uky.edu/ArtsSciences/Classics/wlgr/wlgr-privatelife208.html.
77. IG I³ 574 (= Dedications on the Athenian Acropolis 93). No. 322 in Lefkowitz and Fant, *op. cit.*
78. IG II² 12254. No. 318 in Fant and Lefkowitz, *op. cit.*
79. IG II² 4334. No. 317 in Fant and Lefkowitz, *op. cit.*
80. D. L. Page, *Select Papyri, Vol. III. Literary Papyri. Poetry*, p. 186, lines 18–19 (LCL 360).
81. Euripides, *Medea*, lines 250–251. D. Kovacs, *Euripides, Cyclops, Alcestis, Medea*, p. 317 (LCL 12).
82. Diogenes Laertius, I (Thales) 33. R. D. Hicks, *Diogenes Laertius, Lives of Eminent Philosophers, Vol. I. Books I–V*, p. 35 (LCL 184).

SUGGESTIONS FOR FURTHER READINGS

Blundell, Sue. *Women in Ancient Greece.* Cambridge: Harvard University Press, 1995.

Cameron, A., and Kuhrt, A., eds. *Images of Women in Antiquity.* London: Croom Helm, 1983.

Cantarella, E. *Bisexuality in the Ancient World*. New Haven and London: Yale University Press, 1992.

———. *Pandora's Daughters: The Role and Status of Women in Greek and Roman Antiquity*. Baltimore and London: Johns Hopkins University Press, 1987.

Diotima: Materials for the Study of Women and Gender in the Ancient World. An Internet site with source materials, translations, bibliography, archives, and many links to related sites; URL: http://www.uky.edu/ArtsSciences/Classics/gender.html.

Dover, K. J. *Greek Homosexuality*. Cambridge: Harvard University Press, 1989.

duBois, P. *Centaurs and Amazons: Women and the Pre-History of the Great Chain of Being*. Ann Arbor: University of Michigan Press, 1982.

———. *Sowing the Body: Psychoanalysis and Ancient Representations of Women*. Chicago and London: University of Chicago Press, 1988.

Fant, M. B., and Lefkowitz, M. R. *Women's Life in Greece and Rome: A Source Book in Translation*. Baltimore, Md.: Johns Hopkins University Press, 1992. Some sections available electronically at: http://www.uky.edu/ArtsSciences/Classics/wlgr/wlgr-index.html.

Fantham, E., Foley, H. P., Kampen, N. B., Pomeroy, S. B., and Shapiro, H. A. *Women in the Classical World*. New York and Oxford: Oxford University Press, 1994.

Foley, H. P. *Reflections of Women in Antiquity*. New York, London, and Paris: Gordon and Breach Science Publishers, 1981.

Garland, R. *The Greek Way of Life*. Ithaca, N.Y.: Cornell University Press, 1990.

Golden, M. *Children and Childhood in Classical Athens*. Baltimore and London: Johns Hopkins University Press, 1990.

Halperin, D. M. *One Hundred Years of Homosexuality and Other Essays on Greek Love*. London and New York: Routledge, 1990.

Halperin, D. M., Winkler, J. J., and Zeitlin, F. I., eds. *Before Sexuality: The Construction of Erotic Experience in the Ancient Greek World*. Princeton: Princeton University Press, 1990.

Hawley, R., and Levick, B., eds. *Women in Antiquity: New Assessments*. London and New York: Routledge, 1995.

Humphreys, S. C. *The Family, Women and Death*. London: Routledge, 1978.

Just, R. *Women in Athenian Law and Life*. London and New York: Routledge, 1989.

Keuls, E. *The Reign of the Phallus: Sexual Politics in Ancient Athens*. 2nd ed. Berkeley: University of California Press, 1993.

Konstan, D., ed. Documenting Gender: Women and Men in Non-Literary Classical Texts. Special Issue of *Helios* 19 (1993).

Lacey, W. K. *The Family in Classical Greece*. Ithaca, N.Y.: Cornell University Press, 1968.

Lefkowitz, M. R. *Heroines and Hysterics*. New York: St. Martin's Press, 1981.

———. *Women in Greek Myth*. Baltimore: Johns Hopkins University Press, 1986.

Peradotto, J., and Sullivan, J. P., eds. *Women in the Ancient World: The Arethusa Papers*. Albany: State University of New York Press, 1984.

Perseus Project. An Evolving Digital Library on Ancient Greece and Rome. URL: http://www.perseus.tufts.edu/

Pomeroy, S. B. *Goddesses, Whores, Wives, and Slaves: Women in Classical Antiquity.* New York: Schocken Books, 1975.

———. *Women in Hellenistic Egypt: From Alexander to Cleopatra.* New York: Schocken Books, 1984.

———. ed., *Women's History and Ancient History.* Chapel Hill and London: University of North Carolina Press, 1991.

Rabinowitz, N. S., and Richlin, A., eds., *Feminist Theory and the Classics.* New York and London: Routledge, 1993.

Reeder, E. D. *Pandora: Women in Classical Greece.* Baltimore and Princeton: The Trustees of the Walters Art Gallery and Princeton University Press, 1995.

Richlin, A. *Pornography and Representation in Greece and Rome.* New York and Oxford, 1992.

Rousselle, A. *Porneia: On Desire and the Body in Antiquity.* New York and Oxford: Basil Blackwell, 1988.

Schaps, D. *Economic Rights of Women in Ancient Greece.* Edinburgh: Edinburgh University Press, 1979.

Schmitt Pantel, P. *A History of Women in the West,* Vol. I: *From Ancient Goddesses to Christian Saints.* Cambridge, Mass., and London: Harvard University Press, 1992.

Sealey, R. *Women and Law in Classical Greece.* Chapel Hill and London: University of North Carolina Press, 1990.

Sissa, G. *Greek Virginity.* Cambridge, Mass., and London: Harvard University Press, 1990.

Skinner, M., ed. Rescuing Creusa: New Methodological Approaches to Women in Antiquity. Special Issue of *Helios* 13.2 (1986).

Snyder, J. *The Woman and the Lyre.,* Carbondale, IL. South Illinois University Press, 1989.

Tyrrell, W. B. *Amazons: A Study in Athenian Mythmaking.* Baltimore and London: Johns Hopkins University Press, 1984.

Winkler, J. J. *The Constrains of Desire: The Anthropology of Sex and Gender in Ancient Greece.* New York and London: Routledge, 1990.

Zeitlin, F. *Playing the Other: Gender and Society in Classical Greek Literature.* Chicago and London: University of Chicago Press, 1996.

Orant with group of women are shown on a relief from a sarcophagus now in
Rome's Museo Laterano.   ALINARI/ART RESOURCE, NEW YORK.

3

Matres Patriae/Matres Ecclesiae: Women of Rome

Jo Ann McNamara

Women were the agents of change in Mediterranean societies amalgamated under the Roman Empire. Roman empresses created new public roles following the precedents of Hellenistic queens like Cleopatra. Roman law evolved along lines dictated by a new individualism that helped transform the old gender system that rigidly segregated women and men in political life, economic enterprise, and even private power. The Roman patriarchy crumbled as its representatives were subordinated to the power of the emperors, and women found their way into positions of political influence, gained limited control of money, and increased their independence from paternal power. During the first through the third centuries A.D., women showed themselves to be true mothers of the country (a title conferred on empresses) as well as mothers of the Church, contributing far more than we normally recognize to the shape of Christianity as they used it as the vehicle for their own aspirations.

By the fourth century, some of Rome's most distinguished women had converted to the new Christian faith, paving the way for its acceptance as a state religion. This essay discusses the significance of women's role in the cultural changes and religious innovations of the age. In the context of a new belief system, women ceased to define themselves within the limits of the antique gender system that classified them only in relation to men as daughters, wives, and mothers. They discovered a new sense of individual selfhood and common sisterhood.

T he Empress Livia was "male in her powers of reasoning," according to the Jewish philosopher Philo (d. A.D. 50).[1] Romans had a word for people like Livia. She was a virago, a woman with a heavy measure of virtue (meaning "manliness" in classical Latin). After she was safely dead, the historian Tacitus (d. A.D. 117) called her a "female bully" who lorded it over her humiliated subjects.[2] On the whole, ancient biologists were somewhat uncertain about the very existence of a female gender. They professed to have mythological evidence that men could produce babies if necessary. Hippocrates saw conception as a war between strong male seed and weak female seed in a child's composition. Aristotle conceptualized a continuum running from perfect to defective manliness with most females on the lower end. He argued that women, being deformed men, were unsuited by nature for any task but nourishing male seed.[3]

The Romans did not dispute Aristotle's conclusion that women's imperfections marked them for subjection to men, but nor did the Romans agree that quarantine was necessary.[4] They boasted of women's descent from the goddess Venus and placed noble matrons high among their heroic ancestors. Women's standing even improved somewhat in the biological universe. Soranus (ca. A.D. 100) tamed the "wandering womb," by tying the uterus firmly to the cervix—by implication providing women with inner organs commensurable to those of men. Galen (ca. A.D. 150) saw women as men inside out and admitted that there was a maternal seed that joined with the father's in producing a child. Romans therefore tended to arrange individuals along a gender continuum according to their varying degrees of virility and effeminacy. Thus patrician Roman women would be more generously endowed with virtue than men of lesser races and classes. Though apportionment was largely determined by heredity, the odds could be considerably improved by carefully controlling the conditions of conception—climate, position, and above all the sobriety of the partners.

Training enhanced natural manliness and kept natural effeminacy in check. Thus women who disciplined their intellectual and physical qualities could achieve near parity with the best of men. Livia's only practical equal was her husband, Augustus, who had completed the Roman conquest of the Mediterranean after five centuries. Last to fall was the Roman Republic itself, torn throughout the last century before Christ by civil wars between emperors (generalissimos) at the head of professional armies that were increasingly manned from conquered peoples. First century A.D. emperors used foreign guards to subdue and periodically decimate the old Roman ruling class. Their empresses became their closest partners in organizing the royal household, with its legions of slaves and freed persons, into an efficient and overarching bureaucracy. Tacitus the scandalmonger depicted Livia as domineering even over Augustus and poisoning his natural heirs to advance her own son Tiberius.

Thus the victorious Romans themselves joined their subjugated enemies, who struggled in different ways to resist, accommodate, or take advantage of their political feminization. Meanwhile, at the lower end of the spectrum, an unmarried Jewish girl in a conquered province conceived Augustus's most famous contemporary, a son, Jesus of Nazareth, who preached a new kind of virtue that flourished best among the humble and the poor in spirit. Shaken by external violence and internally menaced by the loss of cultural identities, women and slaves, the outcasts and the traumatized, listened. Christian recruits coalesced around the households of wealthy women, many of whom made bold to renounce the sexual and procreative roles that defined them as female in favor of lifelong virginity. Their critics called them hysterical; their coreligionists called them virile. The Pauline epistle promised: "In Christ, there is neither Jew nor Greek nor bond nor free nor male nor female (Gal. 3:28)."

For the next three centuries, the imperial government and the Christian religion followed separate but converging tracks, ultimately merging in a Christian empire. Out of the psychological and social stress of a hundred cultures seeking new foundations for their individual and their group identities, women came into their own as active public agents. Leaders in the worlds of Caesar and God alike, women broadened the boundaries of their lives. In the palace, empresses claimed royal partnership as a wifely prerogative, and in the Church, virgins claimed to transcend the gender system. By the fourth and fifth centuries, although patriarchy was reaffirmed by mutually reinforcing male political and religious hierarchies, the new social contract included queenly consorts and consecrated virgins in visible and public roles. And all were rooted in the Christian family, where the close bond of married couples and their children was envisioned as a haven from a sinful world.

THE ROMAN REPUBLIC

Romans remembered their Republic as a perfect patriarchy, a golden age when all men set a heroic standard of virtue and even women strove successfully to meet it to the best of their natural abilities. Nearly all the original sources have been lost in favor of the nostalgic and highly romanticized narratives written in the early imperial period. Livy (d. A.D. 17), Vergil (d. 19 B.C.), and Plutarch (d. A.D. 120) gave posterity examples of heroic, austere women and men who built a city out of nothing, overthrew their own tyrants, and proceeded methodically toward a divinely appointed destiny to rule the world by right of their own respect for law and justice. Men ruled women, but women served with dedication and ability. Their chroniclers shaped a collective vision of the Roman Republic as resting firmly on the decorum of their great patrician families. They paid respects to their heroic mothers even while they idealized a patriarchy designed to keep woman out of the arena of power.

The Dominion of Virtue (Fifth to First Centuries B.C.)

At first, says Livy, Rome was a city without women. When her men could not obtain wives in a peaceful manner from their neighbors, they arranged to kidnap the neighboring Sabine women while they were bathing in a stream. The women bore their forced marriages with dignified resistance for a year until their dilatory relatives finally came to the rescue. Then

> with loosened hair and rent garments they braved the flying spears and thrust their way in a body between the embattled armies. They parted the angry combatants; they besought their fathers on the one side, their husbands on the other, to spare themselves the curse of shedding kindred blood. "We are mothers now," they said, "our children are your sons, your grandsons: do not put on them the stain of patricide." . . . The effect of the appeal was immediate and profound. Silence fell and not a man moved. A moment later the rival captains stepped forward to conclude a peace. (Livy I.13)

The Roman matron, grave and resolute, was a worthy partner. The legionaries pursued their destiny of world domination secure in the knowledge that their wives, mothers, and daughters would serve as effective surrogates in the government of their homes. The Republic itself was founded on the integrity of Lucrezia, a faithful wife raped by the tyrannical King Tarquin. To safeguard the honor of Roman matronhood forever, she stabbed herself after revealing the crime to her husband and her kindred, who killed the rapist and vowed that Romans would never again bow to a king. Shamed, the rebel Coriolanus withdrew his invading army, which threatened the city with a new tyranny, after his mother Veturia publicly spurned his embrace and cursed the son who had violated the soil of his motherland. When the African invader Hannibal threatened the city, the matrons gave their jewels to save it. Centuries later, when Lucrezia's descendant Brutus was defeated by Caesar's heirs, his wife Portia killed herself rather than live under a new tyranny.

Romans were well aware that women were capable of both fighting and governing if given the opportunity. The knowledge challenged them to maintain the highest standard of virtue among the senate and people of Rome (practically defined as the army) who governed the Republic. The senate was closed to all but the "conscript fathers" of the patrician class, which was periodically enriched with men whose merit had gained them consular office and periodically purged of unworthy individuals by a censor. The "people" were regularly tested under military discipline, and their victories spoke for them. Women, by definition secondary in virtue, were barred from public office and were not taken into the army. Indeed, they were forbidden to enter the senate chamber, and senators were instructed to control their impulses to share the manly secrets of government deliberations with women.

To qualify for office, a senator had first to prove his manhood as a *paterfamilias*, ruler of one of the small polities of younger siblings, children, concubines, slaves, and dependents who made up the Roman *familia*. Every woman was legally defined as a child who was guided and brought to her full potential by a prudent and stern father and kept under his tutelage for life. In practice, the *familia* was a monarchy, not a republic. Like Alcestis of old, the Roman wife was a stranger in her husband's house, but this did not make her insignificant. The matron was a consort queen in the domestic domain and a resident ambassador for her paternal kindred.

Patria Potestas

The Roman ruling class was held together and systematically reconstituted by a complicated system of marriage, adoption, and inheritance that was increasingly governed by personal testament rather than legal custom. Though the Romans rarely interfered with the private laws of their subject peoples, the upper layers were gradually knitted together over the centuries. In the sixth century A.D., the Emperor Justinian collected surviving practices into a single coherent code and ordered all copies of the older laws to be destroyed. Few fragments survived beyond the precedents that reflected the imperial nostalgia for the old family values of the Republic. Central to this vision was *patria potestas*, paternal power, which enforced the *mos maiorum* (the ways of the elders). Theoretically, fathers had the right of life and death over their children, as over their slaves, and this right generally continued over married daughters (even in cases of adultery). As we might expect, however, few fathers ever seem to have exercised the right, and, indeed, it is generally held that paternal power protected women from the hasty violence of their husbands. A good daughter, in turn, was an active partisan in healing political rifts and forging alliances for their fathers with their husbands and sons. After his death, the father became a god. If he kept his wife long enough, she eventually transformed her character from daughter to mother and found a place of her own in the ancestral pantheon.

Except for a handful of young virgins temporarily serving the goddess Vesta, all women with status or dowry were supposed to marry. There was little room for frivolous preference. Membership in the senate was mainly hereditary and dependent on appropriate marriages. Established families renewed their blood through marital unions with rising men distinguished by wealth, political skill, or military success. Stoic ideals inspired women as well as men to strive for self-control, to master inner passions and shape outward demeanor to the dignity befitting a ruling class and a ruling people. Ideally, a Roman couple fulfilled their sexual duties judiciously to supply healthy progeny of good stock for the Republic. Women ineligible for marriage theoretically helped preserve the dignity of Roman matrons by indulging their husbands' less dignified pleasures as concubines or prostitutes.

Patrician men who were serving Rome abroad in the army or in exile depended on their mothers and wives to run their estates and their family affairs and to keep their political lives from disaster, as we see in Cicero's letters. The physical chores of child care were left to slaves or to anyone else who happened to be in the house, but a mother assisted or replaced an absent father in educating children for their adult duties. Because of divorces, which reflected the shifting patterns of Roman politics, children often grew up in their fathers' houses under the supervision of stepmothers. Nevertheless, in adult life they counted on their mothers for social and political support.

Romans recognized several marital arrangements, but the most popular was marriage *sine manu* ("without the hand"), which ensured that legal control of a married woman would remain at her father's disposition and that he could order her divorce at will. Fathers gave property directly to their daughters (with themselves or a designated relative as guardian), not to their sons-in-law. As women aged and their fathers died, their ability to control their guardians and dispose of their own bodies and property grew. Clodia (called Lesbia by her poet-lover Catullus) was one of the more vivid beneficiaries of the system. A woman of many lovers who was suspected of murdering her husband, she was an active political partisan of her brother Clodius, one of the demagogues whose ambitions added to the turmoil of the dying Republic.

Roman writers refused to blame their undisciplined soldiers for the collapse of their virtuous polity. Instead, foreign women, so unlike the digni- fied matrons of Rome, embodied the old threats of obliteration and chaos em- bedded in Sirens, Furies, and Amazons. Vergil remembered the seductive Dido, queen of Carthage, who almost diverted Rome's founder, Aeneas, from his destiny. Even her pitiful suicide following his desertion only provoked her descendants to fight the Punic wars, which thwarted Roman expansion for nearly a hundred years. Livy immortalized the Etruscan sorceress Tanaquil, who nagged her husband Tarquin into imposing himself upon the gullible Romans as a divinely chosen king. Tacitus added the first century British queen, Boudicca, who sacrificed every citizen of the captured Roman town of Colchester to her thirsty goddess. And all these writers were haunted by the ghost of Cleopatra, queen of Egypt, who seduced their consul Antony from his respectable Roman bride, coupling the powers of rampant female sex- uality with the emasculating threat of monarchy that lowered free men to the effeminate condition of slaves.

THE PAGAN EMPIRE

Civic disorder complemented foreign menace. While the triumvirate (rule of three men) quarreled over Caesar's inheritance, the republican constitution collapsed. First century writers unanimously attributed its failure to loss of old- fashioned virtue; selfish men had neglected their duty to control the women of Rome, whose unguided energies had broken loose in sexual license and politi- cal intrigue. Juvenal (ca. A.D. 100), Tacitus, and Suetonius (d. A.D. 140) called the remnants of the Roman ruling class the withered fruit of a once noble tree.

Augustan Renovation (First Century A.D.)

Half sincere and half fraudulent, Augustus followed his defeat of Antony and Cleopatra by proclaiming the restoration of the Republic. Obsessively reiterating this rhetoric of restoration, he and his successors designed laws and institutions to impose an ancient Roman vision of the right order of society upon an empire exhausted by war and civil strife. If they could, they would have sent men back to the plow and occupied their wives with annual pregnancies. Instead they conspired to glorify old-fashioned paternal power and patriotism and divert Rome's attention from Augustus's and his successors' usurpation by urging Rome's renewal. Behind this makeshift façade, they supported a *de facto* monarchy with the army and a household bureaucracy.

Claiming that Roman fathers had failed to do their duty, Augustus used his imperial powers as an all-encompassing *patria potestas*, infantilizing men while bringing women under the scrutiny of public law. He penalized persistent bachelors with loss of offices and status, restrictions on inheritances, and the right to make wills. He offered women who bore three children recognition as legal persons in their own right, adults capable of controlling their own lives and property without a legal guardian. Freed women, who had been emancipated from slavery but not promoted to the full rights of free-born women, could achieve the same status after bearing four children. Augustus ordered married men to shoulder their responsibilities as guardians of their wives and daughters and to enforce marital chastity. The *Lex Julia de Adulteriis* in 18 B.C. transferred jurisdiction from the family to the state and established a permanent court to hear cases against married women and their lovers. The wronged husband could be punished as his wife's accomplice if he failed to prosecute her adultery. Other laws forbade upper-class women to register as prostitutes in order to consort freely with men. Men were to be prosecuted if they consorted with women who had not registered as prostitutes. Over the next three centuries, emperors reissued and strengthened these laws. They attempted vainly to force marriage upon an increasingly reluctant population and to stem the high divorce rate by transferring some of a father's power over women to their husbands.[5]

Augustus's own private life exemplified the ambiguity and contradictions in his public policies. He had passed his daughter Julia around as a wife to one potential political successor after another. But when he discovered that she had taken a series of private initiatives, he was obliged to send her into exile in conformity with his own law on adultery. His second wife, Livia, had but one child, Tiberius (her first husband's son), but Augustus freed her from *patria potestas* and granted her the Right of Three Children in 9 B.C. This meant that no one could interfere with her administration of her vast personal wealth or subject her to the laws restricting women's inheritance.

Livia's private power was hidden by the façade of Republican institutions: she was never allowed to enter the senate, the sanctuary of the antique patriarchy. As head of the palace household, however, she made the empress an intrinsic part of the imperial structure, routinely rewarding service on her personal staff with promotion in the imperial administration. In his will, Augustus adopted her into the imperial family, and she became high priestess of his cult, which entitled her to the insignia of public office. Her son Tiberius, fearing to enhance his mother's power, vetoed the senate's resolution to award her the title *Mater Patriae*, Mother of the Country. In time, however, the emperor Claudius proclaimed his grandmother a goddess.

The unbridled use of personal power by women and men alike still casts a shadow over the early Roman Empire. The imperial office and the government that supported it were essentially undefined and their limits untested. With no constitutional sanction, the privatization of power inherent in the monarchical principle favored the ambitions of women in the imperial family. Agrippina the Elder, for example, strengthened her son Caligula's imperial claims by cultivating his popularity among the soldiers. If we are to believe scandalmongering second-century chroniclers, the politics of the bedchamber and the poison cup replaced the politics of the forum and the battlefield. Without constitutional restrictions, emperors pursued their caprices until assassination ended their careers. Emperors who no longer listened to the senate or its officials took the advice of their wives and mothers. Fearful of enhancing the power of their rivals, they entrusted unprecedented governmental powers to their slaves.

This was not necessarily an evil course. From Tacitus and Suetonius in the second century until modern times, historians have attributed the untimely deaths of Augustus's immediate heirs to Livia's ambitions for her son Tiberius. They have accused Claudius's empress, Messalina, of every sexual excess and sadistic cruelty imaginable and have blamed Nero's mother, the younger Agrippina, for producing his psychotic symptoms by manipulating him with both sexual and maternal wiles. But, in fact, there is no particular reason to suppose that the influence of these and other women was malevolent. Certainly, the Julio-Claudian empresses used both charm and intelligence to achieve their ambitions. They were often ruthless and, like their husbands, often needed every resource to stay alive and prosper once they had entered the dangerous imperial sphere. In their turn, they inspired fear in others.

We must beware the historian's cliché. Whenever women manipulate their private positions to gain a share of public power, nervous chroniclers blame the lustful weaknesses of men or the unnatural powers of feminine sorcery. Livia the poisoner, Messalina the sexual athlete, and Agrippina the devouring mother are their fantasy creations. Madness stalked the Julio-Claudian emperors, and most of their women died violently. Whether they were really mad and depraved themselves, we will never know. In the second century, peace and prosperity were restored with a line of "good" emperors happily partnered with a succession of "good" empresses, mutually devoted to that virtuous self-control they learned from Stoic philosophers. But even as empresses grew in manly virtue, their subjects feared that loss of freedom and political potency would force them to the feminine end of the continuum. These subjugated women and men turned inward to cultivate that individual self-control that enabled them to resist humiliation and temptation. The manly woman became a metaphor for triumph in adversity.

Christian Innovation (First Century A.D.)

The peoples roughly digested into Rome's empire suffered from severe alienation. Their ethnic gods had failed to protect them and were carried away to sterile honor in the Roman pantheon, leaving the individual psyche vulnerable and bereft. Rural populations became increasingly isolated by language, customs, and religion from their cosmopolitan neighbors, and their cultures withered without the stimulation of urban spectacles and national success. Peasants who enlisted in the army or emigrated to the city fell out of family networks and local cults. People from many lands mixed promiscuously in polyglot cities, where the secular ideals of Roman patriotism did little to heal their spiritual wounds.

Inevitably city life fostered individualism with all its self-involved preoccupations. Despite legal and social pressures, men failed to marry and women resisted childbearing. In the wake of the wars, mobs of veterans and refugees filled the cities: men too restless to farm and widows too poor and friendless to maintain themselves. In a public expression of *patria potestas*, the emperors treated their male *proles* ("children") to an increasingly generous dole. Women without male providers did not share this public charity but were forced to fend for themselves. Alone and unprotected, they sank all too often into the desperate masses of the Roman state's unwanted children.

Not all widows were poor, and not all women failed in their endeavors. Slaves became freed women and free women heiresses. Literary references and epitaphs testify that many women commanded wealth and used it in a variety of ways to benefit family, friends, or favored institutions. Jewish inscriptions, scattered over the empire, praise the generosity of women benefactors of the synagogues. Rich women traveled with Jesus and supported him and his disciples. Some women pushed into the marketplace. Petronius's *Satyricon* ridiculed the freed man Trimalchio who made a fortune on capital amassed by his enterprising wife when she was a slave. Lydia, who owned a thriving business in purple dye, contributed to Saint Paul's mission. Such women, whose wealth did not command commensurate public prestige, seized the opportunity to influence the shape of society offered by new religions that proliferated outside the male power bastions of the early imperial centuries.

Many cults competed for worshippers, and many of them offered women prestige and public activity. The Egyptian goddess Isis and other goddess religions were noteworthy, but even in so patriarchal a religion as Judaism, there is evidence that women widened their devotional roles and enjoyed positions of influence that we do not today associate with the synagogue. Other cults, called "mysteries" because they subjected new candidates to secret initiation rites, were more radical. Their individualistic nature, stressing secret knowledge and personal salvation, posed a subversive challenge to both family and state. Satirists like Juvenal saw women as the unguarded gates through which the unsavory cult leaders gained entrance to the upper reaches of Roman society.[6] Shocked observers saw a nightmare world where women ran loose, their most destructive powers unshackled, threatening the future of the Roman race and the ruling class itself by their refusal to bear children on the one side and their refusal to abide by a sexual code that would certify the paternity of the children they did bear on the other. In A.D. 83, when the empire had suffered several reverses, three of the six vestal virgins, the only Roman women recognized as free of paternal or conjugal authority, were executed for behaving unchastely.

This is the world of the women who heeded the call of an itinerant preacher from Galilee to leave home and family and follow after him to Judaea. Critics despised Christianity (as well as other "mysteries") for its appeal to lower-class men and women who had given way to inherently unstable emotions. The men were generally described as humble folk and even slaves. However, the women mentioned in the New Testament (the Gospels, the Pauline letters, and the Acts of the Apostles) spanned the entire social range. Rich or poor, what the female disciples shared was a general sense of isolation from the safe centers of society. They often lacked the only badge of respectability antique society conferred on women: the matronal guardianship of a patriarchal household. Though Jesus's mother was related to the wealthy Joseph of Arimathea, she was married to a humble carpenter, and critics of Christianity explained this arrangement as a makeshift resolution for an untimely pregnancy. Jesus first revealed his divine claims to a Samaritan woman whose shady lifestyle hardly redeemed her despised origins. An anonymous sinner "who loved much" anointed him before his death. He cured several female companions of demonic possession and one from chronic hemorrhaging, which had subjected her permanently to the stigma associated with menstruation.

These were his companions when the Roman soldiers executed him in the reign of Tiberius (A.D. 14–37). His male followers had run away after his arrest fearing that they too might be executed. Three days later, however, the women announced that Jesus had risen from the tomb where they had laid him. The men filtered back into Jerusalem, where a fierce religious awakening flung them as missionaries throughout the Mediterranean world. The message that they recalled and embedded in the written record of Jesus's preaching was that the last shall be first and the first shall be last. Widows and separated wives, women mourning the loss of a protective brother, a woman about to be stoned for adultery, all attested the failures of the legal patriarchy to support or even control women. Women helped to shape and spread Christianity as a validation of individual worth separate from worldly social status. To heal their alienation, they preached union with God himself and in his name defied the *patria potestas* of their fathers and even their emperors.

By the end of the apostolic generation (ca. A.D. 70), there were Christian churches in Egypt, Syria, Asia Minor, Greece, and Italy. Subsequent sources register their appearance across the Roman world from Britain to Mesopotamia and even beyond into India. Such a vast reach could have been accomplished only by an equally vast multitude of agents. Yet only one record survives in the canonical record; it centers on the work and teaching of Paul. The passionate discussions and experiments that engaged other communities are all but forgotten except in fictional and legendary traditions of the second century that recount the efforts of missionary women. In addition to the women who prophesied and presided over house churches in the New Testament, many women heard the message of wandering Christians and rooted it within their household and among their friends. In some communities there were only women keeping the faith and practicing their religion unassisted by priest or teacher.[7]

Fearing that the political system as well as the gender system was under attack, the emperors often responded to the spread of this religious passion with persecution. In A.D. 19, according to Josephus, a matron was accused of having allowed herself to be seduced in Isis's temple by a lecher masquerading as the god Anubis. As a result, Tiberius had the priests of Isis crucified and their worshippers—four thousand in number—exiled to Sardinia, to kill the brigands there or be killed by them. Along with the worshippers of Isis, he banished a number of Jews who had been accused of cheating a matron by pocketing alms she had given for the community in Jerusalem.[8] In A.D. 57, Nero tried the wife of the Roman general in Britain for "addiction to a foreign cult." A few years later, he accused the Christians of setting fire to the city of Rome, possibly to divert suspicion from himself. He used the burning bodies of Christians for torches in his gardens and forced some of their women to play the leading roles in violently pornographic spectacles.[9] This imperial savagery was not without purpose. The public cults of Rome, culminating in the worship of the emperor himself, focused the loyalty and devotion of Caesar's subjects; the personal religions of the new age were aimed at diverting their devotees away from the fatherland and its concerns.

Women Under Roman Law (Second Century A.D.)

In the second century, a long period of peace and the growing common culture of the provinces fostered rapid communication of new ideas that were given concrete shape by developing Roman law and the spread of eastern philosophy and religions. Most of the emperors of the age came from outside Italy and spent the bulk of their time in the provinces. The benefits of Roman citizenship gradually spread to all the free people of the empire. The ruling class slowly yielded to a humanitarian perspective that encouraged the emancipation or partial emancipation of the unfree. A growing class of freed women and men occupied an intermediate place in the social scale between the free-born and the slave.

Legislation, however, remained traditionalist. The new emperors remained committed to the old family system, periodically reinforcing the Augustan laws on marriage and adultery. They sought to impose monogamy on everyone, though they did not prohibit divorce. They encouraged childbearing but did not prohibit fathers from exposing unwanted children to death or any other fate that might await them in the public streets.[10] They put more emphasis on the element of consent in marriage (though this was probably intended to encourage men to marry, not to free women from male control). Christian morality often simply extended the direction of Roman law. It strengthened monogamy by prohibiting divorce, limiting men's freedom to abandon their wives. Christians wrote treatises in the late second century praising the virtues of conjugal love and parental affection for children. They went on to oppose the exposure of unwanted children, mostly girls, to death or prostitution. Where the Roman dole was restricted to men and their families, Christian charity aimed at widows and orphans in the community.

Roman law also sought to protect the class structure of the empire and viewed cross-class marriage as a deadly threat. Men who wanted a relationship with women of a lower social status could take them as concubines, who enjoyed legal protection for themselves and their children. However, women who wished to enter a union with men lower in the social scale were seen as the instruments of class degradation. In A.D. 52, Claudius sponsored a law reducing to slavery any free-born woman who lived in concubinage with a slave if she had acted without the knowledge of the man's master. If the master had known, she would be degraded to freed woman status and her children were to be slaves. A century later, Hadrian modified this law so that the child was free if the mother remained free. In the early third century, Septimius Severus decreed that a Roman woman could not free a slave in order to marry him.

These prohibitions aimed to control both women and men in the civic spirit of Roman morality. But they fell hardest on women who lacked freedom either to choose or reject sexual experience or childbearing. At the end of the first century, the Emperor Domitian exiled his kinswoman, Flavia Domitilla, for unknown crimes. Later Christian tradition held that after two of her slaves converted her to Christianity, she defied her family and refused to marry. She was far from the last Christian woman to suffer death rather than sacrifice virginity to the population needs of the empire. More traditional women, however, benefited from the extended protection of marriages in third-century Roman law. Eventually, the relations of Roman soldiers with their provincial concubines were transformed into legal marriages and their children were recognized as legitimate.

The Acts of the Apostles remarks that Paul was fortunate in converting "leading women" in many cities, and second-century sources confirm that this continued to be the case. Such women used their wealth and freedom to establish house churches where they and their slaves and the poorer members of the Christian congregation could share their religious feasts. Roman lawyers of the second century took an increasingly liberal view of the capacities of women to own and manage property, freely bestowing the Right of Three Children on growing numbers of applicants. By a decree of A.D. 212, the Emperor Caracalla extended the economic and social privileges of citizenship to all free men and women in the empire. Henceforward, women would enjoy legal protection of their inheritance rights and personal liberty, but not, of course, the privileges reserved for men.

Philosophers began to reconstruct the concept of virtue as gender-inclusive, recognizing the value of courageous women as well as charitable men. The sources for both groups reveal an increasing awareness of independent female agency and male autonomy reduced by imperial power. Stoic philosophers boasted of women in their ranks, and Christian women instructed their neighbors. The Christian theologian Clement of Alexandria, arguing that women commanded the same virtues as men (though always, of course, to a lesser degree), owlishly reminded his readers of the fierce Amazons who fought in barbarian armies beyond the frontiers of civilization. "Manliness is to be put on in order to produce confidence and forbearance, so as to give the other cheek to him who strikes on the one cheek, strongly restraining anger. So we do not train our women like Amazons to manliness in war since we wish men to be peaceable."[11]

The Female Imperium (Second and Third Centuries)

Throughout the history of the Roman Empire, each successful dynasty sought to obscure the brutal truth that their power rested upon their soldiers' arms by emphasizing the familial quality of monarchy. This encouraged second- and third-century empresses to create a public presence that reinforced their husband's military offices. The five "good emperors" (Nerva, Trajan, Hadrian, Antoninus Pius, and Marcus Aurelius), whose reigns spanned the second century, were all adopted at the peak of their military careers by their childless predecessors, a policy which, by co-opting the most threatening rival, secured the pax Romana for nearly a century.

Much of this happy period in the empire's history was secured by Trajan's wife Plotina, along with his sister and aunt, Marciana and Matidia. The seat of empire gradually moved away from Italy, and few of the second- and third-century emperors came from the old Roman families. Plotina acted in her own name, within an hour of her husband's death, to secure Hadrian's succession to the imperial throne by signing a decree adopting him. In exchange, he married Matidia's daughter, Sabina, whom he kept with him through all his travels even though they did not like each other very much. These empresses were not chosen for sexual allure. Power moved steadily upward, centralizing in the emperor's hands. Only the empress, as his divine alter ego, shared his prestige. She was given the imperial title "Augusta" and, like her husband, became a goddess at death.

Their constant travels became a sort of nonmilitary version of the triumphs that had once expressed the warlike capacities of republican emperors. The empress and her entourage became central figures in these elaborate public ceremonials with which the empire focused the loyalty of its subjects. In A.D. 100, Pliny the Younger delivered a panegyric for Plotina, calling her a fit partner for the emperor. Hadrian himself delivered Matidia's funeral oration. Faustina, the wife of Marcus Aurelius, shared the imperial prerogative of having a town named after her. She was commemorated with a coin issue, and a maintenance allowance for poor girls was endowed in her name.

The third century began with renewed conflict over the succession. A provincial military leader, Septimius Severus, emerged triumphant with the formidable assistance of his wife, Julia Domna. The four Severan women, Domna, her sister Maesa, and Maesa's daughters, Soemias and Mamaea, grasped the office of empress firmly and extended it broadly through the next generations. Julia Domna's name appears on inscriptions and coins, and she was publicly acclaimed as Mother of the Army (*Mater Castrorum*). She was swift to destroy the men who challenged her influence over the emperor and had one son killed to secure the throne for another, Caracalla, who was more susceptible to her influence. After Septimius's death in 211, as Caracalla's mother, she held the reins of government while her son distracted himself with gambling. In 214–215, while he was with the army in the East, Domna answered petitions and other official correspondence and sent dispatches to the senate under both their names.

Domna's sister Maesa was equally decisive. After Caracalla's death, she seized command of the army in the name of her daughter Soemias's son, Elagabalus. She and Soemias stemmed a rout by leaping from their chariots to make an appeal that turned the tide of battle. Soemias won the honors for which Livia and Agrippina had striven: a seat beside the consuls in the senate with power to join them in signing decrees. Like Domna before her, Maesa did not hesitate to put her daughter and grandson to death when she saw that Elagabalus could not maintain the power she had won for him. She successfully conspired with Mamaea, her second daughter, to promote Mamaea's son, Alexander Severus. Maesa died four years later, and Mamaea, after fending off Alexander's bid for independence, took charge. She presided over a senate of women intended as a complementary body to the senate of men, which established a complicated code of etiquette for the women of Rome. Though dissolved on Alexander's death, it was revived by Aurelian and possibly other emperors on various occasions.

Led by the Severan empresses, women encroached on the public preserves once sacrosanct to men. Plotina took an active part in religious and philosophical speculation, being particularly influenced by Epicureanism, a school that explored the possibilities of gender equality through philosophy. In moments of insecurity and political danger, Domna also turned to philosophy for support, establishing a following of learned people who called her Julia the Philosopher. These learned ladies from the east probably also knew the work of Clement of Alexandria, one of the principal creators of Christian theology. He maintained that only their sexual and reproductive equipment defined women differently from men. Their spiritual abilities and intellectual capacity was equal in every respect.[12] His Egyptian metropolis later gave rise to the myth of Saint Catherine of Alexandria, a learned martyr whose forceful logic convinced her first panel of judges to convert and share her fate.

According to a plausible Christian tradition, Julia Maesa toyed with Christianity as an alternative source of prestige to Domna's epicureanism, patronizing Origen, Clement's successor in the school at Alexandria. Mamaea also invited Origin to preach at the palace, and the Empress Olalitia Severa, with her husband Philip the Arabian, carried on a joint correspondence with him. Eusebius, the fourth-century historian of early Christianity, said that Origen castrated himself so that no fear of scandal would prevent the admission of women to his school. It was he who suggested that the immortal soul, disembodied, would eliminate the distinctions of gender from the heavenly kingdom.

The Severan women came from a priestly Syrian family serving the sun god Elagabalus, for whom Soemias's son was named. While the empresses of his family moved aggressively into the masculine end of the gender continuum, Elagabalus adopted a distinctly feminine identity. He worked with wool, sometimes wearing a hairnet, and painted his eyes with feminine cosmetics. He held a special festival to mark the day he shaved his beard, and afterwards he had the hairs plucked out so as to look more like a woman. Believing himself to be the God, Elagabalus married Aquilia, a vestal virgin. He dispensed her from her vows in order to join their two religions, but it is highly probable that the union remained symbolic. Aquilia has been tentatively identified as the "Severina" to whom the Christian writer Hippolytus dedicated a treatise. Perhaps she had a special sympathy with Christian values and the contemporary ideal that some of their women drew from the Clementine analysis that virginity was a "manly" condition that transcended gender. In any case, we know that Roman women acted as conduits for the ascent of Christianity from the lower levels of society to its upper reaches.

Female Christianity (Second and Third Centuries)

Women found two things in Christianity that they found nowhere else. First of all, they found their own selfhood. Second, they found one another. These enterprising women embraced and propagated a Christianity that was institutionally different from the Roman Catholic church that consolidated after the persecutions ended. For a long time, many Christian communities were isolated and autonomous. Even in established centers like Alexandria, the schools were not yet subordinated to the authority of bishops, and women could cultivate a wide range of religious experience. Christian virgins and consecrated widows did not isolate themselves from the life of the cities in which they lived. Clement said that the women of Alexandria spent their days running from church to church to meet their friends. Alternatively, they entertained wandering preachers and religious visionaries in their homes, though Clement promoted church worship by family units.[13] In Africa, virgins attended the baths at fashionable hours and danced at other people's weddings. On Sundays, some of them prophesied in the churches after the liturgy.

The developing concept of virginity threatened to destroy gender barriers by rejecting the traditional sexual and procreative roles that restricted women solely to relationships with men. Communities of widows and virgins appear wherever Christians are visible to us. They, or someone writing for their benefit, composed a body of historical fiction, known as the Apocryphal Gospels, whose heroines treated conversion to Christianity as synonymous with a vow of strict chastity. They afforded their readers examples of valorous and intelligent women defying menacing husbands, parents, and imperial troops, role models for a spreading culture of women, married and single, in revolt against their traditional matronal roles. The Apocrypha also express rejection of a class system that separated women from one another. One of the most popular story lines involves the joint conversion of noble women with their slaves and the subsequent union of these converts against husbands, fathers, and public authorities. The story may end in martyrdom for all concerned or in the successful conversion of the male persecutors to Christianity and asexuality, but from the author's point of view, either resolution represents a happy ending.

An eyewitness account of the sufferings of a group of second-century Gallic martyrs confirms that the apocryphal fictions reflected a grim reality. A slave girl had been arrested with her mistress. Both women suffered bravely, but the witness concentrated on the inspiration of Blandina, the female slave, the least virtuous position possible on the Aristotelian continuum. The persecutors accordingly thought that she would be the weakest link in the Christian chain. To induce her to deny her faith and thereby degrade her whole community before the assembled spectators, the soldiers subjected her to a series of ferocious tortures. Day after day, they prolonged her suffering, hanging her on a cross to watch the games below. Daily she inspired her martyred companions with her example and her admonitions. A witness said she had "put on Christ," vividly overcoming her deficiencies of class and gender.[14]

About twenty-five years later, at the beginning of the third century, the prison diary of the martyred Perpetua provides direct insight into the mind of such a woman.[15] She was an aristocratic matron, a recent mother, who was arrested with a group that included the pregnant slave Felicity, who gave birth during their imprisonment. Perpetua turned a deaf ear to the pleas of her respectable pagan family that she recant her faith and save her life. Estranged from her husband, she surrendered her baby to her parents and turned instead to her companion Felicity, who was sentenced to die with her. Perpetua and Felicity formed a revolutionary union, attacking the patriarchal Roman family from both ends of a social scale that had formerly obscured their mutual interests as women. Perpetua's diary stresses the additional pain that she and her companion suffered in childbearing and in thwarted mother-hood before their final ordeal. At the end, Perpetua overcame this anguish and broke through the barriers of her gender. She dreamed that she entered the arena of combat, where she was transformed into a man. Perpetua's meta-phor expressed a revolution in female consciousness.

Second-century women who preached Christianity, nurtured it in their homes and villages, and ultimately died for it had taken up the religion as an instrument of their own liberation from the constraints of pagan tradition and pagan sensibility. As prophets and deaconesses entrusted with the instruction and baptism of women, they found a new role to absorb their energies and creative imaginations. As the directors of "house churches" where communal meals were organized, charity was dispensed, and hospitality was given to itinerant preachers, they could put themselves at the center of a new social grouping. As virgins or chaste widows they could set themselves outside of the gender system. If they were wealthy, they could use their power to bring their former slaves out of the class system.

By the end of the second century, male Christian writers were increasingly attentive to this female challenge and began to take steps to repair a gender system that had deteriorated too much for their comfort. Irenaeus of Lyon and other orthodox writers began to criticize women who joined various cults in which they prophesied and led the ceremonies. Clerical writers became in-creasingly articulate and increasingly exclusive in defining the doctrines of their religion. They tried ruthlessly to brand persons of variant opinions as heretics and to remove prophets of both genders whose preaching was guided by their inner mystic vision from the flock. Particularly obnoxious to them were sects led by female prophets or by men and women performing joint liturgies. Even as orthodox writers were condemning the sacerdotal activities of women, they were co-opting the concept of virginity and trying to reduce virgins to episcopal authority. Tertullian offered the ideal symbolic vehicle in refuting virgins who claimed that they were not subject to the restrictions tra-ditionally placed on women. Indeed, he maintained, they were brides of Christ and must conduct themselves as a model to all matrons.

From apostolic times, while many Christians were pursuing these alter-native visions, a church was developing with a male hierarchy resembling the old republican institutions. Bishops, priests, and deacons gradually were sep-arated from the laity and given a monopoly of the emerging sacramental sys-tem. Women were excluded from all clerical orders except that of deaconess, which covered charitable and instructional services to women. Gradually, deaconesses lost their single sacramental function of conferring baptism upon women when a modest sprinkling with water replaced immersion. Married clergy made self-conscious attempts to avoid the imperial dynastic model for their priesthood, excluding their own wives from the female diaconate. Only widows, who had long enjoyed special status in Christian communities, and virgins of suitable maturity could be consecrated.

If women resented the pretentions of clerical authorities to assume a new *patria potestas* over them, we have only the faintest echoes of their protests. In spite of Christianity's growing institutionalization into a church that excluded them from intellectual, administrative and liturgical leadership, women still clung to it fiercely and continued to number significantly among the volunteers for martyrdom. Women immersed in the charitable and instructional aspects of the diaconate may have underestimated the seriousness of their limitations. Other women may have been too engrossed in preaching Christ's message of equality to give their attention to the practical inequalities that were multiplying under clerical leadership. Their experimentation with new gender roles may have slowed and become muted in the face of outside persecution, while martyrdom enhanced their claims, however elusive, to transcend the gender system altogether by gaining first place in another world.

The final force of pagan Rome, dramatically, was pitted against a religion that boasted that it was strong in its women. The Great Persecution, launched at the beginning of the fourth century by the Emperor Diocletian, finally snapped the long tension between the Augustan ideal of renovation and the hopes of the alienated for Christian innovation. The all-conquering empire and its soldier-ruler faced a legion of virgins, widows, and slaves who made their own suffering the implement of victory for a God who offered a kingdom in which there would be neither bond nor free, male nor female, neither marrying nor giving in marriage.

THE CHRISTIAN EMPIRE

Helena, the Emperor Maximian's Christian concubine, had been repudiated in favor of a wife eligible for the office of empress under the old status-conscious laws. Her son Constantine repudiated the old pagan empire and decreed tolerance for his mother's religion. As emperor he was less radical than the Christian writers, who sought to discourage all sexual relationships outside of permanent and indissoluble marriage; instead, Constantine encouraged cross-class marriages when they guaranteed harmony of religion and sexual virtue. Constantine did, however, sponsor laws respecting the marital rights of slaves, and he strengthened the rights of concubines. He forbade unilateral divorce. Most radically, he allowed women to refuse marriage if they chose to live independently.

The Conversion of the Empire (Fourth Century)

In legitimating his regime, Constantine employed his mother as a principal agent in his effort to use religion as a complement to military power. He translated the cult of imperial divinity into patronage of the Christian church. He put great wealth at his mother's disposal, which she used to establish churches containing inscriptions in her honor. Constantinople, her son's new Christian capital in the east, blossomed with statues of Helena. She erected churches in Bethlehem and on the Mount of Olives to mark the holy sites for later pilgrims. Building on the religious roles that had enhanced the public positions of earlier empresses, she promoted popular devotions that emphasized sacerdotal liturgies, particularly processions and pilgrimage.

When she traveled to Jerusalem, Helena repaid the hospitality of the community of virgins by waiting on them at table. Many people followed her example in visiting the holy places, but women in particular sought to change their lives by physically departing from their accustomed environment. Wealthy widows deserted the unsympathetic milieu of aristocratic Rome to travel in the Holy Land and ultimately settle there. Egeria (or Etheria; manuscripts differ) from Spain made a systematic tour of the places mentioned in both the Old and New Testaments and wrote a record of the devotions she practiced there for her religious sisters at home.[16] Melania the Elder and Paula, matriarchs of two of Rome's greatest families, formed religious communities in the Holy Land and left the old pagan city forever.

Excluded from the clergy, women often turned to the cult of saints to satisfy their religious ambitions, collecting relics and establishing shrines at the tombs of martyrs. Helena was one of the first promoters of the cult of relics. Claiming to be guided by a vision, she demolished a temple to Venus that covered the site still honored as the Holy Sepulchre. There she found a cross and nails, which she brought to Constantinople. Under imperial patronage, the fragments were ultimately dispersed to hundreds of shrines. Indeed, it became a distinctive mark of Western queenship to install wood from the true cross in a suitably imposing church.

The fourth-century Church was moving away from the fluid gender system of the Pauline promise. The implications in Origen's philosophy that the triumphant soul would transcend the body and its biological definitions were rejected in the theological controversies of the age. The immortal soul was to be forever gendered, tied to its resurrected body. Still, the Church did not yet have the earmarks of a male citadel. Efforts to commit the clergy to celibacy at the Council of Elvira (between A.D. 312 and 324) came to nothing. Deacons, priests, and bishops still had conjugal partners. Documents written by men, often of a critical nature, reveal a metropolitan world in which women daily congregated at the churches—sometimes traveling in litters from one church to another—to pray, to meet with their friends, to dispense charity, and to refresh themselves with picnics in the midst of their devotions. The growing popularity of the cult of the Virgin Mary symbolized the dual focus of this early Church. Mary had long been a central figure in the female communities for whom the apocryphal gospels were written, but there was no Marian shrine until Helena built one in Nazareth to commemorate her pilgrimage in 325. Thereafter the cult spread rapidly. In 350, through a vision, the Virgin demanded a church in Rome, sending a summer snowfall to mark its boundaries. Ever since, the shrine of Santa Maria Maggiore has rivaled St. Peter's for the devotion of pilgrims.

Throughout the fourth century, men of the senatorial ruling class routinely continued to conduct pagan rituals while organizing the games, taking omens, or simply doing obeisance to the god-emperor in the ceremonies of public life. Soldiers worshipped their standards, and aristocratic notables tended the altars of their forefathers. But while these men clung to their satisfying old ways, women explored the possibilities of the new religion. By the middle of the fourth century, the story of an obdurate pagan man converted by a pious wife or persistent mother became a Christian stereotype.[17] The history of Christian men in the fourth century tends to be a history of the developing hierarchy and its relationship to the imperial state, and of the creation of orthodox doctrine. Women were excluded from the ecclesiastical orders, but in the fourth century the clergy was vastly inferior in status to aristocratic matrons. Helena could depose a bishop of Antioch whom she regarded as a dangerous theologian. Her successors entered into contests of power with the greatest bishops without hesitation.

The Church still kept its distance from the state, offering a separate sphere of power in which the wealth and rank of aristocratic women might be deployed to advantage. The women of the imperial family and of the great aristocratic houses involved themselves on both sides of the great theological quarrels with fanatical enthusiasm. They lobbied the emperors and his officers, supplied money to their partisans, and demonstrated in the streets. They were as ideologically involved in the politics of orthodoxy as the clergy themselves. But they must also have enjoyed the opportunity to use their political and intellectual skills. The clergy, for all its claims to superiority, flattered and courted women who had political power and economic resources. These women controlled appointments to church offices, the construction of church buildings, and patronage for scholars and preachers. A heroic literature developed with biographies of Macrina, Melania the Elder and her granddaughter of the same name, Paula and Eustochium, Olympias and Gorgonia, and a host of others, all viragos whose admirers sought to hold up as rivals to the fighting heroes of antiquity.[18]

The Cult of Virginity (Fourth and Fifth Centuries)

From apostolic times, women had set themselves apart from the world by pursuing a life of celibacy. Late in the third century groups of women and men began to move out of the cities into the deserts of Egypt and Syria to live in colonies devoted to the rejection of all worldly ties and interests. Some were hermits, like the legendary Mary of Egypt who roamed the wilderness like an animal, far from humanity, seeking God without benefit of priests or sacraments. Others entered formal communities like those established by Pachomius and his sister Mary in the Egyptian deserts near Thebes. There the men lived on one side of the river and the women on the other, strictly secluded from all other men, dependent on the monks to provide for their subsistence from donations solicited from admirers and the sale of their handiwork.

The sources commemorating the people of the desert are full of sexual tension. It is not clear whether the sisters chose their cloistered way of life or whether the monks (who were probably their relatives) imposed it on them.[19] The desert communities loved stories of beautiful courtesans like Thaïs, who was converted to religious life by the desert monk who saw the soul within her well-tended body. But they equated her conversion with confinement, the screening of her fatal beauty from a vulnerable world. At the same time, they reported other stories of women who infiltrated the lairs of men in the wilderness and lived with them harmoniously in male disguise. The legends of these "transvestite saints" demonstrate the confidence of contemporaries that chastity empowered women to compete equally with men for the laurels of self-imposed martyrdom.[20]

Not all women exchanged the older urban forms of celibate life in favor of the desert. Many continued to enjoy a less regulated ascetic experience in their own houses. From Asia Minor to Gaul, fourth-century women formed small religious communities or joined study circles devoted to the study of virginity's philosophical aspects. Basil, generally credited with the foundation of Greek monasticism, was converted to the ascetic ideal by his sister Macrina, who headed an establishment with her mother, brother, former servants, and other compatible women and men. Melania the Younger also institutionalized the cross-class aspect of female Christianity by claiming to be the equal of her former slaves in her new community. Paula's monastery in Bethlehem included women of every class, though she retained her superiority over the whole community. Marcella organized a circle of Roman aristocratic women who studied the ascetic life together and occasionally assisted Jerome with his biblical exegeses. In Gaul and Spain ascetic women lived at home and attended bishops in a body on ceremonial occasions. These communities and networks still live in the correspondence of the Fathers of the Church. The letters written by their female correspondents have not been preserved.

In the last age of the western Roman empire, the *materfamilias* began to emerge in her own right. Mothers and daughters, mistresses and slaves united to resist the last pressures of the old classical *familia*. Widows often helped their daughters to evade marriage and motherhood, and then joined them in the monastic life. Melania the Elder helped to rescue her granddaughter from the dynastic ambitions of her family. Paula took her daughter Eustochium with her to Bethlehem, abandoning her son. Jerome rejoiced that Eustochium's virginity brought one of Rome's most ancient houses to an end. Women turned vast estates into communities under their own direction. As the barbarians advanced, the women gave thanks that they had dispersed their wealth to the poor before it could fall to marauding armies. The Roman world was falling, and its patriarchal structure, the failed design of Augustus, was being buried beneath the rubble.

Classical writers had argued that heterosexual friendship was impossible because all friendship must be grounded in equality. Christians found a new base of equality in the elimination of sexual tensions. Wives, like Therasia, wife of Bishop Paulinus of Nola, persuaded their husbands to forego their conjugal rights. A whole circle of such self-denying couples corresponded with one another and exchanged insights into the deep friendship opened up by their radical way of life.[21] Among celibate Christians, virile women and virtuous men met face to face. Chaste widows and a few consecrated virgins made firm and lasting alliances with bishops and other leading ecclesiastical figures. The women contributed money and political connections to doctrinal or political causes espoused by the men. The men in turn brought their female friends into the inner councils of the Church. Women like Paula and Eustochium funneled their experience through writers like Jerome to evolve a theology of virginity as the conqueror of death, the true road to ultimate salvation. Paula was wealthy enough to build Jerome his own monastery so that they could live in separate establishments, meeting constantly. Young virgins without the independence derived from wealth sought to live chastely in joint households with sympathetic clergymen. This syneisactism (cohabitation without sex) idealistically sought to make reality conform to the ancient Christian formula "In Christ there is neither male nor female."

This mingling of men and women so far beyond the boundaries of the established gender system sounded some deep atavistic chord in the most sympathetic men. Chrysostom, the tempestuous bishop of Constantinople, spoke for gossiping neighbors and scandalized officials. Though sympathetic and supportive of the religious life established by his friend Olympias, he denounced mixed, holy, and celibate households as a source of scandal, regardless of the purity of the participants. By the end of the fourth century, the women who led such daring lives and the men who abetted them suffered a stinging backlash. Christianity was becoming respectable and no longer smiled sympathetically upon its radicals. Thus Jerome says that even in Bethlehem critics hounded Paula and threatened to confine her as insane. Virginity had moved women far along the continuum of virtue. Perhaps few of their contemporaries cared to see the social effects of the new ranking, so unfavorable to the men who continued to live by the rules of antiquity.

Christian Queenship (Fifth and Sixth Centuries)

At the end of the fourth century the Emperor Theodosius declared Catholic Christianity to be the only recognized religion of the empire. Fifth-century empresses of the Theodosian house systematically enhanced their office by imitating Helena. One princess, Pulcheria, used her virginity and the legal freedom it gave her to take control of the empire. In youth, she consecrated herself to virginity and thus escaped subordination to the powers of a husband. She promoted feasts and celebrations honoring virgins, putting herself at the center of the ceremonies. She patronized churches and controlled bishops as she dominated her brother Theodosius. When her brother died, she seized control of the government and married a soldier publicly dedicated to guarding his wife's virginity. While delegating imperial military duties to him, Pulcheria applied herself to directing the ecclesiastical hierarchy. She was an enthusiastic promoter of the cult of the Virgin Mary and influenced the council of Chalcedon (451 A.D.) to condemn the Nestorians, who denied that Mary had given birth to God but called her a mere vessel for a human baby.

The freedom to experiment with the ascetic life and the wealth and power to intervene in both secular and ecclesiastical politics depended finally on the security and prosperity of the Roman Empire. Increasingly through the fifth century, women and men alike suffered from growing violence as barbarian armies began to pillage the cities of the empire. Jerome's correspondent Marcella died in the sack of Rome in 410. The imperial princess Galla Placidia Augusta was carried away as a hostage to marry the Visigothic prince Ataulf. The days of pilgrimage and retreat were ending. But before the final collapse, the Christianized classical heritage received a final increment. In the sixth century, Justinian presided over the exhaustive codification of the Roman law that was destined to dominate the western legal tradition.[22] There, he enshrined many of the rights won by Roman women during the five centuries of the empire. The law guaranteed women's right to control their own property after the age of twenty-five and to leave it where they liked when they died. Justinian extended Constantine's recognition of virginity as a way of life by paradoxically granting consecrated women the Right of the Three Children. He clarified the ambiguity of classical jurists and ratified the Christian view of marriage as a contract between consenting individuals.

In public and in private life, Justinian was inseparable from his wife Theodora, whose image faces his in commemorative mosaics at Ravenna. Theodora came from the underworld of entertainers and prostitutes. To enable her to marry his heir, the Emperor Justin was obliged to revise the laws forbidding a senator to marry a harlot. Once married, her power was institutionalized. As joint ruler of the empire, she fulfilled Livia's dream of participating in all the imperial functions. The *Secret History* of her scurrilous contemporary Procopius attributed her influence to her unreserved sexual prowess.[23] He sneered at her efforts to use the monastic system as a refuge for women who started life as she had done with no alternative but prostitution, claiming that the prostitutes she placed in monasteries were so unhappy that they flung themselves into the sea rather than submit to her virtuous regime. In church affairs, she encouraged Justinian's preference for theological positions that ultimately contributed decisively to the growing rift between east and west. Even Procopius, however, acknowledged that no one equalled the virility she displayed when she confronted a rebellious mob and refused to let the emperor flee, reminding him that "purple makes the best shroud."

CONCLUSION

From Livia to Theodora, from Mary of Nazareth to Mary of Egypt, through the first five hundred years of our era, women wove their way through a loosened social fabric to form dramatic new patterns of life, new relationships on earth and even with heaven. Some of them wielded enormous power, and others voluntarily suffered torture for the sake of the kingdom to come. Released from the confinement of the antique *familia*, they transformed the conjugal partnership and gained economic and legal rights that continued to mark the most influential law code the world has ever produced. Perhaps their proudest legacy was the autonomous woman, the virgins, martyrs, and sainted queens who joined the priesthood at the head of the Christian hierarchy. Unfulfilled still is the dream of the syneisactics, who began to define a new and more equal domestic relationship with men.

Roman law and Roman Christianity would link the dying empire with the emerging West. In the new world, to be sure, men would still be dominant, and most women would still be defined in terms of their relationship with men. But the women of the Roman world had gained a firm foothold in the public world of work and worship. Law and letters recognized their influence. They crossed through the dark passage from the ancient to the medieval world guided by a bright vision of themselves and of one another.

NOTES

1. Philo of Alexandria, *Speculum Legibus*, 319f., in *Works*, ed. and trans. F. H. Colson and G. H. Whitaker, Harvard University Press, Cambridge, 1962.
2. *Annals of Imperial Rome* 1.3, trans. Michael Grant, Penguin Classics, Baltimore, 1962, p. 31.
3. Aristotle, *On the Generation of Animals* 1.3, trans. D. M. Balme, Clarendon Aristotle Series, Oxford, 1972.
4. *Ibid.*, 2.1.
5. The problem of reconstructing these laws and a summary of their history can be traced in Leo F. Raditsa, "Augustus' Legislation Concerning Marriage, Procreation, Love Affairs and Adultery," *Aufstiege und Niedergang der Römische Welt* 2 (1980), pp. 278–339.
6. Juvenal, *Satires* 6:525–30, ed. and trans. G. G. Ramsay, W. Heinemann, London, 1924.
7. Pseudo-Clement of Rome, *On Virginity* 2, 1, *Ante-Nicene Fathers* 8:63.
8. Josephus, *Jewish Antiquities*, 18:81–84, ed. and trans. G. A. Williamson, Penguin Books, New York, 1981.

9. Tacitus, *Annales* 15, 43.

10. Justin Martyr, *Apologia* 1, 29, trans. T. B. Falls, *Works,* Fathers of the Church, New York, 1948 said that most exposed children were picked up by people anxious to exploit them as slaves or prostitutes.

11. *Stromata* 4.8, ed. A. Cleveland Coxe, *Ante-Nicene Fathers,* vol. 2, Eerdmans, Grand Rapids, 1975.

12. *Paedagogus* 1.4, *Ante-Nicene Fathers,* vol. 8 Eerdmans, Grand Rapids, 1975.

13. *Paedagogus* 3.12.

14. Eusebius, *Historia Ecclesiastica* 5, 1, 7, trans. Roy J. Deferrari, Fathers of the Church, New York, 1955.

15. *The Martyrdom of Saints Perpetua and Felicitas,* in *Acts of the Christian Martyrs,* ed. and trans. W. H. Shewring, Sheed and Ward, London, 1931.

16. *Egeria's Travels,* ed. and trans. John Wilkinson, Society for Promoting Christian Knowledge, London, 1971.

17. For extended examples, see Peter Brown, "Aspects of the Christianization of the Roman Aristocracy," in *Religion and Society in the Age of Augustine,* Faber and Faber, London, 1972, pp. 161–182.

18. The Life of Macrina, by her brother Gregory of Nyssa, can be found in his *Ascetical Works,* tr. V. W. Callahan, Catholic University of America, Washington, 1966. Melania the Elder is treated at length in Palladius's *Lausiac History,* (*Ancient Christian Writers,* 34), and Melania the Younger's life by Gerontius is translated into French in *Sources Chrétiennes,* 90. Paula and Eustochium appear frequently in the letters of Saint Jerome, whose letter no. 108 is a lengthy autobiographical eulogy of the latter. The life of Olympias may be found in Elizabeth A. Clark, *Jerome, Chrysostom and Friends,* Edwin Mellen Press, New York, 1979, pp. 107–157.

19. See Palladius, *Lausiac History* and the *Lives and Rule of Pachomius,* trans. Armand Veilleux, *Pachomian Koinonia,* Cistercian Publications, Kalamazoo, 1980.

20. These lives have been translated in Benedicta Ward, *The Harlots of the Desert,* Cistercian Publications, Kalamazoo, 1987.

21. The letters of Paulinus of Nola form a particularly rich source for these relationships; see *Ancient Christian Writers* vol. 35–36, Paulist Press, Mahwah, 1966–1967.

22. See the English translation and edition of Justinian's code, *The Digestive Justinian,* Theodar Mommsen with Paul Krugeur. English Translation Alan Watson, Philadelphia University of Pennsylvania Press, 1985.

23. Procopius, *The Secret History,* Penguin Classics, 1966. Harmandsworth, Middlesex, England.

SUGGESTIONS FOR FURTHER READING

Scholars have been generous in furnishing translations for the use of readers who do not command Latin or Greek. Most of the major classical works of the period are obtainable in several editions. The *Loeb Classical Library* is the most comprehensive series. Similarly, the works of early Christian writers have been translated often. One easily accessible collection is the *Ante-Nicene Christian Library* and the *Nicene and Post-Nicene Fathers,* and individual pieces have been collected in *The Fathers of the Church* and *Ancient Christian Writers* series. In general, I have drawn upon the letters of Jerome, Ambrose, Augustine, Basil, Paulinus of Nola, and Sulpicius Severus, as well as the works specifically referred to in the notes.

The following are available in separate editions:

Brock, Sebastian P., and Susan A. Harvey, eds. *Holy Women of the Syrian Orient.* Berkeley: University of California Press, 1987.

Egeria. *Travels to the Holy Land.* Ed. and trans. John Wilkinson. Ariel Publications, London, Society for Promoting Christian Knowledge. 1984.

Hennecke, Edgar, and Wilhelm Schneemelcher. *New Testament Apocrypha.* Philadelphia: Westminster Press, 1963–1965.

Ward, Benedicta. *Harlots of the Desert.* Kalamazoo: Cistercian Publications, 1985.

Feminist scholarship in all the areas covered by this chapter has burgeoned over the last two decades to almost unmanageable dimensions. Among books covering non-Christian Rome, the first path breaker was J.P.V.D Balsdon, *Roman Women* (New York: John Day Co., 1963). Sarah B. Pomeroy's, *Goddesses, Whores, Wives and Slaves* (New York: Schocken, 1975) has become the acknowledged classic in the field, supplemented by many subsequent articles by the same author and *Women in Hellenistic Egypt* (Schocken, 1985).

The period of the New Testament continues to attract scholars of high caliber, and a feminist dimension has added electricity to their work in recent years. I have myself used many of these works and included them in an extensive bibliography in my book, *A New Song: Celibate Women in the First Three Christian Centuries* (New York: Haworth Press, 1983) and in two subsequent articles dealing with the fourth and fifth centuries: Jo Ann McNamara, "Muffled Voices: The Lives of Consecrated Women in the Fourth Century," in *Distant Echoes: Medieval Religious Women*, ed. John A. Nichols and Lilian Thomas Shank (Kalamazoo: Cistercian Publications, 1984), pp. 11–30; and Jo Ann McNamara, "Cornelia's Daughters: Paula and Eustochium," *Women's Studies* 11 (1984), pp. 9–27.

For further reading, the following books (and other books by the same authors) will provide an introduction to special subjects:

Bauman, Richard A. *Women and Politics in Ancient Rome.* New York: Routledge, 1995.

Bradley, Keith R. *Discovering the Roman Family.* New York: Oxford University Press, 1995.

Brown, Peter. *Authority and the Sacred: Aspects of the Christianization of the Roman World.* Cambridge: Cambridge University Press, 1995.

Bynum, Caroline W. *The Resurrection of the Body.* New York: Columbia University Press, 1994.

Clark, Elizabeth A. *Ascetic Piety and Women's Faith.* Lewiston: Edwin Mellen, 1988.

Davies, Stevan. *The Revolt of the Widows: The Social World of the Apochryphal Acts.* Carbondale: Southern Illinois University Press, 1980.

Dixon, Susanne. *The Roman Mother.* Norman: University of Oklahoma Press, 1988.

Elliott, Dyan. *Spiritual Marriage.* Princeton: Princeton University Press, 1988.

Fiorenza, Elizabeth S. *In Memory of Her: A Feminist Theological Reconstruction of Christian Origins* New York: Crossroad, 1983.

Holum, Kenneth. *Theodosian Empresses.* Berkeley: University of California Press, 1980.

Kraemer, Ross. *Her Share of the Blessings.* Oxford: Oxford University Press, 1994.

Meeks, Wayne A. *The Origins of Christian Morality.* New Haven: Yale University Press, 1994.

Scholer, David M., ed. *Women in Early Christianity.* New York: Garland Press, 1993.

Treggiari, Susan. *Roman Marriage.* New York: Oxford University Press, 1991.

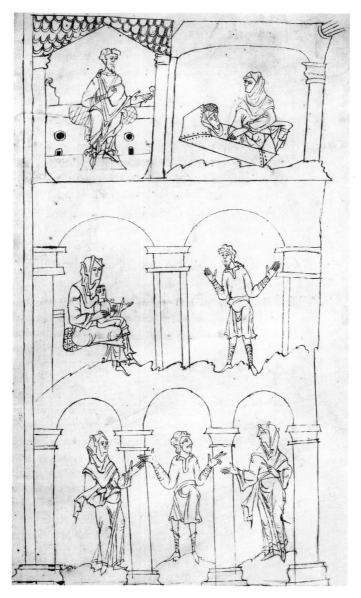

Women as wives and mothers, as conceived by a tenth-century Anglo-Saxon Gospel illustrator. Top panel: Irad and his wife, attended by a midwife; middle panel: Maviael's wife and infant Mathusael, with Maviael on right; bottom panel: Lamech and his wives Adah and Zillah (Gen. 4:18–19).   BODLEIAN LIBRARY, MS JUNIUS 11, F. 53.

4

Women in Early Medieval Northern Europe

Lisa M. Bitel

The people of early medieval Europe had diverse ideas about women, their nature, and their proper roles in society, economy, and politics. Classical literature, early Christian theology, and barbarian tradition all influenced the men who recorded these concepts in written form. Christian theologians and other religious writers, for instance, often taught that women were physically, spiritually, and intellectually inferior to men. Likewise, secular legal codes defined women's status as dependent upon, and subordinate to, that of their male guardians.

Yet other writers, such as the biographers of female saints, clearly believed that women could provide behavioral models for all Christians, male or female. Poets and composers of secular tales wrote vividly of fierce, powerful queens and warrior women who were, nonetheless, headstrong, oversexed, and virile in the most negative sense.

At the same time, literature of all genres suggests that the normative social and economic roles for women were those of wife, mother, and domestic laborer. In the intensely rural subsistence economy of early Europe, women's most important tasks were the production of babies and the maintenance of family homes and farms, where they clothed and nourished the members of their households. Even the greatest Carolinian queens were managers of the royal household and its riches; and famous Christian abbesses were, first and foremost, nurturers to their followers and secular neighbors.

Modern observers must try to make sense of the complex ideas and attitudes of the period in relation to women's actual experiences. How did women perceive themselves and each other? Did they think of themselves as wives, mothers, and household managers or as seductresses, queens, saints, laborers, or any number of other things?

At about the time Charlemagne had himself crowned emperor of a revived empire, a mighty queen stalked warriors in the hills of Ulster in northern Ireland. One of her victims described her as

> a tall, fair, long-faced woman with soft features . . . she had a head of yellow hair, and two gold birds on her shoulders. She wore a purple cloak folded about her, with five hands' breadth of gold on her back. She carried a light, stinging sharp-edged lance in her hand, and she held an iron sword with a woman's grip over her head—a massive figure.[1]

She was Medb (Maeve), queen of the Connacht men and women, battle leader, wife of seven husbands, mother of seven warriors, and probably originally a Celtic territorial goddess of destruction and fertility. Her domain was not real life, but the pages of the saga *Táin Bó Cúailnge* (Cattle Raid of Cúailnge), an eighth- or ninth-century tale of cattle rustling and tribal warfare. This and other tales of Medb, popular throughout medieval Ireland, came from the pens of monks, who preserved and recopied them in monastic manuscripts.

Medb was a powerful character. Although her fame was largely Irish, she was not unique in the European literature of the period. Brunhild of the Germanic tales, heroines of Old Norse sagas, queens of the Frankish histories, and saints of hagiography from many different regions displayed similar strength and authority. These dominant, fictional females may have been what the author of the *Táin* called "devilish lies" and "poetical figments." But real women also ruled territories, took up arms, participated in Christian governance, established churches, guided communities, and judged. Like Medb, they also occasionally lived and loved in contradiction to the strict rules of behavior that permeated medieval culture.

Yet all of these women existed—whether in reality or in people's imaginations—in an age when the laws of European societies formally restricted the status and rights of women. Christian and Jewish theorists of the time preached at best an ambivalent definition of women's nature. Writers of laws and theological texts often assumed that women were weaker, more stupid, and more sinful than men. At the same time, the stories that men wrote about women acknowledged this strange discrepancy between a fairly limited set of formal ideas about women and the mind-boggling variety of actual and fictional women. Although authors sometimes explained away prominent women by describing them as manly, monstrous, or extraordinarily virtuous, they took for granted that ordinary women could be useful, welcome, and even influential members of the community.

How are modern historians to comprehend such a contradiction in attitudes toward women, depictions of women, and women's experience? Three points can help us understand both ideas about women and women's own experiences in early northern Europe. First, although historians have traditionally tried to explain the lives of women in the early Middle Ages by defining a normative status and experience for them, the evidence reveals that women gained no single status or set of opportunities. European women did not undergo a general rise or decline in their status, nor did they enjoy a particular "golden age." Neither women nor men expressed a consistent attitude toward women. Instead, women and men participated in a variety of complex social roles, gender relations, economic opportunities, spiritual possibilities, and political strategies.

Second, whereas medieval gender ideologies were sophisticated and various, women's formal economic and social roles remained theoretically simple and few. Men and women both valued women's labors in the slowly developing economy of the West. Nonetheless, whether they made a living as farmers, seamstresses, abbesses, artists, scholars, whores, or other things, all women were also measured by their two most important social roles; either they were wives and mothers, or they failed or chose not to be wives and mothers. Throughout the early Middle Ages, some women managed to evade, manipulate, or subvert these two roles, especially at times of great social, economic, or political change. But from the fiercest queen to the lowliest slave, women nevertheless were defined in relation to the men who were their fathers, husbands, sons, or other formal protectors. Even Medb was a much-married woman and mother, although also an adulteress.

Third and finally, we must try to comprehend women through their own perspective, as well as that of the men who wrote the documents. When men called them wives and mothers, did women think of themselves in these two ways? Did they use the same vocabularies as their men, but interpret their roles and opportunities differently than men did? Were their economic and political goals the same as men's, and did they experience religion as men did? Because medieval women produced very few of the historical sources necessary for studying them, this is the scholar's hardest task. Yet attempting to stand among the women of early medieval Europe may be the only way that we can conscientiously approach the confusing, irreduceable variety of individual idea and experience in so distant a past.

WOMEN'S NATURE AND STATUS

Early medieval people's ideas about women came from several sources. Christian missionaries brought to northern Europe an already well-articulated system of ideas about women. As an earlier chapter in this book has shown, formal Christian concepts of women were based on the philosophies of the Greeks, Romans, and Jews, and developed into a formal body of thought as the early churches of the Mediterranean world organized themselves. But northern Europeans also drew on traditional Germanic and Celtic ideas about women's capabilities and rights, which they had long before incorporated into custom, law, and oral literature. As soon as missionaries taught them to write, the peoples of the north began to record their laws and literature, and with them, statements about women's status. The Frankish peoples recorded their laws as early as the sixth century, the Anglo-Saxons and Irish in the seventh century, and the Visigoths of Spain in the eighth. Jews maintained their own laws and theories about women wherever they went, blending them with local custom. Of course, both religious texts and legal codes were only the written norms by which people navigated their days.

Christian writers in the early Middle Ages pretty much agreed with the ancient Greeks that women were weak, defective versions of the human standard—men. Like Isidore of Seville, the seventh-century Spanish encyclopedist, most early medieval thinkers were functionalists when it came to the body. Their ultimate, indirect intellectual ancestors were Aristotle and the second-century physician Galen, who wrote that woman's physical and mental deficiencies made her naturally fit as a procreative partner for man. Her inability to practice moderation in all things made her uncontrollably eager for the sexual play that impregnated her. Her inferior physical strength ensured that, even when unwilling, she was vulnerable. Although Isidore had a limited familiarity with Galen, he demonstrated his belief in women's physiological inferiority by quoting his favorite patristic source, St. Augustine, who was certainly influenced by late antique medical thinking: man (*vir*) was named from his *virtus* or power; woman was *mulier* from her *mollitia* or softness.

When Isidore and other churchmen read the Bible, they found divine confirmation for a hierarchy based on sex. The Genesis story of Adam and Eve, for instance, which played a small part in Jewish theology, became for Christian writers the ultimate justification for women's natural subservience to men. Already in the sixth century, Gaulish ecclesiastics gathered in a council to decide whether, when God created "man" redeemable from sins ("human," Latin *homo* in the Vulgate Bible), God meant to include women. By the tenth century, when the Irish translated the Genesis story into their vernacular, Eve explained it all:

> I am Eve, great Adam's wife,
> I that outraged Jesus of old,
> From my children Heaven I stole,
> by right 'tis I should have gone on the Tree [crucifix] . . .
> I that plucked the apple
> which went down my narrow gullet;
> for that, all the days of their lives
> women will not cease from folly.[2]

The travail of childbearing—women's very reason for being, according to Isidore and others—became their punishment for Eve's first sins of greed and curiosity. Eve's guilt also revealed why men must master women: to help women strive for goodness and to avoid being implicated in women's evil, as Adam had been.

Whereas the theorists of antiquity and the later Middle Ages used Aristotle for systematic discussions of gender, early medieval thinkers drew heavily on Scripture and its interpreters for their ideas about women. They recorded their thoughts in practical guidelines for behavior, such as canons (church laws) and penitentials, rather than in philosophical treatises. Penitentials, which were lists of the appropriate penances for assorted sins, emphasized sexual transgressions, suggesting the dangers of contact with women. For instance, when unmarried men and women admitted bathing together, according to the St. Hubert penitential, their penalty was a year's fasting (no meat or wine). A nocturnal emission resulting from a sexy dream meant the recitation of psalms or a short fast; intercourse with a married woman could cost a layman five years' fasting or a period of forced abstinence.[3] The lesson to priestly readers of penitentials, who conveyed it to their parishioners, was clear: if you want to avoid sin, avoid sex, and to avoid sex, steer clear of women.

The texts of ancient churchmen moved with missionaries throughout northern Europe and were recast in local vernaculars to suit local custom. But regional traditions about women also infected Christian thought and practice. Historians once thought that Germanic tribes brought more primitive, sexist customs with them to Gaul when they invaded, thus lowering the status of Christianized Gallo-Roman women. Similarly, English and Irish historians argued that the arrival of Christianity on their islands made the rude Celtic natives more sensitive to the fragile nature of women, thus raising men's esteem for them. More likely, as we shall see, formal Christian ideas and indigenous custom melded in a process of mutual assimilation.

STATUS, MARRIAGE, AND KIN, 600–900

One of the best records of native customs and principles appears in the legal codes of the early Middle Ages. All early medieval codes were composed of civil laws or precedents, often deriving from ancient practices kept orally by an elite of professional judges and lawyers. Four legal principles mattered most to the peoples of northern Europe. First, every human was born with a material value—a certain number of cows or coins. Individuals did not normally ascend a social ladder, but usually remained in the same social class and retained the same relative worth for their entire lives. When someone committed an infraction against a person, the damage to the victim was estimated as a proportion of his or her worth, called an honor-price (*wergeld, lóg n-enech, sarhaed,* etc., in vernaculars). Robbery, trespass, assault, insult, murder, and other crimes all brought a payment to the victim and/or his or her kin based on standard fees plus honor-price. In some codes, such as the Frankish and Anglo-Saxon laws, criminals also paid fees to the king. In all the laws, refusal to pay up branded the evildoer literally an outlaw whose kin no longer had any legal obligation to protect him or her from infuriated victims and their kin.

Infractions against women, children, slaves, and foreigners usually brought different fees than those against the legal norm, the free adult male. Secular laws suggest more or less the same sexual hierarchy as that proposed by ecclesiastical theorists and rule makers. From northern Italy to northern Ireland, from Spain to the eastern edge of Christendom, women were disenfranchised. They were not full citizens of any kingdom or tribe. Their position in a community depended upon that of their male kin, husbands, or other guardians. Their status, as well as their legal and property rights, was calculated according to the worth of their men. However, wergelds varied by region. In some codes, such as the Alemannic and Bavarian laws, premenopausal women's wergeld was double that of men of similar status, reflecting women's worth as childbearers. In Irish law, a woman was worth only half the amount of her guardian. By contrast, Salic Franks tripled the value of a woman when she reached adulthood and was able to bear children.

The second principle important to early medieval Europeans was the distinction between arms-bearing and unarmed members of the community. Only free men could lawfully wield axes or swords. Thus the gender bias of early medieval laws that restricted women also aimed to protect them. As a child or unmarried girl, a female remained under the authority of her father or another male kinsman, who acted for her in all legal matters. At marriage, her guardianship transferred to her husband, as in ancient Roman law. Not only assaults against women, but violations of any kind brought penalties in many early medieval cultures. In Welsh law, for example (which was recorded later in the Middle Ages), a woman had to be compensated with sarhaed when her father gave her in sexual union to a man; when she first went to bed with her husband; and when she arose the next morning and re-entered the public community. Hence, laws protected her honor even in officially sanctioned marriage. In several other codes, penalty fees rose as the insult and harm to a woman escalated. For shaming a free woman by cutting off her hair, a Burgundian owed twelve *solidi* to her guardian, but for sexually molesting her he paid nine times her wergeld plus the twelve solidi. Class was a factor in such cases, too; to rape a slave woman cost the offender much less because, although the slave bore no arms, she was less valuable to her society than a free woman.

The third and fourth legal principles dear to early Europeans concerned property and kin. Legal authorities aimed to preserve both because they were the bases of an individual's identity. As legal incompetents, women had fewer property rights than men. Further, since laws dealt mostly with the processes of contract and crime, and since lawyers assumed women to be unarmed and legally incompetent, women ordinarily entered the legal texts only when men involved them in their negotiations or offenses. Only a few offenses were deemed to be typically female: brewing magic potions for love or poison, infanticide, and eloping or having sex with the wrong man.

In the very early Middle Ages, women's property was under the control of their guardians, at least theoretically. In most cases, women's contracts were invalid without their men's consent. Women rarely inherited the family's lands, which instead went to male heirs—sometimes even distant kin rather than daughters. Families feared that women, whose children belonged at least as much to their husband's relatives, would give away kin land to outsiders. In societies governed almost completely by material worth and constant negotiation, women's rights to manage their own affairs were thus considerably limited. Widows regained some ability to conduct their business and control their property; heiresses also escaped limitations on legal maneuverability. In Ireland, for instance, a woman who had no male relatives and so inherited family property literally "went in place of a man"; she could buy and sell as she wished, hire laborers, even muster dependents for an army. But when she died, her lands (except those acquired by gift or purchase) returned to some distant member of her blood kin, rather than to her sons or daughters. This was a general rule throughout Europe.

Of course, in all early medieval societies, women and men found ways around legal limits. One Frankish will recorded the wishes of a father who was annoyed at sexist property laws and purposely left his lands to his daughter. Undoubtedly, others managed to give their daughters land and other property as premortem inheritances. What is more, restrictions on women's ability to own and manage property eased somewhat during the early medieval period. Especially after the ninth century, when monogamous marriage became increasingly popular, more women were able to control their dowries and other personal property and to give or will it to whomever they wished. English women's rights aptly illustrate this development. In the seventh-century laws of King Ethelbert, childless women's property, including gifts from their husbands, reverted to their blood kin upon their deaths. By the ninth century, King Alfred was discussing the whole theoretical problem of male and female inheritance in his will, demonstrating logically why it was possible for him to leave estates to both female and male descendants. Alfred did arrange, however, that his male heirs have the option to buy back his female heirs' inheritance.[4]

Kinship, the last of the four main legal principles behind the codes, was the organizational axiom of medieval Europe. Hence, the laws treat women mostly as daughters, wives, or more distant kinswomen. Like laws about status and guardianship, women's position as kinswomen was a two-edged weapon, both benefitting and restricting them. Most of what we know about women's legal status comes from rules against harming women, especially pregnant women. But lawmen also ruled on the abduction (*raptus*) or violation of nubile women. They detailed the proper and improper kinds of marriage ties. Laws also paid much attention to women's sexual infractions. Men's sexual activities rarely entered secular legal texts except when they damaged the property (women, slaves, or animals) of another man, but women's sexual misconduct endangered the family bloodline. Finally, legal codes focused on the processes of betrothal, marriage, and concubinage by which a woman was officially handed over to a man along with some property, a household created, and a new branch of the family begun. Laws regulated the amount of dowry, bride price, or bride gift. They decreed who should receive the property and set up penalties for abducting brides or abandoning them, either with or without the goods that accompanied them.

Some legal writers, particularly Celtic and Bavarian, also listed different kinds of allowable sexual unions and the ways that such unions might be dissolved. In other early medieval societies, unions other than marriage or official concubinage went legally unlabeled. Yet, in all the Christianizing societies of Europe, secular laws allowing different kinds of unions and simultaneous unions for men (polygyny or polygamy) were in conflict with Church rules, which emphasized the ecclesiastical preference for monogamy. Christian theorists believed that marriage should be a joining of two souls and two bodies for purposes of companionship and procreation. But, though they recognized the utility of sexual intercourse, some ecclesiastics held that sexual acts were rooted in carnal sin. As Pope Gregory I wrote to St. Augustine of Canterbury, the missionary to Britain, in response to his questions about sex, polygyny, and incest among his new flock, "The very lawful company of man and wife cannot be without pleasure of the flesh . . . for that pleasure itself can in no way be without blame."[5]

Secular thinkers agreed that the wrong kinds of sex were bad. They believed that sex between a free woman and a male slave was socially disruptive, as well as sex between two people of the same sex, or between those married to others. But they did not have much to say about pleasure. In fact, in Iceland and Ireland, a woman could divorce her husband if she believed that they were sexually incompatible.

Jurists agreed that procreation was the main purpose of sex, but their laws concerned contracts and social order, not morals. The basis of social and political order was the family. Jurists worked primarily to ensure that a man obtained heirs who lived to adulthood, to facilitate the orderly passing on of estates and offices. Given infant mortality rates, this sometimes meant impregnating more than one partner. Only wealthy men of high status could afford to support more than one woman and her babies, and many noblemen continued to keep secondary wives or mistresses throughout the medieval period. In England, several kings maintained official concubines on whom they sired legal heirs. One charter of King Edmund lists an *Aelgifu concubine regis* (king's concubine) as a legal witness. Frankish rulers, too, had practiced the much-studied custom of *friedelehe*—something like concubinage or marriage with no strings—until the Carolingian reforms of the ninth and later centuries. Indeed, several Merovingian kings discarded wives like old clothes, sometimes bothering to cloister, divorce, or kill them, and sometimes just taking mistresses. It may have been easier to bring a new woman into a court already packed with queens and queen mothers without introducing her as another official wife; Frankish and English kings customarily took concubines in their youth before they married and inherited the kingship. Children born out of formal wedlock were still able to inherit; royal concubines thus bore the next generation of kings and were often powerful political players. But no early medieval society allowed polyandry. The patrilineal principle underlying the social organization of sex was just too important to permit women to sleep around (another reason why sexually independent literary characters, such as Medb, are so intriguing).

Eventually, politics-playing churchmen persuaded kings and nobles to discontinue official polygamy and find heirs by other means. They began by eliminating legitimate reasons for divorce, exhorting widows not to remarry, and narrowing the definition of legitimate offspring. In the early seventh century, St. Columbanus got into a serious argument over the question of legitimacy with the Frankish king Theoderic II and his grandmother, Queen Brunhild. The saint denounced the royal successors as bastard children of harlots who were, needless to say, not married to Theoderic. The saint condemned, the king resisted, and Brunhild raged. As a result, Columbanus was tossed out of the country.

Nonetheless, churchmen eventually gained the support of the Frankish emperors, although the latter did not always follow their own dictums. Reform-minded clergy in England worked through legal colleagues by gradually broadening the definitions of, and increasing penalties for, adultery and bastardy. By the tenth or eleventh century, sex with any woman besides one's monogamous wife was considered a moral offense everywhere in Europe. Just because rule makers, both secular and ecclesiastical, condemned these practices, however, does not mean that they disappeared. Only medieval society's official ideas about polygyny and illicit sex changed. Ecclesiastical councils and synods never stopped thundering decrees against multiple marriages, divorce and remarriage, and sex with more than one legal partner.

Lawyers and those they served were most concerned that the public know who was joined to whom, who produced the children, how the children were affiliated with each parent's kin group, and who owned what property. There was only so much land to go around, and no one wanted to give it away to outsiders. Hence laws attempted to prevent a woman's marriage to a man from outside the community by refusing her what little inheritance she might normally have and by denying him full rights as a member of the community. Franks were not to marry Gallo-Romans; Irish women were to keep away from men of another tribe; English ladies were to avoid Anglo-Danish settlers.

Lawyers were less concerned with a woman's responsibilities and rights within kin groups, however. Like men, women could expect their kinsmen and affines (in-laws) to avenge them when they were harmed or killed. Unlike their men, women could not participate actively in feuds or formal negotiations aimed at righting wrongs. They might help start feuds or incite revenge, as they often did in Scandinavian literature, but, as everyone was well aware, they could not take up a sword to right a wrong on behalf of a brother or cousin.

This was one reason that women occupied a tenuous place in both blood and affinal groups. When a woman married, she left one family and house for another. In most areas of Europe, women continued to rely on their natal kin for certain kinds of support. When her husband needed some extra help on a military campaign, when the couple wanted loan of a cow, when their children went out to fosterage or required a godparent, a woman could often turn to her parents' families. In the saints' *vitae* (written saints' lives), pious young novices often interned in the nunneries of maternal kin. But very few laws specified any obligations on the part of a woman's own family after she had left for a new life. In the earlier, less formal relationships of concubinage and secondary marriage, women retained more ties to their natal kin, since their mate's family was unwilling to take them on without some guarantees of dowry and legal contract. But to an official wife of another man they owed little or nothing unless they wished to offer her support.

Hence a woman had the responsibility of connecting her children to their cognates. Ultimately a child's chances for affiliations with both sides of its family, and thus for inheritance, depended upon its mother's connections. The less formal a woman's union with her mate, the more dubious the paternity of her child, and the less likely her baby would achieve full status within its father's family. If the mother were lucky or affectionately linked to her own kin, the child might find a refuge as a poor relation among his maternal kinsmen. In fact, as all the early medieval histories demonstrate, determined and fortunate noblewomen did sometimes acquire property to pass on to their sons, perpetrate revenge on their behalves, and in all ways play the political game for them; the result was wealth and political security for their babies. Similarly, the boy of a peasant mother might become a worker on a maternal kinsman's farm or fighter in his mother's family. But if a woman could not find a place for herself among her own or her husband's kin, she might do no more for her sons. Sometimes, with all the best will in the world, a woman could do nothing to unite her family with that of her husband. The Anglo-Saxon poem *Beowulf* told of a Queen Hildeburh whose in-laws and blood kinsmen came to blows in her husband's feasting hall; no matter how she struggled to connect her children, her blood kin, and her affines, she ended up placing her son and her brother on the same funeral pyre. A woman had even less chance to create a stable social network for her daughter, whose value lay in her labor and her potential ability to make a good marriage.

MATERIAL LIFE AND ECONOMIC ROLES, 500–900

Laws and religious literature draw the crude outline of women's place in early medieval Europe. Material evidence—such as bones, house sites, pots and pans—along with bits of textual evidence, helps fill in the motion of daily lives. Material remains were not authored by literate Christian men, and thus do not display the biases of formal attitudes toward women. For instance, the laws' protection of polygyny and the theory of sexual interactions proposed by Christian canons seem more complex in light of mortality rates, demographic patterns, settlement, and domestic architecture. Women's legal opportunities and property rights make more sense given archeological evidence about what women actually owned, wore, and used. And ideals of kinship and ownership become more three-dimensional when we consider how women made a household, a family, and a living.

Bones in old graveyards show, for example, that women in the early Middle Ages could expect to live only thirty or forty years. However, if they survived the first twenty or so years, their life expectancy increased dramatically to fifty, sixty, or even more. Cemeteries at convents contain a much higher proportion of middle-aged and elder female bodies than mixed-sex graveyards in secular communities. Such evidence suggests that childbirth and its associated fevers and complications were killers of young women. Yet women did not die at the appallingly primitive rate previously assumed by historians. Data from several northern Gaulish cemeteries of the fifth through seventh centuries show that only about 10 percent of women were likely to die in their childbearing years (before age 30), with the rate approaching 15 percent in times of famine or migration. This was true for women of all classes, from royalty to migrant peasants, in the early Middle Ages. The rate mirrors that of modern Third World populations. On the other hand, when disease or violence added to their troubles, women were eating less and dying earlier. They also shrank in average height by a greater percentage than men during tough times, a sign of chronic malnourishment.

Epidemic, famine, warfare, the movement of peoples, poverty, and social restrictions—any environmental or political disruption could prevent the expansion of the narrowly dynamic population by killing either its baby makers or its babies. Women who survived their childbearing years could expect to bear four or five children, although half of those might die before living a whole year. Estate censuses (*polyptyques*) suggest that babies did not always die naturally, either. On some Carolingian estates, the sex ratio soared as high as 156:100 (men to women). No population normally produces so many more men than women. Further, the sex ratio rose in proportion to the number of individuals per household dependent upon a single estate. When a particular piece of land was extremely crowded, most of its inhabitants were men. Historians have explained the disparity in a couple of ways. One has suggested systematic female infanticide and neglect, and another believes that estate officials counted many men twice; still others believe that these frontier estates housed more male agricultural workers while their women remained behind to run family farms. But penitentials and canons, which consistently ruled against abortion, contraception, and infanticide, confirm the practice of infanticide, if not necessarily gender-specific infanticide. The *vitae* told many tales of babies left to starve or freeze, rescued fortuitously by a kindly priest. Many more must never have been found.

Although every woman was part of a larger corporate kin group, her daily interactions were mostly with the four or five people who composed her household. Women looked at the same faces, day after day, working, eating, sleeping, dressing and undressing, having sex, growing pregnant and bearing babies, and dying. A peasant girl might grow up in a one- or two-room hut with her parents, or maybe a father and stepmother, possibly a grandparent or aunt or uncle, and maybe a couple of siblings. But any of these relations could succumb to death at any moment. Given the average size of houses across early Europe, only four to eight people could sleep in one building at a time, and sometimes families brought the farm animals in for the night, too, for human warmth and the animals' protection. Huts were dispersed in isolated farmsteads in much of Britain, Ireland, and Scandinavia. Elsewhere, huts clustered in Roman-inspired townlets, or small villages attached to larger estates. But the population was sparse everywhere before the year 1000. As a result, women had few opportunities to see many people besides the family members they lived with and near.

However, unlike men, most women did not spend their entire lives in the same house. They trained for adulthood in their parents' home or the house of foster relations. When they reached maturity, estimated by most law codes as somewhere around thirteen or fourteen, they were eligible to join a new household and start a long life of staring across the hearth fire at a new set of familiar faces.

Privacy as we know it did not exist. People went outside for three reasons: to work, to meet other people on special occasions, and to have illicit sex, which they could not conduct in front of their housemates. Celtic laws refer to prostitutes literally as "women of the bush" and "women of the road." Generally, everyone in the early Middle Ages tended to stay at home. Travel was difficult and dangerous, especially for the unarmed. But even when people did gather, women were often formally excluded from entering public spaces to conduct legal negotiation, participate in community defense, or attend the local lord. This is not to say that women never traveled. The saints' lives and chronicles tell of women pilgrims venturing as far as Rome and Jerusalem. Indeed, in the eighth century, St. Boniface complained famously of the number of English women who had left for the Holy City and ended up as roadside harlots in Francia. Women must have moved from estate to estate with royal courts and assembled at feasts and rituals with their men. Women also traveled, abruptly and involuntarily, when they were kidnapped or taken prisoners of war.

But work, more than any other single factor, determined where people spent their time. Early medieval Europe was supported by a subsistence economy; most people had to labor all day, almost every day, to survive. The numerous famines that cut short women's lives and, as we have seen, made women short, provide ample evidence that early Europeans constantly teetered on the edge of starvation. The majority of people farmed and herded to make a living. The documents mention plenty of women who performed seasonal agricultural chores. Gregory of Tours mentions women in sixth-century Francia drying grains, winnowing, and helping to harvest. Laws also declared it a wife's responsibility to assist her husband when agricultural tasks were most pressing, at ploughing and harvesting.

More often, though, people divided their labors by sex. Women's work was normally in the farmyard and house, close to children and spinning, while men's was in the fields. This was as true for noblewomen, who managed the labor of others, as it was for the slaves and servants who ground the grain in querns or at the mills, and herded the animals. In fact, one Carolingian commentator, in his job description for the queen, declared that "the decor and decorum of the palace and especially the regal robes, and also the yearly gifts for the knights, apart from goods, drink and horses, belong especially to the queen, and under her to the treasurer."[6] Whether her household was a hut with a few sticks of furniture or the entire Carolingian empire, a woman was primarily a housewife, overseer of the family's supplies, and manager of the domestic domain. One tenth-century rabbi wrote of Jewish women, as well, that "it is the custom of men to appoint their wives as masters over their possessions."[7]

A woman's chores usually consisted of feeding the other members of the household, managing the store of food and other reserves, clothing the family, and caring for barnyard animals and the vegetable garden. Although they might, if their farm were not too remote and their harvest provided a surplus, trade for a little of what they needed, most women had to manufacture their own supplies. Cooking meant keeping track of the food reserves, transforming the raw stuff into finished food—the grain became the flour that was kneaded into bread to be baked or brewed into beer—and actually serving the meals. Providing clothing meant herding the sheep, shearing them, combing and carding the wool, spinning the thread, weaving or knitting the cloth, and constructing and decorating the garments. On large estates, such as that of the Carolingian monarchs, entire workshops of servant women labored to produce clothing for their wealthier masters and mistresses, an arrangement that Frankish monarchs borrowed from their Roman models, rulers of the old empire. But on every farm in Europe, and in the monasteries and nunneries, too, women worked to produce shirts and tunics and cloaks for everyone else. Their toil did not always go unnoticed; more than one woman won sainthood for her exquisite embroidery, and in Iceland cloth became the most popular means of exchange with Norse traders.

By far the most important of women's labors was reproduction. More precious than any other commodity were the babies they produced, which not only ensured the survival of the family and its properties, but of the entire tenuous society. Medieval people were well aware of mortality rates and the slow growth of the population. No wonder that canonists and penitentialists chastised those who tried to prevent conception with *potationes diabolicas* (devilish potions or abortifacients) and assigned heavy penalties to infanti-cides. In stories of the saints, couples begged holy intercessors for help in con-ceiving. Husbands and wives also pleaded for saints to ensure the carnal desire of their mates, so that they might get to the point of conceiving. St. Columba, the Scottish exile, for instance, helped a sad soul who disgusted his own wife; she was determined to leave him for the convent until the saint miraculously turned her revulsion to lust and love.

Throughout the early Middle Ages—as well as before and after the period—women were responsible for domestic labor and reproduction. From the fifth and sixth centuries, when the Germanic tribes moved south across the Continent toward Italy and Spain and north through Gaul, to the years approaching 1000, women performed the same roles of childbearer, nurturer, housekeeper, cook, and cloth maker. Yet their experiences varied by period, by region, and even by season and local circumstances. Some historians have argued that the "frontier" mentality of the ninth and tenth centuries, when Europe was experiencing a demographic revival and agricultural expansion, allowed women more economic opportunities. They moved out of the house to help clear land and plant it, and thus earned the right to participate in other profit-making ventures, such as trade. A few even have pursued more spe-cialized vocations, such as praying, healing, or crafts. How they managed all this vigorous economic activity while producing more babies who lived longer, thus enlarging the population, remains problematic.

WOMEN'S POLITICAL INFLUENCE AND AUTHORITY, 600–900

When women left the house for larger gatherings and public activities, they were dogged by restrictions on their social roles and economic opportunities, by the ambivalence of laws and theories regarding their very nature, and by men's suspicions of what, exactly, they were up to. And yet, their very roles of mother and wife enabled a few women to acquire a powerful influence as rulers, leaders, and administrators. Some wielded this power as queens or local rulers. Others, from the same social class as their secular sisters, governed and politicked from religious communities. Either way, their access to author-ity lay in maneuvering around cultural hindrances rather than rebelling against them.

The queens of early medieval Europe were not, alas, all like Medb. But Medb came from the pages of the *Táin*, an epic and a satire in which it was possible for highly sexed, former goddess-queens to govern their own prov-inces, carry weapons, marry and discard husbands, and confer power on men simply by sleeping with them. Legends of ancient Celtic queens such as Boudica and Cartimandua lingered into the early Middle Ages, but not neces-sarily as positive examples. It is unclear even whether women conceived of political power as men did, since power itself was defined by its exclusivity: women, among others, could never have it. When women sought male-defined power, they did so through their husbands, children, and other male relations. Other kinds of female-defined power, such as that of the best embroideress or the wisest old lady in the village, were not of much interest to male authors of our sources, which are silent on the subject.

Yet tales of medieval politics can inform us about women's abilities. Likewise, stories of medieval queens and noblewomen can help us learn more about political structures and personal relations in past periods, as Janet Nelson has shown in her study of Balthild and Brunhild, two Frankish queens. Like any other wife, a Merovingian Frankish queen of the fifth or sixth century was entirely dependent upon her husband for status and wealth. Unlike peasant women, who married locally, a queen often came of a people distant from her new home and possibly hostile to her new husband. Her role was theoretically that of what the Anglo-Saxons called "peace-weaver" (like Hildeburh in *Beowulf*), someone who bound unfriendly peoples together in a political alliance. Her best chance at success was that of any wife: production of sons who could succeed to their father's position and property, and who could draw on the support of both of their kin groups, which would then necessarily unite behind him. The royal wife was a facilitator and negotiator—if she could charm her husband into keeping her. She also had to retain her husband's affections, no easy thing with fickle Merovingians. If she managed to outlive her husband and remain queen, and had borne an acceptable son, then she might achieve new kinds of influence as regent. Of course, she needed the backing of kinsmen, affines, and anyone else who had an army to help her.

Brunhild and Balthild both managed to survive and prosper under this system. Brunhild was a Visigothic princess born around 550 who married King Sigibert of the Frankish kingdom of Austrasia in 566. She governed together with him until his assassination, then later as regent for her son, Childebert, and even later for her two grandsons. She allowed or rejected matches for her offspring and arranged for their accessions to royal power. She also maintained her own connections with Byzantium to the east and the Visigothic kingdom to the west. She corresponded with the bishop of Rome, told other bishops what to do, and carried out a long-standing vendetta against another mighty queen, Fredegund of Neustria, who had once conspired to have Brunhild's sister killed.

Balthild, of a slightly later generation, also governed through her offspring and with the help of sympathetic ministers and bishops. When her presence at court was no longer tolerable to the magnates of her kingdom, she retired to a convent and eventually became a saint. Brunhild, Balthild, and other queens of early Europe relied on churchmen as allies, and vice versa. High-ranking churchmen were often kinsmen of noblewomen, who helped place bishops and abbots in power and endowed their churches with estates and goods.

Bishops, in turn, advised noblemen to support their queens' agendas, working as messengers and councilors, and pulling strings to support their benefactresses. In kingdoms such as early Anglo-Saxon England and Ireland, where inheritance customs allowed distant male relations to inherit the royal office, underage sons of kings did not accede to the kingship. Queens were thus unable to become regents. Bishops also carried less weight in secular and ecclesiastical politics. Likewise, where bishops lacked authority to participate in local government, queens' participation in governance tended to diminish.

When the collaboration worked, the ruling dynasty, through its queens, also maintained contact with saintly patrons, which supplemented its already considerable authority. When a queen failed to manage her personal connections, donations, and politicking properly, however, she got herself retired to a monastery, as Balthild did. From there she might continue her peacemaking efforts, as they were euphemistically called by hagiographers. She could still command interviews with passing magnates or order bishops around, as St. Radegund did in the sixth century and the royal Anglo-Saxon abbesses of the seventh and eighth century.

After Brunhild and Balthild, wives and mothers continued to access power via their men, sometimes even sinking to the level of assassination in order to secure a throne. The Anglo-Saxon princess Ethelfleda, daughter of Alfred the Great, ran her ailing husband's kingdom of Mercia, assuming all the public powers that went with governance: she maintained the laws, oversaw the army, and played politics with other rulers of England. Still, her subjects called her "Lady of the Mercians," not queen of Mercia. When it came time to pass on her power, she made sure that her kingdom devolved to her brother, king of Wessex, rather than her own daughter. Hers was a singular, representative power, not something she had inherited as a property to be bestowed on her female offspring in her own name. Another Englishwoman, Elfreda, mother of Aethelred the Unraed (d. 1016) of England, gained a crown for her son by having his half-brother Edward murdered.

By the Carolingian period, though, the public role of queens was changing throughout Europe. Women were adding ritual status as crowned queens to their actual political influence. Charlemagne's father Pepin had his wife, Bertha, crowned beside him to reinforce his own position and that of his anticipated offspring. By 866, the Carolingians were calling their wives *consors imperii nostri,* "our imperial consort," and kings elsewhere may have picked up the custom. It was only after 900 that Irish women were fashioned queens of territories, rather than wives of kings: queen of Leinster rather than wife of the king of Leinster.

But the model Frankish kingship itself suffered some setbacks in the ninth and tenth centuries, as historians have observed. While English and Irish kings were consolidating their territories and jurisdictions, the Frankish empire split into pieces under the force of divisible inheritance and unruly magnates who played sides with Charlemagne's descendants. Women who derived their power from the personal charisma of monarchs could no longer ride to authority on their men's impetus. But women who governed as wives and kinswomen of local lords—managing households, estates, and the local peasantry—were able to assume a little of the power to govern, judge, and tax that nobles began to grab in this period. Political and juridical power became steadily more local, so that the wife of a man willing to share his authority could attain influence among her neighbors near and far. Although women's status remained formally lower than that of men, the right combination of wifely authority, economic opportunities, and local political influence might prove magnificently empowering in the hands of the right individual.

At the same time, the family itself was evolving in shape, size, and direction. Early medieval families were cognatic groups, in which kinship derived from both mother's and father's sides, and focused horizontally on an individual; later, many families became agnatic groups, deriving descent almost exclusively from the father's side. Women both gained and lost from the slow, massive social and political change that resulted. In general, what little and rare inheritance of family lands a woman might have gained in the very early Middle Ages disappeared as families became more concerned about consolidating estates and passing them on to eldest sons. By 1000, the age of genealogies had arrived: a man begat his son, who begat his own son, who inherited the family lands. Women rarely entered the genealogies except as historical details or heiresses.

PROFESSIONAL RELIGIOUS WOMEN AND THEIR COMMUNITIES, 500–900

If women could not or preferred not to seek power as political leaders among men, they could always retreat to the company of women—that is, as long as they were Christian, had the connections or goods to ensure their acceptance in a religious community, and obtained enough land and friends to establish a new Christian settlement. The women of northern Europe have long been praised (or blamed) as the earliest and most enthuasiastic converts to Christianity and to the ascetic life. Bede tells the story of Bertha, the Frankish princess who persuaded her husband, Ethelbert of Kent, to interview the outlandish monks who first came to England, and even to give them a piece of land for a monastery at Canterbury. St. Pátraic (Patrick) wrote of the "countless virgins" who responded to his call in Ireland. Despite their parents' threats and pleadings, the women vowed their lives to chastity. And dozens of hagiographers wrote of women who created lives as religious professionals either at home or in communities designed for that purpose.

A woman had to be as determined as a Frankish queen to conduct a successful religious life, especially if she wanted to begin a new community. Some of the earliest churches were *eigenkirchen* or family establishments, where a couple of kinswomen and men set up a little church or shrine, maybe a cemetery, and a couple of houses, and called it a sacred place. There they existed by farming, just like everyone else or, if they were lucky, by the labor and donations of others. They practiced as much prayer and education as their subsistence allowed. If they attracted the patronage of a queen like Brunhild or even a local noblewoman, they might flourish. Some women's communities supported hundreds of inhabitants, costly buildings, impressive libraries, farmers and tenants, and arrays of scholars, artists, craftswomen and men, and other laborers.

Cell Dara (Kildare) of St. Brigit is a good example of a mixed-sex community of the kind prominent in the early Middle Ages. Brigit's story followed a formula common to the saintly, wealthy women who founded communities across Europe. She supposedly settled on the plains of Leinster in the sixth century, after attracting a retinue of holy virgins and a companionable bishop, Conláed. After the saint herself died in 524, women continued to govern Cell Dara as abbesses with Conláed's successors as their bishops. Normally, Cell Dara's governors came from the local aristocracies who patronized the community. By the seventh century, it was a regular *urbs* or city, in one hagiographer's eyes: it had a massive church, divided into halves for male and female celebrants, and decorated with tapestries and painted panels. At the front of the shrine in tombs topped by golden crowns reposed, on the women's side, Brigit and, on the men's, Conláed. Irishmen and women came from across the island to invoke the saint, ask her nuns for intercessory prayers, celebrate Brigit's feast, and just to gather and watch. And, of course, there was always the chance of a miracle. Penitents and devotees gathered to see the giant millstone that had magically rolled down the hill to land at the church door, where rainwater gathered in its depressions and cured the ill.

Cell Dara lasted through Irish tribal wars, Viking invasions, the Normans, and the dynastic conflicts of the later Middle Ages. Its abbesses were among those listed by the Irish laws as worth more wergeld than the average woman. Their status came from their ability to "turn back the streams of war" as political negotiators with kings and chieftains. The abbesses were still influential in the twelfth century; one was kidnapped and symbolically defiled by rape so that she and her family had to yield the monastery and its estates to another dynasty. The worship of Brigit, "Mary of the Gael," sustained the Irish through centuries of hard times.

Other religious communities differed in size, function, and gender composition. After the eighth century or so, English and Frankish churchmen began to suspect mixed-sex communities of irregularities. Already in the eighth century, Bede was complaining about nuns who painted their nails, curled their hair, and had too much fun with their religious brothers. Throughout Europe, the misogynist strain of Christian writing intensified in the eighth and later centuries, with stories of nuns who ran off with seductive monks. Charlemagne and his successors sponsored religious reforms that ordered religious women to stay where women belonged—at home, in their convents—and to stop politicking, as earlier generations of Frankish abbesses had done so skillfully.

The notion that nuns should enclose themselves in a sacred space with walls of stone and silence was not necessarily imposed upon religious women. Women themselves may have adopted it as one aspect of a rich and varied feminine spirituality. Saints' lives described women like St. Monenna, who refused to go out in daylight without a veil to protect herself from men's gazes, and who sourly moved her community to a more remote spot when disturbed by the "sounds of the secular world"—that is, joyful wedding songs. Another story, told in the seventh-century life of St. Rusticula, describes how King Chlotar's supporters accused her of treason. One of the king's officials arrived at Rusticula's enclosed settlement to conduct her before the king, but she declared that she would rather die than transgress the nuns' rule of Caesarius of Arles, which stated that women should resist going out of the monastery "even to death." She was eventually blackmailed into emerging by death threats against the local governor, leaving behind sisters and cloister resounding with "groans ululating for their absent mother." After being exonerated and performing numerous wonders en route home, Rusticula returned, though, to her "holy sheepfold."[8]

However much independence religious women occasionally gained, they never enjoyed a golden age of power and influence. Wherever Christianity appeared, some women were able to choose life as religious professionals. If their kinsmen allowed them to alienate a bit of property, they might set up a place for other women in the family and live out their lives in modest contentment as tenders of a shrine or devotees of a local saint, making a livelihood with a piece of embroidery or living off the kindness, not of strangers, but of familiar neighbors. If they were extremely wealthy and well connected, they joined ancient houses of aristocratic women, as did the Anglo-Saxon royalty. From these places, women not only advised their kinsmen in secular politics, but exercised influence over church organization, as well. Hild, daughter of a king, was a famous seventh-century abbess in England who hosted an international conference on the dating of Easter and weighed in on the matter very decisively herself. Leoba, another English abbess, kinswoman and confidant of the missionary Boniface, went off to Germany to convert the natives and found nunneries. She also maintained a learned correspondence with Boniface until he died; long after, she was buried near his bones.

Women's communities were the primary, although not the sole, site of women's scholarship and artistic expression in the early Middle Ages. Hrotswith of Gandersheim (d. 1000) is possibly the most famous of the learned abbesses of the period. She is the earliest known poet in Germany, a dramatist, historian, and classicist, whose poems and plays have been thoroughly examined by modern scholars for evidence of a uniquely feminine spirituality. Like her own dramatic character, the harlot-saint Mary, Hrotswith worked "with all her strength to become an example of conversion."[9] But others practiced arts and learning, too, even if they did not always mark their creations with their names. And some women managed to become literate outside the convent. Some Jewish women may have been able to read rabbinic Hebrew; the daughter of Rashi, the foremost Talmudic scholar of the Middle Ages, recorded her father's dictation of his biblical analyses.

Did women feel and think religion as men did? Men did not think so, at least not all men. The Torah required Jewish men to praise God every morning for *not* making them women. In Christian communities, even women who practiced extraordinary devotion were primarily supposed to be mothers and sisters to male colleagues. Women hostessed traveling clerics while sitting at home in their monasteries; even Leoba waited for Boniface to visit, rather than traveling the German territories with him. By and large, religious women gained reputations for sanctity not by heroic miracles, as men did, but by the quiet, homely miracles of refilling the pantry and healing those who came to them. Brigit, who preached to an assembly of male clerics and was accidentally ordained a bishop, was an exception. Genovefa, the savior of Paris from the Huns, was another. Radegund, who left her husband to run the abbey at Poitiers as the mother of her nuns and peacemaker to the Franks, was more typical. She dispensed advice to male colleagues while secretly lacerating her own flesh with a burning iron. She was nurturer to others, yet, for her own part, was completely repulsed by the demands of the carnal life. Mother and chaste recluse all in one, she was the Christian man's ideal.

CONCLUSION

It is practically impossible to stand among the women of the early Middle Ages. They hide behind so many screens of centuries, languages, and textual hindrances. Their experiences come to us translated by men. Only the rare woman, like Hrotswith, left us her own story, and even then she was speaking a language rich with its own premodern nuances, colored by the conventions of literate male colleagues. We can never fully appreciate their sensibilities, their affections, their biases, their jokes.

The few individual women whose lives are recoverable remain exceptional in myriad ways. Queens and abbesses formed a tiny number among the women of early medieval Europe. Perhaps the access to power and sanctity described here had echoes among women of lower classes. More likely, most women organized their lives around their daily work, which was defined by the roles of wife and mother. These roles changed in detail throughout the period but also remained the same in general contour. Women knew of themselves as wives of men, mothers of men, and daughters and kinswomen of men.

They may also have recognized themselves as leaders, manipulators, sources of inspiration, lovers, artists, and a million other things. And there are some suggestions of separate female values and of women's solidarity at the community level: women blessing each other's weaving, lending each other household equipment, visiting the well together, sitting together and apart from men at feasts. Jewish women may have bonded at the *mikvah*, ritual bath, or in each other's homes on Sabbath. But did this little solidarity, however sustaining to women, represent any consciousness as a social group or class? For all we know, Medb may have been the darling of a thousand Irish girls, who admired her surprise attacks on slow-witted warriors and her sexual freedom. Radegund, who abandoned Medb's life for the sacred enclosure, may have been the role model for another thousand. Brunhild, Brigit, Leoba, Hrotswith, and Rashi's daughter may all have had their female followers and imitators.

All we can say for certain, at this point, is that the diverse experiences of women, and the complicated ideas that people had about them, were often in conflict. The documents admitted that women were legally disenfranchised and yet that some women ruled vast territories in their sons' and husbands' names. Women expected to become wives and mothers, and yet some became leaders of Christian settlements or noble estates. Women were theoretically inferior, and yet some, like the saints, shone with superior knowledge and grace. Perhaps this is why the figure of Medb, the warrior-queen, remained so popular from the Iron Age, when she first took narrative shape, to the twelfth century, the time of transition to a new feudal age, when scribes recorded her story in the manuscripts that still exist, to today, when children in Irish schools still learn of the men she seduced, killed, and conquered.

NOTES

1. Cecile O'Rahilly, *Táin Bó Cúailnge: Recension I*, Dublin, 1976, p. 97; trans. Thomas Kinsella, *The Tain*, Oxford, 1970, p. 208.
2. Kuno Meyer, ed. and trans., "Eve's Lament," *Ériu* 3 (1907), p. 148; trans. P. L. Henry, *Dánta Ban: Poems of Irish Women, Early and Modern*, Cork, 1991, p. 81.
3. James Brundage, *Law, Sex, and Christian Society in Medieval Europe*, Chicago, 1987, pp. 165–166; Ludwig Bieler, *The Irish Penitentials*, Dublin, 1963, pp. 114, 218.
4. Dorothy Whitelock, ed., *English Historical Documents, c. 500–1042*, London, 1955, pp. 359, 492–495.
5. J. E. King, ed. and trans., *Baedae Opera Historica*, vol. 1, pp. 144–147.
6. David Herlihy, *Opera Muliebria: Women and Work in Medieval Europe*, New York, 1990, p. 43; David Hincmar, *De ordine pal.*, cap. 5.
7. Louis Ginzberg, *Ginzei Schechter*, repr. New York, 1969, p. 275, no. 6; trans. Irving Agus, *Urban Civilization in Pre-Crusade Europe*, New York, 1965, vol. 2, p. 607.
8. Jo Ann McNamara, John E. Halborg, and E. Gordon Whatley, ed. and trans., *Sainted Women of the Dark Ages*, Durham, 1992, pp. 127–131.
9. Elizabeth Petroff, *Medieval Women's Visionary Literature*, New York, 1986, p. 135.

SUGGESTIONS FOR FURTHER READING

The historiography of medieval women has become abundant since the first and second editions of *Becoming Visible* were published. Historians have focused particularly on women's social and economic roles and religious lives. Below are some selected readings used in this essay.

On social and economic roles: Suzanne Fonay Wemple, *Women in Frankish Society: Marriage and the Cloister, 500 to 900* (Philadelphia: University of Pennsylvania Press, 1981); Mary Erler and Maryanne Kowaleski, eds., *Women and Power in the Middle Ages* (Athens, Ga.: University of Georgia Press, 1988); David Herlihy, *Medieval Households* (Cambridge, Mass.: Harvard University Press, 1985); David Herlihy, *Opera Muliebria: Women and Work in Medieval Europe* (New York: McGraw-Hill, 1990); Joel Blondiaux, "Le Femme et son corps au haut moyen-âge vus par l'anthropologue et le paleo-pathologiste," in Michele Rouche and Jean Heuclin, eds., *La Femme au Moyen-âge* (Ville de Maubeuge: Diffusion J. Touzot, 1990), pp. 115–138.

On religious lives: Jane Tibbets Schulenberg, "Strict Active Enclosure and its Effects on the Female Monastic Experience," in John A. Nichols and Lillian Thomas Shank, *Medieval Religious Women*, vol. I: *Distant Echoes* (Kalamazoo, Mich.: Cistercian Publications, 1984): pp. 51–86; Jo Ann McNamara, John E. Halborg and E. Gordon Whatley, ed. and trans., *Sainted Women of the Dark Ages* (Durham: Duke University Press, 1992); Caroline Bynum, "Introduction: The Complexity of Symbols," in Bynum et al., eds., *Gender and Religion: On the Complexity of Symbols* (Boston, Beacon Press, 1986), pp. 1–22.

For more specialized studies of particular groups of women: Judith R. Baskin, ed., *Jewish Women in Historical Perspective* (Detroit: Wayne State University Press, 1991); Henrietta Leyser, *Medieval Women: A Social History of Women in England, 450–1500* (New York: St. Martin's Press, 1995); Roberta Gilchrist, *Gender and Material Culture: The Archaeology of Religious Women* (London and New York: Routledge, 1994); Lisa M. Bitel, *Land of Women: Tales of Sex and Gender from Early Ireland* (Ithaca, N.Y.: Cornell University Press, 1996); Pauline Stafford, *Queens, Concubines, and Dowagers: The King's Wife in the Early Middle Ages* (Athens, Ga.: University of Georgia Press, 1983).

Medieval technology for manufacturing noodles. ÖSTERREICHISCHEN NATIONALBIBLIOTHEK, WIEN (BILDARCHIV NEG. 4743).

5

The Dominion of Gender or How Women Fared in the High Middle Ages

Susan Mosher Stuard

Although stereotyping affects women's lives, there have been only a few opportunities to see how and why new stereotypes arise and to follow their course as they gain acceptance. The years from the eleventh to the fourteenth century afford us the opportunity to view that process at a time when Europe was coming of age as a separate and distinctive civilization. Changed attitudes toward women, which employed notions of polarity juxtaposing woman's nature to man's, accompanied and supported significant changes in the economy and society. Out of this process a more systematic social construction of gender emerged, one sanctioned by leading intellects of the day.

At the beginning of the age women contributed leadership and creative skills to the major movements that promoted growth in European communities. As wealth and power concentrated into fewer, typically male, hands, women saw their social and legal rights, their access to institutional support, and their opportunities erode. The newly systematic gender system affected abbesses, queens, and others exercising political power. Soon polar notions of gender changed the lives of women in towns and in rural areas. However, these notions were not applied in a wholly consistent manner. Where women's work was deemed essential, notions of gender might not be brought to bear at all, so arbitrary were they as justification.

U sing the Song of Solomon as authority, young clerks at the cathedral school in Beauvais, France, praised woman in the early twelfth-century *Play of Daniel:* "Woman's value is like that of a strong man come from afar for the eloquence of her words overcomes the wisdom of the learned."[1] The clerks' thoughts on gender, the system of relations between women and men, favored likeness, not difference, when they linked the sexes. In the course of the next two centuries, theologians reconstructed gender on the authority of Aristotle, not Solomon, featuring polar oppositions of woman to man, not likenesses. This profound change in thinking helped set women's history on a separate trajectory from men's in the West, with implications down to the present day. The new thinking on gender accompanied and strengthened fundamental changes in Western society. Because gender became a more inflexible system, often affecting women's work and social roles, women's experience bears earlier and clearer witness than does the experience of men to the West's transformation into a complex civilization during the medieval centuries. When the popular *Play of Daniel* was first performed, women still contributed to all the major movements that spelled success for an emerging European civilization. In the next two centuries, women were successively closed out of opportunities to profit from Europe's increasingly complex institutions, even though their contributions remained essential to society's well-being.

The new thinking about women consisted of notions of polarity rather than rigorously argued ideas; these ideas arrived in the twelfth and thirteenth centuries embedded in classical arguments devoted to entirely different questions. Theologians employed notions of polarity between woman and man as part of a greater apparatus of thought that purported to explain God's rational plan of a dual human creation, that is, one both female and male. The notions served as a cog in an abstract system that holy scholars used to explain to themselves why the creation of man alone was not enough in God's benevolent scheme. But scholastic theologians taught as well as wrote; their students—the priests, lawyers, and doctors prepared at universities—served later in powerful positions where they, and others, employed these revived notions on woman's nature to justify new practices and the elimination of some traditional ones. How learned opinions carried over into generally accepted commonplaces, that is, moved from the scholar's page to conventional wisdom uttered in the streets, forms a complex story. This essay addresses the question of how and why that transference took place.

TENTH- AND ELEVENTH-CENTURY OPPORTUNITIES FOR WOMEN

Before that transference occurred, women inhabited a different world. Of course, gender assumptions existed in that world and affected women, as previous chapters have noted, but, as historians have discovered, gender differs markedly by time and place. It may be an informal and flexible set of assumptions that do not figure particularly high on the scale of social priorities, or it may be rigid and formulaic, a significant component of the intellectual apparatus of an age, one that overrides other considerations when evaluating a person's worth. While medieval Europe would become contested ground between these very different manifestations of gender, people in tenth- and eleventh-century Europe still lived according to flexible, more informal concepts about what women were and should be.

After the breakup of the Carolingian Empire, when Europeans entered the tenth century, an age so filled with war it has often been called "the age of iron," women had encountered opportunities to act decisively. They were equipped with property and inheritance rights and were sustained by gender assumptions that were flexible and which even, at times, stressed similarities between women and men. Institutions of centralized authority painstakingly constructed by Charlemagne and his successors had disappeared. The new, more fluid conditions favored forceful persons who possessed strong family backing. Women fit these qualifications as well as men, and in the contest for land, power, and title sometimes achieved impressive gains. A growing number of women appeared in the tenth and eleventh centuries as chatelaines, that is, mistresses of landed property and castles with attached rights of justice and military command, as feudal custom decreed. Powerful women, like powerful men, were the actual proprietors of churches, and women were recognized participants in both secular and ecclesiastical assemblies. Feudal institutions intended for the conduct of war adapted to women's participation, and religious orders produced an impressive line of women administrators and learned authorities. But women's most consequential long-term contribution in this era lay in the anonymous work of peasant agriculture. This age produced two breakthroughs in technology that turned the seasonal lands of Europe to surplus production: the three-field system (crop rotation) and the use of nonhuman sources of energy—the horse and the mule, the water mill, and then the windmill. Europe's peasant women as well as its peasant men produced Europe's agricultural revolution.

Women and men worked closely together in peasant households, so that tracing the anonymous achievements of women peasants and separating their accomplishments from those of anonymous men proves nearly impossible. Still, some tantalizing shreds of evidence remain from these early times. On the ninth-century manor of St. Germain-des-Prés, women headed farm households in settled and developed areas; in fact, large farms included proportionally more adult women than men. Men dominated on the newly established farms, where assarting (slashing and burning to clear fields) increased the arable land by opening formerly wooded lands for planting. Because peasants constantly expanded their arable holdings, men left to gain new lands, often leaving women at home to produce the agricultural surplus that provided families with their livelihood. Brides traditionally received farm implements and tools for cloth production as wedding gifts. Wives, who with their kin were often referred to as the "distaff" side of the family, practiced cultivation and crafts (the distaff used in spinning symbolizing production). A husband and his kin were referred to as the "sword" side of the family, recalling men's roles in warfare or as protectors of families.

This customary division of labor gave women responsibilities in agricultural administration at all levels of society. The treasurer of the Carolingian court had answered to the queen about taxes on agricultural produce. The king was likely to be off in seasonal campaigns when taxes came due, and few kings showed much interest in agricultural development, so queens assumed responsibility for this essential activity, and this continued through the tenth century.

Chronic warfare postponed the aggregate effects of this practical sexual division of labor except where feudal powers provided a measure of peace. Germany and northern Italy, united under the Saxon dynasty in the tenth century, succeeded first. We have often allotted too much credit to the sword side of that dynasty and overlooked the distaff, that is, the social roles and productive economic roles played by its royal women. Not so the contemporaries of Empress Adelaide, wife of Otto I, whose coins bore her portrait. They respected and applauded her rule. Adelaide's daughter, Matilda, saw women's dynastic power institutionalized in the vast endowments assigned her monastic house at Quedlinburg. While her brother Otto II fought in northern Italy, Matilda brought peace to Germany and earned the title *metropolitana* (overseer of bishops) from her biographer after presiding over an episcopal synod. Quedlinburg and its sister convent at Gandersheim lay at the heart of the "Ottonian system": the use of church office to provide secular rule and pacify the land. A traditional division of labor that associated women with the productive arts expedited this Saxon policy, and earlier advances in agriculture began to yield identifiable surpluses in these lands.

Ottonian Germany prospered under Matilda's guidance, but even greater benefits lay in store for northern Italian lands after she and her warrior brother Otto II died. Responsibility for the empire's welfare fell to their surviving mother, Adelaide, and her new daughter-in-law, the Byzantine princess Theophano. They established a joint regency to sustain the election to the throne of the 3-year-old heir of the family, Otto III. Proud, mutually jealous, quarrelsome, and as overbearing as other members of this brilliant dynasty, Adelaide and Theophano nonetheless put aside their personal animosities and worked for a lasting peace. Together they achieved two critical decades of stability in northern Italy that permitted commerce and industry to establish a foothold in the region. Towns flourished, and the pace of development quickened.

Since kings, lords, and great bishops had yet to discover how to wring the most out of their subjects through tax or tribute, a surplus-producing agrarian economy and peace combined to create growth and towns. Flexible work patterns within urban artisan families, in which an imprecise line between women's and men's work accommodated uneven labor demands, drove this economy. Those patterns warrant a place alongside other more frequently acknowledged factors—agricultural surplus, trade over the Mediterranean Sea, and a fortunate geographical setting—in explaining the remarkable success of towns and commerce in northern Italy. Throughout these decades women in towns seized the opportunity to work and became shopkeepers, artisans, and craftswomen. Families staffed the earliest commercial enterprises and workshops, much as they had formed the essential working unit on manors and farms. While husbands peddled goods, wives watched over stores and purchased or produced supplies, or, in another flexible arrangement, women sold wares in markets or at fairs while their husbands produced goods in home workshops. Enterprising women followed lucrative crafts, such as wool working, textiles, felt making, and hat manufacture, which became mainstays of the export trade.

These informal and home-based initiatives yielded some remarkable results. Anonymous but important technical innovations in manufactures came out of home workshops: mechanical fulling of cloth and mills for tanning or laundering, for crushing anything from olives to ore, for polishing, or for reducing pigments to paints or pulp to paper.[2] These innovations should be credited to artisan women as well as to artisan men; both profited from improved manufacturing processes. In Genoa, brides from laboring families listed stock and tools comparable to those of their husbands when entering marriages. Their marriage contracts sound as much like business partnerships as pacts to establish a household and family. Family workshops in emerging towns throughout Europe produced a whole range of trade-worthy products. Women worked as brewers, glass makers, and textile workers; or in sales as fishwives; or as associates of their husbands in the heavier industries of coopering, smithing, tanning, and salt panning.[3] A flexible division of labor between women and men populated towns with industrious inhabitants who accommodated their skills and labor to tasks in a highly supple and elastic fashion.

Although the most dramatic results in economic growth appeared in northern Italy in cities within the Saxon dynasty's authority, soon Spain, France, England, and the Low Countries saw changes as well. Ruling families throughout feudal Europe made little or no distinction between public and private authority. With rights to lands and resources went sovereign rights of military impressment, justice, minting, taxation, and other responsibilities of rule. Abbesses sent their knights to war. Noble ladies sat in judgment of their vassals and peasants, and held the castles when lords fought in the field. Some made laws. The Countess Almodis of Barcelona coauthored the *Usages of Barcelona*, one of the earliest written law codes of the age. Women acted decisively in all walks of life, helping to create a more peaceful era.

Adela (d. 1138), daughter of William the Conqueror, decorated her bedchamber with scenes of the Norman Conquest of England, perhaps much like those in the great Bayeux Tapestry that had been sewn by women loyal to the Norman cause. Before he disgraced himself as a crusader by fleeing a besieged city, Adela's husband, Stephen of Blois, had written to Adela saying "govern your land excellently, and deal with your sons and your men honourably."[4] Had he lived much into the twelfth century he might have been quite surprised at his wife's understanding of excellence and honor. Her program was to dispose of her oldest son to a minor holding, place the second as his father's heir and Count of Blois (later also of Champagne), the youngest as a monk and later bishop of Winchester, and save the throne of England for her third son, Stephen, king from 1135 until 1154. Since King Stephen had to then fight for that throne with his own cousin, the Empress Matilda, who was the sole legitimate heir of Henry I, England faced two battle-torn decades. But these two branches of the royal family, led by fierce women, finally compromised, making Matilda's young son Henry King Stephen's successor. No wonder the new King Henry II called himself "Henry, son of Matilda"! Through war, then through compromise, and then through surrendering her own dynastic right, she made him king. In the meantime Adela retired as a nun to the Cluniac priory of Marcigny-sur-Loire. A literate and pious woman, Adela was rated high on the scale of success in secular as well as spiritual affairs by her contemporaries, although neither the principle of primogeniture nor her husband's values played much of a role in her strategies.

Not all feudal women stayed home to administer lands and family as Adela did. In the eleventh century, when the Normans entered the Mediterranean area and carved out a kingdom in Sicily and southern Italy, women fought along with men. Gaita, a Norman and Robert Guiscard's wife, accompanied her husband on campaigns on horseback, helmeted and armored. Gaita fought "like another Pallas, if not a second Athena," commented Anna Comnena, the historian of Constantinople.[5] If any of her Norman knights proved timorous, Gaita rallied them back into the line of battle. No wonder that the next generation of Christian women were as enthusiastic about going on crusades as Christian men. They sailed (or, in the case of the First Crusade, walked) to the Holy Land and fought, settled, or returned with new tastes for spices and light fabrics bearing such tantalizing new names as *muslim*.

By the middle years of the eleventh century in most of Europe, the results of efforts at peacekeeping had produced quite a settled world. Population increased steadily, assarting and improved cultivation continued to produce marketable surpluses, and commerce and towns expanded. Historians bemused by the late, but swift, rise of Europe to global prominence tend to regard Western society as pluralistic, adaptable, and free of the shackles of tradition.[6] To an extent they are wrong: Europe possessed its own long-standing traditions, among them, on the practical level, a fluid rather than a static sexual division of labor. Europe's start down the road of development relied heavily on the contributions of women, only to see women's power and opportunities erode over time.

Contemporaries associated feudal women with the administration and defense of land resources, and their husbands with acquiring new lands; however, no absolute rules governed this division of responsibility. Peasant women tied their efforts and fortunes to cultivation, and peasant men tied theirs to assarting; again, no clear-cut line mandated this division, and the labor-intensive but still sparsely populated manors of Europe profited from this elasticity. In towns, women often produced cloth rather than iron tools, but because families formed small workshops, even this distinction could be ignored when a widow wished to keep the family business for her heirs. In convents, women prayed as devoutly in expectation of God's blessing as did men in monasteries. Indeed, their expectation may have been higher because they believed their virginal state more perfect than that of celibate men.

Several considerations, namely, a fortunate birth, a calling to the spiritual life, a recognized skill, wealth, or a particularly forceful personality, overrode habitual or even new assumptions about women's proper roles. In fact, the combination of high birth, an affiliation with an endowed institution such as a royal convent, a penchant for book learning, and a spiritual calling offered the age's best opportunities for self-cultivation.[7] No wonder some well-born monastic women issued learned opinions that carried authority in the day. Often revered as closer to God because of the sanctity assigned to female virginity, these women had also siphoned off a most potent mix of worldly advantages, which they directed toward their own cherished spiritual goals without hesitation.

HOW THE GREGORIAN REVOLUTION AFFECTED WOMEN

As with Adela's and the Empress Matilda's chroniclers, few authorities had seen anything at all remarkable about women in positions of power, but the twelfth century brought changes in opinions about women. New attitudes began to take over, and increasingly the histories and chronicles being written labeled women's political acts as "manly" and exceptional. Clearly the ecclesiastical writers of the day responded to some new notions about sex roles and the differing capacities of women and of men. With its larger literate bureaucracy and new assumptions about women, the Church tended toward restricting the wide variety of roles women had played in the tenth and eleventh centuries. Gregorian reforms affected women in two ways: the attack on clerical celibacy targeted priests' hearthmates rather than priests themselves, while the papacy did all in its power to eliminate the great double monastic houses led by abbesses as examples of lay patronage.

The campaign against clerical marriage and the rights of priests' hearthmates drew the attention of popes and papal reformers first. Pope Gregory VII (1073–1085) and the leaders in reform who preceded and succeeded him vowed to enforce clerical celibacy. This was no new issue in the Church; critics had often mounted attacks on the traditional practice of clerical marriage for parish priests. The tenth-century Bishop Atro of Vercelli had criticized wives of parish priests for diverting revenues to their personal and their heirs' use, taking church land into private hands, distracting husbands from pastoral duties, and involving priests in lawsuits that ended in trials before civil rather than ecclesiastical courts. Although these women's inheritances and their labor contributed to parish welfare, critics chose to ignore that fact. In the eleventh century, voices like Atro's that had drawn little attention in an earlier day found an audience among the higher clergy, fortified now by stronger notions of gender difference.

Popes zealously eliminated lay influence in the bestowal of church offices that culminated in the drive to establish a hierarchical church under the absolute control of the papacy. Aristocratic women of an earlier age had shared with the men of their class in the disposition and protection of ecclesiastical positions. Ironically, the active participation of laywomen who provided interested and energetic patronage allowed the Church to initiate its reforming measures. Then, with the destruction of this lay patronage, women lost that influence. As a case in point, the success of the papal reform movement depended heavily upon the financial and military support of two women, Beatrice of Tuscany and her daughter Matilda. Their castle at Canossa provided the meeting place for the momentous confrontation in 1077 of Emperor Henry IV and Pope Gregory VII over the right to invest, that is, place, churchmen in office. Ultimately Matilda left all her lands to the papacy, providing the substantial base of the pope's landed power.

Papal reforms removed control from the hands of secular leaders and deprived other devout women, like the princesses of the Saxon dynasty, of their former influence. At the same time, the importance of convents in the leadership of society began to decline, although learned and powerful nuns still flourished in the late eleventh and twelfth centuries. After the eleventh-century Gregorian reform, the papacy ordered the dissolution of double monasteries (inhabited by both nuns and monks) in western Europe. Since women led these establishments, their dissolution sharply curtailed women's access to the church hierarchy. However this extended only to Western lands; in Slavic Catholic lands less touched by reform, double monasteries remained, and women played important roles in the management of ecclesiastical affairs. Throughout Roman Christendom nuns continued to study within their convents and to educate girls. But like the monks of the twelfth and thirteenth centuries, nuns tended to turn toward mysticism. Women like Hroswitha of Gandersheim, Elizabeth of Schongau, Herrad, Gertrude, and Hildegarde of Bingen, who in their intellectual curiosity contributed substantially to all fields of human knowledge and never doubted their right to do so, disappeared in time. The last nonmystical literary composition attributed to a nun in the

Middle Ages is the "Hortus Deliciarum," written in prose and poetry in part by Herrad of Landsberg between 1160 and 1170.

Reforming clergy of the twelfth century seldom considered how to support institutions devoted to women's religious enthusiasm, despite the fact that their own reforms depended in no small measure on devout women's patronage and charity. A few of the reform movements, such as Fontevrault, a new popular order in France, gave women access to the religious life and channeled women's energies into reforming activities. But church leaders responded more consistently to men's reforming impulses and demands, endowing men with increasingly complex and well-endowed ecclesiastical institutions. In any event, monasteries no longer remained the center of intellectual ferment after the Gregorian reform. The focus had shifted to endowed cathedral schools and universities, which trained clerks for the priesthood and therefore excluded women. The great age of monastic learning came to a close, and the papacy restricted women's access to new religious institutions. In subsequent decades of the twelfth century, secular institutions swiftly followed the lead of the Church in these matters.

CHANGES IN TWELFTH-CENTURY DOWRY AND MARRIAGE

At first glance, however, women shared in the flowering of the Middle Ages that occurred in the twelfth century. From all walks of life came scattered examples of women valued for their daring or their learning. In the twelfth century, the nun Hildegarde of Bingen, albeit piously protesting her unworthiness, still gave political advice to prelates of the Church, kings, and even the pope. In fables of the day, the wily peasant woman outwitted the monk or the great lord to the audience's great satisfaction. Eleanor of Aquitaine, queen of England, and her royal daughters and granddaughters became the objects of adoration in the new cult of courtly love. The famous romance of the Parisian scholar Abelard with Eloise, niece of a powerful canon of the church, occurred in this century, and Marie de France wrote her popular lays (stories to be sung or recited) in which forthright women took the initiative in solving problems of the heart and of society. In everyday life, women matched their participation in agriculture with roles in new industries and trade that contributed substantially to the economic growth of the era. They counted themselves members of guilds and dominated some guilds, such as that of the silk workers, although they were increasingly excluded from others. Women's wills of the day demonstrate that they shared rather evenly in proceeds from work and joint business enterprises, so that they increased their personal fortunes from the fruits of their own labor. Women continued to own property in their own right, and they still received wedding gifts from their husbands, now often in cash; they could buy and sell property and designate their own heirs in conformance with both law and practice.

Important if quiet changes occurred in commercial towns as well as among that handful of high clergy and powerful feudal families who dominated the emerging institutions of medieval Europe. The family (understood as a chain of generations reflecting a set of inherited values) underwent some of the earliest reactions in response to new conditions. In the towns near the Mediterranean, where urban growth accelerated swiftly and economic success arrived early, the way townspeople arranged their personal lives as well as their commercial networks may be reconstructed from surviving notarial charters or "documents of practice." Businesspeople relied on the same notarial instruments (legal papers) that their families had traditionally used to arrange personal affairs: the *fraterna* (pact among brothers) and *societas* (partnership that often tied family members together), the will or *testamentum*, and the dowry or *dos*, which distributed wealth. In this enterprising manner, families appropriated what they had on hand to use as the building blocks for a commercial economy. The original personal needs that a will or a dowry met expanded to meet the needs of business alliances: to channel capital and to underwrite new ventures. These practices promoted economic growth and figured among the more clever ploys devised by resourceful individuals, but only at a cost to family relations.

For example, awards of marriage gifts or dowries in Italy after 1140 provide a good example of how purposes other than those originally intended could affect the dowry itself, and through it marriage, family relations, and women's lives. The most dramatic changes occurred among affluent urban families because, of course, controlling capital assumed increased importance and the rich could afford to give handsome gifts, albeit with strings attached. Germanic practice had designated a morning gift from husband to wife—a true dowry that transferred goods, land, or money from the groom to the bride. In prosperous towns, new civil statutes passed in the 1140s instituted the Roman dowry (a gift to the groom from the wife's family) and restricted or outlawed other gifts. As in classical times, gifts of linens, jewels, and clothes, which a wife's family also supplied to the new couple, accompanied the cash gift. Legally, the dowry belonged to the wife, but in practice she could only control it if her husband died or if she wished in turn to endow her own offspring. Under most circumstances the husband controlled the dowry and turned it to his purposes.

Since women had owned and disposed of their morning gifts and other marriage portions in earlier times, this revived Roman dowry, although increasingly large, implied a loss of positive legal rights for wives. Over the decades, more and more capital transferred from one family to another through the dowry until it became less a guarantee of a woman's status in her marriage than a system for distributing capital within a developing and vastly more complex commercial economy. A woman's wishes in her choice of marriage partner mattered little because so much rode on this transfer of funds. Still, husbands never legally possessed dowry either. They invested it safely for their wives as their elders dictated. If patriarchy drew strength from the Roman dowry, and it most assuredly did, fathers more than husbands increased their authority over women's lives. By the 1180s, when Pope Alexander III issued directives on marriage, churchmen had begun to regard this new development with alarm. Pope Alexander made consent of the partners the sole valid ground for marriage, intending by this measure to establish the sacred meaning of marriage. Although the right to consent to marriage was a significant right for women as well as men, it was very difficult to enforce for those daughters with huge dowries transferred at their weddings.

In the course of the next two centuries, as dowry awards scaled up, so did a husband's age at marriage, while the age at marriage of a wife dropped. By the economic hard times of the late fourteenth century, plague-depleted families awarded even higher dowries, a practice that lessened the chance to marry for those with small dowries or none at all. The increasing gap in the ages of bride and groom meant that fewer affectionate matches were likely. Less effort was devoted to taking suitability into account when matchmaking. Families inculcated passivity and obedience in daughters in preparation for the delicate negotiations for the proper bridegroom. Wives pleased their husband's kin if they restricted their attention to the domestic household. So dowry, once a gift to the bride that she controlled, became a gift to the groom hedged by restrictions. Over time, fewer marriages occurred, since not all could now afford increasingly expensive marriage, and for a time this trend continued the decline in urban populations that the plague had begun.

The changes in the practice of dowerying transformed the less affluent levels of urban society as well. Affluent families dowered not only daughters but the female servants who found favor with them. This was about the only reliable course for a poor woman hoping to improve her fortune by settling in town. Marriage among artisans soon required a dowry from the bride. Dick Whittington of Mother Goose fame, who ran away to London town with his cat, became in the end Lord Mayor, but his parable does not apply very well to the female experience of moving to town, nor did Dick have to marry to remain there. The very real Draga, enslaved in the Balkan highlands, serving as a slave in a Dalmatian town until freed, dowered and wed, followed a less attractive path into town life.[8] But slavery was a well-trod path into town, and with close to 90 percent of imported slaves female, the slave trade guaranteed domestic servants to Europe's wealthy households. These *ancillae*, as they were called, came from across Europe's frontiers: Muslim women traded in *Reconquista* battles in Spain, women from the Balkans or beyond, from the Crimea ("Tartar" slaves), and later women from North Africa. If manumitted and wed they remained, creating diversity in Europe's bustling towns and cities.

Preachers inveighed against poor urban parents prostituting some daughters as a way to gain a dowry. Still, urban prostitution was lucrative and therefore attracted some to choose this course to earn their dowries. Guiraude of Beziers and Elys of Le Puy, setting up as prostitutes in Montpellier, had money enough from that profession to plead cause for a recognized place to carry on their businesses in town in 1285. Thus they were able to retire rich enough with earned dowries to marry. They were the fortunate ones who did not end their careers, like other prostitutes, with the Repentant Sisters of Saint Mary Magdalene.[9]

Another path into urban life was as a "contract" worker, but as with *ancillae*, such workers were domestic servants in an economy with a high ratio of unskilled to skilled labor. In the later medieval centuries in Florence, *fantine* (girls as young as 8) worked for affluent households. The master owed them only some clothes and sheets to sleep on besides their daily food, because he contracted to provide them a small dowry at 16. There was even a sly carnival song about *fantine*'s availability to men of the household:

> This one, who is a girl to be married
> You keep for your chamber maid,
> And a dowry in five years you will give her;
> But above all we want to beg of you
> That she not have to go to husband before the proper time,
> As is done to all of them today.[10]

North of the Alps, the Roman dowry took centuries to take hold, as it had in the south, but in twelfth- and thirteenth-century England the common law, following its own rhythm, limited women's legal rights in marriage. Feudal custom traditionally disadvantaged the married woman, employing guardianship to restrict the rights she had held when single; therefore, in time, losses of control over marriage gifts reduced already circumscribed legal rights.

With state building an increasingly important concern, royal women's experiences with inherited property set the scene for changes for women in less exalted stations. Queens who had brought into marriage great portions and titles underwent a loss of authority over their own inheritances. In earlier times they had typically continued to rule their possessions by their own right, but in the twelfth century their inheritances were slowly integrated into the Crown's resources and fell under the administration of the ruling monarch's clerks. In the process, the office of queen consort, significant since Carolingian times, changed beyond recognition or, in the case of France, disappeared except in name. In England Eleanor of Aquitaine fought long and hard during her second husband's lifetime for the right of one of her younger sons to rule her inherited possessions in Aquitaine at her death. Her husband, the English king Henry II, who owed his very throne to a woman (see discussion of Adela and the Empress Matilda in text preceding) insisted on keeping Eleanor's inheritance as part of his crown lands, to pass intact through primogeniture to his eldest son and heir.

In the aftermath of this change a queen might still influence a husband or son and his court, or, as the surviving parent, she might be trusted with the power of regent during the minority of her son. But neither her office itself nor her inheritance rights and marriage portion sustained her position. Royal women, except those who could claim the right of primogeniture in the event that they had no brothers, lost authority. If they exerted any power at all, they derived it from their intimacy with, and access to, the reigning king. A royal mistress had the same opportunity to influence monarchical policy as a royal queen.

Dismantling institutions such as double monasteries, eliminating rights that had given women an initial foothold in the complex structures of an emerging European culture, and appropriating family devices like dowry to serve as conduits for an emerging cash economy directed women into more private roles. In the new private domestic sphere, acquiescence brought more approval than the skilled labor and control of property that had previously brought women honor. Changes began among the powerful and affluent, but in time the new priorities affected poorer townspeople, villagers, and even the rural peasantry. In this changed environment, notions that would have been irrelevant or practically unthinkable in an earlier age suddenly had an appeal. They gained a certain cachet that allowed them to be brought forward and offered in justification for action taken. Since changes in women's actual condition corresponded with the general awakening of interest in theology, philosophical inquiry, and classicism, authorities used classical notions, such as those defining "woman," to influence public opinion. Carrying the authority of theology and ancient learning, these notions generally prevailed.

Old axioms about the nature of woman possessed a long history in Western culture. In one guise or another they had appeared in the Bible, in Christian theology, in the treatises on medicine circulated under the name of the second century physician Galen, and in the inherited Roman civil law code. Most ancient pagan authorities had employed polarities that juxtaposed woman's to man's nature in their writings. This system of assigning qualities by sex, with women usually assigned the more negative traits, had not enjoyed much popularity in the early Middle Ages, however, nor had it been politic when abbesses, queens, and other powerful women distributed so much patronage. But when the legal scholar Gratian offered polar notions assigning such qualities in his *Decretum* circulated in the 1140s, they struck a responsive chord. Gratian provided Italian towns legal precedents for introducing the Roman dowry and outlawing other marriage gifts to women; in fact, he stated: no dowry, no marriage (*sine dote nullum conjugium facit*).[11] Gratian taught at the University of Bologna and trained the lawyers who practiced civil as well as church law throughout Italy. When towns decided to outlaw all but the Roman dowry, they had Gratian's great study that incorporated the classical Greek Aristotelian notion that women were passive and men were active to explain why dowry passed through a woman to her husband but not to her.

Notions about men's and women's natures as polar opposites played into other metaphors. In fact, toying with these polarities grew into a rather fashionable intellectual pastime. The twelfth-century Parisian scholar Abelard employed the metaphor that man was the sun and woman the moon, and as the light of the moon shone paler than the sun, woman's frailer nature made her virtue more worthy in God's eyes.[12] Authorities cleverly reversed gender associations to make theological points. Cistercian monks of the twelfth century spoke of Christ as mother; for other writers God was defined by *sapientia,* the feminine noun for wisdom. Even Pope Gregory VII had referred to his benefactor, Beatrice of Tuscany, as "dux," masculine leader and warrior for Christendom. Some women writers of the age showed a fondness for employing polar comparisons when they spoke of women's nature in contrast to men's. For example, twelfth-century Hildegarde of Bingen agreed with the scholar Abelard that women had frailer natures than men, but found this of no advantage to them in finding favor with God.

When polarities became fashionable in the twelfth century, they stimulated imaginations and provided apt images for theological debate. Although these images were by no means consistently pejorative to women, they did depend on a polar construct that first assigned a trait to man, then the opposite trait to woman; thus the construct itself tended powerfully toward misogyny. When opportunity came to the Church to enforce strict enclosure on women's religious orders, to justify women's exclusion from educational opportunities, or to eliminate women from some of the attractive new reform orders or from clerical marriages, those polar arguments could be employed. Those arguments assigned a positive trait to mankind and an opposite or negative trait to womankind; they served now as part of the mental equipment of learned authorities.

GENDER TRIUMPHS IN THE LATE MIDDLE AGES

Concepts with little circulation and consequence in one age have a way of becoming more authoritative over time when they provide a rationale for new actualities. Where twelfth-century thinkers experimented with polar schemes, the thirteenth-century thinker Thomas Aquinas firmly advanced them, on the authority of Aristotle, as essential to natural order. Aquinas placed Aristotle's polar arguments on woman's nature into the first book of his *Summa Theologica.* There *Question 92* defined woman after, and in juxtaposition to, man, to whom Aquinas gave a place in God's universe halfway between the beasts and the angels. Aristotle had developed a systematic polarity in which an arranged set of qualities associated with male—limited, odd, one, right, square, at rest, straight, light, and good—were opposed to a parallel alignment of traits associated with female—unlimited, even, plurality, left, oblong, moving, curved, darkness, evil (see Chapter 2, p. 49). Adapting Aristotle to Christian dogma,

Aquinas defined man in the image of God as active, formative, and tending toward perfection, unlike woman, whom he defined as opposite, or passive, material, and deprived of the tendency toward perfection. The very simplicity of the scheme recommended it. Nothing could be less taxing than finding an opposite quality to man's and assigning it to woman. The axiomatical quality of this thinking eased applying it to everyday life. Laypeople, even the illiterate, could grasp polarities and employ them as unquestioned assumptions sanctioned by theologians; that is, as mere informal thoughts or "notions" polarities were easier to use than more rigorously developed "ideas." Medieval theologians did not themselves subject such notions to the same rigorous logical review they routinely applied to ideas in their philosophical discourse. This new definition of woman passed on an inherited system of notions that remained largely unexamined, in which the polar construct remained constant while any particular comparison (men are at rest, women are moving) could be reconstructed to fit new circumstances.[13]

Gender, which first appeared in Western thought as a notion, slipped into the intellectual baggage of later generations. Expositions of this notion of "woman" may have begun as little more than dry sophistry among male scholars, whose very isolation at cathedral schools and universities meant a separation from society at large, where women might have objected to the exercise. In earlier centuries, women had participated in intellectual discourse. They now found themselves cut off from that opportunity and thus could not comment effectively on this new system of gender. A notion practically unthinkable in earlier centuries went largely unchallenged in the thirteenth century.

The schools and universities that revived these classical notions also taught students, and institutions capable of propagating orthodox theology were staffed by these former students in due course. Professionalization of the disciplines or fields of knowledge had come a long way by the turn into the fourteenth century. The developing fields of medicine, law, ethics, and theology all relied to some extent upon graduates of the universities and upon the same scholastic corpus of thought in which the new more rigid notions of gender figured. Priests, increasingly trained at schools, offered their parishioners expository sermons and writings. They could give their parish congregations the theologians' opinion on woman's nature if they felt the need to do so. In the years after the Black Plague (1348–1350), cities recruited university-trained physicians to care for the sick and the poor. Physicians could prescribe cures according to their own notion of man's and woman's natures in either the Galenic tradition or the rigidly polar Aristotelian tradition. The increased complexity and bureaucracy in church, state, and commerce demanded lawyers. In their hands, causal notions often became legal justifications. Gratian's *Decretals* on woman's incapacity, for example, was offered against women's exercise of certain positive legal rights. Authorities in many fields of knowledge used notions of gender to simplify schemes of thought. They provided rationales for expedient acts using the opposition of female to male as justification.

Europeans began again (as in ancient times) to speak and think of a category rather than of women as they knew them. This tendency became an over-riding consideration in justifying women's roles, responsibilities, rights, and their place in Christian society.

For example, this introduced confusion and conflict into accepted under-standings of sexual reproduction and human sexuality, proving how serious conflicting definitions of gender can be. The long-accepted texts of Galen had assumed that both men and women contributed to reproductive processes, making the sexual response of both parties essential for conception. The vir-ginal nun Hildegarde of Bingen accepted this view, describing the female sex-ual response as "the fluid of fertility with heat." Tro(c)ta, a general practitioner at Salerno, prescribed for her patients out of this understanding of an active female response as well. So great was respect for her practical knowledge that two other medical texts from the University of Salerno were later associated with her general text and became known as the treatise "Trotula." Physicians studied these texts in Latin, and translations into the vernacular reached mid-wives. Jewish, Muslim, and Christian women were recognized as physicians and surgeons in this age; of course, women served as midwives in even greater numbers. All these women advised and prescribed according to Galenic prin-ciples. At times even priests were advised to heed the view that women's active sexual response was necessary for conception, and they were advised to counsel women about its necessity for childbearing.

The newly introduced Aristotelian understanding of sexuality stood at odds with Galen. It simplified conception to man as active and woman as pas-sive, so only men contributed "seed." The passive partner, the woman, served merely as an oven that could botch conception but not add substantially to its "active" process. Hildegarde's "fluid of fertility with heat" would not affect conception at all in this scheme. There were far-reaching implications for med-ical treatment in this new way of thinking: medical concern for women's sexual response and reproductive health—menstruation, or bringing on the "flowers," as it was referred to in medical parlance—was not as significant a concern here as it was for the followers of Galen. Authorities aligned against each other on such questions, so practical concerns like sexual response, conception, child-birth, and nostrums for bringing on the "flowers"—what we today would likely understand as a form of contraception—became contested issues and matters of no little confusion for women and for men. For example, the Aristotelian theory relieved women who had been raped and became pregnant from any accusa-tion that they had actually enjoyed the act, whereas Galenic theory, because it demanded "ejaculation" from both male and female for impregnation, might well find such a victim of rape implicated in the act. But then the Galenic theory of female seed was also used as a justification for giving women pleasure in marital sexual intercourse, since her orgasm ensured fertility.

In the face of confusion, societal attitudes toward women darkened. This may be seen in fear of the polluting effects of women's menses and women's "seed" (bodily fluids). If, according to the Aristotelian tradition, female "seed" had no role in reproduction, then it must play a more ominous role in nature. Since leprosy was understood to be a sexually transmitted disease, women were then understood to transmit it through their bodily fluids while not being affected by the disease themselves. A powerful basis for misogynous interpretations had been laid, with long-lasting consequences.

A GOLDEN AGE?

In the early twentieth century, Alice Clark, an economic historian, looked back on the role of women in late medieval towns and guilds and found the late Middle Ages a "golden age" of opportunity for women, in contrast with early modern times.[14] But we must travel back far beyond the well-documented thirteenth century to find any better times for women. Recent research indicates that thirteenth-century guilds often allowed only the participation of women as wives of masters, and the few women who became guild members in their own right did so as widows who had inherited that status from their husbands. In fact, biographies of women who succeeded and grew wealthy in their occupations turn out to be, in most cases, the biographies of widows who by accident of death and inheritance rights carved out for themselves roles unavailable to other women. Although women still remained active in agricultural and industrial production, their society no longer saw a "natural" role for them in the administrative hierarchy. These roles, for the most part, were reassigned to men. With a revived Aristotelian notion of gender ascendant, women were more likely to find themselves being directed, rather than directing, activities, as they had done in the past.

The economic downturn of the fourteenth century played a crucial part in hardening the roles we have associated with gender expectations until recent times. After more than three centuries of almost uninterrupted economic growth, Europe experienced a disastrous shrinkage in the middle years of the fourteenth century. Many factors caused this, women's lessened opportunity to play active, problem-solving roles numbering among them. Also, the series of famine years from 1317 onward, the closing of the silk route to China, the banking crisis of 1343 to 1345, the Black Death (bubonic plague), which in its first visitation to Europe in 1348 may have taken the lives of one-third to one-half of the inhabitants, all contributed to the crisis. By the second half of the century, cities had lost substantial population, and the economy slowed. Europe entered a period of protracted and costly wars, the plague returned every decade or so, and the population did not recover its late thirteenth-century peak for at least a century and a half.

Popular religious responses to a series of issues that had underlying economic and social causes opened up the monumental problem of popular heresies for authorities in the Church. In a world where the Church responded slowly, if at all, to women's religious enthusiasm and propagated negative views of their nature among the clergy, some heretical groups offered greater participation and equality to women. Albigensians made many converts among women, and Lollardy in England attracted a considerable following of women; in Bohemia the Hussites numbered women among their most dedicated followers and noblewomen among their patrons.[15] Beatrice de Planissoles of Montaillou in the Pyrenees, twice widowed by 1300 and imprisoned as a heretic in 1322, does not appear remarkable for any religious beliefs she held, but still her behavior disturbed her inquisitors. She claimed varied sexual liaisons in her village, admitted to having her four well-loved daughters tutored so they could learn to read and write, and formed close bonds with the peasant women in her community regardless of her noble name and status. This was sufficient to bring her before the inquisitors.[16]

However, charges of heresy did not sully the names of renowned women mystics like Mechtild of Magdeburg; such women were far too popular with ordinary Christians for any authority to venture condemnations. Women mystics became inspirational figures for a lay public who often found the new scholastic language of theologians impenetrable. Such visionary women continued to find opportunities to write as vernacular languages emerged in a late medieval shift from oral to written culture. These visionaries spoke with an identifiable female voice: themes such as the religious significance of illness, or of food, and the clear voicing of the need for charismatic authorization characterized women's mystical writing in the later medieval centuries. These women produced powerful physiological images: of miraculous fasting and more miraculous food, of the gift of lactation, or of receiving the stigmata. Christians sought visionary women as intercessories with God, placing more faith in the power of the visionaries' mystical union with God than in rather arid scholastic proofs for God's existence.

Women crusaders finally won the right to wear the sign of the cross (crucesignata) on their own in the later Middle Ages. Mystics like Julian of Norwich still inspired the faithful, and a few extraordinary women still led, at least in moments of severe crisis and demoralization. Joan of Arc, the Maid of Orleans, claimed that heavenly voices had sent her to lead the French troops in the war against the English king and bring the Dauphin Charles VII to Rheims to be anointed and crowned. Charles believed Joan, and, donning armor, she led the troops to victory. But when her leadership no longer benefited the new king and the army, the Burgundians who had captured Joan handed her over to the English. Among other issues, her failure to conform to gender expectations (at her trial she was accused of wearing men's clothes) brought the charge of acting "against nature." She was charged with demonic possession and burned (see Chapter 6, p. 159).

Gender expectations now figured as critical categories of thought and organizing principles for society. "Womanly" conduct appeared to be ordained by God and sanctioned by earthly institutions. Because gender seemed a component of the natural order of things, it could not easily be challenged. The world of fantasy, play, and humor reveals this tellingly. During the carnival preceding Lent—or "the world turned upside down"—women dressed in men's clothes and walked boldly in the streets. This was a ritual enactment of the unseemliness and absurdity of women failing to uphold their ordained roles—even while women mocked their roles. The system of gender had become conventional wisdom and came to be policed even by the people themselves.

In this period of heightened tension and frustration due to economic hard times, chronic warfare, and continual concern over periodic plague epidemics, people sought answers from authorities. In this way scholastic or Aristotelian notions about gender and about women gained wider acceptance. Yet a deep ambivalence still marked the application of the revived classical gender system, which may be seen where women's work mattered in the economy, and this was the legacy passed on to later centuries. Etienne Boileau, a provost of Paris, in his *Livre des metiers* noted about glass cutters: "No master's widow who keeps working at this craft after her husband's death may take on apprentices, for the men of the craft do not believe that a woman can master it well enough to teach a child to master it, for the craft is a very delicate one." Boileau saw men as "right" or dexterous in the lucrative trade of glass cutting, and women as "left" or clumsy. This belief provided justification for eliminating them from positions of authority within the guild.[17] He disregarded the fact that women practiced the even more dexterous work of lace making. Even the most exquisite, expensive, and fiercely difficult lace making could be fitted in around household tasks and child rearing, so the notion of women's clumsiness did not need to be trotted out. The "traditional" division of labor recognized today had emerged, and notions of gender served wherever they sustained that system.

With a notion of gender in reserve to call upon, Europeans fell into a division of labor between women and men that continued to underlie economic development until the industrial transformation. Women accomplished essential work even though they were denied access to positions of power. A more rigid set of expectations for men's and women's work affected the sharing out of tasks both within the home and in the working place. However, women's contributions remained essential to all kinds of economic endeavors, and women continued to have access to workshops and markets in some, usually subordinate, activities.

In a sense, rigid polar notions of gender battled with an older flexible sense of the proper relations between the sexes. Peering out from behind negative societal norms stood more affirming assumptions about inherent worth that women gained in their natal families and applied to their roles in adult life. These traditions were less amenable to "correction" from intellectual authorities. Among peasants and artisans, in particular, a marriage pattern sustaining productive economic roles that historians have labeled "western European" emerged by the late Middle Ages.[18] Women's choices essentially defined that pattern: women of the popular classes married relatively late, that is, late enough to have put aside savings to provide a stake or dowry. They chose husbands near them in age, sometimes younger than they. Women did not necessarily marry when they became sexually active, but when they had accumulated savings. Some never married at all. The obligations women assumed by viewing marriage as an economic pact to which they were active, lifelong contributors ensured women's productivity to the economy. Working women, that is, all women but a tiny leisured minority, saw themselves as indispensable. Against pejorative views of their nature, this sense of indispensability helped sustain women in the essential work they performed for society.

CONCLUSION

The course of women's history diverged from men's during the centuries from the eleventh to the fourteenth, when gender became an increasingly inflexible category for organizing thoughts about society. This should make us pause and think a moment about transitions in history. The Renaissance has often been presented as an important transition for Europe because revived classical humanism and secular individualism together yielded an empowering new ideal for mankind. The Reformation, too, has been understood as a dividing point in the history of European civilization. The Middle Ages that preceded both eras are seldom understood as such an age for men; rather this period is represented as a time of steady development in which many of the institutions essential to European civilization took shape. But, in fact, the loss of rights accompanying the triumph of a rigid polar construct of gender constituted an important transition for women, and it forced substantial changes in their lives. Certainly for women this era represented as great a change as the Renaissance represented for men later. Women lost ground in the increasingly complex institutions that could enforce a rigid code of gender and in the commercial centers where authority over resources concentrated into fewer, largely male, hands. Perhaps this critical watershed in the course of Western history has been overlooked not only because it requires focusing attention on women. Perhaps it has been ignored because our histories seldom count the costs of development and infrequently acknowledge that progress comes with a price to some, if not all, in society.

NOTES

1. *The Play of Daniel,* ed. Noah Greenberg, Oxford University Press, New York, 1959, pp. 50–53.
2. Lynn White, *Medieval Technology and Social Change,* Clarendon Press, Oxford, 1962, pp. 82, 89.

3. On women as glass makers, see Meredith Parsons Lillich, "Gothic Glaziers: Monks, Jews, Taxpayers, Bretons, Women," *Journal of Glass Studies* 27 (1985), pp. 72–92.

4. Cited in R. H. C. Davis, *King Stephen 1135–1154,* 3rd ed., Longman, London and New York, 1990, p. 3.

5. *The Alexiad of Anna Comnena,* trans. by H. A. Sweter, Penguin, Hammondsworth, England, 1909, p. 66.

6. Among others, Eric Lionel Jones, *The European Miracle,* Cambridge University Press, Cambridge, 1987.

7. Betty Bandel, "The English Chroniclers' Attitudes Toward Women," *Journal of the History of Ideas* 16 (1953), pp. 113–118.

8. Susan Mosher Stuard, "Ancillary Evidence on the Decline of Medieval Slavery," *Past and Present* 149 (1995), pp. 3–28.

9. Leah Lydia Otis, *Prostitution in Medieval Society,* University of Chicago Press, Chicago, 1984, p. 81.

10. Christiane Klapisch-Zuber, *Women, Family and Ritual in Renaissance Florence,* trans. Lydia Cochrane, University of Chicago Press, Chicago, 1984, p. 107. Copyright University of Chicago. "Goes to husband" means getting married.

11. Gratianus, *Decretum,* II, Causa 31, Questio V, cap. VI (Rome: In aedibus populi Romani, 1584).

12. Peter Abelard, *Epistolae 7,* ed. J.-P. Migne, *Patrologiae cursus completus: scriptores latini,* Garnier, Paris, 1885, 178:245a. *"Naturaliter femineus sexus est infirmior eo virtute est acceptabilior et honore dignior."*

13. Ian MacLean, *The Renaissance Notion of Woman,* Cambridge University Press, Cambridge, 1980.

14. Alice Clark, *The Working Life of Women in the Seventeenth Century,* Routledge and Son, London, 1919.

15. Albigensians were thirteenth-century Christians following practices unacceptable to the Church in southern France. Lollards in England followed John Wycliffe,who believed in translating the Bible into English and interpreting Scripture for oneself. The Hussites followed John Huss in Bohemia. Women in this religious sect were famous for their exploits in battle.

16. Emmanuel LeRoy Ladurie, *Montaillou, The Promised Land of Error,* trans. Barbara Bray, George Braziller, New York, 1978.

17. Etienne Boileau, *Livre des metiers,* ed. G. B. Depping, Rene' de Lespinasse et Francois Bonnardot, Paris, 1837, p. 79.

18. J. Hajnal, "European Marriage Patterns in Perspective," in *Population in History: Essays in Historical Demography,* ed. D. V. Glass and D. C. Eversley, Aldine, Chicago, 1965, pp. 101–143.

SUGGESTIONS FOR FURTHER READING

Among general studies, Eileen Power, *Medieval Women,* ed. M. M. Postan (Cambridge: Cambridge University Press, 1979); Derek Baker, *Medieval Women* (Oxford: Basil Blackwell, 1978); Georges Duby and Michelle Perrot, eds., *Silences of the Middle Ages* (Cambridge, Mass.: Belknap Press, 1994); Susan Mosher Stuard, ed., *Women in Medieval*

Society (Philadelphia: University of Pennsylvania Press, 1976); and Barbara Hanawalt, ed., *Women and Work in Pre-industrial Europe* (Bloomington: Indiana University Press, 1986), are valuable.

On dowry, Diane Owen Hughes, "From Brideprice to Dowry in Mediterranean Europe," *Journal of Family History* 3 (1978), pp. 385–411; and Christiane Klapisch-Zuber, *Women, Family and Inheritance in Renaissance Florence,* trans. Lydia Cochrane (Chicago: University of Chicago Press, 1985), provide information on the early and the later period, respectively.

For readings on the depiction of women in literature, Ian MacLean, *The Renaissance Notion of Woman* (Cambridge: Cambridge University Press, 1980), provides a useful introduction to scholastic notions on women. On changes in perceptions of women, see Betty Bandel, "The English Chroniclers' Attitude Toward Women," *Journal of the History of Ideas* 16 (1955), pp. 113–118. See also Peter Dronke, *Women Writers of the Middle Ages* (Cambridge: Cambridge University Press, 1984). On women and sexuality, see Joan Cadden, *Meanings of Sex Difference in the Middle Ages, Medicine, Science, and Culture* (New York: Cambridge University Press, 1993).

A number of books have appeared on medieval women: Carolyn Bynum, *Holy Feast and Holy Fast* (Berkeley: University of California Press, 1987); Heath Dillard, *Women of the Reconquest, Town Women in Castile, 1100–1300* (Cambridge and New York: Cambridge University Press, 1984); Leah Lydia Otis, *Prostitution in Medieval Society* (Chicago: University of Chicago Press, 1984); *Women of the Medieval World: Essays in Honor of John H. Mundy,* ed. Julius Kirshner and Suzanne Wemple (New York and London: Basil Blackwell, 1985); Penelope D. Johnson, *Equal in Monastic Profession: Religious Women in Medieval France* (Chicago: University of Chicago Press, 1991); Roberta Gilchrist, *Gender and Material Culture: the Archaeology of Religious Women* (London and New York: Routledge, 1994; and JoAnn McNamara, *Sisters in Arms* (Cambridge, Mass.: Harvard University Press, 1996).

The three virtues pulling Christine out of bed to begin work on the *Trésor de la cité des dames*, and Worldly Prudence lecturing to women of different classes.

6

Women in the Renaissance[1]

Carole Levin

*The Renaissance brings to mind Italy—and art, architecture, and letters.
But as a period in history it is much more, and this essay suggests that to
understand the period of the Renaissance it is necessary to recognize the wide
diversity of experience of women of different statuses and races. There was no
empowering and positively charged category of humanist "woman" as there
was of humanist "man," although certain women could be highly educated
humanists. Levin discusses the lives of some of these women: Christine de
Pizan, Margaret More Roper, Lady Jane Grey, and Elizabeth I of England.
When the categorical imperative* woman *was employed it generally connoted
negative traits assigned to women, such as susceptibility to witchcraft,
disorderliness, or weakness. Indeed, Levin argues that being powerful and
successful meant in some ways being male, a perception that unfortunately
gravely limited women's potential as* women. *Nonetheless, many women lived
in, worked in, and contributed to the age: women as diverse as an unnamed
African women in sixteenth-century Scotland, or Catherine of Siena, Joan
of Arc, and Margherita Datini. It is the very diversity of women in the
Renaissance that challenges the gendered humanist construction of "woman."
These women proved Christine de Pizan correct in her assertion that women
have the same capacity for virtue and intellectual abilities as men.*

In the first edition of *Becoming Visible* Joan Kelly asked the question, "Did women have a Renaissance?" She was responding to Jacob Burkhardt's classic definition of the Renaissance as focusing on the flowering of a cultural elite and on Renaissance *men* who consciously constructed their multifaceted lives. Kelly looked at women's status and answered her own question with "no."[2] Over the last twenty years people have been responding to Kelly's question of the concept of historical periodization as it applied to women in a variety of ways. The very term *Renaissance* has also become contested, and a number of scholars prefer *early modern*. But if *Renaissance* is a disputed term because it puts too much emphasis on high culture, *early modern* is also not value-free, in that it suggests the importance of the modern age and ties the period of European history from 1350 to 1600 to the period following rather than the era before. For the purposes of this essay I am using the term *Renaissance*, but with a recognition of the complexity of naming historical periods.[3]

Without considering women we cannot truly understand any period, but we need to not only consider women of the elite but also to ask about women of all statuses and races. We cannot speak in this period of the Renaissance woman, nor can we simply talk about the Renaissance Italian woman, or French woman, or English woman. Women's experiences differed across geographic boundaries and according to status. There were greater disparities between women in the same country, city, or even household than between women of the same status in different regions or countries. In the Renaissance, for some few women, there was the opportunity for education and the possibilities of power and autonomy, but generalizing about "women in the Renaissance" ignores the diversity of real women's experience in that era. In this study of the Renaissance there is a place for a wide range of women.

During the Renaissance elite males described woman's nature as morally weak and intellectually feeble. This perspective was challenged at the beginning of the fifteenth century by one of the women we will be discussing: Christine de Pizan, in her *Book of the City of Ladies*, responded to the misogyny of the learned men of the Renaissance by articulating an alternate perspective of women's worth, a view that women had intellect and human dignity.

The period of the Renaissance, roughly 1350 to 1600, included major changes and cultural shifts. The development of humanism, the belief that the ancient Greeks and Romans had a moral wisdom compatible with and helpful to Christianity, profoundly changed how people regarded themselves and their place in the world, including their feelings about the Church. The Protestant Reformation and Catholic revival had political, social, and economic implications as well as religious ones. A more personal sense of self emerged, together with the concepts of national identity and national monarchies. As part of that development different nations were "discovering," exploring, and subjugating "New World" territories. These explorations helped to encourage a growth in trade and to introduce Europe to new products and new peoples; they also aided in the development of more sophisticated capitalistic systems. There was a greater concentration of population and power in urban areas than previously. The invention of the printing press and movable type meant that information could be disseminated at a much faster rate, which led eventually to a growth in literacy.

This essay addresses the variety of women's experience in the period 1350 to 1600, particularly in Italy, France, and Britain. I will be discussing some specific women of the period, such as Christine de Pizan; Catherine of Siena; Joan of Arc; Margherita Datini; an unnamed African woman in sixteenth-century Scotland; Margaret More Roper; Lady Jane Grey; Elizabeth I; and Bellezza Orsini, a woman accused of witchcraft. I will also be discussing the status of women more generally. The specific women whom I will be discussing are in some ways unusual, in other ways representative. Their significance lies not only in themselves but in the ways their lives tell us about every woman's life in this period.

In the Renaissance there was a wide diversity of experience. Many women were wives or mothers or widows, but some women never married, and some of these, but certainly not all, became nuns. Some women were managers of estates; others were servants, and some were slaves. A few women were labeled as saints, and many more were called heretics or witches. A very few were queens, but many more were peasants. Some were highly educated; most had no access to formal education. Some died for their beliefs or for their actions—or simply because they were women at risk. And not all women in western Europe in the period 1350 to 1600 were white or Christian; Europe included racial, ethnic, and religious minorities as well as wide variations among wealth and power within the white majority.

What were the avenues to power, autonomy, and satisfaction for women? Marriage was an economic arrangement, and most women married; how they were treated by their husbands would make a real difference to their experience. For many women, religion was a means to a strong sense of self and sometimes to important roles within society. Some women's direct relationship with God through visionary experience meant a great sense of power and personal achievement. For the women who had the option available to them, education might prove a means to autonomy and self-respect. One woman for whom this was true was Christine de Pizan (ca. 1364–1430), a woman who demonstrates what was possible for a woman of this period to achieve.[4]

Christine de Pizan was widowed at the age of 25. Her marriage had been an exceptionally happy one; not only was she bereft of her life partner, but she was also in a precarious financial situation, which she solved in a novel fashion. Christine became the first European woman to make a living as a writer, and she did so over a half-century before the invention of the printing press.

Christine's unusual background prepared her for dealing with the travails of her life. Her father, Thomas de Pizan, had been summoned from Bologna to the court of the French king Charles V to be his astrologer. Growing up at court, Christine received an excellent education largely through her father. When Christine was 15, her father arranged her marriage with the nobleman Etienne de Castel. (Most women did not marry until they were in their twenties: so marriage at such a young age demonstrates her high social status.) Etienne, 24 at the time of the marriage, was a scholar who knew Christine's father well. Charles V celebrated the marriage by giving Etienne a post as his notary and secretary. Theirs was a very happy marriage; Christine later described Etienne as not only wise, courteous, and knowledgeable, but, even more important to her, loyal, loving and considerate. In turn Etienne had absolute trust in Christine; Christine said of her marriage: "We had so arranged our love and our two hearts that we had but one will, closer than brother and sister, whether in joy or in sorrow."[5] During her marriage, and even more after her husband's death, Christine continued to study and read widely.

In 1380 King Charles V died. Christine's father, now 60 years old, immediately lost his important and well-paid position. Thomas became ill and eventually helpless; he died around 1385. Etienne assumed care of Thomas's family as well as his own; he and Christine had three children, two sons and a daughter. About 1389 Etienne, then 34 years old, accompanied Charles VI to Beauvais, where he suddenly became ill and died. For Christine, "all my good days" were over. Not only her own small children depended on her, but her mother also. Christine, overwrought, wished only for death; she wrote that she considered killing herself, when Fortune came and turned her into a man. She meant, of course, that she had found the courage, strength, and fortitude to make a life for herself and support her family, what Renaissance men and women perceived as "manly" behavior. But this did not mean that Christine did not respect women. In her extraordinary career as a writer she directly responded to male criticisms of woman's nature. Christine decided not to be a victim of circumstance, but to take control of her life and her fortunes.

Christine began to write both poems and prose works that she sent to the wealthy and powerful at court, receiving money in return, as was the custom. With a number of her works she had copies made, each with a separate dedicatory poem. Christine sent these poems to members of the French nobility and received recompense from them. Eventually she began to receive commissions, including a study of the virtues of the late king Charles V.

By about 1400, her financial affairs had straightened out. Her brothers had grown up and returned to Italy. Her daughter became a nun, and her surviving son was placed in the household of the Earl of Salisbury in England. This gave Christine more time to read widely in history, literature, mythology, philosophy, and the writings of the church fathers. She considered herself fortunate "because God and nature had granted to me, beyond the common run of women, the gift of the love of learning."[6] As Christine continued to write, certain themes became clear. One was her ardent patriotism for her adopted country France. Another was the cause of women, the belief that women were not inferior to men simply because they were women.

In 1404–1405 Christine composed her most important work, *The Book of the City of Ladies (le livre de la cité des dames)*,[7] designed to refute the charges that scholarly men had made against woman's nature. She framed the book using the literary device of a visionary experience. Christine had read widely and recognized how negative male authorities were about women. The book opens with Christine sitting in her study wondering why so many male authors, as if all speaking from the same mouth, have written so disparagingly about women. Christine thinks of all the women she knows, and most of them were praiseworthy. But, Christine wonders, could so many authorities be wrong? Fearing not, Christine begins to sink into a pool of despair and self-loathing. Just at that moment three female muses, Reason, Righteousness, and Justice, come to her in a vision and explain that it was the viciousness of men, rather than the faults of women, that led to these attacks.

The spirits tell her that evil is not natural to women; rather, anyone, male or female, who commits sin is evil. "The man or the woman in whom resides greater virtue is the higher; neither the loftiness nor the lowliness of a person lies in the body according to the sex, but in the perfection of conduct and virtue" (24; I.9.3). Women not only have the same capacity for virtue as men, but the same intellectual abilities.

Christine asks if it is true that women's minds can only learn a little. Of course not, responds Reason. If parents would send their daughters to the same schools they could learn just as intently as their male counterparts. Though some men claim that women are good "only for bearing children and sewing" (77; I.37.1), there have, in fact, been great women scholars. Christine wonders why these women scholars have not refuted all this male slander. Righteousness replies that this is to be Christine's task.

Then the three spirits tell Christine she must not only write a book; she must also build a city, "where no one will reside except all ladies of fame and women worthy of praise" (11; I.3.3). This city will protect good women of all times and house them forever. Men have had their cities and, St. Augustine tells us, God has had His. Now it is the women's turn. Thus the story of the book is how Christine, with the help of her three divine guides, constructs a city of ladies.

The book is divided into three sections, with Reason, Righteousness, and Justice each taking her turn to help Christine. In the first, Christine lays the foundations and hears about the active women of the past who led armies and ruled states. In the second section she builds the house for the obedient women who guarded their chastity, honored their parents, loved their husbands, and persevered in their duties; they have lived in righteousness. In her text Christine does not denigrate the married state. She does not want married women to be despised because they are no longer virgins; marriage was not as church Fathers had presented it, a lesser choice. In the third section Christine completes the towers and the roof tops and hears of the women who martyred themselves for their faith and are the handmaidens of the Virgin Mary. They represent the towers and roofs that reach all the way up to God. This city, which Reason assures Christine will never fall, will be the defense of women against all the assaults of men. Christine finishes by addressing the ladies of the city. She warns them that the city is their refuge against their enemies, but she also tells them not to become too proud. Indeed, the more virtuous they are, the more meek they should be. "May this City be an occasion for you to conduct yourselves honestly and with integrity and to be all the more virtuous and humble" (255; III.19.1). Christine not only cares about women of high social status: "In brief, all women—whether noble, bourgeois, or lower-class—be well-informed in all things and cautious in defending your honor and chastity against your enemies!" (256; III.19.6).

Christine de Pizan and her conception of a city for women was remarkable, but there were many impressive women who found means to power and authority in this era. The third section of Christine's city emphasized women who possessed great courage and were martyrs for their faith. One of Christine's contemporaries who would have felt at home there was Catherine of Siena (ca. 1347–1380). Her visions from God, exemplary behavior, and extreme fasting gave her such authority, despite her humble origins, that the city of Florence sent Catherine to Avignon on a mission. The papacy had been moved there seventy years earlier under influence of the French, which caused great distress not only to the Italians but to much of Christian Europe. In 1376 she was able to convince Pope Gregory XI, despite his poor health and the potential wrath of the French king, to leave Avignon and return to Rome. Christine had described how Fortune turned her into a man. Catherine, in one of her extraordinary visionary conversations with God, protested that God was commanding her to do things that she as a mere woman could not do. "My sex, you know," Catherine reminded God, "is here an obstacle for many reasons, whether because men disparage it or because of modesty, for it is not good that a woman consort with men." But God did not accept this excuse. "Isn't it I who have created the human race and divided it into male and female? I dispense where I want the grace of my spirit. In my eyes there is neither male nor female nor rich nor poor. All are equal, for I can work my will through all equally."[8]

Even more at home in Christine's city would have been her close contemporary, Joan of Arc (1412–1431). In a dazzling reversal of gender, status, and age, this young peasant girl, whose authority came from the voices of the saints, turned the tide of war between the English and French and brought the Dauphin, heir to the French throne, to Rheims to be crowned Charles VII. In 1430 Christine de Pizan wrote a poem commending Joan of Arc's triumphs, a final paean to her two themes of patriotism and the worth of women.[9] A year later Joan was dead: captured by the Burgundians, sold to the English, tried for heresy and sorcery, and burned at the stake.

With their visions of God and the saints, their decision to take a public role, and the notoriety that it brought them, Catherine of Siena and Joan of Arc were unusual, but they were also representative of a whole group of women mystics, such as St. Bridget of Sweden, Julian of Norwich, and Margery Kempe of England, who used their personal relationship with God to find a public voice and a sense of self-worth.[10] The direct relationship with God allowed these women to by-pass the constraints that would have been placed on them not only because of their gender, but in some cases because of their status and age as well. Christine not only valued powerful religious women; she had also celebrated in her city of ladies married women who lived righteously.

Most women in Europe in 1350 to 1600 married; usually they did so in their midtwenties. In elite circles young women married much earlier, in their early teens. Marriage provided protection, some measure of financial security, family connections, status and usually, children. Motherhood defined the lives of most Renaissance women for most of their adult years. Except in cases of infertility, this began a cycle of pregnancy, childbirth, nursing, and pregnancy once again. Since elite women put their children out to wet nurses, they became pregnant more frequently. In villages and towns throughout Europe, most adult women may have been nursing a child much of the time. They not only nursed their own, but in some cases the babies of women of high social status as well.

Renaissance women knew that, as wives, their ability to successfully give birth to children was their most important function. But childbirth could be a fearful time. Pregnancy could be a happy time of anticipation, but also one of dread of the forthcoming confinement. It was a time when women could come together and support each other, and this support was needed. Women faced not only great pain but the possibility of death in childbirth.[11] And mothers who themselves survived often had to face the death of their children. Infant and child mortality rates were very high. Estimations vary over how many children women of the period bore. Some demographers suggest that many women experienced between six and eight pregnancies, and others place it as high as eight to fifteen. A number of these pregnancies ended in miscarriages, either spontaneous or perhaps induced in efforts to limit family size. Of live births, as many as half of these children died in infancy and childhood. Mothers suffered real grief over the deaths of their children.[12]

Wives were not only to be mothers; they were also to obey their husbands. Handbooks of the time advised couples to be bound in mutual love and support, and Christine de Pizan's marriage to Etienne certainly followed that model, but sermons and handbooks, such as Leon Battista Alberti, *I Libri della Famiglia,* le Menagier de Paris's book for his wife, and the Elizabethan homily on marriage, also advised wives to obey their husbands in everything, whether the commands were reasonable or unreasonable.[13] Wives should be chaste, obedient, pleasant, gentle, submissive, and, unless sweet-spoken, silent. In marriages where there was affection and respect this might not be so problematic. But the system of submission and obedience meant that those who were beaten or abused had few places to turn. The rights of the husband were entrenched both in custom and in law. It is worthwhile to look at an actual marriage in fourteenth-century Italy to see in what ways real life could support these beliefs and in what ways mitigate them.

Margherita di Domenico Bandini (ca. 1360–1423) married the Tuscan merchant Francesco Datini (ca. 1335–1410) in 1376.[14] Though both were from Italy—Francesco from Prato, Margherita from Florence—they married in Avignon, where Francesco had been engaged in trade for many years. Margherita was about 16 at the time of the marriage, and Francesco over 40. For years he had been under pressure from family and friends to marry, and to marry a home town girl, not a local French woman. Though Margherita did not bring a dowry, she had youth and good looks, and on her mother's side was connected to the Florentine nobility, a cut above Francesco's merchant status.

Once Catherine of Siena had convinced the pope to return to Rome, Avignon was no longer the best place for an Italian merchant, so in 1382 Francesco Datini and Margherita returned to Prato. Because Francesco was frequently doing business in both Florence and Pisa, he was often away from home. He would write at least twice a week to Margherita, who, despite her youth and the dictates of the time, was not always patient and submissive in her responses; sometimes she was outspoken and even critical. Not only Francesco's letters but over a hundred of her letters have survived. For some years Francesco's letters were read to Margherita, and she dictated her letters back to him because she had not been taught to read as a child. In an effort to gain more control over her life, Margherita learned to read and write at about the age of 30; thus there would be no mediating factors between their letters to each other. Like Christine, Margherita understood the importance of education.

Most of Margherita's time was claimed by her domestic duties, which increased with each year, together with Francesco's fortune and the size of his household. Margherita supervised the house, the cellar, the kitchen garden, the stable, and the mill. She had to be up in the morning before the front door was opened, and was the last of the household to retire to her bedchamber.

The relationship was sometimes a difficult one. Margherita was upset by how often Francesco was away. The tone of her letters was at first impatient and self-defensive, later resigned and sad. During these years Francesco was irritable, restless, and often unfaithful. Most of the problems in Francesco and Margherita's relationship can be traced to Margherita's failure at the most important function of being a wife: she was barren. Francesco had several illegitimate children, but despite all the prescribed remedies concerned friends and family members sent her, Margherita failed to conceive.

One can also see in the letters a core of affection and mutual respect. Margherita was as disappointed in not being able to give her husband a household of children as he was. She brought her sister's daughter to live with them and later, when she had given up hope of having a child of her own, eventually agreed to raise Francesco's illegitimate daughter. Ginevra was born in 1392 to Francesco's 20-year-old slave girl Lucia. Apparently at first Margherita refused to bring the child up in her home, and Francesco sent Ginevra off to be nursed and later kept by a foster mother. But when Ginevra was 6 Margherita relented and the child was brought into the household to be raised as their own daughter.

Margherita wrote with pride to Francesco that she was the only one who could control Ginevra. "In my presence she is the best child that ever was, but when I am not there, she will do naught she is told." When Ginevra was ill and Francesco, away from home, was worried, Margherita wrote: "Be assured that I look to her as if she were my own, as indeed I consider her" (186). Margherita bought Ginevra fine clothes and toys and made sure that she—unlike Margherita—learned to read as a child. As Ginevra grew up, Francesco was very concerned that he find his daughter a good husband, someone who would not be ashamed of her since she was a slave's daughter. He provided her with a large dowry, a lavish trousseau, and an extravagant wedding.

Ginevra's mother was a slave, and slaves as well as free-born servants were common in Italian households during the Renaissance. Slavery had never died out in Europe during the Middle Ages.[15] Some of the slaves had similar backgrounds to the Tuscans, but there were also new foreign slaves. After the plague had swept through Italy in 1348, the resultant labor shortage caused a sudden demand for domestic slaves; they were brought to Italy not only from Spain and Africa, but from the Balkans, Constantinople, Cyprus, and Crete, and above all the shores of the Black Sea. In Florence a decree of the Signoria, issued in 1336, officially authorized their importation—provided only that they were infidels, not Christians; this decree, however, was not consistently followed. Below the great merchants, the Guild members, even below the hungry poor, Tuscan cities had another category of people—those with no human or legal rights. We do not even know their original names; we only know them by the names given to them by their masters. There were not only adult slaves, but many young children, and they belonged to a great variety of different ethnic groups: Tartars, Circassians, Greeks, Russians, and Georgians. By the end of the fourteenth century there was hardly a well-to-do household in Tuscany without at least one slave, most of them girls or women. The demand had spread even to the smaller country towns such as Siena, San Gimignano, Pistoia, and Prato. Slaves were used for payment of debts and as part of a bride's dowry.

Francesco had slaves in his household, and he would sometimes oblige friends by selecting a slave for them through his agents in Genoa or Venice; but the most active part of this trade was in his branches in Majorca and Ibiza, where both African slaves bound for Italy and eastern slaves bound for Spain were collected and sold. One should not, however, overemphasize the numbers; usually a few slaves were included in a shipment of other assorted wares, and they were clearly viewed as more goods, not human beings. Both duty and taxes had to be paid on these slaves. Sometimes slaves sent long distances were insured, like other goods, against the perils of the voyage. Francesco insured a slave woman, ironically also named Margherita, but the insurance would not cover the loss if she threw herself into the sea of her own accord, a haunting inference that for many slaves suicide was preferable to servitude.

When slaves were ill, wounded, or pregnant, their value might plummet. Unlike eighteenth-century owners, who viewed pregnancy in their slaves more positively as another potential slave, Renaissance owners and merchants found pregnancy to be a particular irritation, since it reduced the mother's market value. Here is one example of the attitudes of those who trafficked in slavery: "The slave you sent is sick, or rather full of boils, so that we find none who would have her. We will sell or barter her as best we can, and send you the account. Furthermore, I hear she is with child, two months gone or more, and therefore she will not be worth selling." Another letter about a woman who said her pregnancy was due to the priest who had been her former owner is even more brutal: "We spake to the chaplain to whom our slave belonged and he says you may throw her into the sea, with what she has in her belly, for it is no creature of his."[16]

Owners complained constantly about the laziness, dishonesty, and sexual promiscuity of their slaves. This latter complaint is particular ironic, given that the men who impregnated the slaves were often the masters. Despite these complaints, the upper classes of Italy continued to use household slaves as well as free servants because slavery was so much cheaper. Even a fairly expensive slave paid for himself or herself within a few years. Even more pressing, wage or contract servants were difficult to locate or keep on the job because there were other, more attractive opportunities in the cities. How well the slaves were treated depended greatly on the nature of the owners. Just as some wives were treated well by their husbands, so too some slaves were treated well by their masters. But in both cases, there was little recourse for those who were under the control of someone cruel or harsh.

Francesco and Margherita appear to have been decent to their household slaves. Around the time that Margherita agreed to adopt Ginevra, the child's own mother, the slave Lucia, was married off to one of Francesco's servants, Nanni of Prato, and Datini later remembered her in his will. Most of the last nine years of Francesco's life he spent in Prato with Margherita, and thus we have few letters between them. She promised him that if he spent his last years peacefully with her in Prato, he could "live here in a way that will rejoice you" (329). Francesco died in August 1410. In his final will he freed all his slaves. After her husband's death, Margherita went to live with Ginevra and her husband. She died in 1423. Despite the difficulties in their marriage, it seems at the end to have been a relatively successful one. Though they had no children of their own, Margherita raised Ginevra as if she were indeed her mother. And she refused to be passive and submissive to Francesco, even learning to read and write so that she could communicate with him more directly. Their letters give us special insight into an Italian merchant marriage, and also a window into the world of the slaves of Renaissance Italy. Slavery in these households reminds us that options for some women in this period did not mean options for all. And the fact of slavery reminds us also that not all women living in western Europe between 1350 and 1600 were white or Christian women.

The Portuguese and Spanish explorations of Africa and later the Americas drastically changed both those continents and European culture. It also meant a new influx of slaves into Europe itself as well as European participation in a growing slave trade between Africa and the Americas. By the mid-fifteenth century, many hundreds of black slaves were imported into Spain and Portugal. When Columbus "discovered" the New World, he had no compunction about sending hundreds of Indians to be sold in the slave markets of Seville. As early as 1502 Spanish and Portuguese ships were taking Africans to the Americas as slaves.[17]

In the first decade of the sixteenth century, one Portuguese slave ship was intercepted on its way to the Americas. James IV of Scotland ordered it taken in recompense for a Scottish ship that had been taken by the Portuguese. The Africans on board were instead taken to Edinburgh, where they formed a small community. Their status there was unclear, but we do have a brief glimpse of one of the women, though we can only guess her feelings about her situation, since, unlike Christine and Margherita, she could not write, and, indeed, we do not even know her name. We have none of her own words.

James IV loved tournaments and knightly games, and around 1507 he held one called the tournament of the black knight and the black lady. He enjoyed it so much he repeated it the next year. James took on the role of the black knight himself, and the victor's prize in the tournament was the "black lady." She was not, however, like James, a Scottish person in costume, but an African woman. James had a beautiful dress made for the "black lady." It was damask flowered with gold and trimmed with green and yellow taffeta. She also had sleeves and gloves of black leather. She was at the tournament with two female attendants, probably also African women. Two squires, dressed in white damask, carried the black lady to the tournament in a "chair triumphal" made especially for the occasion. We are hardly surprised that the king won all his challenges; the winners were rewarded by the black lady's kiss and close embrace. Contemporaries described the event as a joyous occasion, but today we might wonder how this woman felt, dressed in European finery and expected to kiss and presumably have sex with men not of her choosing.[18]

James's "black lady," however beautifully he dressed her, was forced into the position of a courtesan, and as a result it was she who had the scorn reserved for such women. Because of her race, she contended with an added level of contempt. James's court poet, William Dunbar, wrote that since he had written many poems about white women, he decided to write one about the black woman who had recently landed in Scotland. Despite James setting her up as an object of beauty, Dunbar, in what we in the twentieth century would truly find appalling, wrote a poem that was filled with contempt for how this "black lady" looked, since she did not fit the European model of female beauty. Dunbar tragically demonstrates how some Europeans viewed those who were different as less than human. Used as an object of amusement and derision, forced into sexual service, the "black lady" disappears from the historic record. We do not know her eventual fate. Dunbar critic Tom Scott writes, "It needs little imagination to guess the inner feelings of this wretched creature torn out of her natural and proper environment . . . and subjected to this kind of treatment, and meeting God knows what kind of end."[19]

In the 1570s John Hawkins and Francis Drake were attacking Spanish slave ships, which resulted in more Africans being brought to England. Most became household servants and slaves, but some were also court entertainers, and some African women became the kept women of wealthy English and Dutch merchants. As with many of the slaves in Italy, choice over their sexual behavior was beyond these women's control.

As with Italy and France from the fourteenth century onward, sixteenth-century England was a time of great interest in humanism and reform, a time of cultural flowering, and for some women of the aristocratic and royal classes, a time of high education. Yet for many there was a loss of power. Though the Renaissance flourished in England and on the Continent, and a few women enjoyed a privileged education and potential for power, humanist ideals were not extended to much of the population. No one perceived a dichotomy between the humanist ideals of individual respect and the treatment of Africans in their midst. For the "black lady" of James IV's tournament and other African women in Britain, there were no avenues for power whatsoever.

Sixteenth-century England went through many religious and cultural changes, and women played their role in these transformations. In the 1520s Henry VIII believed the only way to keep England and his Tudor dynasty secure was to have a male heir, but his only surviving child with his first wife Catherine of Aragon was Mary. Henry broke England away from the pope and made himself Supreme Head of the Church so that he might marry Anne Boleyn, an ambitious Protestant. Their child too was a daughter, Elizabeth. Anne's execution for adultery freed Henry to marry Jane Seymour, and this time he had a son, Edward. During Henry's reign, and even more so in subsequent reigns, England rocked back and forth between Catholicism and different versions of Protestantism. Each of Henry's children eventually ruled England, his daughters as well as his son. Mary and Elizabeth, and their cousin Lady Jane Grey, who in an attempted coup ruled for nine days, were all extensively educated.

A century earlier, Christine de Pizan had praised strong women and celebrated her own education that allowed her to learn about them. By the sixteenth century in England there were other women of both impressive education and high courage. Some men in this period argued that women should not learn Latin and Greek and otherwise have a sound educa ion because women were naturally frail and prone to evil and this education would open their minds to unwholesome literature. Humanists, however, argued that learning could benefit women because it would keep their fertile minds occupied; otherwise they might be more inclined to idleness, boredom, and mischief. Learning, in fact, could help guard and enhance women's piety and chastity.

Thomas More, author of *Utopia* and one of the outstanding humanists of the age, is also celebrated for his pioneering efforts to extend humanist training to females.[20] He established a school at his house not only for his son but for his three daughters, an adopted daughter, and other dependents. Thomas More insisted that the girls be treated kindly and gently. Though there were both males and females being educated in More's household, the stars were his eldest daughter, Margaret, and his adopted daughter, Margaret Gigs Clement. Margaret More Roper (1505–1544) grew in time into an excellent classical scholar.[21] Giving daughters an education was not all that unusual, but instructing them to be humanists was. They mastered Latin, Greek, rhetoric, philosophy, theology, logic, mathematics, and astronomy. More believed that a humanist education would prepare men for public employment; for women, it would make them better wives and mothers. More was extremely proud of Margaret, but he warned her that he and husband William were a large enough audience for her erudition, even though More showed her work to others himself.

Margaret was an ideal female humanist—she was a devoted and dutiful daughter, wife, and mother. She was also an outstanding scholar, and not only wrote original prose and poems and but also did translations. Her translation of Erasmus's *Precatio Dominica (Devout Treatise upon the Pater Noste)* was printed during her lifetime in 1523. Unfortunately, most of her writings have been lost. Apparently no one thought to take advantage of the new technology of printing for much of Margaret's writing because Thomas saw it as appropriate for her intimate circle only.

Margaret cared deeply about her father. When her father was imprisoned for refusing to take the oath that Henry VIII was Supreme Head of the Church, she visited him in the Tower and continued to correspond with him. After his condemnation at his trial, she, her brother John, and her adopted sister Margaret managed to break through the cordon of guards to embrace him and say their farewells. The last letter he wrote, the night before his execution, was to her. Margaret Roper and Margaret Clement buried their father's body at the church of St. Peter ad Vincula in the Tower. More's head was exhibited on Tower Bridge as a grisly lesson to all traitors. In what may seem to us grotesque, but was clearly an act of love and of courage, Margaret Roper bribed a constable of the watch to take down her father's head and give it to her; she kept it hidden until it could be safely interred. This illegal action caused her to be brought before the King's Council. Margaret also secretly kept her father's letters and other writings so that they could eventually be published. Her husband William Roper saw to this in the reign of Henry's daughter, Mary I; it was impossible to do so before his wife's death in 1544, that is, while Henry still ruled. Margaret took much more care for the preservation of her father's work than for her own.[22]

With the exception of Margaret More Roper, most of the highly educated women in sixteenth-century England were either royal or had connections to the court. Two who were especially impressive were Lady Jane Grey (1537–1554) and her cousin Elizabeth I (1533–1603). Unlike Margaret Roper, both Jane and Elizabeth were not only educated privately in a humanist tradition, but in a Protestant one as well. For Jane, education meant her intellectual and spiritual liberation. It gave her brief life meaning. For Elizabeth, her education was a tool that helped her reign successfully for forty-five years.[23]

Jane was a grand-niece of Henry VIII, and her parents hoped that she might well play a role in the succession. Though they seemed rather indifferent to the joys of learning themselves, they provided Jane with instruction in Latin, Greek, French, Italian, and Hebrew. The humanist scholar Roger Ascham, tutor to the princess Elizabeth, described visiting the Grey household in 1551. The rest of the household was out hunting, but Ascham found Jane at home reading Plato in the original Greek. When he asked her why she was not out riding with the others, she confided what she was doing gave her much more true pleasure. Jane confided more: her parents treated her with such barbarity "that I do think myself in hell till time comes that I must go to Master Aylmer, who teacheth me so gently, so pleasantly. . . . [that] when I am called from him, I fall on weeping because whatsoever I do but learning is full of grief, trouble, fear, and wholy misliking to me."[24]

Grief and trouble indeed. Jane's parents evidently beat her until she agreed to marry the son of the Duke of Northumberland so she could be proclaimed queen after the death of her cousin Edward VI in 1553. The rationale for the attempted coup was that it would keep England Protestant. She complied under force, and her Catholic cousin Mary I's victory eventually led to Jane's execution the following year. The letters and prayers she wrote in the Tower during her last months exhibit a deep and steady faith and demonstrate a remarkable intellect. Though conversion to Catholicism might well have led to clemency, Jane went to her death a staunch Protestant. An Italian who observed her execution recorded that she "faced her death with far greater gallantry than it might be expected from her sex and the natural weakness of her age." He said that at the actual moment of her death, she "submitted the neck to the axe with more than manly courage."[25]

Henry VIII's last daughter, Elizabeth, came to the throne in 1558. She had had a serious classical, humanist education in Latin and Greek, Italian and French, history, theology, and philosophy. In 1550 Ascham wrote to a friend, "She has just passed her sixteenth birthday, and her seriousness and gentleness are unheard of in those of her age and rank. Her study of the true faith and of good learning is most energetic. She has talent without a woman's weakness, industry with a man's perseverance."[26]

Just as Christine described how Fortune turned her into a man, Elizabeth, ruling as an unmarried woman, presented herself to her people not only as both virgin and mother, but as both male and female, as both king and queen. Elizabeth reigned masterfully and far more successfully than Mary and the other women rulers of her time. During her reign England was preserved from the civil wars that wracked neighboring Scotland or France. She presided over a broadly based religious settlement, and looked only for outward conformity to Protestantism: she had no wish to make "windows into men's souls." Throughout Europe Elizabeth was perceived as one of the leading Protestant monarchs, and her reign was a time of great cultural achievement. For many years Elizabeth kept England out of expensive and dangerous foreign entanglements, and she became in time the symbol of national unity, especially at the time of the Spanish Armada (1588).

But there were also serious potential problems during Elizabeth's reign. One can well understand the terror her refusal to name an heir caused, and the pressure Parliament tried to exert. Had Elizabeth died in the first decade of her reign there might well have been a disputed succession and bloody civil war. One long threat to Elizabeth and England's safety was Mary Stuart. Mary was Elizabeth's Catholic cousin and queen of Scotland; she claimed she was also rightful queen of England since Catholics viewed Elizabeth as illegitimate and thus disqualified from ruling. After the Scottish nobility forced Mary to abdicate, she fled Scotland in 1568; Elizabeth kept her in confinement in England for nineteen years. During that confinement Mary was implicated in a variety of plots to have Elizabeth murdered so that she could assume the English throne. Elizabeth finally agreed to Mary's execution in 1587. The last decade of Elizabeth's reign was also particularly difficult. Inflation and poor harvests caused misery for many of the English, and there was deep fear that the Spanish might attempt another invasion. In 1601, two years before her death, her final favorite, the Earl of Essex, led a rebellion against her, which, although unsuccessful, caused both Elizabeth and England anguish.

Still, Elizabeth cared deeply about the love of her people, and the people as a whole did love and support her throughout her forty-five-year reign. At Tilbury in 1588 at the time of the Spanish Armada Elizabeth gave a rousing speech to her troops that is reported to have included the statement, "I may have the body of a weak and feeble woman, but I have the heart and stomach of a king." For powerful, successful women of the Renaissance, being powerful and successful meant in some ways being male, a perception that unfortunately gravely limited women's potential as women.

The Renaissance did have powerful women; through biological and dynastic accident, the sixteenth century was a century of queens, both regnant and regent. Not only Mary I and Elizabeth I in England, but Mary of Guise (as Regent) and Mary Stuart in Scotland, as well as Catherine de Medici as queen mother in France, exerted royal authority. But the sixteenth century was also the century in which the witch craze was at its height. The intensity of the craze was caused by the confluence of a variety of factors, including anxiety over change, religious wars both between countries and within countries, and the changing values and attitudes about neighborly responsibility and community. If one wants to examine both power and powerlessness, those at the bottom of the scale were the accused witches.

The period we call "the Renaissance," what historians have traditionally seen as the centuries that begin the first phase of the Age of Reason, was also the same time when many thousands of women were burned alive or hung.[27] As Chapter 7 discusses in more detail, in both Catholic and Protestant regions there were some areas of harsh persecution. Though the estimates vary widely, historians agree that probably between 60,000 and 100,000 people died in the period of the witch craze, from the fourteenth to the seventeenth centuries, and out of those approximately 80 percent of the accused and 85 percent of the executed were women.[28] Torture was sometimes used to extract confessions, and indeed, 95 percent of those tortured eventually confessed. The midwife and village healer Bellezza Orsini was accused of witchcraft in Italy in 1528. She denied all charges until she was tortured repeatedly. Then she admitted to killing babies and having sex with the devil. When she was shown the instruments of torture the first time she begged instead for a swift death: "Kill me quickly, don't rack me, don't make me die in torment." Bellezza finally committed suicide in her cell while awaiting execution.[29] The irony is that at the same time some women of high status were receiving fine humanist educations, poorer women were being executed as witches.

CONCLUSION

All of these stories of women in the Renaissance, the lives of queens, writers, saints, merchants' wives, slaves, and witches, tell us not only about these specific women, but about women more generally and about the gender expectations of the period. We can see how the stereotypes about women's appropriate behavior could limit all women. While men of the Renaissance were defined by what they accomplished, women were defined by their sexual status, and their value came from their reputation for chaste behavior, rather than any other accomplishment. Even Christine de Pizan, who carved out an identity as a writer but accepted the values of the day, stated in her *City of Ladies* that chastity was "the supreme virtue in women," and without it all other virtues "would be nothing" (155; II.37.1). Both women and men described successful, brave, powerful women as somehow "male" or "manly" and thus not really women, or appropriate models of behavior for other women. As a result, avenues for power for women were male-defined, leaving most women powerless, especially those at the bottom of the social structure. As we close the twentieth century, we must look beyond such definitions if women are to achieve all of which they are truly capable.

Christine de Pizan constructed a city of ladies, a city for virtuous women of all social classes, but she mentioned neither slaves nor women accused of witchcraft as examples of ladies of her city. Yet if we are to people Christine's city, it needs to enclose not only Christine herself, not only such saints as Catherine of Siena and Joan of Arc, not only the merchant's wife, Margherita Datini, and the elite English women given a humanist education such as Margaret Roper, Lady Jane Grey, and Elizabeth I; it must also have space for Lucia, the slave woman who was the natural mother of Margherita's adopted daughter Ginevra, for the unknown African woman who was the "black lady" of James IV's tournament, and for Bellezza Orsini and all the women who died in the witch craze. Christine's definition of women as worthy individuals with the same capacity for intellect and honor as men is borne out by the courage of these women then and of many more in the following centuries. During the Renaissance one finds many women who led exemplary lives, some of whom made important contributions to political power, religion, and the arts, all of whom as women are worth our study and understanding.

NOTES

1. Writing during the Renaissance, Christine de Pizan described a city of ladies. Instead of a city, I have had a community of friends and colleagues who read drafts of this manuscript and helped in its production in a variety of ways. I very much appreciate the helpful comments of the editors of this volume. I also want to express my thanks to Jodi Bilinkoff, Kit French, Dan Kempton, Edmund Kern, Pamela Nickless, Michele Osherow, AnnMarie Phillips, Jan Schmidt, Marla Segol, Bill Spellman, Deborah Wolkenberg, and especially Jo Eldridge Carney and Elaine Kruse. I appreciate the research assistance of Jean Akers and Kristin Elliott. I am grateful to the New Paltz Foundation and the Folger Shakespeare Library for their help on this project.

2. Joan Kelly, "Did Women Have a Renaissance?" in *Becoming Visible*, ed. Renate Bridenthal and Claudia Koonz, Houghton Mifflin, Boston, 1977, pp. 137–164. Jacob Burckhardt, *The Civilization of the Renaissance in Italy*, 2d ed. rev., Oxford University Press, New York, 1945.

3. For responses to Kelly's question, see, for example, David Herlihy, "Did Women Have a Renaissance? A Reconsideration," *Medievalia et Humanistica* (1985), N.S. Vol. 13, 1–22; Judith Bennett, "Medieval Women, Modern Women: Across the Great Divide," in *Culture and History, 1350–1600: Essays on English Communities, Identities and Writing*, ed. David Aers, Wayne State University Press, Detroit, 1992, pp. 147–175; Margaret L. King, "The Renaissance of the Renaissance Woman," *Medievalia et Humanistica* (1988), N.S. Vol. 16, 165–175; "The Woman of

the Renaissance," in *Renaissance Characters,* ed. Eugenio Garin, trans, Lydia G. Cochrane, University of Chicago Press, Chicago, 1991, originally published in Italian, 1988, pp. 207–249; and *Women of the Renaissance,* University of Chicago Press, Chicago, 1991. See also the discussion of the relative significance of both these terms in Leah S. Marcus, "Renaissance/Early Modern Studies," in *Redrawing the Boundaries: the Transformation of English and American Literary Studies,* ed. Stephen Greenblatt and Giles Gunn, The Modern Language Association of America, New York, 1992, pp. 41–63.

4. For more on Christine de Pizan, see Renate Blumenfeld-Kosinski, ed., *The Selected Writings of Christine de Pizan: New Translations, Criticisms,* W. W. Norton and Co., New York, 1996; Enid McLeod, *The Order of the Rose: The Life and Ideas of Christine de Pizan,* Chatto & Windus, London, 1976; Charity Cannon Willard, ed., *The Writings of Christine de Pizan* Persea Books, New York, 1994; Charity Cannon Willard, *Christine de Pizan: Her Life and Works* Persea Books, New York, 1984; King, *Women of the Renaissance,* pp. 219–237; Maureen Quiligan, *The Allegory of Female Authority: Christine de Pizan's Cité des Dames* Cornell University Press, Ithaca and London, 1991; and Daniel Kempton, "Christine de Pizan's *Cité des Dames* and *Trésor de la Cité*: Toward a Feminist Scriptural Practice," in *Political Rhetoric, Power, and Renaissance Women,* ed. Carole Levin and Patricia A. Sullivan, SUNY Press, Albany, 1995, pp. 15–37.

5. McLeod, *op. cit.,* p. 32.

6. *Ibid.,* p. 77.

7. *The Book of the City of Ladies,* trans. Earl Jeffrey Richards, Persea Books, New York, 1982. All quotations from the text are from this edition. Some translators call Righteousness "Rectitude."

8. Raimondo da Campua, *Vita,* libro II, cap. 1 (ed. Tinagli), p. 169, cited in Herlihy, *op cit.,* p. 15. For more on Catherine, see Caroline Bynum, *Holy Feast and Holy Fast: The Religious Significance of Food to Medieval Women,* University of California Press, Berkeley, 1987; Suzanne Noffke, *Catherine of Siena: Vision Through a Distant Eye,* Liturgical Press, Collegeville, Minn., 1996; and Raimondo Sorgia, *Catherine of Siena,* St. Paul Editions, Boston, 1975.

9. Christine de Pizan, *Ditié de Jehanne d'Arc,* ed. and trans. Angus J. Kennedy and Kenneth Varty, Society for the Study of Mediaeval Languages and Literature, Oxford, 1977.

10. For more on women mystics in the fourteenth and fifteenth centuries, see Katharina Wilson, ed., *Medieval Women Writers,* University of Georgia Press, Athens, Ga., 1984; Elizabeth Alvilda Petroff, ed., *Medieval Women's Visionary Literature,* Oxford University Press, New York and Oxford, 1986, and *Body and Soul: Essays on Medieval Women and Mysticism,* Oxford University Press, New York, 1994; Marcelle Thiebaux, *The Writings of Medieval Women: An Anthology,* Garland, New York, 1995; and Carolyne Larrington, ed., *Women and Writing in Medieval Europe,* Routledge, London, and New York, 1995.

11. Margaret King places the possibility as high as 10 percent; see *Women of the Renaissance,* p. 5. On the other hand, Roger Schofield places it at about 1 percent; see "Did the Mothers Really Die? Three Centuries of Maternal Mortality in 'the World We Have Lost'," in *The World We Have Gained: Histories of Population and Social Structure,* ed. L. Bonfield, R. M. Smith, and K. Wrightson, Oxford, 1986, pp. 259–260, cited in Linda A. Pollock, "Embarking on a Rough Passage: The

Experience of Pregnancy in Early-Modern Society," in *Women as Mothers in Pre-Industrial England,* ed. Valerie Fildes, Routledge, London and New York, 1990, p. 47. Pollock, however, argues that 6 to 7 percent of women ran a cumulative risk of dying in childbirth during their lifetimes and that since childbirth was such a conspicuous single cause of mortality, it would probably cause pregnant women great worry.

12. For more on this topic, see Fildes, *op. cit.,* especially the essay by Pollock (pp. 39–67), and also Patricia Crawford, "The Construction and Experience of Maternity in Seventeenth-Century England," pp. 3–38; Hilary Marland, ed., *The Art of Midwifery: Early Modern Midwives in Europe,* Routledge, London and New York, 1993; King, *Women of the Renaissance,* pp. 2–7; Retha Warnicke, *Women of the English Renaissance and Reformation* Greenwood, Westport, Conn., 1983, pp. 9–10; Audrey Eccles, *Obstretrics and Gynaecology in Tudor and Stuart England* Kent State University Press, Kent, Ohio, 1982; and Jean-Louis Flandrin, *Families in Former Times: Kinship, Household, and Sexuality in Early Modern France,* trans. Richard Southern, Cambridge University Press, Cambridge and New York, 1979, p. 53.

13. Alberti's work has been translated as *The Family in Renaissance Florence,* trans. Renee Neu Watkins, University of South Carolina Press, Columbia, 1969. There is an abridged translation of le menagier de Paris, in *A Medieval Home Companion: Housekeeping in the Fourteenth Century,* trans. and ed. Tania Bayard, Harper-Collins, New York, 1991. See also Carole Levin, "Advice on Women's Behavior in Three Tudor Homilies," *International Journal of Women's Studies* 6, no. 2 (1983), pp. 176–185.

14. For more information on this marriage, see Iris Origo, *The Merchant of Prato: Francesco di Marco Datini,* Jonathan Cape, London, 1957; and Frances and Joseph Gies, *Women in the Middle Ages,* Harper and Row, New York, 1978, pp. 184–209. All quotations from the letters are from Origo.

15. For more on this topic, see Chapter 5; see also Origo, *op. cit.,* pp. 99–101, 194–197; and Susan Mosher Stuard, "Ancillary Evidence for the Decline of Medieval Slavery," *Past and Present* 149 (November 1995), pp. 3–28.

16. Origo, *op. cit.,* p. 10.

17. F. O. Shyllon, *Black Slaves in Britain,* Oxford University Press, London, 1974, p. 1; David Brion Davis, *The Problem of Slavery in Western Culture,* Cornell University Press, Ithaca, 1966, p. 8.

18. Norman MacDougall, *James IV,* John Donald Publishers Ltd., Edinburgh, 1989, p. 294; *The Historie and Chronicles of Scotland, Written and Collected by Robert Lindesay of Pitscottie,* ed. J. G. Mackay, William Blackwood and Sons, Edinburgh and London, 1896, vol 1, pp. 241–244; *Accounts of the Lord High Treasurer of Scotland,* ed. Sir James Balfour Paul, H. M. Register House, Edinburgh, 1901, vol. 3, pp. 506–507, xlix, 258. Paul finds it "well-nigh incredible" that James, "the very pattern of a Paladin [originally one of twelve knightly champions in attendance on Charlemagne; eventually the term came to mean any noble champion] of chivalry," would "set up an absolute negress at a tournament" as an object of beauty (pp. xlviii, xlix). For more on ideas about race and gender in this period, see also Kim Hall, *Things of Darkness; Economies of Race and Gender in Early Modern England,* Cornell University Press, Ithaca, 1995.

19. Tom Scott, *Dunbar: A Critical Exposition,* Barnes and Noble, New York, 1973, p. 68. Scott has rendered Dunbar's poem into modern English, pp. 67–68; it is

available in the original in *The Poems of William Dunbar,* ed. James Kinsley, Clarendon Press, Oxford, 1979, p. 106. Even more horrifying was the belief held by some men during the sixteenth century that intercourse with a black woman was a cure for syphilis. We have no evidence, however, that James IV was aware of this supposed remedy or had any need for it. For a discussion of such medical beliefs, see Winfried Schleiner, *Medical Ethics in the Renaissance,* Georgetown University Press, Washington, D.C., 1995, pp. 189–190.

20. For more on More and humanist education, see Warnicke, *op. cit.,* pp. 16–30; and Maria Dowling, *Humanism in the Age of Henry VIII,* Croom Helm, London, 1986, pp. 219–222.

21. For more on Margaret More Roper, see E. E. Reynolds, *Margaret Roper: Eldest Daughter of St. Thomas More,* Burns and Oates, London, 1960; and Rita M. Verbrugge, "Margaret More Roper's Personal Expression in the *Devout Treatise Upon the Pater Noster,*" in *Silent But for the World: Tudor Women as Patrons, Translators, and Writers of Religious Works,* ed. Margaret Patterson Hannay, Kent State University Press, Kent, Ohio, 1985, pp. 30–42.

22. Thomas Stapleton, *The Life and Illustrious Martyrdom of Sir Thomas More,* ed. E. E. Reynolds, trans. Philip E. Hallett, Fordham University Press, New York, 1966, pp. 91–93; Clark Hulse, "Dead Man's Treasure: The Cult of Thomas More," in *The Production of English Renaissance Culture,* ed. David Lee Miller, Sharon O'Dair, and Harold Weber, Cornell University Press, Ithaca, 1994, pp. 190–225.

23. For further reading on Lady Jane Grey, see Hester W. Chapman, *Lady Jane Grey,* Jonathan Cape, London, 1962; David Mathew, *Lady Jane Grey: The Setting of the Reign,* Eyre Mcthuen, London, 1972; Alison Plowden, *Lady Jane Grey and the House of Suffolk,* F. Watts, New York, 1986; Mary Luke, *The Nine Days Queen: A Portrait of Lady Jane Grey,* W. Morrow, New York, 1986; and Carole Levin, "Lady Jane Grey: Protestant Queen and Martyr," *Silent But for the World,* ed. Hannay, pp. 92–106. Two recent excellent biographies of Elizabeth I are Anne Somerset, *Elizabeth I,* Knopf, New York, 1991; and Wallace T. MacCaffrey, *Elizabeth I,* E. Arnold, New York, 1993. For more specialized studies about how Elizabeth I presented herself, see Susan Frye, *Elizabeth I: The Competition for Representation,* Oxford University Press, New York, 1993; and Carole Levin, *The Heart and Stomach of a King: Elizabeth I and the Politics of Sex and Power,* University of Pennsylvania Press, Philadelphia, 1994.

24. Roger Ascham, *The Schoolmaster,* ed. Lawrence V. Ryan, Cornell University Press, Ithaca, 1976, pp. 35–36.

25. *The Accession, Coronation, and Marriage of Mary Tudor as Related in Four Manuscripts of the Escorial,* trans. and pub. by C. V. Malfatti, Barcelona, 1956, p. 72.

26. Letter to Johann Sturm, April 4, 1550, in *Letters of Roger Ascham,* trans. Maurice Hatch and Alvin Vos, ed. Alvin Vos, Peter Lang, New York, 1989, p. 165.

27. In England witches were hung. For more on witchcraft, see the appropriate notes in Chapter 7.

28. Again, the numbers of males accused versus females varies widely among region and time periods. These are overall averages.

29. King, *Women of the Renaissance,* pp. 154, 155. The full documents of the Orsini case are in Marcello Craveri, *Sante e streghe: biografe e documenti dal XIV al XVII secolo,* Feltrinelli, Milan, 1980, pp. 168–193.

SUGGESTIONS FOR FURTHER READING

The place to begin with further study of this topic is Margaret King, *Women of the Renaissance* (Chicago: University of Chicago Press, 1991). Other significant studies not mentioned in the notes include Pamela Joseph Benson, *The Invention of the Renaissance Woman: The Challenge of Female Independence in the Literature and Thought of Italy and England* (University Park: Pennsylvania State University Press, 1992); Constance Jordan, *Renaissance Feminism: Literary Texts and Political Models* (Ithaca: Cornell University Press, 1990); Ian Maclean, *The Renaissance Notion of Woman: A Study in the Fortunes of Scholasticism and Medical Science in European Intellectual Life* (Cambridge, New York: Cambridge University Press, 1980); and Merry Wiesner, *Women and Gender in Early Modern Europe* (Cambridge: Cambridge University Press, 1993). Hannelore Saches, *The Renaissance Woman* (New York: McGraw-Hill, 1971) has many fine examples of artistic renderings of women in the period. Three collections with a number of useful essays are Natalie Zemon Davis and Arlette Farge, ed., *A History of Women: Renaissance and Enlightenment Paradoxes* (Vol. 3 of *A History of Women in the West,* general editors Georges Duby and Michelle Perot) (Cambridge: Belknap Press of Harvard University Press, 1993); Carole Levin and Jeanie Watson, ed., *Ambiguous Realities: Women in the Middle Ages and Renaissance* (Detroit: Wayne State University Press, 1986); and Mary Beth Rose, ed., *Women in the Middle Ages and Renaissance: Literary and Historical Perspectives* (Syracuse: Syracuse University Press, 1986).

Lucas Cranach d. A., *Women Attacking Clergy* (detail), after 1537.
STAATLICHE MUSEEN ZU BERLIN KD2 (4798).

7

The Reformation of Women

Susan C. Karant-Nunn

In late medieval urban and folk religion, women played quite a prominent part as nuns and beguines, members of many confraternities, endowers of altars and other foundations, and healers who tapped divine power. When the Reformation began, the responses of women, like those of men, ranged from aggressive support to active defense of Catholicism. Wherever the Reformation triumphed, most convents and brothels were shut as Lutheran, Zwinglian, Anglican, and Calvinist authorities struggled to make earthly society conform to their interpretation of God's will as shown in Scripture. Pastors' wives and households held out to Protestant society the new model of the pious family in the parsonage. Women's range of religious and social choices may have declined as marriage, housekeeping, and motherhood were held out as women's only legitimate concerns. In their numerous other roles, women were invisible to those who conceptualized how society functioned.

Likewise, in those areas that remained Catholic, governors of state and church displayed the disciplinary fervor of the day as they set out to reform the populace. They retained female images in the churches but forced into convents those women who tried to imitate the Jesuits and to offer education and social relief to the needy. The Counter-Reformation gave new life to the two proverbial alternatives for women: marriage or the (enclosed) convent. Like Protestantism, it used education as a means of conveying to girls its conviction that women should be subordinate and obedient to men.

The witch trials of the late sixteenth and the seventeenth centuries were another manifestation of rulers', judges', and theologians' determination to root out evil. Whether educated or illiterate, Catholic or Protestant, male or female, Europeans generally shared a fear that women were closer to nature and more vulnerable than men to the wiles of the Devil. The belief that women had a special inclination toward witchcraft was a continuation of medieval misogyny; but this attitude, in combination with the new spirit of determined social disciplining, produced executions on an unprecedented scale.

Although the religious upheavals of the sixteenth century are still usually called "the Reformation," our view of them is very different than it was just twenty years ago. This newer view has several facets and contains implications for understanding women's roles during this tumultuous period.

First of all, we used to think of the Reformation as marking a break between the Middle Ages and the rise of modernity. To this very day, European universities separate medieval from modern history at 1500, chiefly with reference to the Reformations as a cluster of watershed events. A growing number of scholars, however, have shown that both Protestant and Catholic Reformations owed much to that which preceded them, both in theology and social outlook, even though Protestant theologians especially thought that they were returning to the "pristine" Christianity of the early Church. In their attitudes toward women, the men of every evolving denomination showed strong continuity with the late Middle Ages.

A second scholarly insight is that Protestant and Catholic reform movements bear an uncanny resemblance to each other. For centuries Protestants regarded the Catholic church as the very antithesis of reforming ideals, indeed as the fount of abuses that precipitated Martin Luther's revolt. Actually, the Protestant Reformation arose out of well-established, active reforming ideals within Catholicism itself. Unfortunately, perhaps, those ideals lacked the vigorous sponsorship of the papacy until after irreparable divisions had occurred. Now we perceive that, in their goals and methodology, Catholicism and emerging Protestantism were not so far apart. These similarities help to explain why it is possible to come to conclusions about women that have validity for both Protestantism and Catholicism.

Third, modern German historians have put forward the notions of confessionalization and social disciplining. These give us a framework for understanding many men's harsh attitude toward women in these two centuries, and I shall return to them later in this essay. *Confessionalization* refers to the unprecedently close cooperation of church and state in making people identify themselves with a particular religious belief, such as Lutheranism, Calvinism, or Catholicism. During the Middle Ages, when nearly everyone was Catholic, confessionalization was not necessary. Social disciplining pertains to the strict oversight and ready punishment that church and state used in achieving this new identity, and also in attempting to make all their subjects live moral, self-restrained lives as part of the creation of a truly godly society. There is no simple explanation as to why sixteenth-century men in positions of authority were more intent on discipline than their forebears had been. Some historians regard this trend as an accompaniment of spreading capitalism in which narrow regulation aided in economic consolidation and efficiency, but others do not. These two concepts appear, despite qualitative differences from place to place, to be as applicable to Scotland and Italy as to

Brandenburg and Zurich—and thus to both Catholicism and Protestantism. Despite their working together to create what they saw as a godly society, church and state continued to have substantially different interests.

Finally, scholars debate today whether we should go on identifying and evaluating the deeds of women of the past in isolation from those of men. Theirs is fundamentally a discussion about the nature of *gender* studies as opposed to *women's* studies, and it is bound to continue. Among early modernists, Merry Wiesner-Hanks has cogently argued that we must not abandon the effort to add to our still scanty knowledge about the lives of women.[1] By contrast, Lyndal Roper has written, "Even when women's lines of communication seem to run from woman to woman, their male-female context was important."[2] I will take the position in this essay that *both* these approaches are necessary and possible: continuing to excavate the experiences of women *and* acknowledging the inseparability of treatments of women and men. Our endeavor reminds me of the figure-ground optical illusion, often reprinted in introductory psychology textbooks, in which what is the figure and what is the background constantly shifts: looking at it one way, we see the silhouettes of two identical faces, their noses almost touching; from another perspective, we see an urn.[3] No doubt, I must regard the urn as the feminine symbol in this analogy, for sixteenth- and seventeenth-century thinkers and preachers incessantly referred to women, following I Peter 2: 7, as the weaker *vessel.* Each object informs the other. In reality, however, whether of the past or of the present, the lines between ways of seeing are never simple and clean. Women and men had separate and complementary spheres in popular as well as learned stereotypes, but the extent to which they did in real life remains a topic of discussion.

WOMEN AND RELIGION: THE LATE MEDIEVAL SETTING

Every age affords stark contrasts, and the late Middle Ages was no exception. First in cosmopolitan and urbanized Italy, and later elsewhere, the men in power espoused the man-centered, literate culture of first ancient Rome and then classical Greece, finding that it added an appealing dimension to their worldly involvement and personal pride. Yet they were, by the standards of this humanistic cultural milieu, nonetheless men of the spirit, many affiliated with the Catholic church. At the same time, in much of Europe, the evidence of deep piety abounds. People defined their calendars and much of their social and spiritual existence in relation to the parish. Where permitted, women as well as men joined confraternities devoted to one or more patron saints. To the extent allowed, women as well as men took part in the processions of high feast days, such as Corpus Christi. To the limit of their means, women as well as men endowed altars in the larger churches, at which priests were paid to sing masses for the repose of donors' souls. They commissioned pious paintings, statues, and other ecclesiastical decorations. Women as well as men went on pilgrimages to the most distant shrines that they could afford, though probably comparatively few traveled as far as Margery Kempe—all the way to Jerusalem. There were hundreds of local and thus more accessible shrines to which even serving maids could go and return in a day or two.

Where enrollment in convents was declining by the fifteenth century, as in England, we should bear in mind that these establishments were not open to women of just any rank. Both high entry fees, a type of dowry, and social attitudes effectively reserved the greatest of these for noblewomen and rich patricians, with lesser houses receiving the highest-ranking novices that they could command. The urban women of lesser station found avenues of devotion in the small communities of laywomen called *beguines,* living together in normal houses and earning their collective living by such means as taking in washing, nursing the sick, preparing the dead for burial, and making candles. Houses of beguines could be found across northern Europe up until the Reformation. The city of Cologne by itself had at one time over one hundred fifty, and their inmates made up an estimated 7.5 percent of the entire population.[4] These women had a reputation for "enthusiastic" (emotional, sometimes mystical) worship. Religious authorities have always looked askance at mystical expression, for it calls attention to its practitioners and allows them to circumvent the institutional church: they communicate directly with God. Additionally, the beguines were suspect because they were women living and working independently in a society that thought members of their sex should be under the supervision of their fathers, husbands, closest male relatives, or appointed guardians. For both these reasons, most houses of beguines, before the fifteenth century, had come under the supervision of the nearest order of mendicant friars, usually of Franciscans or Dominicans. According to church law, however, they remained laywomen who took no permanently binding vows; technically they were not nuns.

The majority of Christian women had neither the means nor the inclination to leave the world for the cloister. Their piety, which was probably neither more nor less intense than that of the men around them, took mundane and domesticated forms. They prayed at the ringing of certain church bells, envisioned heaven as filled with an array of saints having intercessory powers, fulfilled their annual duty to confess to their priest and receive the sacrament of the Eucharist, and believed in the miracle of transubstantiation.[5] During pregnancy they particularly sought the protective help of the Host, the body of Christ. Supernatural forces surrounded them and could be tapped by means of a wide variety of folk rituals, including incantations that invoked the Trinity, the application of herbs, and the performance of such acts as circling the altar at the new mother's ceremonial return to church after childbirth, or circling the church before burying a corpse. The sacred and the secular interpenetrated.

Women were active in heretical movements such as Lollardy in England. This and other late medieval nonconformist strains bore a theological resemblance to the Reformation that was yet to come.

In the realm of folk religion, women played a prominent part, serving as cunning women and herbalists whose help many people sought in their life crises. In the Iberian Peninsula, *beatas* or holy women devoted their lives to religion but usually lived singly with a maidservant, or with their blood relatives, in the world. Their sanctity attracted their neighbors much in the way that anchoresses and anchorites had; it showed that these devout souls had a special relation to the deity that they could turn to the benefit of others who sought their counsel.[6] In northern Europe, local prophetesses (as well as prophets) occupied a position similar to that of the holy women of the south. In either case, women as well as men not only had access to the divine but were able to use that access in the service of those around them. These informal arrangements obviously did not have the sanction of the Catholic church, within which only ordained male priests could mediate between mortals and God. Nevertheless, the Church rarely took action against individuals with local reputations for sanctity. In practice, many rural priests were willing to share sacred power with others. They often had much in common with the simple people whom they served.

THE EARLY REFORMATION

Urban anticlericalism, that is, fear and dislike of the clergy, was one of the factors that triggered religious revolt. This anticlerical sentiment targeted several aspects of the life of the clergy, including their exemptions from taxes, from many civic duties, and from legal jurisdictions.[7] But one of the reproaches directed at priests (including friars, who were ordinarily ordained and entitled to practice certain aspects of the cure of souls, such as hearing confessions) had to do with women. Catholic clergy were alleged to seduce men's wives and daughters, chiefly through their abuse of confession. Here, it was said, they questioned vulnerable women too closely about their sexual fantasies and practices and corrupted previously innocent people. We today do not see women as passive or opinionless; surely many female victims themselves, and not just their male relatives, objected to these practices even though men were the complaining spokesmen. The women who actually became the mistresses of clergymen were usually of a humble socioeconomic class, indicating society's low regard for their way of life. We may assume that many of the wives and daughters in question reported the clerical attempts at seduction and other abuses when they got home. In 1526, the artist Lucas Cranach the Elder depicted women physically attacking Catholic clerics, including a bishop who lies on the ground in mitred terror as his assailant strikes him with a flail.[8] This is not meant to recount actual deeds but probably men's perception that women were better off with the new creed than they had been under Catholic dominion.

As Martin Luther's celebrity spread in the early sixteenth century, women as well as men found appeal in the call to return to the Scripture as the sole source of Christian truth. This attraction is first noticeable in German-speaking lands, including Switzerland, though intellectuals in France, England, and the Low Countries followed developments with keen interest. A few women participated in the rare but dramatic episodes of iconoclasm (the violent removal and sometimes the outright destruction of works of religious art), which expressed the pent-up popular anger over clerical hypocrisy and the blatant consumption of resources that should have gone—or so some of the rebels claimed—to support the poor. As Ulrich Zwingli, the reformer of Zurich, joined Luther and a growing number of others in calling for the restoration of biblical Christianity, they insisted that monasticism had no foundation in Holy Writ and was based on a belief in salvation through good works; they called for its abolition. Very soon in affected parts of Germany, and by 1540 in England, the closing of monasteries and convents forced many monks and nuns out of their familiar mode of existence and into a precarious world with which the women especially were not prepared to deal. They often lacked marketable skills. Former nuns' pensions were smaller than former monks', and their families often did not wish to take them back. For both genuine spiritual and pressing socioeconomic reasons, nuns often fiercely resisted secularization. Caritas Pirckheimer, a highly educated patrician nun in Nuremberg, stands out for her articulate refusal to leave her convent. She remained there until her death in 1532. Nuns occasionally had the choice of remaining enclosed as long as they lived, on the condition that they agreed to accept Protestant preachers, to lay aside their habits, and not to take in any more novices. Sometimes the men in control permitted the remaining nuns to support themselves by running schools for small children of both sexes or for girls, but on other occasions the men feared that such instruction might still be Catholic under the surface. Rarely, a convent was an official territory and its abbess a princeling of the Holy Roman Empire. Such institutions and their inhabitants could not be touched and remained as anomalies, at least until Napoleon brought the Holy Roman Empire to an end in the early nineteenth century. English and Scandinavian nuns had no such good fortune. But even when forced out of their convents, some former nuns did continue to live together.

Very likely as many women favored the Reformation as opposed it. Members of royal families, such as Marguerite d'Angouleme (also known as Marguerite Queen of Navarre, the sister of King Francis I of France), Renée of Ferrara (daughter of King Louis XII of France, wife of Duke Hercules d'Este of Ferrara), and Katherine Parr (sixth wife of King Henry VIII of England), evidently thought that their privileged station afforded them protection against prosecution for religious nonconformity. They were drawn, respectively, to Catholic reformism and early Calvinism, to more mature Calvinism, and to English Protestantism. To varying degrees they were able to use their positions to support evangelism. Nonetheless, Renée of Ferrara was investigated by the Inquisition, imprisoned at her husband's command, and forced to recant publicly in 1555. She returned to France after her husband's death and lived out her days as a private Calvinist. Catherine Parr was apparently converted to Protestantism by Thomas Cranmer, archbishop of Canterbury. Her activities came to the attention of her still-Catholic husband. Anne Askew, one of her friends, was burned at the stake for heresy. Katherine may have been fortunate to outlive her husband.

Women of high position everywhere, especially if they were widowed, were at greater liberty to follow their inclinations. Vittoria Colonna and Giulia Gonzaga are prominent Italian examples, the latter becoming the head of the underground Protestant circle in Naples after the death of its founder Juan Valdés in 1540. The most common pattern, however, seems to have been for women to convert to Protestantism along with their husbands and other family members. The part that each may have played within the family in fostering that conversion was, unfortunately, private and thus usually undocumented.

All educated women, whether of the princely court or of the city, had the advantage of being able to examine texts for themselves, although most literate women never learned to read Latin. Only the most daring, however, took a stand in writing that drew public attention to themselves. One such woman, Argula von Grumbach, was thoroughly familiar with the Bible. A Bavarian noblewoman and wife of a knight, in 1523 she wrote to the theologians of the University of Ingolstadt defending Luther's teachings and offering to debate with them in person. They had her letters printed in mocking repudiation of her. Violating the prevailing ideal of feminine decorum, she wrote to princes and the city council of Regensburg in defense of the Gospel, which she regarded as the means by which God opened people to His saving grace. Her husband, a devout Catholic, lost his position at the Bavarian court, and the pair retreated to the family estate. In her seventies, Argula was briefly imprisoned for presuming to preside over funerals.

Katharina Schütz Zell was another especially remarkable figure in the period of sometimes tumultuous transition from one faith to another. Married to a priest in Strasbourg in 1523, she took up the pen to defend herself and her husband against the harsh criticism of prominent churchmen and magistrates. She was unrestrained in her accusations, declaring that the Catholic church had a vested interest in maintaining celibacy (*celibacy* technically means refraining from marriage, though now it is often used—incorrectly—to mean refraining from all sexual contacts); it enriched itself with so-called concubinage and cradle fees, paid annually by the many priests who were celibate, to be sure, but who could not live chastely.[9] The Church unwittingly promoted sodomy, she said, the worst sin of all. Even more unusual than the fact that Frau Zell was outspokenly in favor of the Reformation was perhaps that in an era of harsh, *ad hominem* doctrinal disagreements, she fearlessly placed her ideal of Christian love above theology and got away with it. On these grounds she defended Anabaptists—who generally insisted on adult rather than infant baptism because only adult baptism is found in the Bible—including Melchior Hoffmann, one of their most prominent leaders. She befriended Kaspar Schwenkfeld, who went even further than Zwingli in rejecting Christ's presence in the Lord's Supper. She visited a former member of the city council who had contracted the stigmatizing disease of leprosy and been put outside the city wall. She even prepared an edition of the Psalms and a devotional tract based on the Lord's Prayer.

It would appear that when society is in the grip of destabilizing change, whether the French Revolution, the English Revolution, or early phases of the Reformation, some ordinary women depart from the norms that society in quieter times has defined for them. Thomas Müntzer, a leader of the destructive German Peasants' War in 1525, counted women among his followers, and a few even took the liberty of preaching. Women were enthusiastic adherents of Anabaptism in Switzerland, Germany, the Low Countries, Austria, and parts of Europe farther to the east, for Anabaptists often conceded the direct communication of the Holy Spirit with individuals, including women. Every established church, whether Catholic, Lutheran, Calvinist, or Anglican, found Anabaptism abhorrent and persecuted its members. Women were among the martyrs of the faith and sometimes suffered drowning, a method of execution often reserved for women, rather than burning or beheading.

The evidence is growing, however, that Anabaptist men shared the predominant view that women's proper place was in the household raising children and providing for the needs of the family. We have to be cautious in forming conclusions based on the visibility of a small number of women. Although women's temperaments and interaction with family members and neighbors varied as much as men's did, meaning that many women were in practice powerful within their spheres, few became celebrities. And those who did, such as Luther's wife Katharina von Bora (who never tried to gain attention) or Katharina Schütz Zell, maintained that they were simply obedient housewives.

OFFICIAL PROTESTANT ATTITUDES TOWARD WOMEN

Occasionally Italian men traveling in the north remarked with amazement on the freedom of women to be out in the streets, to trade in their own right, and to converse openly with men to whom they were not related. Women of gentility along the Mediterranean were more reserved and cautious about appearing in public. As noted above, wherever Protestantism took hold, monasticism for both men and women came under attack; and the dissolution of convents thrust even more women from the constricted life of the cloister into the world. From one perspective, we may see this as consistent with the existing cultural norm in northern Europe that tolerated women's active visibility.

The reformers were of the opinion that in doing away with clerical celibacy they improved women's lot. In their many treatises against monasticism, they stressed not only that a life of withdrawal could decidedly not earn salvation but also that refraining from marriage went against nature. They argued that God had implanted sexual desire in every person so that the human race would not die out. For that reason, they said, people who did not marry often fell into illicit sex; they could not help themselves. Marriage for everyone was the solution to this problem, for it provided an acceptable outlet for sex and the means of producing the next generation of Christians. Catholics had long regarded women as having a sex drive that was greater than men's, and they often blamed women for seducing men. But Luther noticeably broke with this tradition by insisting that *both* men and women needed to marry in order to provide an antidote for their mutual lust—as well as to provide help and companionship for one another and a structure within which to raise children.

In keeping with this opinion, rulers closed urban brothels at the same time that they were shutting down convents. They might incline toward Saint Augustine in theological matters, but they could not go along with his view that bordellos protected honorable wives and daughters. In the sixteenth century, people were supposed to discipline their bodies, not least by marrying. Ironically, the Reformation changed the lives of both nuns and prostitutes, the sacred and the profane. Despite every effort, of course, unlicensed prostitution continued unabated.

In one sense, then, the Reformation sought to elevate marriage. It elaborated the wedding ceremony and moved it into the churches and before the altars. But at the same time the reformers insisted that marriage was not a sacrament as the Catholic church maintained. It was now merely a civil transaction. Thus, except in England, where it remained illegal, divorce for compelling reasons—adultery, long-term abandonment, or male impotence—was theoretically possible. Yet studies have shown that under Protestantant regimes divorce was nearly as hard to obtain as under Catholic ones, and women were expected to endure even physical abuse "with the patience of Saint Monica."[10] Protestant theology aside, we might conclude that the new faiths made marriage even more sacred than the Catholic church had.

As part of the reformed wedding ceremonies, both Lutheran and Calvinist pastors—the former in wedding sermons, the latter more often by means of pointed quotations from the Bible—conveyed to brides and grooms the ideals to which that they were to aspire. The language of the thousands of homilies (brief sermons) that remain from the sixteenth and seventeenth centuries tells us a great deal about their authors. Wedding sermons reveal that even married Protestant clergymen still regarded women as dangerous because they were, the preachers alleged, particularly susceptible to Satan's wiles. They were prone to a wide range of misdeeds and sinful qualities through their inheritance, as "daughters of Eve," of Eve's "desire to be like God." Whereas the Catholic church had juxtaposed the Virgin Mary to Eve, offering in the person of Christ's mother a model of what women were capable of, Protestant divines no longer promoted Mary, and they removed most of her images, and those of other holy women, from the sanctuaries. In her place, they verbally offered certain Old Testament, apocryphal, and even several classical figures whom the brides and other women among the listeners were to imitate. Sarah, Rebecca, Susannah (but not Judith, who had slain a man!), Esther, Anna the mother of Samuel, and Nausicaa the mother of Coriolanus, to name but a few. The preachers described these as faithful, loyal, obedient, submissive, domesticated, diligent in their housework, silent, and humble. These themes were strikingly constant for several generations. They emphasized that husbands simply had to keep their wives in tow, like horses in harness. Harness images could be found beyond the Protestant world. Paolo Veronese, the Italian artist, painted a scene called "Virtue Restraining Vice" in which a woman ("Vice") wears a bit in her mouth and a man ("Virtue") holds the reins in his left hand and a riding crop in his right, the latter raised as though to strike.

At the same time, the preachers continued, husbands had to provide for their wives' reasonable material needs and to *love* their wives, as Saint Peter had prescribed, remembering always that the feminine capacity for virtue and understanding was smaller than the masculine. Pastors used solar metaphors to describe husbands and lunar ones for wives, noting emphatically that the moon's light was merely the reflected brilliance of the sun.[11] Wives must give up their own wills and assume those of their husbands, subordinating themselves in all matters, including the running of the home. Preachers saw women's loss of independence as a consequence of Eve's disobedience in the Garden of Eden. As pastors and teachers more aggressively defined female roles, they also inevitably defined male ones. For instance, men had to earn a living so that their wives did not have to go out of the house to work, for if women earned money, they thought they had the right to tell men how the family income should be spent.

These messages show us a side of the Protestant pastorate that continued the misogynist attitudes of many late medieval clergy—who were, after all, in their own time attempting to muster devotion to celibate chastity among their peers. But now preachers underscored these themes even as they performed the nuptial rites. Sentiments originally designed to reinforce celibacy were now used to structure marriage, a curious twist. In some sense, the household became the Protestant cloister. The promotion of marriage thinly concealed the belief that women must be kept under control and that the wedded estate was the most effective means of achieving this goal.

The secular counterpart of the lessons from the pulpit in proper marital deportment was the newly founded marriage court. These courts took the place of the late medieval bishops' consistories, which had reserved to themselves as many cases involving faith and morals as they could in their ever more intense jockeying with the expansive state. The Catholic church had regarded private and unwitnessed vows of intent to marry as sufficient to make a binding union. The new committees appointed by city councils and territorial princes forbade clandestine oaths (as princes had begun to do, but usually in vain, beginning in the fourteenth century). Well-off parents may have welcomed the greater control the new regulations gave them over the marriage choices of their children. Beyond this, however, authorities inserted themselves more rigorously and insistently in domestic disputes, viewing the peaceful Christian household as the building block out of which an orderly society was to be constructed. They often brought to an end, for example, the age-old informal practice of incompatible husbands and wives simply living apart. The new policies gave abused women little recourse; even preachers were divided on whether husbands did not occasionally have good reason to beat their wives, with many clergymen insisting that they did. Thus official concern about the threat that women posed to social order also showed itself in the application of existing laws during the sixteenth century.[12] More women were tried and punished for committing infanticide (usually against their own babies). Authorities were more determined than ever before to enforce those principles that earlier ones had often only paid lip service to. We should note, however, that this determination was directed at men as well as women, though with differing consequences. If we disregard the witch craze for the moment, a number of penalties were sex-specific, or more likely to be so. Men were imprisoned and for longer periods than women, and women could be dunked in a pond on a dunking stool or made to wear great stones, painted or carved with the figures of quarreling women, around the marketplace. Men, who more often controlled money, paid fines, whereas women, who frequently had no money of their own, were whipped. Research on the effects upon women of legal changes in the early modern period is still inadequate.

Throughout Protestant Europe, the pastor's wife offered the public a countervailing image. In the Lutheran world, Luther's expressions of domestic bliss with Katharina von Bora filled his correspondence and set a positive tone. Calvin, by contrast, hardly mentioned his wife, Idelette de Bure. After her death, he briefly expressed his sense of loss and remarked that one of her great virtues had lain in never hindering his work. Even though the mistress of the parsonage bore the burden of having to provide the congregation with a paragon of feminine decorum, she might also become a person of prominence within the community. Although some people would have preferred that their pastors were celibate, ultimately Protestants everywhere came to accept the local parsonage with its growing nuclear family plus servants. These wives now came from a social rank that corresponded to the clergymen's own. Even if posted in the countryside, increasingly pastors and their spouses came from cities, and both believed in the schooling of boys *and* girls. These matrons of the parsonages were likely to be literate and to promote literacy in their daughters. Sometimes they even taught the local girls themselves. The curriculum for girls, however, was shorter and more limited, being made up of the shorter catechism (a book which described Christian principles in simple terms), Bible verses, prayers, and hymns; and its purpose was to enable little girls to grow into women who epitomized the Christian virtues that females were supposed to possess. It also conveyed the ideas to them that they in turn, when they became mothers, were to teach to their little children. With these ends in mind, Protestantism specifically advocated elementary education for all girls. Yet women, including pastors' wives, should not have unsupervised access to the whole Bible, for they might interpret it wrongly. By contrast, boys' grammar school curricula bore all the earmarks of intending to prepare future men of affairs.

Pastors' wives were often drawn into informal, and in a few northern cities formal, social relief. They became instruments of the expression of pastoral concern for the well-being of the congregation. Their roles developed spontaneously and were not the result of any denomination's defining public functions for them. Nevertheless, many actively pursued the welfare of their neighbors and even enjoyed a certain authority in their parishes. In villages, pastors' wives occasionally detected improper (negligent or "superstitious") behavior in the local midwives and reported them. Within Calvinist congregations, midwives could no longer administer emergency baptism, and in Lutheran communities, pastors, possibly with the help of their wives, carried out a much closer oversight of midwives and their use of this baptism than before.

Sadly, too many clerical wives were left without means when widowed, until, belatedly, the churches of some German territories began to make modest provision for them. The medieval attitude that widows should forgo material pleasures and devote themselves to a life of prayer continued in the sixteenth and seventeenth centuries.

WOMEN AND CATHOLIC REFORM

Catholic women's lives did not undergo disruption in those regions that remained under the spiritual governance of the Roman church. Monastic institutions and informal convention gave women of every economic class opportunities to foster their personal devotion to the degree that they chose. Images of the Virgin and other female saints, as of male saints, dotted the ecclesiastical landscape and private homes as well, symbolically informing worshippers of women's high station before the throne of the Most High. Femininity was associated with emotional tendencies, with their mingled positive and negative connotations, but in the religious setting, the presence of these figures signaled to the devout of both sexes that affective piety was acceptable to God. It was not the only model of piety available. Perhaps the best summation of pre-Reformation Catholicism is that it offered its adherents, in all their diversity, a wide array of intellectual and pious options, provided only that no one carried any minority option to an attention-getting extreme. The Holy Office of the Inquisition would eventually have labeled such behavior heresy. The lap of Holy Mother Church was commodious indeed. Within her lap, and within a culture that unquestionably valued the female less highly than the male, many women were still able to find satisfying modes of expression.

There is, then, no firm line between pre-Reformation Catholicism and that which is commonly labeled Counter-Reformation Catholicism. There were reform-minded Catholics before the onset of the Protestant Reformation just as there were after, though it is only fair to observe that the falling away from the unity of the Church of great chunks of northern Europe can hardly have failed to challenge Rome to take counteractive measures. Some of these responded to age-old complaints of abuse; and some of them, like the aggressive use of catechisms, preaching, and grammar schools, took methodological inspiration from Lutheranism and Calvinism themselves. But it would be misleading to label as Catholic reform the efforts of Archbishop Francisco Ximénez de Cisneros to regulate the Iberian church simply because Cisneros died in 1517, before the Reformation began, and the observant ardor of Teresa of Avila as Counter-Reformation simply because her career peaked later in the sixteenth century (she died in 1582). In fact, Teresa did worry about the salvation of the "Lutherans," by which she meant the French Huguenots, but this was not the focus of her life work.

What we see in the Catholic lands of the sixteenth century is very similar to what we observe in the Protestant sphere, though more gradual: a growing concern for moral rectitude and for mundane rationalization and orderliness. On both sides—or perhaps *every* side would be more accurate—of the denominational line(s) being established, church and state cooperated more fully than ever before out of their common desire to render human beings truly godly. This cooperation was less thoroughgoing in Catholic areas, where the secular arm never did succeed in taking over the supervision of spiritual matters or the Church itself, a rival corporation. In general, all rulers were convinced that if they did not reform society, God would vent his wrath on collective humanity. Comets, wars, disease, and even abnormal births were evidence of divine anger, which could only be assuaged by the most concerted measures to detect and punish sin. This general tendency had serious ramifications for Catholic women, just as it did for Protestant ones.

The Council of Trent, which met in three clusters of sessions between 1545 and 1563, laid down the essential rules for Catholics to follow. One of the council's fundamental principles was uniformity—of doctrine, ritual, and procedure. The combination of the Church's residual negative assessment of women and its determination to impose uniformity on all led to the narrowing of religious scope for women. Yet the process of introducing the decrees of the Council of Trent was gradual and varied from place to place.

Many new religious orders trace their origins to the idealism and heightened spirituality of the early sixteenth century. The Italian wars left misery in their wake, and many individuals responded to the disaster by renewing their interior commitment and by seeking a means of helping the wretched. It is hardly surprising that, in the age of the formation of new religious orders for men such as the Oratory of Divine Love (a society for elite laymen and clergy), the Barnabites, the Theatines, and the Jesuits, women, too, should have felt called to a religious life that manifested their desire to serve their unfortunate neighbors. Angela Merici, an Italian noblewoman (1470/75–1540), first became a Franciscan tertiary but in 1535 founded the Company of Saint Ursula.[13] Two years later the eighty-one Ursulines elected her their mother general. These Ursulines were remarkable in that, although they took on a religious vocation, they remained in the world, living with their families or in other people's homes as servants. They held regular meetings and dedicated themselves to the ideals of obedience to all those in authority, from their parents through the bishop to God, as well as to the ideals of virginity and of poverty. Their charitable functions consisted of working in hospitals, teaching Christian doctrine to girls, and "bringing souls to God." Their members spread into France as teachers of the Catholic catechism to young children. The clerical hierarchy was most uneasy about these women's freedom to come and go and to govern themselves. Very early it placed them under the rule of men. As the Society of Jesus (Jesuits) became more prominent in the second half of the century, increasing numbers of women, including the Ursulines themselves, imitated their organization and way of life and did not question their right to do so, even though the Jesuits themselves had explicitly rejected the development of a female branch of their order. Finally, in 1618, Pope Paul V imposed enclosure upon the Ursulines, which effectively ended their secular ministry.

A similar resistance and ultimate claustration (enclosure in convents) met the followers of other women, such as Jeanne de Lestonnac (1556–1640), who founded the Compagnie des Filles de Marie Notre Dame; and Mary Ward (1585–1645), who founded the Institute of the Blessed Virgin Mary. Before her imprisonment by the Inquisition in Munich, Ward had founded schools for girls in France, Germany, Austria, and even Rome itself—without permission from the Holy See. Ward even envisioned higher education for members of her "order," but in the short term she was not to see her dream fulfilled.

Women, such as Saint Teresa of Avila, who believed that religious women should indeed be "dead to the world," met with approval during the period of the Counter-Reformation, for their perspective coincided with that of the men who governed them. Although Teresa's early outspoken efforts to reform the Carmelites met fierce resistance from some Spanish prelates, just as they did among many of the nuns whom she was attempting to reform, she did finally succeed in founding the Discalced Carmelites, which had a male branch.[14] The women adhered to the expectation of their day that they withdraw into their convents and unremittingly pursue a life of prayer. Teresa herself turned out to be one of the paramount mystics of western Christianity, compelled to describe her spiritual experiences in writing. She would never have thought of herself as downtrodden or discriminated against, yet she was careful to repeat rather often, as a form of self-abnegation, that she was nothing but a woman.

Although it tapped its considerable power to keep women in what it regarded as their proper place—out of the public eye and subordinated to men—the Catholic church left a number of facets of its former practice intact, in case, as we suspect, these had special appeal for women. The cults of the female saints, and especially of the Virgin Mary, remained, providing feminine models and feminine sources of strength in life's crises. Affective piety continued to be respectable for women and for men; only within this context can we understand Giovanni Bernini's statue of Saint Teresa in ecstasy.

Further, although they were much more closely overseen than before, convents remained as alternatives for women of sufficient means who did not wish to marry. These continued to have at least the midlevel governance of women, and in the privacy of their sanctuaries women's voices still intoned the divine service. Where nuns were allowed any ongoing social function, this usually consisted of helping male clergy to teach the catechism to young children, especially to little girls.

Another feature of Catholicism after the Council of Trent was the spread of religious confraternities and sodalities. Building upon the popularity of these organizations in the late Middle Ages, Jesuits set out to confirm the Catholic identity of people of every rank by seeing them enrolled in societies devoted to the Virgin. Initially women could frequently belong—this varied from place to place—but the growing disciplinary emphasis of church and state soon produced the segregation of women into their own societies or their banning altogether. Wives were seen to be subsumed under their husbands, and their husbands' participation was thus sufficient. There continued to be exceptions, as in Fribourg, a town of only about 5,000 residents, where 900 of 2,000 sodality members were women.[15] In the seventeenth century, a more diverse array of confraternities sprang up under the leadership of the clergy. In France, women of every station could join, for example, the Society of the Good Death (*de la Bonne Mort*), in which they learned to prepare for a Christian death, and ultimately to die in the pious manner that best ensured the salvation of their souls. Although women were instructed to stay in the home and cultivate, along with children, those feminine virtues that all of European society thought fitting, some went on the pilgrimages that continued to be an earmark of Catholic piety.

Within Catholicism, too, a basic education for girls was thought desirable. The curriculum was of the same simplicity as in Protestant territories, and, similarly, its purpose was to foster spirituality, Catholic identity, and submission to those in authority. As the future would show, however, literacy, once gained, may open up the vast domain of unapproved thought. Just as in Protestant England, where an act of Parliament in 1543 barring women (except gentlewomen) from reading the English Bible cannot have been entirely effective, so in the Catholic world no amount of censorship, no Index of Prohibited Books, could prevent the circulation of ideas.

The late-sixteenth- and early-seventeenth-century "ardor for order" affected women in local as well as international ways. The Counter-Reformation popes Pius V (reigned 1566–1572) and Sixtus V (reigned 1585–1590) were determined to curtail the sinful activities of the thousands of Roman courtesans.

These were elegant prostitutes who made their living from the custom of men close to, if not actually within, the papal curia. Pius V forced many of these elite women of pleasure to leave the city. But the demand for their services remained, and punishing only the women could not suppress the flesh trade.[16] As already mentioned, every age presents stark contrasts. Catholic cities in general, like their Protestant rivals, took a less permissive attitude toward sexual transgressions than their ancestors had, but their enforcement of the stricter regulations was episodic.

THE WITCH CRAZE

It might at first appear as if the early modern witch hunts across both Catholic and Protestant Europe in the sixteenth and seventeenth centuries were unrelated to the religious reformations of the time. And indeed religious reform and the hunting of witches were not synonymous. Yet they did have substantial common motivations, and these lay in the dominant worldviews of the day. Renaissance humanism and the religious Reformation were both intensely idealistic movements, both dominated by learned men. The opinions concerning humanity held by these two movements were not the same, to be sure, for the former was optimistic about the power of proper (classical and also religious) education to produce the upright person, particularly the upright man, and the latter was pessimistic concerning people's vulnerability to Satan without the constant preaching of the biblical Word aided by the ever watchful, sword-wielding government. Humanistically educated men felt called to positions of power from which they could ensure that the masses who lacked the fortifying benefits of "good letters" would be held, for the common good, within proper bounds. Those enflamed by the missionizing spirit of religious renewal knew that God's wrath could only be diverted by the application of discipline to the many who, to judge by their sinful acts, did not have the Holy Spirit at work in their hearts. In the worldview of the learned witches were included among those who needed to be controlled and disciplined.

The worldview of the common people also included belief in the existence of witches. Ordinary folk affirmed witches' presence and their powers before, during, and long after the Reformations. As noted above, the more than 90 percent of Europe's population that lived in the countryside, and very likely a noticeable proportion of those who dwelled behind city walls, were convinced that myriad invisible forces surrounded them. These forces were both good and bad, and their manipulation lent humble residents a sense of being able to influence their own fate. The witch was but one of many figures in a fairly animistic, though Christianized pantheon.

Although learned men liked to think of their horizons as vastly broader than those of their lowly fellows, whose practices they tarred with the brush of "superstition," the fact is that the witch craze could not have occurred without the mental, as well as the physical, complicity of theologians, judges, lawyers, and magistrates. From at least the fifteenth century, many high-ranking churchmen shared the popular belief in witches. It was only in the second half of the seventeenth century that the educated people of Europe began to define for themselves an urbane, superior, and "rational" cosmos. Until that trend came to dominate, even those with book learning perceived the Devil and his minions everywhere and were able, with conviction, to accuse their neighbors of entering into pacts with him. Christina Larner has aptly observed,

> Peasants left to themselves will identify individuals as witches and will resort to a variety of anti-witchcraft measures in self-defence; they cannot pursue these measures to the punishment, banishment, or official execution of even one witch, let alone a multiplicity of witches, without the administrative machinery and encouragement of their rulers.[17]

Although reliable statistics can hardly be derived from the surviving patchwork of interrogation transcripts and other judicial records of the second half of the sixteenth and the first two-thirds of the seventeenth century (and later for Massachusetts and parts of eastern Europe and Scandinavia), scholars incline toward agreement that approximately 60,000 alleged witches were executed and that, of these, about 80 percent, with regional variations, were women.[18] A far greater number were accused and underwent some judicial process. The regions of most intense witch hunting were southwest Germany, Switzerland, Austria, Scotland, the Duchy of Luxemburg, what is today southern Belgium and northern France, and parts of England, especially the County of Essex. These "centers" included Catholic and Protestant lands. Martin Luther preached in 1526,

> It is altogether a just law that enchantresses should be killed, for they cause much damage, which is sometimes ignored. They can, for instance, steal the milk, butter, and everything else out of a house. They can do this by milking it out of a handtowel, a table, or a handle [as they] say a certain word or words and think about a cow [while they're doing this]. . . . They can bewitch a child so that it constantly cries and doesn't eat, doesn't sleep, etc. They can also cause mysterious disorders in the human knee, so that the body is consumed. When you see such women, they are devilish in appearance; I have seen some of them. For this reason they are to be killed.[19]

A generation later, the Jesuit reformer, Peter Canisius, wrote to the general of his order, Diego Lainez,

> Everywhere one punishes the witches, which are proliferating astonishingly. Their wicked deeds are outrageous. They envy children the grace that they [the children] have received in their baptism, and they kidnap them. There are large numbers of child murderers among them. Indeed, they have eaten the flesh of some of the children, as they themselves have confessed. One has never before seen the people in Germany so very given over and devoted to the Devil. The godlessness, unchastity, and gruesomeness that these depraved women, under

Satan's guidance, have carried out both openly and in secret, is unbelievable. These are the scandalous deeds that authorities dare to make known from their [the women's] confessions in prison. In many places, these ruinous monsters of the human race, these most extraordinary enemies of the Christian faith, are burned. . . . Nothing is secure against their horrible arts and artifices. The just God allows this on account of the heavy offenses of the people, which they couldn't atone for by any penance.[20]

John Calvin advocated the extirpation of witches from Geneva and the lands under its dominion. In this Calvinist capital, more than thirty executions for witchcraft took place between 1556 and 1570. Scholars have offered theories as to why Catholics and Protestants were equally harsh in hunting and penalizing witches in the sixteenth century whereas Catholics were more determined and executed a higher percentage of the accused in the early seventeenth century. Very likely one has to form conclusions based on the study of each particular context and the personalities involved.

In order for folk beliefs and petty resentments among neighbors to become worthy of the attention of courts of law, authorities had to be convinced that witches engaged in activities that were illegal. Doing harm to the bodies and property of others was, of course, against the law. As the age of intense concern for order took shape, more and more men in high places found it credible that witches—mostly women but also a few men—carried out some of the most horrific crimes that settled humanity has been able to envision: the killing of babies and the use of their body parts in heinous rituals; cannibalism; forming a compact with the Devil (who sometimes took the form of a goat, toad, or black dog), which was sealed by taboo acts such as kissing his backside or having sex with him; and flying through the air to attend witches' meetings or sabbaths and there joining in sexual orgies that included incest. Not all areas of Europe that engaged intermittently in witch trials subscribed to this diabolization of the witch. For instance, England did not as a rule. But everywhere the prosecutors alleged that witches interfered with the smooth functioning of nature by causing bad weather that ruined crops, killing people and livestock, and making women barren and men impotent. Even those who did not link witches to the Devil saw these females as the antithesis of the "good woman." The best of women, too, in European society stood in intimate relationship to nature, that environment that was at once essential to human beings' thriving and yet, if it functioned improperly, threatened to devastate them. All women as the "daughters of Eve" were allegedly more prone to sin. This sinfulness, in view of their closeness to nature, could well show itself in the perversion of nature.

During the fifteenth century, the Catholic church had begun to publicize the view that witches, who it thought were spreading even then, had repudiated their baptism, and with it Christianity, in order to serve Satan. The Church counted as heretics any who falsified or abandoned the true faith to follow an unapproved belief. As such, accused witches now fell under the purview of the Inquisition, which had been founded in the early thirteenth century as a result of the Waldensian and Catharist heretical scares.[21] Pope Innocent VIII announced the dangers that witches posed to Christianity in a papal bull, *Summa desiderantes,* in 1484, and he asked two Dominican friars, Heinrich Kramer and Jacob Sprenger, to draw up a method of proceeding against such women. Both pope and friars were explicit about the preponderance of women in such activities, for the resulting treatise on trying witches, *Malleus malefi-carum* (*The Hammer of Witches*), specifically refers to women, and not to women and men. It was reprinted fourteen times between its publication in 1486 and 1520, followed by a hiatus of fifty-six years, and then appeared in sixteen print-ings between 1576 and 1669, when witch persecutions were most intense.

As a manual to be used by courts, the *Malleus* shocks us today more by its authors' expressions of acute misogyny than by the unpleasant details of procedure, which could include torture. Kramer and Sprenger, who, we must recall, were celibate clergymen as well as inquisitors, quoted the most extreme classical and biblical (such as portions of Ecclesiasticus 25:13–26) vilifications of women. They said that women had, among other vices, an insatiable carnal desire and an immoderate lust for power, which led them to enter into com-pacts with the Devil. They perceived a strong link between midwives and witchcraft. Most modern researchers, however, have not found that midwives were any more likely than other women to be accused of sorcery.

Another striking aspect of witch accusations and interrogations is their sexual overtones. In our post-Freudian culture, we find it hard not to consider the erotic fantasies of accusers, torturers, and judges—as well as the victims, to the extent that without torture a number of them confessed to sexual aberrations—exposed in the transcripts. Witches' alleged misdeeds were often tied to reproductive functions. Today we may regard the search for "witches' teats" and certain processes of torture as sexually sadistic.

Torture and execution occurred less often in areas, such as England and Scandinavia, that were immune to inquisitorial procedure. Farther south, courts were able to prevent the accused from learning who had brought charges of witchcraft and sometimes even from knowing precisely what the charges were. Trial costs were defrayed partly by the confiscation of con-demned witches' assets.

It is important to note that very often women accused other women of practicing witchcraft. Women of the past generally accepted the valuation that their society placed on them. The witch hunts saw little of what one might call "feminine solidarity." It was to be expected that under torture the victims would be prepared to say whatever their tormenters desired. But surprisingly often they did so, both about themselves and other women, without torture, bringing their friends and relatives into mortal danger.

The grimly fascinating phenomenon of witch hunting has attracted much attention, and this attention has grown exponentially since the late 1960s. It has become not only often feminist in nature but interdisciplinary as well, drawing on the perspectives of anthropology, social psychology, and literary analysis. We do not necessarily have to select from among the leading categories of interpretation, for witchcraft prosecution was enormously complex, with roots in several salient features and developments of the day. Because there is no single explanation of the witch craze, we must take each of the following characteristics into account as we seek to understand what transpired.

Most conflicts over the use and abuse of enchantment lay in the village or neighborhood and involved individuals who knew each other. Accusations were class-influenced, with more people from a somewhat higher socio-economic status pointing the finger at people of lower station. They were also age-influenced, with women at or past menopause, and widows, disproportionately vulnerable. Some of the most telling research has consisted of microstudies in which the details of personal relationships have been reconstructed. Some of these have shown, for example, that men coveted the properties or other economic assets of women whom they accused. Psychoanalytically oriented microstudies have attributed Oedipal anxieties to witch accusers.

Early modern villagers had little sense of larger elements that would draw local disagreements to the attention of territorial and interregional authorities, namely, state and church, and cause what was, by our lights, a ghastly outcome. They had little conscious awareness of the expansive spirit of cities or of burghers' growing disdain for the "superstition," and for the seeming disorder and emotion of village culture. Nor did they perceive the urban desire, in this era of emerging capitalism, to incorporate the economy of the hamlet into the city, or that this ambition carried with it a wish to improve and regulate the peasant manner of living.

Witch accusers likewise had little perception—although common people did complain bitterly about a more punitive spirit, not based in custom, in officials' dealings with them—that theirs was what we are presently calling an age of militant confessionalization and social disciplining. As stated above, religion lent its support to politics and vice versa in struggling to achieve the doctrinal conformity and lift the moral tone of *all* the people. In such times, the latent or low-key prejudices that are present in a culture, in this case misogyny, can be reanimated and intensified. In early modern Europe, men's fears about women's familiarity with nature—or, as they would have expressed it, women's greater proclivity to sin—became acute.

The century from about 1550 to about 1650 has been described as "the iron century," one in which wars and other disasters were widespread. Rates of inflation reached unprecedented heights in a society that had no concept of modernization, that refused to raise wages, and that could not easily transfer surpluses of goods to regions where they were needed. Such cataclysms as this "price revolution," the Wars of Religion, recurring epidemics, and revolts demanded explanation and rectifying action. If in fact they were manifestations of God's displeasure over sin, then godly rulers simply had to identify those who violated divine commandments and punish them in order to gain relief. Rulers of both churches and states made their best effort. This conclusion is related to the one about social disciplining, but it is also about a cosmic view according to which the unpunished individual can bring catastrophe. The Turks were invading and capturing parts of eastern Europe and before the end of the seventeenth century had besieged Vienna twice. Western Europeans speculated that such disasters were God's punishment of the entire European subcontinent. Peter Canisius's letter, quoted above, explicitly made a connection between witchcraft and "heavy" sins committed by the populace. This mood found expression in the treatment of a whole range of transgressions, including those that we would agree were crimes, as well as in the persecution of witches, Jews, gypsies, and a wide variety of other nonconforming people. Prominent among the last were adherents of any dissident religious creed, such as Protestants in Italy or Spain, Catholics in England, Huguenots in France during and after 1572, and Anabaptists and anti-Trinitarians just about everywhere. The Spanish Inquisition was less interested in witches than in detecting former Jews who might have made an insincere conversion to Christianity; it burned few of the alleged witches brought before it. But whatever the regional emphasis, educated elites and nonprivileged people alike sought explanations and scapegoats when things went wrong.

Perhaps the most elusive aspect of the European witch craze is why it came to an end. A few dissenting voices could be heard early on, but they were indeed exceptional and met with vigorous refutation. Johann Weyer's *De praestigiis daemonum* (*On the Deceptions of Devils*), published in 1563, insisted that women who were ill with "melancholy" were deluded into thinking that they were witches. Nonetheless, Weyer firmly believed in the Devil, and he also affirmed womankind's inordinate susceptibility to diabolical lures. Many other men in high places, such as King James I of England, propounded the reality of the witch and encouraged witch trials. Until theologians, lawyers, and judges too abandoned their roles in witch persecutions, these proceedings against women and men could not cease.

The spread of science and rational thought offers a convenient explanation of the end of witch persecutions. The theory that the learned men who presided over witch trials came to regard enchantment as a figment of the popular imagination cannot be wholly discounted. They came to reject the ideas of contracts with the devil and witches' sabbaths. In addition, it occurred to some men in positions of power that under torture people would confess to acts that they had not committed. In any case, we cannot help but notice that the dissemination of scientific thought within burgher society did coincide with the subsiding, not of witch accusations among the people, but of witch trials and executions. Lawyers, magistrates, and theologians grew reluctant to try people for sorcery. In general, the mentalities of those who were better educated and those who were less so diverged during the late seventeenth century.

Another partial answer to our question about the end of witch trials may well be found in the gradual uncoupling, at least in Protestant lands, of church and state. During the sixteenth and much of the seventeenth centuries, worldly and spiritual governments had cooperated closely in trying to create an orderly society; and even at the end of the seventeenth century, they both continued to desire calm religious conviction and political docility in all their subjects. But the secular "sword" was increasingly preoccupied with its own triumph in the international sphere. Princely courts were more engrossed in mundane pursuits than they had been, and the pious rituals of members of ruling families became more superficial than in the preceding era of conversion and militancy. In addition, this "sword" had failed, despite generations of bloody attempts to force everyone else to accept its favored creed, to recreate a European-wide unanimity on religion. After this vain exertion, perhaps governments were tired. Certainly they were financially drained. We can detect a certain relaxation at the end of the seventeenth century, continuing into the eighteenth century, in the severity with which those in authority pursued moral infractions.

We might even ask whether the opening up of the world to numerous Europeans by means of colonization had not blunted governors' drive for purity. Initially, Europeans had carried their witch beliefs with them and so "discovered" witches among their own colonists in Massachusetts and among indigenous women in Peru. In Europe, the diversity of peoples gradually made itself ever more widely known through the published reports of travelers, the presence of increasing foreigners, and the introduction of new foods. Under the circumstances, urban leaders—from whose ranks judges and theologians had come—were still convinced of the superiority of their own way of life and cosmic view over those of peasants at home and aliens abroad, but they were content to let countryfolk carry out their witch accusations against each other, undisturbed by trial and judicial torment.

CONCLUSION: THE REFORMATIONS AND WOMEN

European women were everywhere in the sixteenth and seventeenth centuries. This may be self-evident, but it is important to stress that the mistrust with which officialdom regarded them did not produce their withdrawal from view. On the contrary, the fifteenth and sixteenth centuries saw unprecedented numbers of urban laywomen remaining unwed and supporting themselves as day laborers and servants. There are several exceptions to this generalization. Nuns who were forced into enclosure did disappear behind convent walls. In the Catholic world, women were often barred from religious confraternities during the late sixteenth and early seventeenth centuries. During the Reformation era, Protestant and Catholic parish visitors did aggressively punish any woman (or man) found to be a cunning-person (healer and fortuneteller) and succeeded in driving these folk practitioners, or rather their activities, underground; they continued to exist until the nineteenth century.

In addition, from the mid-fifteenth century, men did tend to exclude women from guild membership, and thus from the recognition and better remuneration that accompanied that status. Still, as a rule, women went on "holding up half the sky." I have said elsewhere that early modern women occupied "interstitial space," the space between men. That is, they lived out their days around, among, and in constant interaction with men; but the men usually were the ones who counted, who held official power, who got credit for a job done, who constituted persons for legal purposes, and who were thus, in a figurative sense, truly visible. In the optical illusion that I referred to at the beginning of this essay, men were ever the "figure" and women the "ground," that is, the background.

What has this to do with the Reformations? In an age of growing anxiety over disorder and church- and state-led campaigns to produce a genuinely Christian society, well-established clerical and to a lesser extent popular misogynistic attitudes were revived and articulated with intensity from the pulpit and the judge's bench. Authorities invested these attitudes with new validity as universal norms and bolstered them with the vocabulary of divine will. The Reformations were not coterminous with the age, but they were indeed part of their age and helped very considerably to disseminate its values. From a psychological and symbolic, and to a lesser degree a physical, perspective, the Reformations worsened women's position. It was the spirit of disciplinary anxiety, permeating the whole age, that brought forth the witch trials. Religious men and women contributed to them but by no means uniquely bear the onus of blame for them.

A few educated women and men objected to the denigration of women and engaged in the discussions called *querelle des femmes* (the debate about women). Their writings are quite fascinating though not directly related to the Reformations. In any case, these authors were a tiny minority, writing mainly for each other. We have no idea how great the circulation of their tracts was. At the same time, a number of men (significantly, usually anonymously) wrote satires in which they questioned whether women were actually human beings. They found similarities between women and dogs, cats, swine, snakes, and wolves. This genre persisted into the eighteenth century. Again, probably few people read these.

Most European women undoubtedly went about their business as they always had. They accepted their society's lower valuation of them, believing that their subordination to men was indeed God's punishment for Eve's disobedience. As far as we are able to tell, they did not reflect on this; they were not restive. Their chief concern was probably providing for themselves and their families. At the same time, religion was embedded in their worldview. They practiced their religion with a fervor varying from individual to individual, and they took part in all the movements of their day. It is likely that only a few regretted their marginal status within each creed. The concern for equality, both within religious institutions and in society at large, belonged to the future.

NOTES

1. She made these arguments at a panel discussion entitled "Verhältnis von Frauenbewegung und Frauenforschung: Bilanz und Perspektiven," October 18, 1996, at an international conference, "Geschlechterperspektiven in der Frühen Neuzeit," Zentrum zur Erforschung der Frühen Neuzeit, Johann Wolfgang Goethe University, Frankfurt/Main, Germany.

2. "Gendered Exchanges: Women and Communication in Sixteenth-Century Germany," in *Kommunikation und Alltag in Spätmittelalterlicher und Früher Neuzeit,* Österreichische Akademie der Wissenschaften, Vienna 1992, pp. 199–217, here at p. 208.

3. As, for example, in David G. Myers, *Exploring Psychology,* 3d ed., Worth Publishers, New York, 1996, p. 140, fig. 4-20.

4. Margaret L. King, *Women of the Renaissance,* University of Chicago Press, Chicago, 1991, p. 104.

5. By *transubstantiation* the Catholic church means the conversion of the eucharistic bread and wine into the body and blood of Christ when a priest raises them over his head (elevation) and says the prescribed ritual words. After this, they only appear still to be bread and wine, but they are in *substance*—we might say their inner essence—Christ's body and blood. This belief was rejected by Protestants, though they disagreed among themselves about whether or how Christ was present in the Communion service.

6. Anchoresses and anchorites (also called hermits or eremites) were women and men who lived in isolation for religion's sake. Because of their exceptional piety, they attracted local laypeople who sought their spiritual and personal advice and sometimes brought them food.

7. For a volume of essays surveying the transition from Catholic to Protestant clergy in much of northern Europe, see Andrew Pettegree, ed., *The Reformation of the Parishes: The Ministry and the Reformation in Town and Country,* Manchester University Press, Manchester, England, and New York, 1993.

8. Reproduced as the frontispiece for this chapter.

9. Priests paid the bishop concubinage fees for living in a quasi-wedded relationship with a woman, and cradle fees for the children that were born to them.

10. Saint Augustine's mother, according to her son, had softened her husband's rage with her complete submission.

11. Heide Wunder uses this analogy as part of the title of her excellent survey, *"Er ist die Sonn', sie ist der Mond": Frauen in der Frühen Neuzeit,* C. H. Beck, Munich, 1992; forthcoming in English translation from Harvard University Press.

12. Joel F. Harrington, *Reordering Marriage and Society in Reformation Germany,* Cambridge University Press, Cambridge, England, and New York, 1995) sees the laws governing marriage as changing little during the sixteenth century. Rather, both Catholic and Protestant authorities were more bent on enforcement than earlier.

13. Tertiaries, or members of the Third Order of Saint Francis, led lives of religious commitment but actually remained laypeople and did not take permanent vows.

14. *Discalced* means *shoeless* or *barefoot*. In fact, the nuns wore sandals, but this peasant-style footwear and the word in the name of their order symbolized their complete poverty and humility.

15. Louis Châtellier, *The Europe of the Devout: The Catholic Reformation and the Formation of a New Society,* Cambridge University Press, Cambridge, England, 1989, p. 51.

16. Monica Kurzel-Runtscheiner, *Töchter der Venus: Die Kurtisanen Roms im 16. Jahrhundert*, C. H. Beck, Munich, 1995.
17. Larner, *Enemies of God: The Witch-Hunt in Scotland*, Chatto and Windus, London, 1981, p. 2.
18. Allison P. Coudert summarizes opinion on numbers in "The Myth of the Improved Status of Protestant Women: The Case of the Witchcraze," in *The Politics of Gender in Early Modern Europe*, ed. Jean R. Brink, Allison P. Coudert, and Maryanne C. Horowitz, Sixteenth Century Journal Publishers, Kirksville, Mo., 1989, p. 61, n. 2.
19. My translation from Wolfgang Behringer, ed., *Hexen und Hexenprozesse: Dokumente*, 2d ed., Deutscher Taschenbuch Verlag, Munich, 1993, p. 104, no. 61.
20. My translation from Behringer, *Hexen und Hexenprozesse*, p. 139, no. 89. In the last sentence, Canisius means that the sins of the people are so awful that the sacrament of penance is not adequate to making satisfaction for them. For that reason, in his opinion, God has sent witches as an additional punishment.
21. The Waldensians first came to prominence in France during the second half of the twelfth century and were followers of Peter Waldo or Valdes of Lyon. At first devoted to apostolic poverty, they increasingly attacked ecclesiastical corruption in their sermons. The Catharists were descendants of Manichean dualism. They believed that the physical world was evil and the spiritual world good. Among other heretical beliefs, they denied the incarnation of Jesus. The Catharist movement was so popular that Pope Innocent III called in 1209 for a crusade to suppress it. The persistence of such religious views persuaded the papacy to found the Roman Inquisition, probably in 1232.

SUGGESTIONS FOR FURTHER READING

Ankarloo, Bengt, and Gustav Henningsen, eds. *Early Modern European Witchcraft: Centres and Peripheries*. Oxford and New York: Oxford University Press, 1990.

Bilinkoff, Jodi. *The Avila of Saint Teresa: Religious Reform in a Sixteenth-Century City*. Ithaca, N.Y.: Cornell University Press, 1989.

Cohen, Sherrill. "Asylums for Women in Counter-Reformation Italy." In *Women in Reformation and Counter-Reformation Europe: Public and Private Worlds*, ed. Sherrin Marshall. Bloomington: Indiana University Press, 1989, pp. 166–188.

Coudert, Allison P. "The Myth of the Improved Status of Protestant Women: The Case of the Witchcraze." In *The Politics of Gender in Early Modern Europe*, ed. Jean R. Brink, Allison P. Coudert, and Maryanne C. Horowitz. Kirksville, Mo.: Sixteenth Century Journal Publishers, 1989, pp. 61–89.

Davis, Natalie Zemon. "City Women and Religious Change." In *Society and Culture in Early Modern France*. Stanford: Stanford University Press, 1975, pp. 65–96.

Daniel, David. "Piety, Politics, and Perversion: Noblewomen in Reformation Hungary." In *Women in Reformation and Counter-Reformation Europe: Public and Private Worlds*, ed. Sherrin Marshall. Bloomington: Indiana University Press, 1989, pp. 68–88.

Douglass, Jane Dempsey. *Women, Freedom, and Calvin*. Philadelphia: Westminster Press, 1985.

Harrington, Joel F. *Reordering Marriage and Society in Reformation Germany.* Cambridge, England, and New York: Cambridge University Press, 1995.

Harrison, Wes. "The Role of Women in Anabaptist Thought and Practice: The Hutterite Experience of the Sixteenth and Seventeenth Centuries." *Sixteenth Century Journal* 23 (1992), pp. 49–70.

Hufton, Olwen. *The Prospect Before Her: A History of Women in Western Europe 1500–1800,* vol. I. New York: Knopf, 1996.

Irwin, Joyce. *Womenhood in Radical Protestantism, 1525–1675.* New York: Edward Mellen Press, 1979.

Jacobsen, Grethe. "Nordic Women and the Reformation." In *Women in Reformation and Counter-Reformation Europe: Public and Private Worlds,* ed. Sherrin Marshall. Bloomington: Indiana University Press, 1989, pp. 47–67.

————. "Women, Marriage, and Magisterial Reformation: The Case of Malmø, Denmark." In *Pietas et Societas: New Trends in Reformation Social History,* ed. Kyle C. Sessions and Phillip N. Bebb. Kirksville, Mo.: Sixteenth Century Journal Publishers, 1985, pp. 57–78.

Karant-Nunn, Susan C. "Continuity and Change: Some Effects of the Reformation on the Women of Zwickau." *Sixteenth Century Journal* 13 (1982), pp. 17–42.

————. "*Kinder, Küche, Kirche:* Social Ideology in the Sermons of Johannes Mathesius." In *Germania Illustrata: Essays on Early Modern Germany Presented to Gerald Strauss,* ed. Andrew C. Fix and Susan C. Karant-Nunn. Kirksville, Mo.: Sixteenth Century Journal Publishers, 1992, pp. 121–140.

King, Margaret L. *Women of the Renaissance.* Chicago: University of Chicago Press, 1991.

Kingdon, Robert M. *Adultery and Divorce in Calvin's Geneva.* Cambridge, Mass.: Harvard University Press, 1995.

Marshall, Sherrin. *The Dutch Gentry: Family, Faith, and Fortune.* New York: Greenwood Press, 1987.

————. "Protestant, Catholic, and Jewish Women in the Early Modern Netherlands." In *Women in Reformation and Counter-Reformation Europe: Public and Private Worlds,* ed. Sherrin Marshall. Bloomington: Indiana University Press, 1989, pp. 120–139.

Mentzer, Raymond A. *Blood and Belief: Family, Survival, and Confessional Identity Among the Provincial Huguenot Nobility.* West Lafayette, Ind.: Purdue University Press, 1994.

————, ed. *Sin and the Calvinists: Morals Control and the Consistory in the Reformed Tradition.* Kirksville, Mo.: Sixteenth Century Journal Publishers, 1994.

Merchant, Carolyn. *The Death of Nature: Women, Ecology and the Scientific Revolution.* New York: Harper and Row, 1983.

Ortega Costa, Milagro. "Spanish Women in the Reformation." In *Women in Reformation and Counter-Reformation Europe: Public and Private Worlds,* ed. Sherrin Marshall. Bloomington: Indiana University Press, 1989, pp. 89–119.

Ozment, Steven. *When Fathers Ruled: Family Life in Reformation Europe.* Cambridge, Mass.: Harvard University Press, 1983.

Perry, Mary Elizabeth. *Gender and Disorder in Early Modern Seville.* Princeton, N.J.: Princeton University Press, 1990.

Roper, Lyndal. "'The Common Man,' 'The Common Good,' 'Common Women': Reflections on Gender and Meaning in the Reformation German Commune." *Social History* 12 (1987), pp. 1–21.

———. *The Holy Household: Women and Morals in Reformation Augsburg.* Oxford, England, and New York: Clarendon Press, 1989.

———. *Oedipus and the Devil: Witchcraft, Sexuality and Religion in Early Modern Europe.* London and New York: Routledge, 1994.

———. "Was There a Crisis in Gender Relations in Sixteenth-Century Germany?" In *Krisenbewußtsein und Krisenbewältigung in der Frühen Neuzeit—Crisis in Early Modern Europe,* ed. Monika Hagenmaier and Sabine Holtz. Frankfurt am Main and Berlin: Peter Lang, 1992, pp. 371–386.

Safley, Thomas Max. *Let No Man Put Asunder: The Control of Marriage in the German Southwest, a Comparative Study, 1550–1600.* Kirksville, Mo.: Sixteenth Century Journal Publishers, 1984.

Turner, James Grantham. *Sexuality and Gender in Early Modern Europe: Institutions, Texts, Images.* Cambridge, England, and New York: Cambridge University Press, 1993.

Warnicke, Retha M. *Women of the English Renaissance and Reformation.* Westport, Conn.: Greenwood, 1983.

Weaver, F. Ellen. "Erudition, Spirituality, and Women: The Jansenist Contribution." In *Women in Reformation and Counter-Reformation Europe: Public and Private Worlds,* ed. Sherrin Marshall. Bloomington: Indiana University Press, 1989, pp. 189–206.

Wiesner, Merry E. "Ideology Meets the Empire: Reformed Convents and the Reformation." In *Germania Illustrata: Essays on Early Modern Germany Presented to Gerald Strauss,* ed. Andrew C. Fix and Susan C. Karant-Nunn. Kirksville, Mo.: Sixteenth Century Journal Publishers, 1992, pp. 181–196.

———. "Nuns, Wives, and Mothers: Women and the Reformation in Germany." In *Women in Reformation and Counter-Reformation Europe: Public and Private Worlds,* ed. Sherrin Marshall. Bloomington: Indiana University Press, 1989, pp. 8–28.

———. *Women and Gender in Early Modern Europe.* Cambridge, England, and New York: Cambridge University Press, 1993.

Willen, Diane. "Women and Religion in Early Modern England." In *Women in Reformation and Counter-Reformation Europe: Public and Private Worlds,* ed. Sherrin Marshall. Bloomington: Indiana University Press, 1989, pp. 140–165.

Willis, Deborah. *Malevolent Nurture: Witch-Hunting and Maternal Power in Early Modern England.* Ithaca, N.Y.: Cornell University Press, 1995.

Wiltenburg, Joy. *Disorderly Women and Female Power in the Street Literature of Early Modern England and Germany.* Charlottesville: University Press of Virginia, 1992.

Geertruydt Roghman, *Woman Spinning*, before 1650. D. Parker Collection, Courtesy, Museum of Fine Arts, Boston. Roghman was one of the few women engravers active during the "golden age" of art in the seventeenth-century Netherlands. Her father and brothers were also engravers, but she concentrated more on the daily life of women; this is from a series of engravings of women's occupations. HARVEY D. PARKER COLLECTION, COURTESY, MUSEUM OF FINE ARTS, BOSTON.

8

Spinning Out Capital: Women's Work in Preindustrial Europe, 1350–1750

Merry E. Wiesner

Along with the Renaissance and Reformation, the development of capitalism is often described as one of the key agents in the change from the "medieval" to the "modern" world. Economic and social historians have traditionally emphasized the role of class distinctions as they have traced the gradual, though uneven, development of capitalism, but it is increasingly clear that gender was also an important factor. The growth of capitalism and other forms of economic change had an effect on both the actual gender division of labor and the meaning of the work that women and men performed. Conversely, gender structures shaped economic change, with differences in marriage patterns, laws regulating women's rights to own property, and notions about male and female capabilities and honor all playing a role in the way the European economy developed. The economic changes in the four centuries discussed in this chapter did not affect all women equally. Place of residence, age, marital status, family size, and social class made significant differences in the types of work that women performed. Despite these differences, however, women's work was more likely than men's to be poorly paid and undervalued, defined not as work but as "helping out." Though their work, whether as unpaid household members or wage workers, was essential to the expansion of the European economy during this period, it was often regarded as marginal, and women were only rarely regarded as "workers," an attitude that would carry over into the industrial transformation despite the presence of large numbers of women in the paid labor force.

All societies draw distinctions between men's work and women's work. Cultural norms, technological developments, religious and intellectual currents, economic institutions, and popular beliefs all play a part in drawing those distinctions. The study of women's work has been a major part of the investigation of women's history over the last twenty-five years, as historians have analyzed the gender division of labor and the ways in which it was shaped by and in turn shaped other economic structures. This essay explores women's work from about 1350 to about 1750, a long span of time during which the European economy and prevailing ideologies underwent significant changes. It investigates both the various contexts within which women's work operated and the actual tasks that women performed, analyzing changes in work itself and the way that work was defined and valued.

THE ECONOMIC CONTEXT: HOUSEHOLDS AND CAPITALISM

In the medieval economy, the household was the basic unit of production in most parts of Europe. Peasant families in rural areas raised crops and animals for their own and their landlords' use and traded their surpluses in a nearby village or city for the items they could not produce themselves. Wage labor was generally seasonal or found in areas with extractive industries such as salt or metal mining. Urban households varied dramatically in composition and size, from those of wealthy merchants with many servants to artisanal homes with perhaps a few apprentices, journeymen, and domestic servants, to those of the poor, who often lived alone. Most goods were produced in household workshops, and all stages of production, from the purchase of raw materials and tools to the selling of the finished product, were carried out by members of the household; the goods produced were traded either within that particular city or regionally. Even members of the household who were not family members—the servants, apprentices, and journeymen—stood to benefit from successful production and sales, for this generally brought improved food and clothing, which formed the major part (if not all) of their wages. Large household workshops might also hire outside individuals for wages to do specific tasks, but such pieceworkers and day laborers had no guarantee of regular employment and were generally among the poorest people in any community.

During the thirteenth and fourteenth centuries, craft guilds were established in many cities to organize and regulate production; they set quality levels, terms of apprenticeship, and prices for goods that required a high degree of skill and training to produce. They set standards for the finished product and limited competition between household workshops, but initially they did not regulate what went on within a household.

At the same time that craft guilds were forming to regulate production, a new form of economic organization appeared in western Europe—capitalism. There is great debate among economic historians as to exactly when, where, and why capitalism started, but there is general agreement that it began among merchants, who traded luxury goods like spices and silk in an international market and often made enormous profits. Their businesses often began as family firms, but the opportunity for profit attracted nonfamily investors, and the firms gradually grew larger and more complex. As they grew, more and more of the actual labor was carried out by individuals who were paid wages rather than being rewarded with a share of the profits. This division between capital and labor is a hallmark of capitalism, and this initial stage is generally termed "mercantile capitalism" because it involved merchants and their enterprises in commerce, banking, and trade.

Prosperous merchants throughout Europe gradually sought to expand their investments beyond commerce and began to purchase raw materials, tools, and machinery, hiring workers to produce goods. They then sold these manufactured goods along with their other articles of trade in an international market, using the trading networks, systems of agents, and offices they had already developed. Merchants invested in manufacturing in some parts of Europe as early as the thirteenth century, particularly in cloth production in Florence and Flanders. They hired entire households to carry out one stage of production, such as spinning or weaving, sending out raw materials and often loaning out the necessary tools; this is called the putting-out system or domestic industry. This putting-out system often employed rural households and directly challenged traditional urban methods of production. The household thus remained the production unit, but it was paid wages solely for the labor of its members and had no share in the profits from production. This system is often viewed as a second stage of capitalism and is sometimes termed "proto-industrialization" because workers remained in their own homes or in very small workshops; only much later, in the eighteenth and nineteenth centuries, would industrial capitalism bring workers together into large factories.

Along with the putting-out system, the growth of capitalism brought additional changes to the rural economy. As cities grew, people in the rural areas surrounding them often turned to market gardening, producing fruits, vegetables, and other crops for urban consumers. Because of this development, such a region no longer produced grain, relying instead on imported grain from eastern Europe, where the landed nobility were enserfing the peasants to secure a steady supply of labor for their vast estates. The growth of agricultural capitalism thus had the opposite effect in western and eastern Europe; it brought the decline of serfdom in the west and the simultaneous rise of serfdom in the east.

At the same time that capitalism was changing the economy of some areas of Europe, European exploration and colonization provided new opportunities for trade and investment around the globe. New types of products such as sugar, coffee, and cotton textiles were introduced or sold more widely in Europe, and European products such as wool cloth, straw hats, and lace were in turn exported to an international market. Thus even traditional guild shops might be affected by economic developments thousands of miles away, and the increasing numbers of households dependent on wages were even more at the mercy of international market conditions. Some areas of Europe were not active parts of this international network, however, and remained largely bound to traditional patterns of production and trade. By 1750, then, there were great regional differences in the level of economic development and basic forms of economic organization throughout Europe.

THE SOCIAL CONTEXT: DEMOGRAPHY AND THE FAMILY

Regional economic differences are not the only significant variable when evaluating women's work. Research in all of the world's cultures over the last twenty years has demonstrated that women's work is also shaped to a great extent by marital patterns and family structures, which vary widely both regionally and chronologically, and also vary within a specific culture, depending on an individual's and family's social and economic status.

Historical demographers identify two basic marital patterns in preindustrial Europe. In western and northern Europe, men and women both married in their midtwenties, slightly earlier in rural areas than in urban.[1] This is quite an unusual marital pattern; although in many of the world's cultures men wait until this late to marry, they generally marry women who are much younger, often in their early teens. So it is late marriage for women that is quite unusual, and there are several possible reasons for this peculiar marriage pattern. Married couples generally set up their own households, rather than moving in with the parents of one spouse, which meant that the husband had to be financially secure and the wife able to run a household rather than rely on her mother or mother-in-law. Many crafts forbade apprentices and journeymen to marry, since they generally lived with the master craftsman. Because the guild understood that two people were necessary to run a shop properly, rules required masters to be married. Since the master's wife fed and clothed this large household, craftsmen often preferred to marry an adult women rather than an inexperienced teenager. Whereas in many of the world's cultures men pay a bride price to obtain a wife, in Europe women were expected to provide dowries to their husbands, and delaying marriage gave a woman and her family an opportunity to save that dowry. Even a poor woman was expected to bring something as a dowry to her marriage—linens, dishes, and bedding, for example—which she could afford to purchase only after many years as a servant or pieceworker. In an era before effective contraception, delaying the marriage of women was one way to keep family size smaller. For poorer families, fewer children meant fewer mouths to feed, and for wealthier families, it meant fewer future dowries for daughters or training and education for sons.

This pattern of late marriage was accompanied by a high proportion of the population never marrying, so that there were many adult women who worked, and sometimes lived, on their own. A survey of wills in fifteenth-century York, for example, found that 17 percent of all laywomen who made wills had never been married, and households headed by widows and unmarried women often made up between one-quarter and one-third of all households in many cities.[2]

The marital pattern in southern and eastern Europe was somewhat different from that just sketched for northwest Europe. In eastern Europe, both serfs and nobles married in their late teens or early twenties, with serf couples generally living with the parents of one of the spouses. Wealthier men sometimes waited until later in life to marry, a pattern replicated among the wealthy merchants of Florence and other Italian cities, but they then married much younger women. Girls who entered marriage as teenagers were likely to be more dependent on their husbands and mothers-in-law than the older brides of northwestern Europe, who had perhaps earned their own dowries and developed work skills. Very few women in southern and eastern Europe remained unmarried; in contrast to York, only 3 percent of laywomen in fifteenth-century Florence had never married by age 25.[3]

THE INTELLECTUAL CONTEXT: IDEOLOGICAL AND LEGAL STRUCTURES

Along with economic and family structures, ideology also shaped women's work, both directly and through its influence on the economy and family. As one would expect, the rise of capitalism brought ideological as well as economic change. During the Middle Ages, work was defined as an activity performed to support and sustain oneself and one's family. There were gender-specific tasks, and those that men usually did were more highly valued, but the tasks of women were also considered "work." With the development of capitalism, work was increasingly defined as an activity for which one was paid, which meant that domestic tasks and childrearing were not considered work, unless they were done for wages.

Capitalism and the growth of a market economy cannot fully explain changes in the meaning of work during this period, however, for along with an exclusion of unpaid domestic tasks from notions of "work" came a redefinition of many of women's productive tasks as simply "assisting" or housekeeping. Women's work, including that for which they were paid, such as taking in boarders or sewing, began to be thought of as private, domestic, and reproductive, whereas men's work—even work exactly the same as women's, such as sewing clothes—was understood to be productive.

The reasons for this are complex and involve many other changes that were going on in European society at the time. One of these was the spread of humanist ideas about education, which developed first in Italy. Humanists saw the chief goal of education not as bringing one closer to God but as preparation for a career in the world. Thus women, in their eyes, did not need formal schooling, except perhaps for a few at the very top of the social scale who might be called on to rule territories or countries. At the same time, however, formal training became an increasingly important qualification for certain occupations, so that women—and unschooled men—were no longer able to claim an occupational title. They might heal people, but they could not be "physicians"; they might brew beer, but they were not "brewers."

Along with capitalism and Renaissance humanism, the Protestant Reformation also shaped this gendered definition of work. Some Italian humanists and Christian humanists in northern Europe broke with the medieval Christian notion that celibacy was superior to marriage and asserted that having a family was an important part of a man's civic duty.[4] This championing of family life increased dramatically with the Protestant Reformation, when the value of celibacy was emphatically denied. Sermons and advice manuals created what was in many ways a new vocation for men, that of father and head of household who was responsible for the behavior and ideas of his wife, children, and servants. The Reformation also further exalted western Christianity's already positive assessment of labor because Protestant thinkers, at least theoretically, denied that the work of the clergy was any more important than that of the laity; all occupations became vocations. In Reformation ideology, then, men had two divinely sanctioned vocations, father and worker. Women, however, had only one: mother. Advice manuals and sermons by Protestant clergy, and later in the sixteenth century by Catholic clergy as well, all viewed whatever productive labor women did as simply part of their domestic role, of their being a helpmeet for their husband and an example for their children. That idea was not just found in religious literature, however, but also permeated secular laws and ordinances regulating and defining work. Women's work was called assisting or housework, and men's work was called production or work.

A similar case of other terms masking what was in fact a gender division can be seen in the notions of "skilled" and "unskilled" work, which were supported by guild ordinances and city laws. Guilds often ruled that women were unfit for certain tasks, such as glass cutting, because they were too clumsy or "unskilled," yet those same women made lace, a job that required an even higher level of dexterity and concentration than glass cutting. Historians of the industrial period have pointed to the deskilling of certain occupations, in which jobs that had traditionally been done by men were made more monotonous with the addition of machinery and so were redefined and given to women, with a dramatic drop in status and pay.[5] The opposite process can be seen in the sixteenth century, in the transformation of stocking knitting into a male-dominated occupation. When the knitting frame was introduced, men began to argue that using it was so complicated that only men could possibly learn it; the frame actually made knitting easier and much faster, but women were prohibited from using it with the excuse that they were unskilled. The amount they could earn from handknitting was thus much less than their machine-aided male counterparts could earn, but by the end of the sixteenth century male knitters were pressuring for laws that would exclude women altogether, using the argument that all knitting was so skilled that it should be the province of men alone.[6] (This development has some parallels with the recent switch in gender of those most likely to be found at a keyboard; using a typewriter was gendered female in the early twentieth century—an example of deskilling in secretarial work—but working with computers has been gendered male; advertisements in computer magazines often portray women at the keyboard only if they are emphasizing how easy a computer system is to use.[7])

Laws that divided skilled from unskilled labor and productive from domestic tasks were only some of the types of laws that shaped women's work. Women differed from men in their legal capacity to be witnesses, make wills, act as guardians for their own children, make contracts, and own, buy, and sell property. In addition, the legal status of an adult woman depended on whether she was unmarried, married, or widowed, whereas the marital status of adult men was only occasionally the source of legal distinctions and then only if the man had never married; widowers were never differentiated from married men and were labeled as such only very rarely. The kinds of work each woman could do was thus determined to some degree by her marital status, although this varied from area to area depending on which city, state, or national law code applied.

Generally before the sixteenth century, an unmarried woman or widow had the right to dispose of her own property as she saw fit, using the assistance of a legal guardian only if she chose. When a woman married, she theoretically lost the right to make any contract without the agreement of her husband; she became, in French and English legal parlance, a *femme couverte*. However, married women who wanted to conduct business on a regular basis could appeal to the appropriate governing body for a lifting of this restriction. This was granted fairly easily, and the woman was allowed to act independently of her husband; such a woman was termed a *femme sole* in England and France, and a *Marktfrau* in Germany. In addition to those women who received formal legal approval, urban records indicate that many other married women were carrying out business independently, although the law still allowed anyone to deny a loan or refuse to make a contract with a married woman.

Single women and poor widows had few other options than working independently, and until the sixteenth century city and religious authorities grudgingly left some low-skilled occupations open to them because they recognized that these women would otherwise be forced to rely on charity or public assistance. As tax records indicate, women living independently rarely earned more than enough to survive. Widows were generally better off than women who had never married, for inheritance laws allowed them to keep at least their dowries and any property they brought into the marriage, as well as a proportion of the property or assets acquired during the marriage. Despite this, the household income of a widow was generally much less than it had been when her husband was alive.

In the sixteenth century, civic and religious authorities began to regard the lives of women living independently as a matter of morality as well as economics. Both Protestant and Catholic authorities became increasingly concerned with public order, propriety, decorum, and morality. They toughened laws against vagrants, worrying about what they perceived as an increase in "masterless" persons—wandering journeymen, servants between positions, mercenary soldiers and their camp followers, "sturdy beggars," itinerant actors, and musicians. Whether economic changes were actually causing an increase in people moving from town to town or from household to household is difficult to say, but the perception of an increase on the part of civic and church authorities was very strong.

Migrants were suspect not only because they might engage in criminal activity or become a drain on community charitable endowments, but also simply because they were not part of a household. In a world that appeared to them to becoming increasingly disorderly, authorities viewed the household as an institution of social control. Moreover, they felt that men as heads of household were more effective than women at exerting that control. As these attitudes developed, authorities began to consider women who lived alone as "masterless," lumping them in with other suspect groups. In Germany and France, laws were passed that forbade unmarried women to move into cities, required widows to move in with one of their male children, and obliged unmarried women to move in with a male relative or employer; in England city officials could force any unmarried woman between the ages of 12 and 40 into becoming a servant. In Protestant areas, as convents were closed the nuns were encouraged to marry or move back to their families, and in Catholic areas, unmarried women not living under strict cloister were increasingly suspect.

Despite all their attempts, however, authorities never reduced the number of female-headed households; the factors that favored late marriage in northwest Europe and the demographic realities which meant that parents and husbands often died at a relatively young age throughout all of Europe were stronger than any ideology, so that many women lived alone. The idea that women *should* be married or under the control of a man had a profound and negative effect on women's work, however. Although it was recognized that some women would have to work for wages, authorities always viewed that work as a stopgap or temporary measure until the women could attain, or return to, their "natural," married state. Thus the authorities were reluctant to establish policies that allowed women to practice any highly skilled occupation, and were suspicious when a woman made more than subsistence wages. A woman could work if she needed to support herself and her family, but she had no absolute right to work.

Throughout the sixteenth and seventeenth centuries, because of the increasing emphasis on the household as an instrument of social control, which was strengthened by a rise in the belief that the proper household was headed by a man, the power of (male) guardians over widows and unmarried women increased. City councils or, in England, parishes often appointed guardians for women. These guardians appeared in court on the woman's behalf, although previously women had often represented themselves in inheritance disputes and other cases. In a number of areas, the guardians decided whether a woman should retain control of her children if she remarried. Adult women were not yet the legal minors they would become during the Victorian period, but the laws grew decidedly more restrictive. Women's actual legal and economic activities, however, did not decrease proportionately—an example of the discrepancy between law codes and reality.

WOMEN'S WORK IN RURAL AREAS

With this economic and intellectual backdrop in mind, we can now examine women's work itself, beginning in the rural setting. Agricultural tasks were highly, though not completely, gender-specific, and the proper functioning of the rural household required at least one adult male and one adult female; remarriage after the death of a spouse was more swiftly undertaken in the countryside than in the cities. Women were largely responsible for tasks within or close to the house; they took care of poultry and small animals, prepared dairy products, beer, and bread, grew flax, and made linen and wool cloth. They also worked in the fields during harvest time, particularly in areas where grain harvesting was done with a sickle; manuscript illuminations and woodcuts show women and men working side by side with sickles well into the eighteenth century. Men generally wielded the scythe for harvesting from England to Muscovy (today's Russia), though use of the scythe also created new tasks for women, such as gathering and binding. These tasks were often physically more demanding than the actual cutting but did not require as much upper-body strength.[8] In areas of Europe such as Norway, Portugal, or the Basque region of Spain, where men were gone for long periods of time fishing or whaling, women did all of the farming. Women and children generally gleaned, or picked up grain from the ground after harvesting; particularly when other types of employment was scarce in rural areas, gleaning might provide as much as one-eighth of a family's income.

Women's labor changed as new types of crops and agricultural products were introduced and as agriculture became more specialized. During the seventeenth century, turnips and other root crops were increasingly grown in many parts of Europe. They were crops that were very labor-intensive and that were seen as women's responsibility because they were generally fed to the animals that women tended. Raw materials for manufactured products, such as flax, hemp, and plants for dye, became important commodities in many parts of Europe and were also cared for by women. Women in parts of Italy tended and harvested olive trees and grape vines, and carried out most of the tasks associated with the production of silk: gathering leaves from mulberry trees, raising the silk cocoons, and processing cocoons into raw silk by reeling and spinning.[9] As certain areas intensified stock raising, animals were fed all year in stables instead of being allowed to range freely in the summer—again creating more work for women. In fact, some historians see the late seventeenth and early eighteenth century as a period of the feminization of agriculture, especially in central Europe. In these areas, the demand for female agricultural workers grew faster than that for male workers, and the wives of artisans in many smaller towns were forced to raise food in nearby gardens or fields because the family's income from production was no longer able to support it.[10]

Though we often think of rural households as subsistence producers, they were actually part of a market economy in many parts of Europe as early as the fifteenth century. Serf men and women in eastern Europe produced grain that was exported to western Europe, though they did not control or profit from this trade. Rural women in western Europe did have some control over what they produced and sold. They made soap, butter, and cheese, gathered nuts, herbs, eggs, and manure, raised geese, rabbits, and chickens, and then sold these in market towns and cities to gain cash in order to fulfill their tax and rent obligations; unlike the sale of grain, which was restricted to harvest time, these products were sold year-round, making them a particularly important part of the household economy. Women thus served as an important human link between the rural and urban economies, with rural women traveling to town to sell their products or their labor, and urban women going out to the rural areas to buy products to sell or to work on parcels of land that were often still owned by their families.

Not every family in a village had access to enough land or animals to support itself; many of them also relied on the income of family members as agricultural workers or as artisans, and by the early seventeenth century some rural residents lived by labor alone. Both married and single women sheared sheep, picked hops and grapes, or performed other agricultural tasks. In most areas female agricultural laborers were paid less than men for the same work; traditionally female tasks, such as binding grain, earned less than tasks generally done by men, such as cutting grain with a scythe.[11] Women's wages appear to have been determined more by custom than by the market, for they fluctuated much less than men's both over the life cycle and with shifts in the economy; even during periods of rising wages, women's wages rose more slowly. Married women's wages were also less than those of widows for the same task, a wage structure based on the idea that married women needed less because they had a husband to support them, not on an evaluation of the quality of their work. The difference between male and female wages meant that in families with just a small plot of land women often did all of the agricultural work on the family plot, while men worked for wages on other people's land or in fishing or forestry. Such families had little money to invest in new tools, so women continued to use old hand tools like the spade and hoe rather than horse-drawn plows; women also favored such tools because they could start and stop work with them easily, and so combine fieldwork with care for children or animals.

Along with being hired for specific agricultural tasks, women, especially young women in their teens and twenties, were often employed in rural areas as domestic servants; their tasks were similar to those of their mistresses—care of animals, cooking, dairying, fieldwork. Young women and girls in silk growing areas were often hired in large groups to unwind silk cocoons, a tedious task for which they were paid very little. In mining areas they were hired to wash ore or prepare charcoal briquettes for smelting.[12] In Muscovy, where there was little wage labor, poor rural women sold themselves and occasionally their families (if they were heads of household) into slavery until the eighteenth century; about one-third of the slaves in Muscovy were women, with slaves making up about 10 percent of the population. Female slaves brought lower prices than male slaves, for male slaves were prized both for their managerial skills—that is, running estates for absentee landlords—as well as their physical strength. Female slaves generally worked at a variety of household tasks, and it appears that the Russian Orthodox prohibition of their being used for sexual purposes was generally effective. Women slaveholders were less common than women slaves, although slaves were often included in a wealthy woman's dowry and women bought, sold, and traded them in the same way they traded land.[13]

The impact of proto-industrial capitalism on women's work in rural areas was extremely varied. In areas of Europe where whole households were hired, domestic industry often broke down gender divisions, for men, women, and children who were old enough all worked at the same tasks. Domestic industry might even lead to role reversal, with women producing thread while, in the words of an eighteenth-century German observer, "men . . . cook, sweep and milk the cows, in order never to disturb the good, diligent wife in her work."[14] In other parts of Europe, however, proto-industrialization began in areas where there was a high level of seasonal unemployment, especially among women. In these areas, including parts of France, individual women, rather than whole households, were hired, with men continuing to work at agricultural tasks. In these areas there was no sharing of domestic duties or reversal of roles; since the men's tasks were more highly paid and generally away from the household, the women continued to do most domestic labor. Proto-industrialization in these areas did not lead to great improvements in women's status, for, though the wages women earned gave the family some disposable income, it was the men of the family who decided when and how that income could be spent, and often gathered in taverns and later in cafes to spend it.

WOMEN'S WORK IN URBAN AREAS: PRODUCTION

Because the towns and cities of Europe varied so widely in terms of size, economic base, and pattern of development during this period, it is perhaps more difficult to make generalizations about women's work in urban areas than in rural. Certain trends may be seen across much of Europe, however, though often with very different timing, particularly if occupations are organized by their function in the economy. We will thus look first at production, then at sales, and finally at service occupations.

The craft guilds that were established in many European cities varied widely in terms of structure and level of participation in urban government, but they treated women in remarkably similar ways. Craft guilds were, with the exception of a few female guilds in Cologne, Paris, and Basel, male organizations organized according to the male life cycle. A boy became an apprentice at puberty, became a journeyman four to ten years later, traveled around learning from a number of masters, settled down, married, and opened his own shop, and then worked in the same craft full-time until he died or became too old to work any longer. Because guild members recognized that a master could not run a shop on his own—there were journeymen and apprentices to feed and clothe, raw materials and tools to buy, merchandise to sell in the shop or at the public market—many guilds required that masters be married. Enterprising journeymen also recognized that the easiest way to acquire a shop complete with tools and customers was to marry a master's widow.

Though men dominated the guild structure, a large number of women could be found working in most guild shops. Besides the master's wife, his daughters and maids often worked alongside his journeymen and apprentices. Most workshops were small and were attached to the master craftsman's house so that women could easily divide their time between domestic duties and work in the shop. Households in urban areas were not self-sufficient; it was often more economical to purchase bread or finished clothing so that the women of the household could spend their time in craft production. The clothing and furnishings in all but the wealthiest houses in 1350 were few, simple, and rarely cleaned, so that there was relatively little of what we would call housework.

A woman's work in the craft guilds depended not on her own skill or level of training but on her relation to a guild master and her marital status. A guild master was free to employ his daughter however he wished in the workshop, and she could learn the trade alongside his apprentices. She did not receive any formal apprenticeship certificate, but her skills could make her a more attractive marriage partner. Upon marriage, she could become the most important woman in a workshop, a master's wife. Wives were often responsible for selling the merchandise their husbands made, collecting debts, and keeping the books. Wives as well as husbands were held responsible for the payment of fees and taxes and for the quality of the product; they continued to operate the shop in the absence of their husbands. The wife also distributed salaries and food to the journeymen and this occasionally brought her into conflict with them, for they might complain of being shortchanged and underfed.

After the master craftsman died, his widow confronted restrictions on what she could do, and these increased over time. Though the earliest guild ordinances (thirteenth century) made no mention of widows at all, and though widows ran shops for as much as fifteen or twenty years after the deaths of their husbands even in heavy industries such as iron making and roofing, by the mid-fifteenth century restrictions had begun. The length of time during which a widow could continue operating a shop was limited; she was forbidden to hire apprentices, journeymen, or pieceworkers, and in some cases could not keep the ones she had. This meant that widows' workshops were often so small that they could not produce enough to make a living. Tax records from many cities indicate that over two-thirds of widows were in the poorest income category.[15]

The restrictions on widows were followed by limitations on the work that female servants could do in the shop; even the number of his own daughters a master could employ was limited. Since women were not taught new processes of production like brewing, bleaching, and dyeing, or allowed to use new tools or machinery, such as frames for knitting stockings or ribbon looms, they could not work as fast or efficiently as men.

Because women's participation in guild shops was not guaranteed by guild regulations and ordinances, and because widows had no political voice in running the guilds, women as a group were not able to protect their right to work. Individual women, especially widows, often requested that they be allowed to work despite the restrictions, appealing to the city council or other municipal or parish authorities by stressing their poverty, old age, or number of dependent children while invoking the mercy and "Christian charity" of the authorities. The women who were successful were usually those who could make the most pitiful case. Though this accomplished what they wanted in the short run, in the long run it was harmful, since it reinforced the idea that women's work was temporary, small-scale, no threat to the larger producers, and essentially something to keep a family from starving. Thus authorities increasingly came to view women's work as a substitute for charity or a special privilege, whereas men's work was their right.

The timing of the restrictions on women's work in craft guilds varied from craft to craft, town to town, and country to country. Girls in England were formally apprenticed and then practiced independently in some trades well into the eighteenth century; by the early nineteenth century, however, female apprenticeship in England had also become limited to certain needle-work trades.[16] Since women were excluded from most guilds, state authorities sometimes set up separate guildlike structures especially for them, but still viewed these as charity. In Paris, Louis XIV and his economic advisor Colbert set up an all-female guild of dressmakers in 1675, noting that "this work was the only means that they had to earn their livelihood decently."[17]

Why was women's work in guild shops restricted? To some degree this was part of more general trends; as guilds felt threatened by capitalist pro-duction and other economic changes, they limited membership so as to assure members of a set share of the market for their products. They also attempted to make a distinction between work carried out in a workshop and that car-ried out in a domestic setting, claiming that their products were superior to those made through the putting-out system. Both of these trends worked against women, who were always somewhat marginal as guild members and whose work was always identified with the household.[18] Guilds increasingly regarded workshops and crafts that employed women as inferior, a sentiment made stronger by the increasing number of ceremonies and rituals though which male members bonded with one another.

This symbolic male bonding came exactly at the time that craft guilds in reality were becoming more splintered. When guilds restricted member-ship, journeymen who were not sons or other relatives of masters were often prohibited from opening their own shops; most became permanent wage workers rather than masters-in-training, and many formed separate journey-men's guilds. These journeymen's guilds were totally male in membership and vociferously opposed women's work in guild shops; their members refused to work next to any journeyman who had once worked in such a shop. As their own working conditions became more like those of women, that is, dependent on wages with little hope of advancement and under the control of someone else, journeymen viewed the maintenance of an all-male workplace as a key part of their honor.[19]

Along with guild honor, changing notions of bourgeois respectability and gentility increasingly kept women out of guild shops. By the seventeenth century, master's wives, who earlier had taken an active role in production, increasingly sought to emulate the wives of officials and professionals and concentrated on domestic tasks. More elaborate meals, clothing, and house-hold furnishings became a mark of bourgeois status, all purchased, prepared, and cared for by female family members. Many of these consumer goods came from beyond Europe as new food stuffs such as sugar, chocolate, tea and coffee, and new types of fabrics such as calico increased the range of products available to urban residents with even moderate incomes.[20] Occupations in which the married couple was still regarded as the unit of production and *wife* was still regarded as an occupational label were found only at the bottom of the social scale; the vilifed "fishwife" is a good example. By contrast, earlier, in 1350, even *furrier's wife* would have been considered an occupational label as well as a designation of marital status.

As the guilds restricted opportunities for female employment, women turned to crafts that the guilds had never regulated or to employment in the new capitalist industries. They produced cheap and simple items such as soap, candles, thimbles, brooms, brushes, needles and pins, combs, wooden bowls, and spoons. They often made these items as a secondary occupation after working in the fields surrounding the city or as laundresses or porters, or during winter when there was less agricultural or domestic work available. Because such products required little training, produced a meager income, and could be made by one woman acting alone, guilds and city authorities rarely objected. In fact, authorities often viewed such labor as preferable alternatives to poor relief, and encouraged women to work rather than rely on public or private charity. City and parish authorities often set up small endowments for poor girls to learn a trade or paid their apprenticeship fees in a guild that would still take them in. These opportunities narrowed in the course of the centuries, and by the eighteenth century most girls were learning such things as the making of hats or mantuas (ladies' loose robes, usually worn over other clothing); these trades were unregulated by guilds and were generally regarded as "genteel," because bourgeois ideas of respectability gradually filtered down to shape the work of even those needing public support.[21]

Domestic industry provided a significant source of employment for women in urban areas, particularly in cloth production. In some cities craft guilds controlled wool cloth production and gradually excluded women from most guilds of weavers, drapers, tailors, and cloth cutters. They generally allowed women to continue producing cheaper cloth made specifically for women's clothing, such as veils. Guilds in a few cities allowed only married women or widows to weave veils—an attempt to prevent unmarried women from living independently. In cities such as Florence, where weavers were not an independent guild but were hired by capitalist investors, women as well as men wove; in this setting weaving did not bring high status or financial prosperity.[22] This pattern was replicated beginning in the sixteenth century in linen production and in the eighteenth century in cotton; both rural and urban individuals or households were hired for proto-industrial production.

The initial stages of cloth production—carding the wool (to produce straight fibers), scutching the flax (to produce fibers for linen), and spinning thread—provided ever increasing employment for women. Early modern techniques of wool production—the most common type of cloth in Europe until the eighteenth century—necessitated at least twenty carders and spinners per weaver, whether he or she was an independent guild master or hired by a merchant investor. Each weaver got his or her thread from a variety of spinners. Some of it was spun by female servants who lived in the employer's household, some of it by pieceworkers who worked but did not live in the weaver's house, some of it by pieceworkers spinning in their own homes using wool provided by the weaver or investor, and some of it purchased at the public market from urban or rural spinners who bought their own wool.

Authorities regarded spinning as the perfect female occupation because it required little capital investment or training and could be easily worked around family responsibilities; it could be taken up and put down frequently with no harm done to the work. Women were expected to keep spinning when they were in jail for various crimes, after the rest of their household had been sold to pay off debts, or between customers if they were prostitutes. Poor law authorities in England opened spinstries for poor women, providing women too poor to spin with the needed equipment. Even wealthy or highly educated women were expected to spin; when a young woman who could speak and write Latin, Greek, and Hebrew was presented to James I of England, his first question was "But can she spin?" In Norwich, an 80-year old widow, "a lame woman of one hand," still spun with her good hand, and in Memmingen a suicidal woman was to be chained in her hospital bed "in a way that she can still spin." The Strasbourg city council was offered the prospect of a young woman "with no hands and only one foot, but who can still do all sorts of handwork "like spinning"; the man who found her wanted to show her to the public, and the council agreed, allowing him to charge a penny an onlooker.[23]

As more and more women turned to spinning, wages were held down because the field was overcrowded, a phenomenon economists have discovered in many female occupations in the twentieth century. Spinners could not support a family on their wages, or in some cases even support themselves; as a woman in Frankfurt said, "What little I make at spinning will not provide enough even for my bread."[24] The growth of the putting-out system offered urban and rural women more jobs, but jobs with low pay, little security, and low status.

WOMEN'S WORK IN URBAN AREAS: SALES

If spinning was the perfect employment for women in the minds of authorities, sales was one of the worst, for sales rewarded skills that were viewed as inappropriate in women—independence, verbal dexterity, initiative, and a forceful personality. The marketplace stood at the center of economic life within any early modern city. Whether goods came from far away or close to home, they were usually bought, sold, or traded at the market, often a large open square in front of the cathedral or major church. Women conducted most of the business that went on at this market; they handled almost all retail distribution of food, used clothing, household articles, and liquor— things that made up the major share of most families' discretionary budgets. In addition, the marketplace served as a gathering place for women, who were the majority of customers as well as vendors; men exchanged news, information, and opinions in taverns, while women did this at the marketplace, at church, and at neighborhood wells.

The sales sector of the early modern economy ranged across a wide spectrum in terms of wealth and prestige, from itinerant vendors and hawkers at the low end to major merchants with international trading networks at the top. Though the vast majority of merchants with international connections were men, a few women were able to take advantage of the opportunities offered—able, one might say, to capitalize on capitalism. Most of these were investors in the new trading companies, whose actions were limited to buying and selling shares, but a handful of women actively carried out trade themselves. Glickl bas Judah Leib, for example, better known as Glückl of Hameln, a Jewish merchant's widow, traveled to fairs and markets trading in diamonds, pearls, and gold. She commented in her autobiography, "My business prospered, I procured my wares from Holland, I bought nicely in Hamburg as well, and disposed of the goods in a store of my own. I never spared myself, summer and winter I was out on my travels, and I ran about the city the livelong day."[25]

Glickl was extremely unusual in the scope of her activities, for most women in sales, whether in 1350, 1550, or 1750, were retail distributors who sold from a basket they carried, a small stand at the marketplace, or a small shop bordering the market. They sold pretzels, nuts, wooden implements, firewood, herbs, sausage, candles, hot cooked foods, poultry, vegetables, beer, cider, brandy, and many other types of items; their trade in used clothing and other goods often led to small-scale moneylending and pawnbroking. City officials paid a great deal of attention to these women and what they sold, since they recognized the importance to their citizens of pure products, fair weights and measures, just prices and business practices, and legitimately obtained goods. In many cities they were registered, so that we know that women often predominated among market traders as far east as Poland.

Female vendors continually broke restrictions and ignored regulations. They raised prices, withheld produce from the market in order to force up the price, and forced customers to buy less desirable merchandise before they could buy what they wanted. They sold house to house rather than at the market, a practice authorities disliked because it was hard to control and provided a good opportunity for selling stolen merchandise.

One such vendor, a woman named Anna Weyland, appeared before the Strasbourg city council many times over a thirty-year period. She was first charged in 1573 with illegally selling herring, but she used an ongoing dispute between the city council and the fishers' guild to obtain the council's permission to continue selling. A short time later the fishers' guild complained that she refused to sell herring to people unless they also bought dried cod from her, and that she bought her herring outside the city instead of at the public fish market and then sold it below the established price. She got into the candle business the same year, and was immediately charged with selling candles for less than the official price, as well as with a number of other infractions of the candle ordinance. She answered she "would not obey any ordinance, no matter what in God's name the council made for an ordinance." If she spoke like that again the council threatened that she would be "pinched with glowing tongs and if she works (illegally) she will be thrown in the water."

Those threats apparently worked for a while, for she did not come before the council again for six years. At that point, she was charged with having candles that were underweight. Attempting to anticipate all possible excuses, the council ordered all her scales and weights to be checked secretly, and her candles to be bought "so that she [could] be caught in the act." Her scales and weights were found to be accurate, and the candles too light.

Both Anna and her husband were ordered to appear before the council, but she pleaded some kind of illness, and he appeared alone. Despite his pleading, the council ordered him to shut the shop. His wife was to do nothing, "neither buying or selling, changing money or anything else that has to do with the business" and was not even to let herself be found in the shop. He promised "by the grace of God" never to do anything wrong again. This time the promise lasted two years. In 1582 Anna Weyland was selling Dutch cheese illegally (she simply switched products whenever she was forbidden to sell something). The council sent out a representative to order her to stop or she would be banished. This was effective, for she never sold anything again and was forbidden to do so even twenty-three years later[26]

Their businesses may have been small, but market women such as Anna Weyland were far from helpless or reticent. Not only did they quickly bring anyone to court who they felt was intruding on their territory, but they were also very frequently involved in slander and defamation cases. They called other women and men names—*asshole, whore,* and *thief* were the most common—and then refused to apologize until the case had gone all the way to the city's highest court. Market women developed a strong work identity and described themselves first as "market women" rather than wives or widows; they often played a significant role in urban disturbances, from the iconoclastic riots associated with the Protestant Reformation to those associated with the French Revolution.

WOMEN'S WORK IN URBAN AREAS: SERVICES

The broad range of occupations that may be termed "services" provided the most opportunity for employment for women in the early modern period, as they do today. Part of the explanation for women's relative ease in finding employment in this area, whether in the sixteenth century or the twentieth, is that many of these occupations are considered stereotypically female or "natural" for women. They were and are often viewed as extensions of a woman's function and work in the home—cooking, cleaning, child care, nursing the sick, and caring for the elderly. Such occupations often required little or no specialized training, so women could start and stop frequently, work only when financially pressed, or work part-time if they had a family to care for. Because of this flexibility and fluidity, women working in the service sector were (and are) often underpaid and rarely organized. They seldom protested to get higher wages or salaries.

A large number of women worked in health care, both in institutions, such as hospitals, infirmaries, and orphanages, and as independent practitioners, such as midwives, wet-nurses, and healers. In the medieval period, hospitals, infirmaries, and orphanages were generally run by the Church, but beginning in the sixteenth century secular city governments, both Catholic and Protestant, took over their operations and often centralized all care in one major hospital.

These new institutions employed women in a variety of occupations, from administrative and medical to cooking and janitorial. The hospital mistress, or "keeper," as she was occasionally called, was responsible for the physical and spiritual needs of the hospital and patients. Like male employees, female hospital personnel, no matter what their position, had to swear an oath of loyalty to the city council and agree to follow all directives laid out for the day-to-day operation of the institution. City councils envisioned the hospital as a family that was led by the hospital mistress, who was to treat the patients "as a mother would her children" and do everything "that is appropriate for women to do." The women who assisted her—nurses, cooks, laundresses, and children's maids—were to treat each other as "true and loving sisters."[27] This family imagery meant that such women, even though they had a wide range of responsibilities, were not considered professionals but "family," and were therefore poorly paid, often receiving little more than board and room.

The city orphanages were modeled after the family as well, with a married couple in charge. The "orphan mother" taught the girls to spin, cook, and care for laundry; purchased food and clothing; oversaw servants; and took care of illnesses. She was responsible for the children's spiritual as well as material well-being and instructed them in prayer. Very young children were not admitted into orphanages but were given to wet-nurses living in the city or in the surrounding villages.

Wet-nurses were generally poor women whose own infant had died or who agreed to take on other infants in addition to their own. Most women nursed their own children, but upper-class women increasingly used the services of a wet-nurse so that they could resume their familial and social duties more quickly after the birth of a child. In wealthy households the wet-nurse became part of the household staff, though in most situations she took the infant into her own home. By the eighteenth century women engaged in production in some parts of Europe hired wet-nurses so they could work longer hours without stopping. By this point as well moralists like Rousseau decried wet-nursing as heartless, cruel, and deadly to infants, though we have no way of determining whether infant mortality rates were actually higher for children with wet-nurses than with their own mothers; for orphans and foundlings there was no other choice anyway.[28]

Whereas wet-nursing was generally a very low-status occupation, midwifery was one of the highest-status occupations for women throughout this period. At least until the mid-seventeenth century and until the twentieth in many parts of Europe, childbirth was strictly a female affair that was handled by a woman's relatives, neighbors, and friends and, beginning in the fourteenth century in urban areas, by specially trained midwives. Midwives learned their skill through apprenticeship. They accompanied experienced midwives to births for a period of years and then took an examination with questions ranging from how to handle a breech birth to proper diets for newborns. After passing the examination, the midwife took an oath and received a midwife's license. These oaths illustrate a wide variety of functions. Besides delivering babies, the midwife was to instruct new mothers in child care, perform emergency baptisms if she felt the child might die, and report all illegitimate children and try to discover the identity of the father "during the pains of birth."[29] She swore not to perform abortions, use implements to speed the birth, or repeat superstitions. City councils often called upon midwives to give opinions in legal cases of infanticide and abortion and to examine women charged with fornication or female prisoners who claimed to be pregnant in the hope of delaying their corporal punishment or execution. The midwives also participated in the municipal welfare system, handing out food and clothing to needy women and serving as medical assistants during epidemics. More than women in any other occupation, they defended their rights against outsiders. Their testimony in court shows a strong sense of work identity, for they always proudly note that they are midwives when appearing in court, making an appeal, or acting in any other legal or public capacity.

In the mid-seventeenth century, male medical practitioners began to become interested in childbirth, and "man-midwives" began to advertise their services, first in France and then in England. Gradually the training of these men improved as they took part in dissections and anatomical classes. Since women were excluded from these classes, they appeared more scientific and "modern" to middle- and upper-class English and French women, though there was still a strong sense among rural residents and lower-class urban dwellers that it was improper for male practitioners to actually touch women in childbirth; in any case, poorer households could not pay the fees demanded by male midwives. Male midwives were never accepted in the early modern period in Germany, nor in eastern and southern Europe, where female urban midwives were much more likely to be granted access to formal training in female anatomy and physiology than they were in France or England.[30] In northern Italy in particular, midwifery schools were founded in the mid-eighteenth century to teach women anatomy, though most midwives continued to be educated through apprenticeship.

One of the ways male midwives gained acceptance in northwest Europe was by portraying female midwives as bungling, slovenly, inept, and superstitious, a technique they learned from earlier moves against women in other types of medical practice. Until the late fifteenth century, women as well as men had been listed as physicians on the citizens' lists of many communities. From that time on, however, that title was increasingly given only to men who had received theoretical medical training at a university, a path that was closed to women. As physicians became more clearly "professional," barber-surgeons and apothecaries who had completed formal apprenticeship attempted to identify themselves as also somehow professional. They drew increasingly sharp lines between those who had received formal training and those who simply practiced on their own. Gradually, as these men convinced city and state governments to forbid "women and other untrained people" to practice medicine, female physicians and barber-surgeons disappeared from official records.[31] Some women received permission to handle minor external problems, like eye infections, skin diseases, and boils, if they promised to charge only small fees and not to advertise. Even this was too much for some barber-surgeons, who complained that the status of their profession was irreparably damaged if any women could perform the same operations they did. Some men hinted that the women's skills must be diabolical in origin, for God would certainly never bestow medical talents on a woman.

In most cities women could be found in several other service occupations—running small primary schools; overseeing charities; inspecting milk, grain, or vegetables; and serving as gatekeepers and toll collectors. Such positions were poorly paid, and city governments often rewarded needy widows with them to keep the women from depending on charity, much as they allowed poor women to bake pretzels or sew. In England, poor law authorities in the early eighteenth century paid poor women for laundering, assisting in childbirth, caring for the sick, preparing corpses for burial, and taking in lodgers; they even occasionally paid them to care for their own relatives.[32] Women worked alongside men as day laborers in construction and other types of heavy labor, often traveling to rural areas during harvest time, where, as we have seen, their wages for harvesting, picking grapes, or gleaning were set at one-half those of adult males.

In the later Middle Ages, all major cities had public baths. Here women served as bath attendants, washing the customers' hair and bodies, trimming nails, and beating their backs and legs with branches to improve circulation. During the sixteenth century, public baths went out of style, and respectable people no longer celebrated weddings, christenings, and business agreements with a group bath as they had in the Middle Ages. During the same period, because much of Europe was deforested to provide wood for ships and military equipment, the price of firewood rose, making baths too expensive for journeymen and wage laborers. In addition, the increasing concern with public morality and decorum led city councils to prohibit mixed-sex bathing; this, combined with higher prices, forced most public baths to close.

This same concern for public morality also led to a closing of municipal brothels in the sixteenth century. During the Middle Ages, most large cities and many smaller ones had opened one or more municipal brothels, had hired a brothel manager and prostitutes, and had passed regulations concerning the women and their customers.[33] Municipal authorities protected the women from violence and exploitation, and regarded prostitution as simply a necessary service for journeymen and out-of-town visitors. Such attitudes changed in the sixteenth century, as officials increasingly required prostitutes to wear distinctive clothing and prohibited them from appearing in public. Eventually the municipal brothels were closed.[34] Concern for "public decency" and the spread of syphilis was given as the reason for this action. Illicit prostitution continued, but the women involved were prosecuted rather than protected.

If we use the definition of "work" most familiar to us—a full-time position for which one is paid—domestic service was probably the largest single employer of women in most cities throughout the period. Between 15 and 30 percent of the population of most cities was made up of domestic servants; the larger commercial and manufacturing centers had a higher percentage of servants than the smaller cities, whose economies were more dependent upon agriculture.[35] During the High Middle Ages, many servants had been employed in noble households, and men as well as women cooked, served at the table, and did other domestic tasks; these were simply part of their duties as household retainers, regardless of gender. Gradually, servants' duties were increasingly specialized and divided by gender, with men and boys becoming responsible for the stables and grounds and women and girls for the kitchen and interior household. By the beginning of the early modern period, bourgeois urban households employed the majority of servants in urban areas; since such residences rarely had extensive grounds or stables, more women than men were hired for the indoor domestic tasks that had come to be seen as female; a count of servants in seventeenth-century Florence revealed that two-thirds of them were female.

Service offered young women a chance to earn small dowries that enabled them to marry. In fact, many maids were not paid at all until the end of a set period of service, with the understanding that their wages were specifically to provide a dowry. Service was thus part of the life cycle of many women in the same way that apprenticeship was for men. For other women, service became a career. These women might work their way up in large households from goose girl to children's maid to serving maid to cook. More typically, they remained with a family as its single servant for twenty, thirty, or forty years, doing highly varied tasks. Their wages were low, and inventories taken at the deaths of maids indicate that they usually owned no more than the clothes in which they were buried. Some servants in Europe were, in fact, slaves, purchased from Eastern Europe in Italian households or from northern and western Africa in Spanish and Portuguese ones. Occasionally such women accompanied their owners to the New World, for Spanish records mention both European and African slave women in the American colonies working as housekeepers and prostitutes.[36]

Servants in European artisan homes often spent most of their time in production and ate and slept with the family, for there was rarely enough space for them to have separate quarters. Even in middle- or upper-class households that did have many rooms, servants were rarely separated from their employers the way they would be in the nineteenth century, but lived on quite intimate terms with them.[37] Though they usually came from poor families, they identified in many way with their employers and tended to wear fancier clothing than other lower-class women. This upset bourgeois notions of the proper social order, and beginning in the sixteenth century many cities passed sumptuary laws, in essence urban dress codes that forbade servants to wear fine materials or jewels. Such laws were never very effective, for finer clothing was one of the ways in which servants tried to attract better marriage partners, a key purpose for deciding to go into service.

City officials also tried to regulate the conduct, salaries, and social activities of servants once they were hired. This meant admonishing servants not to leave positions without just cause, stay in public inns, or live independently between positions, and admonishing employers to control the sexuality of their servants.[38] Both male and female servants were regarded as potentially "masterless" persons, and those who tried to live on their own as day laborers could be banished. Servants were to remain dependents under the control of a preferably male head of a household. Wages were strictly limited, and servants in some areas were charged with causing inflation; the authorities in Stuttgart were horrified that "these servants now demand a salary along with room and board."[39]

As opportunities for women to work in other occupations decreased and as domestic tasks became feminized, opportunities in domestic service remained the same or increased, larger household staffs became more fashionable, and maids were used for industrial tasks such as spinning. Men were more free to move in search of employment and opportunities, including those to be found in Europe's new overseas empires, whereas women had to look closer to home. By the early eighteenth century, a greater percentage of the women who worked outside their own homes worked as servants in someone else's home.

CONCLUSION

One of the pioneers of women's history, Alice Clark, investigated the impact of capitalism on women's work almost eighty years ago. Though she saw this impact as negative, with high-status work in a household workshop replaced by low-status wage labor, she also commented that there were "obscure actions and reactions between capitalism and the position of women, worthy of more careful investigation."[40] Clark's call has been heeded in the last twenty years, though in many ways the results of this careful investigation of women's work have been a realization that the relationship between capitalism and the position of women is, if no longer obscure, at least more complex than Clark ever envisioned. As this essay shows, economic change did not affect all women equally or in similar ways. Women's experience varied according to social class, economic status, and geographic region—factors that have traditionally been taken into account when examining men's experience of economic change—and it also varied according to age, marital status, family size, and life span.

If variety is one of the hallmarks of women's work experience during this period, continuity is another. Most women and men in Europe during these four centuries continued to work in agriculture, for at least three-quarters—and in some areas more like 95 percent—of the population remained in the countryside. Even in the cities, much of the economy was still precapitalist, and many occupations, such as domestic service and selling at the public market, changed very little during the period. In addition, dramatic changes in the structure and organization of institutions and industries may also not have been evident to the low-skilled women working in them. Women remained in low-status positions because they often fit their work around the life cycle of their families, moving in and out of various jobs as children were born and grew up or as their husbands died and they remarried. Work for many women during this period was a matter of makeshifts and expedients, a pattern which some historians see continuing until today with only minor alterations.[41]

Despite wide variety and strong continuities, however, there are a few generalizations we can make about changes in the work of many women in Europe during this period. Occupations that required university education or formal training were closed to women. Women rarely controlled enough financial resources to enter occupations that required large initial capital out-lay, and social norms kept them from occupations with political functions. Family responsibilities prevented them from entering occupations that required extensive traveling. These attributes of women's work were true both in 1350 and in 1750, but over these four centuries their meaning changed, for it was exactly those with formal education, political functions, capital investment, or international connections, such as physicians, merchants, bankers, lawyers, government officials, and overseas traders, who were gaining in wealth, power, and prestige.

Indeed, it is in the meaning of work that we can see the most change during this period. Women's productive tasks were increasingly defined as reproductive—as housekeeping—or as assisting—or helping out. Thus a woman who sewed clothes, took in boarders, did laundry, and gathered herbs for pay was increasingly thought of as a housewife, a title that became enshrined in statistical language by the nineteenth century, when her activities were no longer regarded as contributing to the gross national product or relevant to other sorts of economic measurements.[42]

This gender division between production and reproduction was reinforced in the early modern period by parish, city, and state governments, which often allowed women to support themselves and their families with various tasks because these were not really "work," but simply "support." This even included allowing women to sell items that they had produced. Women themselves sometimes adopted the same rhetoric, for they knew that arguing that they had a right to work would be much less effective than describing the children they had to support or how much public money might otherwise be spent if they did not work.

And work women did. A recent study of the London labor market has found that 72 percent of women in 1700 were doing full- or part-time paid work outside the home, most of it low-status work.[43] Historians have posited many reasons for the dramatic development of the European economy and for European expansion around the world. Recently an "Industrious Revolution" has been added to these factors; Europeans are seen as reducing their leisure time and working more in order to have money to purchase consumer goods from around the world.[44] This Industrious Revolution not only involved women; it required their labor. Though it may have been conceptualized as assisting or supporting, women's work provided an enormous pool of labor, in the same way that women and children in developing countries provide the mass of labor for the global market today.

NOTES

1. E. A. Wrigley and R. S. Schofield, *The Population History of England, 1541–1871*, Harvard University Press, Cambridge, 1981; Michael Flinn, *The European Demographic System*, Johns Hopkins, Baltimore, 1981.

2. The statistic from York is from P. J. P. Goldberg, *Women, Work and Life Cycle in a Medieval Economy: Women in York and Yorkshire c. 1300–1520*, Clarendon Press, Oxford, 1992, p. 329. Information on other cities may be found in Barbara Diefendorf, "Widowhood and Remarriage in Sixteenth-Century Paris," *Journal of Family History* 9, no. 2 (Winter 1982), p. 380; Grethe Jacobsen, "Women's Work and Women's Role: Ideology and Reality in Danish Urban Society, 1300–1550,"*Scandinavian Economic History Review* 31, no. 1 (1983), p. 15; Diane Willen, "Guildwomen in the City of York, 1560–1700," *The Historian* 46, no. 2 (February 1984), p. 206; and Mary Prior, "Women and the Urban Economy: Oxford 1500–1800," in *Women in English Society*, ed. Mary Prior, Methuen, London, 1985, p. 105. For details on the lives of unmarried women, see Judith M. Bennett and Amy M. Froide, eds., *Singlewomen in the European Past*, University of Pennsylvania Press, Philadelphia, forthcoming.

3. David Herlihy and Christiane Klapisch-Zuber, *Tuscans and Their Families: A Study of the Florentine Catasto of 1427*, Yale University Press, New Haven, 1985, p. 88.

4. John K. Yost, "Changing Attitudes Towards Married Life in Civic and Christian Humanism," *Occasional Papers of the American Society for Reformation Research* 1 (1977), pp. 151–166.

5. See, for example, Ava Baron, "Questions of Gender: Deskilling and Demasculinatization in the U.S. Printing Industry, 1830–1915," *Gender and History* 1 (1989), pp. 178–199.

6. Merry E. Wiesner, *Working Women in Renaissance Germany*, Rutgers University Press, New Brunswick, N.J., 1986, p. 181. (Many of the quotations and examples that come from Germany are from unprinted archival sources; the specific references may be found on the pages listed here.)

7. My thanks to Phyllis Holman Weisbard, the women's studies librarian for the University of Wisconsin System, and her staff for pointing this out to me.

8. Michael Roberts, "Sickles and Scythes: Women's Work and Men's Work at Harvest Time," *History Workshop Journal* 7 (1979), pp. 3–29; Brit Berggren, "The Female Peasant and the Male Peasant: Division of Labour in Traditional Norway," *Ethnologia Scandinavica* 11 (1984), pp. 66–78.

9. Judith Brown," A Woman's Place Was in the Home: Women's Work in Renaissance Tuscany," in *Rewriting the Renaissance: The Discourses of Sexual Difference in Early Modern Europe*, ed. M. W. Ferguson, M. Quilligan, and N. Vickers, University of Chicago Press, Chicago, 1986, pp. 206–224.

10. Heide Wunder, *"Er ist die Sonn', sie ist der Mond": Frauen in der Frühen Neuzeit*, C. H. Beck, Munich, 1992, pp. 90–95. (This book will soon appear in an English-language edition from Harvard University Press.)

11. Wiesner, *op. cit.*, pp. 92–93; Chris Middleton, "The Familiar Fate of the *Famulae*: Gender Divisions in the History of Wage Labour," in *On Work* ed. R. E. Pahl, Basil Blackwell, Oxford, 1988, pp. 21–46; Pamela Sharpe, *Adapting to Capitalism: Working Women in the English Economy 1700–1850*, St. Martin's, New York, 1996, pp. 71–100.

12. Susan C. Karant-Nunn, "The Women of the Saxon Silver Mines," in *Women in Reformation and Counter-Reformation Europe: Public and Private Worlds*, ed. Sherrin Marshall, Indiana University Press, Bloomington, 1989, pp. 29–46.

13. Richard Hellie, "Women and Slavery in Muscovy," *Russian History* 10 (1983), pp. 213–229.

14. Quoted in Hans Medick, "The Proto-industrial Family Economy: The Structural Function of Household and Family During the Transition from Peasant Society to Industrial Capitalism," *Social History* 1 (1976), p. 312.

15. Same references as note 2.

16. Keith Snell, *Annals of the Labouring Poor*, Cambridge University Press, Cambridge, 1985.

17. French royal statutes, 1675, quoted in Cynthia M. Truant, "The Guildswomen of the City of Paris: Gender, Power and Sociability in the Old Regime," *Proceedings of the Annual Meeting of the Western Society for French History* 165 (1988), p. 131.

18. Jean H. Quataert, "The Shaping of Women's Work in Manufacturing: Guilds, Households, and the State in Central Europe, 1648–1870," *American Historical Review* 90, no. 5 (December 1985), pp. 1122–1148.

19. Merry E. Wiesner, "Guilds, Male Bonding and Women's Work in Early Modern Germany," *Gender and History* 1 (1989), pp. 125–137.

20. The literature on consumers is vast, particularly for the period from the late seventeenth through the eighteenth centuries, and much of it discusses the role of women as consumers. See Carole Shammas, *The Pre-industrial Consumer in England and America*, Clarendon, Oxford, 1990; John Brewer and Roy Porter, *Consumption and the World of Goods*, Routledge, London, 1993.

21. Snell, *op cit.*, Sharpe, *op. cit.*, pp. 38–70.

22. Judith Brown and Jordan Goodman, "Women and Industry in Florence," *Journal of Economic History* 40 (1980), pp. 73–80.

23. Quoted in Patricia Crawford, "Women's Published Writings, 1600–1700," in Prior, ed., *op cit.*, p. 215; unpublished article by Diane Willen, "Women and Poor Relief in Pre-industrial Norwich and York"; Wiesner, *op. cit.*, p. 182.
24. Wiesner, *op. cit.*, p. 184; Alice Clark, *Working Life of Women in the Seventeenth Century*, Routledge and Kegan Paul, London, 1919, p. 9; Donald Woodward, "Wage Rates and Living Standards in Pre-Industrial England," *Past and Present* 91 (May 1981), p. 39.
25. *The Memoirs of Glückel of Hameln*, tr. Marvin Loewenthal, Schocken, New York, 1977, p. 179. Natalie Zemon Davis has recently published an extended analysis of Glickl's life and writings, *Women on the Margins: Three Seventeenth-Century Lives*, Harvard University Press, Cambridge, 1995.
26. Wiesner, *op. cit.*, pp. 124–126.
27. *Ibid.*, pp. 40–41.
28. George Sussman, *Selling Mother's Milk: The Wet-nursing Business in France, 1715–1914*, University of Illinois Press, Urbana, 1982; Valerie Fildes, *Breasts, Bottles and Babies: A History of Infant Feeding*, Edinburgh University Press, Edinburgh, 1986.
29. Wiesner, *op. cit.*, p. 63.
30. Hilary Marland, *The Art of Midwifery: Early Modern Midwives in Europe*, Routledge and Kegan Paul, London, 1993.
31. This process in Germany is described in Wiesner, *op. cit.*, p. 50.
32. Pamela Sharpe, "Literally Spinsters: A New Interpretation of Local Economy and Demography in Colyton in the Seventeenth and Eighteenth Centuries," *Economic History Review*, 44, no. 1 (1991), p. 61.
33. Leah Lydia Otis, *Prostitution and Medieval Society: The History of an Urban Institution in Languedoc*, University of Chicago Press, Chicago, 1985; Ruth Karras, *Common Women: Prostitution and Society in Medieval England*, Oxford University Press, Oxford, 1996.
34. Lyndal Roper, "Discipline and Respectability: Prostitution and the Reformation in Augsburg," *History Workshop* 19 (Spring 1985), pp. 3–28; Stanley D. Nash, *Prostitution in Great Britain, 1485–1901* Scarecrow Press, Metucken, N.J., 1994; Beata Schuster, *Die freien Frauen: Dirnen und Frauenhäuser im 15. und 16. Jahrhundert*, Campus, Frankfurt, 1995.
35. J. Jean Hecht, *The Domestic Servant Class in Eighteenth-Century England*, Routledge and Kegan Paul, London, 1956, pp. 33, 34; Brown, *op. cit.*, Renate Dürr, *Mägde in der Stadt: Das Beispiel Schwäbisch Hall in der Frühen Neuzeit*, Campus, Frankfurt, 1995.
36. Ann M. Pescatello, *Power and Pawn: The Female in Iberian Families, Societies, and Cultures*, Greenwood, Westport, Conn., 1976, p. 141.
37. Sara Maza, *Servants and Masters in Eighteenth-Century France*, Princeton University Press, Princeton, 1983; Cissie Fairchilds, *Domestic Enemies: Servants and Their Masters in Old Regime France*, Johns Hopkins University Press, Baltimore, 1984. For a discussion of the dangers posed by servants (as well as spouses and children) in literature, see Frances E. Dolan, *Dangerous Familiars: Representations of Domestic Crime in England, 1550–1700* Cornell University Press, Ithaca, 1994.
38. Isabel V. Hull, *Sexuality, State and Civil Society in Germany, 1700–1815*, Cornell University Press, Ithaca, 1996, p. 35.
39. Wiesner, *op. cit.*, p. 88.

40. Alice Clark, *Working Life of Women in the Seventeenth Century*, Routledge and Kegan Paul, London, 1919, rpt. 1992, p. 98. Clark's book has seen three recent reprints, in 1968, 1982, and 1992, a clear indication of its continuing importance. The 1992 edition contains an extensive introduction by Amy Louise Erickson discussing Clark's life and ideas and surveying recent scholarship on women's work.

41. Olwen Hufton, "Women, Work, and Family," in *A History of Women in the West*. Vol. 3: *Renaissance and Enlightenment Paradoxes*, ed. N. Z. Davis and A. Farge, Harvard University Press, Cambridge, 1993, pp. 15–45. On the issue of continuity versus change in women's history more generally, see the recent interchange between Bridget Hill and Judith Bennett, "Women's History: A Study in Change, Continuity or Standing Still?" *Women's History Review* 2 (1993), pp. 5–22 and 173–184.

42. Marilyn Waring, *If Women Counted: A New Feminist Economics*, San Francisco: Harper and Row 1988.

43. Peter Earle, "The Female Labour Market in London in the Late 17th and Early 18th Centuries," *Economic History Review* 42 (1989), p. 338.

44. Jan de Vries, "The Industrial Revolution and the Industrious Revolution," *Journal of Economic History* 54 (1994), pp. 249–270.

SUGGESTIONS FOR FURTHER READING

The following discussion includes only works not mentioned in the notes and gives only a small sample of the books and articles available. The best recent bibliography of works in English, especially those focusing on England, is in the 1992 edition of Alice Clark listed in note 40; my *Women and Gender in Early Modern Europe* (Cambridge: Cambridge University Press, 1993) also has a long bibliographic essay on women's economic role.

There are a number of collections of articles that focus specifically on women's work: Barbara Hanawalt, ed., *Women and Work in Preindustrial Europe* (Bloomington: Indiana University Press, 1982); Lindsey Charles and Lorna Duffin, eds., *Women and Work in Pre-Industrial England* (London: Croom Helm, 1985); Pat Hudson and W. R. Lee, eds., *Women's Work and the Family Economy in Historical Perspective* (Manchester: Manchester University Press, 1990); and Daryl Hafter, ed., *European Women and Preindustrial Craft* (Bloomington: Indiana University Press, 1995). Articles that focus on specific aspects of women's work include Maxine Berg, "Women's Work, Mechanization, and the Early Phases of Industrialization," in *On Work: Historical and Theoretical Approaches*, ed. R. E. Pahl (Oxford: Basil Blackwell, 1988), pp. 61–94; and Maryanne Kowaleski and Judith M. Bennett, "Crafts, Guilds and Women in the Middle Ages: Fifty Years after Marian K. Dale," *Signs* 14 (1989), pp. 474–488.

Book-length studies generally explore one geographic area; they include Judith Bennett, *Ale, Beer, and Brewsters in England: Women's Work in a Changing World, 1300–1600* (New York: Oxford University Press, 1996); Martha Howell, *Women, Production and Patriarchy in Late Medieval Cities* (Chicago: University of Chicago Press, 1986); Bridget Hill, *Women, Work and Sexual Politics in Eighteenth-Century England* (Oxford: Basil Blackwell, 1989); and Elizabeth C. Sanderson, *Women and Work in*

Eighteenth-Century Edinburgh (New York: St. Martin's, 1996). Two works that range more widely across Europe and present synthetic overviews are David Herlihy, *Opera Muliebria: Women and Work in Medieval Europe* (New York: McGraw-Hill, 1990); and Louise A. Tilly and Joan W. Scott, *Women, Work and Family* , 2nd. ed. (New York: Metheun, 1987).

Women's work has also been considered in recent broader discussions of women's lives during this period, including Rosalind K. Marshall, *Virgins and Viragos: A History of Women in Scotland from 1080 to 1980* (London: Collins, 1983); Mary Elizabeth Perry, *Gender and Disorder in Early Modern Seville* (Princeton: Princeton University Press, 1990); and Olwen Hufton, *The Prospect Before Her: A History of Women in Western Europe.* Vol. 1: *1500–1800* (London: HarperCollins, 1996).

Works that discuss work more generally and include considerations of women and the gender division of labor include Ann Kussmaul, *Servants in Husbandry in Early Modern England* (Cambridge: Cambridge University Press, 1981); David Sabean, *Property, Production and Family in Neckarhausen, 1700–1870* (Cambridge: Cambridge University Press, 1990); and Sheilagh Ogilvie and Markus Cerman, *European Proto-industrialization* (Cambridge: Cambridge University Press, 1996).

"At the Sign of Minerva," by Léonard Defrance (1735–1805). A young woman is shown reading in the doorway of a bookseller's shop. Defrance puts on the walls of the shop posters announcing works of French Enlightenment writers. Prominent too is the edict of religious toleration issued by Joseph II, Hapsburg emperor and ruler over this territory. Bundles of books piled up in front of the shop suggest how the works of the philosophes, written in Catholic France, were published in the protestant Low Countries and shipped out to areas of Catholic Europe under more repressive regimes (Spain, Portugal, Rome) in order to spread Enlightenment. Off to one side, Christian clerics of various denominations converse civilly and even shake hands. The female reader at the center of the painting embodies Enlightened readership, but she is also the center of voyeuristic attention—as the men to either side eye her. What exactly is the message here for women?   MUSÉE DES BEAUX-ARTS, DIJON.

CHAPTER **9**

Women and the Enlightenment

Dena Goodman

As the Enlightenment's legacy in today's world is debated, historians are asking new questions about the part women played in the Enlightenment and how it shaped their lives: What was the contribution of women to the Enlightenment? How did they participate in and shape the cultural institutions and practices associated with it? What was the impact of Enlightenment ideas on women's role and status in society? How did the languages of reason, rights, and difference that emerged from the Enlightenment contribute to the ideological formation of feminism that emerged in the French Revolution and has continued to develop and change to this day?

Rather than looking at the Enlightenment simply as a set of ideas or political slogans that supported the rise of Western liberalism and democracy, Dena Goodman asks us to view the Enlightenment as both a culture and a project in which modernity took shape. As a culture, it was centered in institutions of sociability—voluntary associations that brought women and men out of families, villages, and traditional relations and into urban communities of like-minded people joined by common values and dedicated to common purposes. As a project, it brought these men and women together to challenge the traditional institutions of church, state, and family and work for social reform and improvement.

In Paris in particular, women who welcomed men of letters into their homes in regular gathering places now known as salons played a significant role in shaping a critical discourse of Enlightenment. There and in the burgeoning world of print, two competing interpretations of gender relations inherited from the seventeenth century shaped Enlightenment discourse: writers both embraced the notion of common sense that demonstrated the fundamental equality of women and men and developed their belief in equally fundamental differences between men and women upon which a well-ordered society was based. These two often conflicting discourses shaped an understanding, not only of gender relations in modern society, but of history and the relationship of a "civilized" Europe to the rest of the world.

If some urban women could participate fully in the enlightened sociability of the age, others contributed to the Enlightenment as writers, and many more

233

were brought into it as readers—both inside and outside the pages of books. In the second part of this chapter, Goodman analyzes major works of the Enlightenment, both male- and female-authored, to suggest both the implications and limitations of Enlightenment criticism for women. And although she concludes that the Enlightenment's legacy for women was an ambiguous one, she sees emerging from the literate, urban woman of the eighteenth century the modern woman we know today.

Since the nineteenth century, the history of Western Civilization has generally been represented either as a struggle between reason and religion or as the inexorable progress of reason and liberty. The intellectual and cultural phenomenon known as the Enlightenment is identified as the turning point in this history. For much of this century the Enlightenment was uncritically accepted by historians and the general public alike as the basis of American political and cultural values. The Declaration of Independence, which proclaimed the belief of the Founding Fathers "that all Men are created equal, that they are endowed by their Creator with certain unalienable Rights, that among these are Life, Liberty, and the Pursuit of Happiness," was considered by most Americans to epitomize the values of the Enlightenment as they were realized in the American Revolution. Beyond the United States, the Enlightenment came to stand for the rationalist mode of explanation that had supplanted the fundamentally religious worldview of the Middle Ages; it came to stand for modernity itself. The modern world that the Enlightenment ushered in—with its greater political liberties and participation, secular culture, and the technological wonders that produced increasingly greater prosperity for all—was the Enlightenment's legacy and its great gift to the rest of the world, which in time would come to share its benefits.

Today, many historians and philosophers look at the modern world with a jaundiced eye and at the Enlightenment with skepticism, if not outright horror. Modern democracy has been countered with modern totalitarianism, secular culture with a loss of faith and spiritual values, and technology's greatest triumph is a war machine of unparalleled destructiveness. In the view of its critics, the Enlightenment legacy is the Holocaust, the atom bomb, and the global ecological disaster to which technology inexorably drives us. Its "gifts" are the political colonialism and cultural imperialism under which subject peoples across the globe continue to suffer. As if that were not enough, feminist scholars have reminded us not only that the fundamental rights declared by the American Founding Fathers and their brothers in revolutionary France were not extended to the sister citizens, but that the universalism of the Enlightenment's claims effaces women in their particularity, demanding that to be a citizen means to be a man—that to be human, in effect, requires denying or discarding one's feminine identity.

To inquire into the question of the relationship of women to the Enlightenment is thus to open a can of very lively worms! Rather than jumping headfirst into the debate about whether the Enlightenment was good for women—or whether it was a good thing at all—I suggest we step back and look at the Enlightenment not simply as a few slogans cast into the political arena of the last decades of the eighteenth century, but as a culture and a project: a set of social and intellectual practices and institutions based on a common set of values that drew together and shaped an expanding group of men and women and gave them a common sense of purpose. Instead of asking what the Enlightenment did for women (or to them), we can ask how women participated in the Enlightenment, how their participation was understood, and how it was circumscribed. We can look at how women were represented and understood by men, but also at how women intervened in and contributed to the conversation that constituted the Enlightenment. For the best way to understand the Enlightenment is as a conversation to whose success women were indispensable.

THE CULTURE OF ENLIGHTENMENT

The Enlightenment was marked by the development of a wide range of voluntary associations in which women and men could meet together on a regular basis to discuss ideas, share their own literary productions, and embark together on projects of social improvement. In cities across Europe and the Americas, the eighteenth-century reading public experienced the pleasures of conversation: both the thrill of encountering and discussing new and daring ideas and the new dignity of being considered by others an equal by virtue of one's ability to read, reason, and converse. In a world whose traditional social structures were hierarchical and patriarchal, in which birth still largely determined social status, marriage prospects, and economic opportunity, men and women created new institutions of sociability in which they established new bonds on the basis of shared tastes, interests, and values. These institutions not only provided new pleasures and the opportunity to interact with a wide range of people; they also established a social basis for the critique of family, church, and state that characterized Enlightenment thought.

Urban Society and Sociability

London was known for its coffeehouses, patronized mostly if not entirely by men, and for the gentlemen's clubs that often met in the upper rooms of the coffeehouses. But men and women also met together around tea tables in the homes of English women. One group of women who were associated with the intellectual life of the tea table became famous as the "bluestocking circle"—a name that arose from a joke about the unfashionable hose worn by one of their male friends, but which eventually was used to refer to the women themselves. They were the wives and daughters of the middle class, privately educated for the most part and dedicated to continuing their education through intelligent conversation. Many were writers. Elizabeth Montagu, the first of the "blues," was the author of an *Essay on the Writings and Genius of Shakespeare* (1769); Hannah More (1745–1833) contributed to the cause of female education by establishing with her sisters schools for the poor and by writing books such as *Strictures on the Modern System of Female Education* (1779). Mary Wollstonecraft, whose *A Vindication of the Rights of Woman* (1792) is considered to be the founding text of modern rights-based feminism, both inherited the bluestocking concern for female education and went beyond the limits of bluestocking respectability by pursuing the political implications of their moral and educational philosophy.

In English cities such as Liverpool and Manchester, whose rapid economic and population growth was spurred by the Industrial Revolution, as well as in port cities such as Bristol that served the booming colonial trade, women joined voluntary associations such as reading clubs, circulating libraries, and charitable organizations. Reading societies brought together members of the local elite who pooled their resources to form libraries and set aside rooms and times for reading and discussion. By the end of the century reading societies were an established feature of the urban landscape in towns throughout Europe. In them, some women were able to expand their horizons beyond the meager intellectual offerings of the home.

In the eighteenth century Paris was a magnet to which those who sought to join the community of the Enlightenment were drawn, and when they got there they sought entrance into one of the salons in which men of letters met to exchange ideas. The Enlightenment salon was a weekly or daily gathering of writers known as "philosophes" and those who wished to associate with them in the home and under the guidance of a hostess or "salonnière." Salon conversation drew upon recently published books, poems, and pamphlets, high-profile trials, and the latest theatrical productions. Writers shared their own works in progress, and letters received from friends and colleagues abroad were read aloud.

The salon was not simply a gathering of men of letters. The project of Enlightenment required that people passionately committed to the truth learn to engage with each other critically and still remain friends. Salonnières used the rules of polite conversation to control the egos and the discourse of men of letters committed to cooperation in the interests of humanity. Marie-Thérèse Geoffrin (1699–1777), Julie de Lespinasse (1732–1776), Suzanne Necker (1739–1794), and other salonnières kept Enlightenment discourse civil; at the same time they engineered their own education in the most progressive thought of their day.

The salons contributed to Paris's reputation as the center of the Enlightenment, despite the fact that many of its most famous books were published in the Netherlands to avoid French censorship. Visitors such as the Neopolitan abbé Galiani, the American Thomas Jefferson, and Stanislas Poniatowski, king of Poland, tried to recreate their Parisian experience through the establishment of "salons" that would spread the Enlightenment to their shadowy corners of the world. Unfortunately, none of these men could find women to "Geoffrinise" them, to use Galiani's rueful term. Without the skilled and dedicated salonnière, polite conversation was impossible and the cooperation that depended on it failed.

The Enlightenment salon was, however, an ambiguous development in the history of women's participation in intellectual life. Although those women who rose to prominence as salonnières acquired dignity, respect, and authority based on their skills and their contribution to a common endeavor, their role was limited to the governance of male conversation. Women enabled men to do their work, but their own voices were largely absent. Why women were assigned (and accepted) the limited role of salonnière can best be understood with reference to seventeenth-century developments in the ongoing debate on "The Woman Question."

The Woman Question

The debate on "The Woman Question" reemerged in the seventeenth century in the salons of Paris, where it was at the center of discussions about society itself and the values on which it stood. The question of woman's nature and of the role and status of women in society was central to the salon for several reasons—not least of which was the fact that women were the hostesses who invited guests into their homes and took charge of the activities in which they engaged. Moreover, in the salon and the handbooks on civility associated with them, women were held up as models for men to emulate. This gave women an authority in the salon that called into question their traditional subordination to men in the world outside the salon. In addition, the salon was both a modern institution and a feminine space. Those who became champions of the salons and the modern values they stood for found themselves also arguing both for the intellectual equality of women with men and for the importance of women in creating a culture in which merit triumphed over birth and men of letters triumphed over men of war. Against the martial values of the ancients and the Middle Ages, they advocated peace and harmony—the values of society over the values of the state.

Two modern ways of thinking about gender relations shaped the debate on the Woman Question in the salons and continue to shape it to this day: the philosophy of René Descartes (1596–1650), who argued for the basis of human identity in a mind freed from the body, and Neo-Platonic thinking, in which men and women were viewed as complementary, that is, as equally necessary for the functioning of society and as equally incomplete without the other.

René Descartes's radical theory of knowledge or epistemology shaped both the Enlightenment and the debate on women. Descartes's approach was to subject all received opinion to methodical doubt, and, having leveled the edifice of knowledge, to build anew on what he considered a more sure foundation: that which could be known by human reason. For women, two important implications followed from Descartes's philosophy: (1) reason is defined as common sense, as a capacity common to all human beings; and (2) reason operates independently of the body—the human being is constituted by reason alone ("I think, therefore I am," as Descartes famously wrote).

In *On the Equality of the Two Sexes* (1673; first English translation 1677), François Poulain de la Barre broke new ground by subjecting the accumulated "knowledge" about women to the same methodical doubt as Descartes had science and philosophy in general. "We are filled with prejudice, and . . . we must renounce it absolutely if we are to have clear and definite knowledge," he wrote.[1] Whereas previous writers had searched the literary and historical record for examples of female virtue, heroism, and literary and scientific achievement, Poulain posited as a starting point the equal capacity of men and women to reason and the irrelevance of differences between male and female bodies to this capacity. The equality of men and women was grounded in the commonality of the reasoning faculty; the historical oppression of women could be explained only by the subordination of reason to force. The triumph of reason would mean the beginning of equality between the sexes.

Poulain's path-breaking pamphlet, written during the heydey of the aristocratic salons, continued to shape the debate on women throughout the eighteenth century in such works as Philippe Florent de Puisicux's *Woman Is Not Inferior to Man* (1750) and Dom Philippe-Joseph Caffiaux's *Defenses of the Fair Sex* (1753). At the same time as this "Cartesian" gender ideology was being elaborated, a second position was being worked out that harked back to the Greek philosopher Plato. Instead of building a notion of the social whole from the combination of discrete, autonomous (reasoning) individuals, this Neo-Platonic theory of gender complementarity held that human beings are by their nature social and sociable, and that only in coming together do they achieve their humanity. Here language, as the means of communication and the basis of society, distinguishes human beings from the beasts.

Rather than focusing on the common ability of men and women to reason, complementary thinkers pointed to the different contributions of men and women to society and history based on their different roles and abilities and emphasized the equal value of these contributions to the progress of civilization. Significantly, their explanation of the historical oppression of women was remarkably similar to that of Poulain and the Cartesians: in the beginning men's brute force had allowed them to dominate women, but over time the civilizing force of women had gradually increased, functioning as a counterweight to male brutality. The triumph of reason would negate men's unwarranted power and lead to a harmonious and peaceful existence in which neither sex dominated the other but each had its own role to play based on its particular nature.

Eighteenth-century philosophes tended to endorse the Cartesian view of common sense, but they also increasingly adopted the complementary view in which men and women were in other important ways different. Rather than contemplating the attributes and rights of the individual, they tended to focus on society as a whole and the different but important roles that men and women had to play in it, both to keep it functioning and as the basis of progress. Indeed, they tended to embrace a philosophy of history in which women played a central role in bringing about a new era of peace, civilization, and "light" after centuries of warfare, barbarism, and "darkness."

From "Barbarous" Martial Middle Ages to "Civilized" Peaceful Modernity

The men and women of the Enlightenment saw themselves as emerging from long, dark centuries of barbarism into a new world of light and reason, a world "civilized" by women and energized by global commerce and trade. A philosophy of history was sketched out by writers such as John Robertson in Scotland, the Marquis de Condorcet in France, and Immanuel Kant in Germany that painted the Middle Ages as barbaric because they were under the rule of force where "might makes right." By contrast, these eighteenth-century writers saw their own societies as just, rational, and civilized to the degree that the rule of law had replaced the law of conquest, where the state saw its mission to protect rather than oppress the weak—or at least to balance the conflicting interests of weak and strong into a harmonious whole. Europe, they believed, was moving ahead toward peace and prosperity after two centuries of religious conflict. The Enlightenment philosophy of history pointed in particular to the rise of commerce and trade as key to these developments, because the social relationships established by trade—like those established by polite conversation—were reciprocal, binding individuals and nations together in a new way that challenged the vertical relations of dominance and deference that defined traditional society.

Over the course of the eighteenth century, Europeans bought goods as never before. They were especially attracted to the new riches streaming in from Europe's colonies: cotton from India and America, coffee and tea from Asia and South America, sugar from the Caribbean, porcelains and lacquerware from China and Japan. No longer was consumption an activity restricted to the aristocrats who sought to display their power through displays of wealth. No longer were goods acquired primarily to increase one's estate, to amass and endow. In the eighteenth century well-to-do families furnished their homes in the latest styles, known to them through magazines and displays in fashionable shops. By the end of the century, middle-class women met around tea tables of exotic woods furnished with Chinese tea sets, and even servants and salesgirls bought new hats and ribbons and dresses in the latest fashion.

According to the Enlightenment philosophy of history, commerce and trade brought about peace and harmony through the medium of exchange and the mutual satisfaction of needs. By contrast, European history was marked by violence and warfare, and religion was generally seen to be the cause, from the Crusades of the Middle Ages through the wars that ravaged all of Europe for more than a century in the wake of the Protestant Reformation. Paralleling this history of religious violence and intertwined with it was a history of religious controversy and disputation, from the scholasticism of the twelfth century to the Protestant Reformation, the Counter-Reformation, and the disputes within both Protestantantism and Catholicism thereafter.

The new values of peace and harmony that were now culturally dominant were traditionally associated with women because disputation and warfare were traditionally the domain of men. The strength by which men had ruled—and had ruled women—was no longer a virtue. The swords they alone wielded were seen as responsible for centuries of misery and oppression. As Mary Wollstonecraft wrote: "Bodily strength from being the distinction of heroes is now sunk into such unmerited contempt that men, as well as women, seem to think it unnecessary; the latter, as it takes from their feminine graces . . . ; and the former, because it appears inimical to the character of a gentleman."[2] The word—in the forms of civil conversation, writing, and print—was now the arena in which women and men would create a new, civilized society, the means by which they could civilize the rest of the world, outside the court, outside the city, outside the bounds of Europe itself.

The self-image of eighteenth-century Europeans as civilized was not a self-contained image. It was constructed primarily in contrast to three other images: the barbarity of the Middle Ages, the innocence of the indigenous American (sometimes called the "noble savage"), and the brutishness of the African. It was constructed by historians who measured the civilization of a culture by the status of women in it. "It is only among nations civilized to the point of politeness that women have obtained the equality of condition that is however so natural and so necessary to the gentleness of society," wrote the French naturalist Georges-Louis Leclerc, comte de Buffon.[3] Antoine-Léonard Thomas put the matter even more bluntly: "More than half the globe is covered with savages; and among all these peoples women are very unhappy. The savage man, . . . having none of the moral ideas that alone soften the empire of force, accustomed to regarding it [force] as the only law of nature, commands despotically those beings whom reason makes his equals, but whom weakness subjects to him."[4]

At the same time that they were refining their manners and congratulating themselves for having emerged from a barbarian past, Europeans were engaging in the largest-scale colonization of the globe that the world had ever seen. With the slave labor of men and women brought from Africa, Europeans established colonial plantations in Asia and the Americas from which they reaped great wealth. Colonial culture, however, was overwhelmingly masculine, and Europeans worried about this. How could men—soldiers, sailors, and priests in particular—establish bridgeheads of civilization when they were the segments of society most in need of civilizing themselves? Rather than bringing civilization to the rest of the world, Europeans were losing the veneer of civilization they had painfully acquired. Without European women, colonists seemed to turn into savages. One commentator pointed to the Canadian trappers who came down to Arkansas in the Louisiana territory and "have taken to themselves wives among the women of the country. . . . From these connections hath soon arisen an almost savage race."[5]

Colonialism created all sorts of contradictions in the European notion of civilization. In the colonial world those who by means of brute force imposed their will upon others weaker than themselves were the Europeans. In addition, missionaries created an identity between the proclaimed truths of Christianity and European civilization at odds with both the Enlightenment philosophy of history and its skepticism toward revealed religion. If Europeans saw ahead of them an end of religious conflict and warfare and a new era of peace, their hopes rested in part on the export of religious fervor and the displacement of warfare from Europe to the rest of the world. The Seven Years' War (1755–1763) brought both colonists and colonized into a European conflict, to fight and die for the interests of Europeans, whose peace settlement entailed redistributing among themselves the lands they had acquired from Asian and North American natives by force.

But the most serious challenges to European identity posed by colonialism were slavery and the slave trade. The commerce that had lifted Europeans out of their own barbarism at the end of the Middle Ages had now plunged them into a new and graver barbarism—the buying and selling of other human beings. "All Europe hath, for this century past, been filled with the most sublime and the soundest sentiments of morality," wrote abbé Guillaume Thomas François Raynal.

> Writings, which will be immortal, have established in the most affecting manner, that all men are brethren. We are filled with indignation at the cruelties, either civil or religious of our ferocious ancestors, and we turn away our eyes from those ages of horror and blood. . . . Even imaginary distresses draw tears from our eyes, both in the silent retirement of the closet, and especially at the theatre. It is only the fatal destiny of the Negroes which doth not concern us. They are tyrannized, mutilated, burnt, and put to death, and yet we listen to these accounts coolly and without emotion. The torments of a people to whom we owe our luxuries, can never reach our hearts.[6]

Raynal recognized what few of his contemporaries were prepared to face: that the civilization of Europe—the gentleness of its manners, the comforts of its life, its morality and its sensibility—was purchased with the wealth generated by the trade in human beings and the free use of their labor. Such a grave contradiction called into question the very idea of civilization as a moral force and weakened the social value ascribed to women, now closely associated with it. If women were indeed the "civilizing force," then were they not also, with their taste for fashion and luxuries, the driving force behind the colonial slave economy developed to satisfy their petty whims? "In short," as Mary Wollstonecraft remarked, "women, in general, as well as the rich of both sexes, have acquired all the follies and vices of civilization, and missed the useful fruit."[7]

The World of Print

The men and women who came together through the writing and reading of printed material, like those who met in salons and other institutions of so-ciability, did so in order to use their common reason to think about and express their views on matters of public concern. In so doing they comprised what his-torians now recognize as.a new public sphere of criticism and debate that be-came the basis of the modern public sphere of political participation. As this new public sphere gained in importance, the publication of books, pamphlets, and periodicals increased enormously, literacy and readership grew apace, and writers—who claimed to represent public opinion—took on a new sense of dig-nity and authority. Not only did they shape readers through their writings, but they claimed to speak for them. Although women constituted a large propor-tion of readers in the eighteenth century, they were much less numerous in the ranks of writers as the profession of writer became an important means for men to achieve social mobility and exercise authority—both literary and political.

In the eighteenth century the majority of women and men were illiterate, as they had been throughout history. Literacy was higher in cities than in the countryside, higher among Protestants than among Catholics, and higher among men than among women, but the eighteenth century saw a significant increase in literacy among all groups. In Catholic France, for example, where the population was overwhelmingly rural, the female literacy rate rose from 14 percent to 27 percent over the course of the eighteenth century. In Protestant Amsterdam, the percentage of women who could read doubled between 1630 and 1780, from 32 percent to 64 percent. And in the brief period between 1755 and 1790, literacy among Englishwomen rose from 35 percent to 40 percent.[8]

As the production of reading material—books, pamphlets, and periodicals of all sorts—skyrocketed, women began to be taken seriously as readers and as consumers of reading material. The novel, which came to prominence as a literary form in the eighteenth century, was so identified with women readers that Jean-Jacques Rousseau saw fit to caution young girls against reading his novel, *Julie*—thus attracting them all the more with the enticement of corrupt-ing their virtue. Men and women alike read these novels, but women were the target audience.

Novels such as Rousseau's *Julie (1762)*, Diderot's *The Nun* (1760), and Samuel Richardson's *Pamela* (1740) and *Clarissa* (1748) placed the heroine at the center of the text. They featured a young woman's struggles to maintain her virtue by reconciling her natural desires for love and freedom with her social duty to be an obedient daughter or wife. The eighteenth-century heroine allowed her readers not only to follow her struggles, but to see herself in them. The letter-novel and the first-person memoir-novel, which were typical in this period, were particularly effective in presenting a male-authored version of a female voice with which women were meant to identify.

Women did not just read novels, however. If novelists encouraged female readership by framing their stories around the moral dilemmas of women and girls and using the female voice, other writers wrote female readers into their texts in order to suggest that they were meant for as broad a readership as possible. Since the Middle Ages, Latin had been the primary language for works of philosophy, theology, and other academic subjects. By the eighteenth century, the triumph of a secular and cosmopolitan Republic of Letters meant that writers aimed not only to transcend the national and confessional differences that divided Europeans, but also, as Joseph Addison wrote, to bring "Philosophy out of Closets and Libraries, Schools and Colleges, to dwell in Clubs and Assemblies, at Tea-Tables, and in Coffee-Houses."[9] To do so meant writing in a language accessible to all readers. The sign of this accessibility was the female reader, because girls, unlike boys, were generally not taught Latin. Indeed, girls received little formal education in academic subjects. To write in English or French or Italian or German, and to write, for example, in the form of a dialogue between a male teacher and a female student, was to convey the message that all human beings possessed the same reason—the same "common sense"; anyone who could read would be as able as anyone else to reason, to learn, and to understand. This was exactly the approach taken by Bernard de Fontenelle is his *Conversations on the Plurality of Worlds* (1686): a series of conversations between himself and an intelligent noblewoman in which he explains to her the new science of the Scientific Revolution. Diderot took the same approach in his *Letter on the Blind* (1749): a treatise on the new empirical epistemology of John Locke in the form of a letter addressed to a woman who is invited to try certain experiments herself. In the eighteenth century, "everyman" of common sense was often represented by a woman.

The naive young girl torn by the conflict of nature and culture, duty and desire, who was the typical heroine of the eighteenth-century novel, and the uneducated but curious and intelligent woman who was the figure of the implied reader of Enlightenment philosophy, were both related to the modern consumer being addressed in the pages of a burgeoning fashion press and other periodicals aimed specifically at a female readership, such as the *Journal des Dames* in France and *The Female Spectator* in England. These were not incarnations of the eternal feminine, but modern, urban women who were learning and making decisions based not simply on traditional concepts of duty but on reading—reading of books and periodicals meant to develop critical taste and judgment.

Yet as the eighteenth century witnessed the significant growth and new importance of women as readers, the door to becoming a published writer did not swing open so wide or so freely. Although it is difficult to determine exactly how many women placed their writing before the reading public in the eighteenth century, one scholar has argued that in France the number of women novelists actually declined from its peak in the late seventeenth century. For England, statistics suggest that the number of women authors did increase over the course of the eighteenth century, and particularly after 1750. Poetry and novels accounted for about half their literary production, but women also published devotional works, memoirs, plays, works of science, and history. They contributed to the boom in works of a practical nature in such fields as cookery, education, household management, travel, and midwifery.[10]

Yet writing for the reading public created problems for women, who were now seen as competing for public attention with their ambitious male contemporaries. As the market for printed works of all sorts expanded and the literary public sphere became more attractive for increasing numbers of ambitious young men, various pressures were exerted on women to limit their writing activity to private consumption. The possibility of making a career, a fortune, or at least a living and a name for oneself through writing and publishing gave male writers an incentive to use the power of the pen to discourage women from competing with them for what were really rather limited opportunities for success. Professional imperatives encouraged men of letters to embrace the gender ideology that stressed the different social roles of men and women based on their complementary natures, rather than their common sense. Ironically, this way of thinking tended to encourage those women who persisted in writing for the public to write in the "feminine" genres of domestic and amatory fiction—the novels which would prove to be the most popular and thus the most lucrative!

The new association of literature with a large, anonymous reading public also placed writing women in a bind, since for respectable women to expose themselves to the glare of publicity was to compromise their virtue. It was as if they were putting themselves on the stage before an audience. The central theme of the eighteenth-century novel—the struggle of a young woman to maintain her virtue—can be seen as a displacement of woman from the position of author and her replacement by a fictional character who suffers and struggles within the circumscribed private sphere of love and family—under the gaze, as it were, of the reading public. Male novelists thus displaced and replaced their female competitors with victimized female characters with whom a female reading public was meant to identify—but whose public exposure a male reading public could enjoy like so many voyeurs.

Despite these developments, there were notable women writers in the eighteenth century: Most famous among them is Mary Wollstonecraft, but also worthy of note are Englishwoman Catherine Macaulay (1731–1791), the author of an eight-volume anti-Royalist history of England; Eliza Haywood (1690?–1756), the editor of *The Female Spectator* (1722–1746), the first periodical written by and for women; Isabelle de Charrière (1740–1805), the Dutch-born author of several volumes of fiction and criticism in French, including the explicitly antimisogynist *Letters of Mistress Henley Published by Her Friend* (1784); and Caroline Schlegel Schelling, who would make her mark in the German Romantic movement after having made a name for herself as the translator of Shakespeare. The works of two French women, Françoise de Graffigny and Louise d'Epinay, will be discussed below.

THE PROJECT OF ENLIGHTENMENT: CHALLENGING TRADITIONAL INSTITUTIONS

In the eighteenth century, religious publishing was on the decline, and novels, science, and history were on the rise. Also on the rise were a category of books known as "philosophy," but which included anything considered threatening or dangerous, from political scandalmongering to pornography to the works of the philosophes. In the expanding public sphere of print and sociability that included both newspapers and talk overheard in coffeehouses and cafés, even ordinary citizens could be heard voicing their criticisms of public officials or policies, demonstrating their ability and their right to hold opinions on matters traditionally held to be the privileged concern of the king and his ministers or the Church and its representatives.

Critical reason defined the Enlightenment, and, in principle, no institution, authority, belief, or practice was beyond its reach or outside its purview. The Enlightenment was a sort of project to which an expanding group of men and women were committed. Its vision was directed toward the future and its hero was Voltaire, the French writer whose motto was *écrasez l'infâme!* (Stamp out injustice!). Its most important publication was arguably the *Encyclopedia* (1751–1777), whose main editor, Denis Diderot, articulated its purpose most simply as "changing the common way of thinking." At its center were the Parisian philosophes and salonnières whose common sense of purpose came from a commitment to seeking and representing whatever truths their reason should establish in the critical and contentious matrix of discussion and debate. From the pens of the philosophes came publications of all sorts that circulated in ever expanding circles of "light" to a reading public across France, Europe, and beyond. These in turn drew to Paris young men and women who wanted to be part of the society of the Enlightenment. Many more men and women participated through subscription to publications and memberships in reading societies, through the reading of books and periodicals, and, in increasing numbers, through the publication of their own small contributions—books, pamphlets, articles—even letters to editors in which they could add their own voices and express their commitment to the project of Enlightenment. Through reading, writing, and associating, the men and women of the Enlightenment began to create a vision of the future and to propose projects of improvement, from the building of turnpikes to the abolition of slavery.

The Enlightenment was limited neither to France nor to a small group of writers. It took different forms in different national and linguistic contexts for three important reasons: (1) because of its embeddedness in the particular social and intellectual institutions that characterized different countries (e.g., salons in Paris, coffeehouses in London, university seminars in the German states); (2) because the critical practice that characterized the Enlightenment as a whole was necessarily directed at particular institutions, practices, and beliefs that differed from country to country; and (3) because the Enlightenment was carried out in language, and language increasingly came to divide linguistic groups from one another and to undermine the cosmopolitan sense of community implicit in a Republic of Letters devoted to truth alone.

There were therefore many Enlightenments, even as there was a common sense of identity among those who have come to be called "philosophes"—whether they were French, Scottish, Italian, German, and so on. What follows is a discussion only of the French Enlightenment as it related to women. We will look first at specific critiques of marriage, the traditional institution that most shaped Frenchwomen's lives; then we will examine the woman question as it was debated by the men and women of the French Enlightenment; and, lastly, we will consider the paradoxes that formed the legacy of Enlightenment thought concerning women. By looking at the French Enlightenment in particular, we will be able to examine the critical project of the Enlightenment as it was carried out: in relation to particular beliefs, practices, and institutions, but with much larger consequences and implications, as ideas spread through the circulation of the printed word.

The Critique of Marriage and Despotism

In the eighteenth century as today, the social institutions that most affected the lives of women and men alike were marriage and the family. It is thus not surprising that marriage and the family should have been a central object of criticism and a central metaphor for the criticism of the political order as well. In Catholic and monarchical France, the king, like God, was seen as a father to his subjects. The royal household was the microcosm of the state. Just as primogeniture (inheritance by first-born sons) was the rule in private families, French law since the sixteenth century determined that the royal succession could pass only through the male line. Thus France in the eighteenth century—in contrast to England, Russia, and the Hapsburg Empire—was ruled exclusively by kings. The Enlightenment critique of the monarchy was therefore couched in a critique of patriarchy figured as despotism. The earliest and most striking example of this critique is *The Persian Letters,* written by Charles-Louis de Secondat, Baron de Montesquieu, and published anonymously in 1721.

As its title indicates, *The Persian Letters* is an epistolary text—a collection of letters written and received by two fictional Persians who come to Paris in the last days of the reign of Louis XIV. Rica is a young man who is fascinated by everything new and different about Parisian society—and particularly by the freedom of Parisian women compared to those of Persia. "It is a great question among males to know whether it is better to deprive a woman of her freedom or let her keep it," he writes in one letter, and then goes on to debate whether or not the subjection of women to their husbands has a basis in natural law, and whether it is worse to have an unfaithful wife or one whose fidelity is forced and whose happiness is therefore sacrificed.[11] Rica later takes up the same issues from a different angle, observing that one of the advantages of the French system is that, although neither husbands nor wives can count on the fidelity of their spouse, jealousy and its consequences are virtually nonexistent. "All of the wise precautions of Asiatics—the veils that cover women, the prisons where they are enclosed, the vigilance of their eunuchs—seem to Frenchmen more apt to encourage rather than tire the ingenuity of that sex. Here husbands accept their lot with good grace and consider the unfaithfulness of their wives as a stroke of some inevitable fate."[12]

Of course, we are not meant to take Rica's comments on either French or Persian social practices literally. Indeed, *The Persian Letters* is less a comparison of French and Persian customs and society than a discussion of issues and debates within French society. Here the harem represents an extreme version— a caricature almost—of the traditional European institution of patriarchy. The idea of the French as completely without morals is just as much a caricature of contemporary Parisian society. *The Persian Letters* uses satire and cultural comparison to suggest the possibility and the dangers of changing from a traditional patriarchal marriage system in which women are deprived of freedom but in which the family itself has order and stability. Rica finds French society attractive, but he also expresses the fear that the freedom of French women will undermine the "natural" authority of men and gut marriage itself of meaning and value.

Rica's companion, Usbek, is older and seemingly wiser. While Rica ponders the Woman Question, Usbek concerns himself with more "serious" issues of religion and politics. The Woman Question, however, turns out to be inescapable, for Usbek has left behind a harem—five wives and several eunuchs to guard their virtue. Over time, Usbek becomes increasingly distant from the harem and its concerns. While he ponders the ideal political system based on a universal concept of justice, his harem—his own personal despotism—falls into anarchy. His wives rise up against their eunuch guards. In an act of desperation, Usbek orders one of the eunuchs to take up the sword of vengeance. The same day he writes to his wives: "May this letter be like unto the thunder that falls in the midst of storms and flashes of lightning! Solim is now your first eunuch—not to guard but to punish you. . . . He is to judge your past actions, and for the future, he will cause you to live under a yoke so rigorous that you will look back regretfully to your freedom even if not to your virtue."[13]

Montesquieu raises questions about France's social and political system by using the two levels of the book—the social commentary and philosophical speculation on the one hand, and the harem plot on the other—to comment on each other. Although Usbek's harem is a caricature of the patriarchal household of eighteenth-century France, his blindness to his own despotism is no greater than that of the head of any household in France—a family headed by a father and husband, or a monarchy headed by a king such as Louis XIV. Usbek's blindness, his failure, is to think that the universal principles that apply to him as a political subject do not apply to his wives (or his eunuch slaves, for that matter). Or, as Roxane, Usbek's favorite wife, and the one who leads the revolt against his despotism, writes in her final letter—a suicide note with which *The Persian Letters* ends: "How could you have thought that I was naïve enough to imagine that I was put in the world only to adore your whims? . . . No! I might have lived in servitude, but I have always been free. I have written your laws after the laws of nature, and my spirit has ever sustained itself in independence."[14]

The Persian Letters was so popular with readers that it spawned a literary genre of books in the form of letters from exotic visitors to France who made the familiar strange by viewing it through their alien eyes. These books, whose titles range from *The Chinese Letters* (1735) to *The Siamese Letters* (1751) to the *Iroquois Letters* (1752), sought to engage the reader's critical spirit as well as her sentimental heart. The most important of them, and the one that can be read most directly as a response to Montesquieu's discussion of women and marriage, is by a woman, Françoise de Graffigny, whose *Letters from a Peruvian Woman* was first published in 1747.

Graffigny's novel is composed of forty-one letters written by Zilia, a Peruvian princess captured during the Spanish sack of the Inca Empire, then recaptured at sea by the French under their captain, the noble Déterville. Most of Zilia's letters are written to her fiancé, Aza, from whom she was separated by the Spanish attack on the eve of her wedding day. Zilia's letters are both love letters and observations on the strange culture of Europeans. Like *The Persian Letters*, the *Letters from a Peruvian Woman* operate simultaneously on two registers: the love/marriage plot and the comparative cultural commentary. Unlike Montesquieu's text, Graffigny's is written entirely in the voice of a woman whose gender and foreignness make her the model subject of Enlightenment: an ignorant being endowed with common sense who learns through her experience, observation, and the ability to reason critically and comparatively.

Whereas Montesquieu's Persians had debated from the male point of view the relative merits of fidelity and freedom in a wife, Graffigny challenges this false opposition with the character of Zilia, who is the embodiment of fidelity (betrayed, not surprisingly, by the feckless Aza) and who learns through her experiences to value her freedom above all else. The institution of marriage looks very different when viewed through the eyes and experience of a Peruvian woman torn away from her own culture and the expectations she had of happiness through marriage in it—just as it would for a European woman captured by "savages" on the eve of her wedding day. As Zilia's curiosity about her new surroundings is awakened, her letters gradually develop from pure expressions of love, grief, loss, and blind faith to an account of her own growth from lovesick girl to mature woman. They shift from a focus on Aza and her undying love for him to the customs and culture of the world in which she finds herself. At the end of the novel, when Zilia has reconciled herself to Aza's betrayal of her, she rejects the marriage offer of the honorable Déterville in favor of her own independence. As she tells Déterville: "Freedom's great sweetness enters my imagination at times, and I listen to it attentively." Although she knows that French customs "do not allow a person of my age the independence and solitude in which I now live," she remains unconvinced of the merits of arguments in favor of marriage.[15] In the end, Zilia remains both faithful and free. She has constructed a self known through writing, defined by a set of universal, Enlightenment values independent of both French and Peruvian cultures. No longer simply the object of a man's desires or even of his thoughts and reflections, Zilia owns both herself and her home.

In the consumer culture of the eighteenth century, the acquisition of objects that both reflect the owner and provide a retreat from family and the world reverses the traditional relationship of women to property. No longer simply the vehicle by means of which property is passed from one generation to another, or shifted from one social group to another, this new woman asserts ownership of herself through ownership of property and through the medium of taste, which gives that self a unique identity. Whereas Montesquieu's ambivalent critique of the traditional institution of marriage had resulted only in the frustrated cry of freedom in the mouth of a woman with no way out but death, Graffigny points to education, consumption, property, and writing as the means by which eighteenth-century women will achieve the autonomy upon which enlightened lives can be built.

The Persian Letters and the *Letters from a Peruvian Woman* reached out to a broad audience with their engaging mixture of narrative and criticism. But the most widely distributed and significant work of the Enlightenment was, surprisingly perhaps, the prototype of the dullest of modern genres: the encyclopedia. The *Encyclopedia* (1751–1765) edited by Denis Diderot and Jean le Rond d'Alembert was anything but dull, however. In it were brought together information and criticism, words and images, history, etymology, and philosophy. What started out as a printer's scheme to translate a popular two-volume English *Cyclopedia* into French was transformed by the young editors into a monument of publishing in seventeen volumes of text and eleven of engraved plates. Just as significant, the project was paid for by the reading public throughout Europe: from the king's mistress to provincial notables, to reading societies and wealthy merchants, men and women signed up as subscribers and waited impatiently for each new volume to appear. This first edition was a luxury item printed on heavy paper with wide margins and good type; soon, however, cheap editions made the *Encyclopedia* available to an even broader public, and volumes of excerpts and anthologies were cobbled together by enterprising men of letters out to profit from the expansion of literacy to people of ever more modest means.

The *Encyclopedia*'s primary aim was to organize the wealth of knowledge that had accumulated as a result of changes in epistemology and technology wrought by the Renaissance, the Reformation, the Scientific Revolution, the invention of the printing press, and the Enlightenment itself. However, it had to be distinguished from mere prejudice, superstition, or traditional belief by viewing all "truths" critically. When Diderot wrote that the purpose of the *Encyclopedia* was "to change the common way of thinking," he meant not only changing what people thought but, above all, how they thought—to subject all received beliefs to their own critical reason or common sense.

The *Encyclopedia* thus constitutes the most thorough critique of the institutions, practices, beliefs, and power structures that defined the Old Regime. Did it, then, expose and criticize the legal subjection of women, patriarchy, and the myriad traditional prejudices, practices, and institutions that flew in the face of common sense and the scientific method? Reasonable as such a conclusion may seem to us, this was not the case. Indeed, when it came to the woman question, many ancient prejudices were reinscribed in the *Encyclopedia* and thus given new authority. In addition, new, "enlightened" views about nature and society became the basis for a new understanding of the difference between the social roles and intellectual capacities of men and women.[16]

The critique of the aristocracy, for example, hammered away at the idea that human beings should be valued for their usefulness to society, rather than for their noble birth or bloodlines. But the utility of women was defined differently from that of men. Whereas men used their reason and their labor to improve upon nature and increase its bounty, women's utility lay in their bodily function of reproduction. Influenced by the physiocrats, a group of men of letters who gave primacy to production and reproduction as the basis of economic growth and social progress, the encyclopedists gave female sexuality a new economic function. They criticized arranged marriages because, love being absent, they did not provide the optimum conditions for reproduction. They also challenged the notion of marriage as a sacrament, and bolstered the state's position that it was simply a civil contract. On this basis, they argued for divorce—once children had been produced and raised. Thus the *Encyclopedia*'s critique of traditional marriage practices, while advocating freedom of choice for marriage partners against the authority of parents and the freedom to dissolve an unhappy marriage against the authority of the Church, also inscribed women within a new, "natural" social and economic order that limited their role and their social value to reproduction.

The encyclopedists, who prided themselves on revealing truths that had been hidden for centuries behind the veil of prejudice, did not indulge themselves in the transmission of mysogynist proverbs. But the "scientific" truths on which the authors based their arguments about women had been around for millenia and yet were accepted without question. Hippocrates' belief that all complaints that beset the female body could be traced to a "wandering womb" was canonized as knowledge rather than exposed as mere prejudice. "All practitioners agree that the various symptoms of the vapors or of the hysterical afflictions which affect young girls and widows are a result of sexual deprivation," readers of the *Encyclopedia* learned.[17] Because the same word, *mariage*, meant marriage and sexual intercourse, these two were linked—but only in reference to women. Men might satisfy their sexual desire outside of marriage, but unquestioned social norms ruled that women could not. The light of reason shone only dimly on the marriage bed.

In its commitment to the conflicting Enlightenment values of freedom and order, nature and progress, autonomous individual and loving, nuclear family, the *Encyclopedia* bears the stamp of Diderot, its main editor. Diderot's novel, *The Nun* (1760), brings these themes together around the story of a young woman forced against her will to take the veil.

Diderot's novel is written in the form of a letter from Suzanne Simonin— an intelligent and virtuous young woman—to the marquis de Croismare—an enlightened reader known for his sentiment (*sensibilité*). Suzanne's story is simple: she has been forced to become a nun because she is the product of an extramarital affair her mother had with an unnamed man. When the time comes for Suzanne to take her vows, she protests that she has no vocation for the Church and asks to return to the world. Her mother's confessor then fills her in on the situation: because she was conceived in sin, her mother must atone by giving her daughter to the Church. Her father, suspecting that Suzanne is not his daughter, has already used every possible means to limit her property rights and thus her marriage prospects. Seeing no escape, Suzanne walks through the ceremony in a daze, waking up later to realize that at 17 she has now made an irrevocable commitment to a life that goes against her reason and her nature.

The Nun recounts the story of Suzanne's life in a series of convents. In one convent the mother superior replaces the nuns' Bibles with hair shirts. The next convent is even worse: there the mortifications of the flesh are replaced by the sins of the flesh. For Diderot, the supreme violation of nature and reason is the lesbianism practiced by the new mother superior, whose love for Suzanne is even more dangerous and corrupt than the hatred of the first. Like the harem, the convent is both a despotism and, in Diderot view, unnatural, because it isolates its members from society—a society naturally composed of people of both sexes.

All of Suzanne's attempts to use the legal system to renounce her vows fail. Finally, with the aid of a sympathetic friar, she climbs the walls one dark night in a final bid for freedom—only to discover that the friar is no disinterested friend. After trying to rape her in the carriage that whisks them off to Paris, he deposits her in a whorehouse, leaving her to the fate of a woman who has no legitimate place within a society in which the power of the state rests on the bedrock of patriarchal families supported by a despotic church.

Diderot's depiction of the convent as a prison or a madhouse full of women who were degraded and perverted because they were trapped there against their wills was as much a caricature as Montesquieu's Persian harem. And, like the harem, it was a powerful figure with which to mount a passionate critique of the authoritarian institutions of the Old Regime in the name of reason, nature, and liberty. Because it is written in the voice of a woman, *The Nun* figures humanity as a woman, endowing her with reason and championing human freedom in her name and as her natural right. At the same time, the horrors of her existence are caused by the fact that the convent violates nature. Despite Suzanne's reason and her right to human liberty, her *nature* is to be a wife and mother. Unlike Graffigny's Zilia, Suzanne seeks only the freedom to marry. Diderot indicts the patriarchal family and the legal, political, and religious institutions that it supports (and that support it), but he does so in the name of a "natural" family that is heterosexual and reproductive.

For women readers, then, the message of *The Nun*, like that of the *Encyclopedia*, was ambiguous. They could see themselves in Suzanne as quintessentially human—as rational creatures endowed with natural liberty and made for society. They could learn from Diderot's novel the injustice of a social, political, and religious system that abrogates their freedom, violates their nature, and makes of them victims. But they also saw themselves as naturally defined by the role of wife and mother and their natural liberty limited to companionate marriage. Finally, however, the very form of the novel—a reasoned plea written by an intelligent woman to an enlightened reader—frames the discussion of freedom and nature within the new media that defined the eighteenth-century public sphere. Pamphlets, periodicals, and trial briefs like those written by Suzanne's lawyer are shown to be the weapons of social and political change.

The Enlightenment Debate on Women: Reason and Difference

If we leave the precincts of fiction, we find that the men and women of the Enlightenment inherited from the seventeenth century two very different ways of understanding women's nature in relation to that of men: the Cartesian view that insisted on the essential sameness of women and men because of their equal possession of reason; and the Neo-Platonic view that valued the differences between men and women and saw them as equally necessary and complementary parts of a greater social whole. To these two modern views were added those of Rousseau, who believed that woman's nature, different from that of man, suited her exclusively to the sphere of the household, where as wife and mother she achieved respect and a new dignity.

A glance at Antoine-Léonard Thomas's *Essay on the Character, Morals, and Mind of Women Across the Centuries* (1772) and responses to it by Diderot and his close friend, Louise d'Epinay, will suggest how the Woman Question was framed in the eighteenth century. Thomas opened his essay with the observation that although society added to the miseries handed out to women by nature, women suffered more in savage societies than in civilized ones, and that the despotism of the Orient was more cruel to women than the moderate regimes of the West. This contrast between savage and civilized, East and West, paved the way for a history of Western Civilization through which "one will see what women have been, what they are, and what they could be."[18] Throughout history, women are shown to have displayed virtue, character, and intelligence, racking up accomplishments both for their sex and for civilization as a whole. These accomplishments, however, are the result of very different strengths and weaknesses, different virtues and vices, than those of men. Women, for example, are strong in imagination, but they lack the ability to reason methodically. They are not suited to govern states, but they are crucial to the smooth running of small groups such as salons, in which men, naturally "impetuous and free," respond only to their subtle manipulations. Men are capable of patriotism and the love of humanity, whereas the sensitivity of women suits them for love and duty in the more immediate arena of family and home. And at a time when female monarchs sat on the thrones of two of France's most powerful neighbors—Catherine the Great in Russia and Maria Theresa in Austria—Thomas warned that women rulers were more likely to be despots than their male counterparts.

Despite the fact that he saw history as an "irresistible march of progress," Thomas saw "the spirit of society" that characterized the modern age as having gone too far in his own day. "With a people in which the spirit of society is carried this far, domestic life is no longer known. Thus all the sentiments of Nature which are born in retreat must here be weakened. Women must thus become here less wives and mothers."[19] To suggest what might be done, Thomas concluded his essay with a portrait of the ideal modern woman. She would cultivate philosophy and literature, but "would love them for themselves, not for the sake of a vain and frivolous reputation." Above all, the ideal woman of the eighteenth century "would know how, within her own home and outside it, to guard her respect for virtue, her disdain for vice, her sensitivity to friendship, and in spite of the desire to have an extensive social circle, . . . would have the courage to make public a way of thinking so extraordinary."[20] Thomas's ideal woman, modeled on his good friend, the salonnière Suzanne Necker, would be the public champion of private virtue. Suzanne Necker herself, however, could not live up to this ideal, for in order to maintain his own authority and reputation as a public figure, her husband had forbidden her from publishing any of her extensive writings.

While Thomas refused to pronounce on the thorny question posed by Poulain de La Barre of either the equality of the sexes or the superiority of one or the other, Thomas's *Essay on Women* was a serious attempt to present a balanced view of woman through the use of Cartesian reason and Enlightenment historiography based on complementary thinking. But no one was happy with the result. Diderot was spurred to write an impassioned response, titled simply, "On Women." As far as Diderot was concerned, the only way to write about women was to write as a man, which is to say, as someone whose very happiness depended on these mysterious creatures. Women were absolutely different from men, determined by their biology and ruled by their passions. Love was as essential to them as fame was to a writer. Paragraph after paragraph, page after page, Diderot contrasted woman with man, hammered home the point that to suggest otherwise was to miss the very point of women's existence. In fact, more so than Thomas but less systematically, Diderot sets out the position that women and men complement each other, are necessary to each other. Their absolute difference is not the basis of an argument for male superioriority or dominance, but for complementarity and the appreciation of women.

Diderot condemns the tyranny of men and the oppression of women, but he rejects the Cartesian claim that because "the mind has no sex" men and women are essentially the same. To appreciate women, he suggests, one must recognize not only their difference from "us," but also the fact that "we" can never really penetrate "their" mystery. For Diderot, virtually the only acknowledged atheist among the philosophes, woman took on the character of the divine—the absolute other by which (male) humanity was defined. He may not have been a good Christian, but Diderot saw the divine as manifesting itself through love.

Diderot's essay was written as a direct response to Thomas, as if the two men were engaged in an actual debate. At the end, he blames Thomas for not acknowledging "the advantages of commerce with women for a man of letters." The dialogue style implies that women's proper role is as an imagined audience or readership for men of letters. "They keep us accustomed to making the driest and thorniest matters pleasant and clear. We address our words to them ceaselessly, we want to be heard, we fear tiring or boring them, and we cultivate a particular way of expressing ourselves that transforms conversation into style."[21] One woman who listened to such debates more than most was Louise d'Epinay, because many of them took place in her drawing room, where Diderot was a regular guest. Also a frequent guest for the ten years he lived in Paris was a Neopolitan man of letters, the abbé Ferdinando Galiani. Epinay's correspondence with Galiani began when he returned to Naples at the end of 1769, and includes a letter in which she shares with him her own thoughts about Thomas's *Essay on Women*. Epinay's letter gives us a rare chance to listen to an actual female reader, rather than the "implied" female readership imagined by Diderot and other male writers.

Epinay's response is as different from Diderot's as can be. In the end, she writes, one doesn't know what Thomas thinks, and whether his opinion of women is anything but received opinion. "He writes with lots of erudition the history of famous women in all fields," she acknowledges. "He discusses a bit drily what they owe to nature, to the institution[s] of society and to education; and then, in showing them as they are, he attributes without end to nature that which we obviously owe to education, institution[s], etc."[22] In other words, despite his attempt to write a history that was not just a catalog of famous women and to use reason to challenge traditional views and prejudices, Thomas had ended up where he began. "So many commonplaces!—Are they more sensitive?—More sure in friendship than men?—Are they more this?—Are they more that? . . . How petty, common, and unphilosophical are all these details!" Epinay exclaims.[23]

Both Epinay and Diderot were asking Thomas to look at himself in relation to his subject, just as Montesquieu and his character Roxane had demanded that Usbek examine himself before pronouncing on the subject of despotism. But whereas Diderot criticized Thomas for attempting to treat in a scholarly and distinterested way a topic that requires all the passion of love, Epinay called on him to abandon the pretense of objectivity that hid the common prejudices of men of his day. Whereas Diderot had pushed the argument for complementarity to its extreme, Epinay argued the Cartesian position in its purity: "It is quite constant," she stated, "that men and women have the same nature and the same constitution."[24]

There are two other points to be made here. First, note how Epinay shifts her reference to women from "they" to "we"—from the male voice to the female one, from object to subject—as she adopts a critical position toward Thomas's argument, revealing in this way the subjectivity of his point of view and asserting her own status as thinking subject. Second, Epinay closes her letter to Galiani with the invitation to continue the discussion. "It was difficult to say anything new on this topic," she reflects, and then suggests that what are needed are "new heads to help us see the problem from different points of view." Galiani is one of them, and she hopes that he will share his thoughts with her on this "delicate question."[25] Galiani did respond to her letter, but he changed the subject, preferring to discuss other matters. The implied reader discovered that despite their praise, men of letters were not really interested in listening to what she had to say, not as committed as she might have thought to her transformation from reader into writer, from passive object into active subject.

Rousseau's Vision of Womanhood

Galiani was a true friend to Madame d'Epinay, but he failed her when it came to understanding the seriousness of the Woman Question and the need for new perspectives on it. That need was especially great because of the tremendous impact the works of Jean-Jacques Rousseau were having on readers, male and female, in France and beyond. In three essays published in the

1750s, Rousseau launched a frontal attack on civilization in which women took an indirect hit. In the 1760s, Rousseau published two books that shaped a new ideal for women that they would carry into the nineteenth century.

In his *Discourse on the Arts and Sciences* (1750), Rousseau challenged the assumption that the progress of civilization brought about an improvement in morals. Knowledge and virtue, he declared, did not go hand-in-hand. In his *Discourse on Inequality* (1754), Rousseau went even further, challenging the Enlightenment belief that human beings are by their nature social and sociable creatures. Rousseau imagined that before the development of families, societies, and states men enjoyed a primitive freedom and happiness now lost to them. His history of civilization was not the history of progress toward greater freedom and happiness, but a new, secular version of the fall, a tragedy in which natural freedom and happiness gave way to misery and oppression. Finally, in his *Letter to d'Alembert on the Theatre* (1759), Rousseau championed the natural innocence of the Swiss against the corruption of their highly civilized French neighbors. He worried that opening a theater in Geneva—banned since the days of John Calvin's Protestant reform of the city in the sixteenth century—would bring with it all the corruptions of the modern city.

Running through all these writings is a fear of women and their influence on men. One sign of the corruption of modern morals and society, according to Rousseau, was the ascendancy of society women as arbiters of taste—the rise of salonnières. Another was the decline of the martial virtues. He praised martial Sparta over "civilized" Athens, and romanticized the solitary, masculine individual, unencumbered by wife or children, unrestrained by social mores or family responsibilities, and deaf to the siren song of love. Whereas writers since the seventeenth century had identified the progress of civilization with the rise of a meritocracy of the pen over a barbarian nobility of the sword, Rousseau feared the loss of masculinity in a society where "every woman . . . gathers in her apartment a harem of men more womanish than she."[26]

Rousseau's critique of civilization was at its core mysogynistic because it denied women the positive role they were thought to play in history and society by denying any positive value to the course of history itself. In Rousseau's view, personal happiness and a just society rested not on a social whole composed of men and women, but on the basic unit of the autonomous masculine individual. What role, then, should women play in a society in which happiness was defined as the maximizing of masculine autonomy? And how were women to achieve happiness when it was defined in such masculine terms? In his writings of the 1760s, Rousseau would address these questions.

In *Emile* (1762), a treatise on education in the form of a novel about a boy and his tutor, the tutor brought the young hero from childhood to adolescence in a radically new way. Emile's tutor encouraged his natural talents and helped him to develop his natural reason as a way to curb his passions, rather than trying to thwart or repress them as educators had traditionally done under the influence of the Christian notion of natural sin. Emile was raised alone, "in nature," rather than in the society of other boys in a school, as was the increasingly common practice throughout Europe. But when he reached adolescence, Emile could no longer live alone: he needed a companion, so Rousseau created Sophie for him.

The final chapter of *Emile* is devoted to Sophie and her upbringing. In creating Sophie, Rousseau adheres to the theory of gender complementary based on sexual difference. He defies the "nature/nurture" controversy by asserting that the radical differences between men and women require that they be educated in different ways: whereas the boy's capacity for abstract reason must be strengthened so that he may become a self-governing, free individual, the girl's lack of it means that she must be taught obedience; her virtue (like that of Usbek's many wives) is a product of constraint rather than freedom and destines her for a life of dependence upon a man. Like Diderot, Rousseau argues that women's talents and virtues result not from education but from instinct, such as a *gift* for observing people which, combined with the social *instinct*, makes them good hostesses.

Rousseau has been criticized for his relegation of women to the realm of nature and the family and for denying them the capacity of reason upon which human freedom must rest. But this view must be placed within the context of Rousseau's critique of civilization if we are to understand it and its attraction for eighteenth-century women. Rousseau differed most from his contemporaries by challenging precisely that which they praised: the rise of civilization through the development of the arts and sciences. He saw the modern world as morally corrupt, driven by a competitive and acquisitive egoism and supported by calculating reason. The masculine focus of Rousseau's history of civilization placed the burden of this moral failure on men (although the competition for women was central to men's hostility toward one another). The point of *Emile* was to demonstrate how men's reason could be cultivated to make them master of these destructive passions and thus free individuals. Women, however, had not developed in the same way. Because they had no capacity for abstract reason, they could not achieve freedom as men could, but they also had the privilege of retaining the natural virtues and happiness that reason could never recapture. Closer to nature, they were also closer to virtue and happiness. By retaining their natural virtue (through strict obedience and constraint, of course), women could more easily achieve the happiness that men, with their calculating reason, could only approximate.

Rousseau's critique of civilization opened up a space of true happiness for modern men and women only in a domestic sphere seen as a haven from the depraved modern, urban world created and dominated by competitive, acquisitive, rational men. Women who sought to imitate men by cultivating their reason or who made a name for themselves in society (writers and salonnières, in short) were not only ridiculous, but foolish, since in defying their nature they ran away from the happiness that they alone could enjoy. Why should women want to imitate men or be jealous of their freedom, when reason and the freedom based on it were merely poor substitutes for the happiness based on instinct and natural virtue available to them alone?

Rousseau took the theory of gender complementarity and used it as the basis of two separate spheres: the moral sphere of the family, whose soul was the natural virtue of woman; and the public sphere of the commercial economy and the state, in which men were driven by rational calculation and self-interest. In *The Social Contract* (1762) Rousseau laid out the democratic political principles by which the public sphere of men ought to be governed; in *Julie, or the New Heloise* (1761), he imagined the private sphere of a patriarchal family in which the husband ruled with the guidance of reason, but the wife was the emotional and moral center around which the family was built.

Rousseau used the form of the epistolary novel made popular by the English novelist Samuel Richardson to paint the portrait of a woman who learns to value herself and becomes a new sort of model of female virtue in her role as wife and mother. Whereas Richardson's heroines, Pamela and Clarissa, had struggled over the course of hundreds of letters and several volumes to maintain their virginity against overwhelming odds, the issue of virginity is quickly dealt with by Rousseau when Julie and her tutor give in to their passion for each other early on. For Rousseau, female virtue is not simply something to be defended by fathers and husbands against male aggression (with high walls and barred windows, for example, as in Usbek's harem). In Rousseau's hands, female virtue is a moral quality and a set of behaviors that are a model for all who come under its sway.

In *Julie* Rousseau sets out woman's new moral role most clearly. In place of both the despotic harem and modern urban and commercial society, Rousseau offers the ideal of Clarens, an economically self-sufficient rural community established by Wolmar, the husband Julie's father chose for her. There, in a world removed from the exchange economy and moral corruption of modern society, Julie is able to blossom as a moral force. This utopian vision is both male-constructed and female-centered: it is Wolmar, after all, who, through his reason, creates the conditions whereby Julie's natural virtue flowers. For her, as Lieselotte Steinbrügge points out, "marriage marks the beginning of the development of her moral capacities and not, as in Wolmar's case, its culmination."[27] Whereas Wolmar retreats to Clarens after having come to know both the corruption of the modern world and its attractions—having struggled, that is, with the conflicts within himself—Julie knows no such conflicts. Once she is placed in a proper (manmade) environment and given her proper role as wife and mother, her nature emerges as the principle of harmony and sympathy that binds the community together emotionally.

Rousseau's influence on readers was enormous. He was responsible, for example, for starting a movement among elite women towards breast-feeding their children instead of sending them out to wet-nurses. Rousseau convinced them—and gave them the credibility to overcome opposition from their husbands—that breast-feeding was a manifestation of their maternal nature.

Emile became a handbook on child rearing and also spawned a wealth of books on education aimed at parents that took a more "natural" approach.

In addition to specific advice to women—which men had been proferring for centuries, after all—Rousseau provided an entire ideology that could be brought to bear on all aspects of culture and society. For example, his criticism of artificiality in the name of nature inspired Parisian editors and designers to promote new fashions of simpler cuts and fabrics that spread across Europe. Most important, by grafting the theory of gender complementarity to a critique of modern, rational, and commercial society, Rousseau took the narrowest conception of womanhood as wife and mother, and revalued it by setting it against all that was corrupt in the modern world. Rather than acting as a civilizing force in the interests of progress, women would stand for and stand up for all that was threatened by the march of progress. They would represent nature and children and family and virtue.

And what of the Cartesian argument for the equality of the sexes based on their equal capacity to reason? Female voices like that of Madame d'Epinay would be drowned out by the overwhelming satisfaction among men and women for this new sort of dignity for women that did not threaten to overturn the traditional relations between the sexes and the social, political, and cultural institutions that had been built on them. It was up to an English reader of Rousseau, Mary Wollstonecraft, to argue that the dignity of mothers was no more incompatible with the rights of citizenship than was that of fathers. Like Rousseau, Wollstonecraft criticized the current state of womanhood, but unlike him, she believed in the Enlightenment philosophy of history. She agreed with the Marquis de Condorcet who, writing also in the midst of the French Revolution, declared that one of the principal obstacles to intellectual progress and human happiness was "the prejudices that have brought about an inequality of rights between the sexes, an inequality fatal even to the party in whose favor it works."[28] Taking up the language of the French Revolution to complete the project of Enlightenment for women, Wollstonecraft explained the main thesis of *A Vindication of the Rights of Woman* in the following terms: "Contending for the rights of woman, my main argument is built on this simple principle, that if she be not prepared by education to become the companion of man, she will stop the progress of knowledge and virtue; for truth must be common to all, or it will be inefficacious with respect to its influence on general practice."[29]

CONCLUSION: PARADOXES OF ENLIGHTENMENT

The Enlightenment legacy for women is thus ambiguous. The critique of institutions such as marriage was overcome by a new formulation that reinstalled it on a firmer basis. If women were no longer to be forced into marriages against their will for economic reasons, if they were no longer to be seen as receptacles for a virtue that had to be guarded against predators at all costs (including their freedom), they were now to find the very meaning of their existence in marriage and child rearing. The world of markets and exchange might be condemned as corrupt, but men continued to flourish in it, and the relationship of women to that commercial world, as consumers and taste makers, would never be completely comfortable after Rousseau asserted the responsibility of women to maintain a moral haven into which men could retreat. The notion of women as a civilizing force, which integrated women into the history of civilization, would give way to the notion of women as a moral force in opposition to the corrosive effects of civilization.

The Enlightenment's championing of freedom and of the commonality of reason was more ambiguous when women were concerned than men. Common sense and increased literacy brought women into the Republic of Letters as readers, real and implied, but men of letters such as Thomas and Rousseau balked at the notion that women, like men, could become writers as well as readers. Women such as Louise d'Epinay learned the hard way that even their most enlightened male friends were unwilling or unable to overcome their own prejudices when it came to the Woman Question. Because women were understood to be oppressed by traditional society, female characters such as Montesquieu's Roxane and Diderot's Suzanne were mobilized to give voice to the humanitarian cry for freedom, but it took a woman writer, Françoise de Graffigny, to suggest that women could only attain that freedom through writing, outside marriage, and with control over their own property.

The Enlightenment gave women and men a language in which to articulate their claims to universal notions of justice, equality, and freedom based on their common humanity and shared history. At the same time, in complementarity it offered another language with which women could express their differences from men without endorsing the subjection of women to men. And the conflicts between these two ways of thinking could be fought out in a new public sphere whose institutions of sociability and varieties of print media would allow women to make their claims before a powerful new public—even if they were discouraged from availing themselves of these means. Finally, the commercial economy and the consumer culture it spawned opened up a world that would never again be limited by the walls of a father's house or a husband's—despite men's efforts to rebuild those walls ideologically. A new, modern woman surely emerged in the eighteenth century who would soon find herself in a new world in which the complex legacy of the Enlightenment would both help and hinder her.

NOTES

1. François Poulain de La Barre, *De l'égalité des deux sexes*, Fayard, Paris, 1984, p. 9.
2. Mary Wollstonecraft, *A Vindication of the Rights of Woman*, Penguin Books, Harmondsworth, 1992, p. 124.
3. Georges Louis Leclerc Comte de Buffon, *De l'homme*, Maspero, Paris, 1974, p. 132.

4. Antoine Léonard Thomas, "Essai sur le caractère, les moeurs et l'esprit des femmes dans les différents siècles," in *Qu'est-ce qu'une femme?* ed. Elisabeth Badinter, P.O.L., Paris, 1989, p. 52.

5. Abbé Guillaume Thomas François Raynal, *A Philosophical and Political History of the Settlements and Trade of the Europeans in the East and West Indies,* London, 1788, vol. 7, pp. 48–49.

6. *Ibid.,* vol. 5, pp. 267–268. This passage was actually written by Raynal's friend and colleague, the philosophe Denis Diderot, who collaborated with him on the writing of this eight-volume compendium on European colonialism.

7. Wollstonecraft, *op. cit.,* p. 153.

8. Roger Chartier, "The Practical Impact of Writing," in Roger Chartier, ed., *Passions of the Renaissance,* vol. 3 of *A History of Private Life,* ed. Philippe Ariès and Georges Duby, trans. Arthur Goldhammer, Harvard University Press, Cambridge, 1989, p. 113.

9. [Joseph Addison and Richard Steele], *The Spectator,* ed. Donald F. Bond, Oxford University Press, Oxford, 1965, vol. 1, p. 44.

10. Joan DeJean, *Tender Geographies: Women and the Origins of the Novel in France,* Columbia University Press, New York, 1992; and Judith Phillips Stanton, "Statistical Profile of Women Writing in English from 1660 to 1800," in *Eighteenth-Century Women and the Arts,* ed. Frederick M. Keener and Susan E. Lorsch, Greenwood Press, New York, 1988, pp. 247–254.

11. Charles Louis de Secondat, Baron de la Brède et de Montesquieu, *The Persian Letters,* trans. J. Robert Loy, Meridian Books, New York, 1961, letter 38.

12. *Ibid.,* letter 55.

13. *Ibid.,* letters 153, 154.

14. *Ibid.,* letter 161.

15. Françoise de Graffigny, *Letters from a Peruvian Woman,* trans. David Kornacker, Modern Language Association of America, New York, 1993, letter 40.

16. The following discussion of the *Encylopedia* is based on Lieselotte Steinbrügge's excellent discussion in Chapter 2 of *The Moral Sex: Woman's Nature in the French Enlightenment,* trans. Pamela E. Selwyn, Oxford University Press, New York, 1995, pp. 21–34. All the quotations are drawn from this fine work.

17. *Ibid.,* p. 30.

18. *op. cit.,* p. 56.

19. *Ibid.,* p. 152.

20. *Ibid.,* pp. 160–161.

21. Denis Diderot, "Sur les femmes," in Badinter, *op. cit.,* pp. 184–185.

22. Letter from Louise d'Epinay to Fernando Galiani, March 14, 1772, in Badinter, *op. cit.,* p. 190.

23. *Ibid.,* pp. 190–191.

24. *Ibid.,* p. 193.

25. *Ibid.,* pp. 193–194.

26. Jean-Jacques Rousseau, *Politics and the Arts: Letter to M. d'Alembert on the Theatre,* ed. and trans. Allan Bloom, Cornell University Press, Ithaca, 1968, p. 100.

27. Steinbrügge, *op. cit.,* p. 78.

28. Marie-Jean-Antoine-Nicolas Caritat, marquis de Condorcet, *Sketch for a Historical Picture of the Progress of the Human Mind,* in *Selected Writings,* ed. Keith Michael Baker, New York, Macmillan, 1976, p. 274.

29. Wollstonecraft, *op. cit.,* p. 86.

SUGGESTIONS FOR FURTHER READING

Barker-Benfield, G. J. *The Culture of Sensibility: Sex and Society in the Eighteenth-Century English Novel.* Chicago: University of Chicago Press, 1992.

DeJean, Joan. *Tender Geographies: Women and the Origins of the Novel in France.* New York: Columbia University Press, 1992.

Gelbart, Nina Rattner. *Feminine and Opposition Journalism in Old Regime France: Le Journal des Dames.* Berkeley: University of California Press, 1987.

Goldsmith, Elizabeth C., and Dena Goodman, eds. *Going Public: Women and Publishing in Early Modern France.* Ithaca: Cornell University Press, 1995.

Goodman, Dena. *The Republic of Letters: A Cultural History of the French Enlightenment.* Ithaca: Cornell University Press, 1994

Harth, Erica. *Cartesian Women: Versions and Subversions of Rational Discourse in the Old Regime.* Ithaca: Cornell University Press, 1992

Jacobs, Eva, et al., eds. *Women and Society in Eighteenth-Century France.* London: Athlone Press, 1979.

Keener, Frederick M., and Susan E. Lorsch, eds. *Eighteenth-Century Women and the Arts.* New York: Greenwood Press, 1988.

Myers, Sylvia Harcstark. *The Blue Stocking Circle: Women, Friendship and the Life of the Mind in Eighteenth-Century England.* Oxford: Oxford University Press, 1990.

Rogers, Katherine. *Feminism in Eighteenth Century England.* Urbana: University of Illinois Press, 1982.

Shevelow, Kathryn. *Women and Print Culture: The Construction of Femininity in the Early Periodical.* London: Routledge, 1990.

Spencer, Samia I., ed. *French Women and the Age of Enlightenment.* Bloomington: Indiana University Press, 1984.

Steinbrügge, Lieselotte. *The Moral Sex: Woman's Nature in the French Enlightenment.* Translated by Pamela E. Selwyn. New York: Oxford University Press, 1992.

Weinreb, Ruth Plaut. *Eagle in a Gauze Cage: Louise d'Epinay, Femme de Lettres.* New York: AMS Press, 1992.

FRANCAISES DEVENUES LIBRES.

Anonymous engraving, probably issued during the summer of 1792. The engraving
bears the caption "French women [who] have become free," and depicts a woman
who boldly faces the viewer, conspicuously displaying on her hat the tricolor cockade,
symbol of French liberty. She bears a pike inscribed with the motto: Liberty or Death.
A medal attached by a tricolor band to her waist, is inscribed with the motto:
"Libertas Hastata Victrix! 14 Juillet" ("Liberty [when she is] armed with her pike [is]
victorious! 14 July.). Contemporaries may have associated this figure either with
Pauline Leon, who had publicly expressed her determination to fight, pike in hand,
during the *journée* of August 10, or with her equally militant friend, Claire Lacombe,
whom the fédérés decorated with a tricolor sash for her role during this *journée*.
BIBLIOTHÈQUE NATIONALE/JEAN-LOUP CHARMET.

CHAPTER 10

A Political Revolution for Women? The Case of Paris

Darline Gay Levy and Harriet B. Applewhite

Women's participation in French revolutionary political culture, the most extensive feminine political engagement in the Western world in the early modern period, raises questions about the meanings of that involvement: did the Revolution bring women irreversibly into a public sphere of contestation and entitlements both in the short term or over the long run, or restrict women ever more narrowly within the domestic sphere? Did doctrines of universal rights mask fundamentally masculinist exclusions and marginalizations of women, or did rights become the foundation of women's claims to full citizenship? Levy and Applewhite focus on multiple meanings of principles of citizenship and of women's political practices and make the case that rights claims became indelibly linked to popular sovereignty and political legitimacy, the touchstones of modern democratic practices.

In the first revolutionary year, the women's march to Versailles (the central event of the "October Days") capped six months of women's political involvement: their active presence in Paris neighborhoods, in electoral assemblies for the Estates General, in the conquest of the Bastille, and in several dozen processions with the newly formed National Guard (demonstrations organized to express thanks for revolutionary innovations and simultaneously to make all authorities fully accountable for supplying bread to Paris and protecting its newly secured liberty). Thousands of marching women empowered themselves as citizens as they confronted the national legislative and the king with demands: bread, royal ratification of the Declaration of the Rights of Man and of the Citizen and other constitutional decrees, and the immediate removal of the king and the government from Versailles to Paris. The women's invasion of the National Assembly challenged representatives who did not represent, challenges that disoriented even supporters of the Revolution because they amounted to claims for plenary citizenship rights for women.

In 1791 and 1792, dramatic additional confrontations between Paris radicals and the National Assembly and king framed popular sovereignty in terms of political rights, eroded monarchical legitimacy, and forged new citizenship identities for women and men of the popular classes. In many instances, women linked their interests and their political identities to universal rights enshrined in the Declaration of the Rights of Man, notwithstanding their formal exclusion from the legal category of active citizenship.

After the fall of the monarchy, struggles for political ascendancy in Paris opened up opportunities for women to organize a single-sex political club, the Society of Revolutionary Republican Women, and to exercise influence in other clubs and popular societies and in legislative bodies. As the Jacobins triumphed, conflicts over the question of women's right to assemble and participate politically reveal that the Jacobins connected the "woman question" to their own grasp on political power in a revolutionary capital torn by internal and international war; they recognized that connection even as they legislated closure of all women's political clubs and sought to restrain women's activism on all fronts.

Women's revolutionary language, indeed the entire range of their political behaviors, can be understood as expressions of the rights of the sovereign people. Women who wrote polemic pamphlets, authored and printed political journals, testified in courts, and answered official interrogators restated rights doctrines to fit their gender specific interests. Levy and Applewhite conclude that universal rights provided one of the principal revolutionary legacies for women, opening up to contestation any issue that can be linked to rights. Although universal rights can mask prescriptive, circumstantial differences of sex, race, religion, and class, rights language also forces onto the defensive those who try to exclude women or any other category of persons from expressing their fullest human definition and from gaining access to fields of power in democratizing societies.

T he French Revolution was arguably the most democratic of all the revolutions in the eighteenth-century Western world. Although the revolutionaries did not live in a world of modern democratic government, with its mass suffrage, political parties, and interest groups, the institutions and principles that the revolutionaries modified and created laid the foundations of the republican tradition in French politics and established the most important precedents for modern democracy. Revolutionaries developed and spread doctrines of human rights, redefined citizenship, and established popular sovereignty both in principle and in practice. They established legislatures, local governing bodies, political clubs, a popular press, and other institutions for political participation; and they involved millions of individuals throughout French society in political conflict and civil and international war.

Women involved themselves in these transformations in many ways: as members of revolutionary crowds, as radical leaders, and as supporters of the French government. Some donated their jewels to the treasury, knitted stockings, made bandages for the armies, or joined revolutionary festivals. Others were victims of revolutionary change: noblewomen who lost rank and privilege, and deeply religious women whose world fell apart when their churches were attacked and their faith declared unpatriotic. Women edited, printed, and distributed journals and political tracts and thereby contributed to both revolutionary and counterrevolutionary ideology. Their revolutionary allegiances were complex and their roles staggeringly diverse. Just as for men, women's experiences and their contributions were conditioned by their situations and their beliefs: Did they live in Paris or the provinces? Were they noblewomen or domestic servants? Did they keep market stalls or write plays? Were they devout Catholics or did they resent the wealth and power of the Church?

As historians have reflected on the meaning of revolutionary democracy for women, they have sharpened the lines of historiographic debate. Did the Revolution irreversibly establish precedents for women's involvement in the public sphere, in political contestations and rights issues? Or did it irrevocably and fundamentally separate women from the arena of political power in ways that normalized their domestic roles? Were "universal" principles in fact fundamentally masculinist ideological formulations that point to the exclusion and marginalization of women? Were these principles necessary and sufficient conceptual foundations for women's claims to equal civil and political rights?

Recently a number of scholars—such as Madelyn Gutwirth and Joan Landes—have interpreted women's revolutionary political activism as heroic but ultimately futile struggles doomed to failure because conducted in a cultural field determined by masculinist values and interests. They argue that as Enlightenment philosophes challenged the hierarchical world of old regime privilege, they undermined the influence of noble and bourgeois women at court and in the salons. They established the model of a society of rational autonomous individuals understood to be male, with interests that the sovereign power was obligated to protect. They either believed women were biologically limited in reasoning capacity and physical strength or argued that their interests were adequately represented by fathers, husbands, or sons.[1] Other historians have questioned this deterministic reading and have emphasized multiple and competing Enlightenment theories about gender roles, including the Marquis de Condorcet's ringing claims for universal political rights that were grounded in the human capacity to reason and to feel and that dissolved gender differences in the political world. Joan Scott has argued recently that when revolutionary feminists connected their interests to univeral rights, they opened a complex and continuing dialogue about the necessary and sufficient conditions of liberty, equality, and autonomy for women as political selves, citizens in the modern world. She views the revolutionary legacy for women in terms of irresolvable paradoxes that nonetheless allow some room for maneuvering: women necessarily must emphasize sexual difference in order to claim the applicability of universal rights to themselves; and they also must deny difference in order to claim equality.[2] In several articles, Lynn Hunt has backed away from the cultural determinism that informed her *The Family Romance and the French Revolution* to emphasize women's self-conscious political organization within "surprisingly open political spaces" to demand their rights.[3]

We argue that links between women's revolutionary political practices and rights issues place the woman question permanently in the modern French political tradition and in modern political culture. We focus here on what women meant when they claimed and practiced citizenship; how those claims were received by their contemporaries; and what their posterity made of those claims. The political language and the acts of women in the revolutionary capital—their political performances—cannot be dismissed simply because the implications of these words and deeds were not realized in French revolutionary politics, or even with the establishment of women's suffrage in 1944 at the beginning of the Fourth Republic, and still have not produced equality in positions of political power.[4] Rights claims, once defined and defended, become indelibly imprinted in a political culture. Revolutionary writers like Olympe de Gouges and Etta Palm d'Aelders formulated their claims as human rights. In doing so they showed that a revolutionary and democratic recasting of relationships between governors and governed dictated a recognition of difference as a condition and ground of common claims for equal rights of citizenship. Other women whose words and thoughts were never recorded made their mark on the Revolution by marching, demonstrating, signing or marking petitions, attending revolutionary meetings, and participating in neighborhood self-government. Thousands of women marched to Versailles from Paris in October 1789, signed petitions concerning the future of the constitutional monarchy on the Champ de Mars in July 1791, and paraded through the halls of the Legislative Assembly and the king's residence in the Tuileries in the summer of 1792. Through these practices, they forged a link between their identities and behaviors as citizens, on the one hand, and new concepts of popular sovereignty, citizenship, and political legitimacy, on the other—the touchstones of modern democratic practices.

THE CHALLENGE TO ROYAL LEGITIMACY AND THE INVENTION OF WOMEN'S CITIZENSHIP

During the 1770s and 1780s, as journalists and other publicists communicated political news and shaped public opinion, they also focused attention on despotic and tyrannical acts of government authorities and thus contributed to narrowing the frames through which the public viewed political issues. In part, the involvement of women of the popular classes in public discourse at this juncture developed out of sociability fostered by their daily routines, like hauling water together and purchasing bread; but it also developed out of their participation in ceremonial functions that both reinforced and subverted order, sometimes simultaneously. The *poissardes* (fishwives) of Paris were required to attend the childbirth of a reigning queen in order to certify the legitimate birth of the royal heir, and were present later when the infant dauphin was presented in a ceremony at the Hôtel de Ville. In the patriarchal society of the old regime, ruled by a monarchy in which a woman could not inherit the throne, this women's occupational group played a central role in validating the future king on behalf of the people; the *poissardes* contributed an important plebeian presence to rituals that legitimated the monarchy.

The legitimacy of Louis XVI and his authority to govern were under challenge from the very beginning of his reign in 1774. These challenges came from many institutions: the parlements, whose power to register laws gave them the power to delay or block royal decrees; provincial estates and assemblies, which had some regional authority over law, administration, and taxes; the Church, with its power to tax, censor, and regulate behavior; and many specially privileged groups of people—army officers, judges, and local administrators—who exploited various opportunities for oppositional political maneuvering.

In addition to these institutional challenges, Enlightenment thinkers had long been questioning, debating, and reformulating theories about the nature and limits of legitimate authority. Enlightenment writers broadcast new doctrines of natural law, natural rights, and social contract. They demanded reforms in civil and criminal law; they challenged the legitimacy of a monarchy based on hereditary right and divine right; and they questioned defenses of privilege based on models of a hierarchical corporate society. Their discourse contributed to eroding the foundations of traditional authority and generating doubts about the legitimacy of one of the strongest monarchies in Europe. Enlightenment debates opened up opportunities for women to participate and, in the process, to acquire new civic identities. Women who presided over Paris salons promoted an antihierarchical sociability reflecting their influence in managing male discourse, but the *salonnières* also heightened male anxieties about women's exercise of real political power.[5]

As ministers and defenders of monarchy joined in the struggle to shape opinion, public opinion itself became a resource available to all parties; inevitably those who formed and exploited it, both elites and plebeians, women along with men, in effect were subverting the traditional foundations of authority. The manuscript journal of Siméon-Prosper Hardy, the Parisian bookseller, provides one window onto women's deployment of oppositional strategies. Hardy reported events like the crowd's failure to shout "Vive le Roi!" ("Long live the King!") as Louis XVI and his queen, Marie Antoinette, reviewed the French Guards and the Swiss Guards on May 8, 1787.[6] He noted that during the Feast of the Assumption in 1787, authorities had to present the *poissardes des Halles* (the fishwives of the Halles market) with a police order to force them to go through with their customary ceremonial offering of bouquets to the queen.[7] In recent close studies of daily life in eighteenth-century Paris, historians have brought into relief a plebeian public sphere and documented circumstances in which women of the popular classes contributed to the erosion of royal legitimacy, particularly in escalating attacks on the person and character of the king.[8]

In May 1788, after failing in a number of attempts to gain support for new taxes from various groups of notables, the king and his ministers decided to convoke the Estates General, an assembly of deputies representing the clergy (First Estate), the nobility (Second Estate), and the common people (Third Estate). The king hoped that the Estates, which had last met in 1614, would consent to the levying of taxes. The announcement generated great excitement and an outpouring of political pamphlets proposing a broad agenda of institutional reform. After the dates for elections to the Estates General had been fixed for the spring of 1789, electors at the local and provincial level drafted *cahiers de doléances*. The Paris electoral assemblies and the *cahier*-drafting process mobilized women along with men. Some working-class women authored *cahiers* in which they defended their economic interests by demanding protection for their crafts and occupations; others made dramatic political claims for rights to political representation.[9] On April 20, 1789, the lieutenant general of police in Paris, Thirout de Crosne, reported the following incident to the king: "I have been assured that women presented themselves for admission to the [electoral] assembly of the Abbaye Saint-Germain. When they were turned down by the Swiss Guards, they asked to see one of the members of this assembly who came to assist them and brought them in. They are twelve in number."[10] No record exists of what these women did or said inside the assembly; nonetheless, the police report documents their striking determination to be included in the process of electing political representatives.

The legal initiatives of the Revolution of 1789 began with the June 17 transformation of the Estates General into a National Assembly whose deputies charged themselves with drafting a constitution. The king initially resisted this legal revolution and then acceded to it, but then, just prior to dismissing Jacques Necker, his popular finance minister, he began massing troops around Paris and Versailles. Parisians, fired up by the writings and speeches of revolutionary leaders and certain that they were about to be invaded by royal armed forces, rushed to arm themselves, seizing weapons from caches all over the city. Women cast themselves as ringleaders in attacks upon the tollgates surrounding Paris where duties were levied; they blamed the king's collectors for raising prices and creating bread shortages in the markets. On July 14th, a crowd of National Guardsmen and other citizens, heavily supported by neighborhood crowds, including women, attacked and conquered the Bastille; immediately afterward, the public, seizing upon the symbolic importance of the deed, proclaimed this victory a triumph of liberty over despotism. In an all-night session on August 4, the National Assembly abolished feudal privileges, and on August 26 passed, and sent to the king, a Declaration of the Rights of Man and of the Citizen.

During August and September, in the aftermath of these revolutionary events, hundreds of women from the central markets of Paris participated as principal players in nearly daily marches that wound through Paris. Ostensibly, these marches were acts of thanksgiving for the liberation of the Bastille, the withdrawal of royal troops from the environs of Paris, the establishment of the National Guard as the city's protective force, and the creation of a reformed municipal administration accountable to electors. The women, accompanied by contingents from the National Guard, marched in formation and to drumbeat. Typically, they proceeded to the Eglise Sainte Geneviève (now the Panthéon), Nôtre Dame, and the Hôtel de Ville (seat of the municipal government of Paris). In passing through these spaces, the participants linked themselves with both traditional and newly designated protectors of the city: Sainte Geneviève, patron saint of Paris; Nôtre Dame, the national church; the Hôtel de Ville, locus of the new elected representative government; and the National Guard, the newly constituted military force composed of property-owning men. Observers detected subversive elements in these ceremonies, and with good reason. The Marquis de Lafayette, commander of the National Guard, the mayor Jean Sylvain Bailly, representatives of the city government, and by extension national authorities and the king himself, were put on notice that women of the popular classes were holding them accountable for provisioning the city and safeguarding its liberty. The bookseller Hardy found these imposing demonstrations of popular allegiance patently ridiculous, but they also made him nervous.

> Many people found there was something terrifying in [the procession's] arrangement, composition, and immensity. Sensitive people found these public acts, which could not be interrupted and of which piety was unfortunately not the full motive, ridiculous. They thought it would have been infinitely wiser for each man and woman citizen to thank the Almighty individually. . . rather than collectively.[11]

These processions continued until a few days before the women's march to Versailles in October 1789. For some weeks, radical leaders and the people of Paris had been concerned about the king's failure to ratify the Declaration of Rights and also about the unresolved constitutional question of a royal veto and the summoning of additional troop reinforcements. All these issues came to a head over news of soldiers' insults to the revolutionary tricolor cockade (a hat decoration with the three revolutionary colors, red, white and blue) at a banquet held for royal bodyguards at Versailles. Just after dawn on October 5, a rainy Monday, the tocsin (alarm bell!) began to ring from the Hôtel de Ville, and then from most churches all over the city. We can hear the stomp of the *poissardes' sabots* (wooden shoes) and imagine the smell of their damp skirts as they swarmed into the Hôtel de Ville and forcibly kept men out. They were looking for ammunition, but also (according to Stanislas Maillard, a National Guardsman) for administrative records; they said that all the revolution had accomplished so far was paperwork. Another eyewitness heard them say that "men didn't have enough strength to avenge themselves and that they [the women] would demonstrate that they were better than men."[12] Late in the morning, they left the Hôtel de Ville and returned to the streets; they drummed the *générale* (a military call to arms), recruited thousands of additional women, then marched off en masse to Versailles. Hardy noted that they left "allegedly with the design of. . . asking the king, whom they intended to bring back to Paris, as well as the National Assembly, for bread and for closure on the Constitution."[13]

When the first group of women reached Versailles, a small delegation was granted an audience with the king . After leaving the royal apartments and returning to the palace courtyard with news of Louis XVI's promise to provision Paris, this delegation was threatened by waiting crowds of women who sent back two among them to obtain a written document sealing the king's commitment. Louise Chabry, one of those who had been granted the royal audience, and thirty-nine other women marchers returned to Paris at 3:00 A.M. in royal carriages; they reported that Stanislas Maillard and women with him were returning to Paris with signed decrees on provisionment.[14] Chabry, allegedly forced to march that morning, took it upon herself (or was assigned) to act as a spokesperson for the royal audience and principal courier bringing the news back to the Paris Commune. Furthermore, Chabry presented the mayor with the orders that the king had given her. This young lace worker had assumed a quasi-official position as emissary for her city and its government.

Other women who marched to Versailles entered the National Assembly and occupied it throughout the night, disrupting procedures, voting on motions, and occupying the speaker's chair. Such political dramaturgy draws upon the French tradition of role reversals on carnival days; however, these were not carnival days. The women's actions were direct interventions in the legislative process and symbolic replacements of representatives who did not represent.

Early on the morning of October 6, the crowd, including women and Guardsmen, broke into the château and killed two royal bodyguards. Fearing more violence, the king agreed to go with his family to reside in Paris. A bizarre procession was formed for the march from Versailles to Paris: the women, some mounted on gun carriages and carrying loaves of bread mounted on pikes; National Guardsmen intermingled with royal bodyguards; the royal family in a carriage from which they could view the heads of the murdered guards impaled on pikes; delegations of deputies; and a host of others.

After October 6, authorities moved to suppress collective demonstrations of popular force. City officials decreed martial law in Paris after the lynching of a baker whom a woman had accused of reserving bread for deputies to the Assembly (the charge implied that deputies had subordinated the public good to their private interests). This event suggests that women and men in the crowd held deputies directly accountable to the people for their actions. Following the proclamation of martial law, two Paris districts protested the prohibition of public gatherings; they also protested the failure of city officials to consult with them before decreeing martial law. These protests amounted to an unequivocal demand for the right of referendum, which authorities did not grant, although they did permit delegations of up to six persons to submit grievance petitions.[15]

The National Assembly, relocated in Paris, began to work in the late fall of 1789 on the details of the new constitution. On December 22, 1789, the assembly set up electoral assemblies and defined the limits of the franchise. Abstract debates about citizenship now yielded a concrete and codified definition. Active citizens were men who could meet a tax qualification: the payment of "a direct tax equal to the local value of three days' labor."[16] The decree did not define a category for those not qualifying as active citizens; however, the question had been discussed in the National Assembly during the October 1789 debates on citizenship.[17] Other people—women, foreigners, domestic servants, and men who did not meet the tax qualification—were considered passive citizens. The deputies construed their definitions to allow for the possibility that men classified as passive citizens might become active citizens should their tax payment reflect an increased income. No such possibility existed for women.

The exclusion of women from the status and political rights of full legal citizenship was never remedied in any revolutionary code or constitution. Nonetheless, many thousands of women in all socio-professional categories pushed past the legal boundaries to claim citizenship in words and acts, to erode acceptance of the constitutional monarchy even as it was being established, and to take their place alongside men in the ranks of the sovereign people, inextricably combining democratic practices with political empowerment and rights claims. In the absence of any preponderant political or administrative authority willing or able to pronounce upon the legality of this de facto citizenship, all these practices together sufficed to keep the question of women's status open and indeterminate.

Publicists and observers promoted this openness as they assigned competing meanings to the October Days. Aristocratic publicists on the extreme right wrote off the October women as mistresses of the former French guards; one pamphleteer called them "the vilest toads from the dirtiest street in the most disgusting city in the universe."[18] Some supporters of the Paris revolution expressed uneasiness about women's initiatives—however strongly they approved the political outcomes of the October Days. Shortly after the insurrection, the radical newspaper *Révolutions de Paris* printed a letter from a priest recounting the classical story of the Spartan mother who, informed that her five sons had all died in battle, refused to mourn her loss since Sparta had won, saying she loved her *patrie* a thousand times more than she loved her sons—indeed she loved them more than she loved her own life.[19] For the journalist, this story taught that women's patriotic responsibilities—their roles as citizens—centered on the rearing of sons and the cultivation of a willingness to sacrifice them, if necessary, for the higher cause of the nation. The Declaration of the Rights of Man and a constitution would not produce good citizens automatically; women must accept responsibility for educating their sons in valor and their daughters in habits of self-sacrifice.

Other pamphleteers celebrated women's achievements on October 5 and 6 in more exalted language; but they assigned women curiously mundane tasks, such as overseeing quality control in the markets. One anonymous polemicist praised the women's daring move to bring the king to Paris, but admonished them to restrain themselves henceforth: they must remain sober, avoid questionable popular entertainers, and keep watch at the tollgates to prevent the importation of spoiled fruit and grain into Paris. In brief, they should abandon insurrectionary politics and limit themselves to narrowly circumscribed surveillance activities.[20]

Some women authors appropriated the language of heroism on women's behalf and demanded their plenary empowerment. In November 1789, the editors of a short-lived journal, the *Etrennes nationales des dames,* published a letter from a "Madame la M. de M," a writer who may have been a man speaking in a woman's voice and who apparently was a collaborator in their enterprise. In a light, bantering tone, teasingly but also pointedly, this writer directly linked the bravery and enterprise of the October women to women's demands for political rights: "Let us return men to the right path, and let us not tolerate that, with their systems of equality and liberty, their declarations of rights, they leave us in a condition of inferiority—let us tell the straight truth—slavery— in which they have kept us for so long."[21] "Madame la M. de M" conjures up scenarios in which women demand representation in the National Assembly, undertake surveillance activities at the Hôtel de Ville, and assume posts in the voluntary National Guard as "amazons of the Queen." The writer holds out to women subscribers the promise of a complete political education—political news, legislative decrees, judicial decisions, extracts from foreign newspapers, military and economic news, and happenings in the world of letters, science, and the arts. For this writer, the achievements of the women of the October days heralded new conquests—plenary rights of citizenship for all women.

During the course of 1790 and 1791, power struggles pitted radicals in the Paris districts and clubs against the municipal leadership and the National Assembly, whose leaders were trying to contain the potential force of the sovereign people by limiting the suffrage, prohibiting collective petitions, and outlawing strikes.

Nonetheless, the Paris sections (neighborhood governing bodies that replaced the districts) met regularly; political clubs actively recruited members and took on an educational mission. Women vigorously challenged restrictions on popular sovereignty, not only as gallery spectators and wives, but also as active members of clubs and popular societies, printers, journalists, political organizers, petitioners, and delegates. Together with men classified as passive citizens, women of the popular classes involved themselves centrally in the spring 1791 crisis over the legitimacy of the constitutional monarchy—a crisis that escalated as Parisians became increasingly suspicious of Louis XVI. As they challenged royal legitimacy, these activists linked the meanings of their protests to rights, sometimes construed as individual rights and sometimes as the collective rights of the sovereign people.

The published minutes of the Cordeliers Club (a radical political club) for February 11, 1791, contained an exhortation to club members by several *citoyennes* from the Rue de Regard. The *citoyennes* characterized themselves as good Rousseauian mothers who taught constitutional principles to their children; but they also threatened to become militant if men did not fight hard enough for the right to liberty.

> We have consoled ourselves for not having been able to contribute anything toward the public good by exerting our most intense efforts to elevate the spirit of our children to the heights of free men. But if you were to deceive our hope, if the machinations of our enemies were to dazzle you to the point of lulling you at the height of the storm, then indignation, sorrow, despair would lead and propel us into public places. There, we would fight to defend liberty; until you conquered it [liberty], you were not men. Then [under these conditions], we would save the Fatherland, or dying with it, we would uproot the memory of having seen you unworthy of us.[22]

On the night of June 21, 1791, members of the royal family, in disguise, were smuggled out of the Tuileries palace into a waiting coach and driven east toward the Belgian border, where they were scheduled to meet up with several French generals, rejoin the Austrian army, and unleash a counterrevolution. At the town of Varennes, local officials recognized them; they were forced to return to Paris, escorted by deputies from the National Assembly. They entered the city surrounded by an escort of National Guards and rode past a silent, largely hostile crowd lining the route.

The National Assembly temporarily suspended the king's executive authority and debated what to do with him. Paris radicals were not so hesitant. Clubs like the Cercle Social and the Cordeliers reached out to other popular societies, many of whose members were men and women of humble rank, and recruited them to sign petitions challenging the legitimacy of both the king and the National Assembly. Women directly involved themselves in this political mobilization. One Mlle. Le Maure, a regular participant in activities of the Cordeliers Club, presented before the assembled club members an address "to the representatives of the French Nation," a systematically argued defense of the right of collective petitioning, a right that the National Assembly had just recently outlawed. The Cordeliers adopted the address, and it was printed in a number of the radical journal *Le Creuset*. Le Maure argued that all individuals of the French nation (a deliberately all-inclusive formulation) had delegated their powers to the National Assembly; however, they had done so without renouncing their rights: ". . . without annihilating the declaration of the rights of man, you could not state as a principle that the right of petition can be exercised only individually. . . ." She argued that the new legislation violated several articles of the Declaration of the Rights of Man, including Articles 3 and 6 (which stated that the source of all sovereignty was in the nation and that the law was the expression of the "general will").[23]

Women were charged with surveillance activities (exposing an arms cache, for example); they incited Parisians to acts of vandalism against statues of the king in Paris, and signed petitions demanding consultation on the future of executive authority in the new constitution.[24] Forty-one "women, sisters, and Roman women" appended their signatures to the "Petition of the 100" delivered to the National Assembly on July 14, 1791. The text of this petition stated: ". . . make this sacred commitment to await the expression of this public voice before pronouncing on a question [the fate of the king] which affects the entire nation and which the powers you have received from [the nation] do not embrace."[25] On this fundamental question of political legitimacy, the petitioners asked the legislators to defer to the will of the nation, expressed concretely in a national vote. They had transformed acts of petitioning from deferential pleas into forceful expressions of the will of the sovereign people.

On July 17, thousands of commoners, women and men of all socio-professional ranks, met on the Champ de Mars and directly challenged the deputies in the National Assembly as well as the Constitution of 1791 that had authorized only the legislature to act in the name of the sovereign nation. They gathered peaceably to sign a petition demanding a national referendum on the question of monarchical authority. The text of the petition read: ". . . the decree [of the National Assembly, reinstating Louis XVI] is null in fact because it is contrary to the will of the sovereign. . . ."[26] The language of these petitioners, and particularly the reference to the "will of the sovereign," again echoes Article 3 of the Declaration of the Rights of Man and Citizen, which located the source of all sovereignty in the nation, and Article 6, which defined the law as the expression of the general will.[27] Late in the afternoon, the municipality declared martial law, following the crowd's summary execution of two men suspected of spying on the petitioners. National Guard battalions, dispatched to the Champ de Mars, fired on the assembled crowds, killing and wounding several dozen people. The mass demonstration had ended in a bloody confrontation between the political leaders of Paris and the crowd of petition signers acting on their claim to the right to express the will of the sovereign in the name of the nation.

Following this violent suppression, authorities arrested a number of participants, including several women. One of them, Anne Félicité Colomb, was the owner of the print works that produced the radical journals the *Ami du Peuple* and the *Orateur du peuple* and a future member of the radical women's political club, the Society of Revolutionary Republican Women. More than half a year before the massacre on the Champ de Mars, Colomb already had made an extraordinary contribution to the practice and defense of republicanism and radical democracy. Her story points to critically important alliances shaping up among political clubs, popular societies, and the printers and editors of radical journals as they stepped up pressure on constituted authorities. On December 14, 1790, Colomb was visited in her shop by a police commissioner and a publicist named Etienne. Etienne had obtained a police order from municipal officers authorizing Colomb's interrogation as well as the removal copies of the journals she was printing, at Etienne's own risk. On the spot, Colomb protested the search of her lodgings and print works as "illegal, damaging to the rights of citizens, whose domiciles could be inspected only by a duly authorized court." She declared that she was reserving the right to initiate proceedings "before the appropriate courts and in full view of the Nation, which is concerned about preserving the liberty of all its members." Furthermore, she stated that she would name the authors of the *Ami* and the *Orateur* "only at the appropriate time and place and to the appropriate persons."[28] On December 18, the court decided against Colomb and ordered her to stop printing and distributing any and all papers. On January 10, 1791, with the Cordelier activist Buirette de Verrières representing her, Colomb appealed before the Tribunal of Police at the Hôtel de Ville. Buirette de Verrières restated Colomb's earlier arguments; asked that Etienne be assessed for 10,000 livres in costs and damages to Colomb's good name and the reputation of her print works; and requested that the sum she demanded be distributed among the poor of the Sections Henry IV and Théâtre Francais. Through her lawyer, Colomb also asked the court to invoke Article 11, the free press guarantee in the Declaration of the Rights of Man, and demanded that her print works as well as the authors of the *Ami* and the *Orateur* and her distributors all enjoy protections accorded to them under law, with the understanding that they would be held responsible for abuses of freedom of the press. The court vindicated Colomb and ordered Etienne to pay a small fine.[29]

On July 20–21, 1791, following the events on the Champ de Mars, authorities arrested and jailed Colomb and others at her print works. The prisoners proceeded to appeal directly to the National Assembly, and on August 16 the Committee on Investigations of the Assembly wrote to the tribunal of the sixth *arrondisement* (an administrative ward) concerning the prisoners' provisional release, claiming that, in at least some cases, arrest and interrogation records did not appear to warrant the court's long delay in reaching a decision. The committee informed the court that it had learned that the grievance of the detained parties would be aired before the National Assembly at any moment. On August 17, an officer of the tribunal replied that he was awaiting the results of further investigation.[30]

Colomb was an extraordinarily sophisticated political activist; during her interrogation of December 14, 1790, that is, even before the Cordeliers club member Buirette de Verrières took on her case, Colomb herself invoked the freedoms and rights of citizenship to defend her professional activities. She and others arrested with her in July 1791 were prepared to go beyond the courts, indeed to go directly to the National Assembly, to do battle for their rights. They may in fact have been trying to discredit the assembly by demonstrating that these newly guaranteed constitutional rights were being violated in investigations ordered by the assembly after the events on the Champ de Mars.

Also detained by the authorities, on the charge of insulting and threatening a member of the National Guard, was Constance Evrard, a cook, later a member of the Society of Revolutionary Republican Women, and a close friend of Pauline Léon (the proprietor of a chocolate shop who cofounded the society in the spring of 1793). The minutes of Evrard's interrogation by the police show that this "passive citizen" and political activist interpreted the National Guardsmen's acts on the Champ de Mars as a betrayal of a new, critically important bond of trust that had been developing between the nation's armed forces and citizens in the Paris sections. The wife of the Guardsman reported that Evrard, Pauline Léon, and Léon's mother had denounced her husband as "an assassin, a hangman, a scoundrel, who was killing everyone on the Champ de Mars"; Evrard had threatened to knife him within three days. Evrard herself admitted that she had returned from the Champ de Mars on July 17 "outraged at the conduct of the National Guard against unarmed citizens," and that, seeing the Guardsman with his battalion passing by en route to the Champ de Mars, she reproached him for going there.[31]

The interrogation of Constance Evrard highlights her extraordinary sensitivity to the potential disaster that the National Guard's treachery could cause. In addition, she identified herself with new concepts, responsibilities, and practices of citizenship and popular sovereignty that the crises of the summer of 1791 had crystallized. She told her interrogators that she had gone to the Champ de Mars and had "signed a petition like all good patriots." While admitting that she did not have the petition read to her on the Champ de Mars, she declared that she "believes that this petition tends to have the executive power organized in another way." She acknowledged that she sometimes went with groups of people to the Palais Royal and the Tuileries gardens (public places where political news was circulated); she also attended the Cordeliers Club, although she was not a member. She reported subscribing to the radical journal *Révolutions de Paris*; she had complimented the editor, Prudhomme, on his article on tyrannicides, and told him how enthusiastic she was about this piece, adding that "had she been a man, she did not know how far patriotism would have led her." She also stated that she read the journals of Marat, Audouin, Desmoulins, and "very often the *Orateur du Peuple*"—all radical journals.[32]

During the summer of 1791, revolutionary activists in Paris, with women prominent among them, legitimated their practice of popular sovereignty by linking it to Article 3 of the Declaration of the Rights of Man and Citizen. Equally significantly, revolutionary leaders, determined to demonstrate the full weight of opposition to the constitutional monarchy, accepted and even recruited women as equal participants. For example, one of the men arrested for sedition on July 16 was accused of carrying a petition to the National Assembly and of reading an invitation to all citizens that included the statement "that all women and children who had attained the age of reason would be received to sign the petition."[33]

Notwithstanding their exclusion from such constitutional rights of citizenship as voting and holding office, the passive citizenry, men and women, identified themselves as citizens. They participated in revolutionary ceremonies; attended political meetings as discussants, petitioners, and delegates; wrote political tracts; formulated and communicated revolutionary ideology; and involved themselves centrally in revolutionary insurrections. They wore symbols of their patriotic commitment like tricolor cockades. These acts escalated pressures on authorities and contributed to transforming the French monarchy into the First Republic. At the same time, these revolutionary actors were crafting civic identities for themselves.

WOMEN AND THE TRIUMPH OF POPULAR SOVEREIGNTY

Between September 1791 and August 1792, revolutionary leaders in Paris tolerated and even encouraged the involvement of women in open challenges to the constitutional monarchy, acts of popular sovereignty expressive of a progressively more democratic understanding of the meaning of citizenship.

The collapse of the constitutional monarchy on August 10, 1792, was the outcome of a battle in the courtyard of the Tuileries between the king's Swiss Guard and a popular armed force. However, it was prepared by a complex series of events that strengthened revolutionary forces and weakened resistance in the king's camp and in the legislature. On April 20, 1792, with the nation threatened with invasion, the Legislative Assembly voted a declaration of war against Austria; that event ushered in twenty-three years of nearly continuous war in Europe. Other principal developments were the king's alienation from revolutionary authorities with whom he was required to work under the Constitution of 1791, and the growing appeal of republicanism. Both of these widened the breach between king and people and sharpened the confrontation between the ministers, deputies, and municipal authorities, who continued to operate within constitutional limits, and the fully mobilized insurgents, who claimed legitimate sovereign authority for the people.

Between March 9 and June 20, 1792, thousands of men, women, and children from all over Paris participated in armed processions through the halls of the Legislative Assembly. In each procession, the participants demanded that the legislature recognize their legitimate power as the sovereign people; they received that recognition from the legislature. In the accompanying speeches, and through signs, exclamations, gestures, images, symbols (like the red cap of liberty and ribbons in revolutionary colors), and the line of march, participants expanded the significance of their actions and linked them to new definitions of citizenship, national sovereignty, and the legitimacy of rulers. Finally, they conspicuously paraded pikes and sabers, which carried the threat that they would deploy armed force. This display of military force, in combination with concrete demands and the symbols and words that colored them with a general significance, produced a second revolution, during which the constitutional monarchy collapsed and a republic was established.

The people in arms reclaimed and rebuilt an alliance with official armed forces that had been shattered by the gunfire on the Champ de Mars in July 1791. Astonishingly, radical leaders as well as authorities first questioned, but in the end tolerated, the presence among the Guardsmen of men and women armed with pikes, the real and symbolic weapons of the sovereign people.

In an editorial, "Des Piques," appearing in a February 1792 number of his *Révolutions de Paris,* the journalist Prudhomme called attention to the symbolic and military significance of the pike: "Universally accessible, available to the poorest citizen," the pike was an emblem for independence, equality under arms, vigilance, and the recovery of liberty. "The pikes of the people are the columns of French liberty." Prudhomme explicitly denied the right of women to bear these arms: "Let pikes be prohibited for women; dressed in white and girded with the national sash, let them content themselves with being simple spectators." In his calculations Prudhomme eliminated the female portion of the 24 million potential pike bearers of France.[34] In fact, women continued to claim and exercise the right to arm themselves with pikes and with other weapons as well. They constructed political identities for themselves that mirrored Prudhomme's definition of the revolutionary citizen: independent, free, equal, vigilant, and armed.

On March 6, less than a month after Prudhomme's article appeared, a delegation of "*citoyennes* from the city of Paris," led by Pauline Léon, presented to the Legislative Assembly a petition with more than 300 signatures concerning women's right to bear arms. The petitioners grounded their claim in an appeal to the natural right of every individual to defend his or her life and liberty. "You cannot refuse us and society cannot remove from us this right which nature gives us, unless it is alleged that the Declaration of Rights is not applicable to women and that they must allow their throats to be slit, like sheep, without having the right to defend themselves." The delegation requested permission for women to arm themselves with pikes, pistols, sabers, and rifles; to assemble periodically on the Champ de Mars; and to engage in military maneuvers. The assembly, after debate, decreed a printing of the petition and honorable mention in the minutes and passed to the order of the day.[35]

While the Legislative Assembly hesitated between dismissing and tolerating women's demands for the right to bear arms, the Paris Commune and the mayor, Jérôme Pétion, took action to honor women's militancy publicly, to reward it officially, and to instate it as a model of women's citizenship. In his speech of April 5 to the commune, Pétion endorsed a petition on behalf of Reine Audu, one of the few participants in the women's march to Versailles in October 1789 who had been arrested and imprisoned. He argued that although French customs generally kept women out of combat, it also was the case that "in the moment of danger, when the *patrie* is in peril," women "do not feel any the less that they are *citoyennes*." The Council of the Commune, acting on the petition, decreed a ceremony in which the mayor would honor and decorate "this *citoyenne*" with a sword as "an authentic testimony to her bravery and her patriotism."[36]

During the weeks preceding the armed procession of April 9, 1792, a concept of female citizenship emerged that dissolved distinctions between active and passive, male and female citizens; combined women's right of self-defense with their civic obligation to protect and defend the nation; and placed both directly in the center of a general definition of all citizens' rights and responsibilities. Thus the armed women, who in spring 1792 marched in imposing processions, giving dramatic and forceful expression to the potent image of a united national family in arms, at the same time embodied militant citizenship, a driving force in the process of revolutionary radicalization. This moving picture is the clean, sharp inverse of the radical journalists' earlier depictions of unarmed families brutally gunned down by Lafayette's troops as they gathered on the Champ de Mars in July 1791 to sign the petition on the fate of the king. In the weeks following the events of July 17, 1791, Jean-Paul Marat had filled the pages of his *Ami du peuple* with provocative images: "The blood of old men, women, children, massacred around the altar of the fatherland is still warm, it cries out for vengeance."[37] The arming of passive citizens, including women, in the spring of 1792 turned upside down this picture of helpless martyrs; it empowered the powerless, and it activated an involuntarily pacific (because legally "passive") citizenry, including the potential force of women within the radical leadership's escalating estimates of the strength of the national family in arms.

The armed procession of June 20, 1792, reflected turmoil in Paris over the king's dismissal of liberal ministers and his vetoes of two decrees, one authorizing harsh sanctions against clergy who had refused to swear an oath of loyalty to the constitution and another establishing a camp for 20,000 French troops beneath the walls of Paris. Four days earlier, on June 16, a delegation from two militant neighborhoods informed municipal authorities of plans to commemorate the fourth anniversary of the Tennis Court Oath—an oath sworn by deputies in the National Assembly not to disband until they had given France a constitution. The key event was to be an armed procession before the assembly and the king to present petitions. The authorities tried to prevent the march, but the mayor, Pétion, realized that nothing could stop it. He developed a strategy of putting all armed citizens under the flags of the National Guard battalions and under the authority of battalion commanders, thereby legitimating a force composed of National Guardsmen and all citizens, passive along with active, women and children along with men.

On the morning of June 20, thousands of marchers were granted permission to parade through the meeting hall of the Legislative Assembly. Marchers included National Guardsmen, light infantrymen, grenadiers, and troops of the line—all interspersed with women ("*dames* and *femmes du peuple*"), men (porters, charcoal burners, priests with swords and guns, veterans), and children. The marchers carried long pikes, guns, axes, knives, paring knives, scythes, pitchforks, sticks, bayonets, great saws, and clubs. Armed women were described as wearing liberty caps and carrying sabers and blades. The marchers' signs and banners proclaimed loyalty to the constitution,[38] and they meant what they said. In addition, their actions made it clear that the constitution, along with the government, was only the instrument of the will of an armed sovereign people.

Through these practices of citizenship, the insurrectionary crowds symbolically subverted the king's legally sanctioned executive authority, his right to veto laws, and his role as representative of national sovereignty. The marchers, constitutionally prohibited from exercising sovereignty, were doing just that.[39] When the marchers left the assembly, they charged into the Tuileries Palace and for six hours paraded, armed, before the king, displaying the banners and symbols that identified them as the sovereign nation. The king, in turn, refused to bend his will to that of this "sovereign people," and the mayor and other officers finally persuaded the demonstrators to leave the palace.[40]

Several witnesses were quick to seize the larger import of the day's events. An official of the Department of Paris (the national administrative unit for Paris) commented: "The throne was still standing but the people were seated on it, took the measure of it; and its steps seemed to have been lowered to the height of the paving stones of Paris."[41] These armed marches, repeatedly legitimized by the assembly's votes to permit and honor them, were successful ceremonial demonstrations of the breadth, scope, and power of a fully mobilized democratic force in revolutionary Paris. The alliance between the women and men of the radical faubourgs (neighborhoods) and their National Guard battalions, an alliance shattered on the Champ de Mars in 1791, was reforged on foundations of rebuilt trust and restored unity of purpose. On June 21, a police commissioner reported that in the Faubourg Saint-Antoine people were saying that ". . . the people is the only sovereign, it must make the law WITHOUT CONSTITUTION AND WITHOUT SANCTION [from any higher authority]."[42]

Pétion, the mayor, called particular attention to the significance of women's involvement in the events of June 20. Under attack for having failed to use force to prevent or disperse the procession, Pétion rushed into print with a self-defense: *Conduct of the Mayor of Paris on the Occasion of the Events of June 20, 1792.* Pétion insisted that neither he nor anyone else could have commanded the force capable of stopping the march of "such an immense crowd of citizens." "Where was the repressive force capable of stopping the torrent? I say it did not exist." All battalions from the two faubourgs had marched with cannon and arms, followed by large numbers of armed citizens and a multitude of unarmed citizens, Pétion explained. Any force mobilized against the marchers could only have been composed of National Guardsmen, who, in that case, would have been opposing fellow Guardsmen; combating fellow citizens armed with pikes; opposing unarmed men, maybe even their neighbors; confronting women—their sisters, their wives, their mothers; and battling with children, possibly their own. "Who would have been able to answer for the lives of these persons who are the most precious to the nation [and] whom it is most important to preserve?" On whom and where would this attacking force have fired? "The very idea of this carnage makes one shiver." "And to whom would this bloody battlefield have been left?" Three-quarters of the National Guard would have refused to fire on their fellow citizens, given that they all shared the marchers' motives, and given that the Legislative Assembly already had set precedents when it "tolerated" earlier processions.[43]

The officials of the Department of Paris, who suspended Pétion from office for his failure to prevent the march, acknowledged that he was right about June 20: the presence of women and children in the ranks of the National Guard had paralyzed it.[44] In short, authorities of all convictions, that is, those who would have had to give the orders, perceived that the participants in the processions of June 20—precisely this particular combination of National Guardsmen and their commanders, armed and unarmed men and women and children, their relatives, friends and neighbors—symbolized a new political and military force, a national family in arms, that could be vanquished only at unthinkable cost.

Furthermore, the conjunction of women's claims to the rights of citizenship, especially the right to bear arms, with their incorporation into the marching revolutionary "nation" endorsed by radical male leaders, ran radically counter to the Rousseauian model of the woman citizen as a civic educator. Women had appropriated radical, alternative discourses of rights and responsibilities as well as dramatically broadened agendas of political action.

After the fall of the monarchy on August 10, the new republican authorities moved quickly to regulate the women and men who had helped bring them to victory, yet even those controls illustrated recognition of women's full political and military engagement. The General Assembly of one neighborhood government printed a decree that all male citizens aged 15 and over and all female citizens over the age of 13 had to take an individual oath before the section assembly. The wording of the oath was similar to one decreed by the Legislative Assembly on August 14: "to uphold liberty and equality and to die, if necessary, for both. . . . " The section assembly declared that it would regard as "bad" citizens and *citoyennes* those who would not swear it, and that it would refuse entry into its sessions to anyone who had not fulfilled this "civic duty." These authorities recognized that the armed men and women who had just brought down the monarchy could not be dissolved or repressed. The administrative requirement was to regulate them: "It is important to know who are the good citizens and *citoyennes* who want to bring about liberty and equality, and who are the cowards and traitors who still would dare to yearn for despotism."[45]

In the spring of 1793, a group of *citoyennes*, petit-bourgeois and sansculotte women who wanted to "bring about liberty and equality," organized themselves into the first exclusively female interest group in Western politics, the Society of Revolutionary Republican Women. Pauline Léon, who had been involved in the violent events on the Champ de Mars in 1791, and Claire Lacombe, an actress from the French provinces, were among the organizers; Constance Evrard and Anne Félicité Colomb, whose radical political activities in 1791 we review above, were members. Initially the society met under the aegis of the Jacobin Club, which provided a meeting hall; it formed close ties with the Enragés, radical men active in neighborhood politics. Members of the society were instrumental in helping to evict the Girondins (a loosely organized "party" of liberal deputies) from the National Convention in late May 1793. Throughout the summer, they pressured the convention to apply more extreme curbs on aristocrats and to pass decrees regulating supplies and prices in Paris and supporting revolutionary armies. They strongly supported the Constitution of 1793 decreed by the National Convention on June 24. In the summer of 1793, a group of women describing themselves as *citoyennes* of the Section Droits de l'Homme came to the society to present a martial standard. Their speech, honoring the society's members, explicitly stated that "the Declaration of Rights is common to both sexes. . . ."[46] In late summer, the society's radicalism evoked protests from market women, who opposed price controls and who accused the society of ruining their commerce.

Despite heroic defensive maneuvers by Claire Lacombe and others, the convention voted to close the society in October 1793 on the grounds that its members threatened public order. Jacobin leaders who presented and debated the proposed repression of the society and the more general question of women's place in the new republican regime also exposed serious tensions and fissures in republican ideology. André Amar, who spoke for the Committee of General Security before the convention on October 28, began with specific complaints about market disorders near Saint-Eustache, which the Revolutionary Women allegedly incited, and reported the request of the Section des Marchés (a self-governing municipal unit) for a prohibition of popular societies of women. Amar then posed the general question: Should women exercise political rights and meddle in political affairs? His negative answer no longer addressed the specific issue of the society's responsibility for market disorders; rather, in his rationalization of the legislation, Amar cited women's reproductive responsibilities, their moral weakness, their inadequate political education, and their nervous excitability. He thus developed a full-blown misogynist theory of the biological, psychological, and moral determinants of women's incapacity for political action. In contrast, another deputy, Charlier, identifying and separating out from one another principles of universal rights and matters of public security, argued that the police ought to be able to deal with disorder and that women should not be denied their right to assemble peaceably: "Unless you are going to question whether women are part of the human species, can you take away from them this right which is common to every thinking being?" The deputy Bazire brought the debate to a close; he declared that he did not want to hear any more about principles; public order was endangered; that situation called for the absolute prohibition of women's associations.[47] Bazire was not endorsing Amar's argument; he was being pragmatic: every political system had the authority to suspend rights in times of dire emergency. These deputies were fully aware of the political implications of defining gender roles either narrowly or broadly; women's status and rights were one factor in the power equation in a city and nation that was caught up in the throes of revolution and war and where the locus of sovereign authority was being contested continually. Even as they outlawed the Revolutionary Republican Women and all women's clubs, the legislators exposed deep conflicts within the republican camp about whether the rights of man could be denied to women.

In the short run, the Jacobin leaders tried to eliminate women's institutional power bases by proscribing clubs and popular societies of women and barring them from sessions of the Paris Commune. These restrictions did not silence women's voices. Mixed-sex popular societies in the sections continued to provide channels for women's influence. Immediately after the repressive legislation of October 28, a deputation from the Fraternal Society of the Two Sexes of the Panthéon-Français section, led by a woman, came before the section's General Assembly. Citizens protested the presence of women: ". . . a woman does not have the right to speak, to deliberate in assemblies, according to the law."[48] Again in February 1794, the Fraternal Society of the Section Panthéon-Français protested vehemently against accusations in the press that it was a hermaphrodite society that violated nature by offering men and women equal access and rights of participation. Two women officers of the fraternal society signed that protest.[49] A few days earlier, the society's Committee of Purification, composed of women and men, voted to exclude members who argued that women "ought not to have been admitted to deliberate on the affairs of a section or to purify its members "; in the short run, they prevailed, notwithstanding the protest of a woman in the section who argued that women should not be sitting on the Purification Committee, that they were voting illegally.[50]

Women of the popular classes were principal participants in the last great revolutionary uprising, the *journées* of Germinal-Prairial, Year III (1795). However, these insurrections were doomed to failure; by that time, women and men in the sections had lost the popular societies and assemblies that had functioned as the common people's organizational base of influence. In May 1795, the legislature ordered women to remain in their homes and decreed that groups of more than five women in public would be dispersed, forcibly if necessary.[51]

CONCLUSION

The Napoleonic Code, the French code of laws completed in 1804, is some-times offered as evidence that the overtures made by revolutionary women were brave but brief efforts that ultimately worsened conditions for women well into the nineteenth century. Under the terms of the code, women could not sign contracts, buy or sell, or maintain bank accounts in their own names. Divorce, legal since September 20, 1792, became more difficult. But if we look beyond legal restraints in the code, we recognize that links between women's revolutionary practices of citizenship and principles of universal rights have turned out to be indelible, as well as complex.

A handful of women writers reformulated definitions of citizenship to address women's gender-specific needs and interests in the language of the Declaration of Rights of 1789. Olympe de Gouges, playwright and publicist, drafted a *Declaration of the Rights of Woman*. It appeared just as the first con-stitution was being ratified in September 1791. Adopting the form and lan-guage of the Declaration of the Rights of Man, de Gouges called for full political equality for women, and in addition drafted articles that addressed women's gender-specific struggles to secure property and inheritance rights and to establish the right of the mother to legitimate her children regardless of her marital state. De Gouges had addressed her *Declaration* to Queen Marie Antoinette; she was arrested in 1793, accused of royalism, tried and found guilty by the Revolutionary Tribunal, and guillotined on November 3, 1793. The Dutch-born revolutionary writer Etta Palm d'Aelders addressed the issue of equal rights for women, focusing on marriage laws, educational opportu-nities, and admission to civil and military positions.[52] Ideas counted in mak-ing and legitimating the revolution. Women like De Gouges, d'Aelders, and Anne Félicité Colomb, in roles as journalists, pamphleteers, speechmakers, printers, petitioners, club members, and witnesses, contributed to the ideolo-gies supporting the liberal tradition in France. We suggest that a common-sense logic informed these women's efforts to restate rights so that they addressed gender-specific interests: if women could recognize themselves in the nation, they could grant its government support and legitimacy.

Women and men involved in marching, petitioning, and other political ac-tivities that brought them into confrontation with authorities linked these practices to universals; they recast their acts as the nation's expression of its sovereign will and rights. The threat and use of force turned out to be particu-larly effective in forging links between practices and rights. On June 20, 1792, armed men, women, and children from the radical sections of Paris co-opted the National Guard and scored a symbolic victory over the legislature; on August 10, they overthrew the constitutional monarchy. All these acts of force prevailed only because the duly constituted authorities in the end accepted these acts as legitimate exercises of the rights and powers of the sovereign nation as these were defined in the Declaration of the Rights of Man.

Links between women's political practices and rights debates were forged not only in Paris but throughout revolutionary France and well beyond its boundaries. Women who founded Jacobin women's clubs in the French departments developed political visions, broad agendas, and practices in the public sphere, including endorsements of the Constitution of 1793, protests against women's political nullity, and demands for the right to vote.[53] In the age of the democratic revolution, the "woman question" was placed squarely on the agenda not only throughout France but also in England, America, the Dutch Republic, Belgium, and elsewhere in the Western world—all revolutionary political cultures in which neighborhoods and communities became caught up in broad democratizing processes and cultural transformations that opened up possibilities for women to claim political identities in the polity, that is, the rights, responsibilities, and powers of citizenship.[54]

The theory of universal rights stands as one of the most vital positive legacies of the French Revolution in the modern world. Because women's ad hoc practices of citizenship were linked to rights issues, the precedent-setting power of these practices was not canceled out by the Jacobins' decrees outlawing women's organized political activities, or by legal restrictions written into the Napoleonic Code, or even by later nineteenth- and twentieth-century exclusionary legislation. [Revolutionary women who took up arms, for example, grounded their action in universal claims: the right to self-defense, the right to assemble, the right to free expression, and the right to full political participation. Once such rights have been legislated for some and appropriated and enacted de facto by many, any issue that can be connected to rights is opened up to contestation and remains on the political agenda, notwithstanding the force of repressive laws and other sanctions.] In fact, in societies in which rights traditions have been established, the burden of proof is on those who wish to exclude specific categories of persons from the enjoyment of rights.

[However, along with these liberal principles (like Condorcet's belief that women enjoyed natural and political rights "common to every thinking and sentient being"), legacies of the Enlightenment and the Revolution relating to the woman question included persuasive and persistent formulations of women's biologically and culturally determined incapacity for assuming roles as equals in a world of power and conflict.] Viewed critically and historically, rights talk itself, even as it reveals the commonalities of human identity, also masks particular or exclusive interests grounded in class, race, sex, ethnicity, religion, age, and national or national-imperial ideologies. Furthermore, rights claimants must state their claims from a base of historically specific, situated interests; women risk the obstruction of those interests when they invest uncritically in the language of universal rights. All historically situated interests—those of rights legislators and adjudicators and those of rights claimants—must be exposed and addressed if universal rights are to be made operable as guiding principles in actual political cultures—for example, to reshape the nature of political conflict or to maximize equality.

Inevitably, meanings of universal rights, such as the right to self-defense, will change with the changing circumstances of individuals and groups: for the revolutionary generation, women and men, the right of self-defense meant the right to use arms for the protection of person, family, and property; today, at the historical juncture at which we stand, the concept of self-defense might include principles of bodily integrity that enabled the United Nations to define rape as a war crime. It is this expansive nature of rights, that is, the way rights work to narrow exclusions to the vanishing point, to embrace, over time, a plenum of concrete positions, that constitutes their irreplaceable value as an ever receding, ever approachable horizon of women's aspirations as human beings.

In the age of the democratic revolution, women of all social and professional ranks took up positions on fields of power and principle; they demanded recognition as citizens; in the historical conjuncture, these demands necessarily reidentified them as subjects of universal rights. The conquest of a permanent place on those fields of power and principle may turn out to be, for them, the most critically important legacy of the French Revolution.

NOTES

1. Madelyn Gutwirth, *The Twilight of the Goddesses: Women and Representation in the French Revolutionary Era,* Rutgers University Press, New Brunswick, 1992; Joan B. Landes, *Women and the Public Sphere in the Age of the French Revolution,* Cornell University Press, Ithaca, 1988.
2. Joan Wallach Scott, *Only Paradoxes to Offer: French Feminists and the Rights of Man,* Harvard University Press, Cambridge, 1996.
3. Lynn Hunt, "Forgetting and Remembering: The French Revolution Then and Now," *American Historical Review* 100 (1995), pp. 1119–1135; quote from p. 1131; "Introduction: The Revolutionary Origins of Human Rights," in *The French Revolution and Human Rights: A Brief Documentary History,* ed. Lynn Hunt, Bedford Books of St. Martin's Press, Boston, 1996.
4. See the comments of Joan Scott concerning 1990s proposals for gender quotas in the French National Assembly, in Scott, *op. cit.,* p. 2.
5. Dena Goodman, *The Republic of Letters: A Cultural History of the French Enlightenment,* Cornell University Press, Ithaca, 1994.
6. Siméon Prosper Hardy, "Mes Loisirs, ou Journal d'événements tels qu'ils parviennent à ma connoissance," vol. 7, May 8 1787, fol. 475, in Bibliothèque nationale, MSS, fonds français, no. 6687.
7. Henri Monin, *L'Etat de Paris en 1789: Etudes et Documents,* Jouaust, Noblet, et Maison Quantin, Paris, 1889, p. 637.
8. Nina Gelbart, *Feminine and Opposition Journalism in Old Regime France: Le Journal des Dames,* University of California Press, Berkeley, 1987; Arlette Farge and Jacques Revel, *The Vanishing Children of Paris: Rumor and Politics Before the French Revolution,* trans. Claudia Miéville, Harvard University Press, Cambridge, 1991; Arlette Farge, *Subversive Words: Public Opinion in Eighteenth-Century France,* trans. Rosemary Morris, Pennsylvania State University Press, University Park, 1994.

9. See, for example, *Doléances particulières des marchandes bouquetières fleuristes chapelières en fleurs de la Ville et faubourgs de Paris* (1789), in Charles-Louis Chassin, *Les Elections et les cahiers de Paris en 1789*, 4 vols., Paris, 1888–89, vol. II, pp. 534–537; translated in *Women in Revolutionary Paris, 1789–1795*, ed. Darline Gay Levy, Harriet Branson Applewhite, and Mary Durham Johnson, University of Illinois Press, Urbana, 1979, pp. 22–26.

10. Letter from Thirout de Crosne to Louis XVI, 20 April 1789 in AN, C 221/160/146, fol. 67.

11. Hardy, *op. cit.* vol. 8, September 14, 1789.

12. *Procédure criminelle instruite au Chatlet de Paris*, Baudouin, Paris, 1790, Part I, witness 81, p. 118.

13. Hardy, *op. cit.*, no. 6687, fol. 502, October 5, 1789.

14. *Ibid.*, and testimony of Chabry, No. 183, *Procédure criminelle*, Part II, pp. 23–25. In her account, Chabry says she and the other women arrived back in Paris at 2:00 A.M.; the secretary of the Commune puts it an hour later.

15. Arch. nat. C 32, no. 271.

16. John Hall Stewart, *A Documentary Survey of the French Revolution*, Macmillan, New York, 1951, p. 129.

17. J. Mavidal, E. Laurent, et al., eds., *Archives parlementaires, de 1787 à 1860*, First Series (34 vols., Paris; Imprimerie nationale, 1867–1890), 9, (October 20, 1789), p. 470.

18. B.N. Lb 39 2412. *Relation très exacte des événemens du 5 et 6 octobre*, Paris, 1789.

19. *Révolutions de Paris*, no. 19 (November 14–21), p. 46.

20. Anonymous, *Les Héroïnes de Paris ou l'entière liberté de la France, par les femmes . . . police qu'elles doivent exercer de leur propre autorité. Expulsion des charlatans &c. &c., le 5 octobre 1789* (n.p., n.d.).

21. *Etrennes nationales des dames*, no. 1 (November 3, 1789), 8 pp.

22. Club des Cordeliers, Société des amis des droits de l'homme et du citoyen, *Extrait des délibérations du 22 février 1791*, Paris, 1791, in Bibliothèque historique de la Ville de Paris, 10,065, No. 67.

23. *Le Creuset*, no. for June 9, 1791.

24. *Ibid.*; Levy, Applewhite, and Johnson, *op. cit.*, pp. 78, 79, 83, 84.

25. *Ibid.*, p. 79.

26. Petition of July, 17, 1791, in Stewart, *op. cit.*, pp. 219–220.

27. "Declaration of the Rights of Man and Citizen," in Stewart, *op. cit.*, p. 114.

28. Dossier of Anne Félicité Colomb, Archives nationales, F[7] 2624. plaq. 1, fols. 52–69.

29. *Ibid.*

30. Section de la Place Vendôme, 20–21 July 1791, Procès-verbal of the seizure of manuscripts and printed works by Marat and others . . . arrest and imprisonment of Dlle. Colomb, Redelé de Fl [illeg.] and Verrières , in Archives nationales, W. 357, no. 750; Letter of the Comité des recherches to the Tribunal of the 6th Arrondissement, 16 August 1791 in Archives nationales, DXXIX[bis]31b, no. 324; letter from the Interim President of the Tribunal of the 6th Arrondissment to the Comité des Rapports, 17 August 1791, in DXXIX[bis]34, no. 352.

31. Procès-verbal of the interrogation of Constance Evrard and witnesses, Section de la Fontaine de Grenelle, Sunday, 17 July 1791, in Archives, Préfecture de la Police, Paris, Series Aa, 148, fol. 30.

32. *Ibid.*

33. Mathiez, *Le Club des Cordeliers*, p. 363.

34. Prudhomme, "Des Piques," *Révolutions de Paris,* vol. 11, February 11–18, 1792, pp. 293–298.

35. *Archives parlementaires* 39 (March 6, 1792), pp. 423, 424.

36. *Extrait du registre des délibérations du Conseil général de la Commune de Paris,* Vendredi, 5 avril 1792, Paris, 1792.

37. Marat, *Ami du peuple,* no. 524, July 20, 1791, p. 2.

38. *Archives parlementaires* 45 (June 20, 1792), pp. 406 ff, and esp. 411–419.[Madame Rosalie Jullien], *Journal d'une Bourgeoise pendant la Révolution, 1791–1793,* published by Edouard Lockroy, Calmann-Lévy, Paris, 1881), pp. 134–147. *Le Mercure universel,* June 21, 1792, as cited in Laura B. Pfeiffer, "The Uprising of June 20, 1792," *University Studies of the University of Nebraska* 12, no. 3 (July 1912), pp. 84, 85.

39. Stewart, *op. cit.,* p. 234.

40. Pfeiffer, *op. cit.,* pp. 284–323.

41. P.L. Roederer, *Chronique des cinquante jours du 20 juin au 10 août 1792,* Paris, 1832, p. 63.

42. Dumont, commissaire de police, Section de la Rue Montreuil, to the Directory of the Department of Paris, June 21, 1792, in "Journée du 20 juin 1792," *Revue Rétrospective, ou Bibliothèque historique,* 2nd series, vol. 1 (1835), p. 180.

43. Jérôme Pétion, *Conduite tenue par M. le Maire de Paris à l'occasion des événements du 20 juin 1792,* in "Journée du 20 juin 1792," *Revue Rétrospective, ou Bibliothèque historique,* 2nd series, vol. 1 (1835), p. 180.

44. *Extrait des Registres des délibérations du Conseil du Département de Paris,* 6 juillet 1792, Paris, 1792.

45. *Extrait des Registres des délibérations de la Section du Pont Neuf, Réunie en Assemblée permanente, le 15 août 1792, l'an 4e de la liberté, le 1er de l'egalité.* Paris, n.d. See also F. Braesch, ed., *Procès-verbaux de l'Assemblée générale de la Section des Postes, 4 décembre 1790–5 septembre 1792,* Paris, 1911, pp. 198, 199, no. 2.

46. Marie Cerati, *Le Club des citoyennes républicaines révolutionnaires,* Paris, 1966, p. 73; and Pauline Léon, Police Dossier, Archives nationales, F7 4774 9, translated in Levy, Applewhite, and Johnson, *op. cit.,* pp. 158–160.

47. *Réimpression de l'Ancien Moniteur,* National Convention, Session of 9 Brumaire, Vol. 18, pp. 298–300; translated in Levy, Applewhite, and Johnson, *op. cit.,* pp. 213–217.

48. Dominique Godineau, "Femmes en citoyenneté: pratiques et politique," *Annales Historiques de la Révolution française,* no. 2 (1995): p. 204.

49. Robert Barrie Rose, "Symbols, Citizens or Sisterhood: Women and the Popular Movement in the French Revolution. The Beginning of a Tradition," *Australian Journal of Politics and History* 40 (1994), p. 308.

50. Godineau, *op. cit.,* p. 204, citing from Archives nationales, W 191, 14 pluviôse; Archives, Préfecture de la police, AA 201, 121–139; B.N., MSS, nouvelles acquisitions françaises, 2713.

51. Dominique Godineau, *Citoyennes Tricôteuses. Les Femmes du peuple à Paris pendant la Révolution française* Alinea, Aix-en-Provence, 1988, pp. 319–355.

52. Etta Palm d'Aelders, *Adresse des citoyennes françoises à l'Assemblée nationale* (n.d.[Summer, 1791]); *Archives parlementaires,* 41 (procès-verbal, April 1, 1792) pp. 63–64; both translated in Levy, Applewhite, and Johnson, *op. cit.,* pp. 75–77, 123.

53. Suzanne Desan, "'Constitutional Amazons': Jacobin Women's Clubs in the French Revolution, "in *Recreating Authority in Revolutionary France,* ed. Bryant T.

Ragan and Elizabeth A. Williams, Rutgers University Press, New Brunswick, 1992, ch. 1; Suzanne Desan, "The Family as Cultural Battleground: Religion vs. Republic under the Terror," in *The French Revolution and the Creation of Modern Political Culture,* Vol. 4: *The Terror,* ed. Keith Michael Baker, (Pergamon, Oxford, 1994, pp. 177–193.

54. Harriet B. Applewhite and Darline G. Levy, eds., *Women and Politics in the Age of the Democratic Revolution,* University of Michigan Press, Ann Arbor, 1990; paperback, 1993.

SUGGESTIONS FOR FURTHER READING

Abray, Jane. "Feminism in the French Revolution." *American Historical Review* 80 (February, 1975), pp. 43–62.

Applewhite, Harriet B., and Darline Gay Levy. *Women and Politics in the Age of the Democratic Revolution.* Ann Arbor: The University of Michigan Press, 1990, 1993.

Chartier, Roger. *The Cultural Origins of the French Revolution,* trans. Lydia G. Cochrane. Durham: Duke University Press, 1991.

Dekker, Rudolf M., and Judith Vega, eds. "Women and the French Revolution." Special edition of *History of European Ideas* 10, no. 3 (1989).

Desan, Suzanne. "'Constitutional Amazons': Jacobin Women's Clubs in the French Revolution." In *Re-creating Authority in Revolutionary France,* ed. Bryant T. Ragan, Jr., and Elizabeth A. Williams. New Brunswick: Rutgers University Press, 1992.

———. "The Family as Cultural Battleground: Religion vs. Republic under the Terror." In *The French Revolution and the Creation of Modern Political Culture,* Vol. 4: *The Terror,* ed. Keith Michael Baker. Oxford: Persimmon, 1994, pp. 177–193.

Differences: Journal of Feminist Cultural Studies 7, no. 1: Universalism (Spring 1995).

Farge, Arlette. *Fragile Lives: Violence, Power and Solidarity in Eighteenth-Century Paris.* Cambridge, Mass.: Harvard University Press, 1993.

———. *Subversive Words: Public Opinion in Eighteenth-Century France,* trans. Rosemary Morris. Cambridge: Polity Press, 1994.

Faure, Christine. *Democracy Without Women: Feminism and the Rise of Liberal Individualism in France.* Bloomington: Indiana University Press, 1991.

Fraser, Nancy, and Sandra Lee Bartky, eds. *Revaluing French Feminism: Critical Essays on Difference, Agency, and Culture.* Bloomington: Indiana University Press, 1992.

Goldsmith, Elizabeth C., and Dena Goodman. *Going Public: Women and Publishing in Early Modern France.* Ithaca: Cornell University Press, 1995.

Goodman, Dena. *The Republic of Letters: A Cultural History of the French Enlightenment.* Ithaca: Cornell University Press, 1994.

Gutwirth, Madelyn. *The Twilight of the Goddesses: Women and Representation in the French Revolutionary Era.* New Brunswick: Rutgers University Press, 1992.

Hafter, Daryl. *Women and Preindustrial Craft.* Bloomington: Indiana University Press, 1995.

Hufton, Olwen. *The Prospect Before Her: A History of Women in Western Europe,* Vol. I: *1500–1800.* New York: Knopf, 1996.

————. *Women and the Limits of Citizenship in the French Revolution.* Toronto: University of Toronto Press, 1992.

Hunt, Lynn. *The Family Romance in the French Revolution.* Berkeley and Los Angeles: University of California Press, 1992.

————, ed. *The French Revolution and Human Rights: A Brief Documentary History.* Boston: Bedford Books of St. Martin's Press, 1996.

Kaplan, Steven L. "Religion, Subsistence, and Social Control: The Uses of Saint Geneviève,"*Eighteenth Century Studies* 13, no. 2 (Winter 1979–1980), pp. 142–168.

Landes, Joan B. *Women and the Public Sphere in the Age of the French Revolution.* Ithaca: Cornell University Press, 1988.

Levy, Darline Gay, and Harriet Branson Applewhite. "Women and Militant Citizenship in Revolutionary Paris." In *Rebel Daughters: Women and the French Revolution,* ed. Sara E. Melzer and Leslie W. Rabine. New York: Oxford University Press, 1992.

Levy, Darline Gay, Harriet Branson Applewhite, and Mary Durham Johnson, eds. *Women in Revolutionary Paris, 1789–1795* Urbana: University of Illinois Press, 1979, 1980.

Moses, Claire Goldberg. *French Feminism in the Nineteenth Century.* Albany: State University of New York Press, 1984.

Moses, Claire Goldberg, and Leslie Wahl Rabine. *Feminism, Socialism and French Romanticism.* Bloomington: Indiana University Press, 1993.

Proctor, Candice E. *Women, Equality and the French Revolution.* New York: Greenwood Press, 1990.

Rose, Robert Barrie. *The Enragés: Socialists of the French Revolution?* Sydney, Australia: Sydney University Press, 1968.

————. *The Making of the Sans-culottes: Democratic Ideas and Institutions in Paris, 1789–92.* Manchester, England: Manchester University Press, 1983.

Rudé, George. *The Crowd in the French Revolution.* New York: Oxford University Press, 1959.

Scott, Joan Wallach. *Only Paradoxes to Offer: French Feminists and the Rights of Man.* Cambridge, Mass.: Harvard University Press, 1996.

Stoddard, Julia C. "The Causes of the Insurrection of the 5th and 6th of October." *University of Nebraska Studies,* 4, no. 4 (October 1904), pp. 267–327.

Match-makers at the East End. *The Graphic,* vol. 3, May 20, 1871, p. 469.   *HARPER'S WEEKLY,* 1871.

CHAPTER 11

Doing Capitalism's Work: Women in the Western European Industrial Economy

Laura L. Frader

Gradually, over the course of the nineteenth century, thanks to capital gained through European colonization and international trade, industrial capitalism expanded and amplified. New machines, technologies, and large factories altered the landscape of Britain and Western Europe. Women's labor in factories and workshops proved to be central to capitalist development. However, industrial capitalism was fraught with contradictions. At the same time as it profited from women's labor, capitalism continued the process of devaluing women's economic contribution that had begun at least a century and a half earlier through a combination of structural changes, new technologies and ways of organizing work, discourses and ideologies about women's work, and the new power relations of the industrial workplace. In spite of this, women benefited from the availability of new jobs in fields like nursing, postal and telegraph work, and department store sales. Moreover, women resisted the exploitation of the workplace, along with its unequal power relations, by organizing in unions and leading strikes and protests.

T he development of industrial capitalism from about the mid-eighteenth century through the late nineteenth century brought dramatic changes to the European landscape. Capitalist entrepreneurs began to invest in large-scale manufacturing, and large factories, the hallmarks of industrial capitalism in nearly every country, belched forth soot and smoke, blackening urban centers like Manchester, Stockport, and Leeds in England; Lille, Roubaix, and Tourcoing in France; Berlin and Hamburg in Germany; and Milan and Turin in Italy. In many parts of Europe, growing numbers of wage workers labored in factories rather than in the household or in small workshops, which earlier had been their primary place of work. As industrial capitalism developed across Europe and in other parts of the world, workers and their families became increasingly dependent on the wage as their primary means of subsistence. Women made a major contribution to this transformation by providing much of the cheap labor that enabled industrial capitalism to expand. The transformation of work and workers' growing dependency on the industrial capitalist system led to the emergence of a working class. But both industrialization and class formation were profoundly gendered.

A long, uneven process, industrialization occurred with fits and starts over a century and a half all across Europe. Moreover, even though industrial capitalism developed first in Western Europe, much of this industrialization depended on connections with the world outside Europe. It was no accident that the development of an industrial capitalist economy coincided with the peak of European imperialism and colonization abroad. In some cases trade with colonies facilitated the capital accumulation that enabled manufacturers to start or expand businesses. Colonies also provided the raw materials and markets that sustained the industrial system, but at enormous cost to the indigenous inhabitants of colonized areas. Industrial capitalism also had complex and uneven effects on the lives of Europeans. The new technology produced extraordinary wealth and profits for the middle class, but the members of the industrial working class often struggled to eke out an existence as capitalism passed through alternate phases of prosperity and depression. All of these developments had consequences for women's place in the industrial economy.

This chapter addresses working women's experience of the process of industrialization between 1750 and 1914. It shows that, in spite of gendered cultural discourses that promoted women's activities in the private realm of the family and men's activities in the public realms beyond the household, women played a very public role through their contribution to the industrial economy. As industrialists attempted to reproduce the paternalistic relations of the family in the public world of the workshop and factory, industrialization confronted women with new sets of power relations.

The chapter examines how, in contrast to an earlier period when contemporaries acknowledged and accepted women's productive contribution, during the development of industrial capitalism in the nineteenth century, employers, social observers, and working men came to question the legitimacy of women's work and to consider it as inferior to men's work. The chapter argues that several factors—technological and structural changes in the division of labor; cultural discourses and practices, including those of political economists, laboring men, and social reformers; and state policies—led to the devaluing of women's work and rendered women inferior players in the labor market and workplace. However, the process through which these factors operated was complex and often contradictory. Even though some women shared common experiences under industrial capitalism, it is impossible to speak of "the woman worker" as a single category. Women differed significantly according to their age, class, race, and ethnicity or nationality. Moreover, although industrialization indisputably had negative effects on women, women were not only or merely the victims of industrial capitalism. Living standards for women improved over the period, and working women became consumers as well as producers of goods for the growing household market. Although the new power relations of industrial capitalism (as well as of the male-dominated labor movement) relied on cultural constructs of women's and girls' passivity and/or inferiority and made women more vulnerable to exploitation, including sexual harassment, women also confronted employers with protests and strikes to claim rights and defend themselves from discrimination in the workplace. Thus employers' efforts to maintain women's inferior position so that they could profit from women's low wages stimulated women's public mobilization against this subordination. This was the paradox of industrialization for women: while conspiring to devalue the labor of working women, at the same time it spurred women's mobilization.

INDUSTRIAL CAPITALISM, STRUCTURAL CHANGE, AND NEW TECHNOLOGY

The examples of Britain, France, and Germany illustrate the ways that individual national histories and conditions shaped the specific developmental paths that industrialization took across Western Europe. Britain's industrial development occurred at a steady pace between roughly 1750 and 1850.[1] Britain was blessed with a wealth of natural resources, a strong system of banking and credit, and capital to invest in industry acquired from the slave trade with Africa and North America. In complex ways, European working-class women's and men's livelihoods were linked to the labor of African and African-American slaves on the plantations of the Americas. Britain's immense colonial empire also provided material resources and markets necessary for industrial growth. Beginning in the seventeenth century and continuing into the nineteenth century, powerful farmers all over Britain put up fences and enclosed common pastures, driving off small peasants who had farmed or pastured their livestock on this land. Many of these uprooted peasants flocked to cities and became the "free" labor force that allowed industrialization to proceed. At the same time, the application of scientific techniques to farming improved agricultural production and created food surpluses that could feed urban workers. Finally, the bourgeois ideology of individual rights and freedom in the market, along with a parliamentary system that ultimately permitted middle-class industrialists to influence government policies, all promoted industrial capitalism.

In France, the process of capitalist industrialization began later, from about the 1840s. The existence of numerous small-holding peasants solidly attached to their land, a legacy of the French Revolution of 1789, prevented the creation of the free labor pool necessary to large-scale capitalist development. Other factors delayed industrialization: the disruptive effects of the revolutionary and Napoleonic wars, entrepreneurs' reluctance to invest in industry and new technologies, a limited banking and credit system, an underdeveloped internal transportation network, and high protective tariffs. By the 1860s, the upper middle class had gained enough influence over state policy to build railways, negotiate free trade agreements, and open banks, all of which stimulated industrial capitalist development. Even then, however, far more than in Britain, agriculture dominated the French economy until well into the nineteenth century, and the scale of French enterprises remained small. Artisanal forms of production and domestic production persisted far longer than in Britain, and the majority of workers labored in small shops of under twenty employees.

The German process of industrialization illustrates yet a third path of uneven development. The fragmentation of German states with different tariffs posed obstacles to trade and industrial development, as did the persistence of guilds and feudal rights into the nineteenth century. A preliminary phase of industrial development began in the 1830s in textiles and consumer goods. The gradual decline of the guilds by the 1850s, the unification of Germany in 1871, and strong government support for industry all led to an intensive phase of industrialization from about 1870 that involved mining and the iron, steel, and metalworking industries. But many industries continued to rely upon both factory labor and domestic labor either simultaneously or according to seasonal demand. Thus, while factory industry in British textiles had begun to replace domestic production by the 1840s, at that same period in Prussia and Saxony, two-thirds of industrial workers labored in domestic production in home-based workshops.[2]

In spite of these important national differences, women and men experienced industrial capitalism in similar ways nearly everywhere. First, all over Western Europe industrialization meant the appearance of factories and new forms of work discipline. Factory conditions differed radically from those of home-based production. Whereas family-based domestic production allowed parents to supervise the work of children, now shop foremen supervised workers. Children often worked in different shops from parents until child labor legislation banned them from factories altogether. Moreover, where machines regulated the pace of work and shop foremen supervised workers, a worker could no longer take time from the loom or spindle to tend to children, plow a field, or work a vegetable garden.

Second, industrialization intensified the division of labor and the fragmentation of the labor process. In factories, workers who had been responsible for a variety of skilled tasks in the production of finished goods in artisanal or domestic production now worked at a more narrow, specialized range of semi-skilled or unskilled tasks and quite possibly never saw the finished product. Third, notions of skill became more clearly gendered in factories. In cotton textile production, male handloom weavers lost jobs when employers introduced steam-driven power looms into the factory in the 1840s and hired young, unskilled boys or women to supervise the new machines. Eventually adult men appropriated the maintenance and repair of machines, considered skilled labor, as "men's work." Women, whose dexterity and accuracy were prized in the hand-spinning of silk thread, eventually moved to unskilled work tending bobbins on mechanized spinning frames in large workshops. As men fought to retain control over skills and the high wages they brought, they more aggressively attempted to exclude women from skilled jobs.

Overall, in moving from their homes into the factories or workshops and in obeying the rhythm of the machine, workers relinquished control over the timing and pace of work and found themselves more subject to the power of employers. These developments did not occur all at once, however. Even in so leading an industrial sector as cotton textiles, the transition to factory production occurred gradually, with different manufacturing structures existing simultaneously: large factories, small workshops, and domestic (cottage) production all thrived well into the late nineteenth century.

Women could be found in all types of manufacturing structures, though their place in industrial capitalism differed significantly according to their class position. Until well into the nineteenth century all over Europe, middle-class manufacturers and small shopkeepers such as textile producers, clothiers, butchers, and bakers, who combined production and sales, relied on family labor. Often the factory or shop stood on the same grounds as the owner's home. Women assumed a substantial proportion of selling, managing, and accounting in early workshops, bakeries, and dairies. As these enterprises expanded, male assistants with training in management and accountancy gradually replaced wives and daughters. Prosperous middle-class businessmen bought homes in pleasant, green suburbs far from the factory or workshop, where their wives created havens from the dirty, unhealthy world of industrial capitalism. These women's lives often involved considerable work in household management or in organizing charity for the poor. But even if middle-class women retreated from the world of industrial labor, they did not retreat from the labor force. By the end of the century, many who were armed with education took jobs in service sector occupations that were opening for women in nursing, office work, and retail sales. These social class differences between women appeared striking, however, when the first factories emerged across Europe.

BETWEEN AGRICULTURE AND INDUSTRY: MAKING THE TRANSITION TO THE FACTORY

All across Europe women tilled the soil, planted, harvested, and sold the products of their labors. In some regions, the appearance of more rationalized methods of agricultural production in the eighteenth century and new landholding patterns had serious consequences for women. Through a slow process of change marked by important national and regional differences, many women gradually found themselves displaced from traditional rural pursuits, or took on new activities to supplement the income of rural households. Already existing gender divisions of labor grew sharper with the emergence of capitalist relations. Even before the appearance of the factory, women's low wages in agriculture or in rural domestic production testified to the way in which their work was valued less than that of men's.

In Britain, the enclosure movement (Britain's Enclosure Act of 1801 allowed prosperous landowners to take over commons land with impunity) made life especially hard for single women or widows who depended on the cultivation of common land for subsistence. Not only were these women deprived of the land on which they had raised potatoes or vegetables for their own consumption, but the same improving farmers now forbade them from the traditional practice of gleaning after harvests and gathering wood.[3] Women's protests against enclosures were of no avail.

Women and children who worked as seasonal or part-time workers hoeing potatoes, harvesting, weeding, stone picking, or haymaking joined agricultural "gangs" that were subcontracted for farmers by gang masters. Working from sunup to sunset and sometimes in pouring rain or biting frost, they hoed, planted, and harvested for less wages than men earned for the same work. The powerful position of the gang master enabled him to sexually harass and sometimes physically punish his workers, since both women and children were already seen as an inferior and powerless form of expendable labor.[4] Thus, over the late eighteenth century and the beginning of the nineteenth century, the capacity of British rural women to either satisfy their family's subsistence needs through production or to contribute wages to the family economy diminished considerably.

The patterns of rural British women's work were even more complex, however, than this sketch suggests. In northwest Ireland, for example, some rural women routinely combined agricultural work with domestic textile production. Women not only cultivated food but also grew flax and prepared it for weaving (cleaning, treating, and finally spinning it). Yet, even the most productive spinners earned two and a half or three times less than male weavers, despite the fact that their labor accounted for about half the value of the cloth.[5] Eventually these households by-passed local women's spinning altogether by importing cheaper yarn from other parts of Ireland. No longer necessary to household production, these women found factory jobs, where they made up almost 70 percent of all employees in the Irish flax-spinning mills in 1838.[6]

The situation of French rural women differed substantially from that of their counterparts across the English Channel. France never experienced the scale of enclosures that the British saw, nor did large numbers of improving landlords consolidate large farms at the expense of smaller peasants. In contrast, the auction of aristocrats' estates during the 1789 Revolution multiplied the numbers of peasant proprietors. Small family farms that relied heavily on the agricultural labor of women (and resisted modernization) remained characteristic of the French rural landscape until well into the twentieth century. As Table 11-1 shows, three to five times as many French as British women worked in agriculture. However, regional variations within France meant that, even in a single country, women's experiences of agricultural work could be markedly different. Whereas in some areas, for example, farm women sold their butter, cheese, eggs, chickens, and rabbits at local markets, in the wine-producing south, women worked as wage laborers on large vineyards by the beginning of the twentieth century under a rigid gender division of labor.

Moreover, rural women's activities in France outside of agriculture also varied considerably according to region. In the region around Le Puy in the southwest, rural women made lace and sold it at local markets to earn extra income, while men were the principal farmers. And in the linen-weaving households of the Choletais in the northwest of France, conditions somewhat similar to those of the Irish linen weavers prevailed: men took the prestigious, skilled job of weaving and confined women to the ancillary tasks of warping the loom and winding bobbins. Although French social observers such as Albert de Mun and Frederic Le Play, writing in the 1870s, sang the praises of industrial homework as an ideal solution to the evils of factory exploitation, the gender division of labor in rural domestic linen production contributed to women's status as "secondary" workers.[7] Though steam-driven looms were introduced in France around the turn of the century (roughly eighty years after the first steam-driven looms appeared in Ireland), large factories did not immediately displace handloom weaving, even though they rendered it less competitive. By the beginning of the twentieth century, increasing consumption of linen goods like towels and bedding led entrepreneurs to subcontract much of their work to small country producers on a piece-rate basis. In the Choletais wives and daughters took jobs in nearby shoe and slipper-making workshops or did embroidery to earn extra income. In this way French rural women's industrial labor allowed male handloom weavers to survive.[8]

TABLE 11-1

Percentage of Women Out of All Workers in Each Major Branch of Activity

	BRITAIN							
	1841	1851	1861	1871	1881	1891	1901	1911
Agriculture	5.3	11.2	8.3	7.5	7.0	5.2	5.8	7.3
Mining/Quarrying	3.1	2.8	1.3	2.1	1.3	0.9	0.6	0.7
Manufacturing	26.0	35.0	35.8	35.5	36.1	36.7	34.7	34.6
Commerce, Banking, Insurance[1]	1.1	0	1.5	2.3	3.0	5.5	11.3	17.5
Transport/Communications[2]	2.0	2.9	1.9	2.4	1.7	1.8	1.9	2.4
Service[3]	69.4	72.0	73.2	73.5	73.4	72.9	69.1	65.3
Domestic Service as Percentage of Service	95.0	91.4	91.5	91.3	88.1	87.9	84.9	83.1

	FRANCE					
	1856	1866	1886	1896	1901	1906
Agriculture	29.6	29.7	33.1	32.5	32.3	37.6
Mining/Quarrying	8.8	8.8	11.9	2.6	2.2	2.1
Manufacturing	35.4	34.2	38.2	37.2	38.5	39.7
Commerce, Banking, Insurance[4]	30.9	33.1	35.6	39.4	54.0	39.8
Transport/Communications[5]	4.5	4.8	7.1	22.6	26.1	27.6
Service[6]	43.1	40.2	41.3	40.2	42.8	42.6
Domestic Service as Percentage of Service	77.5	74.6	69.0	56.8	55.4	54.9

Of all three countries, Germany saw the largest proportion of women in the labor force working in agriculture over the nineteenth and into the twentieth centuries (see Table 11-2). Rural German women's work also varied according to the sharp regional contrasts of the German economy, the results of centuries-old political divisions. In eastern Prussia (Pomerania), the emancipation of the peasants in the early nineteenth century and enclosures permitted massive farms to dominate the landscape. In western Prussia (Westphalia), on the other hand, small family farms remained. In the nineteenth century, the production of grain for the market on the large estates of the east demanded a large and cheap work force. Here, many women worked as full-time agricultural wage workers to supplement the low wages of their husbands or fathers, performing the same tasks as men but for lower wages, whereas in the west, labor-intensive crops like potatoes and beets meant that small family farms needed women's unpaid labor. However, whatever gender division of labor existed on German farms often disappeared during periods of intense seasonal work such as planting or harvest. Overall, farmers recognized the essential contribution of both men's and women's work.[9]

TABLE 11-1 (*continued*)
Percentage of Women Out of All Workers in Each Major Branch of Activity

	GERMANY		
	1882	*1895*	*1907*
Agriculture	30.8	33.2	46.5
Mining/Quarrying	3.7	3.9	3.9
Manufacturing	21.1	22.8	23.9
Commerce, Banking, Insurance[7]	20.6	24.4	30.5
Transport/Communications	3.23	2.9	4.2
Service[8]	27.4	31.8	35.9
Domestic Service as Percentage of Service	26.2	24.5	26.1

[1]Includes women who worked in family-run shops, who did not earn wages.

[2]Women who worked in post offices or as telegraph and telephone operators were most likely included in the government services grouped under "service."

[3]Includes governmental services, liberal professions (teaching), armed services (no women), personal and domestic services.

[4]Includes women who worked in family-run shops. The persistence of small family-run shops in France through the nineteenth and early twentieth centuries meant that considerable more women worked in this sector than in Britain.

[5]Telephone and telegraph workers in France are included in this category.

[6]Includes governmental services, armed services (no women), liberal professions, hotel and cafe workers, and personal domestic service. The smaller proportion of female domestic service workers in France accounts for the small size of this sector by comparison to Britain.

[7]Includes family-run shops in which wives worked.

[8]Includes government services, armed services (no women listed), "services not elsewhere classified" (probably liberal professions such as teaching), and personal domestic service.

SOURCE: Paul Bairoch, *La Population active et sa Structure* (Brussels: Institut de Sociologie de l'Université libre de Bruxelles, 1969), pp. 136–137, 173–175, 189–191. Used by permission of the author and the Université libre de Bruxelles.

In Prussia, where primary school was compulsory for all children after 1763, farm work could also be a rite of passage once a girl had completed her primary school education. From the age of 13 or 14, young girls typically worked for prosperous farmers as domestic servants in return for an annual wage, food, and housing. Although young women saved some of their wages for a dowry or a wedding dress, much of their income was turned over to their families. Single daughters of farmers and rural weavers also increasingly found work in factories, notably in textiles or in the clothing or tobacco industries.[10]

The foregoing changes, however, occurred gradually and very unevenly. Even from the standpoint of new technology, the transition to the factory was far from automatic. In the spinning industry in England, for example, important technological innovations such as the water frame and spinning jenny were first used in domestic production, not in large factories.[11] However, as

TABLE 11-2

Women's Representation in Specific Economic Sectors as Percentage of the Entire
Female Labor Force

	BRITAIN				
	1841	*1861*	*1881*	*1901*	*1911*
Agriculture	4.5	5.0	3.1	1.8	2.2
Mining/Quarrying	0.4	0.2	0.2	0.1	0.2
Manufacturing	35.2	44.7	43.3	44.7	44.9
Commerce, Banking, Insurance	0.1	0.1	0.3	1.6	2.9
Transport/Communications	0.2	0.3	0.4	0.6	0.7
Service[1]	57.4	47.2	50.6	49.6	47.2
Other	2.2	2.2	2.1	1.6	1.9
Domestic Service as Percentage of Service	54.5	43.2	45.2	42.2	39.3
	FRANCE				
	1856	*1866*	*1886*	*1901*	*1906*
Agriculture	48.9	48.0	46.0	37.9	43.3
Mining/Quarrying	0.4	0.3	0.5	0.1	0.1
Manufacturing	24.8	25.7	22.2	27.4	26.7
Commerce, Banking, Insurance	5.2	5.6	8.9	11.3	8.3
Transport/Communications	0.2	0.3	0.4	3.0	3.1
Service[1]	20.1	19.8	20.9	20.3	18.5
Other	0.4	0.4	1.1	0	0
Domestic Service as Percentage of Service	15.6	14.8	14.4	11.6	10.4
	GERMANY		
	1882	*1895*	*1907*
Agriculture	59.5	52.3	55.8
Mining/Quarrying	0.5	0.6	0.6
Manufacturing	23.4	25.7	22.7
Commerce, Banking, Insurance	4.2	5.7	6.7
Transport/Communications	0.3	0.3	0.5
Service	10.4	14.2	13.0
Other	1.7	1.2	0.7
Domestic Service as Percentage of Service	2.7	3.5	3.4

[1]Includes domestic service, cafe and hotel service, government services and the professions. The
majority of women's jobs in this area in Britain and France were in domestic service.

SOURCE: Paul Bairoch, *La Population active et sa Structure* (Brussels: Institute de Sociologie de
l'Université libre de Bruxelles, 1969), pp. 131, 136–137, 167, 173–175, 183, 189–191. Used by permission of the author and the Université libre de Bruxelles.

capitalist manufacturers accumulated capital from rural domestic industry, the slave trade, and other overseas commerce, the temptation to build large factories to house machines, where employers could impose a regular and disciplined rhythm of work, became irresistible. Even women and young girls who initially resisted working on the new machines and altering their work patterns eventually accepted jobs in factories as wages in domestic production declined. But now, instead of being primarily the work of adult women, unskilled, mechanized spinning became the work of adolescent girls and children.[12] Thus the female labor market divided between the labor of adult women and that of younger women. Because all women's work was already considered less valuable than that of men and boys, factory owners could exploit them as a source of cheap labor.

Over the course of the nineteenth century, then, more and more women left household-based production for manufacturing (see Table 11-2). Most worked primarily in areas that were extensions of their traditional household activities, such as textiles. Most of them were single and relatively young, between the ages of 16 and 25.[13] In working-class families, where men's low wages kept the family perilously close to the poverty line, women's and adolescent girls' work was absolutely necessary for survival.

Women supporting families in France sometimes traveled considerable distances to work, leaving home for months at a time, or even permanently, to work as spinners in the cotton-producing city of Lille, in the silk-producing center of Lyon, or as laundry workers and housekeepers in the southern city of Nîmes.[14] Moreover, women traveled across national borders to find work: Belgian women migrated to the textile cities of Lille, Roubaix, and Tourcoing in northern France, and Irish women left Ireland during the "hungry forties" for work in British industrial cities. Around the turn of the century France became a magnet for Jewish immigrant workers fleeing persecution in Poland, Rumania, and Russia. Although contemporary observers feared that female migration was a sign of family breakdown, in fact, family need for income determined women's or girls' decisions to migrate, family ties determined individuals' migration strategies, and resident relatives or friends helped newcomers find work. When Jeanne Bouvier, exhausted and demoralized by thirteen-hour days in a French silk factory, left her job, a cousin helped her to find work as a maid in Vienne, seventeen miles away from home. Similarly, relatives and friends helped Irish women coming to London to find work and lodgings.[15]

Married or single women with children, however, could not easily migrate long distances to work. And unlike women in industrial homework, they had a more difficult time balancing income-producing activities and child care. A homework spinner could watch a child as she spun or could stop work when she needed to nurse an infant. Women who labored in factories, however, had to time factory work more carefully to coincide with periods when they did not have the responsibility of young, dependent children. Women who lacked informal child care occasionally brought their infants into the mills in baskets, and while they worked, they kept their little ones drugged and sleepy with brandy-soaked rags or opiates.[16] Overall, the appearance of factory labor made women's work more public, visible, and the subject of debate among social reformers and state officials. Social observers began to identify the woman worker as a problem.[17] Their discussions of the problematic nature of women's work contributed to devaluing women's work and competence in the industrial age.

DEBATING WOMEN'S WORK: IDEALS OF WOMANHOOD AND GENDERED DIVISIONS OF PUBLIC AND PRIVATE SPACE

Seemingly paradoxically, at the very moment that large numbers of women entered factory labor and became more visible in the industrial labor force, criticism from social reformers and state officials condemned women's industrial labor as "unwomanly" and argued the virtues of a private, domestic role for women in contrast to a public role for men. In the late eighteenth century, middle-class observers had already questioned the femininity of German women agricultural laborers, "who seemed to belong to both sexes" and behaved in a most "unladylike" fashion.[18] By the 1830s and 1840s in Britain, Victorian writers likewise deplored the "utter absence of grace and feminine manners" among women factory workers. An explosion of guidebooks and manuals of domestic economy glorified women's domestic and maternal activities, praised women's supposedly delicate nature, inherent submissiveness, and piety and virtue, and prescribed a role for women bounded by the four walls of the home.

Parallel to the idealization of women's domestic activities, critics deplored working women's alleged "abandonment" of the home and predicted the family's decline. Left-wing social observers participated in this attack on women's wage work. Thus Frederich Engels condemned the exploitation of women in factories and deplored the decline of the home and the inversion of the "natural" social order that resulted from women's wage work.[19] Likewise, some nineteenth-century British and French working men raised the demand for a "family wage" that would be sufficient to enable a working man to support an unwaged wife and child at home. Although French tailors in the 1840s accepted women's productive contribution as tailoresses working at home, printers repeatedly sought to exclude women from their trade and called for a family wage to enable male printers to support their families without the extra wages of their wives.[20] Middle-class political economists in Britain in the late eighteenth century and in France in the early nineteenth century supported these views. Although some accepted certain kinds of wage work as appropriate for women (industrial homework, for instance, was acceptable because it occurred within the home), they deplored the fact that many working women (especially single women) lived apart from their families in order to earn wages. Others argued that women's wages were destined to remain inferior to men's wages and that therefore employers should pay men a family wage.[21] Embedded in both middle-class reformers' critiques of women's work and working-class men's demands for a family wage were assumptions about how gender determines the right to work in the "public" domain. Both assumed that the right to provide subsistence to the family was a male right, and that women's work was either "unnatural" or a perversion of women's maternal duties.

The idealization of separate and gendered public and private realms embedded in many nineteenth-century critiques of women's work was far from the reality of working women's experiences, as Tables 11-1 and 11-2 show. However, this ideal nevertheless had ideological power and did not merely reflect the new conditions of industry, but strongly influenced cultural and entrepreneurial practices as well as definitions of men's and women's work, skills, and wages. Housework, and what historians call "social reproduction," that is, bearing and rearing children and feeding, nurturing, and caring for household members, involved serious effort, but because women received no wages for these domestic "labors of love," such tasks failed to fit into the logic of political economy as "work." And because contemporaries persisted in viewing these tasks as women's "natural" activities, they could easily view any women's wage work as "unnatural," supplemental, and therefore not "real work." From here it was but a short step to claim, as many employers did, that the tasks that women did perform for wages need not be rewarded as highly as men's. Moreover, in some countries (England, for example), this ideal was translated into legislative attempts to limit women's factory labor. The product of middle-class reformers' efforts to restrain women from working in unhealthy conditions, these efforts received the support of male workers eager to protect their own jobs. Thus representations of working-class women as inadequate mothers and homemakers and contemporary views of their work as merely supplemental to family income both contributed to the devaluation of women's work.

GENDER, WORK, AND WAGES IN THE FACTORY, HOME, AND WORKSHOP UNDER INDUSTRIAL CAPITALISM

We have already seen that a gender division of labor and gender differences in the valuation of labor existed in rural production, well outside of the factory gates. However, accentuating the division of labor within industrial capitalism encouraged people to think of women's work as inferior to men's. For both working men and women, the shift of production into factories marked an important moment in the process of redefining certain forms of wage work as "male" and in the devaluation of women's labor. New definitions of work, skill, and wages had a central role in shaping the new power relations of the factory.

The sharper division of work between women and men appeared at two levels. At one level, the entire industrial labor market became segmented according to gender. This meant that entire industries came to be perceived as "female" and others as "male." For example, in many Western European countries for most of the nineteenth century, employers believed that women were especially suited for textile work, whereas they tended to hire men for work in the capital goods industries that developed later—steel, iron, mining, and machine goods. In Britain and Germany, the garment industry also became feminized, and in France, certain sectors of the garment industry came to be seen as typically "women's work." Gender segmentation prevailed in nonindustrial work as well. Women made up the vast majority of service workers in Britain and a large percentage in France (see Table 11-1), because employers believed that women's "natural propensity" for caring and serving made them desirable as domestic servants (see below).[22]

The gender division of labor operated at a second level as well: within a single industry or factory. Partly on the basis of ideologies of gender difference that proclaimed women's weakness and general inferiority to men, employers allocated unskilled work to women and children and reserved skilled work for men. Eventually boys received training in the skilled tasks they would perform as adults, but such training was not available to girls.

The case of British hosiery making shows how the reorganization of production in factories accentuated gender divisions already present in domestic work and how the accentuated division of labor contributed to the devaluation of women's work. In Leicestershire in the 1840s, for example, women made a vital contribution to domestic production in sock- and stocking-weaving households. But because they divided their time between framework knitting and care of children and the household, they simply could not produce as much as men. This allowed contemporaries to insist that women's productive work was merely supplemental to men's.[23] In addition, employers' practice of making husbands responsible for wives' and children's production and paying them a "family wage" reinforced women's status as secondary producers. Men often gave their wives, aged women, or young girls the less remunerative jobs such as seaming and kept the better-paying jobs for themselves. Thus, "under the domestic system, men knitted for the capitalist and women knitted stockings within the family economy."[24]

Conditions like these in British domestic industry influenced the way employers evaluated women's work in factories. When women knitters entered factories to operate power frames in the 1860s and 1870s, the notion that women's work merely supplemented men's work carried over and allowed employers to pay them less: men earned from twelve to fifteen shillings per week and women about nine shillings. Fearful that women's low wages would drive them out of work, male knitters proposed the gender segregation of machines.[25] By the turn of the century, the majority of men worked on power frames and women worked on smaller and cheaper knitting machines. The shift to factory production not only involved a more acute gender segregation of tasks, but it also involved changes in the nature of wages and in authority relations. In domestic production, employers paid the husband for the family's work; husbands and fathers supervised wives and children. In factory production, however, even where husbands and fathers directed their wives' and children's work, employers paid workers individually, thus removing some of the father's control. For women these developments were mixed. Women now earned their own wages, but "women's status as secondary workers contributed to beliefs that they were dependent upon their husbands and fathers for subsistence and that they needed male supervision when working on complex tasks."[26] Thus employers could pay women at well below the levels men earned.

In Germany, a gender division of labor also developed within both entire labor markets and specific industries. Seventy-five percent of the female labor force worked in the linen and cotton textile industries and in garment manufacture by the end of the nineteenth century. Within textile factories, a gender division of labor emerged as employers redefined skill and as mechanization made it possible for women to work at jobs that had previously been considered "men's work." The cotton industry followed this pattern. When the first cotton-spinning mills appeared in the Rhineland at the end of the eighteenth century, most women in the cotton industry worked in spinning. With the mechanization of cotton weaving, women also prepared looms and finished the woven cloth. Men, on the other hand, who had been employed primarily in handloom weaving in domestic production, tended to be employed largely in weaving in factory production. But cotton had no strongly entrenched guild traditions and customs, and by the end of the nineteenth century women also began to run the mechanized looms and began to displace men; women now made up one-half of the weaving work force.[27]

The gradual feminization of cotton textiles in the Rhineland did not occur in other areas where guild traditions were stronger. In wool cloth weaving, strong craft traditions led male weavers to firmly resist the feminization of weaving. Ultimately, although men could not keep women from working on mechanical looms, they did succeed in limiting women to smaller looms and to the production of inferior grades of cloth. In addition, the finishing of woolen textiles involved a new gender division of labor. By the end of the nineteenth century men worked at finishing operations within the factory that involved chemicals and dyes, whereas women performed other skilled finishing operations (napping and darning) as industrial homework. Thus industrial homework, far from disappearing, remained an important complement to factory production.[28] The female domestic homeworkers who performed finishing work in German woolen production earned especially low wages because they worked in their homes and were paid by the piece—a condition that also occurred elsewhere. This form of industrial homework differed, however, from earlier forms of family household production because it did not depend on the cooperative labor of family members but now fell largely to women.

THE PERSISTENCE OF HOMEWORK

In many parts of Europe, in the shadow of the urban factory, both married and single women worked in the "sweating system" of home-based production, doing "slop work" in bookbinding, dressmaking, and millinery, sewing lingerie, shoes and gloves, embroidering decorations for dresses, or making silk flowers for hats. In fact, industrial homework in France expanded by the turn of the twentieth century along with the growth of leather goods, shoe, and garment industries. A number of developments promoted this expansion. First, department stores sold sewing machines on credit in the 1880s and made it possible for women to purchase their own machines for homework. Mechanization allowed women's home sewing to spread to regions where other traditional home industries had declined. Second, following the passage of legislation that limited women's working hours in factories in 1892, French clothing factory owners subcontracted sewing of dresses, trousers, and shirts to women sewing in their homes for piece rates, in order to continue to benefit from women's intense labor at low wages and to save overhead costs. Third, the demand for ready-made lingerie and clothing by working-class as well as middle-class consumers fueled the expansion of industrial homework in the garment trades. Although social observers thought that sewing machines, marketed as quintessentially "women's machines," would permit women to return to making their own families' clothes, their need to sew for piece rates and the availability of relatively cheap ready-made clothing determined women's priorities.[29]

Married women, who made up a majority of French lingerie homeworkers, favored this form of wage earning. Some argued that they even saved money because they didn't have to dress for work or eat out. As a single woman, Jeanne Bouvier enjoyed the relative independence of homework and alternated sewing at home with work in small Parisian workshops, which provided a certain camaraderie and sociability. But not everyone could earn enough to live in this way without extreme hardship, as Bouvier herself recognized later when she attempted to organize France's numerous industrial homeworkers. As one historian has remarked, "Sweatshops and putting-out were sustained in the capitalist economy only because of the extreme hardship produced by inequities in the system itself."[30] Parisian women who sewed suits by hand in Paris in the 1850s could earn more at home than in a factory, but at the price of laboring 365 days a year, working themselves to exhaustion. Although the sewing machine certainly made it possible for women to work faster with less fatigue, it did not change the unequal structural relations of production. Moreover, because sewing at home remained identified as house-work, employers could feel justified paying women low wages. In homework as in factory work, the gender division of labor allowed employers to profit from women's cheap labor and sustained the notion of women's work as in-ferior to men's.

POWER AND SEXUALITY

Gender divisions at work and segmented or segregated labor markets accentuated the unequal power relations between employers and workers and men and women. They allowed employers to pay women lower wages than men, even when men and women performed the same tasks. Generally, women earned between one-third and one-half of what men earned, but the forces that kept women at inferior wage levels were ideological as well as structural. In order to justify paying women low wages so that they could profit from women's cheap labor, employers used the beliefs that women worked only for "pin money," and that their true vocation was marriage, motherhood, and housekeeping. A British parliamentary subcommissioner even argued in 1833 that paying women low wages would discourage them from remaining in the labor force. Women did not leave work because of low pay, however. On the contrary, their need to earn wages kept them working in the most abysmal conditions.

Unequal power relations between women workers and male employers or overseers in industrial factories produced different forms of exploitation. In some factories, women and girls worked twelve- and thirteen-hour days in unsafe and unhealthy conditions as machine tenders, spinners, and weavers. Those who worked at wet spinning in British flax mills in the 1830s spent most of their working day drenched by a constant spray of water from the spinning frames. Overseers sometimes beat women and their children if they failed to come to work on time, as Hannah Goode and Eliza Marshall testified before the British Parliamentary Commission investigating working conditions and hours in 1833. Other women described the horribly crushed limbs or dislo-cated shoulders they suffered at work on large carding or spinning machines when clothing or hair caught in the machine shafts.[31] In small water-powered factories in France, women and girls labored in spinneries whose darkness and dampness contrasted sharply with the sunny landscape surrounding them. From dawn to dusk, they worked without artificial light, up to fourteen to fifteen hours a day in summer, in workrooms whose close, wet air hung thick with cotton dust. Women and girls who worked in silk spinning and weaving suffered from respiratory and lung diseases, including tuberculosis, brought on by the dampness of the workrooms and poor ventilation.

Nowhere, however, did the unequal power relations of the factory appear in sharper relief than in the sexual harassment and sexual coercion of women workers. Middle-class beliefs about the dubious sexual morality of the woman worker provided the basis for such practices. The same cultural constructs of the woman worker that portrayed women as destined for a domestic vocation provoked questions about the morality of working-class girls who ventured into the factory. Social observers often confused them with prostitutes, and in England, after the passage of the Contagious Diseases Acts in the 1860s, police routinely detained working-class women, assumed to be "women of ill repute," and sent them to "lock hospitals" to be examined for venereal disease. Early-twentieth-century British social workers assumed that working-class women in port towns who had relationships with black sailors were really prostitutes.[32] Indeed, working-class women, who labored at subsistence wages, sometimes did work as prostitutes, and others turned to prostitution as their primary means of earning income when out of work.

Sexual harassment went beyond the factory. The Austrian socialist and labor activist Adelheid Popp worked at home around the turn of the century making pearl and silk trimmings and decorations for the fashionable dresses of wealthy middle-class women. When a traveling salesman promised her higher wages in return for sexual favors at the age of 15, Popp began to see unequal power relations intruding on her personal life with frightening intimacy. Men's use of their physical power over working women and girls threatened female workers' security as much as work accidents.

Working women's sexuality cannot be reduced, however, to their confrontation with sexual harassment at work. Working women sometimes developed their own standards of morality or engaged in sexual horseplay on the job in defiance of the power relations of the factory. Young women who worked in the wet spinning rooms of a French linen factory took off their clothes and danced in a circle around the young factory director to embarrass him. In a German spinning mill, women defied the order of the factory by undressing on the shop floor rather than using the dressing rooms.[33] On more than one occasion, women in France and Germany went on strike over the rape of a woman worker by a male overseer. But even their protests, subversive sexualized displays of the body, or the raucous sexual jokes and stories women workers recounted in a German weaving mill do not by themselves adequately depict working women's own views of sexuality. We must be skeptical of assertions of middle-class social investigators like Marie Bernays, who, when observing the mills of Mönchen-Gladbach in Germany, argued that working-class women were as "sexually liberated" as the men, and noted their exceptional tolerance of unwed motherhood. Although working women wrote about sexual experiences, they also expressed concern about the propriety of precocious sexuality and the effects of "sexual emancipation" on their personal lives, even when they were not the product of the unequal power relations of industrial work.[34]

In spite of social observers' criticisms of women's industrial work and the very real exploitation that women experienced, women nonetheless flocked to manufacturing, enticed by wages higher than those in agriculture or domestic labor. In fact, the wages of most industrial workers rose over the course of the nineteenth century, and workers increasingly had disposable cash to spend on clothing, food, and nonessential items like decorative objects for their homes. Young women who worked in the London match-making trade formed clubs to purchase clothing. More than ever before, the diet and material culture of working women and their families in Western Europe reflected the growing internationalization of the economy and the growing connections between Europeans and the colonial subjects they dominated. By the middle of the century the diet of British workers included imported foods such as rice and curry from British India and a more extensive use of spices from other colonies as well (available on the British market since the fifteenth century). Working women in France, Germany, and Britain drank tea imported from India and increasingly drank coffee produced by the labor of colonized Africans. By the end of the century British working-class wives decorated their homes with bric-a-brac like carved figurines produced by artisans in colonial India.[35]

Contrary to observers' fears, industrialization did not destroy the family. Families relied heavily on all members' contributions. Even young women who migrated long distances to work used family ties to locate jobs and lodgings. These women regularly sent wages back home. New job opportunities for women appeared in the food, electrical, and chemical industries and drew women away from the textile and garment trades. Moreover, increasing numbers of women found jobs in the growing service sector of European economies.

BEYOND THE FACTORY GATES: WOMEN IN SERVICE WORK

Despite the striking visibility of capitalist industry on the European landscape, factory work did not occupy the majority of women in any of the countries we have examined (see Tables 11-1 and 11-2). Industrialization was not a linear process that automatically displaced previous forms of production. Homework persisted and coexisted with industrial work up to World War I, and industrial capitalism also stimulated the growth of a "service sector," which produced no goods but rendered services. Wealthy businessmen could afford to hire servants to relieve their wives from domestic drudgery, and working-class women readily found jobs as servants and laundresses in the homes of the middle class. Women also increasingly worked in offices, banks, post offices, department stores, and schools, although in almost all of these areas, gender divisions rendered women's work inferior to men's.

In the early nineteenth century, "service" was practically synonymous with domestic service. As Table 11-1 shows, women made up the vast majority of domestic service workers; in Britain until 1861, domestic service was the most important employer of women overall (see Table 11-2). Fewer women worked as servants in France and Germany, partly because of the demand for women's work in agriculture in those countries (see Tables 11-1 and 11-2).

Most servants did not envision their jobs as lifelong occupations, however, but rather passed through service en route to marriage or other occupations. Thus, in generational terms, the labor market for servants drew primarily on young, single women.[36] Moreover, in contrast to factory workers, not all of these girls and young women were white. Some were migrants from Africa or the Caribbean who had come to Europe after slavery ended and for whom service offered one of a few opportunities for employment. Whether white or black, women worked as chambermaids, cooks, and maids, performing the household chores that white middle-class "ladies" would not deign to touch. Here too, a gender division of labor prevailed: although men also worked as servants or butlers, women tended to be hired for cooking, cleaning, and laundry work.

Domestic service attracted some young women with the promise of working in a home rather than a factory and with the prospect of wearing a proper dress rather than dirty factory clothes. In reality, however, the servant's position was unenviable. Servants had little rest in fifteen- to eighteen-hour days spent in an endless round of cooking, cleaning, and child care. In addition, deference to employers' whims and the fact that maids often worked in intimate proximity to their employers made young servant girls and women, white and black alike, vulnerable to sexual harassment from male employers. One study of nineteenth-century prostitution, in fact, found that the majority of women who sold sex for a living came from the ranks of domestic servants who had lost their virginity on the job. Overall, domestic service embodied one of the most glaring contradictions of the domestic ideal: the exploitation of working-class women of all races by middle-class women and men whose wealth could buy them leisure and respite from domestic labor.

Over the nineteenth century, however, fewer and fewer women worked as servants in middle-class households, as the industrial capitalist economies of Western Europe changed. Three developments explain this shift. First, capitalist economies experienced a series of depressions in the last third of the nineteenth century which, combined with inflation, made it more difficult for middle-class households to indulge in luxuries like servants. Second, compulsory education laws requiring school attendance until the age of 14 meant that young girls now remained in school longer. Armed with a diploma or certificate, women over 14 were better educated and could take jobs that demanded literacy. Simultaneously, the new educational requirements created a demand for teachers. Large numbers of women entered teaching by the end of the century. In Germany, for example, where primary schooling had been compulsory since the end of the eighteenth century, Prussian primary schools and girls' schools hired women, and by the turn of the century over half of the teachers were women.[37] Women's increasing literacy broadened the range of jobs open to them in other service occupations as well.

As industrial capitalism expanded, the growth of large corporations and cartels and banking and retail trade raised the demand for office personnel.

Postal and telegraph and telephone systems grew in the second half of the century and required workers. This constituted the third development that affected women's shift into white-collar occupations. Men moved into managerial jobs and women moved into offices as clerks and secretaries. Convinced that young women possessed "nimble fingers" and would be especially adept at filing papers or using typewriters and adding machines, which made their way into offices in the 1880s, employers hired women for filing, typing, accounting, and taking minutes at meetings. Thus offices that had been dominated by male clerks in the early nineteenth century underwent a striking transformation. At the same time, more women took jobs in post offices and as telegraph and telephone operators; in France, women made up the vast majority of telephone operators by the turn of the century.[38] The emergence of large department stores all over Europe in the late nineteenth century drew in neatly dressed young women to work behind counters. Department stores like the Bon Marché and the Magasin du Louvre in Paris hired so many women that the retail sector quickly became the largest white-collar domain of French working women.[39]

Finally, the nursing profession opened to women in the second half of the nineteenth century, thanks to the pioneering work of women like Florence Nightingale. Previously, nursing had been dominated by men; contemporaries considered intimate contact with the body improper for delicate middle-class ladies. Nightingale, born into a comfortable bourgeois British family, rebelled against the domestic ideals of middle-class womanhood. In the early 1850s, she trained abroad and in Britain, and then served as an army nurse during the Crimean War (1854–1856). In an aggressive and far-reaching campaign to open nursing to women, she transformed the profession by proving that women could handle the rigors of the work when trained.

The feminization of nursing, postal, telegraph, and clerical work and of retail sales had mixed results. On the one hand, it expanded the opportunities available to women, even if those who worked in offices, banking, and communications constituted a small minority of women in the labor force overall (see Table 11-2). In all these areas women enjoyed higher wages, more regular working hours, and higher professional status. Yet feminization could also result in the downgrading of positions formerly held by men and the segregation of women in low-paying jobs. Working conditions could be strenuous: department store salesgirls in France stood for twelve to fourteen hours a day (until a law in 1900 obligated employers to provide seats for them). The pride that British women took in the relatively high-status occupation of school-teaching could be eroded by the glaring inequalities between men and women teachers. Not only did women earn less than men, but the imposition of a marriage bar for women meant that marriage or even the declaration of intention to marry led to automatic dismissal. Male teachers, on the other hand, could marry freely. In France, women teachers fared somewhat better. Although they earned less than men before World War I, no official marriage bar existed there. From the 1890s, the government even encouraged teachers to marry in hopes that this would make it easier for them to remain in remote French villages.[40] Despite the apparent advantages of white-collar work over factory work, however, manufacturing remained the second largest employer of women up to World War I (see Table 11-2). This form of labor above all provoked endless criticism and efforts at state regulation.

REGULATING WOMEN'S WORK: THE STATE AND GENDERED IDEALS OF WORK AND FAMILY

Influenced in part by the arguments of political economists and in part by the depressing reality of women's industrial labor, legislators and social reformers campaigned to reduce working hours, abolish nightwork, and restrict the kinds of work women could perform. Many believed that women's factory labor constituted a profound disruption of the proper relations between men and women and, like Engels, worried about the disturbing consequences of married women's neglect of their families and homes. Others expressed horror at the unsafe and unhealthy conditions in which children and adult women labored (fewer worried about men's working conditions). All of these concerns found their way into the legislative efforts to regulate women's and children's labor that began early in the nineteenth century. These laws incorporated gendered notions about the right to work and free labor. They encoded a gender division of labor and, ironically, confirmed women's status as secondary workers.

Much factory legislation in Britain targeted child labor. The 1802 Health and Morals of Apprentices Act, which reduced the workday of children apprenticed under the Poor Law to twelve hours, required that employers provide children with education and separate sleeping quarters for girls and boys and ordered that children attend church monthly. In the 1830s, factory workers, with the support of social reformers and some legislators, began a nationwide movement to reduce the working day of all workers to ten hours. This reform effort eventually led to 1833 legislation that reduced the hours for children and to a separate bill in 1841 that reduced the working day of women to twelve hours. In 1847, the Ten Hours Bill established a standard ten-hour day for all workers in the textile industry, and the Mines Act restricted women and children to surface work in coal mines. Still later, in 1874, Parliament reduced the workweek for women and children to 56.5 hours.[41]

Moral considerations often played a role in discussion of restrictions on women's work. In parliamentary debates over the Ten Hours Bill reformers voiced their concerns about the immorality of women's work and singled out young factory girls' reputed sexual promiscuity for special criticism. They condemned the "disorder of women" who had abandoned domesticity and could no longer be "useful as . . . female[s]."[42] Legislators argued that, unlike men, women were not free laborers and needed the special protection of the state. Thus the liberal state justified restricting women's work. By the end of the century, when awareness of infant mortality in industrial towns increased, arguments shifted: now legislators focused on infant deaths and the responsibility of working mothers to their children and the British "race."[43]

In France, one of the earliest nineteenth-century efforts to address the "moral problem" of women's work involved religious orders' establishment of convent workshops. Linking the altar and the machine, young women and girls, usually in the needle trades or in spinning, labored under the watchful eyes of nuns. As late as 1906, some one hundred thousand women worked under this system in the silk-producing region around Lyon. Laws already regulating the work of children and adolescents were now extended to women, who were restricted from night work and limited to twelve-hour days. Resistance to regulation was even stronger than in Britain. The debate on women's work began in earnest in 1848 and continued for almost fifty years. In 1874 a law limited the working hours of young women under twenty-one and outlawed underground mine work for all women and girls. But not until 1892, following the depression of the 1880s, did French lawmakers pass a law that forbade women to engage in night work and reduced the workday of women and children to eleven hours.[44] French concerns about low fertility and high infant mortality in industrial centers were at the center of discussions about regulation, rather than the morality of working girls, with final debates focusing on women's responsibility for the preservation of the race.

As gender-specific legislation, the 1892 law organized women's work differently than men's and deprived women of the potentially lucrative night work that could be found in book binderies and textile and garment factories. It also contributed to the development of industrial homework because many women, deprived of the extra wages they could earn at night, took home sewing, stitching, or bookbinding to earn extra income, and employers subcontracted work to them at low piece rates. Based on the principle that women needed state protection and on concerns about safeguarding women's maternal potential, the French legislation contributed in both practical and symbolic terms to the devaluation of women's work and supported the gender division of labor.[45]

Germany, too, experienced a flurry of regulatory legislation at the end of the nineteenth century that focused specifically on women. German legislation differed from British and French legislation, however, in establishing social provisions that addressed German reformers' concerns about maternity and that marked the birth of the early welfare state. Thus a German labor code of 1878 banned women from mine work and established a three-week maternity leave for women workers after the birth of a child. In the 1880s and 1890s, some reformers and legislators called for an end to married women's work outside the home altogether, evoking the same concerns about maternity and motherhood that drove British and French debates. Ultimately, the revised labor code that emerged in 1891, like the French legislation of a year later, banned night work for women and reduced their working day to eleven hours. Moreover, the German legislation extended maternity leave to six weeks and mandated the establishment of "continuation schools" where young women could learn housekeeping skills and young men would learn arithmetic, reading, and mechanics, for example. Finally, the law differentiated married women and mothers from single women workers, providing an extra half-hour break for those with household responsibilities and limiting Saturday work so that women could clean and shop.[46] Although this legislation did not ban married women from work outside the home, the debate on married women's work continued into the first years of the twentieth century and played an important role in further legislative initiatives.[47]

Overall, then, factory legislation in much of Western Europe "protected" women by encoding the gender division of labor and by treating them as a separate category of worker. In reformers' reactions to women's industrial labor, domesticity and maternity not only appeared as idealized roles for women, but also shaped the social policy of the early welfare state. Although in some cases (such as in Germany) labor legislation provided practical benefits to women, it did so through the gendered lenses of legislators and social reformers compelled to deal with the "problem" of the woman worker.

WOMEN TAKE ACTION

The gender divisions and social discourses that gradually made laboring women "second-class citizens" in the labor market and workplace did not make it easy for women to resist or protest the abuses of industrial capitalism. Organizations such as the Grand General Union of the United Kingdom formed at a cotton spinner's meeting in 1824 specifically excluded women and girls.[48] Men resisted women's participation in labor actions, fearful that women's status as low-wage workers would drive down men's own wage settlements. However, in spite of working men's reluctance to include women in their unions and male labor activists' arguments for a "family wage," women all over Europe undertook militant action to strike against abysmal conditions at work, low wages, or exploitive employer practices. Women proved to be as adept at marching on the picket line as they were at winding bobbins on the factory floor. Moreover, over the course of the century, resistance to women's participation in unions weakened.

Women's labor action in Britain began in the earliest years of industrialization, when in 1799 Lancashire women destroyed mechanized spinning jennies that threatened to displace hand spinners. Although male spinners later successfully banned women from working at the spinning mule (and from their labor organizations), women who worked at power looms with men for the same wages actively participated alongside men.[49] British working women also found temporary support in the socialist labor movement of the 1830s, which welcomed women as partners with men in working-class struggles, that is, before men's concerns about competition led them to reject women's participation. Women tended to fare better in same-sex organizations such as the Lodge of Female Tailors and the Grand Lodge of Operative Bonnet-Makers in the early 1830s.

British women's success in unionizing, like their acceptance or rejection by men, varied, even within a single industry. Moreover, the gender division of labor had consequences for women's labor mobilization. In the stocking-knitting industry in the 1880s, for example, the Leicester and Leicestershire Amalgamated Union admitted women who worked on circular knitting frames (designated as "women's machines") and refused to admit women who worked on the cotton frames ("men's machines").[50] At around the same time, however, the National Women's Trade Union League, formed in 1873, was busily promoting women's unions and by 1886 succeeded in organizing between thirty and forty women's unions. But even if women made up only a small proportion of the officially unionized, they nonetheless took militant collective action, like that of the London match workers, who demonstrated in a massive strike in 1888 to protest a wage cut. Although the young girls who dominated the trade were not unionized at the start of the strike, middle-class organizers helped them eventually form a union of 800 members.

French women, too, predominantly in the textile and tobacco industries, demonstrated exceptional militancy in protesting low wages and poor working conditions. Although by 1911 women made up only 9.8 percent of all organized workers (but some 36 percent of the labor force), women often took action without the benefit of formal organization. Poor bobbin winders in the silk-producing center of Lyon led important strikes in 1848 and 1869, and during the latter strike joined the International Working Men's Association. Others went on strike to protest sexual harassment at work, as did several thousand porcelain workers in the city of Limoges in 1905. These women not only brought to public attention the gruesome conditions of factory labor, but also demonstrated just how deeply interconnected were "public" and "private" in industrial work. In the Parisian garment industry dramatic strikes brought hundreds of working women off the job in 1901, 1910, and again in 1911. Garment workers demanded a voice in setting the prices of the goods they produced, an end to piece rates, the negotiation of contracts, and an end to subcontracting that undercut their work. Usually the mass of women demonstrating in the streets was far greater than the numbers of women in the unions, and occasionally the strikes turned violent, as they did in 1911 when battles between striking women and police shocked an indignant public.[51] If some male activists voiced hostility to admitting women to their unions, others argued for women's unionization as a way to achieve wage parity and to eliminate competition from women as low-wage workers. Moreover, as a whole, the French labor movement became increasingly open to women's work and organization, as the case of Emma Couriau demonstrated. Couriau began work as a typographer in Lyon in 1912 at union wages, but the local printers' union refused her membership on the grounds that women did not belong in the print shops. It even expelled her husband from the union for failing to keep his wife at home. Labor leaders all over France, who realized the importance of women's wage work and their participation in labor struggles, sided with Emma Couriau. Buoyed by their support, she began to organize women typographers separately in their own union.

Like their counterparts in the textile and garment industries in Britain and France, German women also formed unions and made militant strikes. After 1890, working women organized in the powerful German Textile Workers' Union, where they made up over one-third of the membership before World War I, and a woman rose to the position of union secretary in 1908. Like French women resisting the sexual coercion of overseers, German women also participated in violent demonstrations and strikes to protest the assault and rape of women workers and to demand the firing of the rapist. Women in the textile union "recognized women's distinct experiences at work, the particularity of the double burden of waged work and housework or child rearing," in calling for women's units within the union that could effectively address women's specific concerns. These women contested the idea that women's domestic concerns were separate from their working lives and thereby challenged male notions of class and union activism.[52]

Women's varied experience as labor activists, unionized or not, demonstrates that the multiple ways that the capitalist relations of the industrial world conspired to devalue their work and render them subject to the power inequities of the workplace, also inspired indignation and revolt. If the gender division of labor occasionally made it difficult to organize with men, women also formed their own same-sex organizations. They rejected men's right to coerce them sexually and showed that the rhetorical separation between public and private that social observers promoted bore little relationship to the realities of their lives.

CONCLUSION

Although we tend to think of globalization as a late-twentieth-century phenomenon, in fact, a global economy was in the making by the time European countries began to industrialize in the mid-eighteenth century. Imports of cotton, tobacco, spices, tea, and coffee and the capital that Europeans accumulated from the slave trade fueled the industrial expansion in which women played such an important part.

Through the protracted and uneven process by which industrial capitalism developed, the devaluation of women's work that Chapter 8 describes in the early modern economy continued and became more intense. Changes in the gender division of labor and the practices of employers and male workers relegated women to certain kinds of work and machines and men to others. Sometimes mechanization made it possible for women to work at jobs that had earlier been labeled men's work, but at the cost of lower wages. Cultural discourses that proclaimed that women were only really fit for "private sphere" activities of social reproduction contributed to devaluing their work in production. State policies that claimed to protect women also reinforced cultural norms about women's inferiority.

In spite of the inequalities of the industrial world, however, the period of industrialization was not one of unremitting gloom for women. Living standards for workers rose enough so that many women could purchase clothing and the household articles that flooded the market by the turn of the century. Women—including middle-class women—moved into new service sector jobs. Finally, women fought against exploitative working conditions, low pay, and sexual harassment through collective organization, protests, and strikes. These activities show us how, even in the most difficult circumstances, women resisted being swept along helplessly by the waves of economic change. Their militant actions joined those of feminists and socialists elsewhere in Europe who struggled for women's rights on other fronts.

NOTES

1. The recent work of two British economic historians (N.F.R. Crafts, *British Economic Growth During the Industrial Revolution* [London: Oxford University Press, 1985] and E.A. Wrigley, *Continuity, Chance and Change: The Character of the Industrial Revolution in England* [Cambridge, Cambridge University Press, 1989]) has challenged the orthodox interpretation of an industrial "revolution" in Britain by arguing for slow productivity growth between 1780 and 1820 (Crafts) and continuity with limited growth before the middle of the nineteenth century. As Maxine Berg has pointed out, both sets of findings are based on a male labor model that ignores women's work, property holding, consumption, and capital investment. See Maxine Berg, *The Age of Manufactures 1700–1820: Industry, Innovation, and Work in Britain*, 2nd ed., London: Routledge, 1994.

2. See Barbara Franzoi, *At the Very Least She Pays the Rent: Women and German Industrialization, 1871–1914*, Greenwood Press, Westport, 1985, p. 4; Kathleen Canning, *Languages of Labor and Gender. Female Factory Work in Germany, 1850–1914*, Cornell, Ithaca, 1996, pp. 19–20.

3. Deborah Valenze, *The First Industrial Woman*, Oxford University Press, New York, 1995, pp. 32, 36.

4. Ernal Olafson Hellerstein, Leslie Parker Hume, and Karen Offen, eds., *Victorian Women*, Stanford University Press, Stanford, 1981, p. 361.

5. Jane Gray, "Gender and Uneven Working-Class Formation in the Irish Linen Industry," in *Gender and Labor in Modern France*, ed. Laura L. Frader and Sonya O. Rose, Cornell University Press, Ithaca, 1996, p. 43.

6. *Ibid.*, p. 45.

7. Tessie P. Liu, "What Price a Weaver's Dignity? Gender Inequality and Survival of Home-Based Production in Industrial France," in Frader and Rose, *op. cit.*, p. 60; and Liu, *The Weaver's Knot. The Contradictions of Class Struggle and Family Solidarity in Western France, 1750–1914*, Cornell University Press, Ithaca, 1994.

8. Liu, "What Price a Weaver's Dignity?" p. 74.

9. This did not mean that men and women had equal power in the rural household; far from it. As Ute Frevert points out, women were clearly subordinate to

men within the household, and despite their equally important contribution, it was the man who contemporaries saw as the head of the household and the official breadwinner. See Ute Frevert, *Women in German History from Bourgeois Emancipation to Sexual Liberation,* trans. Stuart McKinnon-Evans with Terry Bond and Barbara Norden, Berg, New York, 1989, pp. 23–24.

10. Jean Quataert, "The Shaping of Women's Work in Manufacturing: Guilds, Households and the State in Central Europe, 1648–1870," *American Historical Review* 90 (December 1985), p. 1144.
11. Berg, *op. cit.,* p. 236.
12. Valenze, *op. cit.,* p. 81.
13. Michel Anderson, *Family Structure in Nineteenth Century Lancashire,* Cambridge University Press, New York, 1971, p. 71; Louise A. Tilly, "Individual Lives and Family Strategies in the French Proletariat," *Journal of Family History* 4 (Summer 1979), p. 146; Frevert, *op. cit.,* p. 329.
14. Leslie Page Moch, *Paths to the City: Regional Migration in Nineteenth Century France,* Sage, Beverly Hills, 1983, pp. 186–187.
15. Jeanne Bouvier, *Mes mémoires. Une Syndicaliste féministe. 1876–1935* Editions de la Découverte, Paris, 1983; Lynn Hollen Lees, *Exiles of Erin: Irish Migrants in Victorian London,* Cornell University Press, Ithaca, 1979.
16. Louise A. Tilly, "Structure de l'emploi, travail des femmes et changement démographique dans deux villes industrielles: Anzin et Roubaix, 1872–1906," *Le Mouvement social* 105 (October–December 1978), pp. 43–48; Louise A. Tilly and Joan Scott, *Women, Work, and Family,* Methuen, New York, 1987.
17. See Joan Scott, "The Woman Worker," in Geneviève Fraisse and Françoise Thébaud, eds., *A History of Women in the West,* vol. 4, (Cambridge, Mass: Harvard University Press, 1993) who examines the nineteenth-century construction of the problem of the woman worker.
18. Frevert, *op. cit.,* p. 27.
19. Frederich Engels, *The Condition of the Working Classes in England,* Introduction by Eric Hobsbawm, Panther, London, 1984, pp. 172–173.
20. See Laura L. Frader, "Engendering Work and Wages: The French Labor Movement and the Family Wage," in Frader and Rose, *op. cit.,* pp. 146–151; Michelle Perrot, "L'Eloge de la ménagère dans le discours ouvrier au XIXe siècle," in *Mythes et représentations de la femme* (special issue), *Romantisme* 13–14 (1976), pp. 105–121. On Britain, see, for example, Hal Benenson, "The Family Wage and British Working Women's Consciousness in Britain, 1880–1914," *Politics and Society* 19 (March 1991), pp. 71–108; and Sonya O. Rose, *Limited Livelihoods. Gender and Class in Nineteenth Century England,* University of California Press, Berkeley, 1992, pp. 130–132.
21. On France, see Joan Scott, "The Woman Worker," in *A History of Women in the West;* and Joan Scott, "A Statistical Representation of Work: *La Statistique de l'Industrie à Paris"* and "'L'Ouvrière: Mot impie, sordide . . .': Women Workers in the Discourse of French Political Economy, 1840–1860," in Joan Scott, *Gender and the Politics of History,* Columbia University Press, New York, 1988, pp. 124–134 and pp. 143–145. On Britain, see Valenze, *op. cit.,* chapter 7. As Valenze points out, the "feminization of the female worker" in the discourse of the British political economy contributed to the disappearance of the idea of the independent woman worker as a productive member of society and to the designation of female labor as a problem.

22. The differences between women's domestic service employment in Britain and France on the one hand and Germany on the other hand are striking. They probably have much to do with the relatively larger proportions of women in agricultural work in Germany than in either of the other two countries and with German women's greater presence in the category of "commerce, banking, and insurance" than British women's.

23. Sonya Rose, "Gender Segregation in the Transition to the Factory: The English Hosiery Industry 1850–1910." *Feminist Studies* 13 (Spring 1987), pp. 166–167.

24. *Ibid.*, p. 168.

25. *Ibid.*, pp. 172–173.

26. *Ibid.*, pp. 164–165.

27. Kathleen Canning, *Languages of Labor and Gender: Female Factory Work in Germany 1850–1914*, Cornell University Press, Ithaca, 1996, pp. 39–45.

28. See also Franzoi, *op. cit.*, pp. 124–141.

29. See Judith G.Coffin, "Consumption, Production, and Gender: The Sewing Machine in Nineteenth-Century France," in Frader and Rose, *op. cit.*, pp. 111–141; and Judith G. Coffin, *The Politics of Women's Work: The Paris Garment Trades, 1750–1915*, Princeton University Press, Princeton, 1996. As Coffin points out, women's homework in the needle trades also stimulated popular consumption.

30. Franzoi, *op. cit.*, p. 125.

31. Hellerstein, Hume, and Offen, *op. cit.*, pp. 386–391.

32. See Judith Walkowitz, *Prostitution and Victorian Society: Women, Class, and the State,* Cambridge: Cambridge University Press, Cambridge, 1980; Laura Tabili, "Women 'of a Very Low Type': Crossing Racial Boundaries in Imperial Britain," in Frader and Rose, *op. cit.*, pp. 165–190.

33. See Marie-Victoire Louis, *Le Droit de Cuissage. France, 1860–1930,* Les Editions ouvrières-Les Editions de l'Atelier, Paris, 1994, p. 119; and Canning, *op. cit.*, pp. 309–311.

34. On Bernays, see Canning, *op. cit.*, p. 310. For a skeptical view of the notion of "emancipated" or natural working-class sexuality, see Mary Jo Maynes, *Taking the Hard Road,* University of North Carolina Press, Chapel Hill, 1995, pp. 130–150.

35. See Nupur Chaudhuri, "Shawls, Jewelry, Curry, and Rice in Victorian Britain," in *Western Women and Imperialism. Complicity and Resistance,* ed. Nupur Chaudhuri and Margaret Strobel, Indiana University Press, Bloomington, 1992, pp. 237 and 241. See also Neil McKendrick, "Home Demand and Economic Growth: A New View of the Role of Women and Children in the Industrial Revolution," in *Historical Perspectives: Studies in English Thought and Society,* ed. Neil McKendrick, Europa, London, 1974, pp. 152–210.

36. The market for governesses was an exception in that somewhat older, single, middle-class women tended to be preferred for this job. See Lee Holcombe, *Victorian Ladies at Work: Middle-Class Working Women in England and Wales,* Archon, Hamden, 1973, pp. 12–15.

37. Frevert, *op. cit.*, p. 77.

38. Susan Bachrach, "Dames Employées: The Feminization of Postal Work in Nineteenth Century France," *Women and History* 8 (Winter 1983); Holcombe, *op. cit.*, pp. 165–168.

39. Theresa McBride, "A Woman's World: Department Stores and the Evolution of Women's Employment, 1870–1920," *French Historical Studies* 10 (Fall 1978),

p. 671; Claudie Lesselier, "Employées des Grands Magasins à Paris avant 1914," *Le Mouvement social* 105 (October–December 1978), pp. 109–126.

40. On British teachers, see Holcomb, *op. cit.*, pp. 34–46; on French teachers, see Judith Wishnia, *The Proletarianizing of the Fonctionnaires: Civil Service Workers and the Labor Movement Under the Third Republic*, Louisiana State University Press, Baton Rouge, 1990, p. 52.

41. Sonya O. Rose, "Protective Labor Legislation in Britain: Gender, Class, and the Liberal State," in Frader and Rose, *op. cit.*, pp. 194–197.

42. The phrase "disorder of women" comes from the title of Carole Pateman's book, *The Disorder of Women: Democracy, Feminism, and Political Theory*, Stanford University Press, Stanford, 1989. See also Rose, "Protective Labor Legislation," pp. 201 and 202–203.

43. Rose, "Protective Labor Legislation," p. 205; and Jane Lewis, "The Working-Class Wife and Mother and State Intervention, 1870–1914," in *Labor and Love: Women's Experience of Home and Family*, ed. Jane Lewis, Basil Blackwell, Oxford, 1986, p. 109.

44. On the debates surrounding the French legislation, see Michel Zancarini-Fournel, "Archéologie de la loi de 1892 en France," in Leora Auslander and Michelle Zancarini-Fournel, *Différence des sexes et protection sociale*, Presses Universitaires de Vincennes, St. Denis, 1995, pp. 75–92; and Judith F. Stone, "Republican Ideology, Gender, and Class: France: 1860s–1914," in Frader and Rose, *op. cit.*, pp. 238–259. The law played on women's status as legal minors and grouped women with children in their lack of legal rights.

45. Mary Lynn Stewart, *Women, Work, and the French State: Labor Protection and Social Patriarchy, 1879–1919*, McGill-Queens University Press, Montréal, 1989; see also Scott, "The Woman Worker."

46. Canning, *op. cit.*, p. 139.

47. *Ibid.*, chapter 5.

48. Valenze, *op. cit.*, p. 95.

49. *Ibid.*, p. 96.

50. Rose, "Gender Segregation in the Transition to the Factory," p. 175.

51. Judith Coffin, *The Politics of Women's Work*, pp. 177–183.

52. Kathleen Canning, "Gender and the Politics of Class Formation: Rethinking German Labor History," *American Historical Review* 97 (June 1992), p. 762.

SUGGESTIONS FOR FURTHER READING

The literature on women in the making of industrial capitalism is voluminous. The following are additional, valuable sources that complement the works referred to in the footnotes to this article.

The following explore women's experiences of industrial capitalism in countries that, for reasons of space, could not be included in this article: Patricia Hilden, *Women, Work and Politics: Belgium, 1830–1914* (Oxford: Oxford University Press, 1993); Siân Reynolds, *Britannica's Typesetters: Women Compositors in Edinburgh* (Edinburgh: Edinburgh University Press, 1989); Eleanor Gordon and Esther Breitenbach, *The World is Ill Divided: Women's Work in Scotland in the Nineteenth and Early Twentieth Centuries*

(Edinburgh:Edinburgh University Press, 1990); Lynn Hollen Lees, *Exiles of Erin: Irish Migrants in Victorian London* (Ithaca: Cornell University Press, 1979); Louise A. Tilly, *Politics and Class in Milan, 1881–1901* (New York and Oxford: Oxford University Press, 1992), and "Urban Growth, Industrialization, and Women's Employment in Milan, Italy, 1881–1911," *Journal of Urban History* 3 (1977), pp. 467–484; Barbara Engel, "Women, Work, and Family in the Factories of Rural Russia," *Russian History* 16 (1989), pp. 224–245.

Recently historians have begun to examine the gendered foundations of work, skill, and the division of labor. In addition to the works cited above, see Sally Alexander, "Women, Class and Sexual Difference," *History Workshop Journal* 17 (Spring 1984), pp. 125–149; Harriet Bradley, *Men's Work, Women's Work* (Minneapolis: University of Minnesota Press, 1989); Joy Parr, *The Gender of Breadwinners: Men, Women, and Change in Two Industrial Towns, 1880–1950* (Toronto: University of Toronto Press, 1990); and Helen Harden Chenut, "The Gendering of Skill as Historical Process: The Case of French Knitters in Industrial Troyes, 1880–1939," in *Gender and Class in Modern Europe*, ed. Laura L. Frader and Sonya O. Rose (Ithaca: Cornell University Press, 1996).

Among the works that examine the relationships between industrialization and the family are Elinor Accampo, *Industrialization, Family Life, and Class Relations: St. Chamond 1815–1914* (Berkeley: University of California Press, 1989); David Levine, *Reproducing Families: The Political Economy of English Population History* (Cambridge: Cambridge University Press, 1987); and Ellen Ross, *Love and Toil: Motherhood in Outcast London, 1870–1918* (Oxford: Oxford University Press, 1993). Leonore Davidoff and Catherine Hall, *Family Fortunes. Men and Women of the English Middle Class, 1780–1850* (Chicago: University of Chicago Press, 1987), examines the role of the family in the construction of the middle class. Bonnie Smith's *Ladies of the Leisure Class* (Princeton: Princeton University Press, 1981) discusses middle-class women's domestic alternative to industrial capitalism in France.

Important studies of working women's labor mobilization are found in Charles Sowerwine, "Workers and Women in France Before 1914: The Debate over the Couriau Affair," *Journal of Modern History* 55 (September 1983), pp. 414–444; Patricia Hilden, *Working Women and Socialist Politics in France, 1850–1914* (London and Oxford: Oxford University Press, 1986); Marie-Hélène Zylberberg-Hocquard, *Femmes et féminisme dans le Mouvement syndical français* (Paris: Les Editions ouvrières, 1981); Jean Quataert, "The Politics of Rural Industrialization: Class, Gender, and Collective Protest in the Saxon Oberlausitz of the Late Nineteenth Century," *Central European History* 20 (June 1987), pp. 91–124; and Sonya O. Rose, "Gender Antagonism and Class Conflict: Exclusionary Tactics of Male Trade Unionists in Nineteenth Century Britain," *Social History* 13 (1988), pp. 191–208. Barbara Taylor's *Eve and the New Jerusalem* (London: Virago, 1983) discusses women in early-nineteenth-century British socialist and trade union movements. Ulla Wikander, Alice Kessler-Harris, and Jane Lewis, eds., *Protecting Women: Labor Legislation in Europe, the United States, and Australia, 1880–1920* (Urbana and Chicago: University of Illinois Press, 1995), provides a good comparative perspective on factory legislation.

Les Divorceuses by French lithographer Honoré Daumier depicts a French women's rally concerning the right to divorce.   BIBLIOTHÈQUE DES ARTS DÉCORATIFS/JEAN-LOUP CHARMET.

CHAPTER 12

Contextualizing the Theory and Practice of Feminism in Nineteenth-Century Europe (1789–1914)

Karen Offen

*Although Americans are better acquainted with English suffragists' uncom-
promising insistence on fundamental legal and political equality, Karen Offen
reminds us of the variety of situations and initiatives among advocates of
women's emancipation in other European settings. Across the European
continent, women in militaristic authoritarian states advanced their claims to
education, legal and economic equality, and political participation in relation
to other dissenting movements that worked for national liberation, unification,
and sociopolitical reform. Like the women described by Margaret Strobel who
ventured into the Third World under the auspices of empire, these "relational
feminists" saw their concerns as central to all aspirations for societal change.
Offen examines the many ways in which feminists used the belief in a special
womanly nature as a wedge into public activity. After several generations,
feminists seemed to be making some headway. By the turn of the century, they
faced twin threats from a new direction. Respected geneticists declared women
innately inferior, and demographers spread panic about low birthrates among
the "most desirable" Europeans. This double challenge inspired a new generation
of feminists to defend their vision of freedom and fulfillment. While militant
English suffragettes made headlines, most European feminists also insisted on
an expanded public role for women. Throughout the nineteenth century, the
category "women" served feminists as a unifying category. The thrust of
European feminist argument in these years was for "equality in difference,"
not "equality versus difference," and a broad concept of motherhood provided
a complex and dynamic platform for articulating feminist aims. European*

feminists acknowledged some division of labor between the sexes, but argued against the confinement of women to the male-defined "domestic sphere," even as they insisted on the value of women's contributions in the home. Unlike their socialist counterparts in the Second International, however, most feminists did not consider paid employment the sole criterion for women's emancipation; they argued instead that male domination be confronted in the present, and not postponed in favor of class struggle and solidarity.

Between the French Revolution and World War I the Western world witnessed an unprecedented surge of analysis, debate and action by both women and men on behalf of women's emancipation. These efforts aimed to abolish the privileges of the male sex, uproot the prejudices that disadvantaged women, and restructure the "social relations of the sexes" (to use John Stuart Mill's term) within the family and in society.

Arguments for improvement in women's situation had been in evidence in Western Europe for several centuries before the revolutionary era, and phrases such as "the rights of women" and the "equality of the sexes" were already familiar to educated Europeans. Gender (*genre* in French) was already understood to be what we now call a social construction, and women's ostensible inferiority was blamed squarely on their poor education and men's urge to dominate them. Both the critique of women's education and their subjection in marriage (some said slavery) were central to Enlightenment criticism of the existing order. "I love this sex," wrote Madame de Beaumer, editor of one of the first periodicals for women, the *Journal des Dames,* in 1762. "I am jealous to uphold its honor and its rights. If we have not been raised up in the sciences as you [men] have, it is you who are the guilty ones; for have you not always abused, if I may say so, the bodily strength that nature has given you? Have you not used it to annihilate our capacities?"[1]

However, the eruption of specific demands for women's political rights and representation and for legal reform of their status and education coincided with the outbreak of the French Revolution in 1789. A writer from Normandy who signed as "Madame B*** B***" called for representation of women by women in the Estates-General. "Why is it that the law is not the same for both [sexes]? Why does one sex have everything and the other nothing?" An anonymously published "Ladies' Request to the National Assembly" denounced "masculine aristocracy" and called for the abolition of all the privileges of the male sex. "The masculine gender [genre] will no longer be regarded, even grammatically, as the more noble gender, given that all genders, all sexes, and all beings should be and are equally noble."[2] These were indeed radical demands.

The early 1790s witnessed publication of a number of major feminist arguments, both in Paris and beyond France. The Marquis de Condorcet asserted in his *Plea for the Citizenship of Women* (France, 1790) that "either no individual of the human race has genuine rights, or else all have the same; and he who votes against the right of another, whatever the religion, the color, or sex of that other, has henceforth abjured his own." Olympe de Gouges's *Declaration of the Rights of Woman* (France, 1791) trumpeted, "Man, are you capable of being just? . . . Who has given you the sovereign authority to oppress my sex?" She called for a national assembly of women and for the adoption of a Declaration of the Rights of Woman and Citizen. The Dutch writer Etta Palm d'Aelders's *Appeal to Frenchwomen Concerning the Regeneration of Morals and the Necessity for Women's Influence in a Free Government* (France, 1791), the English writer Mary Wollstonecraft's *Vindication of the Rights of Woman* (Great Britain, 1792), and the East Prussian jurist Theodor Gottlieb von Hippel's *On Improving the Status of Women* (Prussia, 1792) all elaborated unequivocal demands for women's emancipation.[3]

Well after the revolutionary regimes had granted single adult women in France full property (civil) rights, though not political (civic) rights, and had established civil marriage and divorce, a chorus of protest against women's continuing marginalization echoed throughout Europe. In 1797 in a published "Woman's Speech to the Italians," an anonymous Venetian woman remarked that in the new revolutionary republican arrangements men had taken over every function: "You think only of your own advantages and the happiness of the male sex; either you do not consider women individuals of the human race, or you are only thinking of making one half of it happy." In 1798 the unidentified "P.B.v.W." issued a wake-up call to Dutch women and to men like himself: "How could we be happy, while we, who renounced tyranny, are in practice tyrants ourselves?"[4]

The failure of the French Revolution and its satellite revolutions to deliver women's emancipation was sharply denounced by women and men alike. From France, Fanny Raoul issued a direct challenge in 1801:

> Who has been given the exercise of civil responsibilities? Men. Who has been assured the rights of property? Men . . . . Who has been given the right and privileges of paternity? Men. For whom has liberty and equality been established? Again, men. In sum, everything is by them or for them; it is therefore for them also, and for them alone, that political society has been made; women have no part in it.

In 1808 the French social critic Charles Fourier reiterated in his visionary *Theory of Four Movements* the claim made by many eighteenth-century Enlightenment thinkers since Buffon when he wrote that "the extension of women's privileges is the general principle for all social progress." In 1817 the British poet Percy Bysshe Shelley pondered the question, "Can man be free if woman be a slave?" At midcentury Fourier's countryman, the poet Victor Hugo, prophesied that the nineteenth century would proclaim the right of woman, the eighteenth century having proclaimed the right of man. By 1900 advocates of ideas about reorganizing male-female relations and the male-dominated family that institutionalized sexual inequality had stimulated not only the growth of consciousness but also the development of a comprehensive theoretical critique of women's subordinate status and the formation of a loosely organized political movement.[5]

During the 1890s these bold ideas and the movement that sought to realize the emancipation of women became known throughout Europe as feminism. The vocabulary itself was French. The words *féminisme* and *féministe* spread rapidly into other European languages to describe both the ideas and the movement. But the ideas and the efforts at organization preceded the birth of the words, and consciousness of women's oppression through their subordination to men, articulated in the course of the Enlightenment critique of European institutions, preceded both. Throughout most of the nineteenth century, however, Europeans still argued over "women's emancipation" and the "woman question," phrases that aptly suggested the focus of the debate in a still monarchical, authoritarian, and male-centered culture in which an unresolvable tension existed for women between the demands of the family and the siren song of freedom, and where democratic institutions were still only a dream. The new words gave focus and meaning to a preexisting analysis and critique.[6]

European thinkers and activists made vital contributions to the development of feminism throughout the world. The debate over these issues raged in religious and political tracts and speeches and in newspapers, periodicals, poems, novels, plays, and books of every description. By the beginning of the twentieth century, organized feminist movements existed in France, Germany, the Low Countries, the territories of the Austro-Hungarian Empire, Switzerland, Scandinavia, European Russia, and Italy, and had begun to spring up in Spain, Portugal, and Greece.

The very vocabulary of European feminist discourse, along with its forms of political agitation—publications, petitions, demonstrations, and even media events—had migrated to South America, to the Middle East, and to Asia. The majority of member nations of the first international organization of women, the International Council of Women, founded in 1888 by American suffragists, were European. The International Woman Suffrage Alliance, founded in 1904 specifically to promote the cause of woman suffrage throughout the world, enjoyed extensive European participation and attracted interest well beyond Europe's shores. Thousands of women journeyed by steamship and railroad to the conventions of these organizations, held every five years in London, Paris, Berlin, Budapest, and other major European cities. In the absolute and constitutional monarchies and even in the few male-dominated democratic republican nation-states of pre–World War I Europe, both the ideas of the feminists and their political activity conjured up visions of a world turned upside down and precipitated ever more intense backlashes. By the early twentieth century, the Swedish author and women's advocate Ellen Key observed that "the struggle that woman is now carrying on is far more far-reaching than any other; and if no diversion occurs, it will finally surpass in fanaticism any war of religion or race."[7]

VARIETIES OF FEMINISM IN NINETEENTH-CENTURY EUROPE

It is impossible to judge the historical significance of European feminism solely in terms of contemporary American understandings of equal rights and individual liberty, or by viewing it through the dualistic lens of equality versus difference. If feminism is potentially individualistic in theory (that is, committed to the maximum self-realization for every individual irrespective of sex, race, class, religion, age, etc.), it has not invariably been so in historical actuality. Despite common ideological roots and similarities in vocabulary and rhetoric, the Anglo-American arguments for women's emancipation through the exclusive acquisition of personal legal rights appear to be as atypical in the overall framework of Western thought as Anglo-American political theory and institutions themselves.

In the nineteenth century, most Western European feminist thinkers—with some notable exceptions—were still as preoccupied with community cohesion as with individual liberty in the abstract. As they chipped away at male-centered thinking about society, they downplayed, sidestepped, or even rejected formal philosophical individual rights arguments for women's emancipation, instead specifically coupling rights with duties even as they spoke freely of "liberty" and "equality." They emphasized the complementary and interdependent relationship between women and men, and women's distinctive nature and contributions to society as a sex, not only as mothers but also as beings with a capacity for motherliness, for accommodation, for peace-keeping, whether or not they bore children. Even those who argued for greater personal autonomy for women generally cast their arguments in terms of women's relationship to others and their responsibilities to a broader collectivity—in some cases the nation and in others the working class. In either case they considered the family, not the individual, to be the primary sociopolitical unit. And they emphasized what we now refer to as an "ethic of care" over an ethic of competition and conflict.

This mode of argument can be understood as *relational feminism*. Nineteenth-century advocates of relational feminism insisted on the physiological and cultural distinctions between the sexes and adhered to the concepts of womanly or manly "nature" and to a sharply defined sexual division of labor both in the family and throughout society. The premise that there exist distinct and different male and female natures led to a conception of sociopolitical organization that implied distinct and different duties for women *and* for men. Relational feminists insisted on the centrality of the complementary heterosexual couple and/or the mother-child dyad to the analysis of women's plight and the search for solutions. They sought to reconfigure prevailing images of women (notably, the Christian association of woman with sin) through "the rehabilitation of womanhood" and to equalize the power and authority of women and men in society. But they wished to accomplish this without eroding or eliminating distinctive and, to them, desirable gender differences. They wished to preserve cooperation between women and men in all aspects of communal life, even as they sought to dismantle patriarchal institutions and restructure society in its totality. The arguments of most nineteenth-century western European advocates of women's emancipation, including most socialist feminists as well as the "bourgeois" feminists they would condemn so vigorously from the 1890s on, can be classified under the broader heading of relational feminists.

The second mode of argument found in nineteenth-century Europe is more familiar to us. It can be called *individualist feminism*. More radical than relational feminism in its claims and consequences, its advocates focused more exclusively on philosophical demands for women's "natural" rights, for freedom from social restraint and opportunities for personal development for women (and for men), and for self-determination, or autonomy, as the essential condition for the growth and development of human potential. Partisans of individualist feminism tended to minimize or even ignore the sociopolitical implications of women's relationships to children, to men, and to the society in which they lived. This was no doubt because such arguments had first been developed with reference to property-holding male heads of households, which is how theorists in previous centuries had understood "the individual." But to critics, individualist feminism seemed to imply women's complete independence from men and children, even to reveal hostility toward any relationships or responsibilities that might infringe on a woman's personal liberty. Relational feminists in Western Europe identified this approach with Anglo-American thinkers, particularly John Stuart Mill and his successors, and also with Russian anarchists and nihilists, and they distanced themselves from it. They accused the individualist feminists of treating women only as asexual, abstract beings. They viewed such ideas as self-indulgent and anti-social, hostile to the collective interest of a well-ordered society.

Thus the terms *feminism* and *feminist* as used in this chapter will designate a spectrum of advocates of female emancipation ranging from relational to individualistic. Some advocates combined both types of arguments in subtle and inconsistent blends. Overall, however, European women and men who fought for the emancipation of women shared several common points of approach that allow us to employ a historically valid definition of feminism that transcends the particularities of time and place. First, they consciously recognized the validity of female experience and emphasized values that women articulated. Second, they analyzed women's subordination as a problem of institutional injustice (not as a purely personal problem). Third, they sought the elimination of such injustices by attempting both to enhance the relative power of women and to curb the coercive power, whether political, legal, economic, or cultural, available to men. Despite these common attitudes, within a given society the feminists' analyses did not always lead to the same priorities, strategies, or tactics on behalf of remedying women's wrongs. Both intranationally and internationally, they often disagreed with one another about solutions, much as feminists still do today.

Yet they disagreed in rather different ways than we are now accustomed to seeing. For nineteenth-century Europeans, religion long remained a more divisive issue than race, and practices of slavery and serfdom, though strenuously contested, continued to be living realities in some Eastern European countries as well as in the colonies of England and France before midcentury. Indeed, the rhetoric of antislavery was quickly extended to critique both the condition of the growing industrial proletariat ("wage slavery") and that of urban female prostitutes ("white slavery"). Class distinctions based on lineage and wealth retained a significance that it is hard to imagine in an age of relatively greater social mobility. Male dominance manifested itself in a high degree of authoritarianism, militarism and warmongering, as well as in strong resistance to relinquishing control over women's sexuality and fertility. With only a handful of exceptions, feminists in that time assumed heterosexuality to be normative. They asserted that "women" were wholly worthy creatures, that women and men could and should be lovers *and* partners, that "women's work" had value, and that women—single and married alike—had a right to economic independence. They argued that women, as the peace-loving sex, had specific qualities and talents from which the entire society could benefit, if they could only be permitted to develop them fully. For nineteenth-century feminists, "woman" and "women" were unifying categories, not divisive ones. Their target was the destruction of male domination, pure and simple.

THE POLITICAL AND INTELLECTUAL CONTEXT OF EARLY NINETEENTH-CENTURY FEMINISM

The historical development of feminism in Europe is intertwined with the political, intellectual, socioeconomic, and cultural history of Europe. Feminist protest accompanied the growth and democratization of nation-states, the spread of literacy through mass education, and the expansive growth of an urban and ultimately industrialized capitalist market economy. The very vocabulary of feminism—liberty, equality, emancipation, liberation, reason, justice—is, as we have said, grounded in the European Enlightenment and the French Revolution. Thus the course of early-nineteenth-century European feminist thought and action cannot be understood without reference to these developments, the ensuing Napoleonic wars of conquest that carried the revolutionary ideals, including its incipient feminism, throughout Europe, and the counterrevolutionary backlash that followed the final defeat of Napoleon's armies at Waterloo.

Led by Prince Metternich, the Austrian chancellor, the peacemakers initiated a campaign to suppress the revolutionary energies and ideas that had emanated from France, a "public sphere" that seemed to have gotten out of hand. Throughout the 1820s, in Restoration France, the Austro-Hungarian empire, or imperial Russia, whenever tensions increased, authorities watched suspiciously for any signs of hostile political activism; they attempted to exert strict control over the press, quickly suppressing all reformist and radical publications, and they patrolled political meetings and surveyed the exercise of personal liberties. Even England, clearly the most politically liberal of the victor nations, was affected by this climate of repression. Additionally, the continental victors sought to consolidate a return to the old sociopolitical order by strengthening centralized, hierarchical, male-dominated political authority in the family and in the polity, often calling on the coercive authority of state-supported religions to control "antisocial" behaviors. Their efforts were seconded by a wave of prescriptive laws (embodied in the Napoleonic Code, which was adopted widely throughout Europe), "scientific" publications, philosophical and medical treatises, and pedagogical tracts, all of which sought to construct rigid boundaries between the "public" and "private" spheres, to establish new secular rationales for women's subordination in the family, and to justify their exclusion from political life.

In order to gain even the slightest success in this political climate and to avoid prosecution by nervous public authorities, most early nineteenth-century feminists—female and male alike—couched even the most modest claims for women's education in language that did not appear subversive to the existing order.

By the late 1820s and early 1830s, however, the repressive climate was again challenged and feminist claims resurfaced, particularly in Great Britain and France. These calls ranged from pleas for major changes in women's legal status and for their access to substantial formal education to full-blown demands for economic freedom and political rights, moral reform, and sexual liberty. The combined effect of still-menacing repression with the unprecedented socioeconomic change brought by the Industrial Revolution ensured that most nineteenth-century continental European feminists would continue to emphasize the importance of women's sociopolitical roles and insist on women's special nature as a positive force. Even as they appealed to principles of liberty and equality, they took care to reassure (not always successfully) their adversaries that the changes they proposed would improve, not explode, the social order. Many continental feminists elaborated on these principles with reference to the late-eighteenth-century images of the mother-educator and the womanly citizen, and proposed concrete reforms that would enhance women's "equality in difference."

England offered a significant exception to this cautious attitude. During the 1820s agitation for change in the position of women reverberated in radical political and religious circles, accompanying agitation for reform of the parliamentary franchise and, in particular, the extension of manhood suffrage. Harriet Martineau and others began to publish arguments on behalf of equal rights and to critique English marriage laws. In 1825 William Thompson and Anna Doyle Wheeler published their *Appeal of One Half the Human Race Against the Pretensions of the Other Half—Men—to Retain Them in Political and Thence in Civil and Domestic Slavery.* The Anglo-Irish Wheeler persisted in her pursuit of rights for women, by demanding "the removal of disabilities." "We then fearlessly ask for education; equal right to acquire and possess property; equal morals; women themselves responsible for their conduct as members of society; equal civil and political rights." Members of radical Protestant sects known as Dissenters, Unitarians, and Quakers, as well as the disciples (called Owenites) of the textile magnate, social reformer, and trade union organizer Robert Owen, all began to address the woman question in their publications. Owen, in particular, would elaborate a revised code of laws for the entire human race in the 1830s.[8]

The question of political rights for women quickly arose and was as quickly dispatched. In 1832, when the British parliament passed the landmark Reform Act, each paragraph dealing with parliamentary suffrage carried the preface, "every *male person* of full age, and not subject to any legal incapacity. . . ."[9] These words deliberately excluded single women property owners (and taxpayers) and all married women from political rights. Only one significant legal reform, establishing limited rights for mothers to custody of their own children (a reform spearheaded by Caroline Norton), was realized before the 1850s. But a stream of eloquent published protests, such as Charlotte Brontë's novels *Jane Eyre* (1847) and *Shirley* (1849), reminded the educated public that some women were disturbed by the continuing inequities, while other women reformers founded professional schools to train single middle-class women for employment as credentialed teachers and governesses.

On the Continent, feminist theory and action found its greatest stimulus in Paris, where in the early 1830s a new revolution replaced the Bourbon monarchy with a constitutional monarchy complete with a charter of rights. In the ferment of this political upheaval, social critics and Romantic writers once again raised compelling questions about women's subordinate status that would be diffused and discussed by women and men in intellectual circles throughout the rest of Europe. British radicals from Anna Doyle Wheeler to John Stuart Mill introduced new ideas gleaned in France to their contemporaries in England. Despite censorship, this intellectual ferment spread to the German states and to the Scandinavian countries, the Italian states, and Russia. Critics revisited many eighteenth-century Enlightenment feminist arguments, particularly the challenge to the principle of male legal control over women in marriage, which in effect treated all married women, irrespective of class, as a distinct and subordinate group. They also reasserted the earlier critique of marriage itself as legalized prostitution, that is, a strictly commercial transaction of support in exchange for sex. Everywhere feminists reiterated the demand for female education, the reorganization of the household, the defense of women's trades against the intrusion of men, and the assertion of women's right to paid employment. French feminists such as "Jeanne-Victoire" argued that "until now woman has been exploited and tyrannized . . . ; half the human race cannot, without injustice, be in servitude to the other half." She called for all women—the privileged and the poor—to unite across boundaries of class on behalf of their common interests. Clarisse Vigoreux's message was aggressively confrontational, demanding "an accounting from the strong sex" for "incompetent administration" of the world's affairs.[10]

French novelists of the Romantic school, especially George Sand (the pseudonym of Aurore Dupin Dudevant), author of the controversial and widely read novels *Indiana* (1832) and *Lélia* (1836), and the male leaders of the utopian socialist reformers known as the Saint-Simonians and Fourierists once again raised the explosive theme of "free love," building on earlier expressions.

Advocates of free love proposed that men and women ought to form couples according to sexual or emotional inclination rather than according to the dictates of class-based, family, sociopolitical, or economic needs; in the metaphor of the time, free love was couple-based, not clan-based, and might exist beyond the bounds of formalized marriage. Free love enthusiasts, such as Prosper Enfantin, the acknowledged leader of the Saint-Simonian sect, not only advocated free love but also contradicted Catholic doctrine on carnal sin by urging a "rehabilitation of the flesh." Enfantin also called for women to speak out on the conditions of their own emancipation. Even as opponents within the Saint-Simonians denounced Enfantin's doctrine from within, those without viewed it as a coded call for sexual promiscuity and the destruction of the family, by which they meant the patriarchal family, and the French government promptly prosecuted the Saint-Simonian leaders for outrages to public morality.

In response to Enfantin's call, a small group of young Saint-Simonian working-class women founded a women's paper, which was called successively *La Femme nouvelle* ("The New Woman"), *L'Apostolat des femmes* ("Women's Apostolate"), *La Tribune des femmes* ("The Women's Tribune"), and *La Femme libre* ("The Free Woman"). Avoiding the use of fathers' and husbands' last names, they signed their articles only by their first names. They downplayed the controversial free love doctrines, insisting instead on the greater importance of women's economic independence from men (the "right to work"), and they defended traditional sectors of women's employment, such as selling ribbons, from male interlopers.[11]

Both Saint-Simonian women and men emphasized the complementarity of the sexes, in which the male-female couple constituted the *social individual*. But the Saint-Simonian women postulated a radical vision of maternity as the common denominator for female solidarity and emancipation, a unique quality that could be turned to good account in arguments for women's emancipation. "Jeanne-Desirée" made this claim in an early issue of the *Apostolat des femmes*: "Women's banner is universal, for . . . are they not all united by the same bond, MATERNITY?" Suzanne Voilquin felt even more strongly on this count, as is evident from her later *Souvenirs.* Was it not *LA MERE*—the Mother—whose revelation the Saint-Simonians awaited and whom they finally went to the Orient in 1834 to find?

This maternal perspective extended well beyond Saint-Simonian circles; the articulate Flora Tristan, though not directly associated with the Saint-Simonian women or their paper, subsequently emphasized (as had Mary Wollstonecraft before her) the sociopolitical importance of motherhood as a vehicle not only for freeing women, but for liberating men. In her tract, *The Workers' Union* (1843), she wrote: "All the woes of the working class can be summed up in these two words: poverty and ignorance, ignorance and poverty. Now, I see only one way out of this labyrinth: Begin by educating women, because women have the responsibility for educating male and female children." This insistent emphasis on the metaphor of motherhood as the central feature of women's difference, incorporating both the physiological capacity for childbearing and the importance of their role as mother-educators, as civilizers, was one of the most striking features of French feminist thought in the 1830s. The major exception to this surge of motherly enthusiasm was the Saint-Simonian dissident, Claire Demar, whose radically individualist pamphlet, "My Law of the Future," was published following her suicide in 1833. Demar called for "a liberty without rules or limits" and "the law of inconstancy" in love and sex, as well as for organized child care ("social motherhood") to liberate most women from having to raise children themselves.[12]

Demar's arguments notwithstanding, emphasis on the national utility of educating women for the family and the secular state increased throughout Europe during the early nineteenth century. The mother-educator concept was strategically important because it provided women with a serious, dignified—and quasi-political—purpose in life, despite their formal exclusion from politics. Women themselves found the new role appealing because of the power and influence it accorded them; it could counterbalance the devaluation of the many other vital but less inspired chores that fell to them. It also gave women an argument for demanding formal educational opportunities and special institutions for their sex, and for acquiring training as teachers. As citizen-mothers, they could make many claims on the state.

Throughout Europe and the Americas, wherever nation building was in progress, the notion of the educated mother as educator of citizens greatly influenced thought on women's emancipation. In various nationalist movements, Polish, Italian, Ukrainian, and Finnish, women writers repeatedly staked their own claims to full citizenship on the mother-educator's sociopolitical utility to the nation. Theirs was the vital role of keeping the national language and culture alive, or of helping to revive it in the face of suppression. Polish nationalist Klementyna Tanska Hoffmanova urged mothers to teach their children Polish and wrote of Polish women's role and duties. Later in the century, Hoffmanova's disciple, Natalia Kobryns'ka, made similar appeals in the cause of Ukrainian nationalism. By 1906 Alexandra Gripenberg could applaud the successful efforts of Finnish mother-educators in gaining full citizenship, including voting rights, in the charter granted to Finland by the Russian tsar.

Throughout the first half of the nineteenth century, women and men used these appeals and other, more general, arguments to invoke the importance of female cultural influence in advancing women's interests both among secular rationalists and within more progressive sectors of the Judeo-Christian religious tradition. In France, after the Saint-Simonian controversy had died down, supporters of female emancipation felt obligated to emphasize the moral respectability of their ideas. In 1848–1849 the French dramatist Ernest Legouvé summed up the arguments for radical change in the legal, educational, and economic status of women in his *Moral History of Women*. Many German women and men invoked the idea of women's importance as culture bearers and spoke, as did Henriette Schrader-Breymann and Bertha von Marenholtz-Bülow, in terms of "spiritual motherhood" as well as of physical maternity. These arguments proved to be as potent a political tool for religiously identified women in Germany as they had been in France for the secularizers.

Among reform Jews in Germany, liberal rabbis took up the cause of women's emancipation. Rabbi Abraham Geiger understood the importance of including women when he argued, in 1837, that "no distinction" should be made "between duties for men and women, unless flowing from the natural laws governing the sexes." There should be "no assumption of the spiritual minority of woman," "no degradation of woman in the form of the marriage service, and no application of fetters which may destroy woman's happiness." Jewish women must be rendered "conscious of the significance of our faith, become fervently attached to it," and thus could the "beneficial influence" of "feminine hearts" enrich Jewish religious life.[13]

By midcentury, however, partisans of female subordination were also invoking comparable notions about the rehabilitation of womanhood and mother-educators to bolster male-dominated religious institutions. Pope Pius IX, fleeing from the revolution in Rome in 1849, invoked the positive power of educated and influential womanhood for Roman Catholicism when he called for promulgation of the dogma of the Immaculate Conception of Mary. As men defected from the Church, the pope seemed especially anxious to retain women's allegiance in a time of revolutionary upheaval; he understood and hoped to harness the power of Christian mothers in forming souls for the Church. Though they were poles apart politically, both the pope and the ardent secular philosopher-sociologist Auguste Comte testified their belief in the importance of female influence for the regeneration of European political and cultural life. Unlike the feminists, neither was led to argue for women's emancipation by this belief. In the highly politicized atmosphere of mid-nineteenth-century Europe, the reinvigorated and elastic notions of women's influence and separate spheres could and would henceforth serve both revolutionary and counterrevolutionary ends.[14]

FEMINIST THOUGHT AND ACTION IN
THE REVOLUTIONS OF 1848

In 1848 revolutionaries once again challenged the European monarchies, demanding republics, public liberties, and popular sovereignty. Beginning with the ouster of Louis-Philippe in Paris, revolutionary protests also erupted in Berlin, Vienna, Frankfurt, and other major European cities. Once again, feminists placed demands for women's emancipation on the political agenda.

Two women exemplify the possibilities and limitations of continental European feminist thought and action in the years from 1848 to 1851. The Frenchwoman Jeanne Deroin (1805–1894) and her somewhat younger German counterpart Louise Otto (later Otto-Peters; 1819–1895) from Saxony illustrate the ways in which the cause of women's emancipation was integral to the political and intellectual history of the times. Their respective approaches also provide insight into the national differences that emerged in the course of the nineteenth century. Both women took active roles in the revolutionary events of midcentury Europe; both were journalists, publishing feminist periodicals during the revolutionary years, Deroin in Paris, and Otto first in Meissen and then in Gera. Both asserted women's claims to liberty, equality, and justice as staunchly as they insisted on the difference of women from men without perceiving these claims as in the least contradictory. Both were radicals with reference to their respective societies, and both can be viewed as relational feminists. Deroin advocated women's suffrage, and Otto advocated improvement of women's educational and economic situation.

Jeanne Deroin was a Parisian working-class woman, who although married and a mother, used her given name rather than that of her husband Desroches. She had participated in the Saint-Simonian movement during the 1830s and had also absorbed some of the teachings of Charles Fourier. She considered herself a democratic socialist, but her first priority was the cause of women.

Writing in the new women's newspaper, *La Voix des femmes* ("Women's Voice"), founded in Paris by Eugénie Niboyet shortly after the outbreak of the February revolution, Deroin called for women's formal participation in public affairs. The provisional government had established universal manhood suffrage; thus France had become the first ostensibly democratic European nation. But this brand new democracy was quite deliberately male, a fact that the feminists did not hesitate to point out publicly. The leaders of the provisional government balked at proposals to extend the vote to women, and soon thereafter the newly enfranchised men elected an assembly that was unsympathetic to the revolution. In early June 1848 (after weeks of controversy and civil disruption) the First Republic's assembly abruptly closed all political clubs, singling out those organized by women.

Even after the male voters elected Louis-Napoleon (heir of the Bonaparte dynasty) president of the Republic, Deroin persisted in pressing for women's inclusion in political life. In 1849 she founded her own periodical, *L'Opinion des Femmes* ("Women's Opinion"), and in a serialized essay on "woman's mission," she presented her vision of what women's participation in political life ought to accomplish. The first priority of democratic government, she argued, must be to end the struggle between women and men. Only by abolishing male privilege (in this case, male political privilege), she insisted, could the new government achieve the realization of a truly new society. "The abolition of the privileges of race, birth, caste, and fortune cannot be complete and radical unless the privilege of sex is totally abolished," she wrote. Deroin argued that only by achieving full citizenship could women participate properly in the reconstruction of French society.[15]

Deroin based her arguments for women's participation in political affairs on sexual complementarity and women's difference (both physiological and social) from men, in particular, on women's "sacred function as mother" and her "sublime humanitarian maternity." Women had not only a right but a duty, given their maternal role, to intercede in both civil and political life in order to carry out the duty of watching over the future of their children.

The conditions of political life in France had radically changed, Deroin argued; violence and repression must henceforth yield to participatory government. Women must be called on to "teach everyone how fraternity should be practiced," to show men the way of transcending secular quarrels between individuals, between families, and between nations. Women had nothing less than an apostolic mission to "realize the kingdom of God on earth, the reign of fraternity and universal harmony." Given the circumstances of male revolutionary violence, Deroin seems to have considered women's moral superiority self-evident.

In early 1849, Deroin acted on her ideals, petitioning the Democratic-Socialist party to become a candidate for the new Legislative Assembly. She quickly aroused the hostility of men newly active in French political life. Deroin's pioneering feminist candidacy for office under a democratized regime was unsuccessful; not long thereafter she would become one of the first women to be arrested and imprisoned for her efforts to organize "illegal" joint associations of male and female workers. In 1852 Deroin fled to England, in the company of other opponents of the regime of Louis-Napoleon, and there she spent the rest of her life in exile.[16]

In the revolutionary turmoil of mid-nineteenth-century Germany, feminist activists used different arguments, although, as in France, they emphasized women's difference from men as a central tenet. The main themes were German womanliness and spirituality, rather than sociopolitical motherhood. In German feminist discourse, arguments often carried an undeniably nationalist (often specifically anti-French) overtone. German feminists emphasized the distinctive contribution that women, as women, could and must make to the building of the German nation (a very important political goal prior to the forced unification of the many German principalities with Prussia in 1871 under Otto von Bismarck). The arguments put forth by Louise Otto, a well-educated single woman of upper-middle-class background who, like Deroin, had become a political radical, exemplify this particular type of relational feminism.

Based in Saxony, one of Germany's most industrialized regions, Otto edited the longest-lived of several German revolutionary women's publications, the *Frauenzeitung* ("Women's Newspaper"). Since the mid-1840s she had crusaded for systematic reform of the education of middle-class women and for improvements in the condition of working women in the region's industrial cities. Marriage, in Otto's view, was a degraded institution, merely an economic "support institution for the female sex." She scorned women's "characterlessness" in a culture where the building of character (*Bildung*) was considered so extremely important for educated men. Far more than Deroin, and reflecting the idealist spirit of German philosophy since Kant (though Kant would hardly have applied such ideas to women), Otto emphasized "independence," not only of a moral nature ("the exercise of judgment") but also of a material, or economic, nature ("the exercise of action").[17]

Of particular significance to Louise Otto was her oft-repeated concern with "true womanliness," which epitomized for her a quality quite different from, and far more potent than, the characterlessness she objected to in so many German women. Her arguments for "true womanliness" carried a defensive tone, however; she constantly issued disclaimers against those who (as she put it) discredited the emancipation of woman "by devaluing woman to become a caricature of a man." This had become a sore point among German feminists, exacerbated by a recent wave of "Georgesandismus"—the aping by certain self-proclaimed "emancipated women" of the unusual and much publicized habits of the French novelist George Sand. These habits included wearing male dress (illegal in France without a police permit), smoking, and engaging in liaisons with men to whom one was not married. In their reaction to Georgesandismus, German feminists at midcentury often exhibited a peculiarly self-righteous and straight-laced quality. Otto's true woman was, above all else, virtuous, courageous, moralistic, patriotic, and peaceable—all the things German men allegedly were not.

THE DEVELOPMENT OF ORGANIZED WOMEN'S MOVEMENTS

The fundamental elements of a feminist critique of European societies were fully developed well before 1848, but attempts to organize had been sporadic and short-lived because of the recurrent efforts to control public speech and association. The most successful organizational efforts before 1850 were located in the United States, not in Europe. As early as 1851, Harriet Taylor Mill (who had evidently not heard of the now celebrated Seneca Falls Convention in June 1848) expressed her admiration at the activism of American women who had freely convened at Worcester, Massachusetts, in pursuit of their "rights." Not until the late 1850s and 1860s, a period of growing prosperity and uneven political liberalization, did equivalent organization on behalf of women's emancipation begin to develop staying power in Europe.[18]

From that time forth, however, many such initiatives sprang up. In Western Europe, the leaders ranged from upper-middle-class women who were well connected to the governing male elites to writers and teachers, as well as educated progressive (often Protestant) women with international contacts such as Jenny P. d'Héricourt, Marie Goegg, and André Léo (pseudonym of Léodile Bera Champceix). Agitation for women's emancipation among the radical intelligentsia in imperial Russia accompanied the freeing of the serfs (to whose plight the situation of women was often compared). Tsarist absolutism did not allow the possibility of democratic political participation even for men, so no organized Western European–style movement sprang up. Even so, Russian women—significant numbers of whom had migrated to Switzerland in the 1860s to seek higher education—became the first in Europe to obtain government-sponsored access to secondary and higher education; subsequently many of these women joined revolutionary movements dedicated to the overthrow of the tsarist regime.

Although conditions specific to each country governed the shape that political activity on women's behalf would take, the new wave of activism that erupted in the 1860s manifested many features common to all. Concerns for women's secondary and higher education and possibilities for employment had become central. Although individual women often acted unilaterally, some of the most successful initiatives for change in each country ultimately emerged from group philanthropic activity, which raised the consciousness of the institutional causes of women's common plight and contributed to the birth of the social work profession.

Concerted efforts to change women's inferior civil and political status in the law were especially evident in Britain and in France during the 1860s. Although a major reform—the transfer of divorce proceedings from ecclesiastical courts to civil courts—had been enacted in England in 1857, married women still had no legal standing. According to English common law, adult women once married lost all authority over property, whether property they brought to marriage or their own earnings. For instance, at one notable trial, the court charged the thief with "stealing from the person of Millicent Fawcett a purse containing £1 18s. 6d., the property of Henry Fawcett." (Millicent Garrett Fawcett eventually became a leader of the British movement for women's suffrage.) British feminists headed by Barbara Leigh Smith (later Bodichon) established a Married Women's Property Committee, and by persuading sympathetic members to introduce legislation, provoked a full-scale debate on the subject in Parliament. This agitation ultimately led to the passage in 1882 of a sweeping Married Women's Property Law. In 1869 John Stuart Mill published his famous treatise, *The Subjection of Women*. This work, which no one could ignore because of Mill's international reputation as a political theorist, quickly became a landmark in the history of European feminist thought; within just a few years it was translated (in many cases by feminists from other cultures) into many languages, including Danish, Polish, French, and Spanish. At the time it triggered much criticism as well as much acclaim.[19]

In France, the subordinate legal status of married women in the Napoleonic Code provoked concerted agitation for change led by the anti-clerical republicans Maria Deraismes and Léon Richer. Following the liberal-ization of the Second Empire's laws on the press and association, in 1868 Richer established a periodical, *Le Droit des femmes* ("The Right[s] of Women"), which insistently promoted changes in the legal, educational, moral, and economic position of women for well over twenty years. In 1878, under the Third Republic, Richer and Deraismes convened the First Interna-tional Congress on Women's Rights, which attracted representatives to Paris from twelve countries. Despite this promising beginning, however, and the reestablishment of civil divorce in 1882, resistance remained so considerable that no thorough overhaul of the legal status of married women would occur until the middle of the twentieth century.

The development of an organized feminist movement in Italy followed on the heels of efforts to achieve national unification under a constitutional monarchy, which succeeded in the early 1860s. The pioneer reformer Anna Maria Mozzoni focused on promoting a liberal treatment of women in the new legal code, while other women reformers zealously promoted women's education for patriotic motherhood in the interest of the new nation, as well as a campaign against state-regulated prostitution.

Agitation to promote women's suffrage also resurfaced in Western Europe during the 1860s. In England, during consideration of the Second Reform Bill in 1867, John Stuart Mill, then in Parliament, introduced a measure to amend the parliamentary suffrage extension bill by substituting the word *person* for *man* wherever it appeared in the bill. Although this measure failed, in 1870 English women won the right to vote in local elections. In France, discussion of votes for women emerged again during this period, only to be squelched again in the wake of France's defeat by Germany in 1870. The ensuing revolt and the short-lived reign of the Paris Commune, in which many women took part, caused another wave of reactionary fears, including fear among men on the left about the inclusion of women in political life. "Do they think they can accomplish the revolution without women?" asked the feminist journalist and Communard André Léo. "From one point of view our history since '89 could be written under the title, 'History of the Ineffectiveness of the Revolutionary Party.' The woman question would be the longest chapter." Despite the valiant efforts of Hubertine Auclert to obtain the right to vote for Frenchwomen in the 1880s, the suffrage issue remained too controversial to arouse much support before the early twentieth century. Anticlerical men of the French Third Republic resisted women's suffrage because they feared that women would support the monarchist Catholic opposition. After German unification in 1871

and the subsequent establishment of an indirect national system of male suffrage for the Reichstag, Hedwig Dohm and others also argued for women's
vote but did not attract a significant following.[20]

Efforts to establish international links in the women's movement also
blossomed in the late 1860s. In conjunction with a movement to promote
European peace and solidarity across national lines, Marie Goegg of Switzerland attempted to establish an international women's network; her vision was
only realized in 1888 with the foundation of the International Council of
Women. Many of the leading European advocates of pacifism and international cooperation also supported women's rights, as did some women and
men active in the first International Working Men's Association, founded in
1864. A third, dominantly Protestant network formed in the 1870s in conjunction with Josephine Butler's campaign against state-regulated prostitution.[21]

The 1880s—a period of economic depression and psychological uncertainty—witnessed a change in the context of the debate on the woman question
and in the character of the demands made for women's emancipation. In the
course of the nineteenth century, the "woman question," like the so-called social question, had become an integral feature of the vast European debate over
changing sociopolitical circumstances. The complex mixture of interrelated
problems stemming from industrialization, working-class agitation, demographic anxieties, and the emerging political challenge mounted by socialist
factions intensified the debate. During the 1870s and 1880s, European governments had begun to confront issues raised by the employment of working-class
women in industrial manufacturing. But since most working women did not
work in factories, their work was not easily regulated. For these women, employment meant long hours, unhealthy working conditions, and inferior pay
with little sense of personal reward. Especially in France, but increasingly after
1900 in Germany and Great Britain, members of the educated classes, including doctors as well as politicians, began to worry over the possible adverse
consequences for their countries of new population patterns. Birthrates were
falling off significantly, and mortality rates, especially high among infants and
small children of the poor, were becoming a major public concern. In some
countries, especially in Scandinavia, heavy emigration threatened to deplete
the population. National governments were becoming concerned about the
production of future generations of workers and soldiers. Opponents of
women's emancipation interpreted even the assertion of women's right to paid
employment (let alone the demand for women's right to pursue the better-paid
"masculine" professions), as a threat to the demographic and economic well-
being of the nation-state. Work for single women prior to marriage was conceded, but not for married women. Working wives, they argued, did not bear
and could not raise healthy children. Women's claims for rights threatened to
interfere with women's "responsibilities" to society and the state.[22]

In this changing context, European novelists and dramatists began to explore the "new woman" and the problem posed for society by women's "ego-
tism," as women's search for freedom and self-realization was often labeled

whenever it threatened to divert them from child care, household work, and comforting men. In the play, *A Doll's House* (1879), which created a sensation throughout Europe in the years that followed, the Norwegian dramatist Henrik Ibsen sympathetically portrayed a woman caught in marriage to a mediocre man and her decision to abandon husband and children in order to "find herself." The uproar generated by Nora's decision to walk out at the end of Act III epitomized the general touchiness of public opinion on the subject of women's emancipation, and on at least one occasion, Ibsen rewrote the last scene before the play could be produced. In her *Story of an African Farm* (1883), the novelist Olive Schreiner created the character of Lyndall, who boasted that she was "not in so great a hurry to put [her] neck beneath any man's foot." Other "new woman" novels followed, many of which attacked the existing institution of marriage; they attracted an enthusiastic readership, especially among women. In England, Mona Caird's widely read novel *The Daughters of Danaus* (1894) elaborated her blistering critique of marriage in fictional form, as did the widely translated *Una donna [A Woman]* (1906), by the Italian novelist Sibilla Aleramo (pseudonym of Rina Pierangeli Faccio), who also edited an Italian feminist publication, *L'Italia femminile*. Such fictional feminist works were complemented by essays and social criticism by intellectuals such as Karl Pearson, Eleanor Marx, Havelock Ellis, August Bebel, and Friedrich Engels, who reintroduced exploration in print of the linkages between sexuality, socioeconomic and family structures, capitalism, and the state. All these writers probed the social consequences of women's emancipation, and although many authors seemed sympathetic to women's strivings, few of them were optimistic about the consequences for society of women's efforts to achieve independence and self-realization. Nevertheless, their arguments contributed significantly to the diffusion of feminist ideas.

Aside from demands for political equality for women, only rarely before 1880 had any advocates of women's emancipation called for more than moral or intellectual equality for women and for ending their legal and economic subordination in marriage. Metaphors of motherhood and womanliness, as we have seen, lay at the base of most arguments, and concepts of "woman's nature" and "woman's role" continued to foster arguments for radical change. Before 1880, only the Fourierists and Owenites had proposed a non-sex-typed, non-role-based notion of human equality for women, or the sharing of "women's work"—housework or child care—by men. After 1880, this began to change rapidly; even the concept of "woman's nature" found its challengers, and "new women" were charged by their critics of pursuing a "masculine" vision of autonomy.

New, more radical reformulations of the problem and proposals for change engendered a resurgence of overt opposition to women's emancipation and dampened the enthusiasm of some earlier supporters. Social Darwinist writers, such as Patrick Geddes and J. Arthur Thomson in Britain, invoked evolutionary theory to justify the sexual division of labor. "What was decided among the prehistoric Protozoa," they wrote, "cannot be annulled by Act of

Parliament." Opponents of sociopolitical change tried to discredit all argu-ments for women's emancipation by alleging that every claim for women's equality was necessarily egotistic, and that the realization of such claims would lead to social and political anarchy. "Woman wants to become self-reliant," the philosopher Friedrich Nietzsche sneered in 1886, "and for that reason she is beginning to enlighten men about 'woman as such': *this* is one of the worst developments of the general *uglification* of Europe." Indeed, opponents of women's rights obsessively conjured up the threat of "individualist" feminist arguments, including the threat that unmarried "independent" women might become a "third sex"—a sex unresponsive to the overtures of men. To frighten off prospective supporters of female emancipation, other opponents warned that emancipated women threatened men's virility and, therefore, national security. "The German man is manly, and the German woman is womanly," the British Minister of War pointed out in 1910 to an antiwoman suffrage audience in Manchester. "Can we hope to compete with such a nation as this, if we war against nature, and endeavour to invert the natural roles of the sexes?"[23]

THE FLOWERING OF FEMINISM

During the 1890s, when the words *feminism* and *feminist* entered widespread usage throughout Europe, a new generation of feminist theorists and women political leaders also emerged. This generation included increasing numbers of self-assured and often politically radical young women armed with univer-sity degrees in letters, law, and medicine or with teaching credentials, who felt little need to apologize for any presumed intellectual inferiority. It also in-cluded middle-aged, more conservative but well-connected women who had come to recognize, through philanthropic assistance to the deviant and the dis-possessed, the systematic injustices that women suffered in male-dominated societies. These women had acquired organizational skills and a far-reaching network of contacts, not only locally but also nationally and internationally, and they elaborated and sought to realize a new and far more extensive set of claims on behalf of their sex.

Many among this new generation of feminists continued to emphasize women's biological and social difference from men and underscored a radical vision of motherhood as the focal point for female solidarity. They argued for special rights for women—women's rights—as well as for equal rights with men—human rights. Though theoretical and literary feminists articulated ideas that were often extraordinarily individualistic, the activists confronted the need to wrest desired reforms from an often reluctant, even fearful male-dominated political power structure. They faced opposition not only from the men in power but from those with more advanced political views. Already in 1879, for example, Hubertine Auclert had expressed concern about the atti-tudes exhibited by some French socialist men: "Those who deny our equality in the present, will deny it also in the future. Thus we must count on ourselves to achieve our own freedom. . . . Without a guarantee, I am truly afraid that human equality, as preached by every socialist school, will still mean the equality of men, and that the women will be duped by the proletarian men just as the latter have been duped by the bourgeois." The situation had worsened by the 1890s, following the founding of the Second International Working Men's Association. In England, Alys Russell replied in 1896 to the arguments of the socialist theorist Auguste Bebel, author of *Women and Socialism* (1879):

> [Bebel] really asks for no more than is demanded in other countries by those advanced women who are not followers of Marx, and whose suggestions are more practical than Bebel's. There is no reason why women should not attain to a very fair degree of economic independence, for instance, through Trade Unions for the unmarried, and through payment of motherhood for the married. . . . And the equal mental and physical training of the sexes, . . . is certainly possible in an individualistic state of society while equal laws for men and women are more and more taking the place of the old unjust laws.

What might have become a cooperative endeavor between socialists and feminists increasingly became a rivalry, especially where socialist political parties prioritized class struggle. In countries like Russia, where a small but energetic reformist feminist movement emerged in the early twentieth century, the socialist women's groups made every effort to impede it, even attempting to break up feminist congresses. The Second International attempted to outflank the feminists' campaigns for woman suffrage by endorsing complete and unrestricted suffrage, even in situations where such democratization was far from being an achieveable political goal.[24]

By the early 1900s, a cluster of feminist movements were taking on substance and bulk throughout Western and Central Europe, while on the southwestern periphery, in Spain and Portugal, and in Switzerland, Austria, and Hungary, feminist organizations had began to sprout. In the countries of Scandinavia, feminist agitation had become well rooted since the 1880s. Indeed, the growth of a full-blown organized women's movement and the explosion of feminist publications in Western Europe between 1890 and 1914 constitutes one of the most significant features of the European political landscape. The movement's rapid growth can be directly attributed to rising educational levels, especially among women, and to the more relaxed and increasingly open political environment of the late nineteenth century, which permitted, in spite of much official reluctance, more freedom for political association and less constrained public speech.

In addition to continuing demands for legal and educational reforms, feminist groups throughout Europe campaigned for such varied solutions as state subsidies for mothers (married and unmarried alike), protective labor legislation and/or the right to work, maternity insurance and leave, and all-female trade unions for working women. They openly criticized objectionable practices of male sexuality, from wife beating to legalized prostitution, and they worked to combat the spread of venereal disease, to promote a new sexual ethic, and to campaign for family planning. Late-nineteenth-century advocacy of women's emancipation ran the gamut from moderate single-issue campaigns for reform to sweeping radical critiques of the entire sociopolitical, economic, and cultural status quo, including the politics of knowledge. Thus women's suffrage was far from the only political issue feminists had placed on the table by the first decade of the twentieth century. But it was becoming increasingly clear to feminist activists on the European continent, as it had become clear in the English-speaking world, that male-dominated governments, especially newly democratized governments responsive only to male voters and male-dominated political parties, were extremely resistant to making dramatic changes on behalf of women who were politically powerless. The vote seemed to be the key to all the other desired changes.

In the few democratizing states of Western Europe, therefore, feminist women and their male allies worked to obtain formal political power equivalent to that available to men. Finnish women were the first to be wholly enfranchised in 1906, followed by their Norwegian (partial suffrage in 1907, full in 1913) and their Danish sisters (1915). In England, the crusade for women's suffrage—especially the militant campaign led by the Women's Social and Political Union (WSPU)—riveted world attention during the early twentieth century. In this campaign, orchestrated by Emmeline Pankhurst and her daughters Christabel and Sylvia, and supported by many middle-class and working-class women, the prevailing ideal of feminine propriety (though not femininity) was renounced. As Emmeline Pankhurst put it in her court testimony of 1908, "We have tried to be womanly, we have tried to use feminine influence, and we have seen that it is of no use. . . ; we are here not because we are law-breakers; we are here in our efforts to become law-makers." The Englishwomen's campaign for the vote ranks as the feminist movement's first great media event, and the repressive measures instituted by the British government against the suffragettes aroused the sympathy of women around the world. Far more controversial were the arguments of Emmeline Pankhurst's daughter Christabel, a law graduate who became the chief theorist and tactician of the WSPU. She became incensed about the sex scandals that rocked Britain during the period of persecution of the suffragettes and launched a scathing attack on male vice and its consequences for innocent women. Her solution: "Votes for Women and Chastity for Men." But even the spectacular English campaign did not succeed until after World War I, and in 1918 only women over 30 obtained the vote from their Parliament, along with their Irish counterparts.[25]

Elsewhere women rarely obtained the vote by parliamentary vote or democratic referendum. After the 1914–1918 war, in the new Weimar Republic of Germany, and in Soviet Russia, women would become voters by decision of revolutionary governments. In the many postwar successor states of the former Austro-Hungarian Empire, women obtained a somewhat unwelcome suffrage as part of a series of postwar settlements. In the older European nations of France, Italy, Belgium, and Switzerland, women's suffrage would be resisted for many more decades.

The successors of Deroin and Otto were conducting far more open discussions of men's and women's sexual practices as well as the politics of reproduction; some frankly claimed woman's right to exercise independence in matters of love and even to bear children outside marriage. The notions of woman's difference and her educational mission continued to buttress the demands of relational feminists for the development of new educational opportunities for women, but now also served as a basis for a far more explicit, more insistent, and daring attack on patriarchal institutional arrangements, including economic practices that disadvantaged women, and on the "masculinist" state itself. Since it is impossible here to deal in depth with all the variations of this attack, what follows is a brief introduction to two of the most singular and influential new contributions by women to continental European feminist thought between 1890 and 1914.

Swedish writer Ellen Key (1849–1926) made perhaps the most controversial contribution by examining at length the problem posed for women by motherhood. Key did not confine her theoretical work to short articles and newspapers, as had the women of 1848. She published important and widely translated books: *The Century of the Child* (originally in Swedish, 1900), and *Love and Marriage* (originally in Swedish, 1904), which were circulated, quoted, and argued about, and which had a major impact not only on leaders of the women's movements in Germany and France, but as far away as Japan.

Key's arguments gave a distinctive twist to the assertions of the social value of motherhood by Jeanne Deroin and other early-nineteenth-century advocates of women's emancipation. Although she spoke of women's biological nature and the traditional division of labor between the sexes in the family, according to which women were the childbearers and child rearers, she diverged from earlier arguments at a critical point—on the question of state-organized and state-subsidized child care for women in the workforce.

The strategic significance of Key's analysis lay in her attempt to synthesize a rigorously relational approach based on women's difference with deeply felt individualist claims for women's right to fulfillment and self-realization. Key proposed that women could achieve their maximum development as individuals through their contributions to society as mothers. But she also argued that the conditions for motherhood must be totally restructured in order for such a synthesis to occur, and that motherhood must be revalued— sanctioned, as it were—both politically and economically, by the nation-state. Economic support of individual women during their childbearing years by individual men, which she viewed as the immediate cause of women's subordination, should be the responsibility of the government. Child care should take place in the home, supported by the collectivity, but in the biological mother's charge; it should not become a direct responsibility of the collectivity, as others from

Plato to Fourier and Claire Demar had insisted. Indeed, Key argued—expanding upon earlier "republican motherhood" arguments—that the state ought to recognize formal training of women for this role as the equivalent of military service for men. She also called boldly for open recognition of the sexual side of love, including women's sexual pleasure, a feature of her arguments that endeared her to commentators such as Havelock Ellis in England but scandalized defenders of traditional morality.[26]

In the population-conscious political climate of Third Republic France, Nelly Roussel (1878–1922) developed a related line of argument, once again based on women's social position as mothers. Herself married (unlike Ellen Key) and the mother of three, Roussel identified herself as a free thinker. She worked closely with Marguerite Durand, publisher of the French women's daily newspaper, *La Fronde*.

Nelly Roussel emerged as a powerful public speaker and polemicist for the French women's rights movement in 1903. Defying the politicians who urged harsh measures to raise the French birthrate, she eloquently advocated women's right to control their own fertility. She called for a complete revision in the French laws governing marriage, at a time when the government of the Third Republic was becoming increasingly concerned about the decline in the national birthrate. She appealed to women of all classes to "declare war on today's society." In one celebrated oration, she even invoked the threat of a birth strike against the patriarchal state:

> Beware, oh Society! The day will come . . . when the eternal victim will become weary of carrying in her loins sons whom you will later teach to scorn their mothers or daughters destined—alas!—to the same life of sacrifice and humiliation! The day when we will refuse to give you, ogres, your ration of cannon-fodder, of work-fodder, and fodder for suffering! The day, at last, when we will become mothers *only when we please*. . . .

Like Ellen Key, Roussel based her claims for women's emancipation on the sociopolitical value of motherhood, and argued in relational terms.[27]

Roussel was first and foremost a women's advocate. She took every opportunity to criticize *masculinisme*, a term she used (as had Hubertine Auclert and Aline Valette before her) to describe male supremacy. She addressed her arguments to women of every class and worked closely with French proponents of birth control and sex education in efforts to reach women of the working class. Like Auclert, Mozzoni, and Alys Russell, she criticized French socialists who, in their single-minded pursuit of class struggle, objected to socialist women's cooperation on women's issues with the so-called bourgeois feminists. She also objected to the socialists' opposition to birth control. From Roussel's perspective, all women were oppressed—the "eternal victims"—and women of all classes should pursue the same goal—emancipation. Women, she insisted, had far more in common than did men of different classes, because whatever their class, they shared a common oppression at the hands of men.[28]

CONCLUSION

By the early twentieth century, European feminist theorists were exploring in depth virtually every issue we are familiar with today. Feminist activists had organized to work for political, legal, socioeconomic, and cultural change in women's position along a broad front. Both theorists and activists found inspiration for their protests and a vocabulary for articulating a feminist consciousness in the language of liberty, equality, and justice. But the contours of their thought and action in the nineteenth century were bounded by historical circumstances, and they had not yet acquired the formal power to reshape these. This may explain why their most persuasive arguments for the achievement of particular reforms featured a relational logic.

Both nineteenth-century European feminist thinkers and their opponents agreed that male-female relations were the very glue that held organized society together and that marriage and sex and gender roles were inherently political. Although most accepted a sexual division of labor in society, they rejected the public-domestic division of spheres as inappropriate and argued that women's influence must be felt throughout society. Most continental feminists in this era insisted on the importance of biophysiological differences between the sexes and on what Adrienne Rich has since derogated as "compulsory heterosexuality," and in fact many (though by no means all) political progressives who supported women's emancipation also argued for universal marriage as their social ideal. Most viewed motherhood as women's particular responsibility. Indeed, for many, maternity had become not only the strategic common ground for women's solidarity but also the vehicle for their liberation. Most nineteenth-century European feminists also insisted (far more than we find comfortable doing today) on the close relationship between the family and the state; indeed, they held an optimistic view of the potential for harnessing state power on women's behalf. This optimism remained intact even as emancipators envisioned a radical reorganization (through democratic means) of existing heterosexual relations, familial institutions, and the sociopolitical structure—a vision diametrically opposed to that enforced by most late-nineteenth-century states, as well as to that subsequently incorporated in the welfare states of twentieth-century Europe.[29]

European feminist theory and practice remains to this day far more overtly conscious of state power and the political centrality of the family to the state than does its Anglo-American counterpart. Nineteenth-century European feminist theorists questioned the political structure of society from marriage to monarchy and increasingly challenged the practices and assumptions of the new industrial economic order that seemed to bolster male-dominated structures instead of dissolving them. Their own assertions about the way in which the entire postrevolutionary order should be revised and reconstructed were based on their prior understanding of "nature" and "culture," on a successful reinterpretation of women's importance as culture bearers, and on their perception of the seeming fragility of the intricate web of relationships that bound individuals together into societies. They knew that feminism was powerful. "Today, after a century of struggle," wrote Mme Avril de Sainte-Croix in her 1907 history, *Le Féminisme*, "the effort of women to acquire more justice and more independence seems poised on the brink of success. Feminism no longer provokes a smirk. . . . Whether one likes it or not, the forward march of feminism is a fact that no one can deny, a movement that no force can henceforth bring to a halt. Woman. . . has become a factor to be reckoned with. . . ."[30] It would take a war or two to halt feminism's advance, to discredit the term, and to erase its very memory. For the quest to end male privilege and undo women's subordination threatened a far more radical reformulation of the sociopolitical order than ending the reign of kings, which in European history had been envisioned as strictly a male affair.

NOTES

All translations are mine unless otherwise indicated; a number of the commissioned translations quoted in the text were funded by grants from the Marilyn Yalom Fund, Institute for Research on Women and Gender, Stanford University.

1. Madame de Beaumer, "Avant-Propos," *Journal des Dames*, March 1762; in Susan Bell and Karen Offen, *Women, the Family and Freedom: The Debate in Documents, 1750–1950*, 2 vols. (Stanford: Stanford University Press, 1983) vol. 1, doct. 2, p. 28.

2. "Cahier des doléances et réclamations des femmes, par Madame B*** B***, Pays de Caux, 1789," reprinted in *Cahiers de doléances des femmes en 1789 et autres textes*, préface de Paule-Marie Duhet (Paris: des femmes, 1981), p. 51; *Requête des Dames à l'Assemblée Nationale* (1789), reprinted in *Femmes dans la Révolution française, 1789–1794*, présentés par Albert Soboul, 2 vols. (Paris: EDHIS, 1982), vol. 1, doct. 19.

3. Marie-Jean-Antoine-Nicolas Caritat, marquis de Condorcet, "Sur l'admission des femmes au droit de cité," *Journal de la Société de 1789*, 3 July 1790, as translated by John Morley (1870), and reprinted in Bell and Offen, *Women, the Family, and Freedom*, vol. 1, doct. 24; Olympe de Gouges, *Les Droits de la femme* (Paris, 1791), as tr. by Nupur Chaudhuri, et al, in *Women, the Family, and Freedom*, vol. 1, doct. 26. Etta Palm d'Aelders, *Appel aux françoises sur la régénération des moeurs et necessité de l'influence des femmes dans un gouvernement libre* (Paris, 1791).

4. Marie-Jean-Antoine-Nicolas Caritat, marquis de Condorcet, *Esquisse d'un tableau historique des progrès de l'esprit humain* (orig. publ. 1795; Paris: Éditions Sociales, 1966), pp. 274–75; *La Causa delle Donne: Discorso agl'Italiani della Cittadina**** (Venice: G. Zorsi, 1797); republished in *Giacobini italiani*, vol. 2, ed. Delio Cantomori and Renzo De Felice (Bari: Laterza and Figli, 1964), pp. 455–56; unpublished translation by Rhoda Hanafi. The translated text of P.B.v.W., translated by Sarah Lewis, is published in Judith Vega, "Feminist Discourses in the Dutch Republic at the End of the Eighteenth Century," *Journal of Women's History* 8, no. 2 (1996).

5. F.R.*** [Fanny Raoul], *Opinion d'une femme sur les femmes* (Paris: Giguet, 1801), pp. 68–69; Charles Fourier, *Théorie de Quatre Mouvements et des destinées générales* (orig.

publ. 1808; reprinted Paris: J. J. Pauvert, 1967), p. 147; Percy Bysshe Shelley, *The Revolt of Islam* (1817), Canto II, verse 43; Hugo, "Sur la Tombe de Louise Jullien" (1853), *Oeuvres complètes de Victor Hugo* (Paris: Editions Hetzel-Quantin, 1880–89), vol. 44, p. 92.

6. For further discussion, see Karen Offen, "On the French Origin of the Words *Feminism* and *Feminist*," *Feminist Issues* 8, no. 2 (Fall 1988), pp. 45–51. The first known use of the word in French to refer to women's rights advocates (by Alexandre Dumas fils, 1872) was pejorative, but in 1882 the French women's suffrage advocate Hubertine Auclert claimed the word *feminist* to describe herself and other advocates of women's emancipation.

7. Ellen Key, *Love and Marriage*, tr. Arthur G. Chater (New York, 1911), p. 214. Orig. publ. in Swedish, 1904.

8. *Harriet Martineau on Women*, ed. Gayle Graham Yates (New Brunswick, N.J.: Rutgers University Press, 1985); Anna Doyle Wheeler, "Rights of Women. A Lecture delivered by Mrs. Wheeler last year, in a Chapel near Finsbury Square," *The British Co-Operator* 1, no. 1 (April 1830), and no. 2 (May 1830). Quote, part 2, p. 35. Thanks to Maggie McFadden and George Offen for procuring photocopies of the Wheeler texts. For historical analyses of early nineteenth-century British feminism, see especially Barbara Taylor, *Eve and the New Jerusalem: Socialism and Feminism in the Nineteenth Century* (New York: Pantheon, 1983; rev. ed. Cambridge, Mass.: Harvard University Press, 1993).

9. "An Act (2 William IV, c. 45) to Amend the Representation of the People in England and Wales, 7 June 1832," in *English Historical Documents*, ed. David C. Douglas, vol. 11 (1783–1832), ed. A. Aspinall and E. Anthony Smith (1959), doc. 303, articles XIX and XX; "Concordia," "To Robert Owen, Esq.," in *The Crisis*, vol. 2 (Sat., August 10, 1833), p. 254.

10. "Jeanne Victoire," "Appel aux femmes," *La Femme libre*, no. 1 (1832), p. 1; as translated in Bell and Offen, *Women, the Family, and Freedom*, I, doct. 36, pp. 146–47; Clarisse Vigoreux, *Parole de Providence* (1834; republished Seyssel, France, 1993), p. 94.

11. See Chapter 3 of Claire Goldberg Moses, *French Feminism in the Nineteenth Century* (Albany, N.Y.: State University of New York Press, 1984).

12. The article by "Jeanne-Désirée" appeared in *L'Apostolat des femmes*, no. 5, 3 October 1832.

13. Ernest Legouvé, *Histoire morale des femmes* (Paris, 1849), p. 154. Rabbi Abraham Geiger, "Die Stellung des weiblichen Geschlechtes in dem Judenthume unserer Zeit," *Wissenschaftliche Zeitschrift für jüdische Theologie* (Frankfurt/Main), vol. 3 (1837); as translated in W. Gunther Plaut, *The Rise of Reform Judaism: A Sourcebook of Its European Origins* (New York: World Union for Progressive Judaism, 1969), p. 254.

14. For the texts of Pius IX and Auguste Comte, see Bell and Offen, *Women, the Family, and Freedom*, chap. 8.

15. Deroin's "Mission de la femme dans le present et dans l'avenir" appeared in *L'Opinion des femmes*, issues of 28 January, 10 March, and 10 April 1849. All quotations are from the translation in Bell and Offen, *Women, the Family, and Freedom*, I, doct. 77.

16. Deroin's arguments with Proudhon are translated in *ibid.*, I, docts. 84–85.

17. The Otto texts referred to here can be consulted in English in Bell and Offen, *Women, the Family, and Freedom*, I, docts. 48, 78, 89.

18. Harriet Taylor Mill, review essay on *The New York Tribune for Europe* (issue of 29 October 1850), *Westminster Review,* no. 109 (July 1851); reprinted, with J. S. Mill's introduction, as "Enfranchisement of Women," in John Stuart Mill and Harriet Taylor Mill, *Essays on Sex Equality,* ed. Alice S. Rossi (Chicago: University of Chicago Press, 1970).

19. See Lee Holcombe, *Wives and Property: Reform of the Married Women's Property Law in Nineteenth-Century England* (Toronto: University of Toronto Press, 1982), and Mary Lyndon Shanley, *Feminism, Marriage, and the Law in Victorian England, 1850–1895* (Princeton: Princeton University Press, 1989).

20. Mill's 1867 speech to Parliament and the ensuing debate is partially reprinted in Bell and Offen, *Women, the Family and Freedom,* vol. 1, docts. 135 and 136; André Léo, "La Révolution sans la femme," *La Sociale,* no. 39 (8 May 1871).

21. On feminists in European peace movements, see Sandi E. Cooper, "The Work of Women in Nineteenth-Century Continental European Peace Movements," *Peace and Change* 9, no. 4 (Winter 1984).

22. On the importance of population issues for feminism, see Karen Offen, "Depopulation, Nationalism, and Feminism in Fin-de-Siècle France," *American Historical Review* 89, no. 3 (June 1984), pp. 648–676.

23. Patrick Geddes and J. Arthur Thomson, *The Evolution of Sex* (New York: Scribner's, 1889), p. 267; Friedrich Nietzsche, *Beyond Good and Evil* (1886), in *Basic Writings of Nietzsche,* tr. and ed. Walter Kaufmann (New York: Random House, 1968); Evelyn Baring, First Earl of Cromer, speech at Manchester, as reported in the *Anti-Suffrage Review* (November 1910), p. 10.

24. Hubertine Auclert, *Égalité sociale et politique de la femme et de l'homme, discours prononcé au Congrès ouvrier socialiste de Marseille* (1879), as translated in Bell and Offen, *Women, the Family, and Freedom,* doct. 143, p. 517; Anna Maria Mozzoni, *I socialisti e l'emancipazione della donna* (Alessandria, 1892), as reprinted in Mozzoni, *Liberazione della donna,* ed. Franca Pieroni Bortolotti (Milan: Gabriele Mazzotta, 1975), p. 212, as tr. by Claire Lavigna; Alys Russell, "On Social Democracy and the Woman Question in Germany," in appendix to Bertrand Russell, *German Social Democracy* (London: Longman, Green, 1896), p. 183.

25. Emmeline Pankhurst, in *Votes for Women,* 29 October 1908, p. 1; reprinted in Bell and Offen, *Women, the Family, and Freedom,* II, doct. 61.

26. See Key's various books, along with Katharine Anthony's still useful analysis, *Feminism in Germany and Scandinavia* (New York: Henry Holt, 1915).

27. Two Roussel texts are translated into English in Bell and Offen, *Women, the Family, and Freedom,* II, docts. 29 and 42. The quote is from doct. 29, a speech Nelly Roussel delivered in 1904 at a mass meeting called to protest the centennial of the French Civil Code.

28. This was the title of Roussel's best-known public address; republished as *Nelly Roussel: L'Éternelle sacrifiée,* ed. Maïté Albistur and Daniel Armogathe (Paris: Syros, 1979).

29. See Gisela Bock and Pat Thane, eds., *Maternity and Gender Politics: Women and the Rise of the European Welfare States 1880s–1950s* (London: Routledge, 1991), and Seth Koven and Sonya Michel, eds., *Mothers of a New World: Maternalist Politics and the Origins of Welfare States* (New York: Routledge, 1993).

30. Mme Avril de Sainte-Croix, *Le Féminisme* (Paris: V. Giard & E. Brière, 1907), p. 6.

SUGGESTIONS FOR FURTHER READING

The following gives only a brief hint of the vast number of studies now available in English, and does not include anything listed in the notes. More extensive bibliographies may be found in Bell and Offen, *Women, the Family, and Freedom,* and in Karen Offen, *European Feminisms, 1700–1950* (forthcoming 1998).

Akkerman, Tjitske, and Siep Sturman, eds. *Feminist Thought in European History 1400–2000.* London and New York: Routledge, 1997.

Allen, Ann Taylor. *Feminism and Motherhood in Germany, 1800–1914.* New Brunswick, N.J.: Rutgers University Press, 1991.

Anderson, Harriet. *Utopian Feminism: Women's Movements in Fin-de-Siècle Vienna.* New Haven, Conn.: Yale University Press, 1992.

Edmonson, Linda. *Feminism in Russia, 1900–1917.* Stanford, Calif.: Stanford University Press, 1984.

Evans, Richard J. *The Feminists: Women's Emancipation Movements in Europe, America and Australasia, 1840–1920.* London: Croom Helm, 1977.

Fraisse, Genevive, and Michelle Perrot, eds. *Emerging Feminism from Revolution to World War.* Vol. IV in Georges Duby and Michelle Perrot, eds., *A History of Women.* Cambridge, Mass.: Harvard University Press, 1993.

Frevert, Ute. *Women in German History: From Bourgeois Emancipation to Sexual Liberation.* Oxford: Berg, 1989.

Hause, Steven C., with Anne R. Kenney. *Women's Suffrage and Social Politics in the French Third Republic.* Princeton: Princeton University Press, 1984.

Hellerstein, Erna Olafson, Leslie Parker Hume, and Karen M. Offen, eds. *Victorian Women: A Documentary Account of Women's Lives in Nineteenth-Century England, France and the United States.* Stanford: Stanford University Press, 1981.

Hollis, Patricia, ed. *Women in Public: The Women's Movement. Documents of the Victorian Women's Movement (1850–1900).* London: G. Allen and Unwin, 1979.

Kent, Susan Kingsley. *Sex and Suffrage in Britain, 1860–1914.* Princeton: Princeton University Press, 1987.

Lerner, Gerda. *The Creation of Feminist Consciousness.* New York: Oxford University Press, 1993.

Rendall, Jane. *The Origins of Modern Feminism: Women in Britain, France, and the United States, 1780–1860.* New York: Schocken Books, 1984.

Scott, Joan Wallach. *Only Paradoxes to Offer: French Feminists and the Rights of Man.* Cambridge, Mass.: Harvard University Press, 1996.

Clara Zetkin, the German socialist organizer, writer, and editor, addresses a rally in Germany.   FPG INTERNATIONAL.

Socialism, Feminism, and the Socialist Women's Movement from the French Revolution to World War II

Charles Sowerwine

Feminism and socialism originated together, out of the crucible of the new world built on the industrial and French revolutions. During the first half of the nineteenth century, general social concern, increasingly known as socialism, conflated the problems of women and of workers. In the second half of the century, these two concerns were articulated in the distinct movements of feminism and socialism. The needs of working-class women, however, were lost in this focus. Gradually, however, women and men brought European socialist parties to commit themselves to women's emancipation, to political rights, and to building women-only movements within the socialist parties. These movements attracted masses of women, especially where, as in Germany, they were autonomous and took the place of the regular—male—party sections. The integration of socialism into capitalist democracy in the twentieth century also meant the integration of the women's movement into general politics, but the socialist women's movement played a major role in advancing women's rights and in leading women to speak for their rights and to participate in the political process.

F rom today's perspective, feminism and socialism appear outdated. We take them for granted because of their success: few today can imagine a world in which women could not vote; fewer still can imagine a world in which workers could not vote and indeed existed as a caste apart, even wearing different clothing from their middle-class counterparts. Yet such was the world after the French Revolution, when women and men began struggles to extend the human rights that the Revolution proclaimed. In these early struggles during the first half of the nineteenth century, the cause of women's rights was closely linked to that of workers' rights. The foundations for later feminist and socialist movements were laid in this period.

THE ORIGINS OF SOCIALISM AND FEMINISM

During 1837, the English socialist leader Robert Owen spoke at many public meetings in Paris. At one he was criticized for not having a woman leader beside him, an indication of how far early socialism had moved toward equality of the sexes. In this case, however, a woman stood up and, in a dramatic gesture, held out her hand to Owen; turning to the audience, she proclaimed, "I am here." She was Flora Tristan (1803–1844). Tristan was well known to Parisians. The crowd apparently accepted her view of herself as one of the preeminent leaders of both the women's and the workers' movements, of what we now call feminism and socialism.

Feminism and socialism emerged in France and England between the French Revolution of 1789 and the revolutions of 1848. Neither term had its modern sense before late in the nineteenth century. We use the words anachronistically when we apply them to movements before 1848. The word *socialism* then referred to all movements for social justice. In the decades leading up to the revolutions of 1848, most French republicans saw themselves as "democratic socialists": they assumed that the republic would be "democratic and social," by which they meant that real democracy would mean a just and fair society. In England, *socialism* came early in the century to refer to the ideas of Robert Owen, who sought to build model industrial communities.

Even the word *feminism* was not employed in English until 1895, and probably not much earlier in French.[1] What became feminism was born together with socialism as a response to the French Revolution, which articulated human rights and indeed the very concept of citizenship but excluded women and workers from active citizenship. The constitution that followed the famous Declaration of the Rights of Man and Citizen created two categories of citizens: "active," those who could vote—that is, men who paid taxes equivalent to three days' wages for a worker—and "passive," those who could not vote.

The very act of excluding women from the new rights, however, led to debate, especially since the emerging cult of domesticity emphasized women's virtues. From the late eighteenth century, on both sides of the Channel, radicals and visionaries responded to women's exclusion from the public sphere, arguing that they should enjoy the same rights as wealthy men. In these responses, the claims of women and of workers were conflated. Mary Wollstonecraft's *Vindication of the Rights of Women,* published in 1792, constituted "an extended manifesto linking the emancipation of women to the social and political liberation of 'the people' as a whole."[2] And, from the opposite perspective, the founding texts of socialism all assumed that "liberation of 'the people'" had to mean equality for women.

Charles Fourier (1772–1837) was the first theoretician of both socialism and feminism in the new democratic society. His writings influenced all Europeans struggling for the rights of women and of workers. Feminists and socialists from Flora Tristan to Karl Marx repeated the key argument he made in 1808: "the extension of the privileges of women is the general principle of all social progress."[3] The liberation of women was central to his argument: since all should share equally in the work and fruits of the ideal community, only by giving women full freedom to realize themselves would society progress toward justice and equality. Fourier even foreshadowed the modern idea of the construction of gender: in the existing society, boys and girls learned masculinity and femininity from the way they were brought up; in his ideal community, they would be reared in identical fashion to enable them to discover their feminine and masculine traits. To be sure, he supposed that women would find fulfilment more often in the arts than in the sciences, but his legacy built the emancipation of women into all the social movements of the nineteenth century.

Across the Channel, Robert Owen (1771–1858) struggled less successfully toward similar ideas. He emerged early in the century not as a socialist but as a businessman, one of the most successful and respected managers of the new industry; his cotton mill was closely studied for the secrets of managing "human capital." By 1820, however, his concern for workers burst out from the confines of his own factory. He began to write and lecture for the creation of fair and just industrial communities everywhere. His "dream of a New Moral World of class and sex equality captured the imagination of thousands of British women and men for nearly a quarter of a century."[4] He was the founder of the first popular socialist movement, and it was both socialist and feminist.

Among Owen's followers were a number of early feminists, such as William Thompson and Anna Wheeler, who together developed arguments for women's rights that Thompson published in 1825 as the *Appeal of One Half the Human Race, Women, Against the Pretensions of the Other Half, Men, to Retain Them in Political and Thence in Civil and Domestic Slavery.*[5] The title says it all. This became one of the founding texts of modern feminism, second only to Wollstonecraft's.

Owen's ideals led him to develop what Barbara Taylor calls "a combined assault on Christian morality and patriarchal power": he sought to abolish traditional marriage, in which women were "family slaves," in favor of a community in which, as he put it, "men and women will . . . become individually independent of each other in all respects, except that pleasing dependence upon each other which will arise from their natural sympathies." On the practical level, he thought that, thanks to community kitchens, "washing and drying-houses, . . . *one* female will, with great ease and comfort, perform as much [work] as twenty menial servants can do at present; and instead of the wife of a working man, with a family, being a drudge and a slave, she will be engaged only in healthy and cleanly employments."[6] He summarized his arguments in his *Lectures on the Marriages of the Priesthood in the Old Immoral World.* Its publication in 1835 aroused enormous controversy. Widely read and read aloud in local socialist circles, it went through five editions in five years; it was denounced from the pulpit, vilified by critics of socialism and defenders of the family, and on at least one occasion publicly burned. Ultimately, conservative horror at Owen's immorality led to the demise of the movement in the 1840s.[7]

SAINT-SIMONIAN WOMEN

By this time the first popular women's movement had emerged in France from the early socialist movement based on the ideas of Henri, Count Saint-Simon (1760–1825). Like Owen, Saint-Simon began not as a social reformer but as a technocrat. He believed that a better world would emerge from the increased production that the Revolution had made possible by replacing lazy aristocrats with enterprising bankers, technicians, and scientists. Saint-Simon's ideas had special appeal for the technocrats at the *Ecole Polytechnique.*[8] After his death, a number of graduates of the *Ecole* and other professional men came together in a movement that explored the ways to build not only a more productive society but also a more just one. Late in 1829, these men decided to build a popular movement. A few months later, in 1830, a revolt in Paris ousted the restored Bourbons. Although social conservatives quickly took control of the revolt and installed a monarchy under the Duke of Orleans, the Saint-Simonians profited from the brief opening and drew many recruits, including a number of women.

The Saint-Simonians not only espoused the formal equality of women with men, but also debated extensively the place of women in the movement. By October 1830, some 200 women were attending their meetings and a woman, Claire Bazard, was installed alongside the men as one of the leaders of the movement. A year later, 220 workers had been inducted in the new Saint-Simonian religion: nearly half were women. By this time, the movement was debating how to achieve real equality of sex and was openly discussing forms of what we would call free love.[9]

In 1832, the Saint-Simonian women began to publish their own newspaper, *The Women's Tribune*. It appeared over the next three years. Suzanne Voilquin (1801–1877), editor of *The Tribune* during most of its existence, and other socialist women produced a feminism of difference, a precursor to aspects of contemporary feminism. They believed that men and women reflected different virtues, which were found equally in creation: Prosper Enfantin, leader of the movement, argued, "yes, God is male and female"; she or he was "not only *good* like a FATHER, but also *tender* like a MOTHER."[10] *The Women's Tribune* was open only to women: they had to come to terms with Saint-Simonian doctrine "themselves, and no longer according to what men have written, [because] what women have to say is as different as the natures of men and women."[11]

Voilquin published the posthumous book of her friend, Claire Démar (1800?–1833), which extended Enfantin's arguments: women were different from men and deserved the new sexual order, in which changed affection could change sexual partnerships. Equality of difference would make for real freedom: "*the emancipation of the proletariat, of the poorest and most numerous class,* is possible," Démar wrote, "only through *the emancipation of our sex,* through the association *of strength and beauty, harshness and gentleness, man and woman* [italics original]."[12]

Although the Saint-Simonian women began with the idea of difference, their aim was "EQUALITY with man" through association in "a clearly united body."[13] Association meant grouping in solidarity not just for political purposes but to build together a new world. Drawn together by the movement and the newspaper, a number of women began to articulate their own ideas. Among them were Jeanne Deroin (1805–1894) and Pauline Roland (1805–1852), future women's leaders during the 1848 revolution and its aftermath.

Roland was born in 1805 in a small town in Normandy, where her widowed mother had taken over her father's humble position as director of the mails. Roland's Saint-Simonian tutor converted her to these ideas, and in 1831 she began correspondence with a Saint-Simonian "mother"—a woman charged with overseeing her induction into the movement, which was taking on a quasi-religious form. Writing to her "mother," she explained that, "like you, I was struck by the degraded state in which women have been kept, [and] like you, I protested against the inferior position relative to men in which one sought to keep me."[14] Roland was by nature gentle and even timid, but when she became convinced of the cause, she showed unshakeable determination. Defying her mother, she left—alone—for Paris, where she joined the new movement.

In 1832, however, the government closed the Saint-Simonian's lecture hall and prosecuted male leaders of the movement for "corruption of public morals." The movement disintegrated, and, after two more years, the women's newspaper, deprived of its base in the larger movement, ceased publication. What is extraordinary in *The Women's Tribune* is not any particular analysis, but that a group of working women, most of them without formal education, created a public forum and used it to debate issues we have not yet resolved and to articulate ideas we still find modern. It is the first example in modern history of a group of ordinary women debating such issues as part of a public movement. It left a major legacy that lasted through much of the nineteenth century. The greatest fruit of that legacy was the socialist feminism of Flora Tristan (1803–1844).

THE SOCIALISM AND FEMINISM OF FLORA TRISTAN

Tristan is an extraordinarily powerful figure who has long captivated historians—more than a dozen biographies have appeared in the last twenty years—as she captivated the public in her own time. She was the daughter of a Frenchwoman and a Peruvian nobleman. They married in Spain in a religious ceremony. Since the French government never recognized the marriage, upon her father's death when she was only four, her mother was unable to inherit her father's estate in Peru. She was raised in poverty and forced to work as a colorist for engravings. The contrast between her aristocratic origins and her poverty awakened her to social issues. Her marriage to her employer in turn awakened her to what we would call gender issues: she separated from him in 1825 and for the next thirteen years sought to elude him in order to maintain custody of her daughter, which automatically went to the father under Napoleonic law. Only when, in 1838, her husband shot her and was jailed for life did she obtain relief.

Tristan turned to writing. In 1835 she published a plan to enable women to travel freely by a network of protecting houses. In 1838 she published a novel and *Peregrinations of a Paria,* an account of her unsuccessful trip to Peru to claim her father's estate, in which she articulated a profound critique of both class and sex injustice in Peru. The next year, she traveled to England to investigate the condition of the working classes and published *Promenades in London,* which bears comparison with Frederick Engels' classic *Condition of the English Working Class in 1844.* Tristan's book devoted a chapter to the condition of women and cited Mary Wollstonecraft's *Vindication* as one of the best arguments for women's equality.

Building on the fame this book brought her, Tristan continued her whirlwind lecture tours. In 1843 she published the first edition of her most celebrated book, *The Workers' Union,* which she developed in discussions with groups of workers on her tours. Tristan took to its logical conclusion the idea of women's moral superiority. It was women who would enable society to transcend the divisiveness of competition by virtue of women's innate capacity for empathy. This is what Susan Grogan calls "Tristan's theory of a 'female' mode of socialism—one which emphasized love and empathy, and gave weight to the 'female' moral sphere."[15] This idea, like Tristan's racism, translated nineteenth-century stereotypes of femininity, but transformed them into a liberating ideal to which women could aspire. In her analysis of women's oppression and her call for one big union of all the workers, she is the mother of feminism and of popular communitarian socialism.

In her book *The Workers' Union* and in the countless, well-attended public lectures she gave on the subject, Tristan argued that the bourgeoisie had achieved union in 1789 and "succeeded the nobility." As a result, the bourgeoisie had become "so powerful that it can exclusively take over all the country's powers . . . to pose its conditions and commands upon 25 million proletarians." "In turn," she argued, "the workers, the vital part of the nation, must create a huge union to assert their unity! Then the working class will be strong; then it will be able . . . to demand from the bourgeois gentlemen its right to work and to organize."[16]

Despite these words, Tristan did not foreshadow class struggle. Her idea was that the Workers' Union would choose a public defender of the workers and he would use moral suasion to end injustice. To help workers choose, she discussed the strong and weak points of all those she considered possible defenders: Victor Considérant, Fourier's leading disciple; Prosper Enfantin, once the leading figure in the Saint-Simonian movement; Louis Blanc, author of a popular tract on "The Right to Work" and later minister of labor in the 1848 Revolutionary Government; and Gustave Beaumont, author of a book on the Irish struggle against England, which Tristan strongly supported. She managed to find a good word for each of them, in a way characteristic of her eclectic style.

Tristan devoted the third chapter of the book to "Why I Mention Women." She argued that women had not produced leaders so far because of their oppression, and she made an instructive analogy between women and "the proletariat," by which she meant all nonnoble men: once given rights in 1789 and told that man was "the *equal* of his former lord and master, . . . as if by magic, from the ranks of the proletariat surged learned men, artists, poets, writers, statesmen, and financiers who gave France a luster she [France] had never had." "What happened to the proletariat," she went on, "is a good omen for women when their '1789' rings out."[17]

In 1844, worn out by her struggles, Tristan died of a stroke during a lecture tour to promote the third edition of *The Workers' Union*. She was only 41. Tristan's generous spirit, her charisma, and her impassioned defense of women and workers made her the leading public figure of feminist and socialist ideas before 1848. In Tristan, all the currents of socialist-feminism met briefly. It would be many years before either would find so popular a public figure to articulate its ideas. Her death left a gaping void. Perhaps, however, her exoticism, her flamboyance, and her love of color lived on in the person and work of her grandson, the artist Paul Gauguin.

SOCIALISM AND FEMINISM IN THE 1848 REVOLUTION

Four years after Tristan's death, the 1848 revolution broke out. In France, it brought the Orleans dynasty to an ignoble end and installed a republic based on universal male suffrage. The revolution spread to much of Europe and fatally undermined the old order. Democratic states with universal male suffrage followed slowly but inevitably.

In France, many of the Saint-Simonian women took important roles in the revolution. Jeanne Deroin joined in the founding of the Women's Emancipation Club and became the editor of its newspaper, *The Voice of Women,* which continued in various forms from March 1848 to August 1849. From the start, it demanded the vote for women and obtained support from at least one daily newspaper.[18] In April 1849, Deroin made feminist history by presenting herself as a candidate in a legislative by-election because she was "dedicated to establishing that great principle: civil and political equality for both sexes."[19]

Meanwhile Deroin and Roland attended a meeting in February 1849 to set up a teachers' association. Roland insisted that the group be more than just a trade union: it should build the new society. Deroin supported her. With a minority of the first group, they founded the Association of Socialist Primary School Teachers. Later that year, Roland sought to build a workers' union in terms reminiscent of Tristan's book, for the publication of which she had more than a day's earnings: "By the association movement, will be accomplished the total destruction of industrial feudalism, the abolition of the lordly rights of capitalist laziness, that is usury and the exploitation of man by man. By it [the association] the task of emancipating the proletariat will be accomplished."[20]

Together, Roland and Deroin as delegates of the Teachers' Association took the lead in founding a Union of Fraternal Associations, which soon united 104 groups. Deroin wrote the statutes; she, Roland, and two men constituted the leadership. In May 1850, the police arrested all those present at a meeting of the union: Deroin, eight other women, and thirty-six men. Roland was arrested subsequently. She and Deroin were sentenced to six months in prison, which they spent together in Saint Lazare, the prostitutes' prison.

Roland was only free for a year before, in December 1851, Louis-Napoleon Bonaparte, president of the republic, executed a coup d'état to remain in power. In February, Roland was imprisoned—almost certainly falsely—for resistance to the coup. (In all, 26,675 men and 169 women met this fate.) After more than a year in Saint Lazare, Roland and nine other women were deported to Algeria. Released at the end of 1852, exhausted by her sufferings, Roland died on her way back to Paris. Deroin devoted the rest of her life to keeping her memory alive.

The coup d'état meant the end of open political discussion in France for a quarter of a century. In England, the failure of Owenite socialism in the mid-1840s, the failure of the enormous Chartist movement (of which most Owenites were members), and now the conservative reaction that followed the threat of revolution from France all combined to stifle discussion of social issues, including women's equality. Across the rest of Europe, reaction to the revolutions of 1848 had the same effect. At the same time, however, the industrialization of Europe laid the groundwork for new movements and debates.

INDUSTRIALIZATION AND THE VISION OF KARL MARX

As industrialization took off in Europe after the 1848 revolutions, industrial wage labor in the factory increasingly replaced artisan work in the household. As artisans faced the prospect of becoming factory laborers, they found themselves in competition for jobs with women, who were far cheaper since they received less than half men's wages. The entry of women into trades threatened not only men's wages, but also their position as skilled craftsmen and thus as men: skill at their craft was both their capital and their masculinity.[21]

In the second half of the nineteenth century, a new kind of socialism emerged that spoke to the fears of artisans and sought to maintain their way of life. This socialism took the place of the communitarian socialism of Owen, Fourier, and the Saint-Simonians. This new socialism, often known as mutualism, fought to exclude women from the factory and to return to the household economy, in which women were dependent upon men: "Woman's place is in the home [*la femme au foyer*]." Pierre-Joseph Proudhon (1809–1865), theoretician of the new cooperative or mutualist socialism, articulated the sentiment of these artisans. He is remembered for his comment, "Women must be housewives or harlots, there is no other choice."[22] As capitalism took off in Germany, members of the pre-Marxist labor movement led by Ferdinand Lassalle (1825–1864) echoed these sentiments, although in more muted form. The artisans' vision was increasingly shaped by the folk memory of the household economy. As one woman put it at the 1876 Workers' Congress in France, "It would be more natural for men to provide a living for their wives and daughters [as in the small shop or farm] than for all to be dependent on capitalists."[23]

Clear theoretical understanding and acceptance of women's liberation began only when a thinker emerged who could demonstrate the beneficial possibilities of industrialization, the need to use democracy to fight for workers' rights, and the potential for women's independence inherent in their earning wages for themselves. That thinker was Karl Marx (1818–1883). Marx's concentration on the political and industrial struggle of the working class may have narrowed the early socialists' broad vision of the emancipation of women to a narrower vision of political and economic equality. Marx's analysis, however, was well suited to the new world of capitalist industrialization and democratic political structures, and if his vision of women's equality was narrower than that of the early socialists, it was more sharply focused.

Marx and his collaborator, Frederick Engels (1820–1895), together developed an incisive analysis of women's double oppression. They agreed that women were oppressed in their relations with men. Marriage, Marx suggested in his *Economic and Philosophic Manuscripts of 1844,* "is incontestably a form of *exclusive private property* [italics original]."[24] Forty years later, Engels made this point in a famous aphorism: "Within the family, he is the bourgeois, and the wife represents the proletariat."[25]

To this historic oppression was being added another that fell upon women drawn into the economic world created by capitalist industrialization. They were subjected to the same exploitation as men but at the same time to a "double oppression": employers could pay women half the wages of men and depend on the family to keep them alive. In this way women's dependence on men facilitated their exploitation by capitalists and vice versa: their wages were kept low because their husbands helped provide for them, and in turn their low wages kept them dependent on their husbands.

This analysis led Marx and Engels to argue a long-term strategy for women's liberation: first women should obtain political equality; then they should use political equality in the struggle for economic equality and economic independence from men. Only after men and women achieved equality within capitalism could they fight together for the full self-realization that socialism alone would bring.

Marx and Engels both maintained that political equality between the sexes was the necessary precondition to the struggle for full human emancipation. Voting rights in a republic did not constitute social and economic emancipation, but democracy did provide "the clear field on which the fight can be fought out." The possession of political rights would highlight women's oppression. As Engels put it in *The Origin of the Family, Private Property and the State,* first published in 1884:

> The peculiar character of the supremacy of the husband over the wife in the modern family, the necessity of creating real social equality between them and the way to do it, will only be seen in the clear light of day when both possess legally complete equality of rights. Then it will be plain that the first condition for the liberation of the wife is to bring the whole female sex back into public industry, and that this in turn demands that the characteristic of the monogamous family as the economic unit of society be abolished.[26]

Engels, like Marx (on whose notes Engels drew in writing *The Origin of the Family*), believed that capitalism would give women economic independence and thus enable them to become independent of men.

Although theoretically enticing, this strategy posed more problems for working-class women in the nineteenth century than for aspiring women executives in the twentieth. Wage labor may have laid the basis for economic independence, but it caused horrendous hardship. Marx and Engels realized this; they did not preach for or against wage labor for women, but only noted that women's ability to sell their labor would lay the basis for their economic and hence personal independence from men.

However terrible and disgusting the dissolution of the family ties within the old capitalist system may appear, large-scale industry, by assigning an important part in socially organized processes of production, outside the sphere of the domestic economy, to women, young persons and children of both sexes, does nevertheless create a new economic foundation for a higher form of the family and of relations between the sexes.[27]

Laying the economic foundation did not in itself build the "higher form . . . of relations between the sexes"; that required political action, for which women needed political rights on the same basis as men. That required the development of mass socialist parties and socialist women's movements.

WOMEN AND SOCIALISM BEFORE WORLD WAR I

Mass socialist parties developed in the quarter-century before 1914. In Britain, the Labour party obtained a significant following by the turn of the century. The 1918 elections gave Labour 22.2 percent of the vote, and in 1924 its leader, Ramsay MacDonald, became the first Labour prime minister. In Germany, the 1912 elections gave socialists 4.5 million votes and 112 seats in the Reichstag, making it the largest single party; it came to power after the war. In France, similarly, the 1914 elections saw socialists win 1.4 million votes and 103 seats in the Chamber; a coalition led by the socialists came to power in 1936.

The development of socialist women's movements was not so uniform. The socialist parties were in theory open to women, but they constituted a strongly masculine space, often meeting in the smoke-filled rooms of cafés and bars. Socialism attracted women only when socialist women's movements offered special, separate groups for women. In Germany, repressive laws forced the party to develop a separate women's organization that became the largest and most radical women's movement in Europe, if not in the world. In France, where democracy and a greater degree of equality for women allowed the party to integrate women in regular party sections, the party recruited few women and their organization was marginal. The socialist women's movements in other countries fell between these two extremes.

August Bebel (1840–1913), one of the principal leaders of German socialism, provided a platform for the socialist women's movement in his book, *Woman and Socialism*, first published in 1879, five years before Engels' *Origin of the Family*. In 1891 Bebel revised his book to take account of Engels' work. In this form it became one of the most popular works of the socialist movement. It ran through fifty editions and fifteen translations before World War I.

Bebel's book supported all the feminist demands of his day, including the right to vote, the right to enter universities and to practice professions, and the right for married women to own their own property and to initiate divorce proceedings. The book went even further than did most feminists. It posed radical new demands, such as the right to dress freely and the right to sexual satisfaction. And it dismissed the idea that women had a "natural calling" to raise families; that idea, Bebel said, was "twaddle." Even more fundamentally, the book argued that the domination of women by men was rooted not in biology but in history and was thus capable of resolution in history: "conditions . . . finally grow into custom; heredity and education then cause such conditions to appear . . . 'natural.' Hence . . . woman . . . accepts her subordinate position as a matter of course."[28]

The book had a great impact on working-class women: someone had written about them! The book was thick and "scientific." Moreover, it was not written by just anyone, but by one of the two principal leaders of the party: it demonstrated not just individual concern for women's problems but the concern of the whole party of the working class. Clara Zetkin, the preeminent leader of the socialist women's movement, later called it "more than a book, an event—a great deed."[29] The book circulated throughout the party. Increasing literacy meant that thousands of women read it. Ottilie Baader, later a leader of the German socialist women's movement, recalled:

> News came of a wonderful book that . . . Bebel . . . had written. Although I was not a Social Democrat I had friends who belonged to the party. Through them I got the precious work. I read it nights through. It was my own fate and that of thousands of my sisters. Neither in the family nor in public life had I ever heard of all the pain the woman must endure. One ignored her life. Bebel's book courageously broke with the old secretiveness . . . I read the book not once but ten times. Because everything was so new, it took considerable effort to come to grips with Bebel's views. I had to break with so many things that I had previously regarded as correct.[30]

The socialist movement as a whole did not immediately accept the principle of equality for women. When, in the 1860s and 1870s, the International Workingman's Association (or First International: 1864–1876) lay the foundations of lasting socialist movements, it was initially dominated not by Marx and his followers, but by mutualists, men like Proudhon and Lassalle, who were hostile to wage labor for women, at least in the factory, and at best unenthusiastic about allowing women into politics. As industrialization progressed, however, wage earners streamed into the socialist parties. They found Marx's vision of collective struggle more relevant than Proudhon's nostalgia for the old household economy and voted increasingly for Marxists. With their support, Marxist intellectuals and bourgeois feminists introduced women's equality into socialist platforms.

The German Social Democratic party (*Sozialdemokratische Partei Deutschlands* or SPD) was founded in 1875. Its first draft program included the vote "for all citizens," which—it was argued—included women. But when Bebel proposed making this clearer by adding "citizens of both sexes," the congress rejected his proposal by 62 to 55. After 1878, Bismarck's antisocialist laws forced the party to go underground. By the time it emerged after the repeal of these laws in 1890, Bebel's and Engels' books had circulated widely and had helped the party articulate a position in favor of equality for women. Moreover, Bebel now dominated the party, together with Wilhelm Liebknecht (1826–1900) and Karl Kautsky (1854–1938); all three were followers of Marx and Engels and shared their support for women's rights.

Under their leadership, the 1891 SPD Congress at Erfurt voted overwhelmingly in favor of universal suffrage "without distinction of sex" and "abolition of all laws which place the woman, whether in a private or public capacity, at a disadvantage as compared with the man." The "Erfurt Program" became one of the key texts of socialists everywhere. Kautsky predicted that with the coming of socialism:

> woman will cease to be a worker in the individual household, and will take her place as a worker in the large industries . . . By working side by side with man in the great co-operative industries woman will become his equal and will take an equal part in the community life. She will be his free companion, emancipated not only from the servitude of the house, but also from that of capitalism.[31]

The French Socialist party evolved in much the same way. During the Second Empire (1852–1870) and immediately after, mutualists dominated the emerging labor movement. During the 1870s the labor movement slowly reconstructed after the disastrous failure of the Paris Commune of 1871, a revolt supported by the International in which 25,000 insurgents lost their lives. Marxists began to propagandize on the basis of accepting the development of industry, seeking to reform it or collectivize it, and supporting women's rights.

The young militant feminist Hubertine Auclert (1851–1914) became involved with these Marxists, and her small feminist organization became a constituent member of their "Workers' party," which would become the French Socialist party. Auclert went to the 1879 Workers' Congress to fight for women's rights. She not only obtained support for women's suffrage and full legal equality, but she also presented a bold vision for the future:

> Men and women . . . will govern this society together and will share in the exercise of the same rights, in public life as in private . . . in all circumstances, women will have their freedom of action like men. . . . Women will take the roles and the places in society to which their vocations call them.[32]

Auclert and her feminist group did not long remain in the Workers' party. In 1880, the party split between the Marxists and the mutualists. Auclert's group sided with the mutualists: both agreed that private property and the family should be "the basis of society." This seemed more important to them than the mutualists' opposition to women's rights. The split that would separate socialist women from what they called bourgeois feminism was opening up. While the feminists allowed their concern for property to override their commitment to women's rights, the Marxists reaffirmed their commitment to equality for women at their congresses of 1880 and 1882.

THE GERMAN SOCIALIST WOMEN'S MOVEMENT

Whereas such issues could be debated openly in democratic France, imperial Germany repressed socialist activity. Even after the legalization of the SPD in 1890, many provinces severely restricted or even prohibited women's political meetings. Forcing the party to create separate women's organizations proved a blessing in disguise. Party statutes drawn up in 1890 provided for women "to elect female delegates to party conferences at special women's meetings." The 1892 conference provided for permanent women's spokes*people*. This was a pioneering use of inclusive language: hitherto the only word was spokes*man*. Ottilie Baader (1847–1925) was elected "central Spokesperson for the women comrades of Germany" at the SPD's 1900 conference.[33]

The SPD created an organizational structure for women independent from that of men, so that women had their own groups in which they could feel secure and develop their talents without fear of male disapproval or ridicule. This separate organizational structure was the key to the success of the German socialist women's movement. It became the largest in the world, the standard by which all other socialist women's movements were judged. Indeed, it was the largest movement of women of any political coloration on the Continent.

Clara Zetkin (1857–1933) articulated the radical orientation of those who entered the party through its women's organization. A teacher who converted to socialism in her youth, Clara spent the 1880s with her de facto husband in Paris, where he had gone in exile. A decade of grinding poverty gave her a steely determination that she displayed in her subsequent half-century of political activism. Her husband died in 1889, leaving her two young sons, but also making her independent.

Zetkin came to sudden prominence with her speech to the founding congress of the Second International held in Paris in 1889. This speech became one of the key texts of the socialist women's movement. In it Zetkin built on the analyses of Engels and Bebel. She assumed that socialists must support the feminist struggle; indeed, she declared that in Germany, given the weakness of feminist and democratic forces, socialists would have to lead the struggle for women's rights. But working-class women, she reminded her listeners, were not only slaves to men; they were also slaves to capitalists. Since the bourgeois women of the feminist movement shared the class interests of the capitalists, working women must reject any collaboration between socialists and feminists and must seek the destruction of capitalism to attain economic independence, which in turn would lead to full emancipation.

> Just as the workers are subjugated by the capitalists, women are subjugated by men and they will continue to be in that position as long as they are not economically independent. The quintessential prerequisite for their economic independence is work . . . Once women have attained their economic independence from men, there is no reason why they should remain socially dependent upon them.[34]

Returning to Germany and developing contacts with the mass movement of socialism there, Zetkin modified her ideas. An experiment during the 1890s in which separate women's groups were abandoned in favor of equal opportunity for women within the party (where legal) convinced her that women needed separate groups. But she never ceased to proclaim that for proletarian women the vote was only the first step in the struggle. Indeed, when moving her resolution for women's suffrage at the 1907 International Socialist Congress, she made this point in virtually the same words Engels had used:

> The granting of suffrage to the female sex does not eliminate the class differences between the exploiters and the exploited . . . It also does not eliminate the conflicts which are created for women as members of their sex . . . On the contrary: The complete political equality of the female sex prepares the ground on which the conflicts will be fought.[35]

At the Gotha Conference in 1896, Zetkin incorporated these ideas into the party program. On this theoretical basis she undertook the practical task of building a socialist women's movement. By 1908, there were 407 female spokespersons in the party hierarchy, with Ottilie Baader at the top. Nearly 30,000 women had joined the party. Through its newspaper, *Die Gleichheit* (*Equality*), edited by Clara Zetkin, the movement reached even more women: the paper's circulation soared to over 70,000.

In 1908, however, the laws preventing German women from joining political parties were repealed. Since women could now enter the party freely on the same basis as men, the SPD dissolved its separate hierarchy of women's organizations. Zetkin, however, argued that women still needed separate groups. In a compromise solution, the party required all local branches to include at least one woman on the executive and created a women's bureau, subordinate however to the national party executive. Instead of Zetkin or Baader, the party appointed the younger and less-known Luize Zietz (1865–1922) as women's representative on the executive.

Some have suggested that the party expected Zietz to compromise more readily on women's issues. Zietz, however, was ready to work with bourgeois feminists and, probably more importantly, stood in the mainstream center left of the party, while Zetkin had broken with Karl Kautsky and now stood with Rosa Luxemburg and Karl Liebknecht on the extreme left of the party. Zetkin's radicalism and authoritarian control of the movement were no longer appropriate now that the women's movement had become a mass movement.

For the German socialist women's movement did become a mass movement once legality enabled the movement to flourish. Zetkin's band of apostles were well trained to create women's units, and women rushed in. Within a year the number of women in the party more than doubled, reaching over 62,000, or nearly 10 percent of the total membership. At Zetkin's suggestion, the 1910 International Socialist Congress designated March 8 each year for International Women's Day; beginning in 1911, the Germans and Austrians made this day the occasion for major demonstrations that resulted in greater visibility to the socialist women's movement. At the beginning of World War I, *Die Gleichheit* had reached a circulation of 124,000 and the party had registered 174,751 women members, constituting 16.1 percent of the total membership, which stood at an amazing 1,058,905 (of 23,192,000 Germans twenty and older). The separate organizational structure had developed their political skills so that these women formed a nucleus within a party that was ready to attract and welcome large numbers of recruits when party membership for women became legal.[36]

THE FRENCH SOCIALIST PARTY AND THE WOMEN'S MOVEMENT

The French case demonstrates the problems caused by the lack of an autonomous women's organization, a problem already experienced in the small, fragmented parties of the 1890s. The French Socialist party was unified in 1905 as the French Section of the Workers' International (*Section Française de l'Internationale Ouvrière,* or SFIO). It did not create a women's organization until 1913. By the beginning of World War I that organization had attracted three hundred women in Paris, but had not yet reached beyond the capital. Total membership in the party (men and women combined) was only 90,725, pathetic in comparison with the SPD in Germany, but still by far the largest political movement in France. Women composed no more than 3 percent of the membership.

Earlier efforts to organize a French socialist women's movement had failed, often because of party schisms; during the 1890s, there had been as many as five competing socialist parties in France! Only in 1899 did there emerge a Feminist Socialist Group, which prefigured the French socialist women's movement and provided two of its most important leaders: Louise Saumoneau (1875–1950) and Elisabeth Renaud (1846–1932). Renaud, the daughter of a worker in a watch factory, had been a governess in St. Petersburg before returning to France and marrying a printer. The printer died after five years, leaving her with two children and numerous debts. To support herself and her family, she ran a boarding house and gave French lessons to foreigners. By 1897 we find her a significant figure in Parisian socialist circles; her Friday afternoon teas were frequented by many socialist leaders.

Saumoneau was a seamstress who came to socialism on the rebound from feminism. Arriving from the provinces in February 1897, she left her work one Wednesday afternoon (thus giving up half her daily pay) to attend a meeting of a feminist group. Because the other women at the meeting were elegantly dressed, Saumoneau stood out: like other working women of the period, she wore a simple cotton shift she had made herself, and her severe countenance and abrupt manners put off any of the other women who sought to speak to her. She saw them as employers and customers rather than sisters. Ill at ease, she listened to a long debate on the morality of the dowry. In families like hers, she reflected bitterly, there were no dowries. She determined to create a movement for working-class women like herself. Her quest led her to Renaud. Together with two other women in the garment trade, they founded the Feminist Socialist Group in July 1899. Their manifesto called for a socialist women's movement on the lines of Zetkin's. It outlined the "double oppression of women, exploited on a large scale by capitalism, subjected to men by laws and *especially* by prejudice."[37]

Two events destroyed the precarious equilibrium between feminism and socialism implicit in the original manifesto. In the first place, Saumoneau and Renaud attended the 1900 feminist congress as delegates of their group. There they proposed that domestics have a full day off a week. This gave rise to a bitter debate:

> Madam Wiggishoff . . . You're asking for an entire day off. But where will these little girls of fifteen or sixteen go? Where will they eat?
>
> Madam Renaud: At your house.
>
> Madam Wiggishoff: So I'm to cook lunch for my maid? I'm not a saint and it's more than likely that her lunch won't be ready.

This exchange alienated the socialist women, who reported that the congress had "established much better than we could have ourselves the barrier which separates bourgeois feminism from socialist feminism."[38] Ironically, however, the male members of the Socialist party seem to have been more comfortable with middle-class feminists than with these tough working women. The group applied to join the newly unified Socialist party—the SFIO—at its founding in 1905, but after protracted debate, the SFIO refused to admit the group to its ranks, although it did admit youth groups. This result went beyond questions of personality: the party thus rejected the German structure of separate women's organizations. It would accept women on the same basis as men and only on that basis. The absence of a separate organization resulted in the low percentage of women in the party. The party did more for women and women's suffrage than any other party in France, but it did not organize women.

This pattern persisted despite the activities of the gifted feminist socialist, Madeleine Pelletier (1874–1939), anthropologist, doctor, Free-Mason, and outstanding theorist of radical feminism. Pelletier was a pugnacious and tireless speaker for both left-wing socialism and radical feminism, which she incarnated by ostentatiously wearing masculine clothing. She was a founding member of the SFIO. At the national congresses of 1906 and 1907, she obtained the passage of strong resolutions in favor of women's suffrage. (They were not followed by action, but then no other party would have passed them.) She was a member of the Guesdist faction, which increasingly followed the Kautskyist Marxism of the Second International, awaiting the "inevitable" revolution instead of acting. In 1908 she denounced their inaction and joined the "insurrectional" faction of Gustave Hervé. In 1909, as a leader of this faction, she obtained a seat on the *Commission Administrative Permanente* or CAP, the real locus of power within the party. But although she came to meetings in male dress, she never mentioned women's issues or women's groups, nor did she raise the party's failure to act on her resolutions on women's suffrage; her fight there was always against parliamentarianism and reformism. When she broke with the faction in 1911 and lost her seat, she had nothing to show for her time on the CAP.

Although Pelletier fought for the principle of women's suffrage, she was profoundly ambivalent about women's groups in the Socialist party. On the one hand, she realized that separate party sections for women were the only way for women to feel free enough to express themselves and develop their confidence; a woman was bound to feel isolated and intimidated alongside so many men in the smoke-ridden clublike atmosphere of a party section. On the other hand, she believed that it would be a "humiliation for women to be placed apart, isolated" from the regular—male—groups; she expressed this view when opposing separate sections for female Free-Masons.

The latter view ultimately governed her action in the Socialist party. Party meetings were part of the world of fully human activity in which she could find fulfilment; among women she found less reward. When young, Pelletier later recalled, she had reproached Louise Michel, the famous veteran of the Commune of 1871, for not being a feminist. Michel had replied "that she was a feminist, but that the women's movement was too narrow; she had gone along with men because action in the masculine political parties was greater and more interesting."[39] Public space was masculine, and so to project herself in the public arena, Michel had to take part in masculine politics: there was no other. A similar dynamic operated in Pelletier's case. Thus, when the International called for the creation in each country of socialist women's groups, Pelletier limited herself to explaining the psychological need for such groups; she took no action to found or lead such groups.[40] When a French socialist women's group was finally constituted in 1913, she refused two invitations to attend the founding meeting, saying that she feared the group would be "the kindergarten" of the party.[41]

This founding meeting was organized in January 1913 by a newcomer to the French Socialist party, Marianne Rauze (1875–1950). Rauze was a beautiful young socialite married to a career officer in the French army. Her youthful idealism led her to socialism. She brought together all the leaders from the original Feminist Socialist Group and got them to agree to found a Socialist Women's Group. As Patricia Hilden has pointed out, the change in name symbolized the group's "willingness to bury the feminist struggle within the class struggle."[42] Louise Saumoneau, however, suspected Rauze of being soft on feminism. Not surprisingly, the tough seamstress never got on with the young socialite. Saumoneau opposed the formation of a separate group for women. She wrote into the new organization's statutes that membership in the party was a *prerequisite* for joining the group. Thus the group could not recruit women directly; it had to recruit them through the party. As an auxiliary organization for women already in the party, the group could never function as a separate hierarchy, the way the German movement did so successfully. Moreover, Saumoneau's hostility to bourgeois feminism had become so bitter that it soon drove out the moderate members of the group. She refused even to support the case of a woman printer barred from her work by male trade unionists, arguing that to do so would give aid and comfort to the feminists.[43]

Yet Saumoneau won all these battles because a majority of working women in the group, especially seamstresses, identified with her more than with the apparently bourgeois women who opposed her. Saumoneau was able to tap their energies, so that the French socialist women held their first International Women's Day in March 1914, with Saumoneau presiding at a rally where over two thousand men and women heard speeches by various party personalities. To Saumoneau's great delight, Clara Zetkin sent a telegram: "A socialist women's day at Paris, that's good news indeed."[44] But these promising beginnings were cut short by the war.

SOCIALISM AND WOMEN IN ENGLAND

England had no movement comparable to the German socialist women's movement, and yet we cannot speak of the failure of socialism to reach women in the same way as we can in the case of France. Three factors make the English situation particularly complex. First, English socialists did not create a unified party on the continental model. Only in 1900 was the Labour Representation Committee founded, an umbrella organization that gradually drew in the existing parties and trade unions and could, by 1907, call itself the Labour party. Its constituent groups remained independent, however. In 1907 and again in 1910, Britain was the only Western European nation not to send a unified delegation to the International Socialist Congress; instead, delegations went from the Social Democratic Federation (SDF) of H.M. Hyndman (1842–1921), the Independent Labour Party (ILP) of Keir Hardie (1856–1915), the Fabian Society, and the Labour party itself. Moreover, reformist trade unionists far outweighed socialists in the Labour party.

Second, Britain was an effective parliamentary democracy, and the suffrage was therefore of vital significance, but, unlike France (where universal male suffrage had been introduced in 1848), Britain still had a property suffrage, which disenfranchised one-third of the adult male population. The right to vote was dependent upon registration at a fixed residence and payment of at least four shillings a week rent or equivalent. This meant that if women obtained the franchise on the same basis as men, most married women would be disqualified. Sylvia Pankhurst estimated that in such an event only one woman in thirteen would vote.[45]

Third, Britain, unlike Germany and France, had a mass-based, radical women's suffrage movement, known as the suffragettes (so called to distinguish them from the suffrag*ists*, who demanded universal adult suffrage and refused to support women's suffrage based on the existing limited basis, whereas the suffragettes accepted the possibility of wealthy women's getting the vote before poor men and women in order to establish the principle of equality of the sexes). Although bourgeois women dominated the leadership of the British as of the continental feminist movements, the British suffragette movement undertook direct action and mobilized support from working-class women, at least in some areas. Jill Liddington and Jill Norris have demonstrated that significant numbers of working-class women actively supported the women's suffrage movement in Manchester, often combining this with trade union or Labour party militancy. Studies of Germany and France and indeed of Europe as a whole have certainly unearthed nothing comparable. Continental feminists had lived through many revolts and wars; they feared that direct action might undermine the existing social and political order. In Britain the existing order seemed secure: British feminists could undertake direct action without fear of endangering the existing social order.

None of the three parties that later merged into the early Labour party had women's organizations before 1906. In that year, the Women's Labour League was founded, largely upon the initiative of Margaret MacDonald (1870–1911; wife of the ILP leader, Ramsay MacDonald), but it existed mainly to support Labour candidates. Liddington and Norris suggest that working-class women who had been active for the suffrage refused to support Labour until the party made a firmer commitment to women's suffrage. Other women hesitated to join the league for fear that, without the theoretical backbone that characterized Zetkin's movement in Germany, it might only be, as one ILP activist later put it, "a permanent social committee." The league never developed into a significant force. A similar women's committee set up by the SDF in 1906 also came to little.[46]

The British path did not lead toward organizations comparable to continental socialist women's movements, but rather toward an alliance of Labour and feminism, which was dependent on the Labour party's making a commitment to women's suffrage. Before the development of the Labour party, the various organizations that would compose it had a mixed record on women's rights. At one extreme, many thought the SDF, under Hyndman's influence, was hostile to women's suffrage, although a recent study has argued that the party was less hostile than has previously been thought.[47] At the other extreme, the ILP and the Fabian Society supported it; the society, however, was not and did not aspire to be a mass movement. Of parties aspiring to a mass base, only the ILP under Keir Hardie consistently supported women's suffrage, and even that support developed slowly.

Only after the turn of the century did the ILP take a formal position in support of women's suffrage. Isabella Ford (1860–1924), "a prosperous Quaker lady," as Sylvia Pankhurst (1882–1960) described her,[48] and an ardent supporter of women's suffrage, joined the party executive in 1903. In 1904, Emmeline Pankhurst (Sylvia's mother, 1858–1928) also joined the executive. The party instructed the executive to introduce a bill for the extension of the suffrage to women on the same property basis as men already enjoyed (or did not enjoy) it. Gradually, however, the nascent Labour party filled with trade union representatives, who had hardly been anxious to welcome women into their ranks: the problem of male wage supremacy plagued the British as well as the French. As a result, the Labour party shied away from supporting women's suffrage if it meant that only well-to-do women would be enfranchised while many working-class men and most working-class women would remain unable to vote. At the 1905 Labour party conference and again in 1906 an SDF representative defeated the ILP proposal for women's suffrage.

The ILP, nevertheless, at its 1907 conference renewed its support for women's suffrage on the same property basis as men's. This position was taken by no other party, Socialist or otherwise. Ironically, it earned the ILP a rebuke from Clara Zetkin at the 1907 International Conference of Socialist Women; to enfranchise bourgeois women, as she and the conference saw it, was antisocialist.[49] Keir Hardie nevertheless continued to press for women's suffrage: at the 1907 Labour party conference, he even threatened to withdraw from the party because of its refusal to endorse women's suffrage rather than adult suffrage. For Hardie and the ILP, women's suffrage was a question of conscience; even if only propertied women voted while working-class men did not, a partial reform in this direction was preferable to the status quo.

At the end of 1911, the ILP, in Liddington's words "still very much the conscience of the Labour Party," resolved "that proposals for franchise extension which do not confer citizenship upon women should be definitely opposed."[50] This solved the old problem. Those who had hitherto refused to support a franchise for propertied women could not in good conscience accept the government's grant of unrestricted suffrage to men without granting it to women. Thus, in 1912, the Labour party as a whole accepted a resolution similar to that of the ILP. The following year, both the ILP and the Labour party reinforced their commitment to oppose any extension of the suffrage that did not include women. Consequently, from 1912 until the war, the National Union of Women's Suffrage Societies and the Women's Freedom League joined together to support Labour, although the Women's Social and Political Union (WPSU, the Pankhursts' group) remained aloof, having broken with Labour in 1907. Thus, if Britain did not develop a socialist women's movement, it did follow another route, which was equally in keeping with the spirit of Engels' arguments. Engels had certainly approved of alliances between the proletariat and the bourgeoisie to obtain the republic; the alliance between Labour and feminism in the Indian summer of Edwardian England had the same logic behind it.

THE SECOND INTERNATIONAL (1889–1914) AND THE
AUSTRIAN SOCIALIST WOMEN'S MOVEMENT

With the exception of England, all the other European socialist women's movements ranged between the French and the German models. Party policies toward women were worked out within a framework determined by the Second Socialist International, which in turn was dominated by the SPD. From its founding congress in 1889, the International had stipulated "that it is the duty of workers to admit women into their ranks, on an equal footing." This resolution assured women the right to join the Socialist parties (until after World War I no other parties accepted women members, though some non-Socialist parties did accept women in auxiliary groups).

Subsequently, the International sought to resolve the dilemma between equality and protective legislation for women. The founding congress of 1889 accepted the principle of equal pay for equal work, but also argued for special protection for women. Only at the 1893 congress did the International resolve this ambiguity. On the one hand, it passed a resolution put forward by Anna Kuliscioff of Italy demanding "equal pay (for women) for equal work" and specifying that protective measures for women should not result in loss of employment opportunity; on the other hand, it passed a resolution put forward by Louise Kautsky of Germany spelling out the measures it had in mind for women workers; these included the eight-hour day, a prohibition of night work and of work in jobs "which are detrimental to their health," and the prohibition of work by pregnant women two weeks before and four weeks after childbirth.[51]

The socialists did not fully spell out their commitment to equality until 1900, when the Paris congress of the International finally addressed itself explicitly to women's suffrage, which it then proclaimed "a necessity for both sexes."[52] Putting this commitment into practice was still, however, a matter for debate in each national section. Thus the Belgian Socialist party was able to "suspend the movement for women's suffrage." As a result of the Belgians' conduct, the German delegation raised the question of women's suffrage again at the 1904 International Socialist Congress. The congress passed a very forceful and explicit resolution on "universal suffrage for women" so that no party would fall into the Belgian trap. Nevertheless, the Austrian Socialist party soon repeated the Belgian fiasco.

The Austrian socialist women's movement sought to emulate the German, but lacked the vital aspect of the German movement, the separate organizational structure for women. The Austrian movement began in the early 1890s, when a small number of Viennese women began meeting as a "working women's educational society." In 1892, the party began a journal for women, the *Arbeiterinnenzeitung* ("Working Women's Newspaper"), edited by Adelheid Popp (1869–1939), the founder and uncontested leader of the Austrian movement. The Austrian movement still lagged far behind the German one (although it was far ahead of the French) when a crisis occurred. Like Britain,

Austria still had a propertied suffrage: only wealthy men could vote. After the Russian revolution of 1905, the leadership of the Austrian party began a campaign for universal suffrage. Fearing a backlash if it included women's suffrage at the same time, the leadership decided to demand only unrestricted male suffrage for the time being. The women's movement accepted this decision in the interests of party harmony and on the basis of the primacy of class loyalties.

For this Clara Zetkin attacked them violently at the first International Conference of Socialist Women, held in conjunction with the 1907 International Socialist Congress. As Zetkin and Baader put it in their draft resolution, "in the fight for the equality of the female sex," the socialists "must not let themselves be overtopped by any bourgeois party, not even the bourgeois women's movement." To postpone women's claim left the impression that they had less right than men; this women should never accept. Bargaining with principles never worked, she argued. Led by Popp, the Austrian women defended themselves, but the conference supported Zetkin. It passed a strong resolution stating that "the socialist parties of all countries have a duty to struggle energetically for the introduction of universal suffrage for women."[53]

Zetkin went on to put a resolution to the full congress of the International, declaring that "wherever a struggle is to be waged for the right to vote, it must be conducted only according to Socialist principles, i.e., with the demand for universal suffrage for both women and men." "Every voting rights battle," she commented, "must also be fought as a battle for women's suffrage."[54] Madeleine Pelletier forcefully overcame amendments weakening this resolution, and it passed as Zetkin had presented it. Subsequently, no national section could subordinate the struggle for women's suffrage to that for men's suffrage without violating a formal resolution of the International. To ensure implementation of this resolution and to spread throughout the parties of the International the German structure of socialist women's organization, the congress voted to set up an independent women's secretariat with Zetkin at its head.

The International's decision galvanized the Austrian women's movement. The following year, in 1908, the Austrian socialist women held a conference at which they agreed that women's suffrage was an inalienable right. The party leadership, chastened perhaps by the drubbing it had received at the international congress, accepted this and went ahead to establish the system of women's spokespersons that had operated so effectively in Germany. As a result, the movement began to grow very rapidly and attained a membership of 15,000 by 1910.

THE ITALIAN SOCIALIST WOMEN'S MOVEMENT

If the Austrian socialist women's movement resembled the German, the Italian socialist women's movement resembled the French; despite fitful efforts in the 1890s, it was not until the eve of World War I that a serious attempt was made to create a movement modeled on Zetkin's. The Italian Socialist party, however, differed from the French in being founded as a unified party much earlier—in 1892—and in including among its leaders two dynamic women, both Russians. On the one hand, Angelica Balabanoff (1878–1965) was one of the principal leaders of the left faction of the party. She did not, however, concern herself with women's issues, preferring instead to act on the national and international stage. On the other hand, Anna Kuliscioff (1854?–1925) played a central role in the founding of the Italian Socialist party and in all the party's efforts to organize women.

Forced into exile from Russia in 1877, Kuliscioff went to Italy, where she lived with an Italian socialist; they had a daughter in 1881. Finding her companion unable to treat her as an equal, Kuliscioff left him and studied medicine, subsequently practicing in a working-class district of Milan and specializing in gynecology. These experiences and her reading of Marx and Engels led her to socialism. In 1884, she met Filippo Turati (1857–1932), with whom she spent the remainder of her life; they were key figures in the Italian Socialist party from its founding in 1892 until its shift to the left in 1912.

In a paper presented in 1890, Kuliscioff made a profound commitment to socialist feminism, echoing Engels' approach: the family, she argued, "will undergo profound modifications which are not yet able to be defined precisely"; "the former domestic relationships based on male domination and on the nuclear family home will be dissolved and a more elevated form of the family, founded upon spontaneity and equality will be prepared." But this did not lead her to introduce feminism into socialism, for reasons that she articulated more clearly than any other socialist feminist leader. Writing in the party magazine in 1897, she argued, "The present feminism of the middle class is merely a reproduction of the revolutionary movement of the male class a century ago. Freedom for woman, conquered during the period of its [the middle classes'] economic monopoly, can only be freedom for the middle class woman." Like Engels, she did not mean by this that feminism was unacceptable; on the contrary, the conquests of the revolutionary bourgeoisie, as embodied in the French revolution, were foundations on which the working class had to build. But "socialism and feminism, if they can be parallel social currents, cannot be one sole cause."[55]

Kuliscioff's work in Milan led her, however, to see the need for women's groups and to involve herself with the Milanese Socialist Women's Group, founded in 1897. The group organized working men and women in support of Kuliscioff's bill to protect women and children workers. Although this did not lead to the independent organization of women, it did lead to a massive campaign of meetings, well attended by women, that culminated in 1902 in over three hundred meetings throughout Italy and final passage of Kuliscioff's bill by Parliament.

Only after the 1907 International Socialist Congress had passed Zetkin's hard-hitting resolution for women's suffrage did Kuliscioff begin to push the party to support women's suffrage. During 1910, she attacked her partner

Turati and other leaders of the party for failing to support women's suffrage. At the 1910 party congress, she presented a resolution enjoining the party to undertake "agitation for the vote for women . . . as an altogether indispensable, utilitarian and idealist necessity to the life and development of the party."[56] The resolution passed; the next step was to organize women.

Kuliscioff pointed out to the 1910 congress that there were fewer women proportionately in the Italian party than in the German and Austrian parties, although she did not give specific figures. The 1911 congress voted funds for a women's newspaper and designated Kuliscioff as editor. In June 1912, at the national party congress and at the first national conference of socialist women (held in conjunction with the congress), Kuliscioff led the effort to found a National Socialist Women's Union and was the most important personality of the three-woman executive committee elected there.

The same congress, however, saw the victory of the left faction, then led by Balabanoff and the young Benito Mussolini (1883–1945), whom Balabanoff—to her everlasting regret—had installed as editor of the party newspaper (he did not begin his swing toward fascism until the war broke out). The left faction took control of the party away from Turati and Kuliscioff, who resigned both as editor of the newspaper and as member of the executive of the women's group. Balabanoff replaced Kuliscioff on the women's executive, but she did not think the matter important enough to mention it in her autobiography.[57] She had argued in 1904 against creating "a feminist socialism since for us the so-called feminist problem does not exist," and she maintained that position.[58] After the war, fascism brought an end to the movement.

SOCIALIST WOMEN'S MOVEMENTS FROM WORLD WAR I TO WORLD WAR II

Throughout Europe, the war posed a new problem for socialism, and in particular for the socialist women's movements, by cutting across sex and faction lines. Clara Zetkin, on the left of her party like Balabanoff, strongly opposed the war. On November 7, 1914, Zetkin issued an appeal to socialist women to struggle for peace: "When the men kill, it is up to us women to fight for the preservation of life. When the men are silent, it is our duty to raise our voices on behalf of our ideals."[59] In France, Louise Saumoneau distributed Zetkin's appeal in a clandestine brochure early in 1915. Socialist women in other countries soon followed suit.

On the basis of this appeal, Zetkin organized an international conference of socialist women at Berne in March 1915, six months before socialist men of the left held a similar conference at Zimmerwald (also in Switzerland). Although the majority of the twenty-eight delegates (including Balabanoff, who did all the translating for the conference) were from neutral countries, several were from Germany and England, a number from Russia (including four Bolsheviks), and one from France: Louise Saumoneau. The Berne Conference showed the potential power of socialist women, but it was not followed by any further action; instead, the socialist women of the various parties devoted their energies to their factions, in working for or against the war as they saw fit. At the end of the war, the socialist women's movement lay in ruins.

Clara Zetkin had joined the antiwar German Independent Socialist party (USPD) along with Rosa Luxemburg (1870–1919) and Karl Liebknecht (1871–1919). When the government, composed of leaders from the old prowar SPD, put down the left-wing "Spartacist" revolt against the Weimar Republic at the beginning of 1919 and allowed the murder of Liebknecht and Luxemburg to go unpunished, Zetkin became deeply embittered. Joining Lenin's new communist Third International, she gave the remaining years of her life to communism. Popp took over Zetkin's position in the Second—or socialist—International when it was reconstituted, but it was only a ghost of its former self, and, in virtually all European countries except Austria, the reconstituted socialist women's movement was no longer a powerful and independent force on the left of the party but a women's auxiliary of an essentially male party.

Even without Zetkin the German SPD attracted great numbers of women in the euphoria immediately following the revolution that overthrew the Kaiser and installed the Weimar Republic with SPD leaders at its head. In 1919, women made up more than 20 percent of the membership, and the party elected nineteen women members of parliament. In 1931, at the all-time high before Hitler came to power, there were 230,351 women members of the party, or 22.8 percent of the total membership.

In France, the SFIO had voted to join the Third International and thus became the Communist party in 1920. Those who sought to continue the old SFIO had to start anew. Louise Saumoneau, unlike Zetkin, shrank from joining the Third International and returned to the SFIO. She and the other leaders of the prewar women's movement reconstructed it on the old lines and reproduced the old failures. The party's success in the 1936 elections put it at the head of a coalition government called the Popular Front. The women's movement, however, made no effort to seize the opportunity presented by the party's being in government, although three socialist women leaders served as undersecretaries of state. At the beginning of 1938, the number of women in the party reached a high point of 9,568, still only 3.34 percent of the total membership.

In Italy, as we have seen, things went from bad to worse. Only in Austria did the socialist women's movement make progress after the war, because in Austria the party remained largely unified and women enjoyed the suffrage. Under Popp's leadership, the Austrian movement continued to flourish, while the split between socialism and communism significantly weakened other socialist women's movements. By 1925, the Austrian movement had 165,000 members, constituting 29.7 percent of the total party membership. The party was taking advanced positions, with the socialist women fighting not only for protective legislation for women workers, but also for changes in the household and even for birth control and abortion. But the Fascists destroyed the Austrian Social Democratic party in 1934 (Popp was among the leaders arrested) and smashed the last strong socialist women's movement remaining on the Continent.

CONCLUSION

The socialist women's movement did not achieve its program in its own time. Political equality came only after World War I (in some countries only after World War II), and where women had gained the suffrage, fascism often rolled back their gains. Economic equality remained a battle to be fought even after World War II, and complete equality still eludes the grasp of both women and workers. The short-term goals of better wages and conditions were partially fulfilled by the trade union movement, but the long-term goals of socialism—economic independence for women and "higher" forms of work and of family life, transcending "the monogamous family as the economic unit of society" and establishing the freer, more just, and more community-oriented society promised by socialism—seem as elusive as ever.

Yet the socialist women's movement left a positive legacy. First, even in the countries where the socialist women's movement was weakest, it reached more women than the bourgeois feminists ever hoped to reach. To be sure, feminism was weak on the Continent, but even in their strongest moments the feminists were held back by their class background and found themselves unable to make contact with working-class women. The socialist parties did reach working-class women, however few, and even when taking their harshest line against bourgeois feminism, as in France, they nevertheless taught working-class women independence and self-respect by giving them a voice of their own, much as the American abolitionist movement did for the early American suffragists.

Second, the socialist women's movement provided a strategy for equality: in welcoming economic independence, however painful it seemed at the time, the movement foreshadowed the demands of socialist feminism today.

Third, the socialist parties gave women a platform to act effectively in politics, at a time when other parties would not even admit women to their ranks. Even leaders who, like Angelica Balabanoff and Rosa Luxemburg, refused to work in the socialist women's movement still provided inspiration for other women as role models. Luxemburg, for instance, preferred to deploy her enormous intellect on the wider stage of the practical and theoretical issues in the party as a whole, but she nevertheless inspired German socialist women.

The most lasting legacy of the socialist women's movement is thus the development of separate organization for working-class women and a consequent

articulation of their distinct concerns. This is what characterized the most successful national movements. This success bore fruit when women voted: those
parties that had developed effective women's organizations had a head start
on those that had failed to do so. The German and Austrian SPD have often
been in power as part of coalition governments since World War II, partly because of their strong blocs of women members. The French socialists were slow
to follow their example, but François Mitterrand tapped both women's social
concern and their desire for equal rights. The success of his campaigns for
president, an office he held from 1981 to 1995, is often attributed to women's
vote. Mitterrand repaid some of this through the creation of the Ministry of
Women's Rights under the energetic Yvette Roudy from 1981 to 1986. Roudy
ensured the implementation of equal opportunity laws, a network of women's
refuges, and various laws against sexism in advertising and in the media.
Roudy's crowning achievement was to obtain agreement on the principle of a
minimum quota of women elected by the party.

Socialism helped give birth to modern feminism, and now, as the twentieth
century draws to a close, socialist political movements have often distinguished
themselves in giving women formal political structures. If more parties are
addressing themselves to women, they are following the example set by the
socialist women's movement.

NOTES

1. See Chapter 12.
2. Barbara Taylor, *Eve and the New Jerusalem: Socialism and Feminism in the Nine-teenth Century,* Virago Press, London, 1983, p. 5.
3. Susan K. Grogan, *French Socialism and Sexual Difference: Women and the New Society, 1803–44,* Macmillan, Basingstoke, 1992, p. 20.
4. Taylor, *op. cit.,* pp. x–xi.
5. Virago Press, London, 1983.
6. Taylor, *op. cit.,* 183–185; Robert Owen, "Book of the New Moral World," Fourth Part, Chapter IX, in *Selected Works of Robert Owen* ed. Gregory Claeys, 4 vols; London: W. Pickering, 1993, vol. 3, p. 225; Owen, "General Rules and Regula-tions," vol. 2, pp. 34–35.
7. In Claeys, *op. cit.,* vol. 2, esp. pp. 276–278.
8. The Polytechnic School, one of a handful of "great schools" founded by Napoleon to educate an elite, is still today a French equivalent of a Harvard MBA.
9. Grogan, *op. cit.,* p. 98.
10. Claire Goldberg Moses, "'Difference' in Historical Perspective: Saint-Simonian Feminism," in *Feminism, Socialism, and French Romanticism,* ed. Claire Goldberg Moses and Leslie Wahl Rabine, Indiana University Press, Bloomington, 1993, p. 34. Moses points out that the women's newspaper quoted this saying several times (p. 34, n. 38).
11. Grogan, *op. cit.,* p. 100.

12. Démar, *My Law of the Future,* in Moses and Rabine, *op cit.,* p. 181.
13. Grogan, *op. cit,* p. 101, Moses and Rabine, *op. cit.,* pp. 286–287.
14. Edith Thomas, *Pauline Roland: Socialisme et Feminisme au XIXe Siecle,* M. Rivière, Paris, 1956, p 38.
15. Grogan, *op. cit.,* p. 179.
16. Flora Tristan, *The Worker's Union,* trans. Beverly Livingston, University of Illinois Press, Urbana, 1983, p. 58.
17. *Ibid.,* pp. 77–78.
18. *La République,* March 22, April 15, 1848.
19. Translated in Felicia Gordon and Maire Cross, *Early French Feminisms, 1830–1940: A Passion for Liberty,* Edward Elgar, Brookfield, Vt., 1996, p. 69.
20. Thomas, *op. cit.,* p. 129. For Roland's contributions, see the lists of subscribers in Tristan, *op. cit.,* pp. 18, 31.
21. Louise A. Tilly and Joan W. Scott, *Women, Work, and Family,* 2nd ed., Routledge, New York, 1989. Cf. Tessie P. Liu, *The Weaver's Knot: The Contradictions of Class Struggle and Family Solidarity in Western France, 1750–1914,* Cornell University Press, Ithaca, 1994, pp. 231–235.
22. *Women, the Family, and Freedom: The Debate in Documents,* ed. Susan Groag Bell and Karen Offen, Stanford University Press, Stanford, 1983, vol. 1, p. 191.
23. Quoted in Charles Sowerwine, *Sisters or Citizens? Women and Socialism in France Since 1876,* Cambridge: Cambridge University Press, Cambridge, 1982, p. 22.
24. Eugene Kamenka, ed., *The Portable Karl Marx,* Penguin Books, Harmondsworth 1983, p. 147.
25. Frederick Engels, *The Origin of the Family, Private Property and the State,* ed. Eleanor Burke Leacock, trans. Alec West, International Publishers, New York, 1972, p. 137.
26. *Ibid.*
27. Karl Marx, *Capital: A Critique of Political Economy,* trans. Ben Fowkes, Penguin Books, Harmondsworth, 1976, vol. 1, pp. 620–621.
28. August Bebel, *Women Under Socialism,* trans. Daniel De Leon, Labor News Press, New York, 1904; reprint New York, Schocken Books, 1971, pp. 187–188, 216–224; 39, 80, 119, 140, 182; 9.
29. *Clara Zetkin: Selected Writings,* ed. Philip S. Foner, trans. Kai Schoenhals, International Publishers, New York, 1984, p. 79.
30. Quoted by Jean H. Quataert, "Unequal Partners in an Uneasy Alliance: Women and the Working-Class in Imperial Germany," in *Socialist Women: European Socialist Feminism in the Nineteenth and Early Twentieth Centuries,* ed. Marilyn J. Boxer and Jean H. Quataert, Elsevier, New York, 1978, p. 120.
31. Karl Kautsky, *The Class Struggle (Erfurt Program),* trans. William E. Bohn, Norton, New York, 1971, pp. 127–128.
32. Quoted in Sowerwine, *op. cit.,* p. 26.
33. Werner Thonnessen, *The Emancipation of Women: The Rise and Decline of the Women's Movement in German Social Democracy 1863–1933,* trans. Joris de Bres, Pluto Press, London, 1973, pp. 48, 62.
34. Foner, *op. cit.,* pp. 46–47.
35. *Ibid.,* pp. 76, 99.
36. *Ibid.,* p. 100; Thonnessen, *op. cit.,* p. 116.

37. Quoted in Sowerwine, *op. cit.*, p. 85 (emphasis in original).
38. Quoted in *ibid.*, pp. 77, 79.
39. Doctoresse Pelletier, "Memoirs of a Feminist, April 1933," in Gordon and Cross, *op. cit.*, p. 237.
40. Sowerwine, *op. cit.*, p. 119.
41. Letters, Pelletier to Hélène Brion, 27 December 1912, 7, 9 January 1913, dossier Pelletier, BMD; Sowerwine, *op. cit.*, pp. 129–130.
42. Patricia Hilden, *Working Women and Socialist Politics in France, 1880–1914: A Regional Study*, Oxford University Press, New York, 1986, p. 249.
43. The Couriau Affair. Cf. Charles Sowerwine, "Workers and Women in France Before 1914: The Debate over the Couriau Affair," *The Journal of Modern History* 55 (1983), pp. 411–441.
44. Quoted in Sowerwine, *op. cit.*, p. 139.
45. Sylvia Pankhurst, *The Suffragette Movement: An Intimate Account of Persons and Ideals*, Longman, London, 1931; reprint, Virago, London, 1977, p. 242.
46. Jill Liddington, *The Life and Times of a Respectable Rebel: Selina Cooper (1864–1946)* Virago, London, 1984, p. 178; Jill Liddington and Jill Norris, *One Hand Tied Behind Us: The Rise of the Women's Suffrage Movement*, Virago, London, 1978, pp. 235–236; Hannah M.W. Mitchell (1871–1956), *The Hard Way Up: The Auto-biography of Hannah Mitchell, Suffragette and Rebel*, Faber, London, 1968; reprint, London, Virago, 1977, p. 189.
47. Karen Hunt, *Equivocal Feminists: The Social Democratic Federation and the Woman Question, 1884–1911*, Cambridge University Press, New York, 1996, pp. 170–182.
48. Pankhurst, *op. cit.*, pp. 167–169.
49. *Zetkin: Selected Writings*, p. 104.
50. Liddington, *op. cit.*, p. 223.
51. *European Women: A Documentary History, 1789–1945*, ed. Eleanor S. Riemer and John C. Fout, Schocken Books, New York, 1980, p. 92.
52. Quoted in Sowerwine, *op. cit.*, p. 196.
53. *Proposals and Drafts of Resolutions Submitted to the International Socialist Congress of Stuttgart (18–24 August 1907)*, International Socialist Bureau, Brussels, 1907, pp. 567–571; "Anhang: Erste internationale Konferenz sozialisticher Frauen," in *Internationaler Sozialistenkongress zu Stuttgart, 18 bis 24. August 1907*, Verlag Buchhandlung Vorwarts, Berlin, 1907, pp. 128 and passim; *Women, the Family, and Freedom*, vol. 2 pp. 231–232.
54. *Zetkin: Selected Writings*, pp. 98, 105.
55. Quoted in Claire LaVigna, "The Marxist Ambivalence Toward Women: Between Socialism and Feminism in the Italian Socialist Party," in Boxer and Quataert, *op. cit.*, pp. 170, 148–149.
56. Quoted in *ibid.*, p. 159.
57. Angelica Balabanoff, *My Life as a Rebel* (New York, 1938; Indiana University Press, Bloomington, 1973); on the other hand, she deemed the victory of her faction at the congress to be worthy of four pages: *ibid.*, pp. 95–98.
58. Nancy G. Eshelman, "Forging a Socialist Women's Movement: Angelica Bala-banoff in Switzerland," in *The Italian Immigrant Women in North America*, ed. Betty Boyd Caroli, Robert F. Harney, and Lydio F. Tomasi, Multicultural History Society of Ontario, Toronto, 1978, p. 67.
59. *Zetkin: Selected Writings*, p. 116.

SUGGESTIONS FOR FURTHER READING

The following suggestions indicate only works not cited in the notes. On early French feminism and socialism, insight can be gained from Joan W. Scott, *Only Paradoxes to Offer: French Feminists and the Rights of Man* (Cambridge: Harvard University Press, 1996). Most texts of early French feminists are now available in translation. Jonathan Beecher and Richard Bienvenu, eds., *The Utopian Vision of Charles Fourier; Selected Texts on Work, Love, and Passionate Attraction* (Boston: Beacon Press, 1971), gives a good introduction to the work of this pioneer. Moses and Rabine (see notes) present a good selection of writings by Saint-Simonian women, including extensive excerpts from *The Women's Tribune*. Other texts are translated in Gordon and Cross (see notes). Most of Flora Tristan's books have been published in English. For women in 1848, David Barry, *Women and Political Insurgency: France in the Mid-Nineteenth Century* (Basingstoke: Macmillan, 1996) provides a general view.

For Marxian ideas on women, see Lise Vogel, *Marx and the Oppression of Women* (New Brunswick, N.J.: Rutgers University Press, 1983). For German socialist women, see Jean H. Quataert, *Reluctant Feminists in German Social Democracy, 1885–1917* (Princeton: Princeton University Press, 1979), and Chapter 1 of Richard J. Evans, *Proletarians and Politics: Socialism, Protest and the Working Class in Germany Before the First World War* (New York: Harvester Wheatsheaf, 1990).

For French socialist women, see the notes. For Madeleine Pelletier, see Chapter 5 of Joan Scott, *Only Paradoxes to Offer* (see above) and Felicia Gordon, *The Integral Feminist—Madeleine Pelletier, 1874–1939: Feminism, Socialism, and Medicine* (Cambridge: Polity Press, 1990).

A useful comparative article is Gay L. Gullickson, "Feminists and Suffragists: The British and French Experiences," *Feminist Studies* 15 (1989): pp. 591–602. For Britain, see also Brian Harrison, "Women's Suffrage at Westminster, 1866–1928," in *High and Low Politics in Modern Britain*, ed. Michael Bentley and John Stevenson (Oxford: Clarendon Press, 1983), pp. 80–122.

Missionary women.   COURTESY FLEMING H. REVELL CO. *PANDITA RAMABAI: THE STORY OF HER LIFE*
BY HELEN DYER, © 1900.

CHAPTER 14

Gender, Race, and Empire in Nineteenth- and Twentieth-Century Africa and Asia

Margaret Strobel

European women participated not only in the politics of their own nations, but also in the empires acquired by those nations. Around the globe, they played ambiguous roles as members of a sex considered to be inferior within a race that considered itself to be superior. This contradictory position brought ambivalent results. On the one hand, European women advanced the interests of the colonizers by maintaining a social distance between the Europeans and the colonized, particularly in colonies with a substantial European population. On the other hand, European women sometimes identified with the oppressed and, although they rarely questioned the practice of imperialism itself, sought to ameliorate some of its worst effects. In either case, women traveling to the colonies often gained opportunities lacking at home and played a central role in shaping the social relations of imperialism. As missionaries, they modeled what Europeans believed to be appropriate gender roles for indigenous women. Through their writings, they helped construct an image of, and rationale for, empire. As ethnographers and anthropologists, they provided knowledge of indigenous peoples necessary for their more effective administration. As reformers, they intervened in practices on behalf of local women and at times used this maternalistic role as spokeswomen to legitimate their own claims back home for political rights.

Europeam[1] women had a complex, varied, and often contradictory relationship to the African and Asian territories controlled by the European powers in
the nineteenth and twentieth centuries. As members of the "inferior sex" within
the "superior race" (to use contemporary formulations), women were afforded
options by imperialism that male dominance in the colonies then limited. By
the twentieth century, some European women were attacking aspects of the
racial, political, and economic inequalities of the colonial relationship. But the
vast majority of them supported and contributed to the imperial venture. These
women benefited from the economic and political subjugation of indigenous
peoples and shared many of the accompanying attitudes of racism, paternalism, ethnocentrism, and national chauvinism. For most of them, life in the
colonies provided opportunities not found in Europe, where their options were
limited by their social class, a "shortage" of marriageable men, difficulty in
finding adequate employment, or the lack of "heathen souls" to be converted.
At the same time, women continuously experienced, sometimes challenged,
and sometimes reproduced the economic, political, and ideological subordination of women. As wives of colonial officials, they subordinated their lives
to a male-centered administrative environment. As educators of indigenous
women, they reproduced the European notions of bourgeois or Victorian domesticity and female dependence. Even missionary women, whose commitment to career and calling was in some ways a challenge to those very notions,
accepted the patriarchal ideology and bureaucracy of the Church and promoted
conventional European gender roles to African and Asian women.

As an outcome of centuries of economic and political rivalry, by 1914 an
estimated four-fifths of the inhabited portions of the world was under the control or influence of one of the Great Powers. European imperialism in Africa
and Asia reached its height between 1850 and World War II. Following earlier
Portuguese, Dutch, and French economic competition on the South Asian subcontinent, by the nineteenth century India had become the "Jewel in the
[British] Crown." The British government took over administration from the
British East India Company after the army rebellion of 1857. Thereafter Britain
governed two-thirds of the subcontinent directly until it granted independence
to India and Pakistan separately in 1947. From the mid-nineteenth century on,
India had a sizeable European community, although men outnumbered
women. The area between India and China remained an area of European com-
petition, with the Dutch settling in and colonizing the Indonesian archipelago.
Much like the British did in India, the Dutch government took over from the
Dutch East India Company in the late eighteenth century. Britain and France
contested for influence over and/or control of various portions of southeast
Asia ruled by indigenous authorities.

Britain's relationship with Africa similarly began in trade and ended in
formal colonial rule. Following the partition of Africa in 1885, Britain, France,

Germany, Italy, Portugal, and Belgium established colonial administrations by military conquest or co-optation of African political figures. In most areas, a small core of white men administered the colony. Even where the European powers encouraged white settlers (for example, Kenya, northern Rhodesia/Zambia, and southern Rhodesia/Zimbabwe for the British; Mozambique for the Portuguese; Algeria for the French), the European population was tiny and largely male until after World War I. South Africa's history differs. There, Afrikaners (Boers, descendants of the seventeenth-century Dutch settlers) had a demographically balanced population when British capitalists and settlers, disproportionately male, came in substantial numbers in the nineteenth century. South Africa became a self-governing (by whites) country in 1910; most of the rest of colonial Africa gained its independence beginning in the 1950s.

Effective control of the colonies required an ideology, accepted by at least a portion of the colonized, that legitimized colonial rule, namely, the superiority of European, Christian civilization. The spread of Western education and medical skills obscured exploitative economic relations and the absence of political rights for colonized peoples at the same time that it led to some real improvements in their lives. Excluded from the military and—until the very end of the colonial period—from key positions in the political administrative structure, women helped legitimize colonialism as teachers, nurses, the wives of administrators, and/or ameliorators of the worst manifestations of indigenous and colonial oppression. Interestingly, the patriarchal ideology that assigned these helping roles to women also masked the exploitation of imperialism by identifying the imperial power as the "mother country" and, by inference, the colonies as immature and untrained children.

Did European women in the colonies threaten the imperial relationship? Many scholars claim they did. Three components of this myth are relevant: British attitudes toward mixed-race sexual relations; rituals that maintained social boundaries between races; and the subordination of the domestic sphere to the public realm of imperial life. Examination of the sexist bias of the myth reveals the racial and gender dynamics of colonial society. The remainder of the chapter analyzes several roles women played in the colonies—as job seekers, travelers, missionaries, anthropologists, and reformers—and asks how women's activities advanced or subverted the imperial mission and how the imperial context reinforced or undermined female gender roles.

THE MYTH OF THE DESTRUCTIVE FEMALE: SEXUALITY, RITUAL, AND HOME

Until recently, most of the histories that mention European women's arrival in the colonies at all claimed that European women contributed to the deterioration of the relationship between the European administrator and those he governed. According to this myth, "vulnerable" European women provoked the sexual appetites of indigenous men, while as wives they replaced indigenous concubines (from whom male administrators had previously learned much about local society and culture) and drew the attention of the men away from their official responsibilities. In addition, historians have described European wives as racists who distanced themselves from the local population. In the words of a famous historian of India: "As [white] women went out in large numbers, they brought with them their insular whims and prejudices, which no official contact with Indians or iron compulsion of loneliness ever tempted them to abandon. [They were] too insular in most cases to interest themselves in alien culture and life for its own sake."[2] It is true that the arrival of women in substantial numbers made possible the creation of an exclusive social group, and that the women, in their social roles as wives and hostesses, maintained the hierarchy within the European community and its social distance from the indigenous peoples by elaborate rituals.

Rather than blaming European women for the growing rift between white and nonwhite populations in the empires, recent historians tend to see their arrival as coinciding with other developments in colonial society: heightened racial prejudice, the growth of evangelical Christianity with its ethnocentrism and attack on nonmarital liaisons, and the increased size of the European population generally. And, where settlement was the goal (in parts of Africa and, earlier, in North America) rather than rule (in India, most of Africa, southwest Asia, and the Pacific Islands), women's arrival seems to have been valued more by their contemporaries than by later scholars. However, because it is so widespread and unquestioned, the components of this myth—sexist assumptions about sexuality, ritual, and domestic life—merit examination for what they reveal about the dynamics of colonial society.

The myth of the destructive female contains two elements that pertain to sexuality: concubinage and the protection of European women. Officials justified access to concubines and indigenous prostitutes on the grounds of keeping men virile and heterosexual, both essential components of rule that reflected imperial power. Moreover, in interfering with the European male's access to indigenous concubines, European women purportedly contributed to the creation of greater distance between the communities. In the early colonial days, European men commonly took concubines. The perils of transition when one's wife appeared are illustrated by a story that circulated in West Africa about 1910:

> One D. C. [District Commissioner] arrived with his new spouse [at] his boma late at night and promptly went to bed. About four in the morning his cook walked boldly into the room, lifted the mosquito net sheltering the exhausted sleepers, soundly slapped the lady on her bottom and said, "Leave now missy, time to go back to the village."[3]

Concubinage entailed physical proximity and intimacy in a context of inequality. The same can be said of the mistress-servant relationship, but historians have not credited the latter with developing ties between the colonizers and the indigenous community. To single out European women's dislike for concubinage as a cause of increasing social distance is to leave unquestioned the inequality of the colonizing male–colonized female concubine relationship. Only if one ignores the element of subordination in a concubinage relationship can it be read as closeness. In fact, it was the attitude of superiority exhibited by Europeans in the colonies, male and female, that created the social distance. Moreover, as racial prejudice deepened toward the turn of the century, the need to reinforce social distance overcame official concerns about sexual access for European men. Previous measures to limit European men bringing wives were lifted in various colonies. In 1909, when there were still few European women in the British colonies other than India, the British colonial secretary prohibited liaisons between officials and indigenous women. In the Dutch East Indies, about the same time, in 1920, European plantation owners reversed their earlier policies that prohibited the employment of married European males.

According to the myth, not only did European women inhibit the valuable institution of concubinage; they also aroused the sexual appetites of indigenous men from whom they then had to be protected. This situation of sexual competition increased the distance between European and indigenous men. The contradictory nature of this formulation clearly reveals the sexism of the myth itself. If concubinage enhanced the relationship of colonizer and colonized, then why should not voluntary liaisons between European women and indigenous men do the same? Such relationships were not common, but they prompted sharp response. In 1893 the maharaja of Patiala married Miss Florry Bryan; this disturbed Lord Curzon, the viceroy of India. Not only did the marriage transgress against the social distance between Europeans and indigenous people mandated by imperial ideology, but the maharaja's high social status and his wife's working-class background confused even more the racial, sexual, and class hierarchies of empire. Even in the absence of marriage across class lines, such relationships raised concern. In turn-of-the-century South Africa, officials, in order to prevent African migrant workers from frequenting white prostitutes, passed laws that forbade intercourse between black men and white women. Such voluntary relationships offended imperial minds because they forced a contradiction between two notions central to the racist and sexist ideologies of the time: whites should be superior to people of color and men should be superior to women.

The aroused sexual desires of indigenous men, many Europeans feared, might lead to sexual assaults on European women—the dreaded "Black Peril." Ironically, European men seemed to feel more threatened than European women by this "danger." In Papua New Guinea, men, not women, pushed for the passage of the harsh White Women's Protection Ordinance in 1926—the death penalty for rape or attempted rape of a white woman by a New Guinea man. Moreover, former colonial women's reminiscences do not mention fear of indigenous men. On the other hand, in 1907 the Associated Women's Organizations of the Transvaal requested the government to enact segregation as a protection against assaults on (European) women. Indeed, increased concern with the sexual assault of white women typically correlated with tensions within the European settlement and a perceived need to consolidate it. For example, labor protests in Indonesia in the 1920s threatened to split the European male population: low-paid European male employees allied with Indonesian workers in labor protests again European male elites who ran estates. The same period witnessed measures to enhance the safety of white women. Whether or not women participated in efforts to prevent real or imagined assaults, the notion that they needed male protection fit nicely into the racist and sexist ideologies of the day.

Surveying British, French, and Dutch colonial practices and policies related to interracial sexual unions, Ann Stoler notes the complex relationship between sexual morality and race:

> Miscegenation signaled neither the absence nor presence of racial prejudice in itself; hierarchies of privilege and power were written into the condoning of interracial unions, as well as into their condemnation. . . . Sex in the colonies was about sexual access and reproduction, class distinctions and racial privileges, nationalism and European identity in different measure and not all at the same time.[4]

Interracial sexual unions resulted, over the decades, in a hybrid subpopulation, some of whose members successfully claimed European status.

In addition to such ideas about sexual relations between Europeans and indigenous people, the myth of the destructive female embodies the stereotype of petty, frivolous, racist, unproductive, and dependent women who contributed nothing to either the imperial enterprise or to indigenous peoples. Typically, the wife of a colonial administrator, settler, or army officer is pictured as living a life of leisure consisting of dinner parties, banal conversation, and petty jealousies about her own and her husband's status. This stereotype can be challenged in two ways: its inaccuracy, which the portraits in the subsequent sections establish, and its conceptual male-centered bias, which both distorts and subordinates female experience.

Colonial society charged women with enacting the social rituals that defined the boundaries between Europeans and indigenous people and the hierarchy among Europeans, but it subsequently stigmatized such activities as trivial (and, later still, as racist). The social life described here reached its height in the late-nineteenth century in India and between the world wars in the remaining colonies when the colonial enterprise was relatively unquestioned. A regal and commanding style necessarily accompanied political domination, and such rituals as dressing formally for dinner helped Europeans define the differences between themselves and the colonized. The widowed wife of a colonial officer, Sylvia Leith-Ross, describes herself and a colonial official dressing for dinner in 1913 on a steel canoe on a Nigerian river: "When you are alone, among thousands of unknown, unpredictable people, dazed by unaccustomed sights and sounds, bemused by strange ways of life and thought, you need to remember who you are, where you come from, what your standards are."[5] If some rituals helped maintain a sense of cultural identity, others emphasized internal stratification. The apparently trivial pursuit of "calling" can be seen in this light. By beginning from the top of the hierarchy on down, the practice of leaving calling cards at each European household revealed the social structure of the settler community as it inaugurated the rainy season in India, when the British returned to the plains from the cooler hill stations. Thus women performed important functions in organizing and executing the social life that appears, in a less formal time and place, unduly rigid and formal if not silly.

Although a woman's role in colonial society included identifying social boundaries and hierarchy, she did so in a profoundly male world. For many women, a wife's position in the colonial hierarchy derived from her husband's; she had no independent place. This fact has implications that shed light on the stereotypical behavior of colonial women. Colonial administrators' wives often had to engage in trivial conversation, for example, while entertaining to avoid revealing privileged information. Moreover, since a woman's position in the social hierarchy depended on the course of her husband's career, she was limited in the extent to which she could express intimacy or solidarity with other women above or below her, which helps to explain her apparent competitiveness with other women.

The diary of Laura Boyle vividly reveals the implications of having one's status and role derive from that of one's husband. Written in 1916 while her new husband was stationed in a northern area of the Gold Coast (now Ghana), where no white woman had been since the turn of the century, the initial portion of the diary describes their joint travels in the bush and her observations of African society. After the government promoted him and transferred them to the Secretariat in Accra, her observations run to sports and cultural activities. "It is all very different from the daily opportunities in Wenchi," she noted then, "where we both could take a share of the problems in 'bush' administration." In Accra she supervised the servants, while he worked at the office.[6]

In colonial administrative structures, the female hierarchy usually paralleled the male hierarchy. The highest-ranking wife set the standard and tone for the female portion of colonial society. Exercise of this leadership might range from mundane decisions that female dinner guests need not wear white gloves in hot weather to more substantive encouragement of welfare efforts. A wife who did not act in a manner appropriate to her husband's rank upset the entire community by disrupting the social order. Even in smaller European colonial communities, elaborate rituals prevailed. Social control of the behavior of other Europeans through gossip or ostracism helped maintain the sense of security of the outnumbered European community.

As noted earlier, the empire was seen as a man's world. Imperial structures and processes made few accommodations to the female roles of wife, mother, and homemaker, even though these activities both provided material benefits for the husband and children and helped to maintain the social boundaries that separated the European community from the indigenous one. Indeed, the task of homemaker and mother had even greater implications for preserving "civilization" when carried out in the outposts of the empire. Women's reminiscences overflow with tales of housekeeping, while men's deal with the public actions of imperial officers, accurately reflecting the typical social division of labor.

Indeed, homemaking in the colonies, particularly in the early days, challenged a woman's ingenuity and fortitude. Flora Annie Steel and Grace Gardiner's *The Complete Indian Housekeeper and Cook* (1888) offered advice on a myriad topics, from the number of camels it took to move the household to the hills for the hot season, to wet-nursing, to remedies for tropical diseases. Health was a constant concern. Malaria and blackwater fever took their toll of both children and adults. Sylvia Leith-Ross noted that of the group of five with whom she traveled from Liverpool to Nigeria in 1906, she alone remained alive thirteen months later. African and Asian women experienced health hazards and raised families under even more difficult conditions, of course. But the change from a European lifestyle shocked many emigrants, who sought to reproduce it as best they could.

The exigencies of life in the tropical colonies forced changes in family life. Unlike their sisters in Britain, women in Victorian India drew upon nonkin from their community for support. Restricted by Victorian conventions, women frequently chose female midwives over male physicians. Racial prejudice prescribed the use of European midwives, who came from lower-class backgrounds. Indeed, the British colonials believed that non-European physicians were unfit to attend European births. Because of local health conditions, miscarriages were common; tropical diseases caused a high infant mortality rate. Among the British in Bengal, for example, infant mortality more than twice exceeded that of England for the period from 1860 to 1869.

Official attitudes toward the domestic sphere changed over time, but they initially articulated the third element of the myth of the destructive female: the idea that a home and family distracted an administrator from his work. Before World War I, the governor-general for French West Africa claimed that administrators who lived with their families "lost approximately 50% of their efficiency."[7] Not until 1920 did the secretary of state for the (British) colonies decree that married life should be the norm for administrators in colonies other than India (where a substantial British community already existed). Elsewhere, until the 1940s a man expected to marry only after his second or third tour of duty. The practice of sending children back to Britain for schooling continued until after World War II. Thus, although many wives of men in the Colonial Service sought to fulfill the traditional female roles of mother, wife, and homemaker, they did so under severe strains and with little official support.

The perquisites of being a European in the colonies included having servants, a luxury not available in the twentieth century to the largely middle-class group from whom colonial administrators came, and certainly not to the working classes from which some settlers came. Granted, homemaking in the colonies was more difficult than in Europe, but Europeans lived at a much higher standard of living than the vast majority of colonial subjects. Dutch household manuals at the turn of the century recommended seven to ten servants for European families in Indonesia; the typical household had four to six. Even otherwise impoverished white settlers in Africa had servants. Living as an administrator's family in a remote part of present-day Ghana in 1916, Laura and David Boyle had six male and female house servants and twelve men working outside. Having servants not only lessened the burdens of housekeeping; it offered many women their most salient interaction with indigenous people. European women developed a distorted view of local people's lives and culture based upon this profoundly unequal relationship. European women's most intense relationships with indigenous people focused upon a single part of the social structure, because servants generally came from impoverished and low-status or low-caste groups. Moreover, Europeans rarely saw servants in the latters' own surroundings, and servants had every reason to mask their real selves.

Not surprisingly, much of the racism or paternalism found in memoirs of colonial women focuses upon servants and substantiates this aspect of the charge leveled at them as "destructive women." Yet colonial men expressed the same racism through their own work as administrators, business owners, or settlers. Elizabeth Melville's *A Residence at Sierra Leone* (1849) communicates a common attitude toward African servants, found with little variation everywhere and throughout the decades. Concerned with the "trivial matter" of daily life and housekeeping, the narrative bemoans the "indolence, stupidity, and want of tidiness of the African" and the problems of locating and training servants.[8] Where it occurs, such noncooperation is, of course, a standard technique of resistance on the part of subordinates. In many cases, cultural differences made difficult the transformation of indigenous men and women into servants for European households. Many memoirs, while noting difficulties with servants, record a paternalistic affection for particular servants and occasional concrete assistance to them. The author Isak Dinesen, for example, went to unusual lengths to provide for her servants when she left her failed coffee farm in Kenya.

In summary, the sexist bias of the myth of the destructive female obscures the real role played by European women in the empire. To the extent that their arrival inhibited the practice of concubinage, it struck a blow at a racially and sexually unequal relationship that has been romanticized to represent harmony between the colonizer and colonized. In carrying out the social rituals that have been characterized as petty, women identified the boundaries between ruler and ruled and the hierarchy within the European community that lay at the heart of imperial relations. In establishing homes in the face of official disinterest or even discouragement, women contributed to the improved health and happiness of male officials and the solidification of a strong European community. Thus colonial women, far from losing the empire, were central to its continuation. Unfortunately, the rising nostalgia for the Raj that is exhibited in films, television shows, and collections of reminiscences provides little critique of either the sexist nature of empire or its fundamental exploitation of colonized peoples.

The women described above largely represent those who came as dependents to their husbands. But, in addition to the many dependent wives who developed an interest in working with African and Asian people, other women came to or grew up in the colonies with their own agendas, which fit the imperial design to a greater and lesser degree. Patriarchal structures and ideologies shaped their lives as well.

DOMESTIC SERVANTS: WHITE WOMEN
AND THE IMPERIAL MISSION

Particularly after World War I, but earlier in India, women—from prostitutes to doctors—came to the colonies seeking employment to escape economic conditions or sexist discrimination back home. The experiences of one such group of white women, those recruited to South Africa as domestic servants, reveals most clearly the harmony of imperial and gender ideology.

Although most domestic servants in Africa were Africans, many of the women who emigrated from Britain throughout the latter half of the nineteenth century ended up in South Africa as domestics. By the 1880s and 1890s, several groups united under the British Women's Emigration Association (BWEA). Their recruiting propaganda stressed the possibilities for genteel domestic service, potential marriage, civilizing the world, and promoting British values in the colonies.

The causes for female emigration lay in demographic imbalance and limited employment for women in Britain. Because of male migration to the colonies, the ratio of women to men in Great Britain increased steadily from the mid-nineteenth century, from 1042:1000 in 1851 to 1068:1000 in 1911. The notion of "surplus" women of marriageable age is, of course, ideologically determined: a patriarchal ideology that prescribed for women the roles of mother, wife, and household manager could conceive no positive outcome for single women. In addition, lower-middle-class and middle-class single women competed for the same narrow range of employment. The differential in wage levels also helped recruitment. White domestics in South Africa might earn as much in two months as their counterparts in England could earn in a year.

The colonies needed female immigrants for demographic, ideological, and employment reasons. In contrast to the belief elsewhere that European women destroyed the empire, here they were considered essential to it. The successful transplantation of British civilization and the assurance of enough white labor required large numbers of white women. Particularly in South Africa after the turn-of-the-century Anglo-Boer War, the colonial state encouraged the "surplus" women of Britain to immigrate. The rhetoric of the time combined imperial and patriarchal goals. Ellen Joyce, a BWEA pioneer, stated that "the possibility of the settler marrying his own countrywoman is of imperial as well as of family importance." Put more bluntly: "We cannot assimilate the Boers at present if at all. . . . If we cannot assimilate them we must swamp them."[9] In addition, the colonial state sought to replace African male servants with white female servants to free the former for work in the goldfields of the Transvaal.

Although many women emigrated, recruitment ultimately failed to satisfy the demand for servants. Between 1902 and 1912, approximately 1,500 white female domestics came to the Transvaal. Once there, however, the women deserted service for other occupations or for marriage. The racial ideology clearly dictated that the lowest work should be done by Africans, and employment in other typically female occupations as waitresses, clerical workers, or, to a lesser extent, factory operatives attracted emigrants after a year of domestic service. Still, although a servant's marriage represented a loss to the employer, it counted as a success for the colonial state, which sought to increase the English population. For the individual woman, marriage meant entry into a relatively privileged white society.

In the institution of domestic service in South Africa, then, we see imperial and patriarchal forces reinforcing each other. European mistresses, while also oppressed as women, had their condition meliorated by the availability of domestic servants. The mistress-servant relationship, often European women's only significant contact with indigenous people, reinforced the ideology of racial superiority. The colonial state's recruitment of white female labor was based on the patriarchal definition of domestic service as (white) women's work, the patriarchal glorification of matrimony, and the imperialist "ideal" of spreading British values and civilization. Domestic service was, for many white women in South Africa, a way to gain a share of white privilege. For African men and women, it remained, as it does today, an institution of exploitation and oppression.

FEMALE MISSIONARIES

Missionaries preceded formal rule in the colonies. They played a crucial role in dissolving and transforming the societies and cultures of the peoples with whom they interacted, linking colonized peoples to the colonizers socially and culturally. Not that missionaries worked hand in glove with colonial governments;

indeed, they often challenged colonial policies. Where colonial governments, conscious of the need to keep the peace, wished not to disturb local customs, missionaries sometimes forced discussion of such issues as clitoridectomy (the removal of all or part of the clitoris). In this sense, because they were concerned with souls and beliefs, they intruded more than European administrators or settlers into indigenous culture, combining some understanding of their converts' society with a firm commitment to European Christianity and gender norms. For all their ethnocentrism, missionaries lived among their Christian converts. This lifestyle challenged the maintenance of social boundaries and often isolated missionaries from the rest of the European community. For more sensitive missionaries, for example, Elise Kootz-Kretschmer, a Moravian missionary in German Tanganyika, living among indigenous peoples called into question their own notions of Western superiority.

While actively engaged in these cultural aspects of imperialism, female missionaries modeled an alternative role to that of wife, mother, and home-maker by pursuing careers abroad. In addition to sending missionary couples, Protestant denominations debated the wisdom of sending single women to the colonies. The experience of Miss Lilly M. de Hailes, sent to the Belgian Congo (now Zaire) by the Baptist Missionary Society (BMS) at the turn of the century, illuminates how such women negotiated their role and the tensions generated within the mission community by their independence. Never marrying, de Hailes adopted several Congolese children, thereby embracing a familiar maternal role; she challenged gender norms, however, by traveling alone. In 1930, against her will, she was ordered not to return to the field following a reassertion of the BMS's policy restricting such travel.

Although they modeled active work roles for women, as helpers and spreaders of "civilization" female missionaries nonetheless embodied conventional European notions of proper sexuality, conformed to European gender norms, and, indeed, taught European domestic ideology to their converts. Misunderstanding local practices, Dutch Missionary Society missionaries on the Indonesian island of Sumatra in the early twentieth century, for example, assumed that Karo women had low status and little power or influence. Hence they strove to "emancipate" Karo women by teaching them to be proper housekeepers by Dutch standards. Moreover, by Dutch norms, women chose between marriage and a career; Karo women, used to working in the fields and controlling the family's finances, refused to be limited in this way.

Female missionaries played a special role in sex-segregated societies such as India, where male foreign missionaries had little access to indigenous women. Female missionaries reached Indian women by offering education in the homes of prominent families for upper-caste women and in public schools for the lower castes. In Bengal, these efforts in zenana education (titled after the name for the women's section of the house) began in the 1820s. Successful conversion occurred primarily among the lower castes and widows, groups who had the most marginal positions in Hindu society. More privileged Indians correctly suspected missionaries to be interested in education largely in order to gain converts. Christian teachings and handicrafts dominated the content of early women's education. By the 1890s, the first two British female doctors arrived in India, sent as part of the Zenana Mission Movement; they added medical education to the curriculum.

The most famous British female missionary in Africa, Mary Slessor, lived for forty years in southeastern Nigeria. Her career advanced the empire perhaps more than Christianity. Slessor made few actual converts but had enormous influence among the Efik and Ibibio peoples with whom she lived. She opposed such indigenous practices as slavery, human sacrifice upon the burying of an important person, poison ordeals, and the putting to death of twins, whose birth was thought to be dangerous to the community. With the establishment of the British Niger Coast Protectorate, Slessor was appointed vice consul and district magistrate. Since she lived under the same conditions as local people, Slessor's commitment promoted a reciprocal trust and affection. Ironically, this relationship aided the extension of colonial rule, occasioned in 1901 by the military suppression of an important local oracle involved in the slave trade. At the same time that she aided imperial expansion, Slessor worked to undermine discrimination against women both locally and in Britain. Her efforts brought significant change in the lives of women among whom she lived, particularly the unfortunate mothers of inauspicious twins. At home her defense of women's rights extended to support for the role of women within mission work.

Other female missionaries came into direct conflict with the Church over women's issues. Teresa Kearney, who became Mother Kevin, arrived in Uganda in 1903 as a Franciscan nun to join the mission settlement organized by the White Fathers. As she worked establishing schools and convents in the area, Mother Kevin came to disagree with the Catholic hierarchy over the need to provide medical missionaries trained in obstetrics. The Vatican did not lift the ban on obstetrical work by religious missionaries until 1936, after years of lobbying by Mother Kevin and the decisive intervention by an influential male ally.[10]

At times, the proselytizing efforts of female missionaries encountered difficulties because of both their own notions of sexuality and the male-dominated structure of the Church. In Tanganyika in the 1920s and 1930s, women missionaries from the Anglican Universities Mission to Central Africa had less success than their male counterparts. In its efforts to Africanize the clergy, the mission created leadership positions for African men, but not for women. In addition, the male clergy created Christian versions of local male coming-of-age puberty rituals. Indigenous puberty rites for girls, however, were not so easily adapted. Local girls were prepared for sexual intercourse by manipulating and elongating their labia. Socialized to much more conservative sexual mores, the European laywomen charged with Christianizing this activity could not do justice to the form and content of the indigenous rituals. As a result, few African women converted.

Steeped in the patriarchal ideology of Victorian Christianity, European female missionaries in Africa, as in India, generally focused upon providing education for indigenous women who might become appropriate wives for elite, Westernized local men, especially clergy. The Homecraft Village School, established in southern Rhodesia (now Zimbabwe) in 1943, clearly was organized for just this purpose. The potential minister's wife needed to adopt new values modeled on European gender roles: self-reliance and independence as distinct from loyalty to the extended family, monogamy, physical and social mobility, familiarity with a "modern" home, and the use of money. Similarly, Belgian Catholic missionaries in the Congo and Ruanda-Urundi (now Rwanda and Burundi) established *foyer sociaux* (social homes) to train African women in Western domesticity, particularly after World War II. Such training, including instruction in preparing cauliflower with cream sauce and participating in most-beautiful-house contests, contributed to the creation of an African elite.

Even though they furthered the expansion of Western culture and at times directly aided the colonial administration, on the whole missionaries questioned the imperial agenda more than they questioned Victorian gender norms. In their role as self-appointed (or government-appointed) representatives of the "natives," missionaries often criticized imperial officials and such practices as forced labor. On the other hand, although female missionaries performed serious work that was acknowledged by their religious community, mission structures rarely accorded women positions of authority over males and females. In addition, the content of their teachings, even when spiritual equality was stressed, reproduced an ideal of female domesticity imported from Europe. Even the reforms they proposed specifically to aid women, most notably the elimination of polygyny, rarely came from a feminist impulse. More often these reforms reflected missionary desires to establish Christian families along a European model.

The activities of missionaries raise fundamental questions about the morality of externally inducing social change and about the relationship of "humanitarian" work to imperialism. The same issues appear with regard to anthropologists and reformers, discussed in the next section. On the one hand, such humanitarian efforts were part of the process of imperialism, the transformation of indigenous societies in the interest of European economies and politics. Undoubtedly, imperialism distorted the development and history of indigenous peoples; earlier European intervention had even significantly intensified some of the evils that Europeans later sought to stamp out, for example, slavery and the slave trade. Yet indigenous societies generated their own forms of oppression. Women suffered from such indigenous practices as *sati* (the burning of a Hindu widow on her husband's funeral pyre) in India and clitoridectomy or infibulation (the sewing up of the vulva to maintain virginity or chastity) in parts of Africa. At times, European women and men attempted to intervene in these situations or in the relationship between the colonial government and indigenous peoples; such people saw themselves, with more or less arrogance, as helping local people. In many cases, European intervention, combined with local efforts at change, resulted in concrete improvements for women: fewer women were burned or had their genitals cut. At the same time, these and other reforms, like women's education, often caused indigenous people to identify more closely with Western culture. Thus the process of externally induced reform itself can be seen as part of cultural imperialism. Carried out, as they were, in the absence of a critique of colonialism, such reforms mistakenly identified women's problems as the result only of indigenous patriarchal relations, rather than as the result of the interaction of these relations with colonial exploitation and gender oppression.

TRAVELERS

Along with missionary accounts, travel narratives played a major role in constructing for an audience "back home" a picture of the empires of the European powers. From 1870 on, increasing numbers of women traveled abroad to remote places. Mostly middle-aged, some were wealthy, like Marianne North, who painted flora in Latin America, the United States, Asia, and Africa. The wealth of Alexandrine Tinne, a Dutch heiress who traveled up the Nile and in the western Sudan, proved her downfall: plundering Tuareg nomads killed her. Some travel writers argued in support of European presence, as did Isabella Bird, writing about British Malaya in *The Golden Chersonese and the Way Thither* (1883); others criticized it, as did Bird's competitor Emily Innes in *The Golden Chersonese with the Gilding Off* (1885). Some married, as did Florence Baker, who accompanied her illustrious husband Samuel up the Nile River. Others, like North, missionary and traveler Mary Slessor, and Mary Kingsley, remained single.

Kingsley grew up in a family of learned men; nonetheless, she had to educate herself. She stayed at home as a dutiful daughter until 1892. Then, released by her parents' death, she traveled to West Africa. In *Travels in West Africa* and *West African Studies*, Kingsley wrote about fish and African religion. She lobbied on behalf of British traders and in opposition to activities of missionaries and colonial administrators. Challenging female gender roles in some ways, Kingsley nonetheless maintained conventional gender notions in others. For example, on one rainy trek, she insisted on walking behind her male companion because the black bootlace with which she had laced her corset would be visible through her sopping wet blouse. She opposed women's suffrage and the admission of women such as herself to scientific societies. She died in South Africa in 1900, nursing Boer prisoners of war during the Anglo-Boer War.

The influence of some travel writers extends to the present, as their works have undergone various incarnations over the years. Anna Leonowens, who may have been Welsh or may have been the offspring of a British sergeant in the Indian army and a mixed-race mother, exemplifies how a person in the outposts of empire might successfully claim British identity. She traveled to Siam (now Thailand) in 1862 to teach the royal women and children of King

Mongkut. After returning to England, she lectured and published two accounts, *The English Governess at the Siamese Court* (1870) and *Romance of the
Harem* (1872). Her biography, *Anna and the King of Siam* (1927) by Margaret
Landon, became the basis for the Broadway musical *The King and I* (1951),
whose images continue to influence American notions about Thailand.

If some travel writers sought in the empire opportunities closed off back
home by rigid gender roles, and others succeeded in advancing claims to
European identity, still others sought "an antidote to mental anguish, social
malaise, or personal angst, a haven whose facade of social liberation was
underwritten by colonial subjugation."[11] Isabelle Eberhardt, a Russian citizen
of illegitimate though aristocratic Armenian and German descent, traveled to
the Algerian desert at the turn of the century. There she dressed in male Arab
clothing, married a Muslim, took numerous indigenous sexual partners, and
adopted as a spiritual mentor a female Muslim saint and mystic, in the
process transgressing multiple cultural and gender norms.

FEMALE ETHNOGRAPHERS AND ANTHROPOLOGISTS

With the establishment of a foreign mission by a church organization or the
establishment of colonial rule by a European government came the need to
understand the peoples and societies of Africa and Asia. As missionaries or as
wives of colonial officers, women at times became ethnographers, studying
systematically the mores and institutions of an indigenous group, or, more
particularly, of the women of such a group. As a discipline, anthropology in
theory sought to understand a society on its own terms. In practice, particularly in Africa beginning in the interwar period, anthropologists worked
closely with administrators to promote change.

In the first quarter of the twentieth century, the interest in having a
woman's perspective came from two sources. First, the European feminist
challenge to political and social practices prompted intellectual questioning
as well. Writing in the midst of the pre–World War I suffrage struggle in
Britain, D. Amaury Talbot, author of *Women's Mysteries of a Primitive People;
The Ibibios of Southern Nigeria* (1915), saw her study as a way of understanding
changes in women's position. Without aligning herself with the feminist
movement, she notes its challenge to the status quo. Second, anthropology's
claim to view society as a whole made more likely the systematic study of
women's roles. Since local custom generally denied male anthropologists
access to local women, female ethnographers performed essential functions
within the discipline.

The male bias of much anthropological work gives evidence that anthropology did not escape the patriarchal perspectives of the broader European
society. Some female anthropologists who should have become prominent
did not. Daisy Bates, who spent fifty years among Australian aborigines, had
her material appropriated by a famous male colleague, A. Radcliffe-Brown.[12]

Other women aided their husbands' research: the classic works of the period by male anthropologists acknowledge their wives' contribution only in the preface, not on the title page.

Denise Paulme and Deborah Lifchitz were among the first cohort of female professional anthropologists to study French West Africa in the 1930s. Paulme's research resulted in her editing one of the first collections of scholarly articles about African women: *Women of Tropical Africa* (1960).

Some anthropologists combined a concern for social problems with an interest in the study of indigenous women. Audrey Richards produced a number of basic ethnographic accounts of indigenous people in present-day Zambia, one of which, *Chisungu* (1956), ranks among the best studies of female life cycle rituals. Nonetheless, an assessment of her career involves coming to terms with a radical critique of anthropology itself. "If she had greater faith than is common nowadays in the will and the power of governments given the right information to solve these problems [arising from social change]," states her memorialist, "she was by no means their unwitting tool." Yet an African critic less charitably attacks her work: "The neogenocidal implications of the involuntary migration of . . . Bemba males to European mines to earn money for colonial taxes are not considered in her classic study of the deterioration of Bemba nutrition (1939)."[13]

Emerging as a field in the late nineteenth century, anthropology represented a step beyond the bald ethnocentrism of unexamined imperialism. Colonial administrators suspected it to be a leftist ideology because it fostered an identification with indigenous peoples. Indeed, many anthropologists empathized with the plight of colonized peoples and sought to ameliorate their conditions. However, they rarely saw colonialism itself as the root of the problems people faced. Because anthropological analyses aided in the administration, rather than the liberation, of colonized peoples, the discipline became scorned in newly independent Africa.

Anthropology, and its applied form colonial administration, provided exciting work and meaningful careers for a number of women of Paulme's and Richard's generation. Yet gender discrimination limited even these women's opportunities. Dame Margery Perham, as influential as any man in the field of colonial administration, would undoubtedly have been appointed a colonial governor had she been a man. As a woman she served, in her travels in the colonies and in her official training seminars for the Colonial Service, as consultant and guide for male administrators: "a builder of empire builders."[14]

EUROPEAN REFORMERS

If any women can be said to have threatened imperial rule, it is the reformers, such as Annie Besant, who was imprisoned for supporting Indian nationalism. Others participated in less radical reform efforts that at least softened the effects of colonialism and breached the social boundaries that colonialism erected between ruler and ruled. Yet even in these efforts, women reformers could not escape the imperial context; indeed, they often drew upon it to strengthen their arguments for change back in Europe. Feminist reformers' activity in two arenas in particular illustrates the linkage between empire and feminism: the campaign to repeal the Contagious Diseases Act in India, and suffrage in Britain and France.

British and French feminists constructed images of indigenous women as suffering, in need of support from their European sisters. In so doing, they sometimes challenged and sometimes shared the positions taken by colonial administrations. For example, European colonial powers and feminists alike frequently identified the status of indigenous women as a measure of civilization in order to justify European domination as the culturally superior force. In finding indigenous women oppressed by local custom, such ideologies conveniently ignored, for example, the fact that Islamic law allowed married women rights to own property that European women still lacked, or that in matrilineal Nayar society in India women exercised considerable personal, economic, and sexual autonomy unavailable to most European women.

Josephine Butler came to prominence for her campaign from 1869 to 1886 against the Contagious Diseases Acts (CDA) in Britain. Applicable both there and in the colonies, the CDA authorized the detaining and forcible medical examination of prostitutes in the interest of containing venereal disease. Butler and her followers in the Ladies National Association (LNA) objected to the acts as both an infringement on personal liberty and as ineffective in stopping venereal disease. Following the successful campaign in Britain, CDA repeal work in India from 1886 to 1915 provided the members of the LNA with a new arena for their prodigious energies and organization. Butler's representations of Indian women to LNA audiences back in Britain articulated an imperial feminism, in which British women spoke on behalf of indigenous women but also in the interest of maintaining the empire, as she criticized the enforcement of the CDA by the colonial government there. Speaking in 1888, Butler made clear both positions: "We, as women, desire to protest in the strongest and most solemn manner possible against the wrong done to our sisters and fellow subjects in India. At the same time we venture to warn you of the danger to our Indian rule. . . . Nothing so surely produces a spirit of rebellion as trampling on the womanhood of a subject race by its conquerors."[15]

Rather than undermining the colonial enterprise, such reform activities on behalf of indigenous women served to legitimate European feminists' claims to full imperial citizenship, including the vote. In the words of the editor of the British suffrage journal *Common Cause*, "The responsibilities of Empire rest on women as well as men. If it were only for the sake of India, women here in Great Britain would be bound to demand the vote."[16] British women's periodicals routinely carried news of the pitiable state of indigenous women suffering under customary practices that, readers were exhorted, the colonial governments should move to outlaw and eradicate.

French suffragist Hubertine Auclert similarly championed the cause of "our Muslim sisters," employing a familial metaphor while nonetheless envisioning a hierarchical relationship. A radical, Auclert founded the first French suffragist newspaper *La Citoyenne*. Living in Algeria, she published *Les femmes arabes en Algerie* [Arab Women in Algeria] (1900), in which she argued a parallel between sexism against women and racism toward colonial subjects. Furthermore, she exposed how French colonialism had contributed to the debasement of Algerian women, as French colonial administrators and indigenous men conspired to allow the sexual exploitation of Arab women and limitations on their education. Much like British suffragists, she saw the enfranchisement of French (and Arab) women as central to France's being able legitimately to rule Algeria as a culturally superior nation: French women would not allow the degradation of their Muslim "sisters," and, given the sex segregation of Muslim society, only women could have the access to indigenous women necessary to prepare them for assimilation to French culture.

Other European women articulated more fundamental criticisms of the imperial enterprise. Olive Schreiner, a child of missionary parents, was active both as a feminist and as a critic of British imperialism. She denounced British treatment of the Boers in turn-of-the-century South Africa and, later, British involvement in World War I. As political unification of the English and Boers proceeded following the Anglo-Boer War, she moved away from the racial attitudes of most whites to advocate suffrage for Africans, albeit limited suffrage. Although Schreiner's attitude toward Africans was patronizing, she saw the need for white and African workers to unite in the class struggle, which she believed would replace the English-Boer conflict. An ardent feminist, she nonetheless resigned from the Women's Enfranchisement League when, in the first decade of this century, it advocated the vote for white women only. However, her feminism subsequently found its expression basically in terms of white women's issues and lives, not those of African women, whose needs and political expressions differed drastically from her own. Arousing little response among South African white women, she leaned toward intellectual allies in Britain. The culmination of years of Schreiner's thinking on the woman question, *Woman and Labour* (1911), proved to be one of the influential feminist works of the early twentieth century.

Living most of her adult life in India, Margaret Cousins devoted her life to the causes of Indian national independence and women's rights. She and her husband came to India during World War I. A committed feminist, Cousins in 1927 brought together the All-India Women's Conference, originally an organization to discuss Indian women's educational needs. She became its president in 1936. Imprisoned for a year for nationalist activity, Cousins increasingly withdrew from direct involvement, instead entrusting leadership to Indian women.

The 1940s and 1950s mark a turning point in both the involvement of European women in African women's issues and the formation of African women's organizations modeled after European voluntary associations. As World War II hastened the demise of the empire, two important changes occurred within the British Colonial Service. First, the colonial mission shifted to an emphasis on trusteeship and development. In addition, after agitation by British feminists, the Colonial Office in 1938 dropped its ban on admitting women and, in the late 1940s, the Colonial Service significantly increased its recruitment of women as education and social welfare officers. It is likely that both the ideological change and the presence of female development officers spurred the efforts of European women in the colonies to help African women.

In Kenya such efforts supported both the imperial mission and European gender norms. Administrators' wives and female white settlers organized classes in sewing and home crafts for African women in rural areas in the period following World War II. Since African women are farmers, they would have benefited more from agricultural extension services. Whether female white settlers were unable to provide help on agricultural topics or were merely blind to the need for such help because of European gender ideology, African women remained without the kind of assistance they needed most. Nonetheless, the groups prospered. By 1951, existing "Women's Institutes" had become the model for the development of Maendeleo ya Wanawake (Women's Progress), now a major national women's organization. Using European volunteers, the Department of Community Development encouraged the growth of Maendeleo ya Wanawake. By the mid-1950s, the Kikuyu insurrection known commonly as Mau Mau had forced settlers and administrators alike to entertain the notion of independent majority rule for Kenya. Administrators viewed the women's clubs as a key to luring some Kikuyu women away from supporting the guerillas.

The ethnocentrism and maternalism of reformers at the center of the empire matched that of colonial women. An example is the controversy that developed in the 1920s in Kenya over the operation of clitoridectomy performed on Kikuyu girls. The dispute, which led to feminist lobbying efforts in Britain, illustrates the presence of indigenous practices harmful to women, European paternalism on behalf of indigenous women, and European blindness to the colonial political and cultural context. Significantly, within the British community, the controversy pitted local male administrators known for their political sympathy to Africans (who advocated allowing a hygienic form of the operation) against British female feminists without direct experience in Africa (who called for its elimination), with the missionary community falling at various points in between.

Missionaries and their converts among the Kikuyu raised medical objections to clitoridectomy. It was painful; unhygienic operations led to infection; the resulting scar tissue made childbirth difficult. The controversy split the Kikuyu community. Some church elders attacked clitoridectomy. Other Kikuyu leaders denounced mission intervention as a form of cultural imperialism. Jomo Kenyatta, later the first president of an independent Kenya, wrote a defense of the operation in *Facing Mount Kenya* (1938), itself an anticolonialist landmark as the first ethnographic study done by an African scholar.

While the controversy raged among Africans and Europeans in Kenya, British women pressured for parliamentary investigations. The Duchess of Atholl, a member of Parliament with missionary friends, joined Eleanor Rathbone and two nonmembers in conducting investigations based on testimony from medical experts, missionaries, and others, including Kenyatta. The group ultimately did not succeed in prohibiting the operation through legislation.

Eleanor Rathbone lobbied in London on behalf of Indian women as well. However, Indian spokeswomen generally did not appreciate Rathbone's role. In 1918 Rathbone became president of the moderate suffrage organization National Union of Societies for Equal Citizenship (NUSEC). In 1927 she pressed NUSEC to work for the improvement of Indian women's status, notably around the issues of women's suffrage and raising the legal age for marriage. She especially blamed the low status of Indian women on the British government for its refusal to intervene in indigenous customs that hurt women. However, her efforts on their behalf met resistance from female Indian leaders who shared many of her goals but found her to be ignorant of the realities of Indian women's lives. She had visited India only once and derived much of her knowledge from a negative and controversial exposé written by an American woman. Although many appreciated Rathbone's concern, by the 1920s Indian women were prepared to speak for themselves. Moreover, they resented the reinforcement of imperial authority that Rathbone's activity represented. Finally, as nationalists, they disagreed with her strategically, placing greater importance on the goal of Indian independence over short-term gains on women's issues.

CONCLUSION

The women described here all lived through a period of European hegemony—economic, political, and ideological—over most of the world. They operated within institutions, cultural patterns, and personal relationships that were profoundly shaped by notions of male superiority and the reality of male power over females. For all their differences, we can discern the ways in which imperialism and male dominance shaped common patterns in their lives. Their participation in the colonial process brought them benefits. Being white generally meant access to land, a higher standard of living, or the protection of the colonial government. Many came to the colonies seeking jobs that were unavailable back home. The colonial enterprise itself created careers for some as anthropologists and members of the Colonial Service. The vast majority of these women failed to develop a full critique of imperialism, either of its political and economic facets or of the racist and paternalist ideology behind the notion of the "white man's burden." African and Asian women needed their own indigenous institutions; European women could not create these, although they served as midwives to several.

If imperialism gave them benefits as Europeans, male dominance limited their options as women. For the most part, the sexual division of labor that shaped their lives in Britain governed their activities in the colonies. The roles of mother and wife dominated most women's lives. Those who worked outside the home took "female" jobs. Indeed, in the public sphere, only unusual women participated in overtly political activities; the rest rarely ventured past providing charity, a task typical of females in socially superior positions.

In one sense, European women's marginal status within a male-dominated colonial society and structure provided an opportunity. People outside the dominant culture have a different perspective that derives from their different experience and position within the social structure. Perhaps European women's marginal position within the dominant colonial society enabled them to see aspects of imperialism differently. European women frequently saw the needs of indigenous women where male administrators were blind to them. Some chose to use their skills, enhanced power, and status as members of the colonizing society on behalf of indigenous people. In so doing, they contributed, if not always intentionally, to the dismantling of the empire.

In the past decades, the study of imperialism has been transformed, as historians have come to view the European countries and their empires from a more dynamic and mutually interactive perspective. The experience of empire is seen not just as Europeans, largely men, acting upon indigenous peoples; instead, the empires are seen as influencing the colonizers. Arguing in this vein, we see the experiences of European women, too, in a new way. The existence of colonized peoples, especially indigenous women, helped construct European women's identities: both in the mother country and in the empire, many better understood who they were in contrast to who they were not. Moreover, a substantial part of Western Europeans' national identities in the nineteenth and twentieth centuries revolved around their roles as imperial powers. Women contributed to the development of this national imperial identity. In their writings about the indigenous people and colonial society, missionaries, ethnographers, settlers, administrators' wives, and reformers all helped shape European notions about their respective nations' empires and thus about the imperial enterprise.

NOTES

1. Although I use the term *European* to indicate nationality and "racial" identity, it is important to underscore its fluidity and ambiguity. Some women successfully asserted claims to European status that are now questioned by scholars, such as Anna Leonowens, who served as governess to the King of Siam in the nineteenth century.

2. Percival Spear, *The Nabobs*, Oxford University Press, London, 1963, p. 140.
3. L. H. Gann and Peter Duignan, *The Rulers of British Africa, 1870–1914*, Stanford University Press, Stanford, 1978, pp. 241–242.
4. Ann L. Stoler, "Making Empire Respectable: The Politics of Race and Sexual Morality in 20th-Century Colonial Cultures," *American Ethnologist* 16, no. 4 (November 1989), pp. 651, 652.
5. Sylvia Leith-Ross, *Stepping-Stones: Memoirs of Colonial Nigeria, 1907–1960* Peter Owen, London and Boston, 1983, p. 69.
6. Laura Boyle, *Diary of a Colonial Officer's Wife*, Alden Press, Oxford, 1968, p. 156.
7. Quoted in William Cohen, *Rulers of Empire: The French Colonial Service in Africa*, Hoover Institution Press, Stanford, 1971, p. 122.
8. Cited and quoted in Catherine Barnes Stevensen, *Victorian Women Travel Writers in Africa*, Twayne Publishers, Boston, 1982, pp. 16–17.
9. BWEA Annual Report 1900, p. 12, and *The Saturday Review* (September 20, 1902), both cited in Jean Jacques Van Helten and Keith Williams, "'The Crying Need of South Africa': The Emigration of Single British Women to the Transvaal, 1901–10," *Journal of Southern African Studies* 10, no. 1 (1983), pp. 22–23.
10. Caroline Oliver, *Western Women in Colonial Africa*, Greenwood Press, Westport, Conn., 1982, pp. 145–188.
11. Julia Clancy-Smith, "The 'Passionate Nomad' Reconsidered: A European Woman in L'Algerie francaise (Isabelle Eberhardt, 1877–1904)," in *Western Women and Imperialism*, ed. Nupur Chaudhuri and Margaret Strobel, Indiana University Press, Bloomington 1992, p. 64.
12. Ruby Rorhlich-Leavitt, Barbara Sykes, and Elizabeth Rutherford, "Aboriginal Woman: Male and Female Anthropological Perspectives," in *Toward an Anthropology of Women*, ed. Rayna R. Rapp, Monthly Review Press, New York, 1975, pp. 124–126.
13. J. S. La Fontaine, "Audrey Isabel Richards, 1899–1984," *Africa* 55, no. 2 (1985), p. 201; Omafume E Onoge, "The Counterrevolutionary Tradition in African Studies: The Case of Applied Anthropology," in *The Politics of Anthropology: From Colonialism and Sexism Toward a View from Below*, ed. Gerrit Huizer and Bruce Mannheim, Mouton, The Hague, 1979, p. S3.
14. A. H. M. Kirk-Greene, "Margery Perham and Colonial Administration: A Direct Influence on Indirect Rule," in *Oxford and the Idea of Commonwealth*, ed. D. K. Fieldhouse, Croom Helm, London, 1982, p. 139.
15. Antoinette Burton, *Burdens of History: British Feminists, Indian Women, and Imperial Culture, 1865–1915* University of North Carolina Press, Chapel Hill, 1994, p. 148.
16. *Ibid.*, p. 172, citing May 1913 issue.

SUGGESTIONS FOR FURTHER READING

The following are in addition to sources cited in the notes. Several works span various of the categories below. These include Margaret Strobel, *European Women and the Second British Empire* (Bloomington, Indiana University Press, 1991); Nupur Chaudhuri and Margaret Strobel, *Western Women and Imperialism: Complicity and Resistance* (Bloomington, Indiana University Press, 1992); Kumari Jayawardena, *The White Woman's*

Other Burden: Western Women and South Asia During British Colonial Rule (New York: Routledge, 1995); Frances Gouda and Julia Clancy-Smith, *Domesticating the Empire: Languages of Race, Gender, and Family Life in French and Dutch Colonialism, 1830–1962* (University of Virginia Press, 1998); and Y. Knibiehler and R. Goutalier, *La femme au temps des colonies* (Paris: Stock, 1985).

The Myth of the Destructive Female: Sexuality, Ritual, and Home

See Claudia Knapman, *White Women in Fiji, 1835–1930: The Ruin of Empire?* (Sydney: Allen and Unwin, 1986); Janice N. Brownfoot, "Memsahibs in Colonial Malaya: A Study of European Wives in a British Colony and Protectorate 1900–1940," in *The Incorporated Wife*, ed. Hilary Callan and Shirley Ardener (London: Croom Helm, 1984), pp. 186–187; and James Boutilier, "European Women in the Solomon Islands, 1900–1942: Accommodation and Change on the Pacific Frontier," in *Rethinking Women's Roles: Perspectives from the Pacific*, ed. Denise O'Brien and Sharon W. Tiffany (Berkeley: University of California Press, 1984), pp. 173–200.

On sexual relations, concubinage, interracial unions, and social boundaries, see various essays in Gouda and Clancy-Smith, cited above; Kenneth Ballhatchet, *Race, Sex, and Class Under the Raj: Imperial Attitude and Politics and Their Critics, 1793–1905* (New York: St. Martin's Press, 1980); Amirah Inglis, *The White Woman's Protection Ordinance: Sexual Anxiety and Politics in Papua* (London: Sussex University Press, 1975); Charles Van Onselen, "The Witches of Suburbia," in *Studies in the Social and Economic History of the Witwatersrand, 1886–1914*, Vol. 2:, *New Nineveh* (London: Longman, 1982), pp. 1–73; and Ann L. Stoler, *Race and the Education of Desire* (Durham, N.C.: Duke University Press, 1995).

Biographies and autobiographies provide information on life in the colonies. See bibliography in Strobel, *European Women*, cited above, and Violet Powell, *Flora Annie Steel, Novelist of India* (London: Heinemann, 1981); Judith Thurman, *Isak Dinesen* (New York: St. Martin's Press, 1982); Ruth First and Ann Scott, *Olive Schreiner* (New York: Schocken, 1980); and Susan R. Horton, *Difficult Women, Artful Lives: Olive Schreiner and Isak Dinesen, In and Out of Africa* (Baltimore, Md.: The Johns Hopkins Press, 1995).

For discussions of gendered colonial society and culture, manners and mores, and the political functions of pomp and ceremony, see Hilary Callan, "Introduction," in Callan and Ardener, cited above, pp. 1–26; Helen Callaway, *Gender, Culture, and Empire: European Women in Colonial Nigeria* (Urbana: University of Illinois Press, 1987); and Catherine Hall, *White, Male, and Middle-Class: Explorations in Feminism and History* (New York: Routledge, 1992). For household interactions and memsahibs' lives, see Nupur Chaudhuri, "Memsahibs and Their Servants in Nineteenth-Century India," *Women's History Review* 3, no. 4 (1994), pp. 549–562; Nupur Chaudhuri, "Memsahibs and Motherhood in Nineteenth-Century Colonial India," *Victorian Studies* 31 (1988), pp. 517–536; and Elsbeth Locher-Scholten, "So Close and Yet So Far: The Ambivalence of Dutch Colonial Rhetoric on Javanese Servants in Indonesia, 1900–1942," in Gouda and Clancy-Smith (cited above).

Travelers

See Mary Louise Pratt, *Imperial Eyes: Travel Writing and Transculturation* (New York: Routledge, 1992); Dea Birkett, *Victorian Lady Explorers* (New York: Basil Blackwell, 1989); Susan Morgan, *Place Matters: Gendered Geography in Victorian Women's Travel Books About Southeast Asia* (New Brunswick, N.J.: Rutgers University Press, 1996); and Kathleen Frank, *A Voyager Out: The Life of Mary Kingsley* (Boston: Houghton Mifflin, 1986).

Job Seekers

See James A. Hammerton's *Emigrant Gentlewomen; Genteel Poverty and Female Emigration, 1830–1919* (London: Croom Helm, 1979); and Van Onselen, cited above.

Missionaries, Anthropologists, and Reformers

For missionaries, see Meredith Borthwick, *The Changing Role of Women in Bengal, 1849–1905* (Princeton: Princeton University Press, 1984); Charles W. Forman, "'Sing to the Lord a New Song': Women in the Churches of Oceania," in O'Brien and Tiffany, cited above, pp. 153–172; Marcia Wright, *German Missions in Tanganyika, 1891–1914: Lutherans and Moravians in the Southern Highlands* (London: Oxford University Press, 1971); Nancy Rose Hunt, "'Single Ladies on the Congo': Protestant Missionary Tensions and Voices," *Women's Studies International Forum* 13, no. 4 (1990), pp. 395–403; and Rita Smith Kipp, "Emancipating Each Other: Dutch Colonial Missionaries' Encounter with Karo Women in Sumatra, 1900–1942," in Gouda and Clancy-Smith, (cited above).

On domesticity, see Nancy Rose Hunt, "Domesticity and Colonialism in Belgian Africa: Usumbura's Foyer Social, 1946–1960," *Signs* 15, no. 3 (1990), pp. 447–474; and Karen Tranberg Hansen, ed., *African Encounters with Domesticity* (New Brunswick, N.J.: Rutgers University Press, 1992).

For anthropology, see Margery Perham's own *African Apprenticeship: An Autobiographical Journey in Southern Africa 1929* (New York: Africana Publishing Company, 1974). Henrietta L. Moore and Megan Vaughan, *Cutting Down Trees: Gender, Nutrition, and Agricultural Change in the Northern Province of Zambia, 1890–1990* (Portsmouth, N.H.: Heinemann, 1994) discusses Audrey Richards's work and the relationship of anthropology to colonialism. Denise Paulme's work is featured in *Cahiers d'etudes Africaines* 17, n. 1 (1977).

For reformers in India, see Nancy L. Paxton, "Complicity and Resistance in the Writings of Flora Annie Steel and Annie Besant," in Chaudhuri and Strobel, cited above, pp. 158–176; various works by Barbara N. Ramusack, "Catalysts or Helpers? British Feminists, Indian Women's Rights, and Indian Independence," in *The Extended Family: Women and Political Participation in India and Pakistan*, ed. Gail Minault (Columbia, Mo.: South Asia Books, 1981), pp. 109–115; "Women's Organizations and Social Change: The Age-of-Marriage Issue in India," in *Women and World Change: Equity Issues in Development*, ed. Naomi Black and Ann Baker Cotrell (Beverly Hills, Calif.: Sage Publications, 1981), pp. 198–216; and Barbara N. Ramusack, "Cultural

Missionaries, Maternal Feminists, Feminist Allies: British Women Activists in India, 1865–1945," in Chaudhuri and Strobel, cited above, pp. 119–135. See also Antoinette Burton (for Josephine Butler), *Burdens of History: British Feminists, Indian Women, and Imperial Culture, 1865–1915* (Chapel Hill: University of North Carolina Press, 1994); and Mary D. Stocks, *Eleanor Rathbone: A Biography* (London: Victor Gollancs, 1949).

For reformers in Africa, see Julia Clancy-Smith, "Islam, Gender, and Identities in the Making of French Algeria, 1830–1962," in Gouda and Clancy-Smith, (cited above). Deborah Kirkwood, "Settler Wives in Rhodesia: A Case Study," in Callan and Ardener, cited above, pp. 143–164; Audrey Wipper, "The Maendeleo ya Wanawake Movement in the Colonial Period: The Canadian Connection, Mau Mau, Embroidery and Agriculture," *Rural Africana*, no. 29 (Winter 1975–76), pp. 195–214; and Jocelyn Murray, "The Church Missionary Society and the 'Female Circumcision' Issue in Kenya," *Journal of Religion in Africa*, 8, no. 2 (1976), pp. 92–104.

Women's adult literacy class.   SOVFOTO.

15

Women and the Revolutionary Process in Russia

Richard Stites

The history of women in tsarist Russia and the Soviet Union defies generalization. Dramatic contrasts in education and class, combined with the sudden transformation from reactionary monarchy to Communist dictatorship, placed women in diverse situations. For the fortunate daughters of wealthy and noble families under tsarist rule, foreign study offered an escape. But several young women used their privilege to fight for a just society. Unlike the middle-class women discussed by Karen Offen or the Socialist women described by Charles Sowerwine, Russian women had no access to legitimate reformist organizations. Many chose exile or clandestine activities. A few became terrorists. Richard Stites depicts the shock of upheaval in the wake of the 1917 October Revolution. Suddenly everything seemed possible: fair wages, birth control, divorce reform, communal child rearing, and sexual freedom. However, such emancipatory reforms, difficult even in a stable society, proved impossible in a nation facing economic collapse, political turmoil, and civil war. Under Stalin, rapid and forced industrialization left no leeway for social experiments; and World War II brought renewed pressure on women to work in war production and at the same time bear many children to compensate for the devastating loss of life. For the postwar years, Stites draws a complex balance sheet, weighing solid gains for women in wages, education, and family support against early utopian expectations and against women's achievements in other Western nations.

By the middle of the nineteenth century, the Russian Empire, out of which arose an extraordinary range of women's movements, was by most measures a backward country—sprawling in territory, economically primitive, and militarily inferior to the major industrial powers of the West. St. Petersburg, the capital of this immense state, was a Westernized city housing an antiquated autocracy in which the emperor-tsar held sway over the land with the aid of a swollen and occasionally brutal bureaucracy. A tiny portion of the population—mostly from the gentry, or nobility—constituted the educated elite, who dressed like Europeans and spoke foreign languages. The vast majority of the people lived on the land as serfs—unfree peasants—or as servants of the gentry and the state.

When the winds of economic and political change, whipped up in Europe by industrialization and the French Revolution, began to blow over Russia, small groups of alienated members of the gentry class conspired or agitated for a variety of reforms and outright revolutionary transformations. When the autocracy decided to modernize society by abolishing serfdom and launching other reforms in the 1860s, these tiny currents swelled into a big stream of opposition and social rebellion. Women's movements are often born in the midst of general crises or large-scale historical changes. And so it was in Russia that in the 1860s, feminist, nihilist, and radical women appeared on the historical stage, beginning a continuous movement for liberation that lasted down to 1917. How did this happen?

STATE AND SOCIETY

Russian society before 1917 was a world of patriarchal power, deferential ritual, clear authority patterns, and visible hierarchy with stratified social classes or estates. At the pinnacle of the state, the tsar-emperor (called Little Father of the common folk), considered Russia a family estate or patrimony and his subjects children—virtuous, obedient, and loyal. The imperial bureaucratic order of ranks, chanceries, uniforms, and rigidly ordered parades constituted a visual celebration of authoritarianism. To subjects of all classes of the empire, every official building—with its geography of guarded entrances, pass booths, waiting areas, and office gates—represented authority and inequality. In the rural outback, far from the capital and the towns, a simpler absolutism prevailed in the village cabins, where the male head of household wielded domestic power that contrasted sharply with the more or less egalitarian land distribution customs of the village community. The Russian Orthodox church reinforced values of subordination at every level of its liturgical idiom, its symbols, its organization, and its political ethos of support for the conservative order. The women dwelling within this authoritarian world felt the additional weight of male power and endured the sexual division of labor and open inequality between the sexes.

A universalizing doctrine of equality for women is the main focus of this essay. That notion, like most other ideas of social reform, originated with the intelligentsia. But far outside that mental realm, specific forms of resistance to patriarchal power were constantly at work. For example, peasant women resisted oppression—real or perceived—in a variety of ways. On the rare occasions of mass protest in the village against lord or state, female members of the community often stood in the front of the crowds to deter the forces of order from using violence—and sometimes it worked. More often, women employed the "weapons of the weak" against brutalizing husbands or persecuting neighbors. Arson, spouse murder, and accusations of witchcraft or satanism—usually against other females—dotted the records of local courts.[1]

RADICAL WOMEN AND FEMINISTS, 1855–1881

The Russian intelligentsia, which emerged out of the educated gentry class in the early nineteenth century, produced a small but influential core of rebellion against the authoritarian, patriarchal culture. Perceived family "despotism," an archaic political order, serfdom, and the inequality that reigned everywhere inspired the psychological revolt of an entire generation of young people in the 1860s. Young women of the educated classes, heretofore excluded from public life, joined forces with men to mutiny against society. Friend and foe alike called the revolt "nihilism"—a negation of old ways, especially those that demanded obedience and conformity. Nihilist men accepted women as equals, and together they created a symbolic and behavioral counterculture evidenced by rude manners, disrespect for conventions, residential communes for both sexes, common law marriages, generational anger, cultural iconoclasm, and rebellious forms of dress and personal appearance. Nihilism was an unofficial slap in the face to official authority.

Nihilism went beyond negation, however. In the hands of popularizers and shapers of the nihilist outlook such as the radical journalist Nicholas Chernyshevsky, it represented training for the future. In a spectacularly successful novel, *What Is to Be Done?*—written in prison in 1862—Chernyshevsky outlined a rebellious, rational, and nondeferential personality that would change Russia; described a utopian socialist future; and made the emancipation of women the central metaphor of all struggles for freedom. The novel was read as more than just a manifesto of its time. For decades it signaled the power of utopian revolutionary thought in Russia and women's role in it. As did the French utopian socialist Charles Fourier, Chernyshevsky made women's equality central to his socialist vision; provided a concrete plan of labor, life, and residential space in his commune of the future; and granted sexuality a significant place in the cycle of work, love, and rest. Women disciples were genuinely empowered by Chernyshevsky's novel, which pointed the way to stature and dignity. "I want to be independent," exclaims the heroine, "and live in my own way."[2] For some women, professing nihilism brought growth in personal freedom through social rebellion without leading them to revolution. These *nigilistki* (female nihilists) of the 1860s became notorious in society for their short hair, dark glasses, and mannish clothes and manners.

For other rebels, the personal merged with the political, in Barbara Engel's phrase.[3] While rejecting organized feminism, radical women passed through an important phase of women's consciousness that enabled them to connect problems of personal, sexual, or family oppression with the perceived generalized oppression of the regime. In the course of the 1860s, these dedicated themselves to conspiracy and revolutionary work. The Russian radicals of the 1860s and 1870s—loosely known as Populists—fought to overthrow the tsarist autocracy, introduce popular self-government, and establish some form of agrarian socialism on the land. An exceptionally large radical movement in nineteenth-century European history, Populism attracted thousands of young people of the educated classes who dedicated their lives and often gave their freedom on behalf of liberating the people. Their vision of the future was radiant and their standard of personal morality—with some exceptions—very high.

Women were welcomed into this underground profession, accepted as equals, and encouraged to use whatever skills they had acquired. No other radical movement of the time contained such a large proportion of women in its ranks. They embarked with passion onto the path of political struggle, spreading socialist propaganda among the peasants and later turning to individual assassination and terror. Women paid the same price as did their male comrades—with their freedom and with their lives. The hanging of Sofya Perovskaya, the daughter of a general, for organizing the assassination of Tsar Alexander II in 1881 dramatically punctuated this phase of radical women's struggle. Women paid in other ways too: through their dedication to revolution, they often lost the comforts of love and sexuality more often than did men, since it was harder for them to balance underground commitment with family life; and by refusing to add feminism to the Populist agenda, they made it easier for others to forget it altogether.

Although there was some fluidity among nihilist, radical, and feminist women, those women of the educated strata who chose not to challenge the regime and its patriarchal structure as a whole but who nonetheless craved to better the lot of women organized the Russian feminist movement (ca. 1860–1917). Feminists shared the class background (gentry and middle-class) of the nihilists and radicals. But they worked for women's rights—not for the rights of peasants or workers, and not on behalf of a socialist vision. In the decades after 1860 feminists formed legal societies, engaged in charity work, and opened university-level and medical courses for women. The last produced an impressive number of physicians, teachers, lawyers, and engineers. At the dawn of the twentieth century, feminists turned their attention to suffrage and to reforms in property rights, divorce, and other matters that primarily affected women of the educated classes of Russia. From 1905 to 1917, four feminist parties struggled unsuccessfully in the political arena. Thus all women (and millions of men) remained without representation in the central government. Russian feminism, in the words of its most eloquent historian, was "a movement for women's civil and political equality, whose supporters trusted that a better world could be created without resort to violence, and a constitutional solution be found to Russia's ills."[4]

INDUSTRIALIZATION, CLASS, AND GENDER, 1881–1905

The speedup of industrialization in Russia from the 1890s onward generated new social tensions and ideologies on the political landscape of imperial Russia. The peasantry, mostly dormant even in the face of Populist agitation, now began to stir again: sporadic revolts in the early years of the century blossomed into major disturbances by 1905 and 1906. Urbanization and the growth of factories enlarged the still embryonic proletariat and made it the favored target of socialist organizers, who found it far more amenable than the peasantry to its messages of class solidarity and revolt. An important segment of this proletariat—women workers—added a new dimension to the interaction of revolution and women's rights. Men and women of the factories launched strikes and protest demonstrations on an ever increasing scale that culminated in the revolution of 1905, a complex movement that consisted of mutinies, peasant unrest, strikes, and other displays of public disorder and opposition to the tsarist autocracy. By the end of the year, the tsar reluctantly granted a constitution and opened Russia's first parliament in modern history—the State Duma (1906–1917), based on limited male suffrage.

How did all these changes in political and economic life affect the lives of women? Peasants, as usual, were the least affected. Rural families were subjected to a certain amount of destabilization by the pull of industrialization. Wives often remained in the villages to run the household and maintain its economy without the presence of their husbands. Other peasant women—responding to a series of land reforms in 1906–1910—joined their husbands in withdrawing from the village communes and setting up independent farmsteads. Some women migrated to the cities to join the urban proletariat. But the bulk of independently employed urban women were domestic servants, overwhelmingly of rural origin, largely illiterate and unskilled, and frequently victims of economic and sexual exploitation. This neglected stratum of women (32 percent of St. Petersburg's working women in 1900 and 25.2 percent of Moscow's in 1912) predominated among mothers (mostly unmarried) who abandoned children and among prostitutes.[5]

The female proletariat was the object of double exploitation: miserable factory conditions and sexual harassment by bosses; and mistreatment at the hands of their proletarian husbands.

Women workers wrote incessantly and openly about the hostility they endured from male workers, making it clear that this hostility was as much a feature of the normal daily exchange between men and women workers as was the humiliating treatment they endured from male supervisory personnel.[6]

This situation drew the attention of feminist and socialist women, who vied for the loyalties of female workers and tried to mobilize them for their own programs. In this way industrialization had brought about what had been lacking in the old rural order: the possibility of a political alliance between women of the upper and the lower classes.

WOMEN IN THE POLITICAL ARENA, 1905–1914

The political parties of late imperial Russia reacted to the woman question in much the same way as their counterparts in Western Europe—their views on this issue being a litmus test for their outlook on social change and mass interests. Those on the right displayed hostility to any kind of feminist platform, identifying legitimate politics with the male sex and proclaiming as their program Faith, Tsar, and Fatherland. The liberal parties in the center—especially the Constitutional Democrats—initially wavered on women's suffrage in Duma elections, but by 1906 supported the more moderate of the feminist parties. The socialists—like their counterparts in Western Europe—proclaimed support for women's rights across the board: politics, maternity protection, and economic equality.

The socialist parties also included women activists at many levels, some of whom would become prominent political figures during the revolution of 1917. Of the three major socialist parties—Socialist Revolutionary, Social Democrat-Menshevik, and Social Democrat-Bolshevik—the first became the largest and most variegated. Heirs to the Populist tradition of the nineteenth century, the Socialist Revolutionaries focused on agrarian socialism and an alliance of the "social trinity": peasant, worker, and intelligentsia. Loose in organization and weak in theory, this party periodically fell back upon terror as its main weapon. Its best-known women were Ekaterina Breshko-Breshkovskaya (1844–1934), a veteran Populist of the 1870s who tried in the 1905 period to promote "agrarian terror" that included assaults on landlords in the countryside; and Maria Spiridonova (1886–?), a young schoolteacher who achieved fame first by her assassination of a general in 1906 and then in 1917 as the leader of the Left Socialist Revolutionary party. The Socialist Revolutionaries—like the Anarchist groups—could deploy a large number of female terrorists, but women played a minimal role in the party's organizational and theoretical work.

The Marxist Social Democrats had split into Mensheviks and Bolsheviks in 1903. Both enrolled women, but in neither did they rise to top leadership.

Among the more moderate Mensheviks, Vera Zasulich was the best-known woman (she had attempted to assassinate an official in the 1870s), but her political influence remained secondary. The most important Bolshevik women—Roza Zemlyachka and Elena Stasova—were tough organizers, but not leaders or theoreticians. In all the socialist parties the leadership remained in the hands of men who spent most of the years from 1905 to 1917 as emigres in Western Europe. Two of the best-known Bolshevik women, Nadezhda Krupskaya (Lenin's wife) and Inessa Armand (their friend), made their mark as loyal assistants of the party leader, Lenin, in the emigration years.[7]

The presence of women in the major socialist parties did not advance the cause of women's rights in Russia. Less than 10 percent of the delegates to Socialist Revolutionary conferences in the peak years from 1905 to 1908 were women; the percentages were even lower in the Social Democratic parties.[8] Even if more women had risen to the top, the picture would not have changed. Women constituted a third of the Executive Committee of the People's Will of the 1870s, for example, yet those women displayed almost no interest in the woman question as such. The same mood prevailed in the generation of 1905; revolutionary women put the "common cause" above what they saw as lesser issues. A sexual division of labor within the Marxist parties prefigured the second-rate status of Bolshevik women after the revolution of 1917; and the proportional numerical decline of women in the movement when it became proletarianized after 1905 was a precursor of what happened in Soviet society in the 1930s. In terms of female power, women ranked low.[9] Yet, through their skills, women added real power to their parties through practical organizational work; and through an emotional commitment equal to that of men, they helped keep the underground movement alive.

The most notable figure, Alexandra Kollontai, had to fight on many fronts when she tried to combine advocacy of women's rights with socialism: against feminist competitors, against indifference in her own party (she was at first a Menshevik and later a Bolshevik), and against conservative society. A general's daughter, Kollontai had come to a feminist consciousness through a personal conflict of work and family. She opposed feminists as bourgeois, and she preached that women workers should rally to the proletarian banner. But, like some European socialist women such as Lili Braun and Clara Zetkin, Kollontai knew that female proletarians had special problems that Marxist programs did not sufficiently address and that they needed self-awareness— as workers and as women.[10]

Out of this set of beliefs arose the Proletarian Women's Movement in 1905–1908 when Kollontai's socialist-feminist movement sought to win the factory women of St. Petersburg from the feminists who were trying to draft them into an "all-women's" movement that was partly tinged with a separatist ideology. Kollontai and a few associates agitated, taught Marxism, and attempted to show women workers that their main enemy was the bourgeoisie—not men. In this struggle over gender and class, Kollontai opposed the bourgeois (as she perceived it) program of the feminists with her own vision of both gender and class awareness, a recognition of the double exploitation of working-class women, and an honest critique of abusive proletarian husbands and insensitive socialist males. Although Kollontai exaggerated the selfish class character of Russian feminists, she did go beyond them and beyond her own comrades in the socialist movement in trying to raise these issues.

ON THE EVE OF REVOLUTION

Most Russian women remained outside the struggle over women's rights at the level of suffrage politics or revolution. For educated society, prostitution remained a burning issue that received an unprecedented public hearing early in the twentieth century. Young women of the villages who came to town for work, servants, and other lower class females constituted the bulk of the recruits. Motives ran the gamut from allure to economic crunch, with a varied range in between. Seduction, unmarried pregnancy, and abandonment or expulsion played a big role. But so did active recruiting by agents and pimps posted at railroad stations to lure unsuspecting (or sometimes half-unsuspecting) youngsters into the trade. The industry was enmeshed in a system of government control and inspection of prostitutes (but not clients) that made flight from brothels difficult and allowed the practice of a certain amount of what was then called by the lurid term *white slavery*—kidnapping or seduction into forced labor in the flesh trade. Eager journalists and novelists, as well as medical and legal experts, vied in exposing the system to public gaze. Efforts by feminists and others to abolish the police-medical inspection system or to prohibit prostitution yielded no results.[11]

Sex was a very big topic of public discussion before and after the revolution of 1905. Gender issues came under the glaring light of the intelligentsia: abortion, rape, homosexuality, masturbation, and female crime and "deviance." Some women—rape victims, sex offenders, and prostitutes—were ascribed, policed, and juridically segregated from the rest of society; and others, such as peasant women, were mythologized as paragons of virtue. The "clinical" and professional approaches by no means exhausted the modes of discourse about sexuality. The creative intelligentsia of the World of Art circle, the Symbolist poets, the theatrical avant-garde, and some important religious philosophers became obsessed with "decadent" perspectives on life—mystical carnality, sexual inversion, and even outright sado-masochism invaded poster art and cinema particularly after 1907. Moralists of the time, and many historians later, have seen this obsession as a clue to the larger decay of the Old Regime as a system. But it might be argued to the contrary that a full-throated discussion of sexuality—and women's place within it—was a harbinger of greater openness in those last unfathomable twilight years. In the entertainment world, rich patrons and managers still took mistresses from the theater. But female celebrity singers and actresses themselves were now choosing male companions from admiring audiences without suffering in reputation.[12]

The woman question in tsarist society remained a public issue right up into World War I. Thousands of women graduates of universities had entered professional life; hundreds languished in jail or in Siberia for their chosen profession as revolutionaries. The female terrorist was the Russian counterpart to the British suffragette—but far more violent. Organized feminists continued to agitate for important reforms in the status of women and won considerable legislative victories in legal, educational, and property rights, though mainly for women of the middle and upper classes.[13]

Lifestyles and the cultural contours of women in the middle-class, lower middle-class, and in the highest reaches of court and aristocracy have not received much serious historical treatment. Some of the professions (teachers, physicians, and pharmacists), religious women, and those in the creative world have received some attention. Although "covering" every discrete grouping of the female gender does not constitute a history of society or of gender, the neglect of some continues to give a distorted picture of the female experience. Another missing piece is the mosaic of ethnic intermarriage. Jewish assimilation and marriage with Christians may indicate greater ethnic toleration within society among some groups—the intelligentsia, the political Left, and the art world. Less of this occurred in the Muslim regions of the empire; but even there, liberal reform movements were already agitating for an end to the exclusionary practices of Islam, particularly isolation and veiling.

The female work force continued to grow and to feel the rigors of industrial life and of relative neglect by the rest of society. With the revival of the militant labor movement around 1912, Mensheviks and Bolsheviks alike reactivated their efforts to organize women workers. International Women's Day, established in Europe in 1910, was celebrated by adherents of both factions for the first time on Russian soil in 1913, and a newspaper, *The Woman Worker*, was established in 1914. During World War I much of the machinery for organizing women workers was smashed by the authorities, and many leaders were arrested before the monarchy itself fell a victim to the same war.

THE REVOLUTIONARY ERA: HEROIZING
WOMEN, 1917–1928

After three winters of bitter fighting, bloody losses, and patent mismanagement of the war, widespread discontent and hatred of the regime found a focus. In February 1917, cold and hungry women of the capital (renamed Petrograd) rioted, beginning an uprising that led to the collapse of the Romanov dynasty within a week. With the men at the front, the women left behind as workers, breadwinners, and heads of households saw the shortages and deprivations as a menace to their existence. They struck, demonstrated, rioted, and persuaded—by appeals to class solidarity—the garrison troops not to fire upon them. When the tsar abdicated, the revolutionary parties linked up with the masses of women. A band of energetic Bolshevik organizers—including Kollontai—fashioned a network of agitation that was effective in spite of tactical squabbles and the enormous problem of communication in the midst of a major revolt. This network produced mass female demonstrations on behalf of Bolshevik issues, organized women in factories, and enlisted others in political, paramedical, and paramilitary work. Bolshevik leadership and dynamism in this arena proved superior to that of the other radical parties, and Bolshevik hostility to the revived feminist movement was unambiguous.

The Bolsheviks took power on October 25 (November 7 in the modern calendar), 1917, and established a Soviet socialist regime; in 1918 they moved the capital to Moscow, issued a constitution for the world's first socialist state, and made peace with Germany. The first years were marked by ruthless political struggle on all sides, a cruel civil war, intervention by foreign troops on behalf of the anti-Bolshevik forces, and a deepening of the economic hardship set off by war and revolution. How, in this time of dreadful calamity, did the Bolshevik regime approach the issue—seen as marginal by all previous governments—of emancipating women? The answers are complicated; any assessment of their response depends upon how one views revolution in general and the Bolshevik Revolution in particular, and upon one's expectations from an insurgent, culture-changing government that sets out to remake the face of one of the largest countries in the world.

The Bolsheviks (now called Communists) displayed the contradictions inherent in all agents of forced social and cultural change: practicality versus vision, the imperatives of survival versus the dream of transformation. Women had no place in the upper reaches of the party hierarchy; and indifference toward women's issues persisted in the party at various levels. This was an inheritance of the twenty years of underground life of party struggle, of the military mentality of Bolshevism that hardened during the civil war, and of the upsurge within the party of people holding patriarchal views of the female sex. In spite of this, it is astonishing what the new regime accomplished in its early years. The party leader and head of the Soviet state, V. I. Lenin, as both a Marxist and a Russian revolutionary, committed his regime to the educational, economic, legal, and political liberation of women; to the interchangeability of gender roles in a Communist future; and to the protection of woman as childbearer and nurturing mother. Lenin possessed an almost compulsive hatred of the domestic enslavement of women to mindless household work, which he called "barbarously unproductive, petty, nerve-wracking, stultifying and crushing drudgery."[14]

Those of Lenin's male and female colleagues sharing his opinions issued decrees, codes, electoral laws, and land reforms and proclaimed an across-the-board equality of the sexes—the first regime in history ever to do so. All institutions of learning were opened to women. Women got equal status in marriage—including the right to change or retain their own names—divorce, family, and inheritance; and equal rights in litigation and the ownership of property. By separating church and state, the Communists invalidated all canonical and theological restrictions on the role of women in modern life—a sweeping and drastic measure in a land wrapped in the constraining meshes of traditional faiths, particularly Russian Orthodoxy, Islam, and Orthodox Judaism. Abortion was legalized (in 1920) and prostitution made illegal.[15]

To this legal structure of sexual equality the Communists added organizations that would help to erect the new order, and an outpouring of art, culture, symbol, and mythic vision to reinforce it. The organizational work was remanded to the Women's Department of the Communist Party (1919–1930), known by its Russian abbreviation Zhenotdel. Led by Inessa Armand and Alexandra Kollontai in the early years, Zhenotdel worked to transform the new revolutionary laws into reality through education, mobilization, and social work. Understaffed and underfinanced, its agents fanned out to the factory neighborhoods, villages, and remote provinces to bring the message of the revolution to the female population. Instructors and trainees drawn from among workers and peasant women addressed practical concerns. In the towns they monitored factory conditions and fought against female unemployment and prostitution. In the countryside they opened literacy classes and explained the new laws. In the Muslim regions they opposed customs and attitudes that appeared to them to humiliate women. Everywhere they counseled women about divorce and women's rights—and undergirded such lessons with the political values of the regime. Activated by Zhenotdel, women previously untouched by political culture entered into the process of governance. Most crucial of all, the activists of Zhenotdel learned the rudiments of organizing and modernizing and taught themselves the meaning of social revolution.[16]

The most spectacular clash of power over sex and gender took place in the oases towns of Soviet central Asia, where bride price, kidnapping, child marriage, polygamy, female illiteracy, and seclusion had been the norm for centuries. The last was symbolized by a cotton garment covered with a horsehair veil that women had to wear in public, since showing the female face to male gaze was considered an erotic provocation. Zhenotdel activists from Moscow arrived to open schools and counseling centers for women and to agitate in largely female spaces such as wells, markets, and bathhouses. Russian and Muslim women put on plays denouncing sexual slavery and seclusion. In 1927 an estimated 100,000 women gathered on town squares and demonstratively tore off their veils. A ferocious "male backlash" transformed rage into violent action. Muslim men beat, gang-raped, disemboweled, and stabbed sisters, wives, or fiancees. Estimates of those killed in 1927 range from eight hundred to the thousands. The regime retaliated and the violence against women escalated. Finally the government backed off and reverted to a gradual pace of change and eventually to accommodation with local social and gender customs and to a stability that was favored over social revolution and transformation.[17]

Speculation about the future of sex ran rampant in the 1920s. The most articulate Communist on this, Kollontai, advanced a program of egalitarian sexual relations and communal "family" life. She vigorously defended woman's need for independence and a separate income that would give her the dignity and strength required for an equal and open love-sex relationship and would enhance the pleasure and quality of sexual intercourse. Marriage for Kollontai had to be unfettered by economic dependence or responsibility for children. The latter were to be cared for in communal facilities. She believed in parenthood—her ideal in fact for all humans—and in regular contact between parents and children. But the material life of the children was to be in the hands of the local "collective" of work or residence. Housekeeping, an "industrial" task like any other, would be the domain of specialists and never of a wife (or husband) alone. Some of the more daring aspects of Kollontai's sexual theories fell victim to misinterpretation in the 1920s.[18]

Kollontai's vision of equality in life, work, and love matched utopian visions of science fiction writers and revolutionary town planners and architects in this decade of experiment. Science fiction fantasies outlined a future world of social justice and ultramodern technology. They almost invariably revealed a unified, urbanized globe bathed in peace, harmony, and affluent communist civilization inhabited by a near-androgynous population with genderless names and unisex costumes. Sexual tensions no longer tormented the human race, women worked as equals to men in a machine-run economy of universal participation and communist distribution, and healthy children thrived in colonies. Town planners designed communal buildings that would shape the consciousness of their inhabitants. Architectural plans offered private rooms for single persons and couples, easy divorce by changing rooms, and communal child care, cooking, and dining. In some actually functioning communes, students and workers made sexual equality mandatory: males learned how to cook and iron and wash floors under the guidance of women so that all could take their turns at housework on a strictly rotational basis.[19]

Endemic misery and material poverty hampered these experiments, and cynicism and indifference mocked the dreams. Although the experiments and dreams persisted, life for women—and men—was difficult in the early years after the revolution. The rural world presented a vast terrain of disease and superstition, suspicious peasants, archaic tools, and ancient agronomical technique. Towns were filled with unemployed women, deserted and abandoned children, criminals and organized gangs, and conspicuously wealthy businessmen. These last constituted a class created by the introduction of Lenin's New Economic Policy in 1921, which allowed a mixed economy, a limited arena of capitalism and hired labor with enclaves of privileged specialists, government leaders, and foreigners. Women were hit very hard by all of this—and some of them by political repression: dismissal, jail, and exile. About 70 percent of the initial job cutbacks that occurred periodically during this period affected women. The tens of thousands of women in *de facto* marriages possessed none of the financial security or legal protection that might have vouchsafed them with registered marriage.[20]

Sexual equality did not become the norm in the 1920s or any time afterwards. Peasant "lords" held sway in their wooden cabins. In the factory towns, women were fired or laid off before men. Male preeminence continued in all walks of life—including party and state. Old ways, rooted in ancient tradition, died hard in spite of laws, campaigns, organizing efforts, and attempts to create new images and myths. The Zhenotdel was in fact weaker at the end of the decade than when it was formed. The sexual revolution launched by the Communists had gotten out of hand; males abused the new sexual equality by deromanticizing love and exploiting women for easy sex in the name of a "proletarian morality." Moral conservatives among the Communists in the mid-1920s launched a backlash against the new sexual culture, and the voices of peasant and working-class women rose in opposition to the "immoral" divorce laws during the marriage debates from 1925 to 1926.

THE STALIN PERIOD: DOMESTICATING WOMEN, 1928–1953

The ascendancy of Stalin at the end of the 1920s and his revolution from above changed the face of the USSR while retaining certain basic ideological and mythic features of the early Communist period. The political revolution was particularly harsh, marked by Stalin's attempt to eradicate all his enemies (real or imagined), the choking off of critical discourse, and a cult of personality that pictured the leader as an all-knowing secular god. The economic revolution—whose achievements and weaknesses outlived Stalin's crimes—collectivized the peasantry and launched the rest of the population into a gigantic and uneven surge of massive, centrally planned industrialization. The accompanying social revolution promoted workers into management and leadership and transformed Soviet cities by some 19 million immigrants in the years from 1926 to 1939.[21] The scale of urbanization was so great and its force so sudden that it changed the social face of major Soviet cities, rusticating them by peasant influx. Peasant forms of motion and work, living habits, customs, modes of speech, and social attitudes created a rural atmosphere even in those urban spaces that had once been marked by urbane sophistication.

Such an immense revolution produced painful results: unimaginable suffering inflicted upon millions—victims of famine, collectivization, terror, and repression—and, for others, the overcrowding and urban dehumanization with the attendant negative impact on families. Against this must be set the genuine industrial growth, the forging of economic and military sinew that enabled the Soviet people to survive and win the war against the Germans in 1941–1945. The upward mobility for the lower classes, the new social coloration of the cities, increasing isolation of the Soviet Union from the West, and the upsurge of xenophobia that came with it led to a cultural reorientation. The verve and bold experimental tone of the 1920s gave way to a search for *kulturnost,* or respectability, the acquisition of middlebrow tastes by the new elite, and a return to certain traditional values of the old regime. Among these were conservative nationalism, the exaltation of military heroes, and patriarchalism at many levels. Much of the utopian experimentalism of the 1920s was repudiated in the 1930s even at the level of idealistic myths and dreams.[22]

The great transformation of the 1930s affected the lives of women more profoundly than any development in Russian history. With it came a dramatic rise in upward mobility, professionalization, and entry into all sectors of the urban economy. Campaigns promoted women and sent them to technical and medical schools. Since precise quotas required that a certain percentage of women be admitted, this technique pushed a previously underprivileged segment of the population forward—a policy called "affirmative action" in our days. In the 1930s the regime laid down the occupational structure of women in the Soviet Union. In practice as well as theory this represented a huge advance for the Soviet female population into a world once designated as male—the world of the laboratory, construction site, technical college, planning office, and other arenas of a society dynamically engaged in rapid construction and economic development. Between 1926 and 1939 the reported percentage of literate females rose from 42.7 percent to 81.6 percent. The proportion of women at institutions of higher education rose from 31 percent in 1926 to 58 percent in 1940. Moreover, as Krupskaya forcefully noted, this meant education for women, not in lacemaking or embroidery, but in agronomy, animal husbandry, sanitation, and technology.[23]

But women had little say in the larger transformation: the Zhenotdel was abolished in 1930. Stalinism defined women's productive and reproductive roles in an authoritarian way. To promote family stability, protect women from male irresponsibility, and increase the population, the regime tightened the divorce laws and outlawed abortion. Many Soviet women favored divorce law over the sexual lawlessness of the previous decade. The regime expected practically all women to engage in productive work outside the home; but it also exalted motherhood as a patriotic duty, and a sugary image of the mother bedecked with maternity medals and beaming over a large family replaced the revolutionary image of the female warrior. Individual family housekeeping survived the dreams of a communal life, and women were again given the main job of child care and domestic work (including the "esthetic" job of adorning the home). Wives of leaders and executives, however, were not required to work. To justify their existence, managerial wives organized a "movement" to decorate the offices and premises of the enterprises run by their husbands. But the vast majority of women held full-time jobs and then performed a "second shift" of shopping, cooking, housekeeping, and child care. Stalin's economic and social revolution propelled some people up the social scale and opened vistas for education and opportunity, especially in science and technology. At the same time, it exalted power, authority, and inequality.

Women were subjected to a wrenching experience in the war against Germany from 1941 to 1945. Aside from the millions pulled into war production and civil defense, about 1 million women actually served in the war, 800,000 of them in uniform as combat soldiers and officers in auxiliary roles (supply and medical); as antiaircraft gunners, snipers, tankers, pilots, and bombardiers; and as behind-the-lines partisans and underground saboteurs. Thousands died or suffered wounds in battlefield fighting; hundreds of thousands fell before the execution squads of the German occupiers. Soviet Jewish women, left behind when men joined the ranks or were evacuated, fell victim to Nazi atrocities in disproportionate numbers. The female national martyr came to symbolize the struggle against the invader. The fact that the vast majority of women held low or middle ranks, staff jobs, and subordinate positions (as in civilian life) does not diminish the epic quality of this experience.[24]

Writers of the late Stalin period spoke of "the solution of the woman question" in the USSR.[25] In reality, women's roles were frozen into a position defined by the regime. After the tragedy and grandeur of military service, women were sent back to the civilian sector (as in other countries) to resume their heavy double burdens, in the economy and in the home—a home that was frequently bereft of a male breadwinner. The postwar years were among the most difficult that Soviet women have ever had to endure. The hideous bloodletting of the 1930s and World War II had left millions of women lonely, prematurely old, overworked, bitterly saddened, and largely ignored.[26]

AN AGING REVOLUTION: THE SOVIET OLD REGIME, 1953–1985

The death of Stalin in 1953 unlocked many doors in the Soviet system, not the least being the prison gates that had surrounded the inmates in the forced labor camps of the Stalin era. His successor, Nikita Khrushchev (1953–1964), released millions of prisoners and delivered his famous "destalinization" speech in 1956, which furthered the process of Cold War détente, cultural thaw, and domestic reform. Specific changes in women's status began in the Khrushchev period and continued after his fall from power. Following considerable debate, abortion was legalized in 1955. Laws enacted in 1965 and 1968 made divorce easier to obtain. The regime quietly introduced in the early 1960s a system of civil rituals designed to solemnify and make sacred certain rites of passage—including matrimony.[27] Maternity protection entitled the expectant mother to fifty-six days of paid leave before and fifty-six days after the birth.[28] Coeducation, partly abolished in 1943, was restored after Stalin's death. The educational system continued to prepare huge numbers of women for professional, scientific, technical, and higher educational degrees, which allowed many of them to achieve careers in professions.

Policy debates and political actions related to interest groups—including women—became more vigorous and effective. The notion of developed socialism, promulgated under Leonid Brezhnev (1964 to 1982) as an intermediate road to full communism, opened a wide-ranging discussion of welfare and public facilities for all Soviet citizens. The press and public organizations—local Soviets and party groups—lobbied on kindergarten care, flextime, maternity protection, and the availability of health facilities that impinge closely upon women's daily lives. Academic disciplines, such as sociology, that had been outlawed in the Stalin years reappeared. Statistical data about women's lives and the mass of monographs, reform projects, press articles, and fiction created a steady public campaign to improve the lot of women within the parameters of the political and economic system.[29] The continuing growth in the number of civic-minded and politically active educated women sharpened the perception of remaining inequality in the workplace and in the home.

In the workplace, vertical segregation kept women out of top positions in factory, enterprise, office, or laboratory even in occupations—such as medicine—where women outnumbered men. Horizontal segregation or "feminization" channeled women into jobs and professions wherein incomes were held down. Although "equal pay for equal work" existed in law since the beginning of the Soviet regime, women remained economically second-class citizens. The exclusion of women from the high political power was replicated in the economic arena. Why such blatant refutation of earlier revolutionary goals? The disempowerment of women in the state and the workplace has been rightly attributed to continuing male refusal to share their power with women. To this must be added two more things. First was the strongly ascriptive nature of Stalinism, which assigned roles to certain kinds of people. Second was the reluctance of women to challenge male power, a reluctance arising from the demographic imbalance and from the traditional sex-role education girls received. On the other hand, the domestic "double shift" evoked bitterness. Married or not, women had primary responsibility for child care and housework, a job made difficult by the shortage of home appliances and by a retail system that made shopping time-consuming. Official rhetoric urged women to work, manage the household, and do volunteer work on behalf of society (party, Communist Youth League, trade union, or similar activities). The tension inherent in this three-way agenda augmented the high divorce rate, family conflicts, and the relatively low rate of professional advancement of women. Women's departure from unequal marriages, though also arising from sexual incompatibility, was in a way the only avenue of resistance to the domestic system.[30]

These problems—heightened by alcoholism and the insufficiencies in housing and transport—were documented in the Soviet press over the past generation. Detailed reports of foreign journalists and scholars revealed how deeply these problems were felt by many Soviet women. A tiny group of dissident feminists of Leningrad went further by publishing in 1979 a collection of grievances, the *Almanac,* a mélange of lament, description, and protest far beyond anything uttered in the legal press.[31] The secular wing of this group protested the injustice of the regime and its treatment of women in particular. A Christian wing produced a journal named after the Blessed Mother (*Mary*). This may seem surprising to Western readers, but in a country whose government had actively fought against Christianity since its very inception, it was natural that some women should express their grievances and their aspirations in a religious idiom. Some of the most important dissidents in the Soviet Union in the previous twenty years had been committed Christians who posited a return to the values of Holy Russia—even though these included patriarchy and male chauvinism—as the true alternative to Communist rule.

By the time the Soviet Union began to crack in the era of perestroika (1985–1991), it was probably clear to all, including those who denied it, that the "revolutionary process" was long gone. Commentators later looked back on the Brezhnev years as an era of stagnation, for women and for everybody else. There is no simple way to sum up what the Russian Revolution and the Soviet regime has meant to women. The balance sheet described in previous pages must be assessed by each historian and by the women who lived through some of the epochs that unfolded. The feeling of exhilaration about the dramatic forces unleashed, the heroism manifested, and the achievements registered must be tempered by the terrible anguish and pain that so many had to endure for these achievements.

NOTES

1. Christine Worobec, *Peasant Russia: Family and Community in the Post-Emancipation Period,* Princeton University Press, Princeton, 1991, offers the best treatment of women in rural life, and she is doing further work on witchcraft and other matters. Cathy Frierson is examining the role of arson in Russian history.
2. N. G. Chernyshevsky, *Chto delat?* (1863; Moscow, 1963), p. 67. See the excellent edition by Michael Katz and William Wagner: *What Is to Be Done?* Cornell University Press, Ithaca, 1989.
3. Barbara Engel, *Mothers and Daughters,* Cambridge University Press, Cambridge, 1983, p. 125.
4. Linda Edmondson, *Feminism in Russia, 1900–1917,* Heinemann, London, 1984, p. x.
5. David Ransel, "Abandonment and Fosterage of Unwanted Children: The Women of the Foundling System," in *The Family in Imperial Russia,* ed. David Ransel, University of Illinois Press, Urbana, 1978, p 195; David Ransel, *Mothers of Mercy,* Princeton University Press, Princeton, 1988; Laurie Bernstein, *Sonia's Daughters: Prostitutes and Their Regulation in Imperial Russia,* University of California Press, Berkeley, 1995.

6. Rose Glickman, *Russian Factory Women*, University of California Press, Berkeley, 1984, p. 276.
7. Jay Bergman, *Vera Zasulich*, Stanford University Press, Stanford, 1983; N. K. Krupskaya, *Memories of Lenin*, London, 1930; R. Carter Elwood, *Inessa Armand*, Cambridge University Press, Cambridge, 1992.
8. According to Amy Knight's figures cited in Richard Stites, *The Women's Liberation Movement in Russia*, Princeton University Press, Princeton, 1978, p. 271.
9. Beate Fieseler, "The Making of Russian Female Social Democrats, 1890–1917," *International Review of Social History* 34, no. 2 (1989), pp. 193–226.
10. Barbara Clements, *Bolshevik Feminist*, Indiana University Press, Bloomington, 1979; Beatrice Farnsworth, *Aleksandra Kollontai*, Stanford University Press, Stanford, 1980.
11. Bernstein, *op. cit.*
12. Laura Engelstein, *The Keys to Happiness*, Cornell University Press, Ithaca, 1992. Louise McReynolds is presently examining the personal and professional lives of actresses and entertainers under the old regime.
13. Edmondson, *op. cit.*
14. V.I. Lenin, *On the Emancipation of Women*, Moscow: n.d., pp. 61–62.
15. The most learned and thoughtful assessment of these measures and their fate is Wendy Goldman, *Women, the State, and Revolution*, Cambridge University Press, Cambridge, 1993.
16. Gail Lapidus, *Women in Soviet Society*, University of California Press, Berkeley, 1978.
17. Gregory Massell, *The Surrogate Proletariat*, Princeton University Press, Princeton, 1974.
18. Alexandra Kollontai, *Selected Writings*, ed. Alix Holt, Norton, New York, 1982.
19. Richard Stites, *Revolutionary Dreams*, Oxford University Press, New York, 1989.
20. Goldman, *op. cit.*
21. Moshe Lewin, "Society, State, and Ideology During the First Five-Year Plan" in *Cultural Revolution in Russia, 1928–1931*, ed. S. Fitzpatrick, Indiana University Press, Bloomington, 1978, pp. 41–77.
22. Nicholas Timasheff, *The Great Retreat: the Growth and Decline of Communism in Russia*, Dutton, New York, 1946; Hans Günther, ed, *The Culture of the Stalin Period*, Macmillan, London, 1990.
23. Lapidus, *op. cit.*, pp. 95–122, 136–137, 149.
24. Ann Griesse and Richard Stites, "Russia: Revolution and War," in *Female Soldiers*, ed. N. Goldman, Greenwood Press, Westport, Conn., 1982, pp. 61–84; Richard Stites, ed., *Culture and Entertainment in Wartime Russia*, Indiana University Press, Bloomington, 1995.
25. Vera Bilshai, *Reshenie zhenskogo voprosa*, Moscow, 1946.
26. The theme is brilliantly handled in Vera Dunham, *In Stalin's Time*, Cambridge University Press, Cambridge, 1976.
27. Christel Lane, *The Rites of Rulers*, Cambridge University Press, Cambridge, 1981.
28. Details on health and maternity care in Barbara Holland and Teresa McKevitt, "Maternity Care in the Soviet Union," in *Soviet Sisterhood*, ed. Barbara Holland, Indiana University Press, Bloomington, 1985, pp. 145–178. See also Murray Feshbach and Alfred Friendly, *Ecocide in the USSR*, Basic Books, New York, 1992.
29. Mary Buckley, "Soviet Interpretations of the Woman Question" in Holland, *op. cit.*, pp. 24–53.

30. For some personal testimony, see C. Hansson and K. Lidén, *Moscow Women*, Pantheon, New York, 1983.
31. Tatyana Mamonova, ed., *Women and Russia*, Beacon Press, Boston, 1984, a translation of *Almanakh* (Almanac).

SUGGESTIONS FOR FURTHER READING

Aside from titles already cited in the notes, one should also consult the detailed and up-to-date scholarship found in Barbara Clements, Barbara Engel, and Christine Worobec, eds., *Russian Women: Accommodation, Resistance, Transformation* (Berkeley: University of California Press, 1991). Barbara Engel and Clifford Rosenthal, eds., *Five Sisters: Women against the Tsar* (New York: Knopf, 1974), is a vivid collection of memoirs. Other works on revolutionaries are Vera Figner, *Memoirs of a Revolutionist*, ed. R. Stites (DeKalb: Northern Illinois University Press, 1991); Catherine Breshkovsky, *Little Grandmother of the Russian Revolution* (Boston, 1930); and Catherine Breshkovsky, *Hidden Springs of the Russian Revolution* (Stanford: Stanford University Press, 1931). For female creative writers, see Catriona Kelly, ed., *An Anthology of Russian Women's Writings, 1777–1992* and Catriona Kelly, *A History of Russian Women's Writings, 1820–1992*, both New York: Oxford University Press, 1994; and Barbara Heldt, *Terrible Perfection* (Bloomington: Indiana University Press, 1987). For brilliant insights into women's social and cultural roles in the tsarist era, see Alison Hilton, *Russian Folk Art* (Bloomington: Indiana University Press, 1995); Priscilla Roosevelt, *The Russian Country Estate* (New Haven: Yale University Press, 1995); and Helena Goscilo and Beth Holmgren, eds., *Russia, Women, Culture* (Bloomington: Indiana University Press, 1996), which extends into the Soviet period as well.

For the generation of 1890 to 1917, three other radical biographies may be noted: Robert McNeal, *Bride of the Revolution: Krupskaya and Lenin* (Ann Arbor: University of Michigan Press, 1972); Isaac Steinberg, *Spiridonova* (London: Methuen, 1935); and Eva Broido, *Memoirs of a Revolutionary* (London: Oxford University Press, 1967). Newer works of scholarship have branched out into social, sexual, and cultural history: Linda Edmondson, ed., *Women and Society in Russia and the Soviet Union* (Cambridge: Cambridge University Press, 1992); the prize-winning work of Barbara Engel, *Between the Field and the City: Women, Work, and Family in Russia, 1861–1914* (Cambridge: Cambridge University Press, 1994); Beatrice Farnsworth and Lynn Viola, eds., *Russian Peasant Women* (New York: Oxford University Press, 1992); Christine Ruane, *Gender, Class, and the Professionalization of Russian City Teachers, 1860–1914* (Pittsburgh: University of Pittsburgh Press, 1994); Jane Costlow, Stephanie Sandler, and Judith Vowles, eds., *Sexuality and the Body in Russian Culture* (Stanford: Stanford University Press, 1993); and Catherine Schuler, *Women in Russian Theater: The Actress in the Silver Age* (London: Routledge, 1996).

Vivid and optimistic treatments of women in the early Soviet period were written by sympathetic foreigners: Fanina Halle, *Women in Soviet Russia* (New York: Viking, 1933); and Ella Winter, *Red Virtue* (New York, 1935). The darker side is chronicled by Eric Naiman in *Sex in Public: The Incarnation of Early Soviet Ideology* (forthcoming). Among the best of the horrifying memoirs of women in the terror is Evgenia Ginzburg, *Into the Whirlwind* (Harmondsworth: Penguin, 1968). A full account of women's experience in World War II—combat and civilian—has yet to be written. An excellent branch study is Reina Pennington, *Wings, Women, and War: Soviet Women's Military Aviation Regiments in the Second World War* (Ph.D. Dissertation, University of South Carolina, 1993).

Some path-breaking articles on the later decades of Soviet history can be found in *Women in Russia*, ed. D. Atkinson, A. Dallin, and G. Lapidus (Stanford: Stanford University Press, 1977). See also Gail Lapidus, ed., *Women, Work, and Family in the Soviet Union* (Armonk, New York: Sharpe, 1982). For recent years, see Susan Bridger, *Women in the Soviet Countryside: Women's Roles in Rural Development in the Soviet Union* (Cambridge: Cambridge University Press, 1988); Mary Buckley, ed., *Perestroika and Soviet Women* (Cambridge: Cambridge University Press, 1992); Mary Buckley, *Women and Ideology in the Soviet Union* (New York, 1989); Helena Goscilo, ed., *Fruits of Her Plume: Essays on Contemporary Russian Women's Culture* (Armonk, New York: Sharpe, 1993); and Francine du Plessix Gray, *Soviet Women: Walking the Tightrope* (New York: Doubleday, 1990). A comparative perspective is offered in Shirin Rai, Hilary Pilkington, and Annie Phizacklea, eds., *Women in the Face of Change: The Soviet Union, Eastern Europe, and China* (London: Routledge, 1992). Two collections with broad scope and insightful comments on the current scene by Russian women themselves are Marianne Liljeström, Eila Mäntysaari, and Arja Rosenholm, eds., *Gender Restructuring in Russian Studies* (Finland: University of Tampere, 1993); and Rosalind Marsh, ed., *Women in Russia and Ukraine* (Cambridge: Cambridge University Press, 1996).

Käthe Kollwitz, *Never Again War (Nie Wieder Krieg)*, 1924, Gift of Richard A. Simms.

16

Women in War and Peace, 1914–1945

Sandi E. Cooper

For European women, the two world wars of the twentieth century were disasters on an unprecedented scale. Few could escape the impact of mass death, unimaginable privation, the daily terror and uncertainty, torturous pain from loss, physical exhaustion, famine, epidemics, and permanently ruined health. The two world wars forever buried illusions of progress and evolutionary improvement.

Both wars overturned traditional gender roles and distinctions between public and private. Women were pulled into every conceivable male activity and occupation—including combat during World War II. Certainly, the architects of these conflagrations had not envisioned such a convolution of the old social contract between men and women. Then, at the wars' ends, women were expected to "return to normalcy." However, "normalcy" itself became contested territory.

As the twentieth century closes, we are just beginning to grasp the long-term importance of those wars in reshaping traditional social relations. Both wars, their preludes and postludes, inspired a new level of women's antiwar and propeace activism. Women's determination to revise the political contracts in European states that had excluded them from domestic and international life became a permanent feature of modern history.

In peace, children bury their parents. War violates the order of nature
and causes parents to bury their children.

[HERODOTUS]

Twice in the twentieth century, European and Asian leaders unleashed the most destructive wars ever waged in recorded history. Politicians sent their nation's youth to be slaughtered; parents buried their children till nations were numbed by despair; millions of families were left to shift on pension pittances or less. Empires and dynasties crashed while entirely new political orders emerged—mass democracy, socialism and communism, fascism, and colonial revolutions that overturned global empires. Thousands of towns and villages were eradicated; infrastructure and revered ancient monuments were destroyed. The wars demonstrated that state regulations could bring immense profits to capitalist economies as rents, prices, and wages were regulated, and that civil liberties could be suspended and civilian life policed—all in the name of democracy.

When the peace of Europe unraveled in August 1914, not one of the fifteen to twenty gentlemen in charge of issuing the marching orders accurately predicted the catastrophe that ended on November 11, 1918, as the guns were silenced. Those who launched World War II in 1931 in Asia and in 1939 in Europe miscalculated the efficiency of lightning terror tactics. Nor did anyone predict the astounding weapon that would conclude the war in 1945. Both wars mocked the optimistic toasts of the New Year in 1900 and 1901—the promise of a century of ever expanding prosperity, human well-being, and permanent peace. Both wars temporarily suspended the social contract that defined proper masculine and feminine roles, and, despite strenuous postwar campaigns to "return to normalcy," the fundamental illogic of sex-role inequalities remained permanently exposed.

World War I was a profound shock. Its length, its ferocity, its appetite for human sacrifice, and its absurd expectation that masculine notions of honor could confront machine guns forever ended the mythology of chivalric warfare. At the outset official militarism garnered public support. Ironically, as national consensus began to unravel in 1916-1917 in the belligerent states, the war was reinvigorated by the Russian withdrawal and the U.S. decision to intervene. Against all rationality, despite the monumental scale of the slaughter, pleas from the papacy, outbreaks of mutiny, and threats to European survival, no state would move to negotiate a settlement.

The technologies of warfare in the twentieth century extended warfare to terror from the skies and beneath the oceans and against unarmed citizens. In World War II, the added objective, the elimination of so-called *Untermenschen* (inferior peoples)—primarily Jewish people, but also Gypsies, ethnic groupings defined as lower evolutionary types, and unacceptable Germans such as mental defectives, homosexuals, and "useless eaters"—transformed war into systematic mass murder, unredeemed by any presumed military purpose. To tally the dead from both wars is a task that has thus far defied all efforts at statistical accuracy.

Estimates of the damage range wildly. Some statistics are established: most scholars agree that about 9,500,000 to 10,000,000 men died in military combat in World War I from August 1, 1914, to November 11, 1918. Following the war, a flu pandemic created another unknown tally of civilian dead. In World War II, there were fewer military dead but many, many more civilian victims. For World War II, death estimates range from a low of 50,000,000 to a high of 75,000,000, reflecting the difficulty of determining civilian losses.[1]

Total war meant total social trauma. Governments ordered young men to drop their work, put on a uniform, train to kill, and leave old men, women, and children behind in charge of economic and public affairs. Women were invited, cajoled, and even ordered to bring in the harvest; to fill in at factories so that the manufacture of essential goods continued; to provide for the education of children; to organize and staff clinics and hospitals; and to cover posts in banks and offices that had ordinarily been closed to them. At the same time, they were exhorted never to forget their primary obligation—the replacement of the population, even if it might mean bearing a child out of wedlock or, worse, from rape. Women, forbidden in 1913 to work as telephone operators, were deemed capable of conducting trams and military ambulances by 1915.

Thus the wars—the quintessential breakdown of patriarchal law and order—challenged the essence of patriarchy itself. Hoary prescriptions of what "normal" women did in "normal" society evaporated; without warning, women were declared fit for every public activity and, at the end, required to "return to normalcy." Normalcy, traditionally defined, meant that most women were to return to motherhood as their primary reason for being, which, many realized, meant replenishing cannon fodder. Modern war, more than class struggle, revolution, charismatic leadership, or any other vehicle of historical change, fashioned the contours of the Euro-American social order in the twentieth century and opened a new era of gender awareness. For that insistent, vocal minority of women who devoted their lives to campaigning for international peace after the Great War, normalcy had to be profoundly modified to include peace and social justice.

THE GREAT WAR: 1914–1918

In 1885, the French feminist Hubertine Auclert (1848–1914) posed a lasting challenge: Would the French republic become a "minotaur," a state that devoured "the blood and resources of its citizens through taxation and war," or would it become a "motherly" state, one that nurtured "its citizenry offering security and work to the healthy, assistance to children, old people the sick and disabled"?[2] Versions of this question have permeated progressive women's movements ever since.

Up to the eve of World War I, women activists realized that peace and international problems had to be included in their agendas. Marie Pognon, a French suffragist and peace activist, alma dolens ("anguished soul"— pseudonym of Teresita Bonfatti dei Pasini) in Italy, Marguerite Selenka in Germany, and Dr. Anna Shabanova, a Moscow doctor—all urged women to reject the argument that arms were essential to keep the peace. The arms race was more likely to produce bankruptcy and war, Pognon insisted. "Not one woman, not one mother has the right to ignore foreign policy; each time a cloud appears on the horizon, let us take our place alongside the men and remind them that a Tribunal to regulate international conflict exists."[3] Dolens, alert to the malaria in the swamps near Rome and the misery in southern Italy, hammered away at the connection between arms expenditure and barbaric domestic conditions. The enemy is not at the border, she insisted; "it is poverty, tuberculosis, unemployment. The cure for these diseases is the end of formidable and costly weaponry."[4] Dr. Anna Shabanova, who devoted her medical career to poor women and children, helped found the Moscow Peace Society (ca. 1910) and insisted that "we Russian women are earnestly convinced that if women were to take part in political life in the country, the idea of universal peace would be immensely easier to realize."[5] The most eminent woman leader of the pre-1914 peace movement, the Austrian Bertha von Suttner, who won the Nobel Peace Prize in 1907, eventually came to insist on the link between women's political rights and international peace. By and large, national and international women's groups, middle class and socialist, had integrated peace issues into their platforms by 1914.

Simultaneously, during the escalating crises of 1911–1914, a fatalistic conviction that war was inevitable moved some women to speculate on their probable patriotic responsibilities. The sense that women had to prepare to take over from men, that they had to train vigorously for more than the ordinary nursing duties and perhaps begin to imagine themselves managing state agencies, began to grow.[6] In Britain, a women's organization emerged to support the expansionist programs of the Naval League, and in Germany the Fatherland Front of patriotic women loudly proclaimed nationalist values.

August 1914 divided prewar feminists for the duration of the war, and sometimes permanently. It sundered the famous English suffrage family, the Pankhursts. Sylvia Pankhurst[7] realized that the war would be disastrous for the poor community she worked with in East London and immediately began a nonprofit restaurant to help feed the hungry, a toy factory to create employment, and a day care center and a clinic. She never ceased antiwar agitation, continuing even when the government confiscated her papers. Her mother and sister, Emmeline and Christabel, persevered in their prowar campaign, convinced that women's suffrage would be their reward at the end. The Pankhurst split symbolized the breakdown in women's groups everywhere. Mainstream suffrage leaders such as Mildred Fawcett in Britain and Marguerite de Witt Schlumberger in France vigorously supported their governments. British women were urged to recognize their patriotic duty as mothers of the nation and take nurses' training. In the fall of 1914, the French feminist Marguerite Durand revived her famous journal, *La Fronde,* "not to demand rights but to help [women] fulfill their social obligations." "Be courageous," Julie Siegfried urged French women. She proclaimed that women's long experience as women had taught them how to serve and help their fighting men—not to dominate them. The misery that all had suffered had made them "one national family," ending all divisions.[8]

In January 1915, four months before Italy actually entered the war, a Comitato Nazionale Femminile Italiano was formed in Milan "to organize women's work in case of mobilization or war, so that . . . they may replace those who leave factories and offices, to prevent interruption to the social and economic life of the nation."[9] A French minister called on women and children to "replace those from the fields" who had gone to battle. "Arise!" he exhorted women, "To work"![10] Italian regulations controlling women's nighttime work were suspended, but those prohibiting women from voting in local elections were reissued.[11] The prewar debate among German feminists about a compulsory service year for women to parallel men's military service assumed new meaning as feminist leaders promoted schemes to transform household skills into social service work.[12]

For socialist women, the coming of war was catastrophic. The socialist-feminist Russian exile, Alexandra Kollontai, described the sinking feeling that she shared with her friends, Karl and Sofie Liebknecht, as they sat in the Reichstag on August 4, 1914, while the war budget passed, supported by every political party. "The collapse of the German Socialist Party struck me as a calamity without parallel. I felt utterly alone and found comfort only in the company of the Liebknechts," she wrote.[13] Clara Zetkin, an eminent German socialist leader and specialist in women's issues, cried: "We women Socialists must call upon the women of all countries to oppose the prolongation of this insane genocide. From a million voices our irresistible cry must arise: Enough of killing, enough destruction! No total war until our people bleed to death! Peace! Permanent peace!"[14] Zetkin called for a peace without territorial annexations, a peace that would respect the integrity of neighboring nations. In spring 1915 she convened a meeting in Switzerland, but French socialist women refused to attend because so many of their sisters remained unfree under the German occupation of their northern provinces. Zetkin's friend, Rosa Luxemburg, whose scorn for the war was proportional to her anger at her German Social Democratic comrades who had supported it, served a three-and-a-half-year jail sentence. She captured the somber realities manifest by 1916:

> The show is over . . . in the sober atmosphere . . . a different chorus: the hoarse croak of the vultures and hyenas of the battlefield; . . . the patriotic cannon fodder . . . rots on the battlefields of Belgium and the Vosges, while profits are springing like weeds from the fields of the dead. . . .[15] Luxemburg understood

that the moment of social solidarity had passed and the glamour was gone. But why did the fighting continue?

Even in the neutral Netherlands, the shock of mobilization to defend the borders stunned the wives of suddenly mobilized men. With no warning, men departed in August 1914, leaving often penniless families behind. The Dutch physician, feminist, social reformer, and peace activist Aletta Jacobs encountered terrified women at the Vlissingen station, where she had gone to bid bon voyage to the South African writer Olive Schreiner. Schreiner was anxious to return to England before her exit might be stopped by a German invasion. On the platform, the bewildered soldiers' wives were frantic to find out where they would find the money that their husbands had said the government would provide. Jacobs transformed her network, the Association for Woman Suffrage, into an emergency aid group; they raised money, organized Boy and Girl Scouts to scour poor neighborhoods to offer help, and found ways to get credit extended. Although volunteer relief work was crucial to prevent starvation, Jacobs and her allies wondered whether her efforts only served to prolong the war.

Jacobs resolved to contact suffrage leaders everywhere to see whether the international women's movement could not convene a meeting to initiate an end to the killing. Thus was born the idea of the Women's Peace Congress at The Hague in April 1915, and in 1919, in Zurich, of the Women's International League for Peace and Freedom (WILPF). When invitations came to British and French women to attend the conference at The Hague, the official suffrage leadership absolutely refused. Most "respectable" French leaders believed that Aletta Jacobs was a German agent. Those who supported the peace initiative broke irretrievably from their traditionalist sisters. In Paris, Gabrielle Duchêne and her friends, disappointed they could not go to The Hague, courageously published *Un devoir urgent pour les femmes* in 1915. It was one of the earliest challenges to the government's defense of the war and to the view that war was a force of nature beyond human control. Expelled from her position in the national suffrage society, her papers taken by the police, Duchêne embarked on a lifelong commitment to politics on behalf of world peace and social justice. Almost at the same moment, an anonymous pamphlet in England, *Militarism Versus Feminism,* appeared, which transformed feminist analysis. The essay condemned militarism as a curse upon women; war reified domestic as well as international violence and perpetuated a brute male in dominant social positions. Woman become permanently subjected, forced to reproduce the species to make more war.

In 1914–1915, women protesting the carnage were few in number, effectively marginalized by the censorship blackout and the unpopularity of their position. Their message soon proved prophetic: conditions deteriorated everywhere and victory became a promise that generals could not deliver. By 1916–1917, most Germans had only turnips to eat. In March, 1917, cold and hungry women finally took to the streets of St. Petersburg, setting off the greatest mutiny in history. What had been treasonous or utopian musings of marginalized women in 1915 increasingly resembled common sense. A yearning on the home front to end the war was echoed on the front by mutinies and rumors of mutinies.

The vast majority of women accepted the patriotic call, did not lead active protests, and usually carried out tasks defined by their class: the middle class rolled bandages, and a few, such as Vera Brittain, volunteered as nurses. Working-class women began to chafe under the extraordinary pressures of child care and of commuting to tiring factory jobs to earn lower wages than male employees. In 1915 the Women's Committee of the Workers' National Committee in England demanded "equal conditions and equal wages" for salaried workers of either sex. Women working in jobs vacated by soldiers have a heavy burden, stated the manifesto; they must stay healthy, care for children, and repair the ravages of the disaster.[16] The disparity in compensation cut across nations. In Italy, where there was less mass enthusiasm for the war than among other belligerents, southern peasant women reluctantly undertook the heavy farm labor ordinarily performed by men at wages of about one-third those of their absent menfolk. After 1916, large numbers of young peasant women undertook factory work, a relatively new phenomenon in Italy. Young women workers in Turinese factories hated the discipline, refused to accept firings, and walked out en masse. Their protests disrupted production for the front. In Germany, despite the fact that women had been joining the work force for decades before the war, their increased numbers in munitions factories and heavy industrial plants by 1917 was depicted as a novel and threatening development. Poorly protected, they often did more work for less pay than men, adding to the unease about sex-role reversals.

Privations, uncontained inflation, unreliable or nonexistent child care, low wages, and the exhaustion that a working mother experienced at the end of a day when facing household tasks in homes without running water, with communal outhouses, and primitive cooking facilities fueled women's antiwar attitudes. What would happen to all these young women and mothers mobilized into the work force once the war ended? In a prescient insight, the English feminist-pacifist Helena Swanwick pointed out that one of the first moves would be to send women "Back to the Home!" even if they have no homes. She realized that "we must understand the unimpeachable right of the man who has lost his work and risked his life . . . to find decent employment, decent wages and conditions." But Swanwick also understood that some women might have changed, experienced "an enlargement and enhancement of life . . . when they are able to live by their own productive work, and we must realise that to deprive women of the right to live by their work is to send them back to a moral imprisonment . . . of which they have become now for the first time fully conscious."[17]

Swanwick's wartime writings, which were concerned with constructing a permanent peace, did not stop at celebrating the creation of new international organisms—the League of Nations, the World Court, and international labor and human rights organizations. Peace required a totally reorganized society, one wherein women and men shared child rearing, where public health services existed, and where education was funded twice as richly as the military. Her analysis became typical of progressive feminist pacifists after the war—linking the personal, the social, and the international.

Before the war, feminist analysis already had addressed issues such as unwanted pregnancies, too many children, abortion, birth control, and the state's obligations to provide maternity and child benefits to the poor. Notions of voluntary motherhood such as those proposed by the remarkable Norwegian crusader Katti Anker Moller were predicated on progressive ideals of improving social conditions.[18] Outspoken crusaders such as Nelly Roussel in France had campaigned energetically for voluntary motherhood. But the massacre of World War I put a dark spin on the issue. Childbearing for the "needs" of the state and as a patriotic act moved to dominate public discourse.

Ellen Key, Swedish reformer and activist, attacked the bizarre proposals that arose on both sides to commit women's bodies and souls to the service of state and society, to population replacement and continuation of the "race." In some instances, out-of-wedlock births were encouraged, abortions refused to even those raped by enemy soldiers, and waiting periods abolished prior to military marriages, while soldiers were encouraged to start babies. Tax policies against the unmarried were shaped to ensure a military class of 1935. Key, realizing that motherhood would be a matter of great interest to the state, warned women that they must *resolutely resist mass production of children* and not permit their highest instincts to become perverted for military ends.[19] Her fears about state interest in population growth as opposed to state support for healthful family environments were immensely prophetic. Nelly Roussel warned her feminist sisters in 1919 that the problem was not depopulation "but rather the opposite. . . . the great social plagues, especially war, are always engendered by 'overpopulation.'" To Roussel, only intelligent reproduction would prevent future colonialism, imperialism, and war.[20]

MAKING AND LOSING THE PEACE: 1919–1939

Women, "the mother half of humanity" in Jane Addams' phrase, insisted that they would not "endure without protest" the disastrous cruelties unleashed by war. The glamour and delirium of power, as Vera Brittain described the temptation that had initially drawn her generation to the battlefield, were a fraud.

When the diplomatic leadership gathered in Paris and Versailles between November 1917 and June 1918 "to make the world safe for democracy," women who had struggled to end the bloodbath regrouped. Since the French government would not grant visas to German and Austrian women, the successor conference to The Hague women's meeting met in Zurich; however, the French government refused to let its citizens travel to it.

The first order of business at the Zurich meeting was a resolution to lift the victor's economic blockade that had continued after Armistice Day, November 11, 1918. It was killing women, children, and the elderly. The Zurich conference denounced the manmade famine, epidemic disease, and unemployment in central Europe as "a disgrace to civilization." The resources of the globe—raw materials, money, and transport—needed to be routed to relieve this disaster. It was an entirely concrete phenomenon to participants, who included an Austrian woman awaiting news of her dying daughter and another participant who actually died at its conclusion.

Hearing of the proposed terms of the punitive Treaty of Versailles, furious that the secret treaties signed during the war would be honored, that territorial changes would occur denying rights of self-determination, and that the spoils of war were to be distributed to the victors, the Zurich congress attacked the Versailles treaty as an instrument "which can only lead to future wars." The women wanted immediate general disarmament. Economic reparations imposed on the new democratic Germany convinced the women at Zurich to protest to Wilson. The group, headed by Jane Addams, was refused entry.[21]

The women at Zurich wanted a peace that included women's rights in an international charter of human rights, women on the crucial committees to be formed under the League of Nations umbrella, an international code of ethics covering the rights of labor as well as capital, and a charter of labor rights that covered working women. The peace they envisioned would address educational and career rights. In 1919 at Zurich, women from all countries—victor and vanquished—sat and worked together. Despite France's refusal to allow its nationals to attend, Jeanne Mélin from the Ardennes managed to reach Zurich on the last day. To great acclaim, she crossed the platform to accept a bouquet from the German delegate, Lida Gustava Heymann. The symbolic act infuriated the French right, including suffragists, but it made Mélin a heroic figure. The symbolic Franco-German reconciliation led the entire assembly to rise and pledge, "I dedicate my life to the cause of peace." "It was in May, 1919 as at the beginning of the war," Mélin wrote later, "that women from all nations—neutrals and belligerents—had the courage to express an opinion contrary to that of all the governments. From that moment, they have never stopped calling for law and justice [against] the crime that sacrificed so many innocents to vile political and capitalistic interests."[22] When the women left, they went home to found and expand chapters of the Women's International League for Peace and Freedom, to run summer schools, to raise money to lobby the League at Geneva, and to campaign among politicians. Some traveled through the defeated countries, documenting the privations caused by the blockade and organizing aid relief—including rubber nipples to feed starving infants—to Central European victims. The generation of women that had lived through the first Great War of the twentieth century was determined to prevent a successor.

In the revolutionary Russian state, in the Weimar Republic of Germany, in most of the smaller northern European states, in Britain, in the United States, and in the successor states of the Austrian Empire, women won the vote. French, Belgian, Swiss, and Italian women did not. Instead of passing the suffrage bill, in July 1920 the French legislature endorsed the first example of pronatal legislation that would serve as a model for fascist regimes to come. Stiff prison terms and fines criminalized abortion and birth control education. Medals for motherhood—gold for women bearing ten children, silver and bronze for lesser breeders—were coupled with campaigns to remind French women that "maternity is the patriotism of women." The profound fear of depopulation that had obsessed France since 1870, now justified by the war losses, convinced a number of French feminist leaders to back the legislation.

While the drastic war casualties inspired much of the campaign for normalcy, domesticity, and reproduction, the postwar giddiness that manufactured the flapper—the New Woman, the short-haired, flat-chested, nearly androgynous female who freely dated, smoked, wore lipstick, and danced all night—increasingly frightened traditionalists, who feared that women were out of control. Thrilling media images of sophisticated, cigarette-smoking women with marcelled hairdos sweeping across dance floors in slinky, backless dresses hardly inspired women to stay home and sweep floors. Prostitution and loose sexuality might have been barely tolerated as an unfortunate companion of wartime, but a permanent sexual revolution was insupportable to proponents of "normalcy." In contrast to the expectations of the solid, respectable, aging, sensibly shoed generation of women pioneers who opened colleges for women, campaigned for the vote, and struggled for disarmament, the new woman of the 1920s openly flirted with sexual emancipation. Rightwing politicians, particularly Adolf Hitler, worked up traditionalist terrors that the greatness of a modern state would be wrecked if these degenerate, Western half-harlots were not curtailed.

Following Mussolini's ascent to power in 1922, the Italian state embraced a blunt patriarchal family policy. On Ascension Day in 1927 Mussolini delivered his famous speech attacking people who cut down family size to enhance their own creature comforts. This "selfishness" deprived the state of population. Bachelors would pay hefty taxes; families would receive benefits—child allowances, after-school programs, and holiday camps for poor children. Abortionists would suffer mightily. Legislation in 1934 required doctors to report immediately to medical authorities any cases of abortion, including miscarriage, or the birth of any deformed infant. Doctors were prohibited from performing any sterilization procedure. Open state concern for the breeding, feeding, and rearing of children increasingly was tied to undisguised interest in building an army. During the Ethiopian War, the campaign to produce babies frankly appealed for replacements for the dead. State-sponsored campaigns to abolish female work accused working women of promiscuity—of consorting with men on the streets, buses, and trains and in factories and offices. One Fascist intellectual insisted that "with work a woman becomes like a man; she causes man's unemployment; she develops an independence and a fashion that is contrary to the process of childbirth. . . ."[23]

The French and Italian models of pronatalist legislation, copied by the Spanish state after the Francoist takeover, were further legitimized by the Papal Encyclical (1930) entitled *Casti connubi* that was issued by Pius XI. This document rejected birth control and insisted that all sexual relations were intended to occur within marriage for procreation. Church leaders claimed that sexuality for enjoyment was contrary to divine intent, and the so-called emancipation of women was a renewal of pagan enslavement that dumped women off the "truly regal throne" that they occupy in the "walls of the home." In Franco Spain, the overturned republic was denounced for permitting moral degeneracy—working women, divorce, and restricted births.

Ellen Key's worst fears about state management of reproduction were realized in the Nazi German state, where propaganda moved well beyond rhetoric. Pronatalism took on murderous forms through medically controlled euthanasia. The state moved to cleanse itself of Jews, Gypsies, and "inferior peoples," as well as of feminists and pacifists. Among the earliest victims of the Nazi state were Lida Gustava Heyman and Anita Augspurg, eminent feminists and pacifists, who went into Swiss exile in 1933. Minna Cammens, an outspoken socialist in the Reichstag, was murdered; her husband was sent her ashes with orders to remain silent. State-sponsored family policies of the interwar years devoted to driving women from the work force, to increasing population, and to controlling previously private decisions over sexuality were the domestic underpinnings of renewed militarism, perhaps as important as industrial production.

Campaigns to encourage women's fertility and domesticity differed from efforts to build social welfare states that aided families in need and that encouraged human well-being. The best example of such an attempt in the interwar years, with all its limitations, was the Swedish case, inspired in part by the writings of Alva and Gunnar Myrdal. Proposals and legislation developed during the depression to provide low-cost housing or loans, marriage loans, school meals, after-school care, sex education, public nurseries, cheap cafeterias, and clinics and laundries in housing units—all as an effort to use public funding for the private good. One alert woman who was active in Social Democratic politics insisted that "no children on command" be manufactured. Women, she stated, "have other tasks and interests in society besides acting as child producing machines."[24]

The Soviet Union, among the most experimental countries in the 1920s in terms of the legal emancipation of women and the development of collective social services, moved toward a traditional family policy during the 1930s as fears of war with Nazi Germany mounted. The world that Alexandra Kollontai had dreamed of—weaving sexual independence with community responsibility—gave way to repressive policies that state leadership clearly believed were essential to production for military needs.

Resistance to remilitarization of the family, community, and nation survived in peace organizations. Of the peace groups that women joined, WILPF grew most impressively, to about fifty thousand members in forty countries. Headquartered in Geneva to be close to the League, the organization and its national components focused on the disarmament promises of Versailles. WILPF became a stubborn, serious, and unwavering lobby for international peace; several of its national chapters also insisted on domestic justice. Along with the International Council of Women and the International Suffrage Alliance, WILPF campaigned vigorously for the hiring of women at the League. Here and there a government appointed a prominent woman; for example, Helen Swanwick joined the British delegation to the League in 1924, and Dr. Gertrud Bäumer became an advisor on women's issues to the German delegation. Women in the Assembly worked determinedly on committees concerned with child welfare or women's rights. Nonetheless, even a conservative British woman complained in 1927 that at the League "all the stenographers and typists are women. The library staff is entirely . . . women. . . . There is one woman Chief of a section [the Social Section]. . . ."[25]

Outside of organizations, individually prominent women made the antiwar message the center of their lives: Käthe Kollwitz produced riveting lithographs of World War I; Maria Montessori crusaded to eliminate violence and competitiveness from children's socialization; and Madeleine Vernet in France and Helene Stöcker in Germany argued that domestic violence was a major source of national and international violence. "The spirit of peace begins in family life itself," Vernet wrote. "The child must not see his father behave like a despot nor his mother outwit this authority by subterfuge."[26] In 1919, the French journalist Louise Weiss, anxious to make Wilsonian ideas a reality, helped launch the influential periodical *L'Europe nouvelle*. The Swiss biochemist Gertrud Woker and the Swedish chemist Naima Sahlbom undertook lecture tours to alert people to the new threats of gas and chemical warfare that emerged in the late 1920s as rearmament discussions began to surface. They graphically pointed out that civilians could not be safe from aerial warfare and that metro stations would not provide protection against gas warfare. Their campaign underscored WILPF's determination to see the Disarmament Conference of 1932 succeed.

In *The Neuroses of Nations*, the psychological as well as the material bases of war led the English pacifist Carolyn Playne to connect international violence to the emotional stress that unleashed primitive impulses. Stress, she argued, was not merely a psychologically induced phenomenon but a result of the bitter struggle to survive waged by the poor. In her powerful essays and letters, Simone Weil explored the European need to dominate "inferior peoples" and observed that all war really ever did was generate its successor—another war. Virginia Woolf, in her famous *Three Guineas*, ruminated on the educational socialization of men and women and the so-called normal social order it produced, and concluded that women's peace action had to be conducted entirely differently from men's. During the 1930s, feminist peace activists on the Continent and in Britain had to decide whether or not to join in anti-Fascist crusades, to support coalitions including Communists or mixed-sex groups, to shape a position toward Hitler, and finally to resign themselves to the possible use of force. WILPF divided bitterly as some members insisted on defending a "pure" antiwar and antiviolence approach and others insisted on joining political coalitions against fascism, such as the Amsterdam-Pleyel movement in 1933–1934 in which left-wing intellectuals mobilized against war and fascism. In 1934, for example, on the twentieth anniversary of the outbreak of the Great War, an international women's assembly against war and fascism in Paris brought 1500 women together, including workers, housewives, professionals, and representatives of women's organizations. Issues included women's family and work conditions across the globe, but mainstream women's peace groups remained aloof. Gabrielle Duchêne, who had become convinced that a broad anti-Fascist front was crucial to keeping the peace, commented that the gulf between "integral" absolutist pacifists of both genders and "realistic" pacifists was a serious threat to the peace campaign. Pacifist purity misled some people to believe that Hitler was a rational political being. Peace, she believed, would not be ensured by appeasement but by isolating Fascist states, imposing embargoes, and driving them from the international community as pariahs. Women peace activists were furious with the Munich Pact in 1938. At a 1939 WILPF gathering, leaders denounced the so-called government pacifists who confused appeasement with peace action. "Pacifism is not the complacent support of evil. It is a struggle for right . . . a courageous initiative to construct a just policy."[27] Feminists prepared themselves to house refugees.

Despite their unwavering commitment, women peace activists of all political stripes could not stem the remilitarization of European society. When the unprecedented "lightning war"—a stunning air and land attack— exploded on September 1, 1939, in Poland, the waiting and wondering finally ended in Europe. In Asia, war had been under way for most of the 1930s.

WORLD WAR II: 1939–1945

Except by absolute pacifists largely in Anglo-American communities, World War II was viewed as a just war, a crusade against barbarism. The anti-Fascist campaign of realistic peace activists during the 1930s, then vilified as a Bolshevik front, suddenly became state policy in Britain, in the United States, and among the Free French under Charles De Gaulle in London. With the German attack on the Soviet Union in June 1941, the Grand Alliance, or the Big Three (Britain, the United States, and the USSR), committed itself to fight until total victory over the Axis had been won.

Lost in this last half-century of Cold Warriorism has been the spirit of political collaboration of World War II. Axis expansion suspended the relentless anticommunist politics of Western states. From 1941 to 1945, Russians contributed the majority of bodies, the United States provided most of the "arsenal," and the British did some of each. Russian deaths, perhaps close to 25 million at the end, included the largest contingent of fighting women ever mobilized in the history of warfare. In 1941, Valentina Grizodubova pleaded with an anti-Fascist women's meeting in Moscow for a global woman's resistance against the barbarians. She went on to become one of the most famous pilots of the air defense. Nina Kosterina, 15 years old, was less fortunate. In November 1941 she joined the partisans to be parachuted behind enemy lines, and she died a month later.

The impact of World War II on women depended on who and where they were. Rosa Manus, the Dutch woman who had helped organize the woman's meeting at The Hague in 1915 and who had devoted her life to WILPF and international peace, was one of the first to be picked up when the Gestapo followed the German army into Amsterdam. She died in a concentration camp. Russian women, already employed in large numbers in factories, fought and served in the navy and the air force as drivers, mechanics, medical personnel, nurses, snipers, and machine gunners. They lifted bombs onto bombers, repaired propellers, moved huge food cauldrons, and often carried a bullet for themselves to use if captured. Three aviation units were composed of women, and women constituted about 30 percent of casualties. In no other nation did women play as substantial a military role, even though their numbers in Britain, Canada, and the United States were greater than ever before in those nations' histories. One estimate states that 450,000 women served in various military or auxiliary capacities in the British forces.

In France, by June 1940, nearly 1 million women lost their husbands to German captivity. Suddenly, women had to take over the economy and provide for families. Madeleine Fourcade observed that "women were everywhere . . . in the fields, the cities, in business, in factories. France became a nation of women."[28] Those in "unoccupied" France living under the Vichy regime of Marshall Henri Pétain were also subject to his harangues about French women's responsibility for their national humiliation; they had failed to produce enough children after 1919.

By 1943, women in Poland, Norway, Denmark, the Low Countries, Greece, Yugoslavia, France, Italy, and other occupied European states joined the resistance. Women worked as runners, networkers, and observers in the communications systems; they wiggled through sewers, published illicit papers, and served as medics. Former Girl Guides turned their education to use; in Warsaw they trained as assassination squads, planting explosives in officers' quarters. Women were considered better than men when it came to memorizing, responding rapidly, keeping secrets, and following orders. The Yugoslav resistance included about 100,000 women, of whom one-quarter died and about 40,000 were wounded. A young chemist, Jeanne Bohec, parachuted into France to train men to set up explosives even though the Free French military in Britain would not let her train as a jumper.

Lucie Aubrac's daring ruse that freed her captive husband and outwitted the Gestapo chief Klaus Barbie in Lyons became the stuff of legend. Pregnant, Aubrac convinced Barbie (who did not know that she was the wife of his prisoner) that she had been "ruined" by the man in his prison and pleaded to be allowed to "marry him" so her honor could be saved. The Nazis agreed, and on his way to be "married" the resistance attacked and spirited Aubrac's husband off. Shortly after, a British plane landed and evacuated them. The Norwegian pacifist Sigrid Lund continued under Nazi noses to hide and smuggle Jews to Sweden and watched in horror as the Gestapo carried off her 18-year-old son, who had published an anti-Nazi paper in his high school.

Italian partisan women such as Carla Capponi, a young typist, and Marisa Musu, a student, mastered explosives, carried bombs, and finally assassinated a German officer outside the Excelsior Hotel as she snatched his briefcase. Disguises, false papers, and identity changes became daily occurrences. In the mountains of northwest Italy, Ada Gobetti skied, hiked, and slid to preserve the communications network of the partisan army. Shopping baskets and handbags contained letters, explosives, newspapers, medicines, and money. Traditional peasant women in Greece took their missing husbands' hunting rifles in often vain efforts to shoot Nazi occupiers; they saved men by dressing them as women when the Nazis organized mass executions of village men as retribution for resistance action; midwives, pretending to deliver babies in the mountains, carried messages, food, medicines, and weapons in their black bags. In 1942, when a large protest against forced labor exploded in Athens, high school girls helped break into German headquarters to destroy files of workers to be deported; the girls were among the first to die.

In these resistance movements, traditional roles melted away, but postwar accounts reflected historical amnesia. Although Italian women may have accounted for nearly 1 million members of the resistance, until recently, historical scholarship was nearly mute about them. In Lucie Aubrac's analysis, French women were bitter that, despite their involvement in every aspect of the resistance, the prewar political structures resurfaced. Incredibly, even when De Gaulle insisted to the Provisional Government meeting in 1944 in Algiers that French women get the vote, about one-third of his own party refused. Only Communist support created the majority to legalize women's suffrage in France.

Women in unoccupied nations—Germany, Britain, Canada, and the United States—experienced the war differently, and those differences were further shaped by social class. After a decade of propaganda aimed at making women queens in private domestic empires, governments shifted to propaganda campaigns to persuade women of their patriotic duty to go to work and to convince them that their femininity would not be ruined by factory labor.

In 1941, the British government began the obligatory registration of women from 19 to 40 years for "essential labor." The authorities mounted propaganda campaigns to overcome the unwillingness of married women and their husbands to take on a double burden. Overall, promises of a wonderful future that included housing, education, health care, and vacations were intertwined with appeals for women to move into heavy industry.

An Englishwoman, Nelly Last, described the exhilaration of realizing herself as a separate, valued human being, an autonomous personality apart from her demanding husband. As a volunteer, she ran a Red Cross volunteer shop near Liverpool, where she discovered, "I'm a really clever woman in my own line, and not the 'odd' or 'uneducated' woman that I've had dinned into me." Women wearing pants struck her as admirable. She finally told her astonished husband to get his own tea. Reshaping her own reality, Nelly Last concluded that future marriages would have to be "partnerships" if marriage was to have a future.[29]

On the other hand, for a mother of six children who held a factory job, the day began at 5:00 A.M. and ended 16-1/2 hours later when she finished feeding her children and cleaning up. Sunday was no respite, since the factory—a town away—ran on Sunday.[30] The working-class woman did not fit the profile of an emancipated, happier British woman participating in the struggle to save the nation from defeat and occupation. Work was not liberation, despite the pay; for a mother with young children, it was an another way to be bone-tired.

Just as war altered the social position of women and pulled them into public space of all kinds, it overturned presumably normal sexual relationships as well. For some, the price of survival was selling sex. In wartime, women's bodies were always at greatest risk at the moment of conquest. In 1945, when Russian soldiers came hunting for women, German girls were hidden in a hospital in Berlin that claimed to be treating typhoid.[31] In Naples, as Allied troops drove out the Axis, entrepreneurs offered their merchandise to Moroccan, Indian, Algerian, and U.S. soldiers—"two dollars the boys, three dollars the girls!" But when the city was flooded with countrypeople, the price of sex plummeted just as the cost of oil, sugar, flour, and bread climbed. A young woman prostitute who earned $25 in one week saw her earnings fall to $4 in the next week. As the journalist Curzio Malaparte explained to an American officer, "wholesalers had thrown onto the market a large consignment of Sicilian women . . . nearly all of them peasants." The collapse of the price of human flesh undermined the entire economy of the city.[32]

To women, men, and children rounded up by the Nazis and shipped to concentration, labor, or extermination camps, the experience of war was unique in human history. During the 1930s, a foretaste of Nazi policies affected thousands of politically active women or women relatives of men who were arrested, exiled, or executed—women held hostage, for instance, when a husband escaped from prison. But even the most primitive prisons run by the most sadistic matrons did not match the conditions of the killing camps of

Auschwitz, Maidenek, Chemnitz, and even the model, Ravensbruck. Recent scholarship suggests that women who survived seem to have prevailed over the barbaric privations somewhat better than men partly because of their experience with housekeeping, nursing, and caring for others, and even their physical capacity to live on less food. But for a Jewish woman from Greece deported to a camp in northern Europe, survival in a cotton shift in three feet of snow proved impossible, even if she were assigned to a work detail. All the camps had an organized resistance that passed messages to the outside world, and most camps organized an underground cultural life. Women in Bergen-Belsen attempted to create educational and musical activities for surviving children. The world with eyes to see cannot forget the pictures of skeleton humans, tattooed with numbers, who were liberated by Russians in 1944 and by British and U.S. soldiers in 1945.

1945: NORMALCY AGAIN

The return to normalcy following World War II was immensely complicated by the transformation of the Grand Alliance into the Cold War. Once again, governments had to demobilize their wartime work force to make room for returning veterans. Across the European continent, now a vast slum, the extraordinary physical destruction required a clean-up effort of historic magnitude. In the Soviet Union, a stunning population imbalance between men and women as a result of the slaughter required a generation to redress. At the minimum, there were at least fifty-five women to every forty-five men. There women would be needed as workers as well as reproducers. Most of the Soviet infrastructure, laboriously erected in the agonizing Five Year Plans, had been blown apart.

However, May 8 and August 10, 1945, were days of unalloyed joy in the victor and liberated nations. Peace would restore normalcy, and normalcy meant the *status quo ante bellum.*

This status quo was actually not quite what it had been in the 1930s. In Britain, France, Italy, the Low Countries, Scandinavia, and eventually western Germany, the modern welfare state emerged. French, Belgian, Swiss, and Italian women finally won the vote. However, the new social contract that redefined state obligations toward the welfare of citizens was designed to preserve the standard male-headed household.

The nuclear family was to be the basic unit of the nuclear age. This was true in the European welfare state as well as in the United States, which remained closer to the laissez-faire model. In the welfare state, public services did not eliminate women's private dependency.

Barely two years after World War II formally ended, the bitter U.S.-Soviet rivalry was in place. Washington-run campaigns against European Communist parties matched Moscow's moves to shape Peoples Democracies along its borders. In Greece, civil war exploded between left and right by 1947, enabling President Harry Truman to lay out a doctrine that froze the terms of the Cold War. As a result, Greek women supporting the left, heirs to the wartime resistance, paid brutally as the U.S.-sponsored, right-wing government triumphed. Women who had been heroines against the Nazis went to prison, sometimes with infants in their arms. They were tortured, raped, murdered, and sent to island camps; villages were exterminated. If captured, they were asked to sign a Declaration of Repentance. In 1950, Commandant Antony Vasilopoulos, who was in charge of the Makronisos camp, a bleak spit of stone in the Aegean, attacked women prisoners for having dishonored the words *Greek woman*—for having supported the communist side in the civil war: "There is no mercy for you. . . . How can you still dare to raise your scrawny little bodies . . . a mere thousand females . . . against the will of our nation. . . . You will be made to sign, whether you like it or not. You will sign from the stretchers before you die." Those women who signed and repented could keep their children, go home, and be "made whole and Greek" again.[33] The women who refused had children dragged from them to be raised by proper Greek families. The Cold War in Greece was not merely a struggle for the kind of postwar state that would emerge; it was a direct effort to undo the liberation of women that the resistance had engendered and to restore patriarchal norms as the basis for an obedient population in an authoritarian state.

CONCLUSION

A generation of women before World War I had struggled to prevent what they feared would be a catastrophe; after the war occurred, another generation mounted an unremitting international crusade to prevent a successor. The effort to restore "normalcy" that privileged pronatalism and drove women from public life was a desperate effort to push back the genie that had fled the bottle in World War I. In wartime, women could do anything; in peacetime, they had to climb back on the pedestal, descending only to keep the house clean. Peace-minded women—while not directly challenging the motherhood message—nevertheless demanded that social and international policies create the conditions for decent personal and family life. Following World War II, despite a few brave words favoring One World, the Cold War largely silenced peace movements and citizen efforts unless these supported state initiatives. In a bipolar world managed by two elites, normalcy meant that male politicians decided the fate of the human race and married women decided the brand of washing machine to purchase.

This sociopolitical equation began to unravel a decade later when those very mothers realized that their children were drinking milk laced with strontium 90—a result of aboveground atomic testing. The astounding threat of nuclear obliteration reawakened a new generation of peace activists, for whom human survival surpassed Cold War imperatives.

NOTES

1. Statistics on the world wars change repeatedly. For World War I battlefield casualties, the traditional source is Quincy Wright, *A Study of War,* 2nd ed., 2 vols. Chicago, 1965, Appendix B. An effort to determine the civilian and military losses after World War I by W. Woytiski, *Die Welt in Zahl,* Berlin, 1928, proposed about 40 million, of which one-fourth were military. More recent research is in J. D. Singer and M. Small, *The Wages of War,* New York, 1972; B. Urlanis, *Wars and Population,* Moscow, 1971; and for World War II, I. C. B. Dear with M. R. D. Foot, eds., *The Oxford Companion to World War II,* Oxford, 1995. If Russian losses include "unborn" children that the civilian dead might have been expected to bear, one estimate states that over 48 million Russian and Soviet citizens died in World War II. See John Ericson and David Dilks, eds., *Barbarossa, the Axis and the Allies,* London, 1994, p. 258. I am very grateful to my colleague, S. J. Stearns, for his help in locating and interpreting these sources.

2. Hubertine Auclert, "Programme électoral des femmes," *La Citoyenne* (August 1885), cited in Gisela Bock and Pat Thane, eds., *Maternity and Gender Politics,* Routledge, 1991, p. 19.

3. Speech to the Conseil National des Femmes Françaises, *Première Assemblée Générale le 17 mai 1903* (Dôle, 1903), *77 et seq.* She was referring to the voluntary tribunal to arbitrate differences that was set up at the first Hague Peace Conference, 1899.

4. Speeches of 1912–1914 in *La Luce del pensiero* (Naples, 1912) and *Le National bruxellois* (2 juin, 1914) in Clipping file, at the Mundanum, La Fontaine collection (Brussels), box 20.

5. Report by A. N. Shabanova, "General Meeting of the Russian Peace Society, December, 1913" in *Peace News* (Moscow, January 1914); text provided by Rusanna Ilukhina; trans. by Manuela Dobos.

6. A succinct summary of this mood is Margaret H. Darrow, "Women Must Pay the Blood Tax: French Women's Ideas for Wartime Mobilization in the Years Before World War I," paper delivered at the Berkshire Conference on the History of Women, Chapel Hill, North Carolina, June 8, 1996.

7. Barbara Winslow, *Sylvia Pankhurst: Sexual Politics and Political Activism,* St. Martin's Press, New York, 1996.

8. Julie Siegfried, *La Guerre et le rôle de femme,* speech at the Musée Sociale, January 1915.

9. Dott. Angelina De-Leva Serdini De Mari, "Che faremo in caso di guerra?" in *Giovine Europa* Milan (January 1915) 3, p. 8.

10. Appeal of August 7, 1914 in *Le Journal.*

11. Law of August, 30, 1914, on labor, no. 925 in *Donne e diritto: due secoli di legislazione, 1796–1986;* Article 24, February, 4, 1915, no. 148 on elections, in *ibid.*

12. Helene Lang, "Die Dienstpflicht der Frau" (1915), excerpted in Susan Groag Bell and Karen M. Offen, *Women, The Family and Freedom: The Debate in Documents* Vol. II: 1880–1950, Stanford, 1983, pp. 262–263.

13. *Autobiography of a Sexually Emancipated Communist Woman,* with a foreword by Germaine Greer, trans. Salvator Attanasio, Herder and Herder, New York, 1971, p. 23.

14. "To the Socialist Women of All Countries," in *Clara Zetkin: Selected Writings,* ed. Philip S. Foner, International Publishers, New York, 1984, p. 115.

15. Rosa Luxemburg, *The Crisis in German Social Democracy (The Junius Pamphlet)*, Part I: Zurich 1916, in *Selected Political Writings of Rosa Luxemburg*, New York Monthly Review, 1971, pp. 322–335.

16. Cited by Helena Swanwick, *The War in Its Effect upon Women*, orig. London, 1916, reprinted with a new introduction by Blanche Wiesen Cook, Garland Library, New York, 1971, p. 13.

17. *Ibid*, p. 8.

18. Ida Blom, "Voluntary Motherhood 1900–1930: Theories and Politics of a Norwegian Feminist in an International Perspective," in *Maternity and Gender Policies: Women and the Rise of the European Welfare States 1880s–1950s*, ed. Gisela Bock and Pat Thane, Routledge, London, 1991, pp. 21–39.

19. Ellen Key, *War, Peace and the Future*, trans. Hildegard Norberg, orig. 1916; Garland, New York, 1972; introduction by Berenice Carroll, p. 184.

20. Open letter to the founder of WILPF in *Le Néo-Malthusien*, June 1919, and *Libre Pensée Internationale*, May 15, 1919, in Fonds Roussel, "Coupures de journaux, 1915–1922," in Recueil No. 6, Bib. Marguerite Durand.

21. Reported in Jane Addams, *Peace and Bread in Time of War*, 1922. Reprinted with a new introduction by Blanche W. Cook, New York: Garland, 1972; Marie Louise Degen, *History of the Women's Peace Party*, 1939. Reprinted with a new introduction by Blanche W. Cook, New York, Garland, 1972, p. 229.

22. Letter of 30 June 1923 to Féderation Communiste des Ardennes in Jeanne Mélin, Documents, in Collection M-L Bouglé, box 33.

23. Quoted from Ferdinando Loffredo (1938) in Mariolina Graziosi, "Gender Struggle and Gender Identity," in *Mothers of Invention: Women, Italian Fascism, and Culture*, ed. Robin Pickering-Iazzi, Minneapolis, Minnesota, 1995, University of Minnesota Press, p. 40.

24. An Inquiry of the Social Democratic Women's Association (1941) cited in Ann-Sofie Ohlander, "The Invisible Child? The Struggle for a Social Democratic Family Policy in Sweden, 1900–1960s," in Bock and Thane, *op. cit.*, p. 70.

25. D. N. Northcroft, *Women at Work in the League of Nations*, Wadsworth, London, 1927, p. 14.

26. Madeleine Vernet, in *Le Quoditien* 13, December 1920.

27. Yvonne Sée, *Réaliser l'expérance*, Ligue internationale de Femmes de la paix et la liberté, Paris, 1984, p. 26.

28. Guylaine Guidez, *Femmes dans la guerre 1939–1945*, Perrin: Terres des Femmes, 1989, p. 59.

29. Richard Broad and Suzie Fleming, eds., *Nelly Last's War: A Mother's Diary, 1939–45*, Falling Wall Press, Bristol, 1981, pp. 254–255.

30. Report of a 40-year-old woman in Gail Braybon and Penny Summerfield, *Out of the Cage: Women's Experiences in Two World Wars*, Pandora, London, 1987, pp. 235–236.

31. Annemarie Tröger, "Between Rape and Prostitution: Survival Strategies and Chances of Emancipation for Berlin Women after World War II," in *Between Culture and Politics; A Century of Change* ed. J. Friedlander et al., Bloomington, University of Indiana Press, 1986, p. 103.

32. Curzio Malaparte, *The Skin*, trans. David Moore, Houghton Mifflin, Boston, 1952, pp. 8–9.

33. Quoted in Eleni Fourtouni, *Greek Women in Resistance*, Lake View Press, Chicago, 1986, p. 152.

SUGGESTIONS FOR FURTHER READING

Aubrac, Lucie. *Outwitting the Gestapo,* trans. Konrad Bieber and Betsy Wing, intro. by Margaret Collins Weitz. University of Nebraska Press, Lincoln and London, 1993.

Bard, Christine. *Les filles de Marianne: Histoires des féminismes, 1914–1940.* Paris: Fayard, 1995.

Brayton, Gail. *Women Workers of the First World War.* London: Routledge, 1981.

Brayton, Gail, and Penny Summerfield. *Out of the Cage: Women's Experiences in Two World Wars.* London: Routledge, Pandora, 1987.

Bridenthal, Renate, Atina Grossman, and Marion Kaplan, eds. *When Biology Became Destiny: Women in Weimar and Nazi Germany.* New York: Monthly Review Press, 1984.

Brittain, Vera. *Testament of Youth: One Woman's Haunting Record of the First World War.* Orig. 1933; New York: Penguin, 1978.

Bussey, G., and M. Tims. *The Women's International League for Peace and Freedom, 1915–1965.* New York: Macmillan, 1978.

De Grazia, Victoria. *How Fascism Ruled Women, Italy, 1922–1945.* Berkeley, University of California, 1992.

Foutouni, Eleni. *Greek Women in Resistance: Journals, Oral Histories.* Chicago: Lake View Press, 1986.

Hamann, Brigitte. *Bertha von Suttner: A Life for Peace,* trans. Ann Dubsky. Syracuse, 1996.

Higgonet, Margaret, Michel Jenson, et al., eds. *Behind the Lines: Gender and the Two World Wars.* New Haven, Conn.: Yale University Press, 1987.

Isaksson, Eva, ed. *Women and the Military System.* New York: St. Martin's Press, 1988.

Josephson, Harold, Sandi Cooper, Lawrence Wittner, and Solomon Wank, eds. *Biographical Dictionary of Modern Peace Leaders.* Westport, Conn.: Greenwood Press, 1985.

Kamester, M., and Jo Vellacot, eds. *Militarism vs. Feminism.* London: Virago, 1987.

Laska, Vera. *Women in the Resistance and in the Holocaust.* Westport, Conn.: Greenwood Press, 1983.

Liddington, Jill. *The Road to Greenham Common: Feminism and Anti-Militarism in Britain since 1820.* Virago Press, London, 1989.

Offen, Karen. "Depopulation, Nationalism and Feminism in Fin-de Siècle France." *The American Historical Review* 89, no. 3 (June, 1984), pp. 648–675.

———. "Exploring the Sexual Politics of French Republican Nationalism." In *Aspects of French Nationalism,* ed. Robert Tombs. London: Unwin Hyman, 1992.

Oldfield, Sybil. *Women Against the Iron Fist: Alternatives to Militarism, 1900–1989.* Cambridge: Blackwell, 1989.

Pierson, Ruth R. *Women and Peace: Theoretical and Historical Perspectives.* London: Croom Helm, 1987.

Quataert, Jean. *Reluctant Feminists in German Social Democracy 1885–1917.* Princeton, Princeton University Press, 1979.

Rossiter, Margaret. *Women in the Resistance.* New York, Praeger, 1986.

Rupp, Leila. *Mobilizing Women for War: German and American Propaganda, 1939–1945.* Princeton, 1978.

Saywell, Shelley. *Women in War.* New York: Penguin, 1985.

Tillion, Germaine. *Ravensbruck: An Eyewitness Account of a Women's Concentration Camp.* New York, Anchor, 1975.

Weitz, Margaret Collins. *Sisters in the Resistance: How Women Fought to Free France, 1940–1945.* New York, John Wiley, 1995.

Wiltsher, Anne. *Most Dangerous Women: Feminist Peace Campaigners of the Great War.* London: Pandora, 1985.

Winter, Jay M., and R. M. Wall, eds. *The Upheaval of War: Family Work and Welfare in Europe 1914–1918.* Cambridge, Cambridge University Press, 1988.

D. W. Koeppen. *A Woman of 1934.*   FROM THE COLLECTION OF MARVIN AND JANET FISHMAN, MILWAUKEE.

17

The "Woman Question" in Authoritarian Regimes

Claudia Koonz

In the chapters that span the history of European women, there are many high points at which activists battled for social justice, civil rights, and material autonomy. At other times, women as victims persevered against staggering odds. But during still other periods, women rallied to political leaders who swore to restore a strong patriarchal state. These dictators promised equality, not by empowering women, but rather by depriving all citizens, male and female, of their fundamental rights. Instead of struggling to improve women's lives, these women sacrificed for collective liberation and thrilled to effusive praise for their maternal contributions. Whereas feminists championed individual rights, women who willingly served dictatorships placed top priority on the rights of their own ethnic communities and turned against the nonconformists and "outsiders" in their midst. Intense patriotism, of the kind normally experienced in wartime, drove activist conservative women as well as their more passive followers into a frenzy of work for dictatorships. Why, many asked themselves, struggle any longer against insuperable odds to win admission into conventionally masculine spheres when powerful states called on them to expand their own separate spheres? As this chapter makes clear, the Italian, Spanish, German, and French women who made this fatal calculation placed themselves firmly on the side of repressive and even criminal regimes that degraded civil society and invaded family privacy in the name of strengthening what Mussolini, Franco, Hitler, and Pétain called "tradition."

1789 liberated men. The World War has liberated women!" declared a French suffragist. Another exclaimed, "In three years women realized more progress than in fifty years of struggle."[1] A German woman rejoiced, "This war is the grandest hour for women!" After decades of struggling for women's rights in peaceful times, during the first days of August 1914 thousands of activists in all belligerent nations abruptly silenced their calls for equality. During the next four years they abandoned their international sisterhood and labored for nationalist victory. What was it about the experience of terrible deprivation, anxiety, mourning, and physical exhaustion that felt liberating to these activists? In later years several leaders reflected on the extraordinary transformation in their political lives. Gertrud Bäumer, who presided over the 700,000-member Federation of German Women's Associations, recalled in rapturous terms the outbreak of World War I. Suddenly, the drab "materialistic and mechanical order" was swept away. In place of lobbying for women's interests, she wrote, "The life of the nation fills our every breath and pulses in our blood. . . . These weeks have revealed to women more than they could have imagined the extent to which their feelings and fate are rooted in the Fatherland."[2] In all belligerent nations, women labor activists welcomed the expansion of employment opportunities created by war. Socialist feminists found themselves collaborating with their erstwhile rivals from religious, liberal, and conservative women's rights groups. Women who had for years denounced patriarchy suddenly thrilled to find out how much they could accomplish within states led by misogynists.

Perhaps more surprising, the national leaders who for so long had scathingly denounced women's rights movements quickly discovered that they needed women to work for victory on the home front. Before the war, misogynist male politicians had done their best to keep women out of public life. The war, however, taught them that masses of women could simultaneously serve their nation and revitalize feminine roles. The Vatican had already made this discovery. In 1909, Pope Pius X, an archenemy of women's emancipation, endorsed the beatification of Joan of Arc and, in the same speech, urged women to enter public life in feminine roles to defend Catholic values. In 1919 Pope Benedict XV carried this logic to its conclusion and defended women's enfranchisement because he confidently assumed that most Catholic women would vote against women's equal rights (and all other progressive measures). Dictators after World War I answered "the woman question" in a similar way. Rather than preaching the simple return of women to domesticity, they recruited masses of women followers to attend to "feminine" concerns in the public sphere. State-sponsored propaganda and special programs rallied millions of women in support of militarism, political repression, racism, nationalism, natalism (the encouragement of high birthrates), and autarky (economic independence).

Nationalism, together with the militarism that accompanied it, marginalized women so completely that no women participated in policymaking. And yet nationalist dictatorships drew masses of women followers into the public sphere in unprecedented ways.[3] It was this seeming paradox that feminists from the pre-1914 era found so troubling after 1919. Younger women, they observed, seemed to find sacrifice for the national good more attractive than what they regarded as first-wave feminists' "selfish" insistence on women's issues. Some champions of women's equality concluded that liberalism had outlived its usefulness as they watched authoritarian rulers defeat democracy in Hungary (1919), Italy (1922), Poland (1926), Bulgaria (1923), Portugal (1926), Yugoslavia (1929), Germany (1933), Rumania (1938), Austria (1938), and Spain (1938). In the first year of World War II, Czechoslovakia, France, the Netherlands, Denmark, Belgium, and Norway fell to German armies. From this bleak record, many feminists concluded that democracy had little chance of surviving.

Throughout Europe, women leaders, many of whom had a strong sense of women's equal worth, allied themselves to the new nationalist dictators, who praised women as "mothers of the nation" and guardians of ethnic purity. By galvanizing citizens' fears of a common enemy, dictators simulated the atmosphere of wartime and accelerated the militarization of all aspects of national life. Women who feared democracy and hated socialism accepted "second sex" status in order to join the nationalist revival. In other words, belief in women's equality did not in itself immunize women against racial hatred, militarism, state-sponsored natalism, or authoritarianism. Advocates of women's rights could be as racially bigoted, morally corrupt, and opportunistic as their male counterparts. The few women who chose opposition or exile from oppressive regimes were motivated less by specifically feminist ideals than by their fear of ethnic persecution and/or their broad political and ethical values.

In this chapter, I explore the impact of dictatorship on women in Fascist Italy, Franco's Spain, Nazi Germany, and Vichy France. In each setting, democracy collapsed for specific reasons: in Germany and Italy because demagogues, backed by paramilitary force, destroyed democratic institutions; in Spain because an insurgent army defeated the republic; and in France because the army surrendered to German forces. In complex ways, millions of women in these countries experienced a certain kind of equality when their governments deprived **all** citizens, male and female alike, of any meaningful human rights.

The process by which women joined the national body politic differed from the trajectory that had transformed men from subjects to citizens via craft guilds, labor unions, rights associations, and political parties. Women arrived at the threshold of formal citizenship during a later stage of industrialization and entered the national community via participation in wartime mobilization, expanding consumer culture, and new media networks. As industrialization progressed, popular culture reached even tiny villages via newspapers, magazines and posters, radio broadcasts, and cinema. Mass marketing introduced brand names, and mass production made clothing and household items affordable to people of modest means. In the interwar democracies, young and independent women enjoyed considerable freedom to cast themselves as *la garçon,* a flapper, or girl with a *Bubikopf* ("bobbed" hair). Although young women in dictatorships could not openly embrace such "decadent" identities, they participated in a rebellion of sorts by engaging in sports, participating in youth group outings, wearing sporty fashions, and escaping from family control in state-sponsored peer activities. To contemporaries in democratic settings, service in a national work corps or a trip to a national political rally might have seemed utterly conformist, but such experiences freed masses of young women from their regional homes and bonded them to the national cause.

In the absense of a genuine foreign danger, authoritarian leaders brilliantly revived the atmosphere of wartime by mobilizing citizens against supposed domestic enemies. They warned that "soulless" individualism had destroyed spiritual values. Against exaggerated reports of communist plots, racial dangers, cultural decadence, and sexual license, these four dictators summoned patriotic women to close ranks within their ethnic community. Echoing the slogans of World War I, dictators told women how vital they were in the crusade for purity, virtue, and health. Against a tidal wave of modern decadence, mothers alone could save the family by defending traditional "feminine" values. A slogan from Vichy captured the rhetoric of the militarized dictatorships: "The mother creates the family. The family creates France!"[4]

And yet, behind the sentimental appeals to motherhood, all four dictators' success in mobilizing women depended on industrialization. Without highly developed communications, the peasant wife or impoverished mother in an urban slum would not even have heard the call to join the nation. In Spain, with one radio per 90 people and meagre programming, Franco's voice barely entered public consciousness. But in Germany (with one radio for every seven people) state sponsored programming entered almost every home.[5] Advanced transportation systems enabled regimes to organize mass ceremonies, and state-subsidized films conveyed the music and speeches glorifying the regime to even the smallest towns. Coercion, too, depended on an efficient and bureaucratized surveillance system to stifle dissent and imprison or murder opponents. The more secular the culture, the more "available" women became for participation in national projects that claimed energies once absorbed by organized religion. In short, the revival of tradition depended on modernization.

A second and closely related paradox soon became apparent. Despite legislation encouraging motherhood as a full-time profession, modernizing dictators required economic changes that depended on the availability of poorly paid and mobile women in the service sectors and in labor-intensive factory work. Rapid modernization disrupted traditional family and community ties, pulling women into the labor force, urbanizing the population, and undermining the centrality of the family. The hardships of urbanization and demographic dislocation further broke down traditional communities and strained family support networks. This mix of modernity and tradition recalled World War I when generals called on women as patriotic consumers, frugal household managers, factory workers, teachers, nurses, and morale builders. Mussolini, Franco, Hitler, and Pétain appealed to women in maternal roles even as they sponsored modernization that gutted the traditional foundations on which those roles rested.

ITALY

When Italians emerged victorious from World War I under the leadership of constitutional monarch Victor Emmanuel III, it seemed that the liberal reforms that had begun before 1914 would continue. But when socialists, communists, peasant leagues, anarchists, and labor unions organized massive strikes and factory owners refused concessions, the parliamentary system faltered. Amidst a chaotic political situation in 1921, Benito Mussolini founded the Fascist party (*Partito Nazionale Fascista*, or PNF) as a militaristic and populist alternative to both left- and right-wing political movements. Although the PNF sent only 35 delegates (less than ten percent) to the legislature, Mussolini commanded over twenty thousand paramilitary troops who brutally attacked and harassed leftist reformers everywhere, especially in the countryside. In October 1922, with the government in gridlock and mounting labor unrest, Mussolini and his black-shirted paramilitary units staged a March on Rome. Without resistance, Victor Emmanuel capitulated and asked Mussolini to form a government.

Several pragmatic considerations constrained Mussolini from quickly carrying out his Fascist programs. Supported in Parliament by a fragile coalition and backed by a vacillating king, Mussolini proceeded cautiously in his attack on the Italian Constitution. The presence of the Vatican mandated at least the appearance of respect for the Catholic Church, epitomized by the Concordat of 1929. Moreover, national cohesion itself was hampered by persistent regional loyalties and an immense gap between the industrializing North and the peasant South. Despite these obstacles, Mussolini made clear his determination to bring all facets of national life under the control of the Fascist state. "Everything in the state, nothing outside the state, nothing against the state!"[6] As this slogan suggested, Mussolini set out to dominate not only public life but the enclaves conventionally labeled "the private sphere." This meant laying claim to many functions previously performed by the family and the church, such as socializing the youth, influencing parents' decisions to bear children, dominating women's organizations, and creating a popular culture that celebrated Fascist values like *Duce* ("leader") worship, war, racial pride, and nationalism.

Celebrating "virility for the men and fertility for the women," Mussolini routinely insulted feminists (although he supported an international women's rights convention in 1923 in Rome and spoke favorably about women's suffrage to improve his reputation abroad). When asked about women's suffrage,

Mussolini told a German journalist, "Women must obey. My notion of woman's role in the state is utterly opposed to feminism. Of course, I do not want women to be slaves, but if I were to give women the vote, people would laugh me to scorn. As far as political life is concerned, they do not count here. . . ." Women exert no influence on strong men.[7] Foreign reporters remarked that it seemed as if *il Duce* saw himself as the husband of Italian women and they cited as an example the much publicized ceremony in December 1935 when masses of Italian women gave their gold wedding rings to Mussolini in order to offset the financial impact of international sanctions against Italy because of the conquest of Ethiopia. In exchange, Mussolini gave them steel rings. How can we understand their enthusiasm?

In the 1920s, the prospect of an atheist, communist revolution frightened many middle class Italians. Playing on these fears, Mussolini revived the militaristic rhetoric of World War I and summoned women to dedicate themselves "unselfishly" to the "battle" against domestic "enemies." An early Fascist organizer and soldier's daughter, Luisa Brolis, joined the PNF. because she hated pacifism and believed Mussolini defended Italian honor. One-time Marxist Teresa Labriola looked back to the war years as a positive experience and called on Italian women to lead a moral revival by "forcing pure values into every generation of men."[8] The founder of the Fascist women's organization, Elisa Majer Rizzioli, had served bravely as a nurse in both the Italian invasion of Libya in 1911 and World War II. Fascism, to these women, rekindled the spirit of idealism and sacrifice born in war. A more self-interested, dimension of some women's support for Fascism lay in a strategy that has been called "national" feminism. Realizing that the Fascist government would remain in power, many educated and ambitious women adapted to the *status quo* in the hope that they might win a measure of autonomy within their own same-sex cultural, philanthropic, and social sphere. This has been described as, "an endeavor to reconcile two wholly antagonistic political traditions: one was the emancipationist legacy of the early twentieth century Italian women's movement, the other fascist mass politics."[9] Suffragist, egalitarian, individualist, and pacifist ideals gave way to a male-dominated, hierarchical, and militaristic state that claimed to value special feminine qualities.

From the early years of Fascism, middle class women with administrative talents found an outlet for their ambitions within the network of state-sponsored organizations. Many aristocratic women relished their new responsibilities as leaders of, for example, the Fascist Women's Organization (*fasci femminili*). In 1925 **ONMI,** the National Service for Infants' and Mothers' Welfare, was founded (with only two women among the twenty-two board members) to improve the birth rate and to aid children. A decade later over three million Italian women and girls had joined one or another of the dozens of organizations sponsored by the Fascist party and state. In all of these female-centered activities, women volunteers provided an essential cadre of enthusiastic support and, in exchange, gained access to patronage networks and community stature. Although programs for physical fitness among ordinary girls and women foundered on the Vatican's prohibition of "indecent" dress, the PNF sponsored a lavish training school for daughters of wealthy families in Orvieto that emphasized beauty and fitness.[10] Few Italians even knew of this institution, but publicity for international audiences made much of its modern progressive image.

Several constraints severely limited the mass mobilization of women as mothers and patriots. The most obvious of these stemmed from the sluggish pace of Italian industrialization. For all Mussolini's bravado, fascism did not permeate the everyday lives of most women, especially not in the countryside where well over half of all Italians lived. Since less than 10 percent of all villages had electricity, film and radio had a limited impact, and, obviously, illiteracy rates of between 25 and 50 percent constrained the impact of print media.[11] In the absence of a transportation network, Italians could not be taken to mass rallies; and without an efficient bureaucracy, laws could not be ruthlessly enforced. Finally, endemic fiscal shortfalls halted ambitious projects for expensive social welfare projects. For these pragmatic reasons, fascism provided a theoretical model for the nationalization of women, but its practice fell far short of accomplishments in industrialized Germany.

In contrast to Germany, concern with eugenics and anti-Semitism remained marginal in these programs. Although Mussolini summoned all Italians to improve the race, he did not defy the Vatican by supporting eugenic restrictions on marriage or sterilization. Racist propaganda accompanied Italian aggression in Ethiopia, but from the earliest days of the Fascist party, Mussolini remained apathetic toward the Jewish question in domestic politics. A third of the Jewish population belonged to the Fascist party in 1938. After his rapprochement with Hitler in 1938, Mussolini authorized laws excluding Jews from the Fascist party, civil service, military and professions. When Italy surrendered to the Allies in September 1943, about 44,500 Jews (one third of whom were refugees from other countries) lived in Italy. As soon as German armies occupied Italy, deportations to Auschwitz began. Although about 80 percent of the Jews in Italy survived, the Jewish community was shattered.[12]

Like many other interwar regimes (including democracies), the government sponsored natalist projects to improve the birth rate, such as tax exemptions for fathers, a bachelor tax on single people, two-month paid maternity leaves, insurance for mothers, and preferential hiring for fathers of large families. Abortion became treason and punishments for spreading sex education and the sale of contraceptives increased. Publicity for child-bearing accompanied the new laws. For example, a documentary film celebrated a 1940 public ceremony in Rome honoring 58 couples who had produced 1,544 living children and grandchildren. Did these initiatives produce the desired effect? In 1927 Mussolini exhorted families to procreate rapidly so that they would increase the population from 40 to 60 million. But even forgetting such fantasies, natalist programs failed. Although Italian couples married younger, the number of children per family dropped and infant mortality rates remained high.[13]

Industrialization in Italy had barely begun, which meant that large numbers of women worked in agriculture, and that the percentages of women in the work force were among the highest in Europe.[14] The vast majority of women wage earners worked at poorly paid, physically exhausting, and marginal jobs. In 1919, the liberal coalition government had passed the Sacchi Laws, which curtailed a husband's right to his wife's earnings and removed restrictions against women in all civil service jobs except those thought to be associated with national honor—the military, judiciary, and diplomatic corps. However, men working in the tertiary sector retained a hold on the kinds of clerical jobs that were often feminized elsewhere. In 1926 women postal employees lost their job security, and during the depression, the government discouraged the employment of women. In 1938 women were allowed to fill only 10 percent of all public employment, but before the measure could be enforced, wartime labor shortages voided its impact.

Throughout the Fascist period, Mussolini railed against wage earning women who sapped the national strength, and he celebrated work as a sign of masculine virility. But his words did not reverse the demands of a modernizing economy that required poorly paid women workers in office work as well as service and factory sectors. It also became clear that modernization required increasing numbers of women as workers in small rural industries as well as in agriculture. To circumvent legal strictures against female labor, employers hired increasing number of women in part time, temporary and often clandestine jobs. Not surprisingly, contradictions abounded. For example, while Mussolini supported the exclusion of women from "spiritually exalted" occupations such as medicine and law, a Fascist Professional Women's Association was formed and, despite pressure for girls to become full time housewives, the numbers and percentages of women students in higher education increased from 17.4 percent in 1935 to 30 percent during the war because men were drafted. The expanding bureaucracy absorbed ever larger numbers of women workers despite male opposition.[15] For all the propaganda against women in the labor force, nearly half of all Italian families depended on at least two wage earners, and throughout the Fascist regime the percentages of married women in the labor market increased.[16] World War II brought renewed calls for women's sacrifice, as mothers of many children, volunteers, and laborers in industry and agriculture. In the last two years of the war, as all possibility of victory vanished, a small but fanatically loyal cadre of young women donned uniforms and swore to fight to the death for their *Duce* against Allied invasion troops.[17]

Italian Fascism provided the first model for a response to the "woman question" that differed both from progressive demands for emancipation and conservatives' efforts to keep women in their homes. While Fascist doctrine praised women's domestic roles, Fascist organizations recruited women into nationally organized leisure activities, mothers' aid associations, and cultural events. Social workers, teachers, and youth leaders brought Fascist values into the domestic sphere, and the economy drew increasing numbers of women into the work force. Fascism provided a model for integrating women into the public sphere by offering recognition not rights. Despite these innovative programs, however, the slow pace of Italian industrialization meant that Fascist Italy resembled Spain under Franco more than Germany under Hitler.

SPAIN

Spanish women suffered the disabilities that stemmed from a pre-modern economic and social structure as well as from a legal system based on the Napoleonic code. Under Spanish law, for example, a husband could imprison his wife for "disobedience and verbal insults," but a husband could be punished only if he physically abused his wife. Female literacy in Spain remained at about 50 percent (compared to male rates of about 70 percent). Because of the largely pre-industrial economy, women's participation in the work force remained high, especially in agriculture. In sweatshops and factories, as well as in the countryside, women worked at poorly-paid and often dangerous jobs without protective legislation. Prostitution was widespread. Because the birth rate did not fall during the 1920s and Spanish men had not died in World War I, Spanish leaders did not yet share the natalist panic so common elsewhere. But they did worry about the high rate of infant mortality, the number of infants born out of wedlock and near-epidemic rates of venereal disease.[18]

Although Spain had been unified since the 15th century, powerful separatist movements in Catalonia and the Basque Country retained their own linguistic and cultural traditions and, like Catholics in Northern Ireland, fought for autonomy. The contest between Catalan separatism and Madrid-centered Spanish nationalism deepened ethnic solidarity and defined the nature of feminism. Indeed, opposition to Catalan separatism constituted the first priority of the Madrid-based middle class women's rights league, the *Asociación Nacional de Mujeres Españolas*, in the 1920s,[19] while Catalan crusaders for women's rights celebrated mothers' special role in preserving Catalan culture against encroachments from the central Spanish government. Thus Catalan and Spanish feminists balanced their ethnic loyalty against their demands for improved female education and expanded roles in "feminine" public spheres. Because their country remained neutral in World War I, Spaniards did not experience the rush of patriotism of the early war years or the deprivation of the last years.

However, Spanish politics did resemble a familiar Western European paradigm, with a weak parliament, a powerful church, and a vacillating monarch. Finding himself in roughly the same situation as King Victor Emmanuel in 1921, King Alfonso XIII, frightened by Marxist forces, cooperated in 1926 with a *coup d'état* by a populist dictator. Under General Miguel Primo de Rivera's Falangist government, labor leaders and factory owners negotiated a new truce. Inspired by Mussolini, and in contrast to the mainstream conservatives, Falangists called for a separation of church and state, the end of large landed estates, territorial expansion, and the recruitment of women into the public sphere. These plans proved too ambitious, especially after the Great Depression eroded the economy. Voters in 1930 overwhelmingly supported left-wing candidates, King Alfonso abdicated, and Spain became a republic. Spanish Republicans swiftly initiated a legal revolution. Women's suffrage, maternity benefits, no-fault divorce, civil marriage, and full legal rights for children born out of wedlock all passed within the first year. In 1935, as part of the campaign against venereal disease, official toleration and regulation of prostitution ended, and prostitution was made illegal. During these heady days of easy victory, Republicans scarcely noticed the backlash generated by their reforms. A liberal parliament legislated progressive reforms that it could not enforce because it lacked the power to displace powerful conservative structures such as the Catholic church, an entrenched landed aristocracy, and a conservative civil service. For radicals (anarchists, Communists, socialists, and labor union activists), the republic accomplished far too little, but the very threat of reform terrified conservatives (monarchists, Catholics, and landowners). Moderates felt pulled in both directions. This kind of polarization plagued all interwar democracies, but the powerful separatist movements that threatened to dissolve the nation made the Spanish case unique.

Alarmed by conservatives' growing popularity, the many factions on the left collaborated to form the Popular Front, which won the February 1936 election. Meanwhile, conservatives, Falangists, and the Catholic church rallied behind insurgent General Francisco Franco in Morocco. Aided by bombers, motorized battalions, and military experts from Fascist Italy and Nazi Germany, Franco's forces fought their way north through Spain. The defenders of the republic formed a common front against Franco. Putting their crusade for women's rights aside, Republican women from all factions worked in war production and the civil service, nursed soldiers, built barricades, and fought at the front.[20] Crash courses educated the illiterate. Social liberties, unthinkable in peacetime, became habit. Under the banner "Men to the front! Women to the homefront!"[21] legal impediments to women's wage work were abolished. As World War I had introduced masses of European women into public life, so the militarized society of the civil war integrated Spanish women into the national society as never before.

Both the defenders and attackers of the republic featured images of patriotic womanhood. *"La Passionaria,"* Communist leader Dolores Ibárruri, organized the Association of Antifascist Women and proved to be a brilliant propagandist for the Republican cause. Ibárruri eloquently appealed to mothers to support their sons fighting for the republic. To her audience outside Spain, she called out, "Hear the painful cry of our mothers and of our women who walk in their mourning through the bloody paths of Spain, which is fighting for peace and the freedom of the world."[22] Catholic Action, a conservative church organization strongly opposed to the republic, also used the rhetoric of women's suffering and purity to rally 38,000 women. The regular clergy mobilized thousands of women against the republic by publicizing putative atrocities committed by Republican soldiers against women Catholics. Organized women sponsored benefits, defied laws they deplored, led moral purity campaigns, went to jail as martyrs, and even ran as candidates of the right. More modern-minded conservative women organized about 10,000 followers in the Woman's Falange founded by Pilar Primo de Rivera, the sister of Spain's powerful ex-dictator. Inspired by Fascist and Nazi examples, these women vigorously entered public life in defense of conventional feminine roles. Apparently unaware of any contradiction, Pilar Primo de Rivera declared, "The only mission assigned to women by the FATHERLAND is at home," as she recruited women into public life. In 1937 Franco appointed Mercedes Sanz Bachiller to direct the Social Auxiliary (*Auxilio Social*) to care for the wounded, collect food, make clothing, and raise morale. Over a half a million Spanish women joined this initiative.

When the Republican forces surrendered in 1939, women felt the impact immediately. The Charter of Labor mandated that "their [women's] only proper place is the nursery" and declared that the "married woman is liberated from waged work."[23] Maternity bonuses replaced health insurance, and legislation to improve women's and children's health (originally passed by the Republican government) were expanded. As in Germany and Italy, financial incentives encouraged young couples to marry and bear many children, provided the wife not seek employment. After 1941 the fathers of "child-rich" families received special claim to employment opportunities (as long as they had not fought on the Republican side in the war). Marriage loans for newlyweds under the ages of 25 for the wife and under 30 for the husband were offered; as in Nazi Germany, the birth of each child who lived reduced the debt by 25 percent.[24] Although Catholicism was the national religion, Catholic women's organizations were complemented by a new state-sponsored network that supervised women's indoctrination and organization. All women teachers were required to join the Falange. Inspired by Fascist and Nazi examples, the Falange developed a women's labor service, which was mandatory for women who desired to depart even slightly from conventional roles by, for example, attending a university or obtaining a passport or driver's license. The Falange published two women's magazines to promote motherhood for a mass readership, a monthly celebrating physical fitness, and a pedagogical journal for teachers of girls. Reinforcing this rightward shift, the media denounced feminists and women's rights advocates in insulting, sometimes pornographic language. One sign of modernization was the government's promotion of biological research that reinforced Catholic views of motherhood. Biologists made many discoveries that their northern European colleagues had declared as orthodoxy in the nineteenth century: that women experienced a drive to motherhood; that women remained in a dependent state akin to puberty almost all of their lives; that mothers contribute only the "vessels" within which men's creative impetus produced children; and that only with menopause did women become full adults, thanks to "masculine" hormones. Thus Catholic values, nature, and Franco's laws worked in tandem to make motherhood women's only calling.

In contrast to Germany, Spanish authorities explicitly denounced racism based on physical traits because, they said, Spain had always stood proudly at the crossroads of great civilizations. "Racial" traits were spiritual, attributes of the "unique Spanish nature." This nature, in turn, could be nurtured only in the proper milieu, defined as the family. The preponderant influence of the Catholic church precluded even the slightest support for eugenic ideas. "For us children and women have always been more important than their ancestors. A fruitful, demographically rich nation, we are the 'creators of the race' of Don Juan, of gloriously fertile reproduction. We are neither eugenicists nor Malthusians."[25] Because of the slow pace of industrialization, birthrates had stayed high, roughly 30 per 1,000 in the 1920s. But, by the 1940s, the birthrate dropped to about 23 per 1,000, alarming social planners. Early in Franco's regime, new laws increased the punishments for abortion, women's adultery, and prostitution. Fathers' power over their families was reinstated as in the Napoleonic Code, and divorce was outlawed. The age of majority was raised to 25, and women were required to live in their fathers' households until marriage.

Although Franco initiated modest economic modernization (such as encouraging tourism in the 1960s) and prepared for Spain to enter the Common Market, domestic repression stifled even the discussion of reform. Dissident women and men who did not, or could not, choose exile risked serving long prison sentences.

GERMANY

Compared with Italy and Spain, Germany entered the 1920s as a modern, industrialized, and democratic nation. German electrical production, for example, was three times larger than in Italy and two hundred times greater than in Spain.[26] Since 1900 literacy had exceeded 99 percent, and over 42 percent of the work force was industrial. A modern rail and bus transportation system linked towns and villages with large cities, and the telephone network was the densest in Europe. The Weimar Constitution, ratified in 1919, guaranteed women's suffrage and fundamental equality between the sexes. Because of proportional representation, women were included in all of the six major parties' delegations to national and state parliaments. The wave of the future seemed to push Germany toward further reforms in marriage and family law, toward expanding opportunities for women in education and the labor market, and toward a freer social climate. But the appearance of large numbers of women in economic and political institutions, combined with a cultural revolution, unleashed a backlash. In Germany, unlike in Spain and Italy, mass audiences gazed at films that challenged traditional gender stereotypes. They saw Greta Garbo flirt with another woman in *Queen Christiana*. Many were shocked at G. W. Pabst's *Pandora's Box*, which starred a woman driven by insatiable sexual desire; were outraged at Marlene Dietrich, the lethal sex bomb, in *The Blue Angel;* and were horrified at the scathing attack on Prussian values in *Girls in Uniform*. Mass circulation magazines, sensationalist newspapers, and bawdy cabarets attracted the restless young and horrified their staid elders. German culture and democracy departed radically and suddenly from the stifling conformity of the prewar monarchy.

The modernity that spurred rapid cultural transformations alarmed conservatives, who took advantage of advanced technology to mount a powerful backlash against secular values and social liberation. At the margins of this backlash, a few hundred women organized in the name of a disreputable agitator, Adolf Hitler. Because Nazi men so totally ignored their women followers, they unintentionally provided ambitious women with wide scope for their talents. Unlike the aristocrats who predominated in Fascist Italy and Franco's Spain, Nazi women leaders (like Hitler and most of his deputies) came from more humble backgrounds and innovated their own versions of official party doctrine. Some championed women's full civic rights within an entirely separate female political framework capped by a women's legislature, while others established auxiliaries to nurse wounded Storm Troopers and to care for impoverished Nazi families. Until the depression destroyed German economic health, the Nazis remained a fringe movement. But when political paralysis brought democratic institutions to a standstill, the 85-year-old president appointed Hitler as chancellor in January 1933. Although the Nazi party never won a majority in any legitimate election, it had attracted a plurality (a high of 37 percent) in 1932. Within four months of becoming chancellor, Hitler assumed dictatorial powers and Nazified every facet of public life. The police and Nazi Storm Troopers arrested and tortured thousands and thousands of political opponents, outlawed all political parties, established the Dachau concentration camp, incited terror against Jews, and destroyed labor unions. Censorship imposed uniformity on the media.

From his earliest speeches on "the woman question," Hitler described women as inferior, useful only as breeders of the superior race. Race soon became the *Führer*'s central obsession in domestic policy, and the propaganda offices accordingly devoted considerable resources to drawing "racially acceptable" women into the national community. Within a year of Hitler's appointment as chancellor, strong-minded "old-timer" women Nazi leaders had been demoted as thoroughly as "old-timer" men Nazis had been promoted. By late 1934 a very different *Reichsfrauenführerin* (National Leader of Women) appeared. Gertrud Scholtz-Klink had gained the attention of key

Nazi leaders by her deference to male superiors, administrative efficiency, and youthful, "Aryan" good looks. Perhaps equally important, her marital status solved a vexing conundrum. An unmarried woman leader would not have provided a motherly role model; but a respectable married woman ought to obey her husband. As a widow with four children, Scholtz-Klink offered the ideal solution. The fact that her husband had died of a heart attack during the excitement of a party rally two years earlier further enhanced her reputation. As the Gestapo and police destroyed all liberal, pacifist, and socialist women's organizations, Scholtz-Klink "integrated" (i.e., Nazified) every remaining women's association within the Nazi administrative structure. Scholtz-Klink praised selfless dedication to national glory, all the while maximizing her own self-interest as a tough-minded Nazi bureaucrat.

Scholtz-Klink encouraged members of legal civic and religious organizations to join her Women's Bureau (*Frauenwerk*) while retaining their prior affiliations. Each of the middle-class women's movements reacted differently. The leaders of the women's rights organization, the Federation of German Women's Associations (*BDF*) (with 700,000 members in over forty affiliates) disbanded rather than submit to Nazi control. But virtually all of its member associations expelled Jewish members and acquiesced to state control. The federation's monthly magazine, *Die Frau,* published under new editorial supervision, continued until wartime paper shortages closed it. Under a stalwart conservative old guard, the 100,000-strong Housewives Federation joined the new state, ultimately merging with the Reich Mothers Service (RMD), which included over 2 million members. Young, energetic, and compliant Agnes von Grone led the nearly 2 million women in the Protestant federation she directed into the Nazi fold. But the women leaders of the nearly 1-million-strong Catholic women's organization regarded the Nazi regime with deep suspicion and fought for the autonomy promised by Hitler's Concordat with the Vatican in July 1933. By about 1936 all women's associations (including occupational guilds) were integrated thoroughly into the state structure. Scholtz-Klink's mass organization, the Women's Bureau, expanded rapidly, claiming upwards of 5 million members in over eighty affiliates. As Scholtz-Klink boasted years later, she ruled over a separatist "state within a state" for women only, which had its own "ministries" in charge, for example, of propaganda, foreign affairs, home economics, and education. For the "élite" of "true believers," she reorganized the *NS Frauenschaft,* which schooled its 2 million members in ideology, leadership techniques, public relations, and administration. Under Frau Dr. Auguste Reber-Gruber, chief (*Referentin*) of the women's division in the Ministry of Education and the Nazi Teachers' Union, the educational system popularized the notion of "more feminine" girls to complement "more masculine" Nazi boys. While obeying all commands from the Nazi party, Scholtz-Klink, Reber-Gruber, and hundreds of other ambitious women enjoyed considerable administrative authority over their masses of followers in their separate sphere.[27]

Because industrialization had occurred far earlier in Germany than in Italy or Spain, the birthrate had begun to fall during the nineteenth century. But Nazi leaders did not aim merely to reverse the downward demographic trends. Hitler was obsessed with improving the "Aryan" racial stock. To accomplish this, the state advanced a myriad of social engineering schemes to maximize the birth of "racially fit" children and to diminish the population of the "inferior." This meant large-scale state intervention into areas of life previously regarded as within the "private sphere." To all couples who passed the physical examination for genetic health and infectious diseases (such as tuberculosis and venereal disease), the state offered a substantial loan at marriage (provided the wife agreed not to seek employment outside the home). With each healthy birth, the debt was reduced by 25 percent. To spur economic recovery, couples received the loan in the form of coupons to be spent on items related to the household and children. Under Heinrich Himmler's direct supervision, the regime launched an effort to eradicate the twin threats to a high birthrate: male homosexuality and abortion.[28] To eliminate the "unhealthy" population a national genetic health census of every citizen was established. Each citizen was required to report his or her family's genetic heritage to health officials in order to receive a "genetic health passport." In an era before computers, the plan foundered under a mountain of record keeping. The impact of Hitler's order to improve the birthrate of "fit" Germans also remains ambiguous. Although the numbers of "healthy" births disappointed planners' predictions, German birthrates in the 1930s remained higher than in other European nations.[29]

After January 1934, the genetic health laws required teachers and social workers to report the students and clients they suspected of "genetic illness" for screening by a panel of eugenics specialists. The most modern science, publicity declared, enabled experts to weed out racial dangers according to biological standards. But whereas spina bifida, blindness, or deafness was relatively clear-cut, culturally biased behavioral symptoms identified alcoholism, schizophrenia, manic-depression, and feeble-mindedness as "biologically based." Predictably, the "experts" discovered alcoholism in men and schizophrenia in women. Although the program was announced with great fanfare and the interior minister predicted that up to 20 percent of all Germans would be sterilized, by the late 1930s "only" about 300,000 men and women (less than 1 percent) had been sterilized. As forced sterilization slowed in response to widespread opposition, the mass murder of "useless" individuals began under the guise of "euthanasia." Terminally ill, physically deformed, and mentally deficient people (together with prisoners of war and slave laborers) were killed in "hospitals" by female nurses as well as by male physicians. In August 1941, after about 120,000 victims had been murdered, two bishops (one Protestant and one Catholic) appealed to Hitler to halt the program. Although medical murder within Germany ceased, clandestine "euthanasia" continued in occupied Central Europe. Probably the toll of both of these programs will never be known.

During the 1920s, Nazi politicians had sworn to restore traditional family values. But, although Nazi propaganda celebrated motherhood, legal changes rendered marriage less attractive for mothers and wives. Already in 1933 "racial error" (i.e., if a non-Jewish spouse wished to leave a Jewish spouse) became grounds for what we would call "no-fault" divorce. In a 1938 "reform," a spouse's mental illness, "refusal to procreate," contagious disease, or a three-year separation all could become the basis for divorce. Officially, the guiding principle in these and all facets of family law was the interest of the racial community. However, many changes strengthened the rights and prerogatives of husbands over wives. In practice, the vague new laws gave judges broad discretionary power, which, in practice, meant that husbands' wishes prevailed over wives'.[30]

A second source of dissonance on "the woman question" developed in about 1936 when Nazi authorities began to plan for a major war—a turning point that dramatically affected young women's roles. Suddenly, the nature of "appropriate" feminine careers burgeoned. With unemployment eliminated, labor scarcities mandated the hiring of women in factories, offices, and the civil service. To be sure, natalist incentives continued, but mothers and wives did not respond enthusiastically to appeals to enter the labor market. With the declaration of total war in 1943, Nazi planners faced a conundrum. Higher wages might attract more women, but Hitler rejected that option because he feared it would increase women's self-esteem at men's expense. Reducing the substantial benefits paid to soldiers' wives and widows would force them to look for jobs and possibly lower morale. In the end, Nazi administrators chose neither option and instead drafted nearly 8 million forced laborers from twenty-six Nazi-occupied nations.

Both the eugenics policies and wartime labor mobilization demonstrated serious shortcomings. However, the Nazis devoted considerably more energy to their attacks on German citizens of Jewish descent (about 1 percent of the population). A boycott of all Jewish stores on April 1, 1933, failed because of widespread public apathy, but seemingly "legal" measures succeeded in expelling Jewish children from public schools, banishing Jewish professionals from practicing (unless they were war veterans), and dismissing Jews from the civil service. Two years later, the Nuremberg Laws forbade sexual relations and marriages between Jews and Christians. Starting in 1936, state officials itemized all Jewish-owned property (from financial assets and real estate down to household items and clothing). Gradually, this property was confiscated. About half of the roughly 566,000 Jews (as defined by Nazi guidelines) in Germany emigrated before the pogrom of November 9–10, 1938. After that brutal attack, no doubt remained about the danger of remaining in Germany; but entry permits to foreign countries became almost impossible to get.

As public life eroded, family life among Jews took on a new importance, and women assumed major responsibilities for providing welfare, maintaining morale, plotting escape strategies, and preserving Jewish culture.[31] Ultimately, about 137,000 Jewish Germans were deported, of whom less than 9,000 returned. About 126,445 Jews emigrated from Nazi Austria, leaving 58,000 to face deportation or hiding. Although the extermination system targeted Jews for total destruction, as many as 250,000 Sinti and Roma (Gypsies) were murdered and tens of thousands of homosexuals perished in concentration camps. As a consequence of Nazi war policy, millions of unarmed civilians along the eastern front were shot, and millions of prisoners of war died or were shot to death in the camps.

Were women responsible in any way for these death tolls? No woman formulated genocidal racial policies, planned deportations, directed a concentration camp, or commanded the killing battalions (*Einsatzkommando*). This does not eliminate women from the chain of responsibility. As office workers, they drew up inventories of Jewish property and made lists of Jews; as neighborhood spies, they denounced victims in hiding or "suspicious" activities; as camp personnel in charge of women prisoners, they wielded power over victims; as social workers and nurses, they targeted the "genetically" or "racially" suspicious" among their charges; and as "true believers" they spread the racial gospel that made hatred a central part of Nazi society.[32]

FRANCE

On June 22, 1940, after only two months of fighting, Field Marshal Henri Philippe Pétain, the hero of World War I, surrendered. While Nazi forces occupied Paris and large sections of the north, Marshall Pétain ruled over the southern, unoccupied section of France from the resort city of Vichy. Granting Pétain a large measure of autonomy, the Nazis trusted him to collaborate enthusiastically with all facets of Nazi rule, including its racial principles. The nationalist (and often intensely anti-German) conservatives who flocked to Pétain's state defended their support of Nazi rule by scapegoating democracy, women's emancipation, corrupt cultural values, and foreign (i.e., Jewish) influence for having weakened France during the republic. They picked up the refrain of, for example, a best-seller in 1939 that warned, "Our land has become a land of invasion" overwhelmed by barbarians, by which the author meant "hordes of Jews" and "internationalist" (Protestant or Jewish) feminists.[33] When German soldiers and occupation officials swarmed over the land, some conservatives even welcomed the occupation for giving them a chance to correct "the error of intellectualism" (*l'erreur intellectualiste*) and to destroy the corrosive influence of modernism. They rallied to Pétain's call for a return to the past (*retour en arrière*).[34] Instead of the "false idea of natural equality" and rights, Pétain told the nation, the new regime "will rest on all citizens' equal 'opportunity' to . . . serve."[35] Even the memory of the "French Revolution" vanished in favor of the "National Revelation" of 1940 (*la révélation de juin 1940*). "Liberty, equality, fraternity" yielded to "Work, Family, Nation (*Travail, Famille,*

Patrie)." Echoing Nazi ideology, collaborators claimed that the "tragic lesson of democracy" had exposed the hollowness of an "elite of the brain" and revealed the glory of the "elites of the body and the blood (*de chair et de sang*)."

For all this regressive rhetoric, however, France was an industrialized society. At the turn of the century, female illiteracy had virtually disappeared. Although women did not win the right to vote in the 1930s, large numbers of women had begun to enter universities, and a few won public recognition as, for example, members of the Legion of Honor and high government officials. During the 1920s and 1930s, women's share of the agricultural labor force dropped, and by the late 1930s just over a third of all industrial wage earners were women. Unlike in Germany, the Great Depression had a gradual and relatively small impact on the French economy, so unemployment figures did not rise precipitously for men or women.[36]

Vichy intellectuals proclaimed that where once women had felt excluded from the rational materialism of democracy, they could now share deeply felt spiritual and feminine ideals. In flowery rhetoric, one "expert" celebrated "the joys of the hearth that the woman illuminates by her presence and revives by her activity. [T]his ideal has endured for centuries . . . [for] millions and millions of Frenchmen. At last! The Head of the French State has redis-covered the key to the eternal Truths. Against the spirit of pleasure, he calls for sacrifice." A leading educator told women, "If the man is rational thought, you are life." [37] Celebrating the family as the very foundation of the nation, he told "mistresses of the home" that they alone could provide the "affection, tact, patience, softness" that would "inspire our Christian civilization" and give men "a taste for hard work, discipline, modesty, and respect."[38] Against weak pluralistic values of democracy, "l'éternel féminin" offered the promise of rebirth. In a healthy hierarchical society, the father dominated his house-hold much as the dictator ruled his nation.

These values did not arrive with German armies in 1940, but developed from a ground swell of conservative grassroots opinion that had been grow-ing for over a decade. Fighting against a tendency toward secularization in the 1920s, Catholic organizations in the 1930s had rallied masses of women and men to their battle against "decadence and godlessness."[39] Reactionary women's organizations like the Patriotic League of Frenchwomen (PLF), founded at the turn of the century, despised democracy, socialism, and "Jewry."[40] By the 1930s, the PLF had organized over a million and a half women in a strict hierarchy. At the national level, members attended annual conventions; at the grassroots, ten-member "cells" organized local initiatives. For the most part, as in Italy, the national leaders boasted aristocratic titles and substantial wealth. But, unlike its Italian counterparts, the PLF deployed a sophisticated media campaign to popularize its views. It published, in cheap editions, popular romance novels about average women struggling against overwhelming odds to find love. "To move souls effectively, one must advance on them slowly, gradually, sympathize with their weaknesses and woes, and patiently await the right moment."[41] The PLF organized charitable activities, religious meetings, entertainment, infant care classes, and sewing circles. While insisting on the apolitical nature of their concerns, the PLF leaders demanded better housing and health care in the interests of expanding the French population. Also high on their "apolitical" agenda was opposition to any measure that might undermine the father's authority over his family or blur the "healthy" difference between the sexes. Organizations like the PLF, as well as mass Catholic women's associations, welcomed Vichy rule and supplied a vast army to carry out its mandates.[42]

As in Italy, Spain, and Germany, a cadre of well-educated women decided to cooperate with the new reactionary state. Having been active in conservative circles before the war, they now stepped into positions of influence. A few, like Charlotte Bonnin, had been pacifists or, like Jeanne Cherenard, trade union activists. Most came from the ranks of Catholic and conservative women's organizations. Like their German counterparts, French women working with the state had access to a modern and technologically advanced communications network. Between 7 and 9 o'clock in the evenings, three times a week, the network "France-Famille" featured programming for women, including "letters from listeners." German and French feature films, as well as Nazi newsreels and "documentaries" on racial education were shown in over four thousand cinemas throughout the nation. Publishing houses produced for a mass market. When a high-ranking Vichy minister wrote guidelines for girls' education, for example, 200,000 teachers received copies within days.

Although the principle of equal education for boys and girls was never rescinded, girls were "tracked" into feminine areas and had to take courses in home economics and racial science. Teachers revived the lost arts of "housekeeping, family meal planning, and budgeting." Girls practiced motherhood by bathing and caring for dolls. Slick, fashionable magazines like *Votre Beauté* preached a special feminine French aesthetic. *La Révue de la famille* provided practical advice as well as praise for large families. Despite wartime conditions, French citizens were treated to a constant round of celebrations, festivals, and commemorations eulogizing mothers. The Exposition of the French Family 1943, for example, opened with a florid tribute to womanhood: "Oh, radiant and luminous face, triumphant in her modesty. . . ."[43]

Despite the outpouring of publicity for natalism and familialism, Vichy brought relatively minor institutional changes for women. Although the modern French economy opened up a great potential for rapid change, wartime conditions and the brevity of the occupation accounted for the relatively moderate impact of Vichy. In one of its first major laws, the Vichy administration forbade the employment of married women in any government office and established financial incentives (allotments to single heads of households, including unmarried women) for childbearing. The Bounot Law established national organizations for family support. Material aid encouraged women to bear many healthy children, a popular demand among all political parties.

Not only had 1,400,000 French soldiers died in World War I, but the postwar birthrate remained among the lowest in Europe. To reverse the trend, Vichy administrators added negative sanctions to rewards. Abortion, made illegal in 1920, was changed in 1942 from an individual crime to an "act injurious to the French nation." About eight thousand people were found guilty between 1942 and 1944, and in 1943 one woman was guillotined. Although we cannot ascertain the reasons, the French birthrate did begin to rise in 1943.[44]

Family law underwent important revisions. The Family Code, first passed in 1939, was expanded in 1942 to strengthen husbands as "heads of the family." Patriarchal authority was further enhanced by a law that declared adulterous wives of prisoners of war "enemies of the nation," whereas a husband could be charged with adultery only in cases of "notorious concubinage," for example, if he established a household with another woman and abandoned his wife. Divorces became more difficult to obtain. Although eugenic concepts infused natalist discourse, neither forced sterilization nor euthanasia became policy.[45] The few organizations created for women provide a glimpse of what the future might have looked like if Germany had won the war. The National School for Women's Leadership (École Nationale des Cadres Féminins) was founded in October 1940 to prepare promising young women for national roles.[46] Within three years, about twenty thousand graduates staffed positions in the civil service, schools, and women's organizations. Yet at the same time, the newly formed Commission on the Family (Le Commissariat général à la Famille) pledged to restore wives and mothers as the "heart" of their families.

By May 1942, the demands of the Nazi occupation had shifted priorities away from childbearing and toward war production. In addition to the 1,600,000 French prisoners of war (half of whom were married men) taken by the German army, the governments in Vichy and Paris conscripted 700,000 workers (about 44,000 of them women) for service in Germany. Vichy did not actually coerce women who refused conscription into the labor market, but relied on incentives to draw women into the wage labor force. The chaotic conditions of wartime, combined with a large unofficial labor market, make it difficult to ascertain to what degree women responded to the call. For all of its rhetorical power, the Vichy state barely dented long-range trends.

In comparison with the Vichy government's relatively weak social impact, Vichy and occupation anti-Semitic policy succeeded with terrifying efficiency. In August 1940, Pétain nullified a 1939 law against inciting racial hatred. Within a year, racial laws first identified and then separated Jewish citizens. A July 1941 law "to eliminate Jewish influence from the French economy" unleashed the official theft of Jewish-owned property. Of the approximately 350,000 Jews in France, over half were refugees. During that summer in Paris, Jewish men without French citizenship were rounded up. Signs appeared throughout the nation: "Here, in this French house, no entry for Jews" ("Ici, Maison française, entrée interdite aux Juifs,") or "This business no longer accepts Israelites." ("L'Établissement ne reçoit plus les Israélites"). In 1941 a committee of experts on the "Jewish problem" drew up plans for eliminating Jews. Within weeks of a June 1942 law requiring that all Jews display a yellow star on their clothing, full-scale deportations began.[47] These mass deportations, of women and children as well as men, occasioned the first signs of public outrage among ordinary French citizens.[48] To meet Nazi quotas, French police set out to arrest 28,000 Jews from the Paris region in twenty-four hours. Five days later, "only" 12,000 (including 4,000 children) were seized. The victims, packed into the Velodrome d'hiver sports stadium without food, water, or medical attention, had no idea what lay ahead. Within days, the deportations to Auschwitz began, and so did protest from many non-Jewish citizens. But for the next two years French police arrested and deported about 77,000 Jews (one-third of whom had French citizenship). Although short-lived, Vichy rule illustrated a terrifying potential for even a democracy with a strong tradition of civil rights to collaborate with a murderous racial state.

CONCLUSION

Duce. Führer. Caudillo. Maréchal. Their very forms of address underscored the militaristic élan of these dictatorships. None of their governments outlived them. And immediately after these four dictators vanished, the subsequent governments declared a clean break with the past. For the first time, Italian and French women won the vote. The constitutions in both sections of Germany reinstated female suffrage and guaranteed women's equality. Within weeks of Franco's death in 1975, four hundred feminists in Madrid petitioned for rights, and over four thousand women demonstrated in Barcelona. The new constitution enfranchised Spanish women and guaranteed their equal civil rights.

Looking back at the record of these four dictatorships, we can see that militarization and dictatorship were inimical to women's aspirations for equality. Not only did they institutionalize misogyny, but they brought terror, ethnic hatred, repression, war, economic devastation, and social coercion. Yet the institutionalization of a separate sphere for women offered new career opportunities to ambitious women who subscribed to the rhetoric of an essential feminine nature. Like the Italian feminist who "looked at the situation straight on . . . without being discouraged, but without too many illusions," they called themselves realists.[49] Gertrud Bäumer, who had so eagerly lain down her battle for women's equality to join the German war effort in 1914, once again relinquished her commitment to fundamental freedoms when Hitler took power in 1933. "In the last analysis, the form of the state, whether parliamentary, democratic or fascist, . . . is a matter of the utmost insignificance. . . . [Our] basic demand will remain constant. . . to allow the cultural influence of women to emerge fully and become a free and effective social force."[50]

As during World War I, thousands of women activists relinquished their feminist goals in favor of ethnic liberation and consequently ignored massive injustice against members of "outside" ethnic groups. This tendency to place a higher value on communal solidarity than on individual rights remained a powerful force among women long after 1945. Some historians call this "Latin" or "Mediterranean" feminism, but others note how common this version of women's rights is in postcommunist Central Europe.[51] In chaotic political and economic settings, citizens often look hopefully to an authoritarian culture of orderliness and harmony based on clearly demarcated divisions between men and women and between ethnic communities. In the face of rapid change in interwar Europe, powerful masculine leaders promised a return to the past. But once in power, Mussolini, Franco, Hitler, and Pétain accelerated modernization, which meant that they not only called for the restoration of traditional roles for women, but supported economic development that required women to enter the labor market in the most poorly paid and oppressive sectors.

However, another legacy outlasted the demise of these four dictatorships. Ironically, many of the family support programs designed, but not fully implemented, under dictatorship formed the bedrock of social policy in the postwar years.[52] Many social supports for mothers and families promised by Mussolini, Franco, Hitler, and Pétain became part of the concept of social citizenship that entitled women to claim benefits in the welfare state. Moreover, laws against abortion (and, in Germany, sterilization) remained in force until citizens mounted national protests against them. Divorce laws favoring husbands, together with prohibitions against homosexuality, changed only gradually and in response to mass protests.

Ten years ago, I wrote in my essay for the second edition of *Becoming Visible*, "Fascism . . . as an intellectual and political force emerged at the close of World War I and died with the Allied victory in 1945."[53] My optimism was misplaced. At the close of the second millennium, with communism in eclipse, extremist politicians incite xenophobia, oppose abortion, extol ethnic pride, and draw on nostalgia for patriarchal family values. To be sure, vast differences separate Neo-Nazi or skinhead gangs from far right politicians like Jean-Marie LePen or Vladimir Zhirownosky, but they mobilize the same fears that drew Europeans to dictatorships in the interwar period.

NOTES

I would like to thank the following for their critical reading of this essay: Erin Chapman, Chris Converse, Jen Frauson, Rachel Golub, Elizabeth Heller, Megan Huchko, Seymour Mauskopf, Katie McKie, Michael Lessin, Jan Paris, Sheri Sauter, Brian Wise, and David Zorub. Special thanks to Victoria de Grazia for calling my attention to recent scholarship on Italian fascism and to Renate Bridenthal, who tirelessly identified logical, organizational, and stylistic lapses.

1. Steven C. Hause and Anne R. Kenny, *Women's Suffrage and Social Politics in the French Third Republic*, Princeton University Press, 1984, p. 197 quoting Léon Abensour, *Histoire générale du féminisme des origines à nos jours*, (first edition 1921).

Delagrave: Paris, 1983, p. 310. Françoise Thébaud, "The Great War and the Triumph of Sexual Division," in *A History of Women: Toward a Cultural Identity in the Twentieth Century*, ed. François Thébaud, Harvard University Press, Cambridge, 1994, p. 21.

2. Gertrud Bäumer, *Der Krieg und die Frau*, Deutsche Verlagsanstalt, Stuttgart, 1914, pp. 6–8. Bäumer may have rejoiced at feeling included, but she was the only female among over eighty authors of wartime pamphlets in this series edited by Ernst Jäckh.

3. This paradox reappeared on a global scale in the wake of collapsed communist systems and resurgent nationalisms everywhere. Cynthia Enloe, "Feminism, Nationalism, Militarism," in *The Morning After: Sexual Politics at the End of the Cold War*, University of California Press, Berkeley, 1993, p. 237. For an insightful essay on the origins of these paradoxes, see Elisabeth Domansky, "Militarization and Reproduction in World War I Germany," in *Society, Culture, and the State in Germany, 1870–1930*, ed. Geoff Eley, University of Michigan Press, Ann Arbor, 1996, pp. 427–463.

4. Miranda Pollard, "Women in the National Revolution," in *Vichy France and the Resistance*, ed. Roderick Kedward and Roger Austin, Barnes and Noble, Totowa, N.J., 1985, p. 43.

5. The numbers of radios compared to total populations in 1939–1940 were Spain: 281,000 to 25,900,000; Italy: 1,142,000 to 41,177,000; France: 5,200,000 to 41,000,000; and Germany: 9,598,000 to 66,000,000. B. R. Mitchell, *International Historical Statistics: Europe 1750–1988*, 3rd ed., M. Stockton Press, New York, 1992, pp. 753–756.

6. George Seldes, *Sawdust Caesar*, Harper and Row, New York, 1935, p. 432. Alexander de Grand, *Fascist Italy and Nazi Germany: The "Fascist" Style of Rule*, Routledge, New York, 1995, pp. 3–4, 15–31.

7. Emil Ludwig, *Talks with Mussolini*. trans. Eden and Cedar Paul, Little, Brown, Boston, 1933, pp. 112–113, 170 (reprinted in 1982 by AMS Press). Women actually received the right to vote in administrative elections in November 1925, but before the next balloting the Fascist government abolished these elections altogether. Mariolina Graziosi, "Gender Struggle and the Social Manipulation and Ideological Use of Gender Identity in the Interwar Years," in *Mothers of Invention: Women, Italian Fascism, and Culture*, ed. Robin Pickering-Iazzi, University of Minnesota Press, Minneapolis, 1995, pp. 38–39.

8. Quoted in Graziosi, *op. cit.*, p. 35. Labriola called for modern Fascist women with "a maternal heart and yet with a virile mind." Barbara Spackman, "Fascist Women and the Rhetoric of Virility," in Pickering-Iazzi, *op. cit.*, p. 109. Victoria de Grazia, *How Fascism Ruled Women: Italy 1922–1945*, University of California Press, Berkeley, 1992, pp. 249–250.

9. De Grazia, *op. cit.*, pp. 236–237.

10. De Grazia notes, however, that Catholic UDCI's (Union of Catholic Italian Women) 6,000 groups included over 250,000 members in comparison to 5,570 women's *fasci* with only 150,000. See *op. cit.*, pp. 245, 248. For Fascist theorists' views on women, see Ferdinando Loffredo, *Politica della famiglia*, Bompiani, Milan, 1938; and Giovanni Gentile, *La donna et il fanciulo*, (1934) in *Preliminasi allo studio del fanciullo*, 9th edition, Opere, vol. 42, Sansoni, Florence, 1961, p. 75–138, cited in de Grazia, p. 317. On elite education, see Lucia Motti and Marilena

Rossi Caponeri, *Accademiste a orvieto. Donne ed educazione fisica nell'Italia fascista, 1932–1943,* Quattroemme, Perugia, 1996.

11. Mitchell, *op. cit.,* pp. 164, 166. De Grazia comments, "Mussolini's mobilization of women was paper-thin when compared to that of the Nazis," in "How Mussolini Ruled Women," in Thébaud, *op. cit.,* p. 143.

12. Célia Bertin, *Femmes sous l'Occupation.* Stock, Paris, 1993, p. 48. During the war there were about 47,000 Italian and foreign-born Jews in Italy, with a population of 45,000,000; 5,706 Italian Jews converted to Catholicism, and all children of mixed parentage were allowed to identify themselves as Catholics. Of 8,360 Jews who were deported, 611 survived. Alexander Stille, *Benevolence and Betrayal: Five Italian Jewish Families Under Fascism,* Summit, New York, 1991, pp. 72–92.

13. The Italian birthrate, which had been about 32 per thousand in the 1900s, dropped to about 30 in 1922 and to 23 in the 1930s. Infant mortality rates fell from 129 per 100 in 1923 to 101 and 97 in 1935 and 1939, respectively. Mitchell, *op. cit.,* pp. A6, 103. On comparative demographics, see also D.V. Glass, *Population Policies and Movements in Europe,* Cass, London, 1967, pp. 219–268.

14. In 1931, over half of all wage-earning women worked in agriculture, and 24 percent worked at factory jobs. Women comprised just under half of all agricultural workers and about 40 percent of the industrial work force. De Grazia, "How Mussolini Ruled Women," in Thébaud, *op. cit.,* pp. 139–142. De Grazia declared Italy "a uniquely hostile environment for the employment of women"; de Grazia, *op. cit.,* p. 181. See also Paul Corner, "Women in Fascist Italy: Changing Family Roles in the Transition from an Agricultural to an Industrial Society," *European History Quarterly* 23 (1993), pp. 54–58.

15. De Grazia, *How Fascism Ruled Women,* pp. 180–199; Bonnie Smith, *Changing Lives, Women in European History Since 1970.* Heath: Lexington, MA and Toronto, 1989, 461; Corner, *op. cit.,* pp. 53–54 and 57–63. Because women's wage labor enabled most peasant families to remain on their small plots of land, many women gained stature within rural families.

16. The percentage of married women workers rose from 12 percent in 1931 to 21 percent in 1936, and the percentage of women in agriculture dropped more rapidly than elsewhere in Europe. De Grazia, "How Mussolini Ruled Women," in Thébaud, *op. cit.,* pp. 136–137 and 178–200.

17. See the rich array of quotations from these idealistic auxiliaries' letters and diaries in Maria Fraddosio, "The Fallen Hero: The Myth of Mussolini and Fascist Women in the Italian Social Republic (1943–5)," *Journal of Contemporary History* 31 (1996), pp. 99–124.

18. Infant mortality rates in Spain were 123 per 1,000 in 1929, 135 in 1939, 143 in 1943, and 99 in 1944. Mitchell, *op. cit.,* pp. A7, 118.

19. Mary Nash, "Catalan Nationalism and the Women's Movement in Spain," *Women's Studies International Forum* 19, nos. 1–2 (1996), pp. 45–47.

20. Elena Cabezali, Matilde Cuevas, and Maria Teresa Chicote, "Myth as Suppression. Motherhood and the Historical Consciousness of the Women of Madrid, 1936–9," in *The Myths We Live By,* ed. Raphael Samuel and Paul Thompson, Routledge, History Workshop, London, 1990, pp. 161–173. As this article emphasizes, typically the women performing "masculine" tasks later remembered their "feminine" motivations, such as defending their children.

21. Mary Nash, *Defying Male Civilization: Women in the Spanish Civil War*, Arden: Denver, 1995, pp. 101–141.
22. *Ibid.*, p. 58. Robert Low, *La Passionaria: Spanish Firebrand*, Hutchinson, London, 1992.
23. Quoted in Danièle Bussy Genevois, "Women of Spain from the Republic to Franco," in Thébaud, *op. cit.*, pp. 190–191.
24. Marie-Aline Barrachina, "Religion, Biologie und Mutterschaft in der Propaganda des Franco-Regimes 1938–1945," in *Frauen und Faschismus in Europa*, ed. Leonore Siegele-Wenschkewitz and Gerda Stuchlik, Centaurus-Verlagsgeschellschaft, Pfaffenweiler, 1990, pp. 61–63. Nash, *op. cit.*, p. 183.
25. E. Gimenez Caballero, "Los secretos de la Falange," 1939, quoted in Marie-Aline Barrachina, "Religion," 61. The birthrates per 1,000 were 28.3 in 1930, 20.0 in 1938, 20.2 in 1942, and 21.5 in 1949; Mitchell, *op. cit.*, pp. A6, 105.
26. Italy 11.65, Spain 2.90, France 16.40, and Germany 25.66 gigawatt hours. By 1940, German production had leapt to 62.96. Mitchell, *op. cit.*, pp. 547–548. Another index of modernization is telephone service: in 1933 the number of telephones in use were as follows: Spain 281,000; Italy 483,000; France 1,349,000; and Germany 2,954,000. The populations of these countries were approximately 25 million, 41 million, 41 million, and 66 million, respectively.
27. Andrea Böltken, *Führerinnen im 'Führerstaat' Gertrud Scholtz-Klink, Trude Mohr, Jutta Rüdiger und Inge Viermetz*, Centarus, Pfaffenweiler, 1995. Ortrun Niethammer, *Frauen und Nationalsozialismus. Historische und kulturgeschichtliche Positionen*, Universitätsverlag Rasch, Osnabrück, 1996; and Ute Benz, ed., *Frauen im Nationalsozialismus: Dokumente und Zeugnisse*, Beck, Munich, 1993. See Liliane Kandel, ed., *Féminismes et Nazisme*, CEDREF, Université Paris, Paris, 1997.
28. Heinrich Himmler's comments on June 15, 1937, in the Federal German Archives, Coblence, BAK/R18/5518, 89–91.
29. The Italian birthrate in the early 1930s was above 25 per 1,000 and fell to about 23 on the eve of World War II; in France the rate declined from about 18 to 14; and in Germany the rate fluctuated from 17.6 in 1930 to a low of 14 per 1,000 in 1933 to 21 in 1939. The infant mortality in Germany was 79 per 1,000 births in 1933 and 64 per 1,000 in 1940. Mitchell, *op. cit.*, pp. 119, A6, 101–105.
30. Gabriele Czarnowski, "The Value of Marriage for the *Volksgemeinschaft*: Policies Towards Women and Marriage Under National Socialism," in *Fascist Italy and Nazi Germany: Comparisons and Contrasts*, ed. Richard Bessel, Cambridge University Press, Cambridge, 1996, pp. 94–112. If an ex-husband desired to start a new family, for example, the judge could release him from alimony and reduce child support. On racial law, see Nathan Stoltzfuss, *Resistance of the Heart*, Norton, New York, 1996.
31. Marion Kaplan, *Jewish Life in Nazi Germany: Dignity and Despair*, Oxford University Press, New York, 1998. Approximately 15,000 "mixed race" (*Mischlinge*) avoided deportation; about 7,000 Jews were protected by their "Aryan" spouses; and between 3,000 and 5,000 lived in hiding, as "Submarines" (*U-Boot*) in the jargon of the day. About 1,000 successfully hid from the Gestapo.
32. Gudrun Schwarz, "Verdrängte Täterinnen: Frauen im Apparat der SS 1939–1945," and Brigitte Scheiger, "'Ich bitte um baldige Arisierung der Wohnung, . . .' Zur Funktion von Frauen im bürokratischen System der Verfolgung," in *Nach*

Osten: Verdeckte Spuren nationalsozialistischer Verbrechen, ed. Theresa Wobbe, Verlag Neue Kritik, Frankfurt a.m., 1992, pp. 175–227.

33. Francine Muel-Dreyfus, *Vichy e l'éternel féminin,* Seuil, Paris, 1996, pp. 100–111.
34. Bertin, *op. cit.,* p. 24.
35. Maréchal Pétain, 11 Oct. 1940, *La France nouvelle, principes de la communauté. 17 Juin 1940–17 Juin 1941,* Fasquelle, Paris, n.d., p. 78.
36. Christine Bard, *Les filles de Marianne: Histoire des féminismes 1914–1940,* Fayard, Paris, 1995, pp. 313–315.
37. Muel-Dreyfus, *op. cit.,* p. 129, quoting Paul Haury.
38. Pétain, *op. cit.* p. 156. Françoise Thébaud, "Maternité et famille entre les deux guerres," in *Femmes et Fascismes* ed. Rita Thalmann, Editions Tierce, Paris, 1986, pp. 85–94. Pollard, *op. cit.,* pp. 36–47.
39. Eugen Weber,*The Hollow Years: France in the 1930s,* W.W. Norton, New York, 1996, pp. 187–190. Weber points out that although 9 of 10 infants were baptized, only one in three adults regularly attended church.
40. Anne-Marie Sohn, "Catholic Women and Political Affairs: The Case of the Patriotic League and French Women," in *Women in Culture and Politics,* Judith Friedlander, Alice Kessler Harris, Blanche Weisen Cook, and Carroll Smith Rosenberg, eds., University of Indiana Press, 198, pp. 239–240. The PLF logo epitomized subservience and pride by pairing Christ and the Sacred Heart; the emblem placed a daisy against the Sacred Heart. Muel-Dreyfus discusses "la culture Catholique féminine," *op. cit.,* pp. 151–188.
41. Sohn, *op. cit.,* p. 247.
42. Bard, *op. cit.,* pp. 436–442.
43. Muel-Dreyfus, *op. cit.,* p. 133.
44. The rates per 1,000 were: in 1940, 13.6; in 1941, 13.1; in 1942, 14.5; in 1943 and in 1944, 16.1. Mitchell, *op. cit.,* pp. A6, 101. Perhaps this was a harbinger of the "baby boom" that began in 1946 with rates of over 20 per 1,000. Paxton, *op. cit.,* p. 168.
45. Noëlle Bisseret-Moreau, "Biopolitik und Demographie," in Siegele-Wenschkewitz and Stutchlik, *op. cit.,* pp. 72–89. Muel-Dreyfus, *op. cit.,* pp. 277–356.
46. Muel-Dreyfus discusses René Benjamin's inspiration, *op. cit.,* pp. 251–271. Cf. Eck, "French Women Under Vichy," in Thébaud, *op. cit.,* pp. 202–206.
47. Gérard Walter, "Étoile jaune et Croix gammé," in *La Vie à Paris sous l'Occupation: 1940–1944,* Armand Colin, Paris, 1960, pp. 175–194.
48. Michael Marrus and Robert O. Paxton, *Vichy France and the Jews,* Basic, New York, 1981, p. 270. "For the first time since the founding of Marshal Pétain's regime, significant numbers of moderate and conventional French people . . . were deeply offended by something it had done." In dramatic contrast to German clergy, a few brave French priests declared their solidarity with the victims, saying "The Jews are real men and women. Foreigners are real men and women . . . They are part of the human species." Hélène Eck notes this period when "the vast majority of the public" began to make a link between the Vichy state and their hatred of German occupation; see Eck, *op. cit.,* p. 216. Before the war only 40,000 Jews had lived in the south, for example, but 120,000 newcomers arrived almost immediately. Lucien Lazare, *Rescue as Resistance: How Jewish Organizations Fought the Holocaust in France,* trans. Jeffrey M. Green, Columbia, New York, 1996.

49. Paola Benedettini Alferazzi, quoted by de Grazia, *How Fascism Ruled Women*, p. 38.

50. Gertraud Bäumer, quoted in Claudia Koonz, *Mothers in the Fatherland*, St. Martin's, New York, 1987, p. 147 and note 73, p. 462.

51. Sabrina P. Ramet, *Whose Democracy? Nationalism, Religion, and the Doctrine of Collective Rights in Post-1989 Eastern Europe*, Rowman, London, 1997. Nash, *op. cit.* pp. 34–36. De Grazia, *How Fascism Ruled Women*, p. 235. De Grazia, "How Mussolini Ruled Women," in Thébaud, *op. cit.*, pp. 30–31. As Hause notes, Austria, Poland, Ireland, and Belgium enfranchised women between 1918 and 1922, thus emphasizing Latin, not Catholic, as the variable. Hause and Kenny, *op. cit.*

52. Lesley Caldwell, "Women as the Family: the Foundation of a New Italy?" in *Woman - Nation - State*, ed. Nira Yuval-Davis and Floya Anthias, St. Martin's, New York, 1989, pp. 168–182.

53. Bridenthal, Koonz and Stuard, eds. *Becoming Visible, Women in European History.* 2nd ed., Houghton Mifflin: Boston, 1987, p. 501.

SUGGESTIONS FOR FURTHER READING

Barnett, Victoria J. *For the Soul of the People: Protestant Protest Against Hitler.* New York: Oxford, 1992.

Boak, Helen. "'Our Last Hope': Women's Votes for Hitler." *German Studies Review* 12 no. 2 (May 1989), pp. 289–310.

Bridenthal, Renate, Atina Grossmann, and Marion Kaplan, eds., *When Biology Became Destiny: Women in Weimar and Nazi Germany.* New York: Monthly Review, 1984.

Cheles, Luciano, Ronnie Ferguson, and Michalina Vaughn, eds. *Neo-Fascism in Europe.* New York and London: Longman, 1991.

de Grazia, Victoria, ed. *The Sex of Things.* Berkeley: University of California Press, 1994.

Delbo, Charlotte. *None of Us Will Return.* Boston: Beacon, 1978.

Durham, Paul. "Gender and the British Union of Fascists," *Journal of Contemporary History* 27, no. 3 (July 1992), pp. 513–530.

Faludi, Susan. *Backlash: The Undeclared War Against American Women.* New York: Doubleday Anchor, 1991.

Felstiner, Mary Lowenthal. *To Paint Her Life: Charlotte Salomon in the Nazi Era.* New York and San Francisco: HarperCollins, 1994.

Ferderber-Salz, Bertha. *And the Sun Kept Shining.* New York: The Holocaust Library, 1980.

Fraddosio, Maria. "The Fallen Hero: The Myth of Mussolini and Fascist Women in the Italian Social Republic (1943–1945)." *Journal of Contemporary History* 31, no. 1 (January 1996), pp. 99–124.

Frevert, Ute. *Women in German History: From Bourgeois Emancipation to Sexual Liberation.* New York: Oxford Berg, 1988.

Gättens, Marie-Luis. *Women Writers and Fascism.* Gainsville: University Press of Florida, 1995.

Goldenberg, Myrna. "'From a World Beyond': Women in the Holocaust." *Feminist Studies* 22, no. 3 (Fall 1996), pp. 667–682.

Hawthorne, Melanie. *Gender and Fascism in Modern France.* Hanover, N.H.: New England University Press, 1997.

Heineman, Elizabeth. "The Hour of the Woman: Memories of Germany's 'Crisis Years,' and West German National Identity." *American Historical Review* 101, no. 2 (April 1996), p. 354.

Ibarruri, Dolores. *They Shall Not Pass: The Autobiography of La Pasionaria.* London: Lawrence and Wishart, 1967.

Isaacson, Judith Magyar. *Seed of Sarah: Memoirs of a Survivor.* Urbana: University of Illinois Press, 1990.

Jetter, Alexis, Annelise Orleck, and Diana Taylor, eds. *The Politics of Motherhood: Activist Voices from Left to Right.* Hanover and London: University Press of New England, 1996.

Kirkpatrick, Clifford. *Nazi Germany: Its Women and Its Family Life.* Indianopolis, Ind.: Bobbs-Merrill, 1938, reprinted by AMS Press, 1996.

Koonz, Claudia. *Mothers in the Fatherland: Women, The Family, and Nazi Politics.* New York: St. Martin's, 1987.

Martin, Elaine. *Gender Patriarchy and Fascism in the Third Reich: The Response of Women Writers.* Detroit: Wayne State University Press, 1993.

Mason, Tim. "Women in Germany, 1925–1940: Family, Welfare and Work." In *Nazism, Fascism and the Working Class,* ed. Jane Caplan. Cambridge, U.K.: Cambridge University Press, 1995, pp. 131–211.

Morante, Elsa. *History: A Novel,* trans. William Weaver. New York: Random House, 1977.

Owings, Alison. *Frauen: German Women Recall the Third Reich.* New Brunswick: Rutgers University Press, 1993.

Passerini, Luisa. *Fascism in Popular Memory: The Cultural Experience of the Turin Working Class.* Cambridge, U.K.: Cambridge University Press, 1987.

Phayer, Michael. *Protestant and Catholic Women in Nazi Germany.* Detroit: Wayne State University Press, 1990.

Quack, Sibelle. *Between Sorrow and Strength: Women Refugees of the Nazi Period.* Cambridge and New York: Cambridge University Press, 1995.

Sahgal, Gita, and Nira Yuval-Davis, eds. *Refusing Holy Orders: Women and Fundamentalism in Britain.* London: Virago, 1993.

Sanabria, Enrique A. *A Woman and Her Party: A Study of Dolores Ibarruri and the Spanish Communist Party. 1920–1960.* Madison: The University of Wisconsin Press, 1993.

Schopmann, Claudia, and Gunter Grau. *A Hidden Holocaust.* New York: Columbia University Press, 1994.

Schulte-Sasse, Linda. *Entertaining the Third Reich: Illusions of Wholeness in Nazi Cinema.* Durham, N.C.: Duke University Press, 1996.

Sehgers, Anna. *The Seventh Cross.* Forward by Kurt Vonnegut, Afterward by Dorothy Rosenberg. New York: Monthly Review, 1987.

Stephenson, Jill. *Women in Nazi Society.* New York: Barnes and Noble, 1975.

Wilson, Perry. R. *The Clockwork Factory. Women and Work in Fascist Italy.* Clarendon Press, Oxford, 1993.

Zuccotti, Susan. *Italians and the Holocaust: Persecution, Rescue, Survival.* New York: Basic Books, 1987.

Women demonstrating for abortion rights in Paris, France, October 1979. MICHEL ARNAULT/GAMMA-LIAISON.

CHAPTER 18

Friend or Foe? Women and State Welfare in Western Europe

Jane Jenson

After the conflict and destruction of World War II, many Western Europeans hoped to make the world anew. From such optimism and the sense of new possibilities came one of the most important legacies of World War II: the welfare state. Women's lives changed profoundly, and so did their political practice. Women participated in the push for better health care, reproductive rights, and family policy as well as access to legislative assemblies and to the paid labor force on equal terms with men. In doing so, they soon found, however, that "universal" citizenship rights often fell short for women.

This chapter describes the citizenship claims made by women and their allies over the last decades. As second-wave women's movements mobilized against the assumptions about gender relations that underpinned postwar policies, they frequently characterized the postwar welfare state as the foe. It appeared as a set of institutional arrangements that undermined women's capacity for autonomy and equality, for full citizenship. These second-wave movements won important victories, in part because they were finally able in the late 1960s and 1970s to rally their allies as well as governments to a definition of citizenship that took gender relations into account and could begin to generate equality in difference. Nonetheless, before these victories could be consolidated, economic, political, and ideological conditions dramatically changed. By the 1990s women confronted political actors with an agenda that made it much harder to advance their citizenship claims. Welfare states, which had been painfully transformed into more women-friendly institutions, were being cut back, redesigned, and even transformed. Women's movements were forced to mobilize to defend past victories and existing policies, limited as they were.

After the conflict and destruction of World War II, many Western Europeans hoped to remake the world. They were determined to establish the political consensus and economic well-being that had eluded them before and during the war. Victory, liberation from occupying forces, and escape from domestic fascism all served as moments of opportunity to recast social relations. From such optimism and the sense of new possibilities came one of the most important legacies of World War II: the welfare state.

This form of state can be defined as an interconnected set of social programs intended to alleviate the negative effects of economic cycles on national economies and of the life cycle on individuals and their families. The state would heretofore share the burdens of poverty, sickness, old age, and child rearing with individuals and families as well as ease the devastation of unemployment. Programs to do so became social and economic citizenship rights and were added to the civil and political rights that had been previously extended. A new relationship between states and societies came into being. The postwar situation is one of "reproduction going public." The "core is state acceptance of some kind of responsibility for the organization and financing of care for the old, the sick, children and the disabled. This development has not only changed the boundaries between the private and public sphere but also the understanding of what is public and private."[1]

With these postwar changes, women's lives changed profoundly, and so did their political practice. Immediately after the war, women's organizations flowered. Women participated in the push for better health care, family policy, and women's access to legislative assemblies and to the paid labor force on equal terms with men, as well as for reproductive rights. In doing so, they soon found, however, that the "universal" citizenship rights promised by male politicians often fell short for women.

This chapter describes the citizenship claims made by women and their allies over the last decades. By the 1960s and 1970s second-wave women's movements in all Western European countries contested the postwar vision of citizenship and uncovered its assumptions about gender relations and its programs, which often reinforced gender inequities and disempowered women. For example, "in Sweden, the 1950s was the decade of the housewife. More women than ever married and had children but they did not combine work and family, because joint taxation of incomes made it unprofitable. Nor was there daycare for children and paid parental leave did not exist."[2] In Ireland until 1977 a marriage bar prevented married women from working in the civil service. Postwar West German family law reinforced the domestic authority of husbands, and the tax system was heavily weighted in favor of married, one-earner couples.[3] In Italy, the incoherence of the system of social provision left women to pick up responsibility for providing care and managing the family's access to the services that did exist.[4]

As second-wave women's movements mobilized against such practices and the assumptions about gender relations that underpinned them, they frequently characterized the postwar welfare state as the foe. It appeared as a set of institutional arrangements that undermined women's capacity for autonomy and equality, for full citizenship. These second-wave movements won important victories, in part because they were finally able in the late 1960s and 1970s to rally their allies as well as governments to a definition of citizenship that took gender relations into account and that could begin to generate equality in difference. Nonetheless, before these victories could be consolidated, economic, political, and ideological conditions dramatically changed. By the 1990s women confronted political actors with an agenda that made it much harder to advance their citizenship claims. Welfare states, which had been painfully transformed into more women-friendly institutions, were being cut back, redesigned, and even transformed. Women's movements were forced to mobilize to defend past victories and existing policies, limited as they were.

One example illustrates these contradictions. In the United Kingdom after 1945, all women began to receive family allowance benefits. This universal benefit was paid once a week at the post office to any woman with two or more children. Feminists criticized the program at the time it was established. They found it inadequate, simply reinforcing the image of "mother and child." It did nothing to challenge old ideas to recognize that men had responsibility for caring work too. In the 1960s and 1970s feminists called for guaranteed annual incomes and universally available, 24-hour-a-day child care services. They castigated the family allowance as a remnant of the past that reflected traditional gender assumptions. Nonetheless, when in 1973 the Conservative government moved to eliminate the universal family allowance and replace it with tax credits, a feeble form of social provision that would become the preferred instrument of the Thatcher government, women in the Family Allowance Campaign explained to the House of Commons Select Committee why the current system was crucial for their everyday lives and their own sense of independence: "Family Allowance as it stands at present is for many women the only money which we have which belongs to us by right. . . . We need some money we can be sure of, some money we do not have to ask for either from men or from the Department of Health and Social Security. Some money we collect each week from the Post Office."[5]

FULL CITIZENSHIP: AN UNREALIZED IDEAL

Before World War II many states provided pensions for some of the elderly, health care for the indigent or for subscribers to state insurance programs, poor relief for the poverty stricken, maternity benefits and leaves for women workers, family allowances for those with children, and other benefits to relieve financial distress. After 1945, these piecemeal and limited programs became more coordinated and comprehensive. Even more importantly, they gained a new rationale—the right to certain minimum standards of life. For example, when they grew old, citizens had a right to state pensions; when they had children, they had a right to maternity benefits and family allowances; when they were unemployed, they had a right to lost wages in the form of unemployment insurance; when they were sick, they had a right to inexpensive and quality health care; when they could not find affordable housing in the private market, they had a right to safe, sanitary, and inexpensive state-subsidized homes; and so on. This change signaled the arrival of social citizenship.

In a classic presentation of the history of citizenship in Britain, the sociologist T. H. Marshall (writing in the late 1940s) documented the struggles of different social groups, over a period of two and a half centuries, to realize the claim to be accepted as full members of the society, that is, as citizens.[6] The first claims were for *civil rights* that provided protection for the right to work and established a clear sphere of individual liberty. Central to the general notion of civil rights were two specific rights: to make contracts and to have bodily integrity, that is, to be protected from interference by the state or other actors.[7] Next were *political rights,* which were gradually extended to incorporate all male citizens, giving them the right to participate in political life. By the twentieth century, it had become painfully clear that individual freedom and formal equalities were insufficient. *Social rights* were necessary in order to ameliorate excessive inequalities or the failure of formal rights to generate full membership in society. Postwar welfare states that provided social protections for all citizens incarnated such social rights.

Access to citizenship rights was never gender-neutral. For example, whereas virtually full manhood suffrage was won in the nineteenth century in most of Western Europe, women did not gain the vote until much later. Indeed, in France, Italy, and Belgium this basic political right came only after World War II. Social citizenship was also profoundly gendered. For the architects of welfare states, social citizenship was usually thought to derive from the seemingly "universal" condition of waged work. In this formulation the "model citizen" was a wage earner, and everyone was assumed to approximate that condition or at least to aspire to it.

One expression of this discourse can be found in the ambitions for the European Union, whose roots stretch back to the 1950s:

> The Treaty [of Rome, 1957] takes account of the individual citizen viewed as a factor in the economy in the wide sense of the term. Thus, for example, the Community has found itself over the years dealing with highly complex fishing quotas, but also with the working conditions and the specific problems of fishermen. . . . The Convention for the Protection of Human Rights and Fundamental Freedoms drawn up by the Council of Europe in 1950 recognizes individual rights and freedoms: the right to life, to liberty, to respect for family life and so on. . . . The contracting parties look at the individual in his capacity as a worker and commit themselves to action to bring about a number of

conditions: the right to work, the right to safety, the right to a fair wage and the right to vocational training.[8]

This description of the international agreements of the 1950s is very representative of the public discourse of the time. Rights of citizenship were not only civil and political but also economic and social, but these latter rights accrued to citizens by virtue of their relationship to the labor force.

This relationship was construed as "universal," although not necessarily all-encompassing. It was obvious that not all citizens were actually wage earners, and policymakers had to decide how to incorporate those who were not into the state welfare system. Moreover, not all situations related directly to work. Decisions made after World War II about the treatment of workers and of those outside the paid labor force generated a complex system of distinctions. The result was, as Barbara Castle, then secretary of state to the Department of Health and Social Security, said in the House of Commons in 1974, that women were treated like "second class citizens entitled to third class benefits."[9] French feminists described women as "domestic immigrants" (*immigrées de l'intérieur*), thereby indicating that they did not have the same rights as native-born Frenchmen.

In these welfare states, lone mothers, who had no male to support them, posed a particular dilemma. In some countries, such as France and Sweden, they were simply treated as other parents, with the same rights and the same benefits, which encouraged them to combine family care and paid work. In other countries, they were dealt with as a special case, treated as if they were "married to the state." Since they could not be "married twice"—that is, receive support from two sources—they lost their benefits as soon as any male person might be construed as supporting them. Thus the "man in the house," or the cohabitation rule, compelled social workers to police welfare recipients' relationships with men to determine when the state could be relieved of its responsibility for them.

In some countries, married women gained access to the social and economic rights of citizenship through their husbands. In the 1940s in the United Kingdom, many in the Labor and Conservative parties, as well as in the trade unions and in some women's groups, had assumed that the traditional family—that is, a waged male worker and a dependent wife and several children—was the norm to be maintained.[10] Therefore, when new social programs were created, women's access to the system passed via their husbands. They could not be claimants as individuals in their own right.

Lord Beveridge, the architect of the British welfare state, wrote in 1942:

> During marriage most women will not be gainfully employed. The small minority of women who undertake paid employment or other gainful occupation after marriage require special treatment differing from that of a single woman. Since such paid work will in many cases be intermittent, it should be open to any married woman to undertake it as an exempt person, paying no

contributions of her own and acquiring no claim to benefit in unemployment or sickness. If she prefers to contribute and to requalify for unemployment and disability benefits she may do so, but will receive benefits at a reduced rate.[11]

This quotation illustrated the ways that ideas about the gender division of labor structured not only society's assumptions about the place of women but even the new programs themselves. The husband was the citizen whose rights were recognized; women were treated as dependents, as second-class citizens. Moreover, the policies reinforced their dependency. In case of sickness or disability, they received lower benefits than men or single women, and therefore would need their husband's income to survive. The system also encouraged employers to pay lesser benefits to part-time workers, who were likely to be married women already covered by their husband's benefits. Overall, British policymakers continued to work with the long-standing assumption that "marriage means total and permanent economic dependence for most women. . . ."[12]

In other countries, however, gender equality was a stronger theme in postwar political discourse. Both France and Italy inserted clauses into their new postwar constitutions guaranteeing women equality with men. They also decreed an end to the practice that many employers had used of paying women lower wages even when they were doing the same work as men. This emphasis on equality among workers and equal rights for women citizens provided women's groups with a basis for making claims to eliminate unequal treatment and gender discrimination throughout the postwar decades.

In the 1950s and 1960s labor force participation rates rose, especially for married women with children.[13] This social change was driven both by women's desire for economic autonomy and the fact that service-sector economies, such as Europe was building at the time, were staffed by women. Indeed, the very creation of social programs demanded more workers in traditionally female occupations, such as teaching, health care, social work, and clerical work. Divorce rates also climbed, while changes in societal norms made single-parenthood more socially acceptable. The number of lone mothers increased. At the same time, new birth control techniques became available, and for the first time it was technologically possible to control reproduction in a reliable way.[14]

A widening gap emerged between the reality of women's lives and the assumptions about gender embedded in many social programs after 1945. Political changes, especially the appearance of second-wave women's movements in the late 1960s in all Western European countries, gave content to the complaints many women had previously thought to be only "their own" individual problems. Finally, a political movement could name the problem as being the gap between the promise and the reality of supposedly universal citizenship rights. Women's movements set out to eliminate the structured distinctions among citizens that had limited women's autonomy, often disempowered them, and failed to take into account sexual difference. They sought to overcome the gender biases of the welfare state and to achieve a real "equality in difference."

Extending Civil Rights: Sexuality and Equal Opportunities

Even when women carried their own passport and were thereby recognized as nationals of a country, they did not have the same rights as their male compatriots. For example, after 1945 married women in many countries still did not have the right to confer their citizenship on their foreign husbands, although men could do so for their wives. Nor did mothers necessarily endow their children with their nationality. Married women in several countries also lacked basic legal capacity to hold a job without their husband's approval, to manage their own financial affairs, or to make decisions about their children's affairs. In France, for example, several reforms of the Civil Code were needed before women gained full economic autonomy from their husbands and shared responsibility for making decisions about their children. This came only in the mid and late 1960s.

Women's civil rights were also limited by institutions such as labor markets, which restricted women's employment opportunities by channeling them into "female employment ghettos"; by male-only educational institutions, which blocked women from the education and training necessary to enter certain occupations, and by the policies of banks and other institutions that refused to recognize married women as individual economic actors (often requiring that husbands cosign credit notes, for example). These practices all restricted women's possibilities of "freely contracting," a basic civil right that men had gained in the eighteenth century.

Crucial too was the absence, for women, of that basic civil right of bodily integrity upon which autonomy depends. In almost all Western European countries until at least the mid-1970s women faced barriers in their access to contraception and to abortion. They did not have control over their own bodies. Virtually everywhere one of the first targets of women's mobilization was improved access to contraception and the right to choose to end unwanted pregnancies. The struggle to overturn long-standing bans on abortion, in particular, provided an initial occasion for diverse groups and tendencies of the second wave of the women's movement to focus on a common issue.[15]

The politics of abortion took a variety of forms. Women's groups lobbied parliaments for legislative change and sought allies among the parties. They also engaged in more spectacular events, ranging from mass demonstrations to systematic and widely publicized law-breaking. In the Netherlands, for example, a broadly based, single-issue coalition brought together a wide variety of women's groups, both those organized autonomously and those affiliated with left-wing parties, to mount demonstrations, lobbying, clinic occupations, and other actions in an effort to gain liberal legislation guaranteeing women's right to choose.[16] France and Italy also had broad coalitions for reform.[17] In

1971, 343 prominent French intellectuals, politicians, and ordinary women published a manifesto announcing that they all at some point had broken the law by having an illegal abortion. A year later a similarly large number of doctors declared that they also were lawbreakers because they had performed abortions. Such confessions were also used by prominent German women in the early 1970s.[18] Also common were well-publicized bus caravans that took pregnant women to neighboring countries where the law was less harsh. For example, in the early 1960s Swedish women departed weekly for Poland, where they could obtain abortions. Even in the United Kingdom, where abortion was legalized in 1967, in response to mobilization by the medical profession and leftists more than by feminists, political assaults on the right to choose and on access to abortion services meant that "throughout the 1970s, abortion was almost the definitive issue of the movement, with tens of thousands of people supporting demonstrations against the anti-abortion bills of White in 1975 and Corrie in 1979."[19]

All of this law-breaking, accompanied by mobilization for legal changes, was important because it forced into the universe of political discourse a new way of thinking about women's rights and sexuality. Feminists sought to represent women as individuals who were sexually different from men and not defined simply by a family status. When they were successful they gained legislation recognizing women's right to choose. In other cases, of course, many actors were less willing to acknowledge and grant legal space for women to choose. Doctors remained the gatekeepers in those—usually very limited—situations in which women could have access to abortion.[20]

The other area in which women's movements have made major claims for removing distinctions in women's and men's civil rights of citizenship is in policies for achieving economic autonomy. Second-wave feminists, like their sisters who struggled at the beginning of the twentieth century for women's right to engage in paid work, devoted a good deal of attention to the labor market situation of women and the sources of their income. If women's labor force participation was rising rapidly by the early 1960s, women's jobs were nonetheless often very concentrated in a few sectors and poorly paid. To be sure, the explanations for these enduring patterns identified the role women and their families played in socializing girls to limit their ambitions in school and the labor market. But they also pointed to structural patterns of discrimination that made it difficult for women to "contract freely" and to gain access to a full range of employment.

Some of these blockages were located in educational institutions that still did not permit young women to enroll in the programs likely to lead to high-paying and prestigious occupations, and that channeled girls into programs considered "appropriate" for them. Therefore, although girls were "investing in their human capital"—their rate of success in higher education surpassed that of boys—this investment paid off less.[21] Women's movements agitated for opening more programs to both sexes and for developing programs to encourage girls to take up nontraditional training.

The second structural blockage identified was in hiring and in wage setting, both of which processes were accused of being sources of discrimination. Therefore, campaigns for equal opportunity in hiring and for equal pay for work of equal value became a part of movement politics. These struggles were not always easy. In particular, the relationship to the labor movement was often rocky. In countries such as France, where a weak union movement had always sought to protect the working class by raising the minimum wage, it was relatively easy to accept equality politics. Thus the labor movement welcomed state legislation in 1983 that prohibited discrimination on the basis of sex and that gave responsibility for instituting equality to negotiations between employers and unions. In countries such as West Germany and Britain, however, where the union movement had since the nineteenth century followed a strategy of demanding the "family wage," feminists had to struggle hard to convince unionists that attention needed to turn toward discrimination, especially in hiring. Therefore, employers, who had also well-developed employment practices based on the assumption that women's labor force participation was "atypical" (that is, likely to be only part-time and discontinuous because of family responsibilities), faced little organized challenge from the unions seeking pay or employment equity. Another pattern emerged in Sweden, where the unions were both strong and officially committed to gender equality. There the dispute was over the institutional mechanisms appropriate to achieving labor force equality. Unions were reluctant to accept state-mandated policy because their general strategic perspective was to seek resolution of wage issues in collective bargaining.[22] Yet, as many feminists were quick to point out, it was previous negotiations about how to solve labor shortages and the labor movement's pressure for social programs that had led to the situation in which women were overwhelmingly segregated into part-time work and a very limited number of occupations. Therefore, feminists sought to use the power of the state to force the unions and employers into new ways of addressing gender relations. The eventual result was that equality programs were grafted onto existing collective bargaining and corporatist practices.[23]

Extending Political Rights: Greater Democratization

Another target of many second-wave feminists has been the institutions of representation, including unions, parties, and the institutions of corporatism.[24] The goal was to enlarge women's citizenship by entering these central institutions of representation. In almost all countries there have been efforts to feminize the leadership of the trade unions in order to better represent the reality of a feminizing labor force and also to alter the unions' agendas.[25]

In the Nordic social democratic countries, feminists had considerable success as their numbers rose in the legislative assemblies, the ranks of unions and parties, and the institutions of social democratic corporatism.[26] Elsewhere, however, the experience was less positive. In France representative institutions remained a male sanctuary; the percentage of women in parliament is lower in the 1990s (5.7 percent) than at the time of the Liberation. Feminists seeking to become full citizens were appalled when in 1982 the Constitutional Court struck down legislation that had established a 25 percent quota for municipal elections.[27] Ironically, the judges made the decision against increasing women's participation in the name of the French Revolution's Declaration of the Rights of Man and the Citizen.

The politics of representation illustrates the complexities of extending citizenship rights. The citizenship right that appeared most "universal"—universal suffrage—actually remained profoundly differentiated by gender, and women's access to the institutions that were designing welfare state programs was thereby severely limited. Therefore, many branches of the second wave of the women's movement targeted the state and struggled to advance the principle that both women and men had the right to participate in democratic governance and to enjoy full democratic rights at all levels. In doing so, these women's movements have obviously given attention to more than simply the presence of women in representative institutions. Feminists have been in the lead in efforts to alter the ways of doing politics—to make them more democratic, less hierarchical, less leadership-focused, and more "user-friendly." For many groups, the procedures for making decisions were as important as the outcomes. They rejected formal leadership tasks, rotated responsibilities among members, and insisted on full discussion. In turn, these practices fed back into the world of mixed political organizations, where parties such as the Greens and even the Communists began to experiment with other models for organizing their internal activities.[28]

Extending Social Rights: Women as Providers and Consumers of Social Services

Second-wave women's movements in several countries concentrated on exposing the inequities of power within the family and social programs that limited women's ability to achieve full autonomy and equality. Feminists understood that the unequal distribution of caring work made women dependent on men and on the state.

> Attempts to improve women's opportunities and pay within the labour market can therefore have only a limited success as long as women within the family continue to undertake most of the work of caring. . . . On the practical level, changes in social policies which reduce women's claims to maintenance on men but do not recognise that changes in the division of responsibilities for

caring between men and women within the family and between the family and the wider community are also required, may in the end be counter-productive as far as women are concerned.[29]

Women are particularly well placed to expose these interconnections and to propose alternatives because they are not only consumers of state services but also often work within the state. Therefore, their interests in its functioning are multifaceted.

One of the first campaigns that gained popularity was for "wages for housework." The idea was that women should be compensated for their un-paid work, which had no financial recognition and which brought none of the benefits, such as pensions, associated with a lengthy working life. The wages-for-housework movement was particularly strong in the United Kingdom, and Italy. In the United Kingdom, throughout the interwar years reformers had proposed that family allowances be paid directly to women as a way to reduce their dependency on their husbands' wages and therefore as a basis for some economic autonomy and stability for women and their children.[30] The idea resurfaced within second-wave feminism in the following way:

> Our housework goes on behind the scenes, unnoticed, uncounted, uncharted as long as it is unpaid. But if we demand to be paid for it, if we demand Wages for Housework from the State, we are saying first that housework is work . . . we are saying that we women need money of our own. If we didn't have to depend on men for money, we wouldn't have to put their needs before ours, to service them sexually, physically, emotionally . . . we say TO BRING UP CHILDREN IS WORK and we want a WAGE for all the work we do—whether cleaning offices OR homes, producing electrical parts OR babies.[31]

This idea of paying women to do housework, or even caring work, was vehemently rejected by other feminists, however. They saw it as simply reproducing society's unfair gender division of labor, which already relieved men of responsibility for providing care. They always argued instead for pub-lic provision of child care, parental leaves that were sufficiently well paid that men might take them, or a reduction of working time so that all adults would have sufficient time to care for children, the elderly, and themselves. For example, in the 1970s feminists within the French Socialist party convinced both the party and the presidential candidate, François Mitterrand, to support a thirty-five-hour workweek in part to promote gender equality.[32] Swedish feminists, for their part, promoted the six-hour day, for the same reasons.

Failing to recognize the importance of caring work was not the only dimension of social policy that feminists found unacceptable. In Britain, for example, second-wave feminists took as their preferred target the system of state welfare that reproduced in a myriad ways the dependence of married women on their husbands and single mothers on the state. For example, they demanded individualized, separate coverage in social programs (especially pensions) and in tax regimes for all women, irrespective of their marital status.

Feminists' distinctive contribution has been to link the issue of hardship and bureaucratic insensitivity to the wider principle that women should be treated as independent individuals throughout the income maintenance and taxation systems. Feminists have called for disaggregation of needs and benefits such that any man or woman can claim benefits in their own right and be treated separately for purposes of taxation.[33]

Even in the Nordic countries, where such individualization was relatively quickly achieved, the welfare state remained a target of second-wave feminism. Employment policies encouraged women to remain in the caring professions and to identify their family responsibilities as primary. Generous parental leave programs as well as a proliferation of part-time jobs in the state sector meant that the expansion of social programs did little to challenge unequal relations of gender power in the family and society.[34] Rather than accepting more of the same, Nordic feminists agititated for child care and parental leaves programs that would more effectively involve fathers, and a policy of reduced working time for everyone that would really encourage families to renegotiate their gender division of labor. Swedish feminists said that their goal was to negotiate an "equality contract" between women and men.[35]

Feminists also criticized the day-to-day operation of the welfare state as too centralized and bureaucratic. They joined other social forces in calling for decentralization and democratization. Women's movements sought to empower clients and workers by ensuring that they could participate in program design and delivery. In France in the 1980s, for example, several large strikes by nurses (who are public employees) opposed the effects of budgetary restraint in the public sector, which compressed the wages of nurses, at the same time that they demanded better recognition of the professional qualifications of nurses, who are overwhelmingly female. Their major claim was based on the feminist analysis that *because* nursing is done by women it is seen as relatively unskilled, indeed "natural" for women to do. Thus, behind the mobilizing slogan *"ni nonnes, ni bonnes, ni connes"* ("neither nuns, nor maids, nor stupid") these movements became the most important manifestation of feminist politics to be seen in several years.[36]

This targeting of the institutions, both in the state and civil society, that were responsible for the design of the postwar welfare state did result in movement toward equality on civil, political, and social rights. Nonetheless, the agenda for achieving full citizenship was never completed. Even the citizenship status of Nordic women, who so often served as a model in the years of the second-wave movement, remains less than had been hoped for:

After 20 years of equality policies at various levels, women's and men's life patterns have changed but they still differ, and women still have considerably less societal power. Most social clients are women. Most full-time workers—the powerful "indirect citizens" of corporate structures—are men, most voters are women, most representatives are men. Women are the direct participants in an increasing number of citizen roles, men are either represented indirectly or are those who fill representative posts at least in the majority of cases.[37]

REMAINING LOYAL TO A WEAKENED FRIEND: WOMEN'S MOVEMENTS AND WELFARE STATES AT THE END OF THE TWENTIETH CENTURY

In recent decades in several countries—the United Kingdom,, Italy and Denmark come first to mind—there has been an assault on the values and programs of the postwar welfare state. Even if elsewhere there has been less of an outright attack, everywhere there have been moves to redesign postwar programs. All are seeking novel ways to reduce and control state expenditures and limit public responsibility for care, which, as we saw at the beginning of this chapter, was the hallmark of the postwar welfare state:

> Today . . . welfare states are at a turning point. There are political attempts from both the left and the right to restructure the welfare state, to cut public expenditure and to change the relationship between the state and individual citizens, whether as consumers or clients. Whatever it is called—modernization, privatization or decentralization—the aim is to expand the sphere of the market and the family and consequently to limit the sphere of the state.[38]

As in the postwar period, these changes will have implications for gender relations and will complicate women's political struggles for full citizenship. New barriers for gender equality are emerging. Rising enthusiasm for the values of competitiveness and individual achievement, which are the values promoted by neoliberals, challenge postwar commitments to the civil, political, and social rights of citizenship. The idea that economic, political, and social resources should be redistributed has lost many supporters, even on the political left.[39] In such shifts, women have emerged as a major source of support for maintaining commitments to state responsibility for social solidarity in egalitarian ways. A gender gap has emerged in elections, with women more than men tending to vote for the left.[40] At the same time, the political discourse of the new right has encouraged the emergence of challenges to reproductive rights. Women's control over their bodies is being increasingly threatened in several European countries.

A Policy Dilemma: Distributing Working Time and Caring Time

In the postwar years, as we have seen, ideas about work and workers were central to social policy design. In many countries the assumption was that there would be a male breadwinner whose income would be sufficient to support his wife and dependent children. In this model, best exemplified by

Britain, West Germany, and Ireland, care for the family was to be provided by women, and a strong line was drawn between public and "private" spheres. As we have seen, the result was that there was real inequality of treatment within social programs, an assumption that if women were employed it was only part-time and that therefore the state needed to provide neither paid maternity leaves nor child care.[41] Moreover, women bear heavy financial costs in the form of income they do not earn when they stay out of the labor market in order to bear and care for children.[42]

In other countries, such as France and Nordic Europe, the model was transformed in the postwar years into one of dual earners. Both women and men worked for wages, and two incomes were needed to support the family. Single mothers, for their part, were given positive encouragements to enter the labor force, and their child-rearing costs were heavily subsidized. In these countries, care was still provided by the family and within the family by women, but there was also an increase in publicly provided and highly subsidized services, especially for child care and other forms of care. In France, policymakers explicitly assumed that women's jobs would be like men's, that is, full-time. Therefore, they focused on increasing public child care places. In other cases, such as the Nordic countries, policymakers assumed that women would have heavy caring responsibilities, and therefore many jobs were part-time. Nonetheless, they were well paid and had full social benefits. Moreover, they tended to be "long part-time" jobs, with women working over 30 hours a week. Therefore, their incomes were relatively high.

These models have changed dramatically in recent years. Women's labor force participation has risen everywhere. In part this is because throughout Europe there has been a rapid rise in part-time work, and these jobs are overwhelmingly taken by women. Moreover, it is young women, married or unmarried, with children who have begun to fill the part-time positions. The development of the service sector and new employment practices in industry have created demand for part-time employees. At the same time, rising rates of unemployment through the late 1970s and 1980s made governments more interested in encouraging the creation of more part-time jobs. Two people could be employed part-time, rather than having one in the paid labor force and one on the unemployment rolls. Therefore, if they had not already done so, several governments in Western Europe began to pass legislation to encourage hiring part-time workers and to improve their working conditions.

A new intersection of policy realms emerged. This description of the Dutch situation could serve equally well for several countries:

> Flexibility, privatization, and deregulation were the key words in this new vision of the relationship between market and state. Within this framework, part-time work was key, viewed as an instrument to meet several goals. First, to the extent that the need for a flexible labor market has been identified as a

condition for economic expansion, the idea of part-time work acquired new popularity. Part-time jobs with flexible work schedules could permit plants, stores, and offices to remain open the longer hours. No longer are the hours of opening and individuals' work schedules synchronized around a nine-to-five model. Part-time work has been considered a major weapon in the battle against unemployment. Dutch employment policy has increasingly concentrated on encouraging part-time work. Creation of part-time positions as well as splitting full-time jobs became a means for spreading the available work among a larger number of people. Another argument made in favor of the development of part-time work is its contribution to the economic independence of women. Redistribution of paid and unpaid work between men and women will improve the labor market position of women. Many believe that part-time work can play a major role in this issue by offering both men and women the possibility of paid and unpaid work.[43]

Although the intersection of a variety of interests is clear in this statement, all is not rosy. In the Netherlands, the right to equal pay and equal treatment for part-time workers is not yet legally established. Many collective agreements do provide for such equality, but not all. In the United Kingdom, the problem is even more severe, because its labor market is virtually unregulated. Without a minimum wage, without limits on the length of the average workweek, and with very weak unions, labor market "flexibility" has taken hold and the idea of "standard working hours" has collapsed, but part-timers have gained no new protections.[44]

In other countries, which have stronger unions and women's movements and states less committed to neoliberalism, part-time workers have gained more protections. Nonetheless, the issue is not settled simply by prorating wages (so that part-time employees are paid at the same level as full-time ones) or ensuring access to social benefits. Rather, the issue of *how* to reduce working time needs to be addressed directly.

Two strategies for doing so have long been identified. One is to reduce the hours of some workers, such as women with family responsibilities. A two-track labor market is thereby maintained. Part-time work does not necessarily lack social benefits, but it is not part of the core labor market. The other is to reduce the hours of all workers so that a more equal gender division of labor in the family can be negotiated.

We have seen that women's movements (for example, the Swedish women's movement and the French Socialists described above) have tended to favor the second strategy. Nonetheless, the ability to push for this second strategy is weakened by labor market policies that favor part-time work for mothers and by cutbacks to social policies that redirect more and more care back toward the family. As governments move to implement such policies, women, their movements, and their allies find that they must fight to defend their vision of gender equality. They must fight again to claim full citizenship in these redesigned welfare states.

In France, for example, since the 1980s the government has encouraged employers to think of hiring part-time workers. At the same time it has altered its thinking about child care, moving away from the idea that child care would be provided full-time in subsidized municipal centers or in family day care facilities. It has done so in the name of cost saving, as well as to promote the idea that the state should provide families with more choices about how to provide their own care, including by purchasing it in the market.[45]

Since 1985 successive French governments have been encouraging mothers to provide more of their own child care. Paid parental leaves were established in 1985 and have been extended to cover more families. These leaves are not like those of the Nordic countries, however. They are not at all generous, being well below the minimum wage. Nonetheless, they are sufficiently large to compensate a woman who has a low-paying job and lives with a partner. They compensate for wages foregone as well as for what she would have to pay for child care. They do not appeal to single mothers, who use other forms of child care. Over time, moreover, these parental leaves have been redesigned to mesh more closely with part-time employment. Parents can now take a part-time leave combined with a part-time job.

At the same time, the French government has developed other programs to encourage families to hire caregivers. This category of workers has always been overwhelmingly female. The government's goal has been to force such workers off the black market by regularizing their employment situation and thereby guaranteeing them better working conditions.[46]

Such policies for all forms of caring work are beneficial to many people, of course. However, examined from the perspective of women's equality we can uncover several worrying trends. First, the parental leave programs, because they provide low benefits, have become a female ghetto. Fathers very rarely take advantage of them, and the programs do very little to challenge the notion that mothers are primarily responsible for care. Therefore, this is a solution to the working time/caring time dilemma that continues to assign responsibility for care to women, and recompenses them at rates well below real wages. The result is that French feminists have been profoundly critical of this program, arguing instead for continued financing of subsidized public child care.

A second reason to be sceptical of such programs is that they are also a low-paid ghetto for women *workers*. If municipal child care centers are overwhelmingly staffed by women, such employees earn good wages and benefits. If care work is shifted to individual workers hired by individual families, the general or average situation of care workers deteriorates. These programs save a good deal of public money and are therefore popular for cost choppers. Their unintended effect is to deskill and undermine the status of care workers. Nurses in hospitals or visiting services, for example, find themselves threatened with unemployment as government policy shifts care-giving in the direction of unskilled, often part-time, and often immigrant caregivers. Therefore, women's organizations representing state workers are deeply sceptical of such solutions to the fiscal problems of the state. They do nothing to generate gender equality at work or in society more generally.

France is not the only country to which such solutions are appealing. The Swedish government, under pressure to cut costs, has moved in this direction as well. It reduced the rates for parental leaves so that 75 percent rather than 90 percent of salary is now replaced. Given that men tend to earn more than women, a loss of 25 percent of their salary would have a greater negative effect on the family income, and therefore parental leaves remain the mothers' preserve. Moreover, debates have recently surfaced over "care subsidies." These would allow families to choose whether to purchase child care or to provide it themselves, by one member staying out of the paid labor force and using the subsidy to compensate for wages foregone.[47] In Britain, Margaret Thatcher's Conservative party instituted one of the first neoliberal assaults on the welfare state. These included cutbacks to social provision and health care, as well as the failure to develop public child care, all of which resulted in pushing responsibility for care back into "the family," which means of course the women of the family.

Assaults on Reproductive Rights

As we saw above, gaining access to safe and legal abortions had been one of the first claims of second-wave feminists as they sought to expand their civil rights. The legislative victories of the 1960s and 1970s have begun to be undermined by the reemergence of antichoice politics that have put the hard-won laws in doubt. Germany provides the most dramatic example. The unification of East and West Germany after 1989 raised the question of whether the much more liberal law of the German Democratic Republic (GDR) would be immediately replaced by the limited access to abortion that existed in the Federal Republic of Germany (FRG). Efforts to do so were blocked, in part because of a successful interparty alliance of elected women. In addition, many activists considered the moment of unification ripe for actors to press forward, to decriminalize abortion, and to make the FRG's legislation more prochoice by removing restrictions on the circumstances under which abortions were legal. Feminists mobilized behind new legislation, and a much more liberal law was passed in 1992. Nonetheless, an appeal to the Constitutional Court struck down the new law, and in doing so rolled back access even in comparison to West Germany before unification.[48] The intense debate about abortion in these years resulted in a severe blow to prochoice positions, and for the moment German women have *less* access to this crucial civil right than they did before 1989.

But Germany is not alone in having seen a resurgence of antichoice politics. The growing power of religious fundamentalism among Protestants, Catholics, and Muslims in several Western European countries has generated an upsurge in "prolife" campaigns, which include harassment of women and doctors as well as efforts to change the law. In France, for example, violence in clinics where abortions are performed led the Socialist government to create a new crime—interfering with legal abortion. This legislation came only after women's groups had mobilized to publicize the problem and to demand action from public prosecutors who were doing nothing in the face of prolife actions.[49] Right-wing parties have also introduced legislation to eliminate social security coverage of the costs of abortion, and women's groups must remain on the alert against such attacks, which are not likely to end. In the United Kingdom, which was one of the Western European countries that legalized abortion earliest, the antichoice forces have never given up. Through the 1980s they pressured the government to set stricter limits on access and to reduce the time limits for legal abortions. The women's movement had to mobilize frequently and massively to maintain women's right to choose.[50]

In these circumstances, too, we see that women and their movements have struggled to defend the victories made possible in an earlier time. As with the work/care dilemma, the task is simply to protect hard-won prochoice victories. There is very little forward motion. Such defensiveness is likely to be the prevalent stance as long as neoliberalism remains dominant in Western Europe. Restructuring of labor market and social programs, carried out in the name of improving international competitiveness, privileges the market and market relations. As the state retreats from responsibility for overseeing social solidarity and deregulates, it is necessary to defend the kinds of state activities that women's movements have identified as central to overcoming women's economic and social inferiorities. Even more costly are cutbacks in social spending. In struggling against cutbacks and for solidarity, women and their movements have emerged as the most loyal friend the welfare state currently has.

NOTES

1. Birte Siim, "Welfare State, Gender Politics and Equality Policies: Women's Citizenship in the Scandinavian Welfare States," in *Equality Politics and Gender,* ed. Elizabeth Meehan and Selma Sevenhuijsen, Sage, London 1991, p. 179.
2. Siv Gustafsson, "Childcare and Types of Welfare States," in *Gendering Welfare States,* ed. Diane Sainsbury, Sage, London, 1994, pp. 50–51.
3. These examples are all from Jane Lewis, "Introduction: Women, Work, Family and Social Policies in Europe," in *Women and Social Policies in Europe,* ed. Jane Lewis, Edward Elgar, Aldershot, 1993, p. 17.
4. Laura Balbo, "Crazy Quilts: Rethinking the Welfare State Debate from a Woman's Point of View," in *Women and the State,* ed. Anne Showstack Sasson, Hutchinson, London, 1987.
5. Memorandum of the Family Allowance Campaign, in Clare Ungerson, ed., *Women and Social Policy: A Reader,* Macmillan, London, 1985, pp. 30–31.
6. T. H. Marshall, *Class, Citizenship and Social Development: Essays,* Anchor Books, New York, 1965, p. 76.
7. This right emerged first in the form of protection from unreasonable search and seizure, of *habeas corpus,* etc.

8. European Documentation, *A Human Face for Europe,* European Community, Brussels, 1990, pp. 18–19.
9. Quoted in Hilary Land, "Who Still Cares for the Family? Recent Developments in Income Maintenance," in Clare Ungerson, *op. cit.,* p. 53.
10. There were, of course, debates over such matters. For a description of the variety of positions with respect to family allowances in the interwar period, see Clare Ungerson, *op. cit.,* p. 4.
11. Quoted in Hilary Land, "Women: Supporters or Supported?" in *Sexual Divisions and Society: Process and Change,* ed. Diana Leonard Baker and Sheila Allen, Tavistock, London, 1976, p. 110.
12. *Ibid.,* p. 128.
13. Isabella Bakker, "Women's Employment in Comparative Perspective," in *The Feminization of the Labour Force,* ed. Jane Jenson et al., Polity Press, Oxford, 1988.
14. Lewis, *op. cit.,* pp. 6–11, provides statistical information on these social changes.
15. In Italy, the struggle for abortion rights was preceded by one to reform divorce law, which was one of the first actions in which the second-wave women's movement engaged. Karen Beckwith, "Response to Feminism in the Italian Parliament: Divorce, Abortion, and Sexual Violence Legislation," in *The Women's Movements of the United States and Western Europe: Consciousness, Political Opportunity and Public Policy,* ed. Mary F. Katzenstein and Carol Mueller, Temple University Press, Philadelphia, pp. 157–158.
16. Despite this mobilization, the actual law passed in 1980 was quite restrictive. Monique Leijenaar and Kees Niemöller, "Political Participation of Women: The Netherlands," in *Women and Politics Worldwide,* ed. Barbara Nelson and Najma Chowdhury, Yale University Press, New Haven, 1994, p. 500.
17. For Italy, see Yasmine Ergas, "Feminism of the 1970s," in *A History of Women in the West: Toward a Cultural Identity in the Twentieth Century,* ed. Françoise Thébaud, Belknap Press of Harvard University, Cambridge, 1994; and Beckwith, *op. cit.* For France, see Jane Jenson, "Changing Discourse, Changing Agendas: Political Rights and Reproductive Policies in France," in Katzenstein and Mueller, *op. cit.,* pp. 82ff.
18. Christiane Lemke, "Women and Politics: The New Federal Republic of Germany," in Nelson and Chowdhury, *op. cit.,* p. 274.
19. Joni Lovenduski and Vicky Randall, *Contemporary Feminist Politics: Women and Power in Britain,* Oxford University Press, Oxford, 1993.
20. This doctors' "right to choose" coupled with very restrictive conditions was the result of West Germany's reform of abortion law in the 1970s. For a discussion of the Norwegian mobilization to move away from the doctor-controlled model, which resulted in the 1978 legislation permitting "free abortion" for twelve weeks, see Janneke Van der Ros, "The State and Women: A Troubled Relationship in Norway," in Nelson and Chowdhury, *op. cit.,* p. 532.
21. Margaret Maruani, "The Position of Women in the Labour Market," *Women in Europe,* Supplement, 36 (1990) p. 30.
22. E. Haavio-Mannila, et al., *Unfinished Democracy: Women in Nordic Politics,* Pergamon, Oxford, 1985, pp. 148–149.
23. For Sweden, see Mary Ruggie, "Workers' Movements and Women's Interests: The Impact of Labor-State Relations in Britain and Sweden," in Katzenstein and Mueller, *op. cit.,* p. 262. For Norway, see Hege Skjeie, "The Uneven Advance of Norwegian Women," *New Left Review* 187 (1991), pp. 87–89.

24. In several countries, especially the Nordic ones, many decisions are not taken by the government alone. Rather, they are made in institutions that provide representation of the "social partners"—employers and labor. This is called the corporate channel and may include representatives of a variety of associations in civil society.

25. On Italy, see Bianca Beccalli, "The Modern Women's Movement in Italy," *New Left Review* 204 (1994). On Germany, see Elisabeth Vogelheim, "Women in a Changing Workplace: The Case of the FRG," in Jenson et al., *op. cit.* On Sweden and the UK, see Ruggie, *op. cit.* Whereas such efforts have been relatively successful almost everywhere, a surprising holdout has been in Norway. See Skjeie, *op. cit.,* pp. 93ff.

26. Christina Bergqvist, "The Declining Corporatist State and the Political Gender Dimension," in *Women in Nordic Politics: Closing the Gap,* ed. Lauri Karvonen and Per Selle, Dartmouth, Aldershot, UK, 1995, pp. 205–228.

27. Jane Jenson and Mariette Sineau, "The Same or Different: An Unending Dilemma for French Women," in Barbara Nelson and Najma Chowdhury, *op. cit.*

28. On the Green-feminist link, see Myra Marx Ferree, "Equality and Autonomy: Feminist Politics in the United States and West Germany," in Katzenstein and Mueller, *op. cit.,* p. 179. On pressures to change the Italian Communist party, see Stephen Hellman, "Feminism and the Model of Militancy in an Italian Communist Federation: Challenges to the Old Style of Politics," in Katzenstein and Mueller, *op. cit.*

29. Land, "Who Still Cares for the Family?", p. 52.

30. Land, "Supporters or Supported?", pp. 129–130.

31. Quoted in Zoë Fairbairns, "The Cohabitation Rule: Why It Makes Sense," in Clare Ungerson, *op. cit.,* p. 67.

32. Jane Jenson and Mariette Sineau, "Family Policy and Women's Citizenship in Mitterrand's France," *Social Politics: International Studies in Gender, State and Society* 2, no. 3 (Fall 1995).

33. Jennifer Dale and Peggy Foster, *Feminists and State Welfare,* Routledge, London, 1986, p. 108.

34. Anette Borchorst and Birte Siim, "Women and the Advanced Welfare State: A New Kind of Patriarchal Power?" in Anne Showstack Sasson, *op. cit.*

35. Jane Jenson and Rianne Mahon, "Representing Solidarity: Class, Gender and the Crisis in Social Democratic Sweden," *New Left Review* 201 (1993) p. 91.

36. Danièle Kergoat, ed. *Les Infirmières et leur coordination, 1988–89,* Lamarre, Paris, 1992, pp. 19–20.

37. Helga-Maria Hernes, *Welfare State and Women Power: Essays in State Feminism,* Norwegian University Press, Oslo, 1987, p. 141.

38. Birte Siim, "The Gendered Scandinavian Welfare States: The Interplay Between Women's Roles as Mothers, Workers and Citizens in Denmark," in Lewis, *op. cit.,* p. 25.

39. George Ross and Jane Jenson, "The Tragedy of the French Left," *New Left Review,* 171 (1988).

40. Pippa Norris, "The Gender Gap: A Cross-National Trend," in *The Politics of the Gender Gap,* ed. Carol M. Mueller, Sage, London, 1988.

41. Jane Lewis, "Gender and the Development of Welfare Regimes," *Journal of European Social Policy* 2, no. 3 (1992), pp. 159–173.

42. Lewis, "Introduction," p. 20.
43. Janneke Plantenga, "For Women Only? The Rise of Part-Time Work in the Netherlands," *Social Politics: International Studies in Gender, State and Society* 3, no. 1 (1996), pp. 61–62.
44. Colette Fagan, "Gendered Time Schedules: Paid Work in Great Britain," *Social Politics: International Studies in Gender, State and Society* 3 no. 1 (1996), pp. 72–106.
45. In the United Kingdom the government takes no responsibility for child care except in a few cases of child welfare. Asked to explain to the House of Commons why Britain ranked very low in the provision of quality public child care, the minister responsible said: "Our view is that it is for the parents who go out to work to decide how best to care for their children. If they want or need help in this task they should make the appropriate arrangements and meet the costs." Quoted in Lewis, "Introduction," p. 4.
46. Details are available in Jenson and Sineau, "Family Policy and Women's Citizenship in Mitterrand's France."
47. Gustaffson, *op. cit.*, p. 53.
48. For women from the GDR the change was obviously very great. But even in the former West Germany, the Court's stress on the "rights of the unborn life" and prohibition of coverage by health insurance of even legal abortions done for "social indications" (90 percent of legal abortions) constituted a major new limit on access. Lemke, *op. cit.*, pp. 275–276.
49. For example, antiabortion "commandos" who threatened women or invaded clinics were only rarely charged with assault or trespass. Jane Jenson and Mariette Sineau, *Mitterrand et les Françaises. Un rendez-vous manqué*, Presses de Sciences po, Paris, 1995, Chapter 9.
50. Lovenduski and Randall, *op. cit.*, pp. 244–251.

SUGGESTIONS FOR FURTHER READING

Gelb, Joyce. *Feminism and Politics: A Comparative Perspective.* Berkeley: University of California Press, 1989.

Githens, Marianne, and Dorothy McBride Stetson. *Abortion Politics: Public Policy in Cross-Cultural Perspective.* New York: Routledge, 1996.

Lewis, Jane. *Britain Since 1945: Women, Work and the State in the Postwar Years.* Oxford: Blackwell, 1992.

———, ed. *Women and Social Policies in Europe.* Aldershot: Edward Elgar, 1993.

Lovenduski, Joni, and Pippa Norris. *Gender and Party Politics.* London: Sage, 1993.

Moeller, Robert G. *Protecting Motherhood: Women and the Family in the Politics of Postwar West Germany.* Berkeley: University of California Press, 1993.

Nelson, Barbara, and Najma Chowdhury, eds. *Women and Politics Worldwide.* New Haven: Yale University Press, 1994.

Sainsbury, Diane, ed. *Gendering Welfare States.* Sage: London, 1994.

Cinderella: Polish reality meets Western myths of femininity.   RICK GERHARTER/IMPACT VISUALS.

CHAPTER 19

The Great Divide?
Women's Rights in
Eastern and Central
Europe Since 1945

Barbara Einhorn

Women in East Central Europe have experienced two major systemic changes in the period since 1945. In the aftermath of World War II, Europe was divided between the Allies—and between two opposing political, economic and social systems. This divide hardened with the beginning of the Cold War, and was often referred to as the "Iron Curtain." The countries "behind" the Curtain disappeared from Western view, so that for much of the period, little was known about the lives of women there. Within the state socialist system which dominated those countries, women's rights were seen as part of an effort to abolish privilege and establish equal rights for all citizens. Yet women were defined in law as having a dual role, as workers and mothers. Some measures attempted to compensate for this "double burden." In practice, however, gender-based inequalities persisted, both in the workplace and at home.

Since 1989, this region has undergone fundamental change. State socialist regimes have been replaced by multi-party democracies. Centrally planned economies based on the abolition of private ownership have given way to private enterprise within a neo-liberal version of the market economy. From being defined as workers and mothers in state socialist legislation, women are now confronted with an idealized view of motherhood as their primary role and responsibility. In both periods, it could be argued, the image of womanhood was, and is, manipulated for economic and demographic purposes, rather than out of a commitment to social equity, or gender equality. This chapter demonstrates that legislation on its own—even when reinforced by "special needs" provisions—is insufficient to guarantee women's rights in practice. Nor is civil society activism alone a viable route to full implementation of women's rights. What is needed is both grassroots activism, and state provision.

This chapter offers comparative analysis on multiple levels. It allows for a comparison between the approach to women's rights adopted by state socialist

515

*regimes in East and Central Europe, and the postwar welfare states of
Western Europe discussed by Jane Jenson in Chapter 18. As examples of the
implementation of the socialist model for women's "emancipation," as it was
called, these countries can be seen as variations on the Soviet version discussed
by Richard Stites in Chapter 15, and as developments of early articulations of
the ideals of both feminism and socialism dealt with by Charles Sowerwine in
Chapter 13.*

Studying the region of East and Central Europe since 1945 is both complex and illuminating. Not only can we observe the confrontation of two different social, political, and economic models across the Cold War divide, with the German-German border as the zipper that threatened at times to burst apart, but, in addition, the countries of the region have been involved, since 1989, in a process of fundamental transformation in which they are changing a one-party state socialist model, with its centrally planned economy, to a pluralist democratic model based on a capitalist market economy.

The history of the postwar era in East and Central Europe is thus divided into two time periods, before and after 1989. The state socialist period, from 1945 to 1989, was of course neither monolithic nor unchanging. We shall see how there were differences between countries as well as shifts in policy within countries at different stages within this first period. Similarly, the years since 1989 have seen individual countries within the region adapt their economies and polities at differing speeds, some adopting the "shock-effect" rapid process of marketization and privatization, and others opting for more gradual economic change in order to minimize the dislocation and social impact of the paradigm shift. Changes of government during the post-1989 period have also led in some cases to policy changes or modifications. Differences of policy between and within individual countries have meant that different groups of women have been differentially affected by the transformation process, some benefiting from the greater scope for choice and individual initiative, and others becoming impoverished without the secure employment, subsidies, and social provision of the previous regimes.

While acknowledging such differences, both between and within countries, and between women in different countries and different groups of women within individual countries, it is important to acknowledge commonalities. Particularly within the first of our historical periods, 1945 to 1989, the imposition of a political, economic, and social model that stressed universality, equality, and uniformity and that implemented its ideology by means of strongly centralized power structures, meant that women both within and between countries in the region shared large areas of experience. Thus we will show that in the first period, as a result both of the attempt to build an egalitarian society and pressures on individuals to conform to the dominant ideology, commonalities outweighed differences, whereas in the more recent transition period, it appears that differences are becoming more and more marked. Both within and between countries, there are growing income differentials and thus increasing social inequalities.

Overall, then, we can say that women in the countries of East Central Europe have experienced, or, some would say, had to suffer, the application to their lives of two distinct social, political and economic systems, each with quite different views of what role women should play within society. The lived experience of women in this region allows us to evaluate the record of two opposing systems in their attempts to achieve equal status for women.

State socialism started out from a model of universal rights based on the rights of a class, the working class. But the force of traditional norms and expectations in these societies, onto which the policy emphasis on bringing women into the labor force was superimposed, simply meant that women ended up with the much described "double (or even triple) burden,"[1] coming home from a full day at work to another shift at home. Paradoxically, this made state socialist regimes introduce "special needs" legislation, that is, legislation and social provision based on women's specific needs arising from their role as mothers.

The new, democratic regimes, by contrast, have embraced wholeheartedly the return to tradition, and in emphasizing women's role as mothers, rather than as workers, have returned to a social model based on gender difference. Thus an examination of these two periods throws into relief the much debated question, as yet unresolved by either system, about whether definitions based on equality or difference might provide the appropriate basis for empowering women so that they may become citizens on an equal basis with men.[2]

The countries to be covered in this chapter will be (moving from west to east) the German Democratic Republic (GDR, later the New Federal States of Germany), Czechoslovakia (later the Czech and Slovak Republics), Poland, Hungary, Bulgaria, Romania, Albania, Yugoslavia (later Croatia, Serbia, Bosnia-Herzegovina, Slovenia, Montenegro, Macedonia, and Kosov).

The GDR/New Federal States of Germany provides a trenchant example for both periods. As the country situated right on the Cold War divide, face to face with West Germany (the Federal Republic of Germany, FRG), its history demonstrates both the confrontation between two opposing paradigms in the earlier period and the later systemic convergence or, in this particular case, incorporation, rather than transformation into, a democratic country with a market-based economy. As a young East German woman put it soon after German unification took place: "Without having moved, I am suddenly living on the other side of the boundary between the First and Second Worlds. The day of unification was for me a day of sad farewells; not from the political system, but from the land I grew up in. I don't know if I shall find a home in this newly developing country."[3]

POLITICAL RIGHTS: LEGISLATIVE EQUALITY, QUOTAS, CIVIL SOCIETY

Right from the start, the state socialist countries introduced equality in their early constitutions and other pieces of legislation. Although women in Czechoslovakia had enjoyed the right to vote and equal rights since the 1918 Constitution enacted by the newly independent state under its president T. G. Masaryk, in practice there was pervasive and persistent discrimination against them. The May 1948 constitution of the new communist state "enacted principles of equality between men and women in all aspects of social life."[4]

Interestingly, all early examples of state socialist legislation stipulated protection for motherhood and the family. The GDR's 1950 "Law on the Protection of Mothers and Children and the Rights of Women" is an example, although it did deal with a broader spectrum of issues. The act provided for the creation of state child care facilities, for maternity grants and paid maternity leave, for revisions in marriage and family law, and for measures designed to help women improve their level of qualification and gain access to previously male-dominated occupations. Both this law and the 1948 Czechoslovak Constitution removed the stigma attached to illegitimate children, thus eliminating the exclusivity of the marriage bond as the basis of the family.

The Soviet military occupation forces in Eastern Germany had introduced an equal pay order (no. 253) in 1946, even before the GDR came into existence in October 1949, predating by five years the ILO's International Labor Office 1951 Equal Remuneration Convention (no. 100), and by nine years the 1955 equal pay legislation in the Federal Republic (West Germany). The extent to which this legal principle became reality in any of the state socialist countries, however, will be discussed below.

Differences between the socialist and capitalist approaches to equality legislation can be seen in the German case. Although the 1949 Constitutions of both German states provided for men and women to be equal under the law, these could still be overridden in the Federal Republic by the earlier (1896) German Civil Code, up until the new civil law on equality of the sexes was passed on June 18, 1957 (becoming effective only from January 1, 1958).

Later constitutions in several of the state socialist countries recognized the need, over and above gender-neutral legislation, for some affirmative action. Thus Czechoslovakia's 1960 revised Constitution affirmed (article 27) the following: "The equal status of women in the family, at work and in public life shall be secured by special adjustment of working conditions and special health care during pregnancy and maternity, as well as by the development of facilities and services which will enable women to participate fully in the life of society."[5] There has always been debate around the question of whether legislative change is the best, or indeed an effective, way to achieve equality of opportunity for women. Certainly the introduction of equality legislation as well as later gender-specific provisions reflects the top-down approach that was characteristic of state socialism in its dealings with what it called the "woman question." Equality was not something that women achieved through struggle. Rather it was "given" to them in a way that rendered it at best invisible, part of life that was taken for granted until the changes of 1989 made it clear that some rights could be lost. As Fatos Tarifa of Albania put it: "For more than four decades Albanian women remained victims of the party's propaganda, which portrayed even the rights guaranteed to women by the constitution as gifts of the party, not legitimate rights that the party was bound to recognize." Or, in the words of Roumyana Slabakova from Bulgaria, "Emancipation was a gift women had to be taught to appreciate." But equally, as Maxine Molyneux commented aptly as early as 1981, "women's emancipation cannot be achieved 'from above,' any more than can a genuine socialist transformation."[6]

Moreover, as Hilda Scott pointed out as early as 1974, state socialist regimes saw "equality as something that can be given to women without affecting the position of men."[7] This neglect of the reality of gender relations as unequal power relations hindered the achievement of equality. It reinforced traditional patriarchal family structures, resulting in the double burden carried by women, which in turn disadvantaged women in the workplace. Gender imbalances in the domestic division of labor made women into "unreliable" workers, the ones who were often absent to care for sick children, the ones who did not even push themselves forward for promotions because of the difficulties of juggling their double and triple roles.

Legislation alone is not sufficient to improve women's situation; traditional attitudes and the gender divisions that accompany must also shift. Yet the post-1989 transformations indicate that, without a certain level of female representation in the formal political structures, even legislating for equality is jeopardized.

Before 1989, quotas for the Communist parties, the official women's organizations and other mass organizations ensured that women held on average around one-third of the seats in state socialist parliaments. But increasing women's level of representation by means of quotas has often been seen as questionable. It has been argued that in the state socialist regimes it was a mere gesture in the direction of "emancipating" women, which resulted in "token appointees," "the 'yes-women' of the past who always voted as the leadership expected them to and rarely took independent initiatives."[8] Sharon Wolchik points out that in Czechoslovakia, as in other state socialist legislatures, over two-thirds of women deputies (who constituted 25 percent of the total) in the 1986 Federal Assembly were workers or agricultural laborers (compared with only 25 percent of male deputies); in other words, they also lacked the background or training to act effectively in their role as politicians.[9]

Moreover, the parliaments were not the real loci of power. Important decisions were made by the central committees and politburos of the ruling Communist parties. Here there was a quite different scene, with women constituting 24 to 30 percent of total party membership but diminishing in visibility toward the top of party hierarchies. In 1975, 15 percent of the membership of the Czechoslovak party's Central Committee were women. The equivalent figures were 13 percent in the GDR, 12 percent in Hungary, 8 percent in Poland, and only 3.3 percent in the Soviet Union.[10]

The situation in the politburos, the most powerful groups in state socialist regimes, was even worse. Even up to the late 1980s, women were conspicuous by their absence from the politburos of Bulgaria, Czechoslovakia, and Yugoslavia. In the politburo of the ruling PUWP (Polish United Workers' Party) in Poland, there was one woman in 1987. Two women members graced the politburos of ruling parties in Hungary and Romania, but it is unclear whether they were full or candidate members. In the former GDR, no woman ever became a full member of the all-powerful politburo: Inge Lange and Margarete Mueller remained nonvoting candidate members from 1973 and 1963, respectively, until 1989, the former as the much hated state secretary for women's affairs, a clear indication of the low priority accorded this issue by the regime.[11]

With the total rejection of state socialism and all of its mechanisms in the immediate aftermath of 1989 came a rejection of quotas, viewed as a part of the manipulative control exercised by the one-party state.[12] The results were dramatic drops in the level of female representation in the first and second democratic elections. From an average one-third parliamentarians, women accounted in the first postcommunist elections for 10 percent or less of deputies, the equivalent at that time of the worst of Western European levels. In Romania, the percentage of women representatives fell from 34.4 percent in 1985 to 5.5 percent after the elections of May 1990. In Albania, there was a fall from a high of 33.3 percent in 1974 (29 percent in the later 1980s) to 2.8 percent in 1992.[13]

The plethora of new political parties in the emerging pluralist polity boasted almost no female leaders. Nor did they, for the most part, consider it necessary to include policies relating to gender equity in their programs. In 1990, Anna Petrasovits, the only woman leader of a new political party in Hungary, the Social Democrats, stated that "we don't want token women like the Communists had, stupid silly little women who sit there. . . . We want real, strong women politicians, who have to be born themselves." Unfortunately, the chances of finding such women in the immediate post-1989 situation were, in her view, not high, since "this is not a civil democratic society. These are half-feudalistic, agrarian societies which have then had forty years of socialist dictatorship. You cannot see women leaders in either form of society." As if to prove the point, Petrasovits came sixth in her constituency. And her party failed to qualify for the second round of voting in the 1990 elections.[14]

It is historically the case that left-of-center parties tend to promote women politicians and equality issues more readily than those of the right. Yet disillusionment with their recent past meant that, for East and Central Europeans in the immediate post-1989 period, social democracy and all left-of-center parties were seen as tainted by the totalitarian practices of state socialism. It was therefore not surprising, but hardly optimistic for feminist scholars such as Irene Dölling, that in the first all-German elections over 46 percent of women in the eastern part of Germany (former GDR) voted for the conservative alliance of Chancellor Helmut Kohl led by the Christian Democrats.[15]

This political behavior, clearly indicating that many women were out of touch with equality issues and unaware of how to further their own best interests, is attributed by Dölling to a tradition of passivity born of what she has called the "patriarchal-paternalist principle" of state socialist regimes. The state claimed to know best what was right for its citizens, especially for that segment of the population often referred to patronizingly as "our women."[16]

In place of this paternalistic, all-providing but prescriptive state, a yawning gulf has opened up in the post-1989 politics of East and Central Europe. The advent of democracy has brought the civil right to organize and to form free associations. This is a clear advance on the pre-1989 period, where the semi-governmental Women's Councils or Unions were the only nonparty organizations permitted to "represent" grassroots women's interests.[17] Yet it is notable that almost eight years after the "revolutions" of 1989, no large-scale women's movements (not that these are evident in Western Europe at this point in time) and very few self-styled feminist groups have emerged.

This might seem surprising, given the active role of women in the opposition movements of the 1970s and 1980s. Yet often in those movements, women performed crucial work, but in a secondary, supporting role.[18] They provided safe houses for dissidents on the run from the authorities, transmitted information in and out of the country, acted as couriers, and produced and distributed *samizdat* (clandestine) publications. An exception was the *Frauen für den Frieden* (Women for Peace) group in East Germany, which was active in the early 1980s on peace issues.[19] The group's principled opposition to violence as a viable means of conflict resolution influenced other dissident groups prior to 1989 and hence also the organizational stress on nonviolence that ultimately prevented bloodshed in October 1989. Its nonhierarchical structure and grassroots democratic mode of operation (autonomous working groups liaising loosely) influenced not only the theoretical conceptions for democratic renewal in the GDR but also the structure and working methods of the Round Tables set up after autumn 1989.

In a striking omission, given their path-breaking and pivotal role, the Women for Peace tend not to feature in recent accounts of the dissident movements of the 1980s and the 1989 "revolutions" in East and Central Europe.[20]

What has happened, in the new democratic context, is an idealization of the role of civil society associations as opposed to formal party political structures. Clearly, the telephone hotlines set up to deal with exploding levels of domestic violence, the women's centers, the private child care networks, and the care for the elderly springing up in the region demonstrate that women are filling the gap where the state once was through informal welfare provision.

However, this can hardly be seen as representing the promotion of gender equity or the furtherance of women's access to full citizenship rights.

Indeed, the problem with grassroots groups stepping into the gap created by withdrawal of the state from social provision is that the women who run them, far from making political demands, are compensating for the loss of some of the social rights associated in political theory with citizenship. There is also an open question about how the gulf between such usually locally based groups and the national political power structures can be bridged. This endangering of women's access to the public sphere of mainstream politics, and of their claims upon the state for welfare provision, in the idealized name of "civil society" is something I call the "civil society gap" or, more drastically, the "civil society trap."

Many of the small, often explicitly nonfeminist or even antifeminist groups that emerged around 1989 have adopted a maternalist, as opposed to the socialist state's paternalist, stance. An example is the group, formed in 1988, that called itself "Prague Mothers." These young women, many of them Catholics and mothers of several children, formed a group to protest environmental pollution in Prague specifically out of concern for their children's health. In this sense they were exercising their newly acquired civil rights, but certainly not in the name of women's citizenship rights. Rather they were acting to protect others, perpetuating an image of self-denial, a self-sacrificing stance in the interests of their children attributed to mothers in the traditional cultures of many East European societies. Illustrative of the attempt to return to these cultures in the post-1989 period is the sentiment voiced by Milan Vojnovic in 1993 urging Serbian women to "return to the morals of their mothers. . . . The traditional ornament of our woman is sacrifice without limits for her family."[21]

Many of the early autonomous groups emerged not so much spontaneously as in reaction to threats to erode or abolish social or reproductive rights. Thus in Poland, a (mixed) protest group, "Pro Femina," was formed in June 1989 to defend abortion rights in the face of Church-led efforts to make it illegal, and became weaker or ceased to exist after the drastic changes in the legislation went through the *Sejm* (parliament).[22] Explicitly feminist groups like the Polish Feminist Association or the Hungarian Feminist Network had to deal with reactions ranging from ridicule to outright hostility, stances I have elsewhere dubbed an "allergy to feminism."[23]

More widespread, and arguably more successful, have been groups that provide practical support, information, and resources for women, rather than address themselves to issues of gender equity and women's citizenship. These groups, which establish telephone hot lines or women's refuges, can be seen as reactive, not proactive, providing emergency damage limitation in the considerable social upheavals and dislocations engendered by the transformations following 1989, even in those countries not affected by military conflict and war. And in former Yugoslavia, a network of women-run centers offers support and rehabilitation to women refugees and victims of war and mass rape.[24]

What has made a stunning impact, seen from the perspective of 1997, is the large number of new Women's Studies and Gender Studies programs based both at universities and in free-standing women's resource centers all over the region.[25] This growth area reflects a perceived need to reevaluate women's situation and to create a local feminist analysis free of association with the tainted record of state socialist policies for women's "emancipation," and independent of Western feminist theory and scholarship.[26]

THE RIGHT TO WORK? WOMEN AS ECONOMIC ACTORS IN A CENTRALLY PLANNED AND A MARKET ECONOMY

Most theories of women's equality have argued that, for women to become citizens in their own right, they need to gain economic independence from men. Both socialist and capitalist economic models attach rewards only to what the socialists called "productive labor," namely, work that is rewarded by cash payment within the public world of the labor market. Both systems have failed fully to recognize as "work" most of women's "reproductive labor," that is, household work and child care within the private sphere of the family. In this way, much of women's work in the postwar period, in both east and west, north and south, has failed to be either "counted" or recompensed. United Nations estimates put the value of unpaid housework alone at between 10 and 35 percent of the gross domestic product (GDP) worldwide.[27]

Up to now, entitlements, particularly to the social rights of citizenship, have been dependent, in both the socialist and the capitalist models, on labor market participation.[28] This means that for women to become economic actors and thus citizens on an equal footing with men, they have needed—and continue to need—equal access to the labor market and equal rights and opportunities within it. In the region of East and Central Europe in the period 1945–1989, participation in the public world of work was the main focus of state socialist policies for women's "emancipation." There has been much debate about the motives for government encouragement or expectation of women's labor force participation in this period. Was it driven by ideological commitment to women's "emancipation," or rather by the need for additional labor power in the drive to build the socialist economy after the devastation of war?

Women from the region, especially writing with the bitterness of hindsight, have sometimes seen women's labor force participation not as the expression of the right to work but as an obligation imposed on them by cynically manipulative regimes. Thus Anastasia Posadskaya, founding director of the Moscow Gender Studies Center, said in a 1990 interview with Maxine Molyneux: "You are right that this commitment to equality has always existed. But it was absolutely formal and absolutely instrumental, it was not a commitment on behalf of women as such but was pursued only to achieve other goals, economic or demographic."[29] Especially in the earlier part of the period, it was suggested that women could become like men, or certainly gain entry to many formerly male-dominated fields of work. A somewhat simplistic view of the Marxist theories about women's "emancipation" meant that "productive" labor was given priority to the point where women's reproductive role was rendered invisible.

It took some years before the socialist regimes responded to the detrimental effects of the "double burden" this imposed on women by revising gender-neutral legislation to take account of women's special needs. Stereotypes arose about the unattractive, dungaree-clad women of state socialism. For the women themselves, the notion that they could be tough work mates during the day and charmingly feminine as well as exemplary housewives, mothers, and lovers in the evening led to severe exhaustion, anxiety about their identity and role, and feelings of guilt and self-doubt. Women felt inadequate in both roles, competent in neither. A representative sample of men and women physicians in Czechoslovakia in 1970 found that only 18 percent of the women felt able to combine happily their roles as doctors and homemakers, with 41 percent feeling that this required "extraordinary effort," 16 percent feeling that their work suffered, 6.7 percent feeling guilty of neglecting their children, and 5.5. percent worrying about undone housework.[30]

Writing in the 1980s her memoirs of Czechoslovakia in the 1950s, Rosemary Kavan, an Englishwoman married to a Czech Communist who was later imprisoned in connection with the Slansky trials, describes how

> women were struggling heroically against heavy odds. A 48-hour week, plus two hours' commuting, two hours' shopping and five hours' housework per day, was not resulting in the picture of fulfilled womanhood that might have been expected under a system that offered freedom from exploitation by man (except husbands), emancipation (from everything except child-bearing, home-running and the need to take up gainful employment because a man's salary could not support a family), and victory in the fight for equal rights and equal pay (by taking the less lucrative jobs the men were only too happy to leave). . . .

> Proud of my affiliation with the toiling masses, I had discarded make-up, wore only my oldest clothes . . . I wanted humbly to belong. . . .

> Now, seeing thirty colorless women, dedicated but joyless, indispensable but uncherished, I suddenly rebelled. This was not what we had fought for. No wonder the pubs and the divorce courts were full. My next demonstration was going to be against the oppression of Czech women.[31]

"How did you cope with it, Mama?" asks the writer Janina Bauman's daughter about her mother's experiences of the dual role during the same period in postwar Poland:

And here I begin my old tale that she has heard so many times before: three little children . . . full-time work . . . studies . . . Political commitments . . . A constant need to hurry. Sleepless nights. Exhaustion. Yes, things did go wrong sometimes, but somehow it all worked out. . . .

Shall I tell her that my life then was an endless compromise? Yes, I have to tell her that.[32]

The guilt, the conflict, and the stress of fulfilling these two roles were the expression of a juridically defined dual role. Section 3 of the GDR's 1977 revised Labour Code reflects this; it defines women juridically as workers and mothers, without any equivalent definition of men, and it simultaneously recognizes the need for special provisions to take the edge off: "The socialist state shall ensure that conditions are created everywhere which enable women increasingly to live up to their equal status at work and in vocational education and to reconcile even more successfully their occupational activities with the duties they have to fulfil as mothers and within the family." The "compensatory" legislation introduced by the GDR government to alleviate women's double burden has often been derided, in retrospect, as *"Muttipolitik"* ("Mommy politics").[33] Its impact, which will be discussed in the next section, did not fundamentally alter the fact that, of the two roles, it was women's role as workers that was given priority under state socialist policies. Both these aspects, namely, the policies dubbed "Mommy politics" for their attempts to stimulate the birthrate, thereby instrumentalizing women's reproductive labor for demographic purposes, and the prioritization of labor market participation that rendered the private sphere of the family publicly invisible, fed into and reinforced existing, often patriarchal, gendered relations of unequal power within the family.

Nor did the socialist regimes' primary focus on women's "productive labor" succeed in achieving equal conditions for women within the labor market. Some gains were made, especially in the earlier years, in terms of women's entry into formerly male-dominated occupations. However, there was continuing occupational segregation and wage inequality. Women tended to end up clustered in female-dominated sectors of the economy such as light industry and the retail and service sectors. They mostly did jobs involving serving, catering, and cleaning, in other words, jobs that could be seen as a form of domestic labor, extended into the public sphere of work. These sectors held lower status and hence attracted lower pay than industry in general, and heavy industry in particular. Even professions such as medicine and law, which became heavily feminized in this region in the state socialist period, were consequently devalued in terms of both status and pay.

Hungarian economist Mária Ladó has identified a vicious circle whereby those sectors that employed large numbers of women offered less than average wages, and those jobs that commanded low wages were female-dominated. She maintains that "the feminization of a career starts when, following technical, economic and social changes, the status and prestige of a given career begins to fall. Thus cause and effect are interwoven in a self-maintaining and self-reproducing mechanism." As a consequence of feminization in the 1980s, around 80 percent of all Hungarian women were working in occupations in which female workers constituted the majority. And more than 90 percent of workers in clerical and administrative occupations, such as typists, accountants, cashiers, and clerks, were women.[34]

Even within feminized professions, the apex of career hierarchies was dominated by men. In medicine, the senior hospital consultants, medical specialists or surgeons, tended to be men, while in 1989 in the former GDR, 95.5 percent of trainee nurses were women. In Bulgaria in 1989, 90 percent of paramedical personnel but only 35 percent of doctors and dentists were women. Among specializations, there was a stereotypical gender divide: surgery, neurology, and psychiatry were 80 percent male, whereas gynecology and pediatrics were female-dominated. In Czechoslovakia in the early 1970s, Hilda Scott reported that "only two of the more than 300 district national medical centers are directed by women, despite the "feminization" of medicine."[35]

Few women became managers, even in female-dominated sectors of the economy such as retail. Stanislawa Dworzynska, section manager of a clothes department at "Central," a large department store in Lodz, Poland, reveals an interesting double-think here on the part of women themselves: "The top people are mainly women here. The general manager is a man. The section managers are women." Magdalena Niewadomska, businesswoman in a state-run foreign trade company in Poland, makes the situation clearer:

> The important departments are dominated by men, even new employees are mainly men; women are not hired; the less important sections are full of women. The highest positions held by women are vice-managers and if there is a choice between a man and a woman, the man is preferred, no matter what qualifications he may have. This is because . . . it's generally thought that business talks are handled better by men. Also, women bring up children, they take leaves, have more house duties; men can stay at work overtime, prepare themselves better. When children are sick, women stay at home and take leaves to look after them.[36]

The degree of occupational segregation by gender increased over the state socialist period. In the earlier period, socialist realist iconography featuring the woman tractor driver or women engineers wearing hard hats on a building site had, to varying degrees in the different countries, mirrored real changes. Yet Scott reports the predominance in Czechoslovakia even by the early 1970s of the conviction that particularly those occupations "which are an extension of women's 'mothering' role (teacher, nurse) and those which require her 'nimble fingers'" are deemed "suitable" for women.[37]

This tendency became more marked toward the end of the state socialist period. Thus in the period 1970–1989 in Bulgaria, 81 percent of all women workers were employed in light industry, trade, education, finance, and the health service. Over 90 percent of accountants, teachers, nurses, and librarians were women. In Hungarian vocational schools in 1990–1991, only 0.7 percent of apprentices in metallurgy and 1.1 percent in engineering were girls, but 98 percent of apprentices in the textile and garment industries were girls. And in the former GDR, over 60 percent of female school leavers opted for training in a mere 16 out of a total 259 occupations. Girls comprised 95 percent of trainee textile workers and 99 percent of trainee garment workers in 1989. And close to 100 percent of trainee secretaries and salespersons were of course girls. As Dimitrina Petrova described it with reference to Bulgaria: "Today's mainstream stereotypes about women's roles, conservative and right-wing as they are, did not emerge overnight in 1989; they were articulated much earlier. . . . Woman Secretary had been around for at least a decade" [displacing the earlier role model of the 1950s, whom Petrova calls "Woman on a Tractor"].[38]

In the former Yugoslavia too, female popular folk singers from early on pandered to the male "preconception of a 'real woman.'" Later, when Yugoslavia disintegrated into ethnic conflict, pop music became emblematic of the new ethnic-national identities, and pop singers the evangelists of this culture of hatred. While five Croatian women writers and journalists who attempted to oppose this culture were pilloried in the media as the "five Croatian witches" who had "raped" Croatia in their writing, the world's media reported the actual mass rapes of Bosnian and Croatian women as part of Serbian military strategy. The writer Dubravka Ugresic reports that "at the same moment, Croatian music stalls were selling a cassette featuring a cheap folksy with the title *Punish Me Like a Woman*."[39]

As a result of horizontal and vertical occupational segregation, the legislatively ordained equal pay for equal work remained a goal, rather than a reality. One of the disillusioning realizations, as more statistics became available toward the end of the state socialist period, was that the wage gap in Eastern and Central Europe had been not dissimilar to that pertaining in Western Europe. Women had earned on average 66 to 75 percent of men's wages across all branches of economic activity.

The wage differential was not as wide in the GDR as in the Federal Republic of Germany (FRG), where women earned on average 65 to 70 percent of male incomes as compared with 76 to 84 percent on average in the former GDR. In Poland, studies conducted in the early 1980s established that in all occupational categories barring the professions, gender was a far more decisive factor in wage differentials than level of education, occupational position, age, job tenure, or membership in the Communist party. The greatest wage gap in Poland existed among industrial workers, where in 1989 women earned only 70 percent of men's wages. Yet it was almost equally marked in the feminized professions. Hence in May 1990, whereas female lawyers earned 98 percent as much as male lawyers, female doctors and social workers brought home only 72 percent of men's salary, women in administration and management earned 68 percent compared with men, and women bookkeepers scraped together a mere 66.3 percent of men's pay. In Czechoslovakia, too, women earned on average only 68.9 percent of men's wages, and in Hungary it was 73.4 percent (in 1987); Yugoslavia was exceptional in that women earned 86 to 89 percent of men's wages there in 1986.[40]

The transformations that followed the "velvet" and not-so-velvet "revolutions" of 1989 threw all of these issues up in the air for reconsideration. They represented not "simply" a shift from a state socialist to a democratic polity, nor a transition from a centrally planned to a market-based economy alone, as if those changes in themselves could have been simple. Rather, the rejection of state socialism and all of its trappings meant that a vacuum was created around ideas of women's role in society. The next section will discuss the traditional views of women's primary responsibility to the family that sprang into the breach.

In the economic arena, downsizing of the vast state enterprises and fundamental economic restructuring caused large-scale unemployment levels. This was a totally new situation in an economy where there had not been much choice about jobs, and many jobs were in retrospect felt to have been unproductive. Yet there was job security for most people, albeit with some hidden unemployment, shadowy activities in the "grey" economy, and underemployment as phenomena that did not feature in the data.

In most countries of the region, women carried and are still carrying a disproportionate share of the burden of unemployment, accounting for well over 50 percent of those unemployed, with the exception of Hungary. In East Germany in September 1996, women made up 57.5 percent of all unemployed people, with regional variations, so that they comprised 62 percent of those unemployed in the state of Saxony, the textile and clothing center of the former GDR. Female-dominated industries like textiles and clothing, which now had to struggle to compete with even cheaper labor sources elsewhere in the global economy, were particularly badly hit. This led to regional concentrations with alarming high female unemployment figures.[41] In July 1993, for example, over 70 percent of unemployed persons in two districts of Brandenberg in East Germany, were female.

The economic changes were twofold: the transition from a centrally planned to a market economy was accompanied by an economic restructuring process that transformed economies that were for the most part still heavily industrial into postindustrial economies, something that had already been in process for some time in Western Europe. The dual impact was colossal. One might have expected that the transition from heavy to light industry, with an emphasis on consumer goods and the retail and service sectors, might favor women's employment, or at least shield women from the worst effects of the changes. This was not the case, however. Women had been employed in heavy industry in the top-heavy clerical and administrative branches. These branches were decimated, not only in heavy industry, but in the administration of the state and in the large education and research sectors. A recent newspaper report cites the demise of the Gdansk shipyard, cradle of *Solidarnosc* and one-time workplace of former *Solidarnosc* leader and former Polish president Lech Walesa. Katarzyna Rewers, a counselor in the labor office, said that women were the hardest hit by the closure: "Nearly 70 percent of those unemployed in the Gdansk region are women. . . . And women from the shipyard were mostly bookkeepers with no knowledge of computers. They don't even know how to be cashiers."[42]

Women are also experiencing greater difficulties than men in finding reemployment. Part of the reason for this is made evident by the Gdansk example. Despite generally high educational levels, the skills and qualifications women possessed in the state socialist period turned out to be not necessarily appropriate for the new market economies. This in part explains why computer skills are the most ubiquitous retraining program on offer for women. But this in itself represents a narrowing of the apparent choice made available by a free enterprise system. In some cases, for example, where a woman has made it into a formerly male-dominated occupation such as engineering, it also means a process of deskilling.

Another reason why it is harder for women than for men to find new jobs is the emergence of discriminatory hiring practices on the part of private firms.[43] Furthermore, the continuing existence of compensatory legislation acts against women's equality of opportunity, in the sense that it makes it possible for employers to describe women as "unreliable" or "expensive" labor. This arises from the generous provisions in most of the state socialist countries for paid leave that is taken to look after sick children. Such leave was overwhelmingly taken by women, with the result, in Hungary, for instance, that women were off work almost as much as they were there.[44]

A further factor affecting women's unequal chances in the new labor market has been the loss of child care facilities. The shrinkage of the state sector has meant closure of some facilities. Others were previously attached to enterprises. In their efforts to survive in the marketplace, many enterprises saw child care as the first optional extra that they could simply cut. They tended to pass the day care centers and/or kindergartens over to local authorities, which often had no resources to maintain them. Privatized facilities are often priced out of the reach of many women. Without access to publicly provided, affordable child care, many women are denied equal opportunities to become economic actors in the new marketplace. In a situation where the process of democratization is sometimes equated with marketization, it is the economic actor who is seen as the citizen. If women are barred from equal access to this role through a diminution in social rights, then their citizenship rights are affected.

The process of marketization is in turn often regarded as synonymous with its accompanying process of privatization.[45] Entrepreneurship is often seen as the highest form of the new market economy and as a solution to female unemployment. Not only is it unrealistic to expect that the establishment of private businesses could benefit more than a minority of those affected by unemployment; actual figures show that, in fact, women are underrepresented in the process of privatization.[46] In her study of Poland, Hungary, the Czech Republic, and Slovakia, Liba Paukert points out that this does not mean that women are unadventurous, or "risk-shy." Rather, there are structural reasons, located in the gendered patterns of "the occupational structure of the workforce and women's concentration in professions such as teaching, nursing and social care," that have "tied them to the public sector much more than men."[47]

One of the side effects of privatization and economic restructuring, as elsewhere in the global economy, is the growth of the informal sector. It is often women who predominate in this trend towards casualization, working part-time for low pay and without social protection in terms of sick pay or holiday entitlements. An early example of this trend, initially hailed in Russia as an expression of free enterprise, was the huge growth in prostitution across the region.

Even before the notion of prostitution emerged as the expression of a specifically female form of business enterprise, it had sometimes been seen as a strike for self-determination in contrast to the reality of women's harsh working lives. In a first-person narrative documenting the involvement of women in heavy labor of the type officially banned by law, a woman from Petrozavodsk in Karelia (in the former Soviet Union), who worked lifting heavy mail bags, said:

> It should not be surprising that some women leave this "women's work" for prostitution, . . . preferring even that humiliating "profession" because it gives a woman at least some measure of freedom, some degree of choice. . . . Of course prostitution is ruinous for women. I do not want to justify it. . . . Yet, ironically, prostitution has become a euphemism for women's freedom, a freedom that society condemns.[48]

Once hermetically sealed against the world, Albania has been branded by the German feminist magazine *Emma* as the "bargain-basement brothel of the West." Albania illustrates that legislation alone is an insufficient guarantee of women's rights, since prostitution is in fact prohibited by law there. Hence the raw materials for this industry are simply exported. Chris Corrin writes that "many young women between 14–18 years of age are either tricked or physically forced to take up work in Greece and sometimes other neighboring countries. Often the young women believe that their work will be in sewing factories or textiles." More likely, according to *Emma,* they are in fact being sold by their own mothers in return for scarce food, coal, or petrol.[49]

Western findings on the feminization of poverty seem already to be echoed in the transitional economies. Poverty particularly affects the high number of single parents, of whom the vast majority are women. A 1992 report in the newsletter of the UFV, the East German–based Unabhängiger Frauenverband (Independent Women's Association), compared the social support and employment that enabled single mothers to support themselves and their children in the past in the former GDR with the single mothers in the West who are dependent on social welfare and threatened with poverty. In the new Federal states, 20 percent of all families with school-age children have only one parent, compared with what is already considered a high 13 percent in the old Federal states. As of mid-1991, East German women were edging closer to poverty as a result of unemployment and the closure of child care facilities. Every tenth unemployed woman in the new Federal states was a single parent, and in East Berlin, every ninth. And their bargaining position in terms of re-employment was clearly weak. When Ute Pust, a 27-year-old single mother of two in the new Federal states, wanted her job in a hotel kitchen back after her maternity leave, as was her right under earlier GDR law, her boss said simply: "Either you work the late shift, or not at all."[50]

In Poland in 1990, 91 percent of single-parent families were headed by women. Of these, 66 percent had fallen below the poverty line.[51] In Hungary Júlia Szalai commented in the early 1990s that "one-parent families (mainly female-headed) are . . . over-represented among the poor. The resulting feminization of poverty in Hungary has been recently extended by severe cuts in social spending on child-related benefits." But poverty is not confined to single mothers. Szalai also notes the "over-representation of young urban families with children" among the poor in Hungary, and sees the "decreasing real value of the child care grant" as "a major contributor to that fact: women on grant at home are more than twice as numerous among the poorest than the overall population."

More recently, Szalai has pointed to the way that poverty is increasingly being defined as "more or less a 'private affair'" as a "result of the liberalization of the system." She is concerned about what she calls "new traps in the withdrawal of the state" that result from adoption of a neoliberal social policy model. In this model, benefits are granted on an individual basis, stigmatizing the poor and effectively depriving them "of the main personal and political rights they have only just gained—in the interest of expanding the rights of the majority." She concludes that such a development of second-class citizenship represents "one of the most fundamental political dangers threatening the barely institutionalized democracy."[52]

Another group especially prone to poverty are older women. The allegedly positive discrimination in favor of women in the form of their five years earlier retirement age in effect operated against their interests even under state socialism, but even more so in the current situation of surplus labor. Now, one of the largest groups of unemployed people are women around the age of 50, in the so-called preretirement bracket, whose chances of finding new employment, once made redundant or if their enterprise closes, are almost zero. An example is Heide Haack, who worked for 15 years as a shepherdess on a collective farm in the GDR and then took on her own herd of 550 sheep together with her husband. In the past, she was publicly lauded and given medals and bonuses. Sheep breeding was the money spinner of the farm. In November 1991, the sheep were slaughtered. Suddenly she was "ancient," at 49. The job center told her she would never find another job and was "too old" for retraining to "pay off."[53]

It is usually thought that the shift from heavy to light industry, and from industry as a whole to retail and services, is one that favors women's employment, particularly in the service sector. Banking, finance, and insurance services provide an extremely interesting case study, given the marginality of this branch in a centrally planned economy and its central importance in a market economy. However, early case studies from Eastern Germany suggest that as this formerly female-dominated branch grows in importance and status, so it becomes more interesting to men. The female workers at middle management level are faced by double competition, on the one hand from West German women trained in the skills appropriate to this branch under market conditions, and on the other from male managers.[54]

Despite the disadvantaging and overtly gender-based discriminatory practices, the majority of women are continuing to express a strong labor force attachment. This appears to contradict earlier predictions, in part by women themselves, that many women would embrace unemployment as the opportunity to exercise choice, a choice previously denied them. The choice in favor of continuing labor force involvement has multiple causes. On the one hand, newly dominant discourse about the need for women to return home and take care of the family, or calls for a family wage and a male breadwinner/female homemaker family model, cannot hide the fact that two incomes are in most cases necessary for economic survival. And for the many female-headed households in the region, this fact is of course a given. On the other hand, it is clear from opinion surveys conducted in several countries of the region that sheer material necessity is not the only reason why women continue to seek work. Asked whether they would prefer to stay at home or go out to work if their husbands earned enough for the family, the great majority of women stated a clear preference for working outside the family.[55] It is clear that in the forty years in which it was the norm for women to go out to work, this has become a central part of women's sense of identity. Colleagues and the working environment are also perceived as the main source of women's social and personal networks.

SOCIAL AND REPRODUCTIVE RIGHTS: MOTHERHOOD, EQUALITY, DIFFERENCE

Richard Stites describes (Chapter 15 of this volume), how early notions of a revolution in sexual relations had been abandoned in the Soviet Union by the 1930s as a result of the social problems and dislocations of the 1920s. Similarly, by the time the state socialist regimes of East and Central Europe came into power after World War II, the traditional family was reinstated in the name of social stability, simply being renamed the "socialist" family.

The family was seen as the basic cell of society, entrusted with the task of bearing and rearing the socialist citizens of the future. Admittedly, Family Laws in several of the state socialist regimes in the region specified the equal responsibility of the marriage partners within the family.[56] Reality, however, lagged behind the legislation. Thus the formal equality of women "in all spheres of life" guaranteed in the constitutions and family laws of most regimes in the region coexisted in practice with the traditional family practices of an often patriarchal culture in the region.

In practice, then, women continued throughout the state socialist period to shoulder the main burden of responsibility for child care, cooking, and cleaning. And if the juridical definition of women as workers and mothers in the state socialist period had imposed the notorious double burden on women, the Leninist injunction that women should participate in the political life of society added to their stress with a third role.[57]

What the double burden required was superwoman in a hard hat, often depicted on the front cover of *Für Dich*, the official women's magazine in the GDR, as a woman capable of running a factory or a building site during the day and transforming herself into desirable lover and exemplary mother in the evenings.[58] Several ironic stories by women, characterized by a bitter twist in the tale, appeared in the GDR in the late 1970s and early 1980s testifying to the impossibility of becoming this media icon.

One of the many difficulties of "mastering" the double burden during the state socialist period was that of shopping. The working day was often punctuated as well as followed by excursions to buy the wherewithal to feed the family in a situation of chronic shortages. Speaking in the summer of 1990, Grazyna Zawi, head nurse of the Hospital for Polish Mothers in Lodz, says: "Polish women have a hard life. To bridge professional and family life is extremely difficult. Shopping used to be a big problem—now it's improved. Polish women don't have cars so they have to carry all their heavy bags of shopping. Polish women are wonderful, they manage to handle all their duties, but they are tired."[59]

In an ironic play on the title of "heroine" attached to women's roles as exemplary mothers or workers, a story about a young researcher in Leningrad in the early 1980s describes the conflict between work and shopping. It illustrates how, in most of the countries of East and Central Europe as well as the Soviet Union, tropical fruits like lemons and bananas became objects of desire that prompted spontaneous acts of "heroism":

> I was walking along Nevsky Prospect one day, when I saw a huge crowd outside Yeliseevky's. I asked what was being sold. "Bananas!" they answered.
>
> So I immediately got in the queue and started dreaming of bananas. . . . I used to dream a lot about the various exotic fruits. . . . My dream about bananas was a bit different: I didn't just want to taste one little banana, I wanted to eat three or four at once and really stuff myself on them! . . .

I stood for two-and-a-half hours, and then the happy moment arrived. I squeezed my way out of the shop carrying a paper bag with a kilo of bananas! . . .

Lisa's twins weren't five yet. They had been coming down with illnesses ever since they started going to nursery school. It was a good thing they always got ill together, or she would have been completely worn out by it all. She was already getting dirty looks at work because the children were ill so often. Her husband was a good man, but he couldn't help. They don't give fathers medical certificates for looking after children, only mothers get those. I looked at Lisa and saw how exhausted and upset she was over her shopping failures. And then a great heroic feeling rose up in my breast, and I had this noble impulse to give her the bananas![60]

I Quit, by Charlotte Worgitzky,[61] suggests, along with other short stories by GDR women written in the late 1970s, that the only way to become superwoman is with the unscientific, utterly nonsocialist help of magic, the supernatural or the divine, in this case a female angel. The narrator is a young woman so worn out by her studies that she falls asleep one night while her boyfriend is kissing her feet, prompting the reproach that she doesn't love him as much as he loves her. She is relieved from this desperate situation by the appearance of the angel, who grants her one wish. Her wish is never to need sleep so that she can "master" all the roles required of her. As a result, she becomes a star, a real socialist heroine. She manages to combine motherhood—of four children—with a successful career as school principal (while her husband remains a mere grade teacher) and an active public role as member of the city council. The drawback is a deterioration in the domestic division of labor: her husband does not see why he should iron his shirts or mend socks when she has all the night hours available to perform this extra shift. Relations sour somewhat, especially after his envy of her public successes and consequent sense of inadequacy lead him to acquire the first in a series of young, blond girlfriends.

One day, awaiting her turn to be given a medal at a televised ceremony "in honor of our best people," the narrator ponders the question: do the other people honored with her also have a secret midnight pact? With bitter disillusionment, she suddenly realizes that they do not need an angel; they are all men, who have wives at home to perform the extra shift for them. Sobered and disillusioned, she too takes a lover. As the angel had warned, this breaks the spell. The narrator is overcome by the irresistible need to sleep. When she falls asleep in the middle of a teachers' meeting, her colleagues finally give in to her plea to give up being principal. Concerned for her health, they send her to the doctor. But when she decides to come clean and confess the truth about the secret of her success, the doctor sends her off to the psychiatrist. She writes the story, she says, in order that other women should know what it takes to become "superwoman."

In reaction to this evident overburdening of women, several of the state socialist regimes introduced compensatory legislation and social provision.

The triple burden had led to a drop in the birthrate in many countries of the region, with the one-child family becoming commonplace. Measures promulgated in the GDR included the "household day," a paid day off work per month for mothers that was introduced in 1966 and extended in the 1977 Labor Law to include all full-time female workers who were married, 40 years of age or older, or had children under 18 at home. The 1976 extension of maternity leave to a full year off work with a job held open for them became known as the "baby year." In Hungary, the introduction of the child care grant in 1967 allowed women to stay at home until their child was 30 months of age (extended in 1969 until the child's third birthday). In Poland, paid maternity leave was extended to sixteen to eighteen weeks, with a further three years of unpaid leave and sixty days' paid leave to care for sick children.[62]

Again, there is debate about the motivation for compensatory laws and the provision of social services such as child care facilities, workplace canteens, and communal laundries. Those who favor the instrumentalist argument would maintain that the policies of state socialist regimes teetered and shifted toward favoring one or other of the dual roles, depending on their perceptions of whether women's productive or reproductive labor was the more needed at any one time. For Hungary, Júlia Szalai argues that "the development of public child care facilities was driven above all by the employment needs of forced industrialization. Children's needs were painfully subordinated to the political priorities of economic goals."[63]

The record in relation to public child care provision both between and within countries was patchy, reflecting this ambivalence. Clearly, relocating responsibility for the care of young children in the home as a result of the pronatalist policies of the late 1960s and 1970s was also cheaper than providing public child care facilities. Szalai has calculated that the annual cost per child of the extended child care grant was only "about one third of the additional costs of constructing and equipping public nurseries." And since Hungarian women spent 30 to 40 percent of their work time on sick leave for children's illnesses, it was possible to argue that the investment in them as workers with the back-up of child care facilities didn't pay.[64]

Many of the compensatory policies introduced in the 1970s had the additional, perhaps unintended, effect of reinforcing unequal gender roles in relation to the division of domestic labor. The "household day," for example, was explicitly available to women only. Men were entitled to take it only if they were single parents (which remained unusual throughout the history of the GDR) or if their wife were certified ill by a doctor. This ruling manifestly reinforced the notion that women alone were responsible for household work.

After 1989, traditionalist expectations of women's role became stronger, to the point where the prescriptive worker-mother duality of state socialist ideology became replaced with a unitary role, that of mother. The Catholic church in Poland, and conservative politicians elsewhere, emphasized women's primary responsibility for the family. Nationalist politicians in many countries of the region stressed women's duty to "bear babies for the nation." Where state socialist policies had asked women to subordinate their individual hopes and aspirations to the collective project of building an egalitarian society, post-1989 rhetoric all too often asked that they again submerge their identities in the interests of the collective, this time conceived as the good of their individual family first, and then the wider ethnic or national family.

This kind of rhetoric of traditional family values was underlined by the economy's need to shed labor in the transition to the market, with women being the first to be laid off. Privatization has also brought structural changes in the family: As Dobrinka Kostova from Bulgaria put it: "The economic function of the family is being restored through property rights and inheritance. This makes it very likely that the family could turn from a predominantly consuming unit into a more comprehensive economic unit, especially given the development or re-emergence of small firms and farms."[65] Kostova rightly suggests that these material changes could lead to changes in the balance of power in gender relations. First, women may well become involved in farms or small firms as unpaid family labor. Second, the traditionalist discourse explicitly appeals to a traditional family form that was patriarchal in nature and hence could reinforce the unequal gender relations that had never been eliminated during the state socialist period.

Both before and after 1989, it could therefore be argued, women's rights have been instrumentalized in the name of political, economic, and demographic priorities. The year 1989 has brought for women, it might be said, a simple reversal, with state socialism's prioritization of their productive over their reproductive role being replaced by an idealization of their role as mothers.

The distinction between the two political and economic systems at the level of discourse is that, whereas state socialism was framed in terms of a universalist model based on equality, the rhetoric of the post-1989 regimes has often appealed to an essentialist, difference-based paradigm. Thus there has been a rediscovery of the presumed virtues of femininity and masculinity, supposedly lost in the socialist search for equality. Femininity is expressed not only by the newly boosted consumer culture and in the sexualized iconography of Western-style mass media. Rather, in a form of expression particular to the region, femininity is equated with maternity.

An example is the document "Ukrainian Women and Reproductive Function," produced by the Union of Ukrainian Women in 1992, which subsumes reproductive rights to encouraging Ukrainian women to preserve the ethnic Ukrainian population "from extinction as a nation." In an illustration of notions about femininity needing rescuing from the state socialist equality ethic, one section of the paper attributes the "androgynization" of women to their status as workers. Hard labor and the wearing of gender-neutral work clothes are held to alter female behavior and physical movements to the extent that male hormones are stimulated, which make women unwilling and ultimately also unable to become mothers.[66]

It is interesting, too, to note the frequency with which governments, in an era of economic insecurity and uncertainty about national identity, resort to measures designed to control women's sexuality. The record of governments in the region of Eastern and Central Europe has been no exception to this. Unanimously hailing the restoration of "the rule of law," several of the new democratic, and male-dominated, governments first reinstated the private property rights abolished by state socialism's egalitarian project and then rushed to ban or limit abortion.

Abortion is a contentious issue that inflames passions and public debate about ideology, morality, and the family. When male-dominated church establishments, governments, and constitutional courts move to pronounce rulings on it, it also becomes a telling marker of the relative absence of individual women's self-determination. Indeed, one could argue that, standing as it does at the very juncture where private meets public, abortion provides the ultimate test case of women's citizenship rights. Before 1989, abortion functioned all too regularly as the main means of fertility regulation in Yugoslavia and elsewhere in the region. This clearly goes against the guideline laid down at the 1994 UN Conference on Population and Development, namely, that "in no case should abortion be promoted as a method of family planning." In January 1992 in Albania, abortion was not made legally available within the first twelve weeks of pregnancy and to all women over 16, until January 1992. However, in the continuing virtual absence of contraception and sex education, here too abortion continues to be used as the main contraceptive method.[67]

The prime example of abortion as a matter of state was the German case, where disputes over how to reconcile the two diametrically opposed laws pertaining in East and West Germany threatened to hold up the unification process in 1990. Two years and many political compromises later, a new unified abortion law was passed by a sizeable majority in the Bundestag in June 1992, only to be overturned by a group of Christian Democrat and Christian Socialist (Catholic) politicians, who lodged an appeal with the Constitutional Court.

In May 1993, the Constitutional Court came up with a truly bizarre ruling: abortion was indeed unconstitutional (in view of the right-to-life clause of the German Basic Law) and illegal, but would not be punished within the first twelve weeks of pregnancy if the woman underwent compulsory counseling, whose clear purpose was to dissuade her. What the judges (six male and one female) had contrived, in their wisdom, to do was in effect to confirm the law passed by the Bundestag, simply prefixing its terms with the words *unconstitutional* and *illegal*. In addition, they exempted it from health insurance schemes for all but the certifiably poor, thus introducing a two-tier citizenship in respect of reproductive rights.

The new German law, confirmed by the Bundestag in June 1995 after much further debate, represents an advance for West German women, compared with the infamous paragraph 218 that criminalized abortion, but a clear diminishing of rights for East German women, whose 1972 Abortion Law provided for abortion on demand and free of cost within the first twelve weeks, with the woman alone entitled to make the decision.[68]

One of the first products of the opening up of the market and a free press in Eastern and Central Europe was a flood of pornography. This was even hailed by some within the region as a legitimate response to the puritanical attitude toward sexuality during the state socialist period. Voices raised in objection to this reduction of women's bodies to objects of consumption were simply not heard. If the media were not open to the opinions of autonomous social movements in the state socialist period, commercialization does not appear to have given women's groups more than the most minimal access to media channels. It seems that freedom of expression is a selective right in the region. In some respects, however, the advent of democracy in 1989 did appear to usher in a liberalization in attitudes, for example, toward homosexuals and lesbians. Although to be gay had not been illegal in most of the state socialist societies since the early 1960s, in the dominant culture of state-supported heterosexuality it continued to be viewed as an unfortunate affliction. Not until the late 1980s did it surface in public discourse, with groups subsequently emerging throughout the region.[69]

Most recently, however, a newly repressive culture is emerging, presenting itself, in a sort of distorting New Speak, as a consolidation of the new democracies. Examples are the May 1997 ruling by the Polish Constitutional Court that abortion is unconstitutional and, being against the "rule of law," "violates the country's nascent democratic legal order." The contested law, passed in 1996, had replaced "one of Europe's most restrictive abortion statutes by permitting abortions for compelling social and financial reasons until the 12th week of pregnancy." Its repeal makes abortion totally illegal, thus restricting women's reproductive rights. And in Romania in September 1996, the parliament adopted a law making all homosexual acts, including those conducted in private, criminal offenses. Romania is already a member of the Council of Europe and a prospective member of the European Union. Yet this legislation contravenes the European Convention for the Protection of Human Rights and Fundamental Freedoms.[70] In terms of sexuality, then, if the state socialist period could be called publicly puritanical, the post-1989 period and marketization seems to have made (mainly female) sexuality public property, but within the context of an overwhelmingly conservative notion of what is acceptable and the reestablishment of the privatized heterosexual family as the social norm.

CONCLUSION

It has been argued in this chapter that equality legislation alone is insufficient to achieve women's rights.[71] Put another way, without the ability to exercise rights, there is a danger they may remain paper rights. State socialist regimes did go some way toward addressing this dilemma in their attempts, albeit patchy and inconsistent, to socialize some of those tasks associated with domestic labor and child care. However, we have also shown that their relative prioritization of women's labor force participation meant a lack of attention to continuing inequalities in gender relations within the family.

Now, however, along with the transition to democracy and the market, we see a reprivatization of the family, and thus a reinforcement of traditional gender-based role divisions, not only within the family but within society as a whole. This rehabilitation of the family, along with the rhetorical assignation to women of primary responsibility for those traditional values associated with it, is occurring alongside the simultaneous predominance, in practice, of the public spheres of politics and the market. Meanwhile, the shrinking of the state sector means that NGOs (non-governmental organizations) often run by women, are increasingly responsible for the informal provision of social welfare. And what I have called the civil society "trap" arises when there is a potentially unbridgeable gap between women's activism at the local, grass-roots level and the operation of power at the national and global levels.

Clearly, much depends on the shifting boundary between the public and private spheres. In order for women to become full citizens in their own right, they need the ability to access the public spheres of work and politics. This in turn requires that they have social rights. The problem with the currently dominant neoliberal model is that it devolves all responsibility onto the individual, exonerating both state and society from collective social responsibility. It emphasizes the responsibilities of citizenship to the exclusion of the rights. And by minimizing the role of the state, formerly the largest employer of women, regulator of working conditions, and provider of welfare services, it effectively erodes the concept of citizenship, especially for women. The history of women's struggles shows that there is a need for both change initiated by grassroots women's activism *and* for state provision in order for women to enjoy full citizenship rights.

NOTES

1. For early accounts of the "double burden," see Barbara Einhorn, "Socialist Emancipation: The Women's Movement in the German Democratic Republic," *Women's Studies International Quarterly* 4, no. 4 (1981), pp. 435–452; and Maxine Molyneux, "Women in Socialist Societies: Problems of Theory and Practice," in Kate Young, Carol Wolkowitz, and Roslyn McCullagh, eds., *Of Marriage and the Market: Women's Subordination in International Perspective*, London: CSE Books, 1981, pp. 167–202.
2. For feminist debates around equality versus difference as a basis for achieving citizenship, see Ruth Lister, "Tracing the Contours of Women's Citizenship," in *Policy and Politics* 21, no. 1 (1993), pp. 3–16; Shelia Rowbotham, "Knots: Theoretical Debates," chapter 26 in Rowbotham, *Women in Movement: Feminism and Social Action*, New York and London: Routledge, 1992, pp. 284–293; Joan Wallach Scott,

Only Paradoxes to Offer: French Feminists and the Rights of Man, Cambridge, Mass., and London: Harvard University Press, 1996, esp. chapter 6, "Citizens but Not Individuals: The Vote and After," pp. 161–175; Joan Wallach Scott, "The Sears Case," in Scott, *Gender and the Politics of History,* New York: Columbia University Press, 1988, pp. 167–178; Ann Snitow, "The Gender Diary," in Marianne Hirsch and Evelyn Fox Keller, eds., *Conflicts in Feminism,* New York and London: Routledge, 1990, pp. 9–43. In relation specifically to East and Central Europe, see Barbara Einhorn, "Gender and Citizenship in East Central Europe after the End of State Socialist Policies for Women's 'Emancipation,'" in Barbara Einhorn, Mary Kaldor, and Zdenek Kavan, eds., *Citizenship and Democratic Control in Contemporary Europe,* Aldershot: Edward Elgar, 1996; Ann Snitow, "Feminist Futures in the Former East Bloc," *Peace and Democracy News,* 7 no. 1 (Summer 1993).

3. Angela Kunze, aged 27, "Reflections," Leipzig, 25 January 1991, in Mita Castle-Kanerova, ed., *High Hopes: Young Voices of Eastern Europe,* London: Virago, 1992, pp. 51–52.

4. Alena Heitlinger, *Women and State Socialism: Sex Inequality in the Soviet Union and Czechoslovakia,* London: Macmillan, 1979, p.136.

5. *Ibid.,* p. 137; for the Polish Constitution, see Anna Reading, *Polish Women, Solidarity and Feminism,* Basingstoke: Macmillan, 1992, p. 30.

6. Fatos Tarifa, "Disappearing from Politics: Social Change and Women in Albania," in Marilyn Rueschemeyer, ed., *Women in the Politics of Post Communist Europe,* New York and London: M. E. Sharpe, 1994, pp. 133–152, here p. 137; Roumyana Slabakova, "Research on Women in Bulgaria: The Hard Way into the Future," *Women's Studies Quarterly,* nos. 3 and 4 (1992), pp. 136–143; Molyneux, *op. cit.,* p. 200.

7. Scott, Hilda, "Eastern European Women in Theory and Practice," in: *Women's Studies International Quarterly,* vol. 1, 1978, pp. 189–9–199, here p. 198.

8. Both these remarks refer to the past in relation to changes in the Soviet Union following *perestroika.* See Gail Warshovsky Lapidus, "Gender and Restructuring: The Impact of Perestroika and Its Aftermath on Soviet Women," in Valentine M. Moghadam, ed., *Democratic Reform and the Position of Women in Transitional Economies,* Oxford: Oxford University Press, Clarendon Press, 1993, p.155; Mary Buckley, "Political Reform," in Mary Buckley, ed., *Perestroika and Soviet Women,* Cambridge: Cambridge University Press, 1992, p. 57.

9. Sharon L. Wolchik, *Czechoslovakia in Transition: Politics, Economics and Society,* London and New York: Pinter Publishers, 1991, pp. 70–71, incl. Table 2.1.

10. Sources: Sharon Wolchik, "Eastern Europe," in Joni Lovenduski, ed., *The Second Electorate: Women and Public Participation,* London and New York: Routledge, 1981, p. 260; Harry A. Shaffer, *Women in the Two Germanies: A Comparative Study of a Socialist and a Non-Socialist Society,* New York and Oxford: Pergamon Press, p. 89; Vicky Randall, *Women and Politics: An International Perspective,* 2nd ed., Basingstoke: Macmillan, 1987, pp. 97–101.

11. Sources: Renata Siemienska, "Women in Leadership Positions in Public Administration in Poland," paper prepared for conference organized by the Friedrich Ebert Stiftung and the Federal German UNESCO Committee, July 1–4, 1987; Barbara Einhorn, "Socialist Emancipation: The Women's Movement in the GDR," in Sonia Kruks, Rayna Rapp, and Marilyn Young, eds., *Promissory Notes: Women in the Transition to Socialism,* New York: Monthly Review Press, 1989,

p. 287; Mira Janova, and Mariette Sineau, "Women's Participation in Political Power in Europe: An Essay in East-West Comparison," *Women's Studies International Forum*, 15, no. 1 (1992), table 5, p. 122; Buckley, *op. cit.*, p. 60.

12. Attitudes to quotas may be shifting, with them being viewed more favorably by women in Poland according to recent interviews, cited by Malgorzata Fuszara and Eleonora Zielinska in a paper given to the conference entitled "The Meanings of Feminisms in the Reconfigured Public/Private Spaces of Central and Eastern Europe and the Former Soviet Union," held at Rutgers University, New Jersey, 26–28 March 1997.

13. See Barbara Einhorn, *Cinderella Goes to Market: Citizenship, Gender and Women's Movements in East Central Europe*, London and New York: Verso, 1993, pp. 150–158. For the East-West comparison, see Janova and Sineau, *op. cit.*, table 1, p. 117, reproduced in Einhorn, *op. cit.*, table A10, p. 274; for Albania, see Tarifa, *op. cit.*, pp. 147–150.

14. The Anna Petrasovits story was reported by *The Guardian*, 7 June 1990.

15. Irene Dölling, "Between Hope and Helplessness: Women in the GDR After the 'Turning Point,'" in *Shifting Territories: Feminism in Europe*, Special Issue no. 39 of *Feminist Review* (1991), pp. 3–15, here p. 4.

16. On state socialism as patriarchal, see *ibid.*, p. 10; see also Ferenc Fehér, "Paternalism as a Mode of Legitimation in Soviet-type Societies," in T. H. Rigby and Ferenc Fehér, eds., *Political Legitimation in Communist States*, Basingstoke: Macmillan, 1982, pp. 64–81; on "the debt we owe our women," see Hilda Scott, *Women and Socialism: Experiences from Eastern Europe*, London: Allison & Busby, 1976 (1974), p. 197.

17. Fatos Tarifa emphasizes, writing about the Women's Union of Albania: "As it was totally dependent on the party-state, the WUA could not truly represent women's interests. . . . Of course, women were often seen on platforms at solemn meetings, serving the same function as the potted plants: decoration." Tarifa, *op. cit.*, p. 137.

18. On the secondary role of women in dissident movements, see Barbara W. Jancar, "Women in the Opposition in Poland and Czechoslovakia in the 1970s," in Sharon Wolchik and Alfred Meyer, eds., *Women, State and Party in Eastern Europe*, Durham: Duke University Press, 1985, pp. 171–177. For fascinating interviews with many former dissidents, including women like Helena Luczywo, coeditor with Adam Michnik of *Gazeta Wyborcza* in Poland (pp. 40–54), see Eva Hoffmann, *Exit into History: A Journey Through the New Eastern Europe*, London: Penguin Books (1993), 1994.

19. See Barbara Einhorn, "Feminism in Crisis: The East German Women's Movement in the 'New Europe,'" in *A New Europe?*, Special Issue of *The Australian Journal of Politics and History* 41, no. 1 (1995), pp. 14–28, here p.19.

20. See for example, Timothy Garton Ash, *We the People: The Revolutions of '89 Witnessed in Warsaw, Budapest, Berlin and Prague*, London: Granta Books, 1990; and the critique of it along these lines by Barbara Einhorn, "'New Enemy Images for Old': The 'Boys' Debate' Around Timothy Garton Ash's *We the People*," in: Mary Kaldor, ed., *Europe from Below: An East-West Dialogue*, London and New York: Verso, 1991, pp. 130–135. Even some female chroniclers of the historic changes in this region are not free of this tendency to render women's contribution to historical change invisible. See Tina Rosenberg, *The Haunted Land: Facing Europe's Ghosts After*

Communism, London: Vintage Books, 1995; and Jane Kramer, *The Politics of Memory: Looking for Germany in the New Germany,* New York: Random House, 1996.

21. An extreme expression of this self-sacrificing tradition was rhetorically invoked in Serbia during the war in former Yugoslavia, during which "women were not only expected to sacrifice their own interests for their families, but also had to be prepared to sacrifice their children to national needs. . . . The image that was repeatedly evoked was that of the Mother of the Jugovici, the epic heroine whose nine sons died fighting the Turks at Kosovo, who did not weep over her dead, but whose heart burst when she recognized the hand of her youngest son, dropped in her lap by ravens from the field of battle": Wendy Bracewell, "Women, Motherhood, and Contemporary Serbian Nationalism," in *Links Across Differences: Gender, Ethnicity and Nationalism,* Special Issue of *Women's Studies International Forum* 19, nos. 1–2 (1996), pp. 25–34, here p. 29.

22. See Hanna Jankowska, "Abortion, Church and Politics," in *Shifting Territories: Feminism and Europe,* Special Issue no. 39 of *Feminist Review* (1991), pp. 174–182. See also Further Reading list.

23. Sociologist Mira Marody maintained in 1992 that the tiny Polish feminist groups were "usually an object of jokes"; in Hungary, in a debate during summer 1989 with Enikö Bollobas, later her country's ambassador to the U.S., conducted in the literary-political biweekly *Hitel,* Gyula Fekete, then a prominent male politician, accused feminists of being "mother-murderers," involved in the "abuse and devaluation of motherhood." Both examples are cited in Einhorn, *Cinderella,* Chapter 6, "An Allergy to Feminism," pp. 182–215, here pp. 192, 196.

24. For issues of ethnicity, nationalism, and mass rape as an instrument of the war in former Yugoslavia, see Further Reading list. For accounts of women's autonomous peace and feminist and rehabilitation activities in former Yugoslavia, see Further Reading list.

25. On official and autonomous women's organizations, both before and after 1989, see Further Reading list. On women's studies programs, see Further Reading list.

26. On the difficult dialogue between feminists in the east and west, see Further Reading list.

27. See *The World's Women, 1970–1990: Trends and Statistics,* Social Statistics and Indicators, Series K, no. 8, chapter 6, New York: United Nations, 1991. For a wider discussion of the growing awareness on this issue on the part of international agencies, see *Women in a Changing Global Economy: 1994 World Survey on the Role of Women in Development,* New York: United Nations, 1995, pp 53–58. For accounts of the conceptual, theoretical, and methodological barriers to accounting accurately for women's work, see Lourdes Beneria, "Accounting for Women's Work: The Progress of Two Decades," *World Development* 20, no. 11 (1992), pp. 1547–1560; and Marilyn Waring, *If Women Counted: A New Feminist Economics,* London: Macmillan, 1989.

28. On labor market participation as the condition for social welfare entitlements in state socialism, see Júlia Szalai, "Some Aspects of the Changing Situation of Women in Hungary," *Signs* 17, no. 1 (Autumn 1991), pp. 152–170; here p. 153, note 2; in capitalist Western Europe, see Jane Jenson, Chapter 18 this volume, p. 493.

29. Anastasia, Posadskaya, in conversation with Maxine Molyneux, 25 September 1990, published in *Shifting Territories: Feminism and Europe,* Special Issue no. 39 of *Feminist Review* (Winter 1991), pp. 133–140; here p. 135.

30. Scott, Hilda, *Women and Socialism,* p. 9.

31. Rosemary Kavan, *Love and Freedom: My Unexpected Life in Prague,* New York: Hill and Wang, 1988, pp. 68–70.

32. Janina Bauman, *A Dream of Belonging: My Years in Post-War Poland,* London: Virago, 1988, referring to 1955, pp 118–121.

33. Myra Marx Ferree, Hildegard Maria Nickel; See Myra Marx Ferree, "The Rise and Fall of "Mommy Politics: Feminism and Unification in (East) Germany, *Feminist Studies,* vol. 19. no. 1 (Spring 1993), pp. 89–115; and Maria Hildegard Nickel, "Fraven in der DDR," *Aus Politik und Zeitgeschichle,* Beilage zur Wochenzeitschrift *Das Parlament,* B. pp. 16–17 (1990).

34. Mária Ladó, "Women in the Transition to a Market Economy: The Case of Hungary," in *The Impact of Economic and Political Reform on the Status of Women in Eastern Europe and the USSR,* Proceedings of United Nations Regional Seminar, Vienna, 8–12 April 1991, published as ST-CSDHA-19-UN, 1992.

35. For Bulgaria and the GDR, see Einhorn, *Cinderella,* pp. 124–125; for Czechoslovakia, see Scott, *Women and Socialism,* p. 14.

36. Reading, *op. cit.,* pp. 104, 115.

37. Hilda Scott, *Women and Socialism,* p. 2, points out that in Czechoslovakia in 1966, women accounted for more than half of workers in ten out of eighteen branches of the economy, whereas in 1948 they had made up a majority of workers in only two of the seventeen branches of the economy (agriculture and health/social welfare). Nevertheless, she maintains that already by 1972, "the image of the beautiful tractor driver as heroine" had already faded into the "distant past" (*ibid.,* p. 1); for the quote about what is regarded as appropriate work for women, see *ibid.,* p. 15.

38. Source for Bulgaria: Bulgarian National Statistics, 1990, cited in Dobrinka Kostova, "The Transition to Democracy in Bulgaria: Challenges and Risks for Women," in Valentine M. Moghadam, ed., *Democratic Reform and the Position of Women in Transitional Economies,* Oxford: Clarendon Press, 1993, pp. 92–109, here p. 98; for Hungary and GDR: Einhorn, *op. cit.,* table A5.1, p. 267; for "Women Secretary" as opposed to "Women on a Tractor," Dimitrina Petrova, "The Farewell Dance: Women in the Bulgarian Transition," chapter 13 in Eileen Janes Yeo, ed., *Mary Wollstonecraft and 200 Years of Feminism,* London: Rivers Oram, 1997.

39. Dubravka Ugresic, "Balkan Blues," in Joanna Labon, ed., *Balkan Blues: Writing out of Yugoslavia,* Evanston: Northwestern University Press, 1995, pp. 3–37, here pp. 15, 18–20, 22.

40. Einhorn, *Cinderella,* pp. 122–123; see also Barbara Einhorn, "The Impact of the Transition from Centrally Planned to Market-Based Economies on Women's Employment in East Central Europe," in Eugenia Date-Bah, ed., *Promoting Gender Equality at Work: Turning Vision into Reality,* London: Zed Press with the International Labour Office (ILO), 1997; for Czechoslovakia, Hungary, and Yugoslavia, see Monica Fong and Gillian Paull, "Women's Economic Status in the Restructuring of Eastern Europe," in Moghadam, *op. cit.,* tables 10.7, 10.8, p. 228.

41. For comparative statistics, see Einhorn, "The Impact of Transition"; for the textile and clothing industry in Poland, especially the regional concentration of unemployment in Lodz, see Jacqueline Heinen, "Unemployment and Women's Attitudes in Poland," in *Social Politics: International Studies in Gender, State and Society,* Special Issue *Between East and West: Gender in an Era of East European Transitions* 2,

no. 1 (1995), pp. 91–110; for similar phenomena in Eastern Germany, see Rachel Alsop, "Women, Work and the *Wende*: Regional and Sectoral Perspectives, Political and Individual Responses," in Elizabeth Boa and Janet Wharton, eds., *Women and the* Wende*: Social Effects and Cultural Reflections of the German Unification Process*, Amsterdam and Atlanta: Rodopi, 1994, pp. 30–37; Rachel Alsop, *Reversal of Fortunes? Women, Work and Change in Eastern Germany*, Oxford: Berghahn, 1998 (forthcoming); and Kerstin Bast-Haider, "The Economic Dimension of Social Change: Women in the East German Clothing Industry," in *Social Politics, op. cit.*, pp. 51–60; *Neues Deutschland* newspaper report, 19/20 July 1997, p. 4.

42. Katarzyna Rewers was quoted by Jane Perlez, "Ship of Dreams Goes Under in Poland," *The New York Times International*, 29 March 1997, p. 4.

43. See Heinen, *op. cit.*; Irene E. Kotowska, "Discrimination Against Women in the Labor Market in Poland During the Transition to a Market Economy," *Social Politics, op. cit.*, (1995), pp. 76–90; Liba Paukert, *Economic Transition and Women's Employment in Four Central European Countries, 1989–1994*, Geneva: International Labour Office (ILO), Labour Market Papers no. 7, 1995; Einhorn, "The Impact of Transition."

44. See Szalai, *op. cit.*

45. Yudit Kiss, "Privatization and Economic Democracy in Hungary," in Barbara Einhorn, Mary Kaldor, and Zdenek Kavan, eds., *Citizenship and Democratic Control in Contemporary Europe*, Aldershot: Edward Elgar, 1996, pp. 102–116.

46. In Bulgaria, for example, of 87,750 private firms established in 1989, only 1.7 percent were owned by women, despite the fact that the majority of businesses are in the service sector, light industry, education, and consultancy, all fields that might have been expected to attract women entrepreneurs (Kostova, *op. cit.*, p. 105). For Poland, see Aleksandra Dukaczewska, "New Forms of Men's Political Domination in Poland in the 1990s: Women and Power in Poland, or Who Should Strive for Change?," paper delivered to the conference entitled The Meanings of Feminism in the Reconfigured Public/Private Spaces in East and Central Europe and the Former Soviet Union, held at Rutgers University, New Jersey, 26–28 March 1997.

47. Paukert, *op. cit.*, p. 34.

48. Valentina Dobrokhotova, in Tatyana Mamonova, ed., *Women and Russia: Feminist Writings from the Soviet Union*, Oxford: Basil Blackwell, 1984, p. 7.

49. "Verkaufte Kinder" ("Children for Sale"), report in *Emma*, no. 12 (December 1992), p.25 [translation mine, BE]; Chris Corrin, "Creating Change or Struggling to Survive? Women's Situation in Albania," in *Women in Eastern and Western Europe: In Transition and Recession*, Special Issue of *Journal of Area Studies*, no. 6 (1995), pp. 74–82.

50. Petra Drauschke, and Margit Stolzenburg, "Are Lone Mothers Slipping into Poverty?" in *Weibblick*, newsletter of the Independent Women's Association (UFV), 2(1992), pp. 13–15. The case of Ute Pust was cited in an article pointing out that long-term unemployment affects single mothers particularly in the new federal states, in *Der Spiegel* 24 (1992), p. 99.

51. B. Zmijewska, "Born but Unwanted," *Warsaw Voice*, 23–30 December, 1990, p. 10, cited in Gail Kligman, "The Social Legacy of Communism: Women, Children, and the Feminization of Poverty," in James R. Millar and Sharon L. Wolchik, *The*

Social Legacy of Communism, New York: Woodrow Wilson Center Press, 1994, pp. 252–270.

52. Szalai, *op. cit.,* pp. 155, 169; and Júlia Szalai, "Power and Poverty," in *The Social History of Poverty in Central Europe,* Working Papers of the Max Weber Foundation for the Study of Social Initiatives, Budapest, 1995, pp. 203–218, here pp. 205, 213, 216–217.

53. Heide Haack's story was quoted from "Frauen in den neuen Bundesländern," *Stern* 46 (1992), p. 126 [my translation, BE].

54. See, for example, Hildegard Maria Nickel, "Women in the GDR and the New Federal States: Looking Backward and Forward (Five Theses)," in Nanette Funk and Magda Mueller, eds., *Gender Politics and Post-Communism: Reflections from Eastern Europe and the Former Soviet Union,* London and New York: Routledge, 1993, pp. 138–150; for a case study of the retail branch of the service sector in the Czech Republic, see Anna Pollert, "Women's Employment and Service Sector Transformation in Central Eastern Europe: Case Studies in Retail in the Czech Republic," *Work, Employment and Society* 9, no. 4, pp. 629–655; see Eva Fodor, "Gender in Transition: Unemployment in Hungary, Poland and Slovakia" (forthcoming in *East European Politics and Society,* 1997) for an article which argues that women may have a comparative advantage in the development of the service sector because of what she calls their "revalued resources" (qualifications and experience in this sector). However, her own data force her to concede that these assets may well be outweighed by other, gender-specific forms of discrimination.

55. For a range of such public opinion survey results, see Barbara Einhorn, "Ironies of History: Citizenship Issues in the New Market Economies of East Central Europe," in Barbara Einhorn and Eileen Janes Yeo, eds. *Women and Market Societies: Crisis and Opportunity,* Aldershot, UK and Brookfield: USA: Edward Elgar, 1995, pp. 217–233.

56. For Czechoslovakia, see Scott, *op. cit.,* pp. 89–93, 107, 210; for Hungary, see Chris Corrin, *Magyar Women,* Basingstoke: Macmillan, 1994, p. 86; for Poland, see Reading, *op. cit.,* p. 30; for the historical legacy and state socialist practice, see Einhorn, *Cinderella,* pp. 27–36.

57. For a discussion of this and other aspects of Lenin's role in establishing the theoretical framework that formed the basis of women's lives in state socialist societies, see Einhorn, *Cinderella,* chapter 1, here p. 32; also Richard Stites, Chapter 15 this volume; for a fuller account, see Richard Stites, *The Women's Liberation Movement in Russia: Feminism, Nihilism, and Bolshevism 1860–1930,* Princeton: Princeton University Press, 1978.

58. Irene Dölling notes the way women in prominent positions, "'model women' were presented with a demonstrative emphasis on traditional 'feminine' stereotypes" in the GDR women's magazine *Für Dich* before 1989. She also comments on the "astonishing similar" images of women in the magazine before and after 1989, with "stereotypes of 'femininity'" bridging the ostensible gap between the "industrious women" worker of socialism and the "consumer" of capitalism.

59. Grazyna Zawi was interviewed by Reading, *op. cit.,* p. 109.

60. Irishka's story, "describing her own heroic deed performed during a time of great food scarcity" (p. 291), in Julia Voznesenskaya, *The Women's Decameron* (1985), London: Mandarin, 1990, pp. 291–295.

61. Charlotte Worgitzky, "I Quit," in Nancy Lukens and Dorothy Rosenberg, eds., *Daughters of Eve: Women's Writing from the German Democratic Republic,* Lincoln and London: University of Nebraska Press, 1993, pp. 49–60.

62. For the GDR measures, see Einhorn, "Socialist Emancipation," pp. 288, 293; for Hungary, see Szalai, "Some Aspects," pp. 162–168; for Poland, see Jacqueline Heinen, "The Impact of Social Policy on the Behavior of Women Workers in Poland and East Germany," *Critical Social Policy* 10, no. 2 (1990), pp. 79–91; here pp. 87–88.

63. Szalai, "Some Aspects," p. 163.

64. *Ibid.*, p. 165.

65. Kostova, *op. cit.,* p. 95.

66. Elena Suskova, "Nationalism in Ukraine," speech delivered to the Women's Commission of the Helsinki Citizens' Assembly, Bratislava, March 1992; Union of Ukrainian Women document on women's reproductive function circulated at the meeting by her.

67. On Yugoslavia, see Mirjana Morokvasic, "Sexuality and the Control of Procreation," in Kate Young, et al., *op. cit.,* pp. 127–143, here pp. 129–131; on Albania, see Corrin, "Creating Change or Struggling to Survive?," pp. 79–80; for the UN statement, see United Nations, *Reproductive Rights and Reproductive Health: A Concise Report,* New York: United Nations, 1996.

68. For the German abortion law, see Further Reading list.

69. Peter Tatchell, *Out in Europe: A Guide to Lesbian and Gay Rights in Thirty European Countries,* London: Channel 4 Television, 1990.

70. For reports on the recent abortion ruling by the Polish Constitutional Court, see *The Guardian,* 26 May 1997, and the *Los Angeles Times,* 29 May 1997, p. A26; the Romanian law on homosexuality was discussed in the European Parliament in January 1997, as reported in *News from Swedish Lesbian/Gay Politics,* no. 8, May 1997.

71. For a discussion of the role of legislation in achieving women's citizenship rights, with particular reference to the postcommunist constitutions of the region, see Ann Snitow, "Can Constitutions Repair the Damaged Citizenship of Women?," in Irena Grudzinska Gross, ed., *Constitutionalism and Politics,* Proceedings of the Bratislava International Symposium, 11–14 November 1993, Bratislava: Slovak Committee of the European Cultural Foundation, 1994.

SUGGESTIONS FOR FURTHER READING

On Women's Groups,
Both Before and After 1989

Barbara Einhorn, "Where Have All the Women Gone? Women and Women's Movements in East Central Europe," in *Shifting Territories: Feminism in Europe,* Special Issue no. 39 of *Feminist Review* (1991), pp. 16–36; Einhorn, "Feminism in Crisis: The East German Women's Movement in the 'New Europe,'" in *A New Europe?,* Special Issue of *The Australian Journal of Politics and History* 41, no. 1 (1995), pp. 14–28; Katalin Fabian,

"Unexpressionism? Challenges to the Formation of Women's Groups in Hungary," *Canadian Women Studies* 16, no. 1 (1995), pp. 80–84; Eva Hauser, "How and Why Do Czech Women Associate? (Altos, Sopranos, and a Few Discordant Voices)," *Canadian Women Studies* 16, no. 1 (1995), pp. 85–90; Donna M. Hughes, Lepa Mladjenovic, and Mrsevic Zorica, "Feminist Resistance in Serbia," *The European Journal of Women's Studies* 2, no. 4 (1995), pp. 509–532; Eva C. Karpinski, "Do Polish Women Need Feminism? Recent Activity of the Parliament Women's Group," *Canadian Women Studies* 16, no. 1, (1995), pp. 91–94; N. M. Stretenova, "A Sleeping Beauty Is Awakening: The Revival of the Feminist Movement in Bulgaria," *The European Journal of Women's Studies* 1, no. 1 (1994), pp. 111–114.

On Women's Studies Programs

Burton Bollag, "Women's Studies Programs Gain a Foothold in Eastern Europe," *The Chronicle of Higher Education,* December 13, 1996; Irene Dölling, "On the Development of Women's Studies in Eastern Germany," *Signs* 19, no. 1 (1994), pp. 739–752; Dasa Duhacek, "The Belgrade Women's Studies Centre," *The European Journal of Women's Studies* 5, no. 3 (1998); Marianne Grünell, "Feminism Meets Scepticism: Women's Studies in the Czech Republic," *The European Journal of Women's Studies* 2, no. 1 (1995), pp. 101–112; Tanja Rener, "Women's Studies in Slovenia," *The European Journal of Women's Studies* 3, no. 2 (1996), pp. 167–172; Roumyana Slabakova, "Research on Women in Bulgaria: The Hard Way into the Future," *Women's Studies Quarterly,* nos. 3–4 (1992), pp. 136–143.

On the Difficult Dialogue Between Feminists in East and West

Barbara Einhorn, "Feminism in Crisis," pp. 14–28; Dorothy Rosenberg, "Distant Relations: Class, 'Race,' and National Origin in the German Women's Movement," in *Links Across Differences: Gender, Ethnicity and Nationalism,* Special Issue of *Women's Studies International Forum* 19, nos. 1/2 (1996), pp. 145–154; Ann Snitow, "Response to Fuszara, Maleck-Lewy, Gaber, Lang and Petö," in Joan Wallach Scott and Cora Kaplan, eds., *Transactions, Environment, Translations: The Meanings of Feminism in Contemporary Politics,* London and New York: Routledge, 1997.

On Ethnicity, Nationalism, and Mass Rape as an Instrument of the War in Former Yugoslavia

See, for example, *Links Across Differences: Gender, Ethnicity and Nationalism,* Special Issue of *Women's Studies International Forum* 19, nos. 1/2 (1996) for: Wendy Bracewell, "Women, Motherhood and Contemporary Serbian Nationalism," pp. 25–34; Maja Korac, "Understanding Ethnic-National Identity and Its Meaning: Questions from a Women's Experience," pp. 133–144; and Ruth Seifert, "The Second Front: The Logic of Sexual Violence in Wars," pp. 35–44; see also Alexandra Stiglmayer, ed., *Mass Rape: The War Against Women in Bosnia-Herzegovina,* Lincoln and London: University of Nebraska Press, 1994.

For Women's Autonomous Peace, Feminist, and Rehabilitation Activities in Former Yugoslavia

Women in Black, eds., *Women for Peace Anthology,* Belgrade: Women in Black, 1993; Women in Black, eds., *Women for Peace,* Belgrade: Women in Black, 1995; Maja Korac, "Understanding Ethnic-National Identity and Its Meaning: pp. 133–144; Donna M. Hughes and Kathleen Foster, "War, Nationalism and Rape: The Center Against Sexual Violence in Belgrade," in *Links Across Differences: Gender, Ethnicity and Nationalism,* Special Issue of *Women's Studies International Forum* 19, nos. 1/2 (1996), pp. 183–184.

On Abortion Laws in Germany and Poland

Germany: Elizabeth Clements, "The Abortion Debate in Unified Germany," in Elizabeth Boa and Janet Wharton, eds., *Women and the* Wende: *Social Effects and Cultural Reflections,* Special Issue of *German Monitor,* Amsterdam and Atlanta: Rodopi, 1994, pp. 38–52; Eva Maleck-Lewy, "Between Self-Determination and State Supervision: Women and the Abortion Law in Post-Unification Germany," *Social Politics* 2, no. 1 (1995), pp. 62–75; Monika Prützel-Thomas, "The Abortion Issue Since Unification: Are Women the Losers?" *Debatte: Review of Contemporary German Affairs* 3, no. 2 (1995), pp. 105–120.

Poland: Barbara Einhorn, "Polish Backlash," *Everywoman,* no. 91 (April 1993), p. 20; Jacqueline Heinen and Anna Matuchniak-Krasuska, *L'avortement en Pologne: La croix et la bannière,* Paris: L'Armattan, 1992; Ann Snitow, "Poland's Abortion Law: The Church Wins, Women Lose," *The Nation,* April 26, 1993, pp. 556–559; *The Guardian,* May 26, 1997; *The Los Angeles Times,* May 29, 1997, p. A26.

Female immigrant worker leaves a plane after cleaning duty.
Frankfurt/Main airport, Oct. 90.   ULRIKE PREUSS/FORMAT/IMPACT VISUALS.

CHAPTER 20

Women in the
New Europe

Renate Bridenthal

*This chapter examines contemporary trends in women's lives in the light
of new economic and political dynamics affecting the major European states,
whose boundaries have become more porous to movements of people and
capital. The lives of migrant and immigrant women, from the oldest, the
Roma or Gypsies, to the newest, ex-colonials, contrast with the lives of the
majority of settled women, around whom the forces of globalization swirl,
profoundly affecting their family and work lives. Women's increasing political
activity ranges from broad humanistic concerns such as peace and ecology
through self-emancipatory efforts like the "second wave" of women's movements and ever greater visibility in the institutions of the European Union
and of the United Nations. New dangers and new opportunities present
themselves in the new millenium, but never before have women been so
mobilized as women to meet them.*

World citizenship has been a remote ideal in European history. In the contemporary world, which is knitted ever closer together by the communications revolution, transnational economies, and supranational political institutions, it seems both a nearer and yet more elusive goal. Many national and subnational groups react against this globalization by more forcefully asserting their uniqueness. For women, this contradiction is even more true, for despite the wave of feminism that has swept over most of the world in the last two decades, differences continue to loom large over acknowledged commonalities. And yet, the effort to work together continues.

Women in Europe have perhaps a better chance than those in other regions to redefine themselves in a new polity as the European Union takes shape. The European Union is a work in progress whose form and function are still under construction. It began soon after World War II, in 1952, as the European Coal and Steel Community, which name described modest economic goals. Comprising six nations (Belgium, France, Germany, Italy, Luxembourg, and the Netherlands), it also had a political agenda, which was to include West Germany as a peaceful nation within the anti-Soviet bloc crystallizing with the Cold War. Five years later, the member states adopted the Treaty of Rome, which created a more comprehensive economic integration, the European Economic Community. New members were gradually admitted until now it consists of fifteen states, the nine new ones being Britain, Denmark, Ireland, Greece, Portugal, Spain, Finland, Sweden, and Austria. Still others are considering applying for membership: some of the formerly socialist countries such as Hungary, Poland, the Czech Republic, and other nations whose "Europeanness" has been questioned, like Russia and Turkey. In 1992, a Treaty on European Union was signed at Maastricht, in the Netherlands, which set more ambitious goals, namely, to create a more cohesive political union through the establishment of a European citizenship, a single European currency, and a central European bank by 1999.

The new applicants to the European Union raise an old question: what is Europe? Not only have its eastern boundaries on the Eurasian landmass always been fluid, but its social and cultural boundaries are just as ambiguous. The definition of "Europe" is also heavily political: in the twentieth century,

the concept has included Russia up to its 1917 revolution, then excluded socialist Central Europe after 1945, and now, with the demise of the Soviet
Union, is coming to reinclude both. Ironically, one common aspect of "Europeanness" might be the very fragmentation to which each state is susceptible
as microregions within them strive for greater autonomy.

How far can unification go, and what would it mean for women? The
answer depends on three processes: the development of supranational democratic institutions in the European Union, the political will of organized
women, and the actions of European capital in a globalizing economy, which
is a defining context. For European capital has also moved. It has fled steadily
abroad into a global economy whose competitiveness fosters businesses to
seek out ever lower wages and fewer contributions to social benefits. As a
result, the economic foundations of European states have shifted, causing
landslides of unemployment and declining welfare provisions.

Perhaps the greatest fluidity of all is that of population. Not since the
invasions into the old Roman Empire has there been such enormous movement of people on the European subcontinent. Immediately after World War
II, thousands of "displaced persons" streamed out of prison camps, concentration camps, and other areas to which they had been removed by the war.
Then, thousands of "guestworkers" took the place of the dead and injured to
help rebuild from the war's destruction and later to contribute to and participate in Europe's prosperity. In the 1960s, subjects of former colonies, newly
defined as citizens, migrated to the heart of their former empires. Both these
groups of new immigrants brought renewed questions of race and cultural difference to the fore. Finally, in the late 1980s, hundreds of thousands of people
came from Central and Eastern European states that are making the transition
from socialism to capitalism.

Who are the women in this new Europe, and how are they faring under
so much uncertainty? This chapter begins with the tenuous lives of migrant
and immigrant women, continues with settled women's experiences with
globalization, and concludes with women's political organizing.

MOVEMENT OF PEOPLES

Although the new immigrants are a tiny minority of the European population, the response to them has been a major political issue, leading to a general closing of borders to further immigration. No small reason for such
limitation has been the reunification of immigrant families, that is, the growing presence of women and children among them, with all the implications of
their social needs, such as housing, health, schooling, jobs, and potentially
welfare. Arguably, then, despite the small percentage of immigrant population, they—and especially the women among them—loom disproportionately
large on the political horizon. And the extremity of their situation makes it

paradigmatic of some of the new problems confronted by the majority of women in Europe.

Migrating peoples are not new in European history. Perhaps the oldest of wanderers are the Roma, or Gypsies, who have been traveling over the subcontinent for a thousand years, rejected everywhere. Their origins remain mysterious, though most probably they came from northern India, propelled by unknown circumstances to begin a nomadic life that has created a diaspora of perhaps 12 million people in the world.[1] The name *Gypsies* comes from a mistaken notion of their origin in Egypt. Some have organized politically and prefer to be identified as "Roma."

Enslaved for four centuries in the lands that now constitute Romania, they were freed by decree in the mid-nineteenth century and set to wandering again.[2] They have always been unwanted: cargoes of Roma preceded African captives for slave labor in the Americas as France, England, and Portugal shipped them to the West Indies, Louisiana, and Brazil.[3] Nazi Germany's racist laws included Roma and Sinti (the German branch) in Germany's roster of "subhuman races," and the Nazis killed about 250,000.[4] A survivor, Ceija Stojka, has written a book, *We Live in Secrecy,* describing her experience in Bergen-Belsen with her mother, who kept their courage up with the famous Roma gift of storytelling. And among women in the resistance were light-skinned Roma who "passed" as German citizens, even in the military administration.[5]

Yet still today, Roma are persecuted for their different culture and their generally darker complexion. With the fall of socialism in Eastern Europe, where most Roma live, discrimination has intensified: "They throw rocks into our windows, don't let us into restaurants, don't let us ride on buses. This is how they explain democracy." In the Czech Republic, during a recent house search for a robber, one policeman told a Roma woman, "You black ape, shut up."[6] At the other end of Europe, in Ireland, the Travelers (as they are called there) are also regularly harassed, fined, and jailed.

Gypsy women are a stock figure of the European imagination, represented as gold-bangled, skirt-twirling, romantic free spirits—the opposite and envy of solid, settled working folk—or as gaudy and fearful old women with mysterious powers of fortunetelling. In fact, although that image is cultivated by Roma in the entertainment business, the reality is more complex. The lives of Roma women, like those of other women in Europe today, are very much in flux. On the one hand, like women of any migrant group, they have a special task of keeping the family together under extraordinary external pressures. This often means preserving cultural norms that are not only different from those of the host society, but that may seem oppressive toward the women themselves.

On the other hand, some will break away and assimilate. Some have acculturated to their host country and become businesspeople, intellectuals, and politicians. Others, rather than flee from a pariah identity, have taken up the struggle to end discrimination by working through new institutions

dedicated to human rights. A World Romani Union has sponsored international congresses since 1971 and has bureaus in twenty-seven countries.[7]
More and more women have taken active roles in mobilizing their communities and in running Roma organizations.[8] Nan Joyce, for example, an Irish
Traveler, became an activist after long years of hardship. Her father had died
in police custody when her mother was pregnant with her ninth child. Fined
for camping, her mother for the first time stole some scraps of copper waste
to sell, but was caught and jailed for a year, leaving the children, including
Nan, on their own. As a defiant adult, Nan became a political organizer in the
1980s, leading demonstrations, appearing on television, and running for local
election in order to put Travelers on the political map.[9]

Somewhat similar experiences of prejudice are the lot of other migrants
in Europe today. Of the approximately 370 million inhabitants of the European Union today, some 8 million are of non-European descent.[10] Nearly half
of these are women, including naturalized citizens, residents, and undocumented migrants. In the first two postwar decades most immigrants were
men, with exceptions like the women recruited for domestic service and nursing from the West Indies to England and from the Philippines to various
European countries. With the onset of recession in the mid-1970s, most European states severely restricted further immigration and even deported non-
citizens to their country of origin. One defiant response of ex-colonials has
been: "We are here because you were there!" Those who could remain, however, were permitted family reunion, which led to an influx of many women
and children. In addition, uncounted thousands continue to enter Europe
illegally from North Africa through poorly guarded entry points in Italy and
Spain. Most of these clandestine commuters are men, but single women out-
number men coming from the Philippines, Cape Verde, Sri Lanka, Eritrea,
Somalia, Nigeria, and Senegal as domestic servants and sex workers.[11] People
also pour in from Eastern Europe, where the transition from communism to
capitalism is creating great hardship. However, these white newcomers competing for scarce jobs are less likely to be expelled.

Some observers view immigrant families, especially those from non-
European countries, as oppressive for the women because of clearly visible
forms of patriarchy, such as the strict Muslim prohibition against girls socializing with boys or the restriction of married women to the home. However,
immigrants' varying backgrounds and opportunities prevent easy generalizations. Somali Muslim women leave home to work as hospital cleaners and
factory workers in Britain, and Turkish women also go out to work doing
cleaning and dishwashing in Sweden and Denmark, clothing and food pack-
aging in Norway and the Netherlands, chemical, textile, and electronic
factory work in Germany, and seamstressing in France.[12] On the other hand,
sometimes gender roles become a marker of cultural integrity for an ethnic
enclave in an alien, even hostile, environment. For example, homebound
Arabic-speaking women in Berlin in the 1980's monitored the movements of

their Palestinian, Lebanese, and Kurdish husbands and children through a neighborhood network of observation and gossip. Palestinian girls who flee to German women's centers to escape such cultural parental control usually return home again, for fear of being isolated in a discriminatory environment.[13] In contrast, Somali women's networks around the same time worked to integrate newcomers into a sisterhood that eventually became a mutual aid society for negotiating with public agencies and for education.[14]

This extraordinary cultural variety needs to be taken account of before feminist goals are projected for migrant women in Europe. Imperialism in Africa and Asia greatly disrupted sex and gender relations there and continues to have an effect when "the Empire strikes back" and the formerly colonized people land on the doorstep of the former colonialists. Cross-ethnic feminism is hampered by the feelings of resentment that some migrants harbor against Europeans who benefited from colonial exploitation but who have offered neither apology nor compensation and who continue to act as if they were superior.

The second generation of immigrants, born in Europe, feels a much sharper tension between customs of the old country and the new. For young women, this frequently takes the form of conflicts over sexual behavior, especially since European norms have relaxed considerably in the last three decades. Also, the extended family is breaking down in favor of the nuclear family, and young people more often choose their marriage partner, rather than have marriages arranged.[15] Some find this wrenching, like the Indian girl in England who wrote:

> I don't like to be "caught" between two completely opposite ways of thinking. I do know that I will probably either not marry at all, or marry someone of my choice be it Asian, West Indian, English, whatever, and so will have to face the consequences of probably losing my family. Because I love them so much I don't want things to end up like that so I have no idea what I will do.[16]

In general, the generation of daughters expects more role sharing, for example, in housework, from their husbands and is less likely to tolerate physical abuse.[17] But divorce remains problematic: for women who lack independent resident status apart from their husband's, it may result in deportation to their home country. Or they may become outcasts from their community, left alone to confront a racist environment complicated by rising unemployment. In England, an Indian woman worried: "I am sometimes so frightened about English people and feel they don't see anything good in us. Just we are black bastards [sic], that is our only identity."[18]

And indeed, the xenophobia can become deadly. In 1993, in Solingen, Germany, arson killed a Turkish family of five as they lay sleeping at home. Similar acts of terrorism have occurred throughout Europe. One result has been for some immigrant women to defend their men and their culture, whatever its degree of sexism. A common enemy fosters cohesion.

It is thus hard to measure the relative status of immigrant women caught between their culture of origin, with its often very overt and coercive patriarchy, and European society, with its subtler patriarchy and aspiring feminism, but harsh xenophobia. Buchi Emecheta, in her novel, *Second Class Citizen*, describes how a Nigerian woman immigrant in England gains her freedom from an abusive husband through an independent income, but is condemned to permanent second-class status through her race, thereby losing both her status at home and also the extended supportive family that would have helped her to rear her children.

Like most women, those of immigrant societies play a dual role, as both workers and mothers. However, many European states begrudge the costs of reproducing migrant or immigrant labor. Initially, immigrants arrive as cheap unskilled labor or as professionals with ready-made training, paid for elsewhere. But once those immigrants settle, their next generation must be trained at the host country's own expense. This makes them less cost-effective in economic terms and consequently less desirable in social terms. Much of the reaction against immigrants, then, is directed against women, because although their children may be tomorrow's potential work force, they also may be today's beneficiaries of social services. Once immigrants acculturate, have fewer children, and assert worker militancy, employers tend to seek other solutions to keep their profitability high. Often, rather than import more cheap labor, employers move away to low-wage countries, where again the cost of reproducing labor is borne by others and where foreign authoritarian regimes will keep workers under control. Even when companies choose to stay at home, the mere threat of their potential departure allows them to reduce wages and pay lower taxes. Immigrant women, already at the bottom of the employment ladder in terms of skills and pay, earn the least and have double the unemployment rates of native women.[19]

As a result, some resort to prostitution, where they are joined by new global migrants. The International Organization for Migration estimates that as many as half a million women cross borders in Europe to work as prostitutes.[20] In part, this business works through brokers who claim to bring in domestic servants, waitresses, or entertainers, sometimes misleading the women themselves. Marriage brokers specializing in "foreign-exotic" women or employment offices recruiting servants from abroad may also place their "clients" in brothels, where their passports are withheld and their wages docked for the costs of their immigration. Currently, Amsterdam and Frankfurt are the European centers of this modern sexual slave trade from Latin America, the Caribbean, Southeast Asia, and Africa. A two-tier system has evolved, in which white native-born women work in government-approved brothels where customers are often required to use condoms, while Asian and Latin women work in nearby seedy illegal brothels, where customers need not use condoms and where women service three or four times as many men in eighteen-hour days.[21] Brothel owners often rotate their personnel across

European borders to prevent the women from forging longer liaisons.[22] If illegals, they are subject to deportation when caught; few dealers are prosecuted. In Eastern Europe, Budapest has emerged as the center of a criminalized sex industry, in which Hungarian and Ukrainian mafias have vied for control over an estimated 60,000 bar, disco, hotel, and street prostitutes.[23]

To the degree that migrant women are disproportionately poor and discriminated against, they have organized to protect their interests. In Berlin, 50 percent of cleaning women were unionized in 1992. In France, migrant women campaigned for battered women's shelters, against apartheid, and against toxic dumping in Africa. Philippinas, the largest migrant group of single women, have organized in the Netherlands, Germany, and Greece in defense of worker rights. Asian women, confounding their stereotype as being passive and docile, have led strikes in England.[24]

The institutions of the European Union also provide some avenues of transnational organizing, especially the Parliament's Committee on Women's Rights. A Churches Committee for Migrants in Europe, which monitors and lobbies the Parliament has a network specifically made up of migrant women. The Migrants' Forum, instigated by the European Commission as a consultative body, has a Women's Committee that tries to mainstream women's concerns under the forum's general headings like education or employment. The European Women's Lobby, consisting of transnational networks and representatives from women's organizations in the member states, is now striving to facilitate black and migrant women's organizations. An independent Black Women and Europe Network constituted itself in 1993 as an umbrella organization. Other groups include an African Women in Europe Network and a Turkish Speaking Women's Network.[25]

Not all the people crossing borders in Europe come from far away; the majority, about 65 percent, are European Community (EC) citizens moving from their home state to another within the EC, usually for work. Of the female Community citizens so employed, more than half come from three member states: Italy, Portugal, and Ireland. They work mainly in France, Belgium, Germany, and Luxembourg.[26] This shows a movement from the poorer European periphery to what has been called "the golden triangle" of European wealth. Most of these female migrant workers go into domestic service or the hotel and catering industries.[27] However, there is also an elite business personnel being trained to traverse the national boundaries of Europe comfortably. A European business school with campuses at universities in Oxford, Berlin, Madrid, and Paris offers a three-year management course that provides a three-country, three-year trilingual experience, in which students spend one term of each year in a placement abroad. People who live and work in contiguous states are known as "frontier workers," people who commute daily or weekly to work in another member state.[28]

Beyond Europe lies the wider world of international expatriate employees, which has been growing rapidly and includes 12 percent women now, a figure expected to rise to 20 percent by the year 2000.[29] A new class of nomads is jetting through the world, working on portable computers and through cellular telephones. They have some of the same values as the oldest European nomads, the Roma: they are entrepreneurial, flexible in their skills, and highly mobile. The scope of their activities, however, prevents them from being as family-oriented as the Roma.

WOMEN AND GLOBALIZATION

The majority of Europeans remain in their native country, especially women, whose child care responsibilities limit their movement. However, while these settled Europeans may be staying in their home country, the global and European economies swirl around them, creating new instabilities and growing unemployment. Heightened competition since the recession of the mid-1970s has resulted in a "dog-eat-dog" environment for business, in which companies have been fleeing their home states for lower-wage countries and to be near foreign markets as well as to avoid taxes. This movement has been facilitated by the demise of the Soviet Union and the disappearance of the socialist alternative to capitalism. Companies no longer fear expropriation when they invest in low-cost countries, including formerly communist countries in Eastern Europe and in the ex-Soviet Union itself.

A United Nations study estimates that multinational corporations now control a third of the world's private productive assets.[30] Economic analysts have noted: "The big corporations do not live anywhere any more."[31] About 20 percent of European companies invest their assets overseas, for example, car manufacturers like Mercedes-Benz of Germany and Fiat of Italy, which have moved production to Brazil, Argentina, Indonesia, and India, where wages may be as low as 1 percent of a European worker's.[32]

This departure of industry, one aspect of deindustrialization, has been accompanied by mergers and downsizing, resulting in widespread industrial unemployment and lowering of wages. At the same time, shareholders have profited and company directors have improved their own salaries and bonuses. The resulting maldistribution of wealth and power, in turn, has created a revenue problem for nation-states, which collect fewer taxes from a low-wage population and from runaway corporations. Major employers have become very clear about their power over national budgets. In Germany, the president of the employers' association, the Federation of German Industry, said outright that if social security taxes (to which they contribute) were not cut back, "We will vote with our feet and go abroad."[33]

The long-term effects of such changes are seen earliest and most clearly in the United Kingdom, where the government of Margaret Thatcher in the 1980s inaugurated policies that facilitated capital flows abroad and weakened labor unions. Britain is now the world's largest overseas investor after the

United States, yet British wages are the third lowest in Europe (better only than Spain and Portugal). As a result, British employees work more hours than any other in the European Union, and some have gone abroad, where they undercut local wages and compete with other migrant workers, as in Germany. At the same time, these low wages have made England attractive to investors fleeing their own high-wage countries like South Korea, where workers have staged massive nationwide strikes protesting their growing job insecurity.[34] In England, poverty has increased to the point that a United Nations report charged the British government with breaching the spirit of the UN Convention on Children's Rights by its cuts in state benefits and the resultant increase in children sleeping and begging on the streets.[35]

Family

In this global economy, restructuring of all kinds of work, including women's work, tends to affect family relations as well. The increase in men's unemployment and underemployment has forced increasing numbers of married women with children to work for wages. At the same time, women who had been employed in the public service sector are losing those better-paid and more secure jobs, as governments shrink to meet their eroding tax base. The resulting decline in social services compounds difficulties for married women workers, since it means that they have less support for family care work, which still remains largely and often solely their responsibility.

Family life has been changing along similar lines everywhere in the new Europe, if at different speeds. People are cohabiting frequently before marrying at a later age, households are becoming smaller with fertility dropping below replacement level, more children are being born outside of marriage, divorce is more frequent, and single-parent and single-person households have increased. In some ways, these phenomena are reminiscent of early nineteenth century forms practiced by urban working classes experiencing the economic instability of early industrialization. But in other ways, these are new trends signifying more choice and less moral stigmatization for women who reject a double standard of sexuality, practice birth control, and earn a living wage. These changes appeared first in the Scandinavian countries, with their high female employment and generous social services. However, even in Southern Europe the traditional family is waning somewhat, as shown by the referenda approving divorce in 1970 and abortion in 1981 in Italy, seat of the Catholic church. Even Ireland allowed divorce in 1995, though abortion remained illegal there.

Changes in family formation have met with conflicting responses. On the one hand, some deplore the decline in fertility, which, combined with the drop in mortality rates, could impose a greater burden of elder care on the next generation. Xenophobia prevents many from welcoming young immigrants as a population replacement who contribute to the social funds that support an aging native population. And state social policies vary widely.

But cutbacks are on the agenda everywhere; even in Sweden, long considered the most generous nonsocialist European welfare state, lawmakers reduced child allowances, pensions, unemployment, and sickness benefits and planned further cutbacks. Thus care of the elderly, who are mostly women, has become a crisis issue. The current life expectancy for women in the European Union is 79.6; for men, 73.2 years. In 1993, 15 percent of the population was aged 65 or over.[36] In the past, a large family ensured its members against a poor and lonely old age. But with families becoming smaller and more mobile, divorce more common, and many more women working outside the home, this tradition is being eroded. The willingness to support the old and sick who may need costly help is wearing thin, but age discrimination also aims against healthy workers over age 50 who face younger competition in the shrinking job market. Forceful lobbying by both elderly and women's groups and by a younger constituency worried about its own future aging will be necessary to keep states and the supranational European Union sensitive to their citizens' needs throughout life.

Some people argue that a smaller population would reduce competition for scarce jobs and thus relieve unemployment. However, employers prefer a larger labor force competing for jobs and keeping their wage costs low. Thus conflicting interests have so far militated against any coherent social or family policy. In the absence of clarity, women have carried an increasingly heavy double burden of paid and unpaid work. Married women with children still do most of the housework and child care, are losing many social services through cutbacks, and increasingly find that they have to work for wages as well.

Employment

In 1995, women comprised 51.2 percent of the inhabitants of the European Union's fifteen countries. About 45 percent of all these women, and 61 percent of women aged 20 to 59, were paid workers, and they constituted 41.4 percent of the total labor force. About 70 percent worked full-time and the rest part-time. Eighty percent of part-time workers in the European Union were women, though some governments, such as the French and the British, provided incentives to businesses for expanding part-time work to men as well.[37]

What kinds of work are these women doing? The answers are manifold. Some work in factories, some in offices, others do manual or office work at home, and still others labor in women's ancient job of domestic service.

In factories, women are still generally found in routinized assembly-line work, where breaks are few and are timed. One study of a Japanese-owned factory manufacturing microwave ovens in England showed a clear gender and ethnic hierarchy: women assembled the ovens, local men were technicians, male British executives were responsible for purchasing, finance, and personnel, but engineering instructions arrived from Japan in Japanese to keep control in the hands of male expatriate managers. Needless to say, women received the lowest wages, technicians made a third more, and the managing director earned seventeen times as much.[38] Interestingly, women as consumers tended to use these microwave ovens to reheat meals they had precooked for their families, so their housework was little diminished by this new household technology.

Office work, long a major employer of women, has been revolutionized by information technology. Paralleling the path of some industries, routinized work like data entry or payroll has been relocated to "electronic sweatshops" in Asia or the Caribbean. However, more sophisticated work, like computerization of services in finance or retailing, or the customized production of specialized goods configured on computers, has created new skills. The paperless office has polarized women's work, so that simple word processing remains semiskilled and low-paying while a few secretaries have assumed middle management tasks (the ranks of male middle managers having been thinned through cutbacks), although without much raise in pay or authority. Thus the new technology has both downskilled and upskilled the office.

Near the top, women managers still have not shattered the glass ceiling that prevents their rise into high-level management. They tend to be relegated to the areas of personnel and marketing, and excluded from the better-paid areas of research and development or manufacturing and production. One woman deplored the clique that excluded her: "It's always been men at the top of this company and the top of the company I was in before. They all know each other. They've all come up the same route together."[39] This tendency is compounded in multinational companies. A female advisor on senior executive development noted: "Life is very hard for women in multinationals. . . . My client has identified 180 people, 10 of them women. Forty percent of the people available for selection were women and they chose just 10. . . . The system in multinationals has been set up by men for men."[40]

According to a study of five multinational companies in which women held executive positions, family patterns continued to limit their gains: only 73 percent were married, compared to 93 percent of the men, and only one-third had children, compared to two-thirds of the men.[41] Part of the women's salary went to domestic service (sometimes called "self-substitution"), while the men more often had non-wage-earning wives. However, a dual earner family at the highest level makes many times more than one at the lowest, where basic subsistence is at stake.[42]

The worst-paid women can rarely afford to pay for domestic service or child care. In the countries without publicly funded child care, many mothers work part-time and/or at home. More and more employers are looking for this kind of casual or "flexible" labor because it allows them to pay little or no social insurance, health insurance, or other benefits. Home production also saves employers the costs of overhead, such as rent, lighting and heating, and even sometimes tools of the trade, like sewing machines or computers. To the extent that workers carry these costs, their pay is thus effectively lower. The shift from centralized assembly in a factory to decentralized branch plants that may subcontract or "outsource" some of their work is another aspect of deindustrialization. Women, long considered marginal workers when the "model worker" was a man employed full-time outside the home, may well be replacing men as the new "model workers" if these restructuring trends continue.[43]

Another new way in which companies economize is to produce goods "just in time," or soon after an order is placed, rather than to pile up inventory. This method requires a work force to be always available, though not consistently employed, in order to produce quickly on demand. Again, women provide an ideal labor supply of this kind because they are often homebound with care work of children, elders, or the sick. If social services continue to decline, more women will be in that position. Some analysts argue that nations have deliberately cut the public sector, not only to balance their budgets, but also to make this kind of cheap women's labor available. Of course, some women appreciate working at home because they feel that it gives them more control over their time while they are also able to care for their families. Others, on call particularly for office-type work, feel imprisoned in their own homes. "You can't go out for a walk or even wash your hair. They come any time. And if you are not in, they give the work to someone else."[44]

Italy has become the model for just-in-time clothing manufactures, where small firms subcontract to individual entrepreneurs who, in turn, commission work to home workers. Leather goods, long an Italian specialty, now encounter competition from Greece and Spain, where women often labor full-time at home. Thirty-two-year-old Anna, for example, with two children and pregnant with a third, produces eighteen to twenty pairs of uppers for shoes in a day, working from 10 A.M. to 7 P.M. with a lunch break. She does her housework between 7 A.M. and 10 A.M., which includes cooking the evening meal and preparing lunch. Fifty-five-year-old Francesca, who lives with her retired husband and four of her eight children, produces fifty pairs of gloves a day. These items are sold at high prices in luxury stores of big cities like Paris or New York. However, piecework rates are so low that women have to work many hours and as a result hardly meet their family's needs, the oft-cited rationale for working at home in the first place.[45]

In the service sector, jobs such as sales, waitressing, and domestic service remain relatively unchanging staples of female employment, absorbing between one-third and two-thirds of the female labor force.[46] House cleaners and child care workers, the necessary self-substitutes for women employed full-time, are often immigrant women. However, rising unemployment has a cascading effect, and native women are displacing immigrants in those jobs. The unemployment rate among women is on average longer term and higher than it is among men in the European Union.[47]

The struggle to maintain living standards has been fierce in Europe. Labor unions have demonstrated and struck everywhere, but most dramatically in France, where a nationwide strike in the winter of 1995 by public sector workers against government austerity measures tied up the country for three weeks. However, the 1990s have been hard times for trade unions, which have been weakened by recession and by governments favoring employer interests. On average, fewer women join unions than do men, which mainly reflects the fact that they work in less organized sectors. Where they are in unions, they are generally underrepresented at the decision-making level because of their greater family responsibilities and a male-dominated discriminatory environment. However, those women who succeed in becoming full-time union officials do tend to prioritize issues such as equal pay, child care, maternity leave, and sexual harassment.[48]

The many changes in women's work and family life have been accompanied, not surprisingly, by a momentous surge in women's self-awareness and in their attempts to gain more control over their lives. Since the 1960s, more and more women have initiated political movements on local, national, regional, and global levels for their own emancipation and for general humanistic goals. Despite national and ideological differences, they may broadly be called feminist movements.

THE WOMEN'S MOVEMENT

Contemporary feminism, like its historical predecessor, arose in the context of broader social movements for greater equality and democracy. A catalyst in Europe as well as in the United States was the long war in Vietnam, where French imperialism had been decisively defeated but where the United States had assumed the fight against a presumed danger of communist expansion. Anti-imperialist sentiments merged with a youth revolt, led by students but sometimes joined, as in France in 1968, by young workers demanding a more equitable distribution of power and wealth. To their dismay, women who participated in these movements soon found, as their predecessors had in the eighteenth and nineteenth century emancipatory movements, that their male comrades did not see them as equals. They were kept out of decision making, denied an equal voice, expected to limit themselves to providing support services for the militant men, and sometimes sexually exploited.

As a result, some women began to organize separately for causes to which they felt particularly close, such as peace and ecology. In England in 1981, a group of women opposed the deployment of ninety-six new nuclear cruise missiles at a United States military base at Greenham Common by setting up a peace camp just outside it. The first four women chained themselves to the fence, but after their arrest, thousands more joined the camp, which remained in place for the next seven years, constantly replenished by women from all over the world. In 1982, they surrounded the nine-mile perimeter and, "embracing the base," festooned it with photographs, balloons, and other decorations. One woman recalled: "I'll never forget that feeling; it'll live with me for ever . . . as we walked round, and we clasped hands. . . . it was for women; it was for peace; it was for the world."[49] Some women even broke through the fence at dawn one day and danced on top of the Cruise silos, making headlines all over the world. A year later, 30,000 singing, chanting women surrounded the base, holding candles and lighted flares.

Another major political interest of women has been ecology. In Germany, for example, women members of the "Green" party had such a strong presence that they succeeded in getting a 50 percent quota of candidates. Here Petra Kelly, one of its founders, rose to prominence as a member of the German Parliament from 1983 to 1990. A longtime grassroots activist, fired into action against nuclear radiation by the death of her 10-year-old sister from cancer, Kelly mobilized millions with her vision, courage, and unflagging energy on a wide range of issues besides environmental safety and preservation: human rights, peace, social justice, and equality. Born in 1947, strongly influenced by her fiercely antifascist grandmother, and raised in a convent school, Petra developed early on a sense of mission. Brought to the United States in the 1960s by her mother's second marriage to John Kelly, an American colonel, she studied at American University, where she participated in a nonviolent occupation of the university president's office in a protest against the Vietnam War. She marched with Martin Luther King, Jr., and campaigned for Democratic presidential candidates. In 1971, she worked with the European Community in Brussels and there uncovered evidence that its funds were being channeled to right-wing European politicians. At the time, she was a member of Germany's Social Democratic Party, but, incensed by its willingness to allow more U.S. nuclear missiles on German soil, she helped to found the Green Party in 1979. Endlessly meeting with politicians at home and abroad, preparing and giving speeches, writing books, engaging in nonviolent civil disobedience, she was burning her candle at both ends, but felt that "it is better to burn than to stop. The world isn't getting any better, so I can't stop."[50]

Women also mobilized directly on their own behalf in national feminist movements. For the mostly educated women or female students who had been active in the movements of 1968, the key notion of this "second wave" of feminism was "consciousness," specifically that "the personal is political." This meant an awareness that personal experiences, choices, and relationships are shaped by power relations and hierarchies. A heightened sensitivity to the many daily forms of male dominance led to widespread sharing of experiences and grievances as in American consciousness-raising groups. A main goal was to end internalized oppression, that is, belief in one's own inferiority and deserved subjugation. Ultimately, the refusal to accept male dominance any longer led women to organize for a variety of goals. And although only a minority of women actually joined such movements, they eventually affected hundreds of thousands of women confronted with the dual burden of production and reproduction in society.

Feminists disagreed widely about the sources of the women's problems and consequently about their solutions. Radical feminists prioritized gender power differences, which seemed to trace inequality back to biology; socialist feminists prioritized class differences, which were located in the entrenched property relations of capitalism; liberal feminists, while acknowledging the force of patriarchy and capitalism, pragmatically focused on making incremental legal changes.

Country by country, the themes and forms of organizing varied. In England, the first initiative came in the fall of 1968 from working-class women, sewing machinists at Dagenham, who brought Ford to a halt in order to gain the right to better-paid work. This led to a demonstration for equal pay in May 1969, joined by unionists, Labor and Communist party members, and student leftists. In the fall of 1969, a workshop on working-class history followed at Ruskin College in Oxford, at which some women suggested having a similar workshop on women's history. Hooted down at first, that conference met in February 1970, drew over five hundred people, and may be considered the formal beginning of the new organized feminism. Women at the conference made four main demands: equal pay for equal work, improved educational opportunities, twenty-four-hour nurseries, and free contraception and abortion on demand.[51] For many, the meeting itself, the sharing of experiences and the determination to bring change, was revolutionary.

> That sense of sisterhood was so supportive and so powerful for me that it actually replaced everything I felt I didn't have at that time. . . . I don't think I liked women so much when I was a young woman because we were so busy being competitive with each other for male attention. . . . Ruskin enabled me, for the very first time, to see women as powerful people. It made me think maybe I could be one of them.[52]

This excitement permeated movements in other countries as well. In France, the reference point was the Revolution of 1789, which framed the political discourse of claims for the completion of the agenda of citizenship that had emerged at that time.[53] However, some French feminists pointed out that the model Republican citizen had been cast as masculine, and they made claims for a recognition of legitimate differences. A dramatic symbolic act in August 1970 was the laying of a wreath, under the Arc de Triomphe, to a person more unknown than the unknown soldier: his wife. On a more practical level, the fight for the legalization of abortion caused 343 prominent women to publish a manifesto in a weekly news magazine announcing they had terminated pregnancies.[54]

In West Germany, feminists preferred to act through informal networks of local projects, including women's centers, publications, and bookstores. Nationally circulated feminist magazines bound them loosely in a shared consciousness. They stressed autonomous, nonhierarchical organizations addressed to immediate needs, such as shelters for battered women, support groups for single mothers or lesbians, meeting places for prostitutes, classes for immigrant Turkish women, and of course the ongoing struggle to liberalize abortion laws.[55] Although celebrating autonomy, some nevertheless accepted state funding for these projects.

The German feminists' stress on autonomy from male-dominated political parties found an echo in Italian women's extra-parliamentary activity, which kept aloof, until the mid-1970s, from the male-run Communist and Socialist parties, while pressuring and relying on them to secure civil divorce in 1970 and legalized abortion in 1978.[56]

A major difficulty that emerged in feminist organizing was heterosexism. Not only homophobia in the women's movement, but political fear kept many heterosexual women from including the specific oppression of lesbians in their program. "Lesbianism is used as a threat against heterosexual women. Whenever women step out of line, whenever women say 'no' to a man, whenever a woman refuses to smile in the street, she is called a lesbian. People use that threat to keep us in line and doing the work that is expected of women."[57] Partly as a result, separate lesbian organizations emerged. These were greeted by their participants with the same sense of liberation that the women's movement had experienced. Again, political separatism, like that of women from left politics after 1968, was experienced as salutary, at least as a phase of organizing.

> [It] changed a private sexual encounter into a cultural happening, a psychic happening, a way of seeing, a way of being in the world, a life of personal and political exploration, self-realization at a level that was so much more exciting, fulfilling than collusion with heterosexism or what seemed then to be apolitical bisexuality.[58]

But lesbian separatism had its pitfalls, too. Splintering over identity politics could become destructive. Race was another major identity according to which people were organizing in increasingly multicultural Europe. England provided a case example of atomization, where dissatisfaction with the largely white feminist movement led to the establishment of an Organization of Women of African and Asian Descent in 1978. This was abandoned three years later by a group of lesbians who then organized Britains' first black lesbian conferences, Zami I and II, in 1985 and 1989, respectively. The over two hundred women who attended these conferences split again, one group forming out of historically immigrant communities, such as Southeast Asia, Latin America, and Arab countries, and the native group forming into a Black Lesbian and Gay Center. Yet a third group emerged for lesbians of mixed racial heritage, who felt comfortable nowhere, like the Nigerian-Polish woman who complained, "I have been called a half-breed in some Black women's groups" or the Indian-German woman who said, "I don't belong completely to the Asian or European community and I feel like a little island floating around on my own." Political action foundered on particularity: "Suspicion and distrust

of each other has created these tiny factions. . . jealousies, insecurities and para-
noia, all the things that are results of being oppressed."[59]

A more successful tactic has taken European lesbian feminists in the
opposite direction, toward regional and global organization. The International Lesbian and Gay Association (ILGA) was founded in 1978 in Coventry,
England, to monitor, publicize, and campaign against the oppression of
homosexuals globally. It currently includes over four hundred groups in sixty
countries. In Europe, ILGA has actively lobbied the European Parliament and
Commission on behalf of the estimated 5 percent lesbian and gay population,
on the grounds that such a "turn to Europe" helps solidarity, pools resources,
and enhances a sense of strength. A first result, thanks to the support of members of the Green, Socialist, and Communist parties in the European Parliament, was the inclusion of sexual orientation in the 1991 Code of Practice
Protecting the Dignity of Women and Men at Work, which aimed to protect
people from sexual harassment on the job. This was extended in 1996 by a
European Court ruling that the dismissal of a transsexual for reasons related
to a sex change was contrary to the principle of equal treatment for women
and men enshrined in European law. Progress has also been made in member
states toward decriminalization of homosexual practices and a uniform age of
consent. However, activists see that more needs to be done with respect to discrimination in employment, housing, and social services.[60]

Finally, women have also worked through the cumbersome structures of
the European Union. The legal basis for political pressure is Article 119 of
the 1957 founding Treaty of Rome, which stipulated equal pay for equal work.
In 1974 this was broadened to include pay for work of equal value (comparable worth), in 1975 discrimination was prohibited on grounds of sex, and in
1976 the European Commission installed a Women's Bureau. In 1984 the Parliament established a standing Committee on Women's Rights, and in 1990
the commission established a Women's Lobby representing several women's
organizations. By 1997, women comprised about one-fourth of the delegates
to the European Parliament.[61]

This female presence and the strength of the socialist parties has allowed
the Parliament to pass several resolutions on behalf of women. One is expanded reproductive choices, including abortion. Farm women's needs were
addressed in proposals to extend benefits to "helper-spouses" for productive
work and replacement services during pregnancy and motherhood. Women
also gained equal treatment in social security schemes.

However, European-wide social legislation has been hard to implement
because of the great national differences in laws and attitudes, maternity
leave being a case in point. The fear of people in the more generous welfare
states of Europe that a convergence of social programs will tend toward the
lowest (and cheapest) common denominator balances against the hope of
those who look to improvements. And this struggle is happening in the context of a global competition between the European Union and other large

economies with weaker social security systems, which then exert a downward pressure on those in Europe.

As recession deepened, the climate for further progressive Europe-wide change chilled even further. In 1995, the Court ruled that the use of employment quotas giving priority to women over similarly qualified men when selecting candidates for a job or for promotion was incompatible with the European Union 1976 Equal Treatment Directive and therefore unlawful.[62] Conditions had changed: the early successes of the women's movement had depended on the conjuncture of the labor market's need for their work and their own political mobilization. Starting in the 1980s, these faltered. The global economy expanded the labor pool, governments rolled back social supports, and the organized women's movements began to splinter into single-issue politics, diffusing their energies.

Some hope remains that reforms in sexual politics can be implemented through the Social Charter, an annex to the Treaty on European Union signed at Maastricht in 1992. It would allow legislation beyond issues of employment because it extends fundamental social rights also to people *not* in the paid work force, on the grounds of their European *citizenship*.[63] Although a separate protocol allowed the United Kingdom to opt out of implementing it, the other states signed. Among other things, like sponsoring partnership in decision making between workers and employers, the charter reemphasizes the goal of equality between women and men. Most important, it provides a legal framework for further struggle, although control by member states remains supreme, making change difficult.

In other areas, feminists have been more successful, as in calling attention to the sexual traffic in women and children. In 1989, the European Parliament passed a Resolution on the Exploitation of Prostitution and the Traffic in Human Beings, which urged member states to increase and enforce penalities against procurers, to assist victims, and to create a special police force staffed by women to serve victims.[64] The European Commission also initiated efforts to combat traffic in women, including a witness protection program.[65]

Feminists also called attention to sexual harassment. In 1990, the European Union's Commission found that it prevented the proper integration of women into the labor market. A resulting Code of Practice provides the basis for what constitutes sexual harassment in the workplace. It is defined as unwanted and offensive physical, verbal, or nonverbal conduct of a sexual nature or other conduct based on sex that affects the dignity of women and men at work. Lobbying by the International Lesbian and Gay Association extended the definition to include harassment for sexual orientation. Member states have agreed to implement the code in their public sectors, to serve as an example to the private sector.[66]

Attempts to pass legislation against violence in the home have so far fallen on deaf ears, on grounds of privacy. However, the Parliament did pass a resolution, drafted by its Women's Rights Committee, that recognized the importance of shelters for battered women and of national legislation to protect women better. In this, it may have been influenced by a spreading awareness of the problem initiated by a 1976 International Tribunal on Crimes Against Women in Brussels, which brought over two thousand women from forty countries together to testify to abuses suffered on account of rape, battering, and homophobia. As a result, women's refuges were set up in many countries.[67]

Finally, women in Europe may have much to gain from the global mobilization of women. The four United Nations conferences for women, in Mexico City in 1975, in Copenhagen in 1980, in Nairobi in 1985, and in Beijing in 1995, have brought women together from all corners of the earth. Although these meetings have exposed significant and painful differences among women, who reflect the vast inequalities among and within their societies, they have also revealed crucial commonalities and helped to establish strong new bonds of solidarity. For all the disagreements over strategies, women agree that they must continue to fight against the forces that constrain them.

Women stand on the threshhold of the new millenium with a heightened sense of self, facing new challenges and opportunities. We have become fully visible in all our splendid diversity.

NOTES

1. Isabel Fonseca, *Bury Me Standing: The Gypsies and Their Journey,* Chatto and Windus, 1995, p.14.
2. David M. Crowe, *A History of the Gypsies of Eastern Europe and Russia,* St. Martin's Griffin, 1994, pp. 118–119.
3. Fonseca, *op. cit.,* p. 216.
4. State Museum of Auschwitz-Birkenau, ed., *Memorial Book: The Gypsies at Auschwitz-Birkenau,* K.G. Saur, 1993, p. 150.
5. Jan Yoors, *Crossing,* Simon and Schuster, 1971, p. 189.
6. Rachel Tritt, *Struggling for Ethnic Identity: Czechoslovakia's Endangered Gypsies,* Human Rights Watch, 1992, pp. 100, 97.
7. Ian Hancock, *The Pariah Syndrome,* Karoma Publishers, 1987, p. 47.
8. B. Shyamala Devi Rathore, "A comparative study of some aspects of the socioeconomic structure of Gypsy/Ghor communities in Europe and in Andhra, Pradesh, India," *European Journal of Intercultural Studies,* 6, no.3 (1996), p. 20.
9. Nan Joyce, ed. by Anna Farmar, *Traveller, An Autobiography,* Gil and Macmillan, 1985, p. 85.
10. *Europe: Magazine of the European Union,* March 1996, p. 22.
11. Eleanore Kofman and Rosemary Sales, "Towards Fortress Europe?" and Jacqueline Andall, "Women Migrant Workers in Italy," *Feminist Review,* no. 39 (1991), pp. 29–39 and 41–48.
12. Hazel Summerfield, "Patterns of Adaptation: Somali and Bangladeshi Women in Britain," in *Migrant Women: Crossing Boundaries and Changing Identities* ed.

Gina Buijs, Berg, 1993, p. 91. Tahire Kocturk-Runefors, *A Matter of Honour: Experiences of Turkish Women Immigrants*, Zed Books, 1992, p. 93.

13. Dima Abdulrahim, "Defining Gender in a Second Exile: Palestinian Women in West Berlin," in Buijs, *op. cit.,* pp. 62, 70.
14. Summerfield, *op. cit.,* p. 90.
15. Kocturk-Runefors, *op. cit.,* p. 110.
16. *Breaking the Silence: Writings by Asian Women* by Centerprise Publishing Project, Centerprise Trust Ltd., 1984, p. 6.
17. Kocturk-Runefors, *op. cit.,* pp. 119–122.
18. *Breaking the Silence*, pp. 73–74.
19. Mirjana Morokvasi, "Fortress Europe and Migrant Women," *Feminist Review*, no. 39 (Autumn, 1991), p. 77.
20. *The Boston Globe*, August 19, 1996.
21. Dorchen Leidholdt, "Sexual Trafficking of Women in Europe: A Human Rights Crisis of the European Union," in *Sexual Politics and the European Union: The New Feminist Challenge*, ed. R. Amy Elman, Berghahn, 1996, p. 89.
22. Morokvasic, *op. cit.,* p. 78.
23. *Financial Times*, January 28, 1997.
24. European Women's Lobby, *Confronting the Fortress: Black and Migrant Women in the European Union*, European Parliament, Directorate-General for Research, 1995, pp. 84–85.
25. *Ibid.,* chapter 3.
26. Eurostat, *Rapid Reports: Population and Social Conditions: Female Population by Citizenship in the European Community* (1993 - 8), p. 2.
27. Rita James Simon and Caroline B. Brettell, *International Migration: The Female Experience*, Rowman and Allanheld, 1986, pp. 7, 152–177.
28. *The European*, February 1 – 7, 1996. *Social Europe*, March 3, 1996. p. 5.
29. *Financial Times*, May 5, 1995.
30. *Financial Times*, September 24, 1993.
31. Editorial, *Financial Times*, March 20, 1996.
32. *The European*, June 24 – 30, 1994.
33. *Financial Times*, April 25, 1996.
34. *Financial Times*, June 21, 1995; *The New York Times*, October 15, 1995.
35. *Financial Times*, January 28, 1995.
36. Eurostat, *Facts Through Figures: A Statistical Portrait of the European Union* (1996), p. 4.
37. Eurostat, *Women and Men in the European Union: A Statistical Portrait* (1995), pp. 9–15.
38. Cynthia Cockburn and Susan Ormrod, *Gender and Technology in the Making*, Sage, 1993, p. 71.
39. Judy Wajcman, "Women and Men Managers: Careers and Equal Opportunities," in *Changing Forms of Employment: Organisations, Skills and Gender*, ed. Rosemary Crompton, Duncan Gallie and Kate Purcell, Routledge, 1996, p. 274.
40. Jane McLoughlin, *Up and Running: Women in Business*, Virago, 1992, p. 163.
41. Wajcman, *op. cit.,* pp. 268–269.
42. Jill Rubery, "The Labour Market Outlook and the Outlook for Labour Market Analysis," in Crompton et al., *op. cit.,* p. 27.

43. Jane Jenson, Elisabeth Hagen, and Ceallaigh Reddy, eds., *Feminization of the Labor Force: Paradoxes and Promises,* Oxford University Press, 1988, Introduction, p. 11.

44. Ursula Huws, Jenny Hurstfield, and Riki Holtmaat, *What Price Flexibility? The Casualization of Women's Employment,* London Low Pay Unit, 1989, p. 12.

45. Victoria A. Goddard, *Gender, Family, and Work in Naples,* Berg, 1996, pp. 106–113.

46. Anneke van Doorne-Huiskes, Jacques van Hoof, and Ellie Roelofs, eds., *Women and the European Labour Markets,* Chapman Publishers, 1995, table on p. 17.

47. Eurostat, *Facts Through Figures,* p. 8.

48. van Doorne-Huiskes et al., *op. cit.,* pp. 222–223.

49. Jill Liddington, *The Road to Greenham Common: Feminism and Anti-Militarism in Britain Since 1820,* Syracuse University Press, 1989, p. 244.

50. *Vanity Fair,* January 1993, p. 108. Kelly was finally stopped under mysterious circumstances by a gunshot wound to the head as she lay sleeping. Police swiftly concluded that her lover and fellow antinuclear activist, former East German General Gert Bastian, had committed the murder and then killed himself; they refused further investigation, despite requests by some of Kelly's political friends.

51. Sheila Rowbotham, "The Beginnings of Women's Liberation in Britain," in *Once a Feminist: Stories of a Generation* ed. Michelene Wandor, Virago, 1990, p. 22.

52. Interview with Audrey Battersby in *ibid.,* p. 115.

53. Jane Jenson, "Extending the Boundaries of Citizenship: Women's Movements of Western Europe," in *The Challenge of Local Feminisms: Women's Movements in Global Perspective,* Amrita Basu, Centerprise, 1984, p. 413.

54. Claire Duchen, *Feminism in France from May '68 to Mitterrand,* Routledge and Kegan Paul, 1986, pp. 9, 13.

55. Myra Marx Ferree, in "Equality and Autonomy: Feminist Politics in the United States and West Germany," *The Women's Movements of the United States and Western Europe,* ed. Mary Fainsod Katzenstein and Carol McClurg Mueller, Temple University Press, 1987, p. 174.

56. Karen Beckwith, "Response to Feminism in the Italian Parliament: Divorce, Abortion, and Sexual Violence Legislation," in Katzenstein and Mueller, *op. cit.,* pp. 158–162.

57. Diana E. H. Russell and Nicole Van de Ven, eds., *Crimes Against Women: The Proceedings of the International Tribunal,* Les Femmes, 1976, p. 44.

58. Ide O'Carroll and Eoin Collins, *Lesbian and Gay Visions of Ireland: Towards the Twenty-First Century,* Cassell, 1995, pp. 30–31.

59. Valerie Mason-John and Ann Khambatta, *Lesbians Talk Making Black Waves,* Scarlett Press, 1993, pp. 12–18, 35, 53.

60. Kees Waaldijk and Andrew Clapham, eds., *Homosexuality: A European Community Issue,* Martinus Nijhoff, 1993, pp. 5, 74, 141.

61. Catherine Hoskyns, *Integrating Gender: Women, Law and Politics in the European Union,* Verso, 1996, pp. 104–109, 130. European Women's Lobby, *op. cit.,* p. 37.

62. Kalanke *vs.* Freie Hansestadt Bremen, *Women of Europe Newsletter,* no. 57 (January–February 1996).

63. Linda Hantrais, *Social Policy in the European Union,* Macmillan Press, 1995, p. 15. Hoskyns, *op. cit.,* p. 190.

64. Leidholdt *op. cit.,* p. 91.

65. *Boston Globe*, August 19, 1996.
66. Evelyn Collins, "European Union Sexual Harassment Policy," in Elman, *op. cit.*, pp. 23–33.
67. Russell and Van de Ven, *op. cit.*, preface. Jalna Hanmer, "The Common Market of Violence," in Elman, *op. cit.*, p. 133.

SUGGESTIONS FOR FURTHER READING

There is no comprehensive study of women in contemporary Europe as of 1997. Further material on the topics dealt with here may be found in the following:

Movement of Peoples

Centre for Contemporary Cultural Studies. *The Empire Strikes Back: Race and Racism in Seventies Britain*. Hutchinson, 1982.

Ford, Glyn. *Fascist Europe: The Rise of Racism and Xenophobia*. Pluto Press, 1992.

Fraser, Angus. *The Gypsies*. Blackwell, 1992.

Kramer, Jane. *Unsettling Europe*. Random House, 1980.

Phizacklea, Annie, ed., *One Way Ticket: Migration and Female Labour*. Routledge and Kegan Paul, 1983.

Tong, Diane. *Gypsies: A Multidisciplinary Annotated Bibliography*. Garland, 1995.

Women and Globalization

Family

Hantrais, Linda, and Therese Letablier. *Families and Family Policies in Europe*. Longman, 1996.

Jetter, Alexis, Annelise Orleck, and Diana Taylor, eds. *The Politics of Motherhood: Activist Voices from Left to Right*. University Press of New England, Dartmouth College, 1997.

Kiernan, Kathleen E. *Cohabitation: Extra-marital Childbearing and Social Policy*. London Family Studies Centre, 1993.

Prinz, Christopher. *Cohabiting, Married, or Single: Portraying, Analyzing, and Modeling New Living Arrangements in the Changing Societies of Europe*. Avebury, 1995.

Employment

Phizacklea, Annie, and Carol Wolkowitz. *Homeworking Women: Gender, Racism and Class at Work*. Sage, 1995.

Pillinger, Jane. *Feminizing the Market: Women's Pay and Employment in the European Community*. Macmillan. 1992.

Probert, Belinda, and Bruce W. Wilson, eds. *Pink Collar Blues: Work, Gender, and Technology*. Melbourne University Press, 1993.

Stubbs, Cherrie, and Jane Wheelock. *A Woman's Work in the Changing Local Economy.* Avebury, 1990.

Webster, Juliet. *Office Automation: The Labour Process and Women's Work in Britain.* Harvester Wheatsheaf, 1990.

The Women's Movements

D'Amico, Francine, and Peter R. Beckman. *Women in World Politics.* Bergin and Garvey, 1995.

Duchen, Claire. *French Connections: Voices from the Women's Movement in France.* Hutchinson, 1987.

Githens, Marianne, Pippa Norris, and Joni Lovenduski, eds. *Different Roles, Different Voices: Women and Politics in the United States and Europe.* HarperCollins, 1994.

Kaplan, Gisela. *Contemporary Western European Feminism.* New York University Press, 1992.

Lovenduski, Joni, and Pippa Norris, eds. *Gender and Party Politics.* Sage, 1993.

Parkin, Sara. *The Life and Death of Petra Kelly.* Pandora, 1994.

Tatchell, Peter. *Europe in the Pink: Lesbian and Gay Equality in the New Europe.* GMP Publishers Ltd., 1992.

Notes on Contributors

Barbara Switalski Lesko did her undergraduate and graduate work on Egyptology at the University of Chicago's Oriental Institute and has taught in adult education programs at the University of California, Berkeley, Mills College, and Brown University, where she is Administrative Research Assistant in the Department of Egyptology. She has recently produced a new edition of her best-selling *The Remarkable Women of Ancient Egypt,* and she was the organizer and editor of the *Conference on Women in the Ancient Near East* (1997, Brown University), which has been published by Scholars Press, Atlanta, Georgia, 1989.

Marilyn Arthur Katz received her Ph.D in classics from Yale University and is currently Professor of Classical Studies and Department Chair at Wesleyan University. She teaches in the Women's Studies and Judaic Studies programs, as well as in the Classical Studies Department. She is the author of *Penelope's Renown: Meaning and Indeterminacy in Homer's Odyssey* and of "Women, Men and Children," forthcoming in *The Cambridge Illustrated History of Ancient Greece* (ed. Paul Cartledge).

JoAnn McNamara is Professor of History at Hunter College, City University of New York, and an active participant in various organizations of feminist historians. She received her Ph.D from Columbia University. Her interest in gender now extends to masculinities as well as femininities; in *Medieval Masculinities,* edited by Clare Lees, she provides the keynote article. She has recently published *Sisters in Arms, Catholic Nuns Through Two Millennia* for Harvard University Press.

Lisa Bitel is Associate Professor of History and Women's Studies at the University of Kansas. She received her Ph.D. from Harvard University, and she is the author of two books on early Irish Christian settlement and literature in northern Europe: *Isle of the Saints: Monastic Settlement and Christian Community in Early Ireland* and *Land of Women: Tales of Sex and Gender from Early Ireland.*

Susan Mosher Stuard is a medieval historian concerned with social and economic questions. She received her Ph.D. from Yale University and is Professor of History at Haverford College. She is the editor of *Women in Medieval Society* and *Women in Medieval History and Historiography,* and author of *State of Deference, Ragusa/Dubrovnik in the Medieval Centuries.* She won the Berkshire Prize in 1996 for "Ancillary Evidence on the Decline of Medieval Slavery," *Past and Present* 149 (1995) pp. 3–28.

Carole Levin received her Ph.D. in Renaissance history from Tufts University. She is Professor of History at the State University of New York, College at New Paltz, and has received the SUNY Chancellor's Award for Excellence in Teaching. She has held long-term fellowships at the Newberry Library and the Folger Shakespeare Library. Professor Levin has coedited three collections of essays on Renaissance women, and she is the author of *The Heart and Stomach of a King: Elizabeth I and the Politics of Sex and Power* (1994) and *Propaganda in the English Reformation: Heroic and Villainous Images of King John* (1995).

Susan C. Karant-Nunn is the author of *Luther's Pastors: The Reformation in the Ernestine Countryside* (1979); *Zwickau in Transition, 1500–1547: The Reformation as an Agent of Change;* and *The Reformation of Ritual: An Interpretation of Early Modern Germany* (1997). With Andrew C. Fix, she is coeditor of *Germania Illustrata: Essays on Early Modern Germany* (1992). She and Merry E. Wiesner are preparing a volume of Martin Luther's principal writings about women. She has served as president of the Sixteenth Century Studies Conference and has held, among other fellowships, research fellowships from the International Research and Exchanges Board and the Fulbright Commission. She is Professor of History at Portland State University.

Merry E. Wiesner is Professor of History and the former Director of the Center for Women's Studies at the University of Wisconsin, Milwaukee. Her books include *Working Women in Renaissance Germany* (1986), *Women and Gender in Early Modern Europe* (1993), *Convents Confront the Reformation* (1996), *Discovering the Western Past* (3rd edition 1997), and *Discovering the Global Past* (1997). She is the coeditor of the *Sixteenth Century Journal,* is currently working on a study of Christianity and the regulation of sexuality in the early modern world, and, along with Susan Karant-Nunn, is also working on an edited volume of Luther's writings on women.

Dena Goodman is Professor of History and of Women's and Gender Studies at Louisiana State University. She is the author of *The Republic of Letters: A Cultural History of the French Enlightenment* (Cornell University Press, 1994), which won the Charles B. Smith Award from the Southern Historical Association. She has also coedited a volume of interdisciplinary essays, *Going Public: Women and Publishing in Early Modern France,* published by Cornell in 1995. Her current research focuses on the material culture of women's epistolary practice.

Darline Gay Levy received her Ph.D. in history from Harvard University. She teaches French and European intellectual and cultural history in the Department of History at New York University. She is the author of *The Ideas and Careers of Simon-Nicolas-Henri Linguet: A Study in Eighteenth-Century French Politics,* and the coeditor, with Harriet B. Applewhite and Mary Durham Johnson, of *Women in Revolutionary Paris, 1789–1795.* She and Harriet Applewhite coedited *Women and Politics in the Age of the Democratic Revolution.* Their coauthored book, *The Impossible Citizenship: Women, Gender and Power* *in Revolutionary Paris,* is forthcoming in the Duke University Press series, "Bicentennial Reflections on the French Revolution." She is currently working on two projects: an international collaborative project to publish the complete correspondence of S.-N.-H. Linguet; and a book on mentors and protégés in eighteenth-century France.

Harriet B. Applewhite, University Professor and Professor of Political Science at Southern Connecticut State University, received her Ph.D. in political science from Stanford University. She is the author of *Political Alignment in the French National Assembly, 1789–1791.* She edited, in collaboration with Darline Gay Levy and Mary Durham Johnson, *Women in Revolutionary Paris, 1789–1795.* She and Darline Gay Levy coedited *Women and Politics in the Age of the Democratic Revolution.* Their new book, *The Impossible Citizenship: Women, Gender and Power in Revolutionary Paris,* is forthcoming in the Duke University Press series, "Bicentennial Reflections on the French Revolution."

Laura L. Frader is Associate Professor of History at Northeastern University and Senior Associate at the Center for European Studies, Harvard. She is co-editor, with Sonya O. Rose, of *Gender and Class in Modern Europe* (Ithaca: Cornell University Press, 1996) and author of *Peasants and Protest: Agricultural Workers, Politics and Unions in the Aude, 1850–1914* (Berkeley: University of California Press, 1991). She has published articles on gender and work in modern France and is currently working on a book length manuscript on gender, work, and the French labor movement between 1919 and 1939.

Karen Offen (Ph.D., Stanford University) is a historian and independent scholar affiliated as a Senior Scholar with the Institute for Research on Women and Gender, Stanford University. She is a founder and past secretary-treasurer of the International Federation for Research in Women's History, and is past-president of the Western Association of Women Historians (USA). Karen has coedited three volumes of interpretative documentary texts and the 1991 volume, *Writing Women's History: International Perspectives* (with Ruth Roach Pierson and Jane Rendall), on behalf of the International Federation for Research in Women's History. Her monograph, *Paul de Cassagnac and the Authoritarian Tradition in Nineteenth-Century France,* appeared in 1991. She is currently completing books on the woman question in modern France and on European feminism, from 1700 to 1950 and has published several recent articles on the comparative history of feminism and other topics.

Charles Sowerwine received his Ph.D. in history from the University of Wisconsin. He is now Reader in French and Women's History at the University of Melbourne (Australia). He is the author of *Sisters or Citizens? Women and Socialism in France since 1876* and of *Madeleine Pelletier, une féministe dans l'arène politique.* His article, "Workers and Women in France before 1914: The Debate over the Couriau Affaire," *The Journal of Modern History,* was awarded the William Koren Prize by the Society for French Historical Studies.

Margaret Strobel, Professor of Women's Studies and History at the University of Illinois at Chicago, received her Ph.D. in history in 1975 from UCLA. The subject of an NEH fellowship in 1989, her current research focuses on the Chicago Women's Liberation Union. She is on the editorial board for the *Historical Encyclopedia of Chicago Women* (Indiana University Press, forthcoming). Strobel's first book, *Muslim Women in Mombasa, 1890–1975* (Yale University Press, 1979) was cowinner in 1980 of the Herskovits Prize awarded by the African Studies Association. She has also published *Three Swahili Women: Life Histories from Mombasa, Kenya* (coedited, in English and Swahili, with Sarah Mirza, Indiana University Press, 1989), *European Women and the Second British Empire* (Indiana University Press, 1991), *Western Women and Imperialism: Complicity and Resistance* (coedited with Nupur Chaudhuri, Indiana University Press, 1992), and *Expanding the Boundaries of Women's History: Essays on Women in the Third World* (coedited with Cheryl Johnson-Odim, Indiana University Press, 1992). With Cheryl Johnson-Odim, she also coedited a four-volume series on the history of women in Africa, Asia, Latin America and the Caribbean, and the Middle East, forthcoming from Indiana University Press, which is intended to help teachers integrate women's history into history survey courses.

Richard Stites is a Professor of History at Georgetown University. He is the author of *Women's Liberation in Russia* (Princeton University Press, 1978), *Revolutionary Dreams* (Oxford University Press, 1989), *Russian Popular Culture* (Cambridge University Press, 1992), and of numerous articles in Russian history.

Sandi E. Cooper is Professor of History at the College of Staten Island and at the Graduate School, The City University of New York (CUNY), and Chair of the University Faculty Senate of CUNY. She is the author of *Patriotic Pacifism: Waging War on War in Europe, 1815–1914* (Oxford University Press, 1991) and an editor of the Garland Library of War/Peace and of the *Biographical Dictionary of Modern Peace Leaders*. She has written numerous articles on peace movements, women in war and peace, and public higher education.

Claudia Koonz, one of the coauthors and co-editors of the first two editions of *Becoming Visible* and author of *Mothers in the Fatherland: Women and the Family in Nazi Politics,* teaches history at Duke University.

Jane Jenson has been a Research Affiliate of the Center for European Studies, Harvard University, and Professeure titulaire in the Département de science politique, Université de Montréal, since July 1993. She is the coauthor of, *inter alia, Mitterrand et les Françaises: Un rendez-vous manqué* (Paris: FNSP, 1995), *Absent Mandate: Canadian Politics in the Era of Restructuring* (Toronto: Gage Publishers, 1995), and *The Politics of Abortion* (1990). She has also written numerous articles on gender politics and the women's citizenship in Canada and France.

Barbara Einhorn is Acting Director of the Research Center in Women's Studies at the University of Sussex in England. She is the author of *Cinderella Goes to Market: Citizenship, Gender and Women's Movements in East Central Europe* (London: Verso, 1993); coeditor (with Eileen Janes Yeo) of *Women and Market Societies: Crisis and Opportunity* (Aldershot, UK and Brookfield USA: Edward Elgar, 1995); and coeditor (with Mary Kaldor and Zdenek Kavan) of *Citizenship and Democratic Control in Contemporary Europe* (Aldershot, UK and Brookfield USA: Edward Elgar, 1996). She was guest editor for *Links Across Differences: Gender, Ethnicity and Nationalism,* special issue of *Women's Studies International Forum,* vol. 19, nos. 1–2, 1996, and of *The Idea of Europe,* special issue of *The European Journal of Women's Studies,* vol. 5, no. 3, 1998. Barbara Einhorn is Associate Editor of *The European Journal of Women's Studies* and is an editorial board member of the *Asian Journal of Women's Studies.*

Renate Bridenthal is Professor of History at Brooklyn College and at the Graduate School, The City University of New York. She has coedited and contributed to *Becoming Visible: Women in European History* through all three editions (Houghton Mifflin, 1977, 1987, 1997), coedited and contributed to *When Biology Became Destiny: Women in Weimar and Nazi Germany* (Monthly Review Press, 1984), co-authored *Families in Flux* (Feminist Press, 1980, 1989), and authored numerous articles, especially in German women's history.

Index